Register for Free Membership to

solutions@syngress.com

Over the last few years, Syngress has published many best-selling and critically acclaimed books, including Tom Shinder's *Configuring ISA Server 2000*, Brian Caswell and Jay Beale's *Snort 2.1 Intrusion Detection*, and Angela Orebaugh and Gilbert Ramirez's *Ethereal Packet Sniffing*. One of the reasons for the success of these books has been our unique **solutions@syngress.com** program. Through this site, we've been able to provide readers a real time extension to the printed book.

As a registered owner of this book, you will qualify for free access to our members-only solutions@syngress.com program. Once you have registered, you will enjoy several benefits, including:

- Four downloadable e-booklets on topics related to the book. Each booklet is approximately 20-30 pages in Adobe PDF format. They have been selected by our editors from other best-selling Syngress books as providing topic coverage that is directly related to the coverage in this book.

- A comprehensive FAQ page that consolidates all of the key points of this book into an easy to search web page, providing you with the concise, easy to access data you need to perform your job.

- A "From the Author" Forum that allows the authors of this book to post timely updates links to related sites, or additional topic coverage that may have been requested by readers.

Just visit us at **www.syngress.com/solutions** and follow the simple registration process. You will need to have this book with you when you register.

Thank you for giving us the opportunity to serve your needs. And be sure to let us know if there is anything else we can do to make your job easier.

SYNGRESS®

YNGRESS®

DEPLOYING
Citrix
MetaFrame
Presentation Server 3.0

With Windows Server 2003 Terminal Services

Connie S. Wilson   (CCEA)

Anthony "Andy" Jones   (CCIA, CCEA, CCI)

Paul Stansel   (CCEA, CCA)

Ralph "JJ" Crump   (CCEA, CCSP)

Chris Broomes

Melissa Craft (CCA) Technical Editor

Travis Guinn (CCA) Technical Editor

KEY	SERIAL NUMBER
001	HJIRTCV764
002	PO9873D5FG
003	829KM8NJH2
004	HJB4377883
005	CVPLQ6WQ23
006	VBP965T5T5
007	HJJJ863WD3E
008	2987GVTWMK
009	629MP5SDJT
010	IMWQ295T6T

PUBLISHED BY
Syngress Publishing, Inc.
800 Hingham Street
Rockland, MA 02370

Deploying Citrix MetaFrame Presentation Server 3.0 with Windows Server 2003 Terminal Services

Printed in the United States of America
1 2 3 4 5 6 7 8 9 0
ISBN: 1-932266-50-X

Publisher: Andrew Williams
Acquisitions Editor: Jaime Quigley
Technical Editors: Melissa Craft,
  Paul Stansel, Andy Jones, Travis Guinn
Cover Designer: Michael Kavish

Page Layout and Art: Patricia Lupien
Copy Editor: Beth Roberts
Indexer: Rich Carlson

Distributed by O'Reilly Media, Inc. in the United States and Canada.
For information on rights and translations, contact Matt Pedersen, Director of Sales and Rights, at Syngress Publishing; email matt@syngress.com or fax to 781-681-3585.

Acknowledgments

Syngress would like to acknowledge the following people for their kindness and support in making this book possible.

Syngress books are now distributed in the United States and Canada by O'Reilly Media, Inc. The enthusiasm and work ethic at O'Reilly are incredible, and we would like to thank everyone there for their time and efforts to bring Syngress books to market: Tim O'Reilly, Laura Baldwin, Mark Brokering, Mike Leonard, Donna Selenko, Bonnie Sheehan, Cindy Davis, Grant Kikkert, Opol Matsutaro, Steve Hazelwood, Mark Wilson, Rick Brown, Leslie Becker, Jill Lothrop, Tim Hinton, Kyle Hart, Sara Winge, C. J. Rayhill, Peter Pardo, Leslie Crandell, Valerie Dow, Regina Aggio, Pascal Honscher, Preston Paull, Susan Thompson, Bruce Stewart, Laura Schmier, Sue Willing, Mark Jacobsen, Betsy Waliszewski, Dawn Mann, Kathryn Barrett, John Chodacki, Rob Bullington, and Aileen Berg.

The incredibly hardworking team at Elsevier Science, including Jonathan Bunkell, Ian Seager, Duncan Enright, David Burton, Rosanna Ramacciotti, Robert Fairbrother, Miguel Sanchez, Klaus Beran, Emma Wyatt, Chris Hossack, Krista Leppiko, Marcel Koppes, Judy Chappell, Radek Janousek, and Chris Reinders for making certain that our vision remains worldwide in scope.

David Buckland, Marie Chieng, Lucy Chong, Leslie Lim, Audrey Gan, Pang Ai Hua, Joseph Chan, and Siti Zuraidah Ahmad of STP Distributors for the enthusiasm with which they receive our books.

David Scott, Tricia Wilden, Marilla Burgess, Annette Scott, Andrew Swaffer, Stephen O'Donoghue, Bec Lowe, Mark Langley, and Anyo Geddes of Woodslane for distributing our books throughout Australia, New Zealand, Papua New Guinea, Fiji, Tonga, Solomon Islands, and the Cook Islands.

Technical Editors

Melissa Craft (CCNA, MCSE, Network+, CNE-5, CNE-3, CNE-4, CNE-GW, MCNE, Citrix CCA) is director of e-business offering development for MicroAge Technology Services. MicroAge is a global systems integrator headquartered in Tempe, Arizona. MicroAge provides IT design, project management and support for distributed computing systems. Melissa is a key contributor to the business development and implementation of e-business services. As such, she develops enterprise-wide technology solutions and methodologies focused on client organizations. These technology solutions touch every part of a system's lifecycle, ranging from network design, testing and implementation to operational management and strategic planning.

Melissa holds a bachelor's degree from the University of Michigan, and is a member of the IEEE, the Society of Women Engineers and American MENSA, Ltd. Melissa currently resides in Glendale, Arizona with her family, Dan, Justine, and Taylor.

Travis Guinn (MCSE, CCA, A+) has been a contributing author to several Citrix books and is now a senior systems engineer with Softricity, Inc. Travis currently provides senior-level implementation and diagnostic services to customers implementing SoftGrid Virtual Application services. Prior to Softricity, Travis worked for JP Morgan supporting Citrix, and five years with a leading Citrix Platinum integrator where he provided consulting services to Fortune 500 companies. Travis lives in Frisco, Texas with his family, Crystal, Travis, and Sarah.

*Authors **Andy Jones** and **Paul Stansel** also contributed to the technical editing of this book.*

Contributing Authors

Connie S. Wilson (MCSE, CCEA, CNA, CCNA) is the Information Services Operations Manager for CNA National and has ultimate responsibility for design, implementation, and ongoing oversight of multiple Microsoft and MetaFrame Presentation Servers. Her specialties are troubleshooting, new product testing, and Citrix consulting. Connie has a broad technology background with 18 years in progressively challenging IT work and a B.S. in telecommunications. Before joining CNA National Warranty, Connie was employed by GE, bringing a chronically problematic MetaFrame Server farm to a high level of reliability.

Anthony "Andy" Jones (MCSE+I, MCT, CCIA, CCEA, CCI, CCNA, CCDA, MCIW, Network+, A+,) is the services director for MTM Technologies, previously known as Vector ESP. He provides comprehensive solutions focused on Citrix and Microsoft technologies for clients ranging from 50 to 50,000 users, focusing mainly on architecting and deploying Access Infrastructure solutions for enterprise customers. One of Andy's primary focuses is developing best practices, processes and methodologies surrounding Access Infrastructure that integrate with virtually every part of a customer's infrastructure.

In addition to field work and business development, Andy regularly teaches Microsoft and Citrix courses. Andy holds a master's degree from Morehead State University.

Andy also contributed to the technical editing of this book.
I would like to thank my family, Amy, Julia and Jocelyn, without your patience and support my contribution would not have been possibly. I would also like to my fellow consultants who have helped in ways that cannot be expressed. Finally, I would like to thank the editors for this project for their assistance in helping me "refine" my work. I would like to dedicate my contribution to this work to my brother Jeremy and my mother. I love you both and miss you dearly.

Paul Stansel (MCSE, MCSA, CCEA, CCA, CNA, MCP+I, A+), co-author of *Citrix MetaFrame 1.8 for Win2K,* is a consultant specializing in the design and implementation of the Citrix Access Suite for environments of any size. Paul has consulted at a variety of major corporations including The Hartford, GlaxoSmithKline, and Pfizer Pharmaceuticals.

Paul holds a bachelor of science degree in information technology from the University of Phoenix. He has contributed to other books and online articles, and served as the Technical Editor for the *A+ Certification Study Guide, Third Edition* from Syngress. Paul also contributed to the technical editing of this book. Paul currently resides in Manchester, Connecticut with his wife Rachel and their two children, Abby and P.J.

Chris Broomes (CCNA, CCDA, MCSE, MCP+I, MCT) is a senior network engineer with USERS Inc. His current responsibilities include security and infrastructure management and support of the company's ASP Internet and thin-client Intranet networks which host the company's flagship Internet and Intranet products. Chris is a seasoned IT veteran who has held numerous senior engineering and management positions over his thirteen-year career at companies like Staples, EXE Technologies Inc., and Devon IT Inc. His areas of expertise include all versions of Microsoft Windows, Citrix MetaFrame, Cisco network design and support, IPSEC and SSL VPN design and support on a number of devices, computer forensics, and technical project management. Chris has contributed to a number of best-selling Syngress titles such as *Email Virus Handbook, Configuring Citrix MetaFrame XP,* and *MCSE Designing Windows 2000 Web Solutions.* Chris recently completed a master of science degree in information science from Penn State Graduate School of Engineering. Chris lives in Lansdowne, PA with his wife Keisha, son Jared, daughter Jordan, and ten tropical fish.

Ralph "JJ" Crump (Citrix CCEA, CCNP/CCDP, CCSP, MCSE, HP ASE) manages an advanced solutions consulting firm in Atlanta, GA. His firm provides senior design and technical guidance for major clients focusing on enterprise deployments of thin-client, VoIP, network, and security solutions. He has worked extensively in enterprise organizations designing and building infrastructure services and specializes in enterprise Citrix solutions, networking design and implementation, and security solutions. He has written several other books on similar topics including Microsoft Windows 2000, Network+, and Citrix CCA.

Contents

Chapter 1

Introduction to Microsoft Windows Server 2003 and Terminal Services

Solutions in this Chapter:

- Overview of Terminal Services
- History of Terminal Services
- Capabilities of Microsoft Windows Server 2003 Terminal Services
- Limitations of Microsoft Windows Server 2003 Terminal Services

☑ Summary

☑ Solutions Fast Track

☑ Frequently Asked Questions

Introduction and Overview of Terminal Services

The concept of users sharing computing resources is not new. The practice of this computing model dates back to mainframes with green-screen terminals. While computing has evolved dramatically since those early days, the basic premise of "centralized" computing hasn't changed a great deal. Centralized or server-based computing originally sprang out of the need for many users to have access to very expensive computing resources without actually placing a computer on each user's desk. This was the right approach for the time due to two primary reasons. First, computers then cost hundreds of thousands, if not millions, of dollars to acquire and typically cost even more to maintain and operate. Second, computers were at best the size of large cars, so placing one on each user's desk would pose a serious space issue to any corporation. The benefits of centralized computing weren't as pronounced then as they are today. Centrally managed end-user devices weren't *an* option then, they were the *only* option. The ability to have a single point of update for applications and operating systems was the norm in the "good old days." Providing hundreds of users access to a new application was instantaneous—again, only one computer to "upgrade."

Popularity for centralized computing waned for several years as the advent of the personal computer (PC) allowed end users to have the power of the mainframe on the desktop without the expense of the mainframe. Individual PCs gave rise to the need for networking, so we began to tie PCs together to allow sharing of files and printers. Over time, our use of computers went from a centralized to a decentralized model. Decentralization occurred for several reasons. PCs were cheaper to maintain and purchase than mainframes and mini-computers. A host of new applications allowed for much greater range of computing uses, such as word processing, spreadsheets, and e-mail. We slowly moved from the point of placing computers on engineers' desktops to placing computers on everyone's desktop. We moved the majority of our computing power to the edge of the network, along with the majority of support issues. Anyone who has ever managed a network knows that purchasing the computer is the least expensive part of owning a computer. Maintenance, training, upgrades, viruses, and spyware all add up to the bulk of the cost over time for PC ownership. Several studies are available that indicate that the initial capital outlay for the purchase of new computing hardware and software only accounts for about 10 percent of the actual cost over a three-year period (then you get to start all over!). This process of suburban sprawl inside our networks continued unchecked for several years. Then, one day, a bright engineer named Ed Iacobucci sat up at IBM and thought, "hey, wouldn't it be great if we could put all those applications and tools that users run on their desktops back on the mainframes!"

Now, we're sure that Ed Iacobucci never actually uttered those words, but the principle is the same. Let's take the "network sprawl" and reconsolidate back to the data center where we can more effectively manage it. While we're doing that, let's eliminate some of the major "reasons" for moving away from centralized computing in the first place. We will create highly available server "farms" to allow for reliable user connections instead of single points of failure in our mainframes. We'll install and manage the applications centrally on controlled, reliable, enterprise-grade hardware to increase our uptime. Create a single seat from which all information in our enterprise can be controlled and access granted based on role. Oh, and by the way, we would like this all to be an end-user device and network agnostic! A pretty tall order, but with that thought the basis for Terminal Services was born.

What Is Terminal Services?

"What is Terminal Services," you ask? For anyone who has used VNC, Timbuktu, PC Anywhere, Remotely Possible, X Windows, or even the new Remote Desktop for Microsoft Windows XP, you have some idea of what Terminal Services enables you to do. Terminal Services is the multiple simultaneous use of a Microsoft Windows computer remotely by the user population. This can occur as a user gaining access to his Microsoft Windows XP Professional desktop while working at a satellite office halfway around the world. More typically, this is the access of many users to a centrally located and managed server farm running the Microsoft Windows Server 2003 operating system. Each user's connection is "virtual" and remote. Whether users are accessing the terminal server from their local area network (LAN), or remotely from a Windows Mobile Powered handheld while waiting for a flight, it is all about access. Terminal Services allows users of virtually any device (Windows PCs, Apple Mac OS X workstations, Linux servers, etc.) to be able to access the same applications and data from anywhere internal and external of the network, anytime.

All applications are installed on the terminal servers, creating a single easy to manage point of upgrade. All applications and code execute exclusively on the terminal servers, allowing devices to execute the latest and most feature-rich applications, even when the device would not natively support these applications. The terminal servers present the *interface* to the user's device. The end user interacts with this interface via his local keyboard and mouse, transmitting these signals to the terminal servers. This transfer of the *interface* of the application and the input from the user occurs via a presentation layer protocol. Presentation layer protocols exist at the presentation layer of the OSI model. Sandwiched logically between the application and the session layers, presentation layer protocols primarily perform the roles of translation and, to a lesser degree, encryption. To put this into perspective, presentation layer protocols allow computers to *understand* something that they cannot understand out-of-the-box. Logically, presentation layer protocols' primary functions are translation and encryption. Let's use a Windows 9x workstation with IPX installed and a NetWare 3.12 server to better understand the relationship of the presentation layer protocols in computing. Is the Window 9x workstation capable of accessing shares on the NetWare server simply because of the IPX network layer protocol? No, IPX really performs the routing and transport of requests on the network. IPX doesn't know how to properly ask the NetWare server for access to the share; the NetWare Client installation provides this feature. When you install the NetWare client, you are installing a *redirector* that allows your Windows 9*x* workstation to successfully "talk" with the NetWare server "in a language it can hear." The same is true of the presentation layer protocols used in Terminal Services to allow user connections. Microsoft Terminal Services natively uses the Remote Desktop Protocol (RDP), and Citrix MetaFrame Presentation Server uses Independent Computing Architecture (ICA) as the presentation layer protocols of choice. The protocols and the software that is installed on the client devices act as the redirector that allows for translation and understanding of the Terminal Services *language*, whether ICA or RDP.

History of Terminal Services

As previously stated, Terminal Services began life as a concept created by Ed Iacobucci while working on the OS/2 project at IBM. After gaining no interest from IBM on including this technology in OS/2, Ed left to found Citrix Systems, Inc. Ed and his team at Citrix Systems had signed an agreement with Microsoft allowing Citrix to modify the code and create a multiuser version of Windows NT 3.*x*. This modification to the kernel became known as *MultiWin*, and Citrix Systems sold the solution as a product named WinFrame. WinFrame was in every sense a completely capable and functional Windows NT 3.*x* server. WinFrame could function in any capacity that a "standard" Windows NT 3.*x* server could. In addition, WinFrame could host multiple user sessions and allow users remote access to their applications and information. More information on Citrix will be forthcoming in Chapter 2." For now, let's cut to the chase of Terminal Services.

The Dark Ages: The Birth of Windows NT 4.0 Terminal Server Edition

In February 1997, Microsoft informed Citrix that it would be pursuing its own version of WinFrame, which would be based around the Windows NT 4.0 platform. Both Microsoft and Citrix knew that the older file manager interface of Windows NT 3.*x* and WinFrame needed to be replaced with the current Windows 9*x* Explorer interface used in the recent release of Windows NT 4.0. Microsoft decided to consolidate the product offerings and base the next version on the Windows 9*x* Explorer interface. Many speculations exist as to why Microsoft chose to end the code-sharing agreement and pursue the centralized computing model directly. Some say that Microsoft perceived that the Windows NT kernel stood a good chance of becoming "fractured" into many camps, similar to the versions of UNIX, if Microsoft didn't maintain tight control over the source. Others claim that Microsoft wanted to have a "quick" entrance into the emerging centralized computing market space. Whatever the reasons, Microsoft chose to go it alone and announced Project Hydra, the codename for the upcoming release of Windows NT 4.0 Terminal Server Edition (TSE).

After several tenuous months, Microsoft and Citrix reached a new agreement. In August 1997, Microsoft agreed to license the MultiWin technology from Citrix for inclusion in Windows NT 4.0 Terminal Server Edition. While the core function of Terminal Services would now be under Microsoft's control, Citrix played and continues to play a large role in the product roadmap. As part of the agreement, Citrix would continue to have access to the source code. A new feature of the agreement was that Citrix would place developers onsite at Microsoft's campus in Redmond to work side by side with the terminal server development team. Citrix would retain rights to develop clients for all non-Microsoft Windows platforms. Additionally, Citrix would develop an add-on product, MetaFrame, which would provide ICA Services to Windows NT 4.0 TSE.

NOTE

The agreement that was reached in August 1997 has since expired. A new agreement was signed that continues the same kernel source-code sharing. The current agreement is set to expire in 2005, but conventional wisdom is that this also will be renewed. If you are wondering as to the "status" of the relationship between Microsoft and Citrix, ponder no more. Microsoft named Citrix Systems "Partner of the Year 2003," Microsoft's highest partner award… so things must be pretty good.

In the summer of the following year, 1998, Microsoft released Windows NT 4.0 TSE. TSE was built on the MultiWin technology licensed from Citrix Systems through a collaborative development effort between Microsoft and Citrix. However, beyond that, several changes were made to licensing and connectivity to TSE. Since ICA Services were part of the Citrix solution, and the ICA protocol for client-server sessions was part of those services and not of the base terminal server product, Microsoft needed to develop its own presentation layer protocol for user sessions. Microsoft leveraged an existing technology that it had recently acquired in its product NetMeeting. NetMeeting contains a feature that allows users to "share" their desktop or applications with other users during the meeting. This capability is based on the T.120 or "T-Share" protocol. Microsoft adapted that presentation layer protocol for TSE and named it the Remote Desktop Protocol, or RDP.

RDP version 4.0 contained two pieces. First was the server-side component. The terminal server would run a *terminal server* service, similar to other services such as workstation, server, or messenger. This terminal server service basically listened to the network for incoming terminal server sessions, created the sessions, managed the sessions, and tore the sessions down on exit. The client-side component consisted of an RDP Client.

Users could choose to install the RDP Client on a Windows 16- or 32-bit operating system to allow them to connect to the terminal server directly. RDP, being based on the T.120 protocol, requires TCP/IP as its transport protocol stack. RDP rides inside the payload section of a TCP packet. The list of initially supported clients was rather thin, no pun intended. With the release of TSE, Microsoft included client support for Win16, Win32, and WinCE operating systems. The WinCE client and support was originally only available from the manufacturer of the client device. Eventually, Microsoft would release an ActiveX-based plug-in for Internet Explorer 4.0 and higher and a client for the Apple MAC OS.

In addition to the *terminal server* service that ran on each TSE server, a new service was introduced to server-based computing by Microsoft known as the Terminal Server Licensing service. This service's job was to enforce Microsoft's license model for users connecting to terminal servers. The Terminal Server Licensing service maintained an Access or Jet Database on each terminal server to track the issuance of terminal server client access licenses, or TSCALs. The original implementation of this service had several flaws. The database and service were dependent on the version of the Microsoft Data Access Components (MDAC) that was installed on the terminal server. Occasionally, when you installed an application or upgraded the terminal server, it would "break" the database, causing the service to fail to start. Additionally, the database was maintained on *each* server and no mechanism existed to "reconcile" the issued licenses between the servers. The license issuance was based on the client's computer name or NetBIOS name. If the helpdesk rebuilt a user's computer, a *new* license would be issued and decremented from the total count available, without the original license ever being returned to the database. Due to these and other issues, many administrators chose to disable the Terminal Server Licensing service on the TSE servers and enforce the TSCAL requirements manually.

NOTE

Microsoft's TSCAL requirements are in addition to any Citrix licensing requirements. Both Microsoft and Citrix MetaFrame Presentation Server must be licensed correctly for user sessions to function. For a user session to be correctly licensed for a Citrix connection, several licensing requirements must be met. Microsoft will require a File and Print Client Access License and a Terminal Services Client Access License. These Microsoft licenses are in addition to the Citrix connection license consumed during the ICA session.

By many in the industry, especially those deploying the platform, TSE was viewed as a completely separate product offering from Microsoft with its own design considerations and support needs. Microsoft certainly viewed the platform as such. To that end,

Microsoft created and maintained a separate Hardware Compatibility List (HCL) for TSE. In addition, Microsoft issued separate service packs and hotfixes specifically for TSE. Third-party vendors had a difficult time adapting to this new mainstream platform offering of terminal servers. Many applications that were developed to run correctly on Windows NT 4.0 Workstation or Server, failed outright to execute on the Windows NT 4.0 TSE platform. Many applications required modifications or tweaks to enable them to run correctly on TSE. With these kinds of disparities among versions of the same platform, one can see why support and design issues arose. Microsoft rose to the challenge.

The Renaissance: The Light of Windows 2000 Terminal Services

In December 1999, Microsoft released Windows 2000 to manufacturing. Some major steps in the right direction were made for the Terminal Services platform. The foremost change was the inclusion of Terminal Services into the Server product line. The perception of why Microsoft included Terminal Services in the platform is based on two lines of reasoning: 1) simplicity, allowing for the creation of a single kernel; and 2) administration, as Microsoft (as the rest of the server-based computing community already knew) discovered the invaluable benefit of remote administration. With this single change, Microsoft cemented the destiny of centralized computing. Now Terminal Services was part of the mainstream distribution of the platform available as a selectable service to install, similar to Windows Internet Naming Service (WINS) or Dynamic Host Configuration Protocol (DHCP). This allowed for the creation of a single HCL. A single service pack offering existed for servers built with Windows 2000 Server regardless if they were installed as file servers or terminal servers. Hotfixes, as is the nature of such updates, continued to be maintained somewhat separately based on the services installed on the server. In short, there were and continue to be hotfixes developed specifically for terminal servers that would not and most likely should not be applied to file servers, for example. The inclusion of this feature as a component allowed third-party integrators to more easily support their software on the platform, as the platform could then be viewed as one product instead of two separate products from the previous version.

NOTE

Unlike Microsoft Windows XP Professional, Windows 2000 Professional could not run the terminal server service or remote desktop function. A Windows 2000 Professional computer could only function as a client in the Terminal Services process and could not accept connections from other RDP clients. Windows XP Professional supports a single connection via Remote Desktop. Windows XP Home does not support this feature.

Another major change for Terminal Services under the Windows 2000 Server platform was the ability to select the role of the terminal server during the addition of this service. For the first time, administrators could choose between two modes of operation for their terminal servers, *Remote Administration* and *Application Server*. Remote Administration was a groundbreaking feature that included much of the benefit of Terminal Services' session speed and ubiquitous access simply scaled down to support only two simultaneous administrative sessions. For Windows administrators then and now, Remote Administration mode (or what has become known as Remote Desktop for Administration) is a lifesaver.

Remote Administration mode did not require any special or additional licensing to install and use. Microsoft *gave* us two free connections to the server for the purposes of remote administration. Application Server mode was reserved for true terminal servers (the focus of the remainder of this book). Application Server mode allowed for the unlimited connections (platform prohibiting) to the terminal server, and is the mode that all terminal servers are configured for today.

In addition to the change to the terminal server service, Microsoft heavily modified the Terminal Services Licensing (TSL) service. Gone are the days of being able to simply disable this service; as part of the new platform, Microsoft required the terminal server to be able to *talk* to a TSL server. Additionally, the TSL service no longer is installed and running on each terminal server, as with NT 4.0 TSE. Installation and configuration of TSL is discussed in more detail in Chapter 3, but typically, one or two TSL servers will suffice for most organizations. The new TSL service allowed Microsoft to enforce the new licensing model. The basic premise of this new model was that clients that were equal to or greater than the terminal server platform would not be charged a TSCAL, but instead would be able to use the client operating system's built-in TSCAL. For all down-level clients or non–Microsoft clients, a TSCAL would be required and charged against the total TSCAL pool available from the TSL server. Table 1.1 demonstrates this licensing concept.

Table 1.1 Windows 2000 TSCAL Requirements

Terminal Server OS	Windows 2000 Pro or Newer [2]	Windows Pre-2000 [3]	Non-Windows Clients [4]
Windows 2000 Server [1]	Built-in	TSCAL required	TSCAL required

1. All versions of Windows 2000 Server, including Standard, Advanced, and Datacenter

2. Includes all versions of Windows 2000 (Professional and Server), Windows XP Pro, and all versions of Windows Server 2003

3. Includes all Windows platforms before Windows 2000 (Windows Me, Windows 9x, Windows 3.x, Windows CE, and Windows NT)

4. Includes all non-Windows clients (MS-DOS, Mac OS, Linux, UNIX, etc.)

Improvements to the RDP protocol on the server side and client side were made to take advantage of the improvements to the server. Redirected printing (the ability to make use of client-based print resources while in the session) was added to the Terminal Services platform. Clipboard redirection, or the ability to cut, copy, and paste text between the local client and the Terminal Services sessions, was added. Shadowing (the ability to remotely control a session), disk bitmap caching for improved session speed and performance, and the RDP Advanced client were also included as updates for Windows 2000 Terminal Services. The RDP Advanced client was also known as the Terminal Services Advanced Client (TSAC). This specialized client was a plug-in created for Internet Explorer to allow users to browse a Web site to start a Terminal Services session.

The Future and Beyond: Capabilities of Windows Server 2003 Terminal Services

In March 2003, Microsoft released to manufacturing the current flagship for Terminal Services in the form of Windows Server 2003. Great advancements in security, scalability, and manageability were the bedrock of this release. With these improvements to the core platform, several major changes were made to the Terminal Services portion of that platform. Taking a queue from the Windows XP platform, Microsoft changed the name of Terminal Services to Remote Desktop—although most practitioners continue to refer to the feature set as Terminal Services. Remote Desktop is a feature available to all versions of Windows XP and Windows Server 2003, with a few minor differences.

On Windows XP Professional machines, Remote Desktop allows a single user to connect to the "console" of the target machine and assume control of it (similar to VNC or PC AnyWhere). The ideal is that a user could be away from his or her desktop and remotely access it via the Remote Desktop client on another machine, whether in the office or away. The capability to perform this function is already installed but disabled out-of-the-box for security reasons.

Remote Desktop is also installed out-of-the-box on Windows Server 2003, but is disabled. The primary difference on the server platform is that enabling Remote Desktop is functionally equivalent to Remote Administration mode in Windows 2000 Server. By enabling Remote Desktop on Windows Server 2003, an administrator is allowing two simultaneous remote connections to this server and one login at the console (where Windows XP only allows a single session to the console). Application Server mode, the mode typically associated with Terminal Services, requires a trip to **Add/Remove Programs** to install this additional functionality. Application Server mode is available on Windows Server 2003 editions, except for the Web edition, which is limited to the Remote Desktop for Administration mode. Enabling this feature is easy, as you can see in Figure 1.1. Open the **Start** menu, right-click **My Computer**, and then select **Properties**. From the **System Properties** dialog box, select the **Remote** tab and place a check in the **Remote Desktop** box that states **Allow users to connect remotely to this computer**.

Figure 1.1 Enabling Remote Desktop for Windows Server 2003

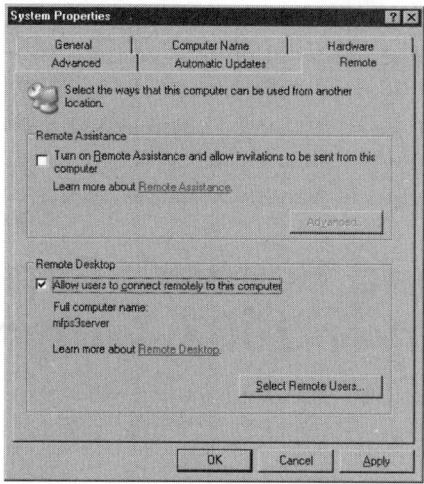

When the **Remote Sessions** dialog box appears, read the information concerning security and the requirement for a password on all accounts that will use Terminal Services, and click **OK**, as shown in Figure 1.2.

Figure 1.2 Remote Sessions Dialog Box

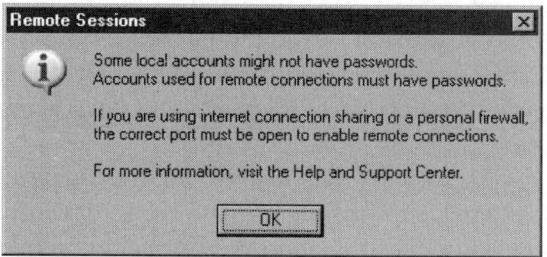

NOTE

The method described to enable Remote Desktop is similar to Remote Administration mode in Windows 2000 Server, and thus does *not* provide the full functionality of Application Server mode. Application Server mode can only be enabled through **Add/Remove Programs,** and is discussed in more detail in Chapter 3.

In addition to the installation differences between Windows 2000 Terminal Services and Windows Server 2003 Terminal Services, major changes occurred in TSL, and a new feature has been introduced called Session Directory. TSL became much easier to manage and understand. Quite simply, now everything is a TSCAL. No longer do the built-in licenses of Windows 2000 Pro and Windows XP Pro matter. All connections to Windows Server 2003 Terminal Services (when in Application Server mode) require and consume a TSCAL. The other big difference is that there are now two licensing modes to choose from on the terminal servers themselves. Now a terminal server can ask a TSL server for a per-device or a per-user license. We discuss TSL installation, configuration, and best practices in Chapter 3.

Session Directory is a new feature designed to allow for a more consistent experience when user devices disconnect from active Terminal Services sessions. The Session Directory stores session information, such as users, devices, terminal servers, and so forth in a "directory." If users want to disconnect and reconnect later, their session will be reconnected to the already running disconnected session based on the information the Session Directory maintains. There are some pretty steep requirements for implementing Session Directory, including the use of a load-balancer (either Windows Load Balancing Service (WLBS) or a third-party hardware load-balancer such as F5 Network's BigIP devices). Additionally, the Session Directory requires Enterprise or Datacenter editions of Windows Server 2003 on the terminal servers in order to function. The Session Directory itself can run on Windows Server 2003 Standard edition. Since Citrix MetaFrame Presentation Server already has this functionality and doesn't require the expense or complexity of hardware load-balancers and Windows Server 2003 Enterprise Edition, most production networks will opt not to install this feature. Instead, we will use load balancing as a function of Citrix MetaFrame Presentation Server 3.0 Advanced and Enterprise Editions.

A new client has also been introduced to leverage the new server-side features' functionality. Remote Desktop Client (RDC) (the replacement for Remote Desktop Protocol Client (RDP Client)) is supported by Microsoft on Win32, Web Client (ActiveX for Internet Explorer), Mac OS X, and Windows CE, including the newer Windows CE .NET. Several third-party RDC clients are also available to allow Linux/UNIX distributions to connect directly to terminal servers without Citrix. These RDC clients were not created by Microsoft, nor are they supported. However, we've used various versions for years and they seem to function well, if not feature-complete. Citrix develops, maintains, and supports clients for many of the mainstream UNIX and Linux distributions.

Many improvements were made to RDC client versions 5.1 and 5.2 over the previous Windows 2000 version, RDP 5.0. RDC 5.1 ships with Windows XP and is preinstalled ready to use on every Windows XP machine, to include all editions. RDC 5.2 ships with Windows Server 2003 and is preinstalled on all versions of Windows Server 2003. The differences between RDC 5.1 and 5.2 are practically nonexistent, the one noticeable exception being the automatic reconnect feature of the RDC 5.2 client (see Figure 1.3). Administrators wanting to use this feature might want to update the RDC client on their Windows 32-bit clients, from Windows NT 3.5*x* through Windows XP.

Figure 1.3 RDC 5.1 vs. RDC 5.2 Differences

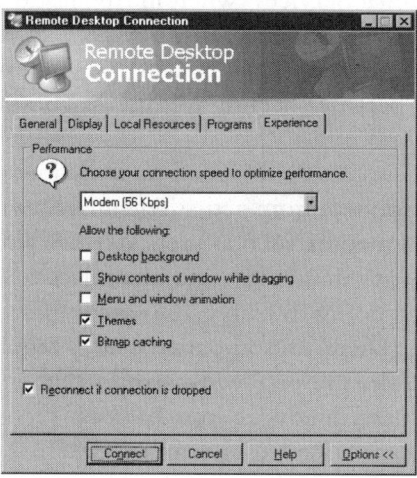

RDC 5.*x* also has improvements in color depth and performance optimization over the RDP 5.0 client of Windows 2000. RDC 5.*x* now supports True Color (24-bit) via the Terminal Services session. While this may seems like a trivial improvement on the surface, more and more developers are creating applications assuming that the target computer has the capability to "see" more than 256 colors (as we were restricted to in Terminal Services on Windows 2000 and Windows NT 4.0 Terminal Server Edition). Try running Publisher or Visio through a Terminal Services session at 256 colors, then increase to 24-bit, and you'll see the difference.

Microsoft has also included in the RDC 5.*x* interface the ability to "tweak" the performance characteristics of the client to allow users to optimize their Terminal Services session based on their network connection. This is a huge step forward for out-of-office and remote office users and a much-needed addition, albeit a feature that requires manual modification. An example of these settings can be seen in Figure 1.3.

System configuration and automation has been greatly improved in Windows Server 2003 with the expansion of the Windows Management Interface (WMI) Providers. Currently, a great deal of the underlying functionality of Terminal Services has been exposed to various scripting languages that WMI and the Windows Script Host (WSH) support. In addition, Microsoft has exposed the Terminal Services attributes for user objects in Active Directory with this release. For the first time, administrators are able to create scripts to modify the Terminal Services properties for users' accounts without the need for third-party products.

The following is a piece of sample code to demonstrate the capabilities of WMI in Terminal Services. This code simply queries the server on which it is executed to determine if Terminal Services is in Remote Desktop for Administration mode or Application Server mode.

```
Set objWMIService  = GetObject("winmgmts:" &
"{impersonationLevel=impersonate}!\\.\root\cimv2")
Set cItems = objWMIService.ExecQuery("Select * from
Win32_TerminalServiceSetting",,48)
For Each oItem in cItems
    Wscript.Echo "This server is in " & oItem.LicensingName & " Mode."
Next
```

Security of the Windows Server operating system has been improved. Out-of-the-box, Microsoft disables many unnecessary services that pose security issues to Terminal Services, such as Internet Information Services. Additionally, Microsoft has improved the security of Terminal Services itself. Windows Server 2003 now leverages a Remote Desktop Users built-in group to manage access rights to the terminal servers. Moreover, additional system rights are restricted based on membership in this group. No longer does every user account automatically have rights to access the terminal server remotely. RDC connections now default to 128-bit RC4 symmetric key for encryption of session information. This encryption setting can be adjusted on the connection properties or through group policy to allow for legacy clients, particularly older versions of Windows CE to connect to Windows Server 2003 terminal servers.

Figure 1.4 demonstrates the process to "decrease" the encryption level to allow legacy Remote Desktop Protocol clients to connect to Terminal Services in Windows Server 2003.

Microsoft also has included support for the Federal Information Processing Standard (FIPS), meeting both FIPS 140-1 (1994 revision) and FIPS 140-2 (2001 revision). FIPS is a security standard for cryptography that many governmental agencies (federal, state, and local) are required to meet. Broader support for the use of smart cards to authenticate to Terminal Services sessions has been introduced. The file system and registry have also been secured more tightly with this release. Microsoft has made extensive use of the Authenticated Users built-in group to assist in assigning NTFS permissions and Discretionary Access Control Lists (DACLs) to files, folders, objects, and registry keys. Microsoft's security initiative is certainly a step in the right direction for all parties concerned through decreased vulnerabilities, less administrative burden patching systems, and greater system uptime due to decreased patching. Currently, there are no service packs in release for Windows Server 2003, although there is a release candidate for Service Pack

1 for Windows Server 2003. This is quite a statement to make, considering that the platform is nearly two years old as of the writing of this book.

Figure 1.4 Lowering the Encryption Requirements of RDP for Legacy Clients

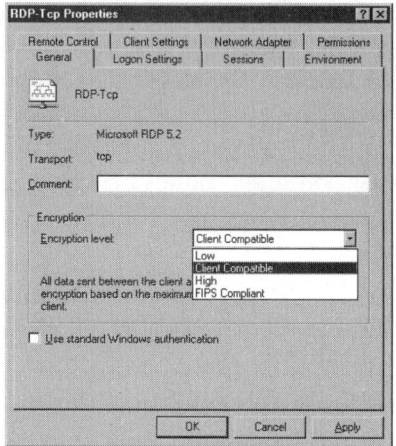

Limitations of Windows Server 2003 Terminal Services

Microsoft has truly brought a great platform to market with Windows Server 2003 Terminal Services. However, as with any product, there are certain limitations or situations in which Terminal Services by itself doesn't fit the bill.

The limitations can be broken down in a few key areas:

- Load balancing
- Secure remote access solution
- Lack of an enterprise toolset for management
- Lack of a built-in application deployment solution
- Small list of supported clients
- Limited client-side functionality

Load Balancing Limitations

Microsoft has two options for load balancing in a Terminal Services environment. The first option is to implement the Windows Load Balancing Service (WLBS) that is now available in all versions of Windows Server 2003 (Windows 2000 Advanced and Datacenter Server previously had this feature). WLBS uses a *virtual IP* for the group of servers participating in the service. Up to 32 nodes may aggregate to form a single vir-tual IP that users can connect to for sessions. When a user session comes in, the servers that are part of the cluster (not true clustering) determine which server will service the incoming request. A user's session will continue to be serviced from that server until the session is terminated through a process known as *affinity*. If the user terminates his or her session, subsequent connections to the virtual IP will most likely redirect to one of the other available nodes. What then, are the true limitations of WLBS? First, it is a user-load based algorithm. As users start sessions, they are "loaded" onto the servers in the cluster "evenly," the old "one for me, one for you, one for me, and so on." If a user on ServerA launches a process that consumes a high percentage of the resources for an extended duration, WLBS is "unaware" of that situation and will continue to load users proportionally on the servers. This process continues despite the fact that ServerA may be nearing 100-percent resource utilization with 50 users, while ServerB and ServerC are at 30 percent with 50 users. WLBS would allow the 51st session to start on ServerA.

The second major limitation of WLBS is that it uses a "fabricated" Media Access Control (MAC) (hardware) address for the virtual IP. Certain enterprise switches do not allow a single MAC to be associated with more than one switch port at any time. The situation arises as follows:

1. ServerA boots to production with local IP 192.168.0.1 and converges in the WLBS cluster as NODE1 with virtual IP 192.168.0.100.

2. ServerA is plugged into switch port 1.

3. The switch "listens" to network traffic to allow it to build an Address Resolution Protocol (ARP) table (to know where to send packets).

4. The switch associates Port 1 with ServerA's real MAC and the virtual MAC from the convergence.

5. ServerB boots to production with local IP 192.168.0.2 and converges in the WLBS cluster as NODE2 with virtual IP 192.168.0.100.

6. ServerB is plugged into switch port 2.

7. The switch continues listening.

8. The switch associates port 2 with ServerB's real MAC and then associates the virtual MAC with port 2.

9. Since the virtual MAC isn't associated with both ports, only one of the servers will actually be able to respond.

Workarounds include updating switch code, trying various combinations of multicast and unicast with WLBS, statically entering the virtual MAC in the ARP table for each port necessary, or plugging all the servers that are "converging" into a hub and then uplinking that to the core switch. Beware of switch port flooding that can occur by allowing your switches to propagate the ARP broadcasts as a result of the convergence required for WLBS to function correctly.

Let's look at the second method of load balancing Windows Server 2003 Terminal Services without Citrix MetaFrame Presentation Server 3.0. This method of load balancing involves third-party hardware from vendors such as F5 Networks, Cisco, and Foundry Networks. Each of these vendors creates hardware that can more intelligently route incoming Terminal Services sessions (and other traffic types) to the least busy server. Some of the devices are more intelligent that others. Typically, the prospect of creating a redundant hardware solution just for Terminal Services is prohibitively expensive, often costing tens of thousands of dollars.

If your goal is to use the session directory feature of Windows Server 2003 Terminal Services, Microsoft recommends you implement one of the previously discussed technologies, WLBS or Hardware Load Balancers. We will see in later chapters how Citrix MetaFrame Presentation Server's built-in load balancing is much more elegant and easy to implement than either option available to Terminal Services alone as a solution to high availability. Presentation Server's load balancing is far more dynamic and can direct user sessions based on a myriad of criteria. In addition to the standard user-load criteria that WLBS uses, Presentation Server can also load balance based on CPU utilization, memory utilization, time of day, and the subnet from which the client is establishing the session, just to name a few.

Secure Remote Access Solution

One of the biggest challenges that we face as administrators of Terminal Services solutions is providing users with secure remote access. Simply providing the user with remote access isn't enough these days. Access must be simple to use, adaptable to the user's connection, and totally secure for both the session data and the servers running the sessions. Various options exist to attempt to meet these needs. Virtual private networking (VPN), Remote Authentication Dial-In User Service (RADIUS), SecureID, and Server Publishing with ISA and Network Address Translation (NAT) are a few of the more popular methods to provide secure remote access to your Terminal Services deployment. Let us examine each of these options in more detail.

Server Publishing with Microsoft's ISA Server and NAT are very similar concepts as far as a remote access solution to Terminal Services is concerned. The idea is to place a device or service between the "outside" and the Terminal Services. This device or service will screen incoming requests specifically for the types of traffic you are expecting to receive on the terminal servers. While this goes a long way in helping to protect the servers from attack where system vulnerabilities or missing patches are concerned, the terminal servers are still exposed to the outside with only a username and password between the "bad guys" and your servers. If one of your users wants to access the terminal servers from a kiosk computer at the trade show, you may still be out of luck. Even if the kiosk computer has the RDP client, do they have the correct ports open to allow it to traffic out? Can you install a VPN client?

Virtual private networking is a popular method to allow users to gain remote access to the internal network. Depending on how they are implemented, VPN tunnels can provide secure access across virtually any connections. Issues with VPN solutions typically center on user configuration of the client-side piece to establish the tunnel, portability of the VPN solution from platform to platform, and split-tunneling. RADIUS and SecureID can provide an additional layer of security through confirmation that the device trying to establish the connection is legitimate. VPN client configuration can be challenging even for some of the best engineers in the business. Depending on which vendor you implement, the configuration and supportability can vary widely. Some VPN clients don't work well or reliably across digital subscriber lines (DSL). Some VPN clients don't work well with software that already exists on the client's computer. Some VPN solutions don't have client software for Mac OS X, Linux, and so forth. And of course, our personal favorite situation: you send a user home from work with the VPN client software, detailed directions on how to install and configure this software, and the next morning you arrive at your office with the user standing at your door with his computer in his hands explaining how *your* VPN client broke it and it won't boot.

The biggest problem from the standpoint of the VPN is that it allows any clients (that successfully connect) to bring all their problems to the corporate network. Split-tunneling is the capability for the VPN client to "interact" with other networks while in the active process of maintaining a VPN tunnel into your network. If split-tunneling is enabled, it allows the client that establishes the VPN tunnel to maintain connectivity with nonsecure networks, such as public LANs or the Internet. This exposes the private network to the possibility of attack via the client that establishes the VPN tunnel. Split-tunneling is a decidedly bad thing. To clarify, the possibility of split-tunneling can theoretically provide "bad guys" on the Internet the ability to route through the user's computer at home and into your production network. Viruses on home computers, spyware, unpatched operating systems, and more are now "on" your network attaching to your servers—hope you didn't have any plans for the weekend. One possible fix for this is to issue the user a company controlled device, something you can lock down with your own security measures. Secure Socket Layer (SSL)-based VPN with Client and Server certificates promises to help eliminate a good deal of these kinds of headaches, but it doesn't go very far in the portability category. Unless the user can "bring" her certificate to the device, she will not be able to establish a session.

We can see how secure remote access can be a real challenge. In Chapter 10, we discuss in detail several methods of providing secure remote access to users leveraging a feature included in Citrix MetaFrame Presentation Server 3.0. This feature set includes Secure ICA, SSL Relay, Web Interface, and Secure Gateway. We will see how users can be anywhere they have an Internet connection and be able to securely and easily access their applications and data.

Lack of an Enterprise Toolset for Management

Windows Server 2003 has some tremendous centralized and remote management capabilities built in. From group policy to security templates, from Remote Desktop for Administration to WMI, the toolset is vast. However, there is a chink in the armor. There are several tools to do several jobs inside a Terminal Services-only world. No single toolset has been created by Microsoft to assist Terminal Services administrators in centrally managing their servers. In fact, the Terminal Services Manager tool found on every Windows NT 4.0, Windows 2000, and Windows Server 2003 is based (almost entirely) on the WinFrame Administrator (later MetaFrame) tool (MFADMIN.EXE). For those of you still running MetaFrame Presentation Server 1.0 or older, try launching the Terminal Services Manager and the Citrix Server Administrator and do your own comparison.

The point is that we have several tools that we have to master in order to perform our job as a terminal server admin without Citrix. A single framework for managing large-scale Terminal Services deployments is missing. Citrix MetaFrame Presentation Server provides that Enterprise Toolset through the existing Presentation Server Management Console and the new Access Suite Management Console, both part of the Citrix MetaFrame Access Suite that includes Presentation Server 3.0.

NOTE

The Presentation Server Management Console is the new name for the Citrix Management Console tool from MetaFrame Presentation Server 1.0.

Lack of Built-in Application Deployment Solution

Windows Server 2003 provides a good foundation for installing and managing software on servers, whether remote installation routines for application install, Group Policy based application package installs, or just the basic functionality that exists thanks to the Windows Installer Service 2.0. However, two major features are missing when it comes to enterprise-level application deployment.

The first issue relates to the ability to schedule the deployment and removal of applications or updates to servers centrally. Now before you drop us a note, yes, we have heard of Microsoft's SMS and the various other technologies that exist as third-party software to perform this function. However, there again, we are purchasing more software, creating more infrastructure, and creating more support burden to be able to perform this function. In addition, we may be involving more vendors to manage. In our efforts to reduce complexity, we inadvertently created more.

The second issue is the ability to create a package or modify an MSI. Some excellent products exist on the market today from InstallShield and Wise Solutions to allow developers and administrators alike to create and modify MSI packages. We strongly recommend both of these products to any Terminal Services administrator out there. However, we're looking, again, for something more "built in" to the product, which is where Installation Manager for Citrix MetaFrame Presentation Server 3.0 comes in. Installation Manager provides a complete solution for packaging, distributing, and removing applications, hotfixes, service packs, and more, all integrated into the Presentation Server Management Console.

Small List of Supported Clients

While the majority of the computing ecosystem is a Windows 32-bit world, broader support for a heterogeneous client base is needed for a successful Terminal Services infrastructure. Currently, Microsoft supports the following list of RDC (and older RDP) clients:

- Win32
- WinCE (certain versions direct from Microsoft, others via OEM)
- Pocket PC (also known as Windows Mobile)
- Web Client (ActiveX plug-in for Win32 version of Internet Explorer)
- Mac OS X

The level of functionality varies widely based on the client version. Many advanced functions (such as drive, print, and com port redirection) exist only for the Win32 client. As administrators and enterprises embrace centralized computing, eventually the question arises as to how to continue to reduce costs and complexities. Replacing the Windows Desktop PC with a thin client or Windows-based terminal can provide substantial return on investments. Having greater feature set support on non-Win32 clients will become necessary.

Citrix MetaFrame Presentation Server 3.0 has a very long list of supported clients, everything from Win32 to MS-DOS, from Mac System 7.1 to OS X, Windows CE, UNIX/Linux and OS/2, just to name a few. And for those hard-to-please operating systems, Citrix offers the Java client. To give you a glimpse into how long Citrix Systems has been building clients for their MultiWin technology, let's examine the MS-DOS client in more detail. What is the oldest version of MS-DOS supported with a Citrix Client? Give up? MS-DOS 3.3. How old is MS-DOS 3.3, you may ask? Well, let's answer that question with another question.

What was the largest physical or logical partition size that the file allocation table (FAT) version of MS-DOS 3.3 could support? Another stumper... the answer is 32MB (no, that is not a typo, it is 32MB). Remember the good ole days of 32MB hard drives?

Limited Client-Side Functionality

While the RDC 5.x client has come a long way since its inception in 1998, several critical areas leave something to be desired when running a remote session via Terminal Services alone. Drive redirection, or the ability to access your local client drives inside the session, is only supported on the RDC client while running on Windows XP desktops. Citrix supports this functionality on all versions of Windows, Mac OS, and UNIX/Linux.

Printer redirection, or the ability to print to your (logically or physically) locally attached printers on the client device while in the session, is only supported on Windows XP desktops with the RDC client. Citrix supports all their clients with redirected printing, even MS-DOS and Windows CE (with some limitations of the client OS, of course).

The RDC client provides no mechanism for delivering role-based access to applications, data, and information. Additionally, there is no mechanism to integrate such access into the client's desktop to provide easy access to the Terminal Services infrastructure. If a user wants to execute a calculator installed on the terminal servers, he will have to navigate the desktop of the terminal server or adjust to the "window within Windows" phenomenon. RDC lacks a feature that Citrix leverages called *seamless windows*. This feature removes the "window-wrapper" around applications to allow the client to work within the application as if it were locally installed. Refer to Figures 1.5 and 1.6 for examples of the "window within Windows" available via Terminal Services.

Figure 1.5 Navigating a Terminal Services Desktop to Launch an Application

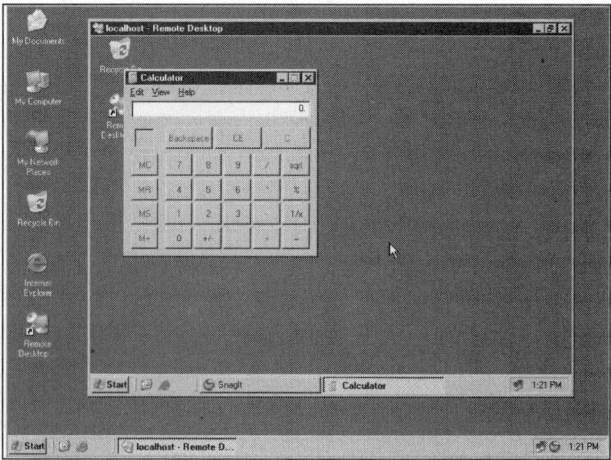

The last two features focus on *perception of performance* within a Terminal Services session. The first feature is the lack of support for multiple monitors. More and more technical and high end users are requiring multi-monitor support to more efficiently

accomplish their jobs. The second feature is really more of an area of features concerning multimedia acceleration.

Figure 1.6 "Window within Windows" when Launching an Application

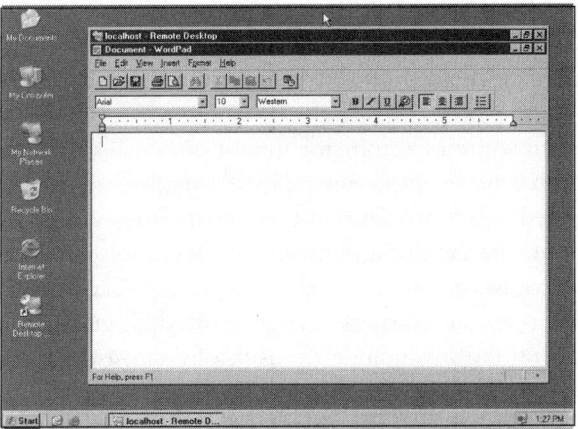

Administrators and users of server-based or centralized computing expect to be able to centralize nearly all of the applications that they use on a regular basis. As deployments of this technology increase, the integration of multimedia rich applications increases. Users expect to have the same experience use Flash and Shockwave animations through their Terminal Services session as they would if they executed the application locally on a fully functional desktop. Terminal Services is not optimized by default for such operations, nor does the RDC client offer such options. Citrix has created a series of technologies included in the MetaFrame Presentation Server 3.0 platform that greatly enhance the multimedia experience through a Presentation Server session. Citrix refers to the various technologies as SpeedScreen, which allows for better handling of multimedia through the session. More details on this and other Citrix performance increasing technologies are covered in Chapter 2 and throughout the book.

Summary

In this chapter, we examined the history, features, and limitations of Terminal Services. We started with an introduction to Terminal Services, examining the logical basis of Terminal Services and how it works. We gained a basic understanding of presentation layer protocols and their critical role in the Terminal Services computing world.

Next, we shifted our attention to the history of Terminal Services. We learned about MultiWin, the core technology built by Citrix Systems and licensed back to Microsoft for inclusion into what we use as Terminal Services today. We discussed the features and limitations of previous versions of Terminal Services to allow us to have a firm understanding of the forces and trends that continue to shape the product. We looked at

Windows 2000's Terminal Services and its multiple modes of operation, to include a first look at Terminal Services Licensing.

We looked in greater detail at the features of Terminal Services in Windows Server 2003. Some of the most striking new features are the improvements made to RDP on the server side and the RDC client, such as the native ability to redirect client drives, printing, audio, and so forth. We discussed the changes made to Terminal Services because of the Microsoft security initiative, the result being increased uptime and a more secure platform out-of-the-box.

Finally, we reviewed some of the major limitations of Terminal Services. We dug into the challenges of load balancing and reviewed the various ways of implementing the Microsoft recommended solutions. One of the major issues with a Terminal Services only solution centers on the lack of an enterprise-level toolset. Terminal Services has no centralized single seat toolset to assist in managing larger Terminal Services farms. We also looked at the client-side limitations such as limited client platform support. Additional client-side limitations include the lack of a consistent feature set across the Remote Desktop Connection Clients and the Remote Desktop Protocol Clients. This inconsistency in the feature set includes drive redirection and printer redirection, to name two. We also discussed desktop integration issues, such as the "window within Windows" and lack of role-based access to the Terminal Services farm and the applications it hosts. We closed with a review of multimedia support issues such as Flash animation and multiple monitor support and how it is lacking in the native Terminal Services solution and client. In the following chapters, we will explore how Citrix MetaFrame Presentation Server 3.0 can "embrace and enhance" Windows Server 2003 Terminal Services to create a truly enterprise solution.

Solutions Fast Track

Hardware Planning

☑ Deciding whether to scale up or out is the first step and usually scaling out wins the day.

☑ Determining what redundancies to build in.

☑ Consideration for applications to be deployed.

☑ Options around Server Virtualization.

Platform Deployment Options

☑ Manual Installation – good for one off servers or test labs.

☑ Unattended or Scripted Installs – good for dissimilar hardware or pre-existing process.

☑ Server Cloning – Excellent for large deployment with identical hardware.

☑ Server Provisioning – the most flexible single method but involves additional complexities and costs.

☑ Hybrid Approach – the most flexible method of all, but requires the greatest level of technical expertise as it encompasses techniques from all platform deployment options.

Microsoft Windows Server 2003 Hardware/ Software Requirements and Recommendations

☑ Dual Processor Pentium 4 Xeon (fastest available with most L1 and L2 cache).

☑ 256–512 MB for the Operating System then plan for 64MB to 128MB per session (depending on applications).

☑ SCSI RAID 1 Ultra-320 15K drives.

☑ Teamed 100Mbps or faster NICs.

Citrix MetaFrame Presentation Server 3.0 Initial Farm Planning

☑ Where to place the terminal services licensing server.

☑ Where to place the Citrix Licensing server.

☑ Home Folder and Terminal Services Profile selection and placement.

☑ Choosing the version of Presentation Server 3.0 needed (Enterprise, Advanced or Standard).

☑ Data Store selection for the Citrix configuration database.

☑ Dedicated Data Collector placement.

Citrix MetaFrame Presentation Server 3.0 Hardware/Software Requirements and Recommendations

☑ 400MB for Enterprise Edition of Presentation Server.

☑ Windows Installer Requirements (2.0 or greater).

☑ JRE 1.4.1_02 or higher.

☑ Web Interface will require IIS 5 or 6 with ASP.

Frequently Asked Questions

The following Frequently Asked Questions, answered by the authors of this book, are designed to both measure your understanding of the concepts presented in this chapter and to assist you with real-life implementation of these concepts. To have your questions about this chapter answered by the author, browse to **www.syngress.com/solutions** and click on the **"Ask the Author"** form. You will also gain access to thousands of other FAQs at ITFAQnet.com.

Q: I am considering running Windows Server 2003 Terminal Services without using Citrix MetaFrame Presentation Server. Due to the lack of an enterprise management toolset, what would be the largest number of servers (thereby users) that you would recommend?

A: The answer to this question depends heavily on what types of users and applications you will be running. If the user population has similar needs as far as the application list, the servers could be built nearly identically, and therefore a larger farm of terminal servers without Citrix would be manageable. If your goal is to deploy a single application, the farm of terminal servers could be quite large to support this, upward of 10 to 20 servers, supporting 500 to 2000 user sessions. If the users have different application needs, this number would decrease sharply.

Q: Is there an updated RDC client for my Win16 users?

A: No. Microsoft hasn't created a newer version of the RDC client for Win16 platforms. However, users who still have the Win16 client from previous versions of Terminal Services will be able to connect to the new terminal servers (with decreased functionality).

Q: I have been around Terminal Services and Citrix for quite some time. There has always seemed to be a debate over whether to use dual processor or quad processor servers. Which is best for a Terminal Services implementation, with or without Citrix?

A: The answer to this question lies in whether the applications you are running on the terminal servers are multithreaded and behave well on the third and fourth processors of a quad. Typical applications found on users desktops and subsequently moved to the terminal servers do not scale well on the third and subsequent processors. The reason is simple: applications are written for workstations that at best have two processors. How many of your workstations in the past have been quads or eight-way processor machines? The real answer would be thorough testing of your application set to determine the benefits, if any, that advanced multiprocessor servers may bring.

Chapter 2

Introduction to Citrix MetaFrame Presentation Server 3.0

Solutions in this Chapter:

- **History of Citrix MetaFrame**
- **Understanding the MetaFrame Architecture**
- **Capabilities of Citrix MetaFrame Presentation Server 3.0**
- **How MetaFrame Fills the Gaps in Terminal Services' Capabilities**

☑ **Summary**

☑ **Solutions Fast Track**

☑ **Frequently Asked Questions**

Introduction

Citrix MetaFrame Presentation Server 3.0 (MPS 3.0) is the latest in a line of products from Citrix Systems. Building on the many versions of software before it, MPS 3.0 provides the latest enhancements and features for remote computing. Citrix chose to re-brand the MetaFrame server line as MetaFrame Presentation Server in 2004, to go along with their new MetaFrame Access Suite label. The MetaFrame Access Suite encompasses both the original server software and several other products, including Password Manager and Conferencing Manager that have been developed or purchased by Citrix over the last few years. Together they expand the reach of remote computing.

What is MetaFrame Presentation Server? As the core technology to Citrix's product suite, it is the foundation for the rest of the MetaFrame Access Suite products. As a third-party add-on for Microsoft's Windows Terminal Services, it provides advanced remote access capabilities for system administrators. It interacts with the underlying architecture of Terminal Services to improve the remote application process

Citrix MetaFrame groups their servers into *farms*, a group of Citrix servers with a common set of information, referred to as the *data store*. Within a farm, servers can be broken into different subsets based on everything from function to location.

In this chapter, we look at the history of the MetaFrame products. We also explore how they fill the gaps in Microsoft's Terminal Services technology, and why you might prefer to add MetaFrame to your Terminal Services environment. The decision to add Citrix is not without cost, and understanding the gains involved is critical in deciding to add MPS 3.0 to your environment.

History of Citrix MetaFrame

Citrix has been a driving force behind Microsoft's development of remote access technologies. In the early years of server software development, remote access was a relatively low priority for Microsoft. In 1989, a small third-party company developed a remote access protocol named Independent Computing Architecture (ICA). In 1991, they shipped their first product called Citrix Multi-User.

The field was a fairly niche market, and so Citrix decided to be bold. In 1992, they worked out a licensing agreement with Microsoft for their NT Server software. Over the next few years, they modified the underlying operating system (OS), and in 1995, they released their own OS, Citrix WinFrame.

Based on the NT Server 3.51 OS, WinFrame was in fact an entirely individual system. It incorporated proprietary Citrix technology such as the ICA protocol. It also allowed multiuser remote access in a way that Microsoft had never addressed. WinFrame was an excellent product given the times and the hardware. It was relatively stable, and provided a new level of accessibility to remote users.

Microsoft was never one to ignore a good possibility, so when they released their NT4.0 server software, they also began the process of creating their own multiuser remote application software. When Citrix went back to negotiate the license rights for the NT4.0 server platform, they were told about Microsoft's own plans for remote access.

It was a difficult time for Citrix. Without the license to Microsoft's technology, they could not create a version of their ICA technology compatible with NT4.0. Moreover, with Microsoft having decided to release their own remote access platform, they would lose the advantage of being the primary player in the marketplace. After some intense negotiations, Citrix and Microsoft came up with a partnership for the marketing and development of the Citrix MultiWin technology.

Microsoft incorporated the MultiWin Citrix technology in its release of Windows NT4.0 Terminal Services Edition while Citrix retained the rights to their ICA architecture. In addition, in conjunction with the release of NT 4.0 TSE, Citrix released a new version of their technology known as Citrix MetaFrame 1.0. MetaFrame 1.0 was an add-on technology that expanded the reach of NT4.0 TSE. NT4.0 TSE used RDP as its client technology, and had many holes that prevented many administrators from using it exclusively.

Citrix soon released MetaFrame 1.8 and various upgrades for it. They eventually expanded their support for Windows 2000 Server, and in 2000, they released Citrix MetaFrame XP. Microsoft changed their Terminal Server technology to become a service, and continued adding features to it in an attempt to fill the gaps that remained in Terminal Services.

When Citrix renamed their MetaFrame 1.8 software to MetaFrame XP, they also decided to provide three different levels of the software so that administrators could purchase only the features they needed. And in 2002, Microsoft and Citrix signed a new licensing agreement that gave Citrix access to key underlying Windows software for the development of their next MetaFrame release, MetaFrame Presentation Server 3.0.

With the release of Windows Server 2003, Microsoft again expanded their remote access technology platform to try to fill the gaps in Terminal Services. Citrix continues to restructure and acquire more technologies that will position them as a valued add-on for Microsoft. The rest of this chapter deals with the features of MPS 3.0, and the advantages it gives you over using just Terminal Services.

Understanding the MetaFrame Architecture

MetaFrame Presentation Server uses server farms to organize and manage servers. This allows you to manage many settings as a unit, rather than apply them individually to each machine. Servers in a farm all connect to the same data store, and generally have some features in common that makes grouping them together logical. Farms also provide a method for application publishing. Publishing an application means to provide it to remote users from the server installation. Figure 2.1 shows a basic MetaFrame farm configuration.

Figure 2.1 MetaFrame Farm

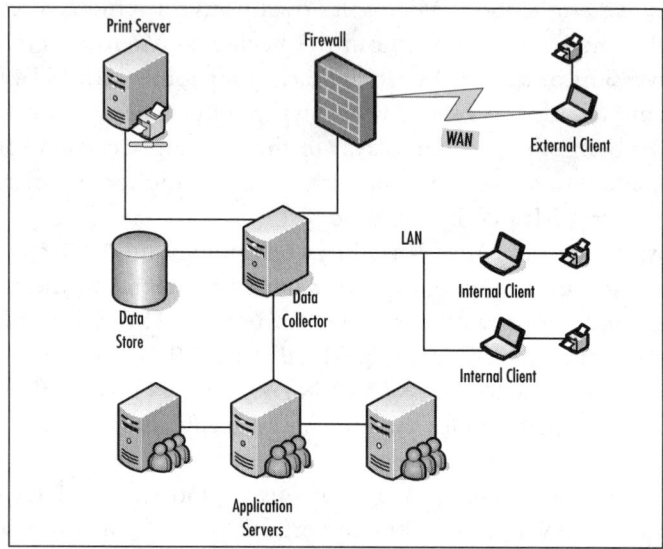

Within the farm model are the two technologies that make the on-demand enterprise function: Independent Management Architecture (IMA) and Independent Computing Architecture (ICA).

Independent Management Architecture

IMA provides the basis for MetaFrame Presentation Server. It is a centralized management subsystem that allows you to define and control the elements of your server farm. In essence, it is the technology that allows you to group servers based on design decisions and not necessarily location.

IMA runs on every server in the MetaFrame farm. It communicates through TCP ports 2512 and 2513 by default, although they can be changed to fit your network's needs. The IMA service allows users to connect to the server for published applications, and can be started and stopped from the services manager. When IMA is stopped, users are no longer able to connect to the server; however, current connections are maintained.

Independent Computing Architecture

ICA is the communications protocol used by the ICA client software and the MetaFrame servers. It provides optimized transport of data between the devices, and can function even on low-bandwidth connections such as slow dial-up. ICA works by essentially piggybacking on top of other protocols such as TCP/IP. The TCP/IP header encapsulates the ICA packet, and on the receiving end, the ICA software handles the functions required. ICA can be run over several other protocols such as UDP and IPX/SPX.

At its heart, ICA intercepts and transports screens from the server that a published application runs on to the client PC. It then takes the user's return input and transmits it back to the server for processing. The data is transmitted on standard network protocols such as TCP between the client and the server.

On the client side, ICA intercepts user's interaction with the presented application and sends it back to the server. This includes mouse movement, clicks, typing, and anything that would cause a screen refresh. The ICA client is a minimal application, and requires few resources on a workstation to run. Citrix provides ICA clients for a variety of technology platforms.

The ICA client works by queuing and transmitting anything the user does to affect the state of the application. The transmission rate can be modified on the client side to happen with each mouse movement or keystroke, or to queue up a certain amount of data before sending. If you use the queue feature, be aware that it does impact the seamless feel of the session. Because the keystrokes and mouse movements are queued, the user will not have instant indication on the screen that they happened.

The ICA client also can cache frequently used graphics such as icons and menu items. This improves the client response because they do not have to be downloaded from the server each time they would occur. The client can simply call them from the cache. The size of the cache can be set by the administrator to limit the impact on local storage.

Capabilities of MetaFrame Presentation Server 3.0

MetaFrame Presentation Server 3.0 is a valuable extension for the Windows Terminal Services environment. Although Microsoft has improved on Terminal Services through various upgrades and hotfixes, it still lacks some of the enterprise functionality and ease of use that MPS 3.0 can provide. Here are some highlights of MPS 3.0:

- Enterprise-level management and scalability
- Improved load-balancing criteria
- Published icons that link to server-side software
- Local application interaction with remote files
- Remote software updates and deployment
- Improved printer compatibility and creation
- Real-time monitoring of both MetaFrame and Terminal Services components in a single view
- Resource monitoring for historical data and reporting

Additionally, Citrix uses its own proprietary technology to improve the overall remote experience for users. Together with the Terminal Services architecture, MPS 3.0 can provide a complete end-to-end solution for almost any deployment.

MPS 3.0 Version Information

MetaFrame Presentation Server 3.0 is packaged in three different versions. In theory, this allows administrators to purchase only the tools they require for their environment. In reality, many administrators simply purchase the highest tier to gain access to all of the application functionality. The decision about which version you will purchase is driven more by the feature set you require, and generally not the label. Table 2.1 lists the different MetaFrame Presentation Server editions.

Table 2.1 MetaFrame Presentation Server Versions

Version	Features
Standard Edition	Designed for the small farm environment, the Standard Edition provides many of the common features required by administrators.
Advanced Edition	Provides small and medium-sized installations with advanced scalability and manageability software such as workstation control, session reliability, and advanced Speedscreen acceleration techniques.
Enterprise Edition	Designed for the most demanding installations, Enterprise Edition gives administrators access to all of the tools Citrix provides. The most important improvements are the addition of Resource Management and Installation Management technologies.

Management and Monitoring

Citrix MetaFrame Presentation Server provides a significant level of management and monitoring capabilities for your remote application access. Within the Citrix Management Console (CMC) tool, administrators have access to almost every function of monitoring and reporting they might need. It also allows for role definition, which gives users and groups limited rights within the CMC itself.

Management can be handled on an individual application level, individual server level, or by groups of applications and servers. You can perform hierarchal grouping to keep large environments organized into easily defined areas. You can also connect directly to your servers as either a remote user or a console user. The CMC gives you total control over your MetaFrame Presentation Server architecture. For example, within the CMC you could look up where a user is connected. Once you have him located, you could message that user to log off. If the user's session was hung, you could disconnect it and log it off yourself. You could even remote to that user's connection and shadow him to see what the problem was. Your CMC could warn you that a server is down, or that an application is exceeding the threshold levels you set for it. You can deploy new software fixes through the CMC, or define Citrix-based policies. It really is a one-stop tool.

If you have Citrix's Resource Manager software installed, the CMC can provide real-time status information on your servers and applications. Counters can be set that will alert the monitors in a variety of areas, and can provide paging and e-mail escalation of issues that occur in your farm. If configured correctly, Resource Manager can also provide statistical reporting on everything from individual user access to farm-wide application statistics. It can also provide real-time graphs and data about the current status of the farm.

With the release of MPS 3.0, Citrix also provided a snap-in for the Microsoft Management Console (MMC) platform. The MMC snap-in allows you manage user sessions, monitor the server health, create reporting, and even perform trace analysis. It also lets you launch the CMC for additional functionality, as well as the Web Interface Console and the License Management Console.

Additionally, Citrix provides plug-ins for popular third-party monitoring programs such as Microsoft Operations Manager. This allows you to extend your monitoring to data center staff without the need to provide the CMC. You can also use other third-party tools such as Crystal Reports to access the Citrix data and provide staff with precise reporting information.

Beyond the CMC and plug-ins, the Software Development Kit (SDK) from Citrix provides even more ideas for tools that you can deploy in your environment. In addition, several popular Web sites exist that have even more user-developed scripts and tools to give you more granular control over your servers and user community. Today, there is a wealth of resources available to Citrix administrators from both official and user-driven sources.

Application Publishing

Perhaps the key feature of MPS 3.0 is the ability to publish applications to your user community. When an application is published on a MetaFrame server, it becomes available as an icon to the users and groups defined for it. This can be displayed as an application within a Web page, within users' client software, or even pushed to their desktop.

Application publishing opens up a whole new world for remote computing. Because you can provide a single point of access for all the remote applications, it creates the impression that they are local for the user. Remote and local apps can be blended on the same desktop, and can be managed through appropriate policies and groups. Applications can be launched from different servers without the users realizing that they are touching more than one machine. These multiple connections only consume a single Citrix license as long as the applications are in the same MetaFrame farm.

Along with application publishing, administrators can also load-balance their applications across multiple servers in the farm (or even multiple farms if architected correctly). With a load-balanced environment, administrators can plan for increases in user capacity, take servers out of the farm for upgrades and repairs without impacting the users, and provide fault tolerance in case of server failure.

Published applications are executed entirely at the server level, and the screen data is transmitted back to the clients. Other client components, referred to as *channels*, can also be enabled between the client and the server. Typical channels are local printers, sound, and COM or USB port mapping. With these channels, an administrator can create the illusion that the application is executing locally.

Printer Management

Printer management is also a key function of Citrix's toolset. Keeping track of print drivers in a remote environment is a headache for any administrator; drivers can cause hang-ups and crashes, and poorly implemented print strategies can consume both time and bandwidth. MPS 3.0 gives you the ability to define specific driver mappings, push driver sets to servers that do not have them installed, and define settings for Citrix's Universal Print Driver (UPD). The UPD allows clients that connect with a printer that is not in the allowed list to use the universal driver instead. This driver gives a decent range of functionality to most printers commonly used by clients.

Printer mapping can be controlled in a number of other ways as well. It can be defined in individual user properties for their Terminal Services settings in Active Directory. It can also be defined on a per-connection basis on each server. In addition, using Citrix's policy management, an administrator can also define printer mapping for role-based users.

Within the CMC, it is possible to check each server and see what print drivers are installed. If one is missing, it can be pushed to that server in a relatively quick fashion. Your servers can also be set to propagate any and all print drivers amongst themselves without the need for you to constantly monitor them. Keep in mind, though, that if a rogue print driver gets in to this process, you could spread it to every server in your farm.

Citricks...

A Look to the Future...

The next release of MetaFrame Presentation Server provides a new type of "universal" print client. This new client will be based on EMF technology and provides many of the same features commonly found in third-party print solutions.

Deploying Service Packs and Hotfixes

Keeping your servers up to date is another problem farm administrators frequently face. With the constant stream of hotfixes coming from both Microsoft and Citrix, managing your patch levels and guaranteeing deployment is an important part of your day-to day-activities. Citrix tries to bridge that gap by providing packaging technology to administrators known as Installation Manager (IM).

IM allows administrators to package applications, registry changes, and even hotfixes for deployment. It can create entirely new packages, or use those already created by other install programs such as Windows Installer files with an MSI extension. These applications can be imported into the IM database and executed from a common share.

The benefit in using IM is control over the distribution process from the same tool as your administrative tasks. Servers can be grouped within the IM tool to provide managed distribution of applications. The distribution process can be scheduled to occur at specific times, allowing the gradual rollout of new software and patches. IM is a useful tool for Citrix administrators to keep servers up to date and in good order.

Security Improvements with MPS 3.0

A significant advantage to using remote technology such as MetaFrame Presentation Server is that it provides an increased level of security for both users and administrators. Because of the way access is designed, both the server and client machines are safe from data interception both inside and outside your networks. Here are some features of MetaFrame security:

- **SecureICA** SecureICA allows you to encrypt the ICA transmissions between the client and server machines. Even if the encryption were broken, all the attacker would get is meaningless screen information.

- **Citrix Secured Sockets Layer (SSL) Relay** Usually used with smaller farms without the need for a demilitarized zone (DMZ). It does not provide end-to-end encryption between the servers and clients.

- **Citrix Secure Gateway** Using a gateway server provides complete encryption and firewall transversal. This is the most secure method for access with a public Internet site. It uses two-factor authentication and hides all internal IP address schemes from the user.

- **Virtual private network (VPN) solutions** A dedicated VPN solution is also a good way to provide security for your users. It provides a complete end-to-end tunnel between the user and server, and is the most secure method for access.

Because there is always an element of risk in allowing remote access, administrators should assess what their requirements are for security and plan appropriately. The best solution is always the one that limits exposure to risk from outside forces such as viruses and attackers. With good planning, a Citrix installation can be almost completely secure.

Beyond the security of the connection, there are other considerations for server administrators as well. By allowing or disallowing certain channels to connect, you can provide greater security to your network and servers. For instance, not allowing your users to map their local drives or clipboards will often prevent most virus attacks.

Still, for every feature you disallow, it becomes more of an inconvenience for your users. Often, administrators will be forced to choose between convenience and security. These choices are difficult, and need to be negotiated and explained to the user community.

How MPS 3.0 Fills the Gaps in Terminal Services

We've covered the basics of Microsoft Terminal Services and Citrix MetaFrame Presentation Server. They both offer an impressive feature set, and MetaFrame builds on top of the existing Terminal Services architecture. For some environments, Terminal Services alone might fill the needs for remote access. So why would you decide to choose MPS 3.0 over native Terminal Services?

The unfortunate fact is that Terminal Services has gaps. Despite years of design and upgrade, it still fails to perform some client-server tasks as well as MetaFrame can provide. For the rest of this chapter, we'll address where those gaps are and how MPS 3.0 fills them for you.

Improvements in Terminal Services

Windows Server 2003 provides a number of improvements in Terminal Services capabilities over Server 2000. Microsoft has continued their commitment to improving the basic Terminal Services functionality, and with the improvements of Windows Server 2003, many administrators are considering only using Terminal Services. Citrix is a very useful product, but it is also an expensive one. When you consider licensing costs for Terminal Services Client Access Licenses (CALs), application licenses, and then MetaFrame license costs, it starts to add up to a lot of money.

The improvements that Windows Server 2003 provides lie chiefly in the area of its RDP client. The new RDP 5.2 protocol is thinner and now supports more virtual channels than ever before. RDP can now support clipboard, audio, printer, Component Object Model (COM), and Line Printer (LPT) mappings. It also provides full color depth to 24 bit at 1600x1200, and has clients across almost all platforms (Win32, Win16, DOS, Java, Macintosh, Linux, and others). Windows Server 2003 also supports technology such as smart cards for user authentication.

Windows Server 2003 also provides limited load-balancing capabilities and improved scalability. Load balancing in Windows Server 2003 is limited to node balancing only, which means that you can only balance the servers based on a narrow set of conditions and only with other comparable servers. Windows Server 2003 allows for more users per box than Server 2000 did, and gives remote management capabilities through the Windows Management Instrumentation (WMI) provider. New enhancements to roaming profiles, Group Policy Objects (GPOs), and application compatibility make Windows Server 2003 a valuable improvement over Windows 2000 Terminal Services.

So, Where Are the Gaps?

For all of the advances Windows Server 2003 has made, gaps do still exist. They are primarily in some client functionality, and more importantly with Terminal Services load balancing and application publishing processes. Citrix tries to fill these gaps to provide a reason for using their software.

Application-Level Improvements

Citrix has taken application publishing to a whole new level. With MPS 3.0, administrators have the ability to create applications and publish them to specific groups or users. Although Terminal Services allows you to provide a simple redirect of the RDP client to specific applications on the terminal server, it does not provide direct application publishing. With MPS 3.0, you gain the full capability of MetaFrame's publishing software.

Application publishing is an extremely valuable tool for administrators. When an application is published, your users are presented with an icon that corresponds to the program. That application is tied to an ICA file that contains the information needed for the client to connect to the application. This is everything from the security settings specified to the address information of the server that hosts the application.

Because application publishing gives your users a simple icon to launch a connection, it is much easier to integrate with their existing desktop. As mentioned before, you can provide this application to your users in several ways. Because the ICA client can integrate with your desktop, applications that are published to the users can be pushed to the desktop. This means that they will see an icon on the desktop that will appear to be a local application but will instead launch a remote connection.

Another method of providing applications is with the Citrix Program Neighborhood. The Program Neighborhood will display all of the icons published to a user in a single window, or separated into folders based on application groups. The administrator has complete control over the presentation of the applications, which require a single login for all applications to be displayed.

The third method is to use Citrix's Web technologies and provide the application icons through a Web interface. With Citrix's secure access technology and their Web interface software, you can design and present a Web page with all of your published applications. Users will see only the applications assigned to their ID, and those applications can again be grouped into folders by application suite.

Another advantage to application publishing in Citrix is the ability to use seamless windows. With a seamless window, there is nothing to indicate that the application is not running locally besides the small ICA icon in the taskbar. Users can interact with the application exactly as if it was running locally. They can maximize or minimize it, copy data to or from the application (assuming you have the clipboard channel enabled), and even use drag and drop to move data to and from the application.

Citrix Speedscreen

Both the RDP client and the ICA client use "thin" technology. This means that they are designed to be as streamlined as possible. The goal is to make the user feel like the application is actually being executed locally. This is relatively easy with simple applications, but applications that use many graphics (especially animated graphics) put a strain on the ICA channel. Not much compression can be done on these graphics to speed their presentation.

Citrix developed a proprietary technology called Speedscreen to help address this problem. It allows you to define some settings that improve the presentation speed of heavy graphics in applications. It is especially important with Internet browser applications. In MPS 3.0, Citrix has taken Speedscreen a step further.

The bane of Speedscreen has been streaming applications such as multimedia or flash animation. In MPS 3.0, new virtual channels can be defined that allow you to stream the content untouched between the server and the client. This stream is outside the ICA channel, and can consume quite a bit of bandwidth.

Because the stream is being passed intact to the client, it does require that you have the appropriate codecs and client software installed to handle it. There is a significant trade-off here. The quality can be much better than accessing a streaming video that is being executed on the MetaFrame server itself. However, bandwidth concerns may make this an impossible choice.

MPS 3.0 also allows administrators the choice to use *lossy* compression, a JPEG-based compression scheme that can significantly reduce the size of graphics-laden material prior to transmission to the client. The client interpolates the missing data. In many situations, most clients will never know that lossy compression is being applied. It is not appropriate, however, for applications that require extremely accurate graphics representation.

Using this compression can speed up the client interaction significantly. Web pages with heavy graphics can load up to 10 times faster with compression enabled than without. Obviously, this solution would be less than ideal in situations where reference quality is needed for the graphics such as photo-editing, medical imaging, and so forth For instance, this author implemented a medical imaging package on a Citrix server for a radiology group. Although the images where huge and the load time was 10–15 seconds per image, it would not be appropriate to enable compression to speed up the connection. You wouldn't want your radiologist looking at anything but the highest quality pictures, would you?

Session Disconnections and Reliability

One of the drawbacks of allowing remote users access is the stability of the connection. When users connect to applications across a wide area network (WAN), latency and link reliability become a real concern. It doesn't do any good to provide all sorts of published applications if your users can't reliably access them. Moreover, when remote access is their only means of working, it becomes critical that their sessions are as reliable as possible.

Regardless of the steps you take, there will be hiccups in the connection. Unfortunately, RDP does not handle these hiccups particularly well. Sessions end up disconnected with no warning to the user, and information can be lost. When an RDP session drops to disconnect, it fades to a gray screen and attempts the reconnection process in the background. Citrix has implemented the auto-reconnect in a different fashion with the ICA client. There is no indication to the user that the link has failed, and to the user it looks like a seamless experience. When the session reconnects, it continues as if nothing happened.

Citrix also has implemented keep-alive technology between their clients and servers. A special keep-alive packet can be transmitted at a defined interval from the server to the client. This keep-alive packet does exactly what it says: it lets the client know that the link is still alive and well. By default, the packet is sent once every 60 seconds. This can be increased or decreased to meet your needs.

Citricks...

Using the Keep-Alive Packet

The keep-alive settings can really improve the overall stability of your client sessions. If you maintain connections across a WAN, you will want to lower the default setting. Many administrators with high latency environments lower it to one second.

Yes, that does mean that a packet is sent every second to every client from each server to which they are connected. That might be a concern to your network team. However, the size of the packet is so small that the impact is nonexistent unless your network is already oversaturated. At one second, your disconnected sessions become much more manageable and can usually be traced to a significant network event.

Web Interface

As mentioned previously, Citrix provides a Web interface to their platform. This allows you to display a Web page to your users that contains icons for the applications published to their IDs. These applications can span the farm, or even multiple farms if configured correctly. The Web interface can be configured to run separately on a Web server in your DMZ, and secured with Citrix technologies such as Secure Gateway to provide complete encryption of the data between the client and server. Unfortunately, Terminal Services lacks these advanced features.

When users log in to the Web interface, they are presented with a page containing their application lists. This page can be customized if necessary, or can be left in the default state. Icons will be displayed in the Web interface in the same way they are shown in the Program Neighborhood, complete with folders.

When the user clicks on an icon, an ICA template file is generated and the Citrix client is called. The template file contains all the data required for the Citrix client to make the connection to the published application. This can include color depth, security settings, address schemes, and so forth. If you are using Web Interface and Secure Gateway, your gateway server(s) function as a tunnel through which all traffic flows. Using session tickets and security keys, the integrity of the information is maintained in a secure fashion (Figure 2.2).

Figure 2.2 Secure Gateway Diagram

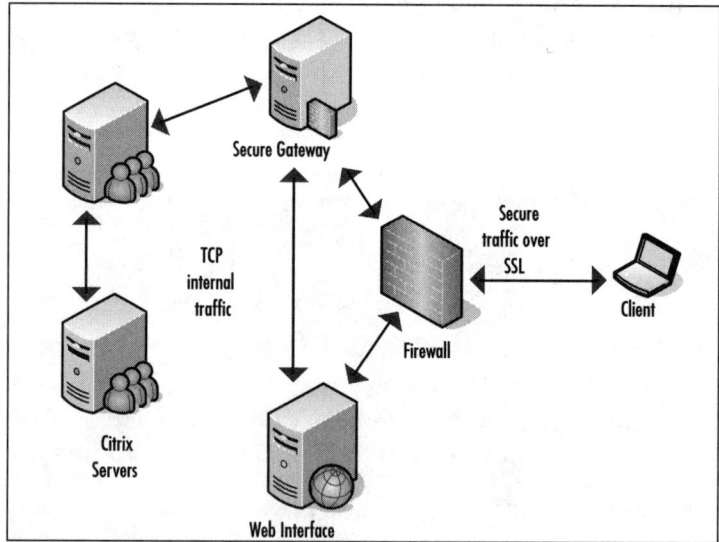

Performance Issues

Microsoft has improved the speed of the RDP 5.2 client significantly. It is now on par with the speed of the ICA protocol, which is a big step forward. ICA maintains its advantage, however, in dealing with the virtual channels. Because of the advances that Citrix continues to make with the ICA protocol and related technologies, in many situations it could still be called "faster." For instance, with its new graphics acceleration and compression technology, pages can load up to 10 times faster in ICA than in RDP.

Printing through ICA using the universal client is usually going to be less bandwidth intensive than the local printer mapping method used by RDP. Because print jobs can cause significant bandwidth consumption, it is a good idea to pay attention to your users' printing habits. Citrix also allows you to engage bandwidth throttling for printers so that they do not lag the sessions of everyone else connected to the server.

As mentioned earlier, Speedscreen technology improves the performance of graphics-intensive applications and Web pages. By using Speedscreen's compression technology, application response can be significantly faster on an ICA connection as opposed to RDP. You can also use the streaming functionality to provide unaltered streams to your users.

Load Balancing

The last major improvement that Citrix provides over Terminal Services is the ability to load balance in a variety of ways. Microsoft's load-balancing technology is entirely dependent on node-to-node balancing. It is network-based only, and to be most effective requires the expensive Windows Server 2003 Enterprise Edition. It also is limited to 32 nodes at most. That is a lot of expense to achieve a limited load-balancing functionality.

Citrix handles load balancing differently than Microsoft does. Any application that is published to multiple servers can be load balanced between them, and the administrator can choose the method of load balancing. Default counters include CPU load, memory usage, and number of connected users. Far more granular counters can be set that allow you to customize load balancing on everything from an application level to a server utilization level.

When an application is load balanced and a user requests a session, MPS 3.0 will look at the current load information for every server defined as part of the load-balanced environment for that application. It will then assign the user to the server with the least utilization as defined by the load-balancing parameters. If a user launches additional applications, the load-balancing technology will try to provide them from the same server to prevent the need for multiple logins.

Because administrators have such advanced control over the load-balancing functionality, it is far easier to use than Microsoft's implementation. Even if you leave it at the default counters, it provides a level of load balancing that is tough to beat for the price. Citrix has a definite advantage when it comes to load-balanced servers and applications.

Summary

MetaFrame Presentation Server 3.0 is a technology platform that runs on Microsoft Windows Server 2003 servers with Terminal Services enabled. Microsoft and Citrix have a long history together and have co-developed much of the underlying technology that allows multiuser remote access to occur on Windows servers. For some administrators, Terminal Services alone will provide enough functionality for their environment. For more demanding installations, Citrix adds value with their MPS 3.0 product.

MPS 3.0 addresses gaps that exist in Terminal Services. These gaps deal primarily with load balancing, client access methods, and application availability. Citrix expands on the very limited options Microsoft gives you in these areas to provide a more seamless experience for both users and administrators.

Beyond the gaps it fills, Citrix also provides some additional features that Terminal Services lacks. Depending on the version of MPS 3.0 you have installed, Citrix can provide everything from role management to advanced reporting and application packaging. By choosing the feature set that is right for you, you can add value to your Terminal Services environment without breaking the bank on Citrix.

Solutions Fast Track

History of Citrix MetaFrame

☑ Citrix developed their ICA technology in the early 1990s.

☑ Through a licensing agreement with Microsoft, Citrix released a stand-alone OS called Citrix WinFrame, which was based on NT 3.51.

☑ Starting with NT 4.0, Citrix became a technology that ran on top of Windows Terminal Services.

Understanding MetaFrame Architecture

☑ MetaFrame is based on two core technologies known as ICA and IMA.

☑ IMA is the underlying technology of the MPS 3.0 servers. It allows multiuser remote access to occur with all of Citrix's advanced features.

☑ ICA is the protocol technology that links together the client and the server. It uses virtual channels to improve the client's seamless experience.

Capabilities of Citrix MetaFrame Presentation Server 3.0

☑ Advanced client connection options for mapping local resources.

☑ Administration through both a Java-based tool and an MMC snap-in.

☑ Advanced monitoring and reporting capabilities.

☑ Improved client printer experience, with advanced printer mapping options.

How MetaFrame Fills the Gaps

☑ Provides advanced load-balancing options over Microsoft's basic node balancing.

☑ Gives administrators more options to improve the speed of the client's experience.

☑ Has increased session reliability features to prevent remote users from being disconnected.

☑ Provides for published applications and access to them through a variety of methods, including Web-based access.

Frequently Asked Questions

The following Frequently Asked Questions, answered by the authors of this book, are designed to both measure your understanding of the concepts presented in this chapter and to assist you with real-life implementation of these concepts. To have your questions about this chapter answered by the author, browse to **www.syngress.com/solutions** and click on the **"Ask the Author"** form. You will also gain access to thousands of other FAQs at ITFAQnet.com.

Q: I keep reading about these license agreements between Microsoft and Citrix. When do they expire?

A: Citrix and Microsoft just announced that they renewed their deal through 2009.

Q: Will the Web Interface protect my servers from external hacking attempts?

A: Web interface alone will not, but you can add on other Citrix components such as Secure Gateway to provide the added security. If used in conjunction with a good firewall, you can isolate your servers from outside attacks.

Q: What if I don't use the new streaming technology in Citrix, and my users access a video stream?

A: Depending on the bandwidth, it's going to be really choppy. You are taking a data stream, converting it to ICA traffic, and then shoving it down the ICA pipe. Playback is seldom flawless and frequently unusable.

Q: I only have the Standard Edition of MPS 3.0. Can I use the Web Interface?

A: Yes, Web Interface is included as part of the basic package. Other Citrix products may not work without Advanced or Enterprise Edition.

Q: I already use SMS to push my applications. What would I gain from using Citrix's Installation Manager?

A: Depending on how advanced your SMS infrastructure is, not much. Installation Manager does not have the full range of packaging options that SMS can provide, and the interface is not as easy to use. However, you do gain the benefit of having the data in the same management tool (the CMC) and you can use it to publish SMS–created packages that are in a .msi format.

Chapter 3

Installation Planning and Requirements

Solutions in this Chapter:

- **Hardware Planning**

- **Platform Deployment Options**

- **Microsoft Windows Server 2003 Hardware/Software Requirements and Recommendations**

- **Citrix MetaFrame Presentation Server 3.0 Initial Farm Planning**

- **Citrix MetaFrame Presentation Server 3.0 Hardware/Software Requirements and Recommendations**

Introduction

Planning the deployment of Citrix MetaFrame Presentation Server 3.0 is a very in-depth process. Since Presentation Server and the underlying Terminal Services platform will be required in many deployments to integrate into nearly every process an organization may have, careful consideration and forethought must be given as to how best to introduce the technology. As with any major initiative undertaken in our current information technology shops, much thought is given on how to provide the greatest chance for success of new deployments that leverage as many features of the new products being introduced as possible, while reducing risk to the current environment—and doing all this as inexpensively as possible. Careful planning is frequently the difference between a successful implementation and a failed deployment. Careful planning can be the difference between happy users and unhappy ones, as it can affect the performance of the overall network even if we are only conducting a project on one aspect of the network. This is a very serious issue.

In this chapter, we look at the various pre-installation tasks that must be considered in order to minimize risks to our deployment, while allowing for easy expansion and growth in the future. Our first topic in this chapter is hardware planning. Hardware planning is a very large process that includes everything from selecting a vendor to evaluating user session load on the various platforms we are testing. Next, we turn our attention to platform deployment options, allowing us to investigate exactly *how* we are going to deploy Windows Server 2003 and configure our newly selected hardware. Deployment method selected, we begin a thorough review of the requirements and recommendations for hardware and software when installing Windows Server 2003. We complete the chapter with a look into the concepts surrounding Citrix MetaFrame Presentation Server farm design and the hardware and software required thereof.

Hardware Planning

Hardware planning is the process of selecting and testing the actual computer hardware from which our Windows Server 2003-based Citrix MetaFrame Presentation Servers will operate. Hardware planning is a cyclical operation. Typically, the process involves selecting hardware that is compatible with the operating system, estimating the size of the servers required and then performing adequate load testing. Load testing, or stress testing, involves loading the server with sessions until a bottleneck is reached. Correct the bottleneck and then retest. Repeat this process as necessary until the desired number of connections per server is reached or you have exhausted the capacity of the hardware. The last step would be to plan for future growth, so scale your hardware with an eye on what would be expected of this solution six months, 12 months, and two years from today. We are going to look at hardware planning from an architect's viewpoint. We will look at the "big picture" pieces such as horizontal vs. vertical scaling and platform deployment options.

Horizontal vs. Vertical Scaling

The argument as to whether it is better to scale up or scale out our Citrix Presentation Server farms is nearly as old as the concept of server-based computing itself. Scaling up is the process of servicing more user sessions on the same hardware or increasing session density within the server through internal upgrades, such as four processors instead of two. Scaling out is the process of servicing more user sessions by adding more physically or logically separate servers to accommodate an increase in user session load. For a given number of user sessions, is it better to service them on more "smaller" servers or fewer "larger" servers? The argument arose shortly after Citrix introduced the Load-Balancing Option License for WinFrame nearly a decade ago. Today, load balancing is built into all versions of MetaFrame Presentation Server except Standard (or "S"). We will explore the differences between Presentation Server versions later in this chapter. Additionally, we should consider the "type" of session that our users will leverage. Accessing the farm from an internal ICA thin client will require less resources and planning typically than external access.

The ability to service user session load across more servers, or scaling out, has its advantages. Lower user session density on a given server translates to less impacted user sessions in the event of hardware failure. This also allows for greater flexibility during hardware or software maintenance windows, again with fewer users impacted. However, there are disadvantages to scaling out. More servers with lower user session densities mean more servers to license and maintain. More power requirements, more rack space, more components to replace when they fail, more Windows Server 2003 licenses to purchase—in general, just more to support and maintain. Increased cost in both hard and soft dollars, due to these factors, can make scaling out prohibitively expensive.

The flip side of higher user session densities on fewer, larger servers also has certain advantages. Less hardware to support and maintain, possibly less rack space, probably fewer Windows Server 2003 licenses to purchase, and overall, better utilization of software and hardware costs through the economies of scale.

The argument seems on the surface to be decidedly one-sided. Scaling up is the way to go, or so it seems. In the cruel, unforgiving reality of a production deployment, however, scaling out nearly always wins the day over scaling up. There are several reasons for this, but really none is "logically based." One would think that a four or quad processor server would be cheaper than two dual processor servers, when in fact that is usually not the case. A typical 2U rack-mount Dual Xeon server with 4GB of memory costs about 1/3 to 1/4 as much as a typical 4U rack-mount Quad Xeon server with 8GB of memory. Therefore, from a hardware standpoint, you can buy two to four times the number of dual processor servers as you can quad processor servers. For those of you who are interested, eight-way processor servers are even more skewed. Vendors produce even fewer eight-way servers than quads, so the economies of scale are even at a greater loss. Hopefully, money will not be the determining factor in the long run. A single eight-way processor server simply doesn't have the "oomph" that four dual-processor servers have.

The second issue with scaling up instead of out is due to design considerations within the operating system that is installed on the target hardware. Terminal Services' purpose in life is to "virtualize" a desktop computer for the remote user session. A typical desktop workstation contains a single processor, and hopefully enough memory for the operating system and an adequate amount of memory remaining for the applications that a single user would use. If the workstation processor becomes overwhelmed due to the demand the user places on the system, overall performance only affects the single user of that workstation. If we take the user desktop environment and "virtualize" it via a Terminal Services session, we can see how this can compound the problem. We can look further into this scaling discussion by comparing the differences in *roles* that can be placed on a given server. A typical terminal server will have many more active processes running in the operating system than the same server hardware functioning as a mail or database server. To expound upon this point further, consider a typical Windows Server 2003 in the role of domain controller running on a dual processor server with 4GB of memory. The domain controller has roughly 30 processes actively competing for the hardware resources at any given time. That same server functioning as a terminal server may have thousands of processes competing for the resources at any given point. Now, one could argue that the single process, WINWORD.EXE, for a user executing Microsoft Word on a terminal server has far less impact on a server than the single process NETLOGON.EXE running on the domain controller to facilitate the authentication of the domain services. Therein lays the crux of the matter. Typically, it is not the single process that causes the load on the terminal server, it is the juggling act that the operating system must maintain to service the user sessions as evenly and quickly as possible. Occasionally, however, that single process *may* impact the overall performance of all user sessions on the server if the process demands a disproportionate amount of system resources either through user action or faulty application design. The result is that during planning, we as architects must plan for normal load that a server would incur during typical operations. We must also plan for the occasions when abnormal load is introduced to the server or server farm.

NOTE

The ability to perform load balancing at the user session level is provided as a base function of the operating system in Windows Server 2003 called Windows Load Balancing Service (WLBS, previously known as Network Load Balancing). Citrix MetaFrame Presentation Server 3.0 Advanced and Enterprise editions provide much greater control over load balancing through techniques Citrix developed years ago for larger WinFrame server farms. Today, larger Terminal Services implementations leverage the powerful load-balancing features of Presentation

> Server due primarily to the greater degree of control and lack of certain noted limitations of the WLBS.

To assist us in planning for and selecting the appropriate hardware for our Presentation Server 3.0 farm, we must explore some of the possible bottlenecks that can occur in a typical Presentation Server deployment. The following list presents basic information for consideration and is not an exhaustive compilation of all potential scalability concerns for terminal servers. Primarily, the following list of bottlenecks is to aid in selecting a hardware platform through the basic components of that platform, namely central processing unit (CPU), memory, disks, network interface cards (NICs), and the limitations of the operating system. An exhaustive pilot should be conducted to determine the baseline for a given server platform prior to introducing that platform into production.

CPU performance obviously has the greatest impact on user perception of performance during periods of intense processor utilization on the server. When users start a session on a Presentation Server, there is a great deal of processor time required to complete the authentication, apply the group policy objects, run the various login scripts, redirect the appropriate user devices (for example, drives and printers), and present the user session with the desktop or published application. Similarly, during logoff, the processor resources of the server are in greater demand than during a typical session. Periods of disproportionate logons or logoffs can cause a greater load on the servers than at other times. These periods of peak login/logoffs are typically associated with shift changes and start of the business day times. Additionally, lunch period and formalized break times can cause similar resource utilization issues, due to the frequency of logon and logoff operations. Multiple higher performance processors can assist with overcoming some of these issues. A solid recommendation would be to start with a server capable of dual processors and perform very detailed testing of your specific application needs to determine if scaling up to a quad processor server (or higher) will provide further benefit.

We must also consider the relationship between memory and disk subsystems on the server. A server can become memory bound through a variety of ways. If user session density is too high, available memory will be too low to adequately service the user sessions on the server. If flaws in applications, system drivers, or the operating system are present, these memory leaks can result in a similar memory-bound situation. Insufficient memory can masquerade as other system resource issues. If a server is low on available memory, the operating system will *swap* information from physical memory to virtual memory in the page file of the operating system. A memory-bound server in this case may actually report excessive disk times indirectly caused by the low system memory situation. Additionally, you will see this performance issue arise if the page file is not configured to be large enough, is placed on a volume with limited space, or on a volume that does not use the NT File System (NTFS). Memory minimums should be considered when detailing the specifications of the server platform for testing or building your production solutions. Consider the first 256MB to 512MB of the server's memory as reserved for the operating system. An average user session today using Microsoft Office 2003-based products, Internet Explorer, and a few line-of-business applications can easily consume 64MB to 128MB of memory. With that being said, consider any "special" applications that you know are greater consumers of memory in your environment and plan accordingly.

Disk subsystems can be a challenge to diagnose and overcome. Typically, disk utilization should be low on Presentation Servers. The logic behind such an assertion is that Presentation Servers typically access application data across the network and really shouldn't "store" information locally. The use of the network file shares translates into lower disk times, typically, for the Presentation Servers. We have several options when it comes to selecting the disk subsystem for our servers. We have Integrated Drive Electronics (IDE), Small Computer Systems Interface (SCSI), Boot from storage area network (SAN), and solid-state memory drives from which to choose. Which is the best option? Which solution will produce the best bang for the buck? Let's consider IDE-based systems. IDE drives are very inexpensive compared to the other solutions. They typically don't require expensive controllers to run them, and the new Serial Advanced Technology Attachment (ATA) devices are bursting at 150MB throughput. IDE sounds good on the surface, but in reality, the Achilles heel of this platform is also what makes it so affordable. IDE (whether Parallel ATA or Serial ATA) on a Windows platform only supports multiple operations when they are spread across multiple channels. On a terminal server, there will undoubtedly be multiple simultaneous read and write operations, thus exposing this limitation, so… IDE is out as an option for most.

SCSI disks with a hardware Redundant Array of Inexpensive Disks (RAID) controller typically provide the best cost to benefit ratio. SCSI (especially RAID) controllers support the multiple input/output requests that characterize a terminal server. SCSI-based RAID drive sets provide a vast improvement over IDE and ATA drive sets. The RAID controller (not the CPU and IDE chipset) controls all the disk operations. The RAID card controls the drives via its own on-board CPU and memory. This allows the server CPU(s) to continue servicing requests without wasting time reading and writing to disk. Think of the RAID control as the "administrative assistant" to the CPU(s). In addition to the performance benefits gained through SCSI-based RAID controllers, there is the obvious fault tolerance benefits gained from creating RAID 1 Mirrored Sets or RAID 5 Fault Tolerance stripes.

Boot-from-SAN and solid-state memory drives can be excellent solutions to environment-specific needs. Boot-from-SAN allows you to leverage your considerable investment in your SAN and lower the cost per server (since there would be no local disks) for implementing your terminal servers. Boot-from-SAN may, however, prove slower than some of the newer faster SCSI RAID-based hard drives and can be prohibitively expensive if the SAN doesn't already exist.

Solid-state memory drives have come a long way since their inception a couple of decades ago. A few companies today make random access memory (RAM) drives that fit into most standard hot-plug device slots. These devices, while a little pricier than conventional disks, provide amazing throughput and make for great solutions to disk-bound servers. If you have servers that are disk-bound, a RAM drive can go a long way to improving performance by reducing and in some cases eliminating this bottleneck.

Network bottlenecks can occur anytime an application that is executed by Presentation Server doesn't actually exist on the server itself. For instance, Microsoft Word will typically install locally on the Presentation Server, but the data normally exists somewhere else on the network. This is even more true for client server applications such as Peoplesoft or SAP. While the bandwidth used by the sessions the server is hosting is relatively low, the network requirements for those sessions will be substantially higher. There are several ways to address this issue: teamed cards to increase available bandwidth, colocation of the application and data on the Presentation Server, and multihomed servers with network connects that separate session bandwidth from application bandwidth.

Teaming network cards for redundancy is almost always a good idea. This concept is covered in the next section, so we will wait until then to discuss that aspect in more detail. Teaming for increased bandwidth is really more what we are talking about in this section. By aggregating multiple network cards together, their "physical" bandwidth can be logically totaled to provide for more "pipe." Most network cards today support teaming (in various forms), and in some cases the ability to team dissimilar network cards (such as a 10/100Mbps card with a 1Gbps card) if the need arises. We recommend that you always attempt to team identical cards to reduce the complexities and supportability issues that could arise otherwise.

Placing the application and data on the Presentation Server will certainly decrease the amount of traffic required to service the user request, thus eliminating the network as the potential bottleneck. However, this action means we have indirectly created a single point of failure for access to this application. If the data is located on a single Presentation Server, we will most likely not be able to "load balance" the application across the farm; therefore, this option isn't really a viable solution except in certain circumstances.

The last option of multihoming our Presentation Server presents many opportunities to increase performance and in a more limited way to increase fault tolerance. The concept of multihoming servers of all kinds has been around the networking world nearly as long as the network itself! Multihomed servers presented solutions to allow for fault tolerance, increase bandwidth, and in some cases, "private" networks for backup and authentication services. However, historically, Citrix Presentation Server's ancestors had issues with multiple "paths" to a server. In the past, a Citrix server may inadvertently direct a user session to the "wrong" card in a multihomed server scenario, thus creating a denial of service. This problem has been long since fixed, so today we can discuss the benefit of multihoming our Presentation Servers to improve quality of service (QoS). By multihoming our Presentation Servers we can segment our session traffic from our data traffic (and possibly the authentication and backup traffic as well). Placing two "legs" or "routes" to the network also can provide some measure of fault tolerance for access to the specific Presentation Server (although typically this is not as reliable or automatic as teaming). The situation arises due to the nature of application and network access. Let us consider the following scenario. Suppose we have a single Presentation Server that has a single NIC for all user sessions and network data access. The server is servicing 50 user sessions. The applications are all well behaved with the exception of our in-house database system for order tracking. When the application running on the Presentation Server (or client workstation) accesses the database for queries, large amounts of traffic are generated between the server and the database until the request is fulfilled. This translates into periods of slowness for the other user sessions on the server (even though the CPU, memory, and disk performance may be fine). Why? Because all the user sessions and the application data access are contending for the same network link. Consider separating the user sessions and database access onto two separate network cards. Figure 3.1 demonstrates this concept of isolating the "data" network from the "session" network.

Figure 3.1 Multihomed Presentation Server

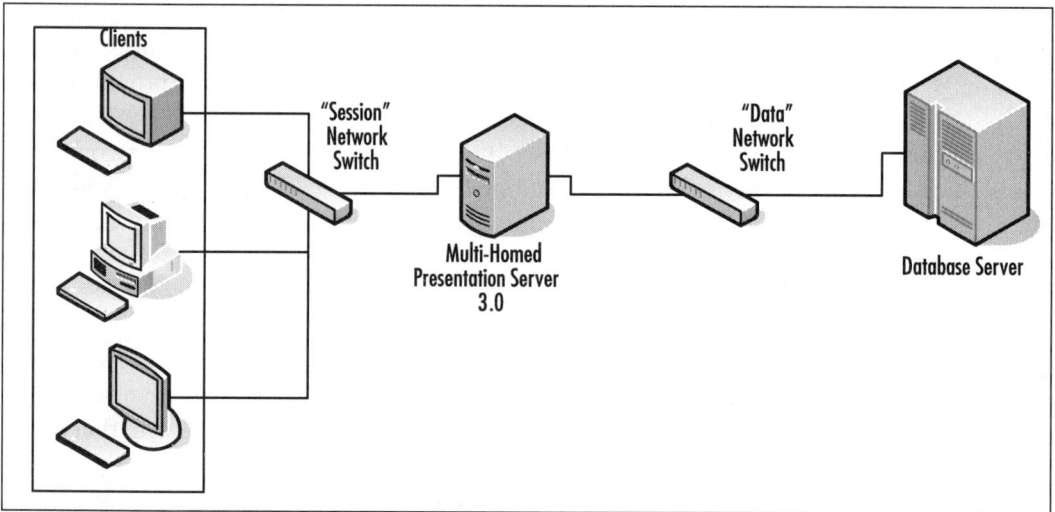

Build In Redundancies

One of the many decisions that face Citrix architects is what types and how much redundancy to build into our production Presentation Servers. The goals of redundancy are to improve uptime and availability of the system where the redundancies are implemented. Redundancy comes in two flavors: high availability and fault tolerance. High availability is concerned with the availability of the system regardless of the status of fault. Citrix Presentation Server 3.0 Advanced and Enterprise editions include the feature of load balancing that provides high availability. A server that is servicing the user session may fail, but the user could simply reconnect and start a new session with limited downtime. Fault tolerance is the ability of a system to overcome the failure of any component of the system without a break in service occurring. Consider a set of hard drives connected to a RAID controller to provide redundancy. If a single disk fails, the remaining disks, through the controller, can provide the fault tolerance without interruption of service. If the controller to which the disks are attached fails, the system will fail. Thus, high availability is about minimizing the downtime associated with fault, and fault tolerance is about preventing the fault from occurring. The process of building in redundancies is the practice of selecting the appropriate components that are more likely to fail and balancing the cost of building in redundancies vs. the lost opportunity created when a nonredundant component of the system fails. In simpler terms, is the cost of the lost productivity greater than the cost of the redundancies?

Building in these redundancies can be a slippery slope. Where to begin building them in is fairly easily, we will start with the physical hardware of the individual Presentation Servers. The issue arises after we complete building the redundancies into the server and logically leave the server and touch the network. How far do we go toward creating a highly available and fault tolerant "system" depends entirely on how you define "system." Is the system the physical Presentation Server hardware, the Citrix farm, or is it the entire local area network/wide area network (LAN/WAN) space in which our Presentation Server farm will serve? This definition is up to you and your organization and typically correlates to the dependency on the solution in your environment. For the purposes of this chapter, we will look at the typical redundancies that we can build into our Citrix Presentation Server's hardware to assist us in increasing server fault tolerance and availability.

Any typical Presentation Server farm can benefit from the recommended hardware redundancies as outlined in Table 3.1.

Table 3.1 Recommended Hardware Redundancies

Redundancy	Recommendation	Benefit
RAID level	1	RAID 1 will provide mirror disk sets at a lower cost to implement than RAID 5. Additionally, some studies suggest that five to seven disks are required in a RAID 5 stripe before you will begin to regain the performance lost from the overhead of striping. Since our Citrix Presentation Servers are typically smaller 1 or 2U servers, the additional size and costs associated with RAID 5 typically fail to provide the return on the investment. When creating a RAID 5 stripe, 1/n (where n is the number of drives) of the total capacity of the set will be lost to "overhead." In a mirrored set, a full 50 percent will be lost to overhead. Additionally, it is strongly discouraged to use the "built-in" RAID capability of the Windows platform.

Continued

Table 3.1 Recommended Hardware Redundancies

Redundancy	Recommendation	Benefit
		Although Windows Server 2003 supports creating "software-based" RAID arrays, the performance benefits and fault tolerance are substantially less than a true "hardware-based" solution. Final thoughts are that additional (thereby redundant) controller cards for the RAID drives may prove beneficial to eliminate the card as a single point of failure. A card with multiple "channels" is not sufficient, as the card itself may fail.
Network interface cards	TEAM	Teaming network cards provides benefits of both fault tolerance and increased network capacity through bandwidth aggregation. Teaming with two or more physically separate cards is recommended instead of teaming two ports on a multiple port card (as the card is still a single point of failure).
Power supplies	2 or more	Most servers in the class have the capabilities of redundant power supplies, and this should be leveraged. Additionally, uninterruptible power supplies or conditioned power should be considered.
Memory	Spare row	If your server hardware supports "spare row" memory, the additional expense of a "spare" piece of memory can provide greater server availability in the event of memory failure. The "spare row" memory stick will not be used until one of the regular sticks fails.

NOTE

The redundancies listed in Table 3.1 are based on a generic sampling of server hardware typically implemented in server farms as of the writing of this book. New technologies and hardware choices should be given consideration, as they may provide more redundant solutions at a lower cost. Additionally, some of these recommendations may not be available in all hardware platforms.

Effective Usage Strategies

Now that we have a basic understanding of some of the best practices surrounding server hardware, let's look at a few scenarios or strategies where Presentation Server can be a good fit. These strategies are not meant to be a complete list of all possible solutions that could be architected using Presentation Server. Instead, these scenarios will provide some ground rules and further the best practices discussion surrounding server hardware selection and implementation.

Standard Office Usage

The standard office usage scenario has become the bread and butter of Presentation Server deployments. Most deployments are implemented entirely for this purpose or as one of the major driving factors. The standard office scenario would be for organizations that want to deploy their line of business applications via Presentation Servers. These applications typically include the primary office productivity application suite (MS Office), the organization's primary e-mail client, and any other applications that are required for a typical office employee to function. This application list may also include terminal emulators and host connectivity software such as Attachmate or IBM's Client Access.

The standard office usage scenario typically benefits from scaling out instead of up. Since session per server density is typically higher than other implementations, we begin to reach the breaking point of the operating system that simply throwing more hardware at can't fix. Moreover, we will most likely want to lower the impact of a failed server by spreading the load around as much as possible. A typical server solution would be similar to the following:

- Dual processor P4 2.8GHz or faster
- 4GB of RAM (limitation of Windows Server 2003 Standard Edition)
- Teamed network cards or possibly multihomed to allow for separation of network traffic
- RAID 1 for system
- Redundant power supplies

This server would typically service 75 user sessions (or greater) in the standard office usage scenario. Your session density numbers may be much lower or higher depending on the application versions and how they are used.

CAD and Graphically Intensive Applications

Computer Aided Design/Computer Aided Manufacturing (CAD/CAM) and graphically intense applications bring a very special set of design considerations to the table. These types of applications are "heavy" for two primary reasons: first, they are typically very

CPU and memory intensive with frequent page file usage, and second, they will consume more network bandwidth than a simple text editor running through a session will. The CPU and memory usage is driven by the needs of the application itself, for picture rendering or 3-D modeling. The increased network traffic will be due to the increase in screen session resolution (1024x768 or higher) and the increase in color depth (65,536 or higher) required to service the user sessions.

CAD/CAM and graphically intense applications are a good example of when scaling up instead of out can be useful. Session density is typically much lower on a server hosting these applications when compared to other applications. The memory "footprint" required for a single user session is much greater, sometimes approaching 512MB per session (much greater than, say, Word sessions at 16MB). A typical scaled out server would start to look like the following:

- Quad processor P4 2.8 or higher

- 8GB of RAM (or higher depending on application needs)

- Teamed network cards

- RAID 1 for OS, RAID 1 for Applications, RAID 5 for Application and Operating system "scratch space"

- Redundant power supplies

This setup would probably accommodate 30 or more simultaneous AutoCAD or similar application users. Additionally, the RAID 5 volume set for scratch space could be replaced by the RAM drives previously described and dramatically increase the performance and scalability of the server (possibly nearly doubling the sessions per server count).

Internet Usage

Internet usage is a tough scenario to describe, primarily because the "solutions" implemented this way vary nearly as much the Internet itself. The types of applications vary widely, from a standard Web browser to file transfer protocol (FTP) based applications to Java applets/applications. Even within these types of applications, there are huge disparities. Look at the Web browser example. Depending on the site you are leveraging, the impact of the browser (thus the server) can be very different. Consider a user who uses Internet Explorer via Presentation Server to browse the company's online inventory and order management system vs. a user who uses a Java-enabled Web site the company uses as their primary asset tracking application. The difference in impact on the server is substantial.

Some engineers in the field argue that allowing sessions "Internet" access via Presentation Server is a poor practice that invites calamity. With all of the viruses, worms, spyware, and malware that exist today, browsing the Internet through a session can have catastrophic effects on the reliability of your servers. As an engineer who has stood on both sides of this battleground, this author can offer one solid piece of advice. It is easier to control Internet usage and protect a handful of Presentation Servers than it is to control and protect the hundreds or thousands of client devices. Additionally, it means that there is a (mostly) single Web browser version to support, thus allowing internal developers to target home-grown Web resources to a single browser version instead of having to support the myriad of browsers available today. If you elect to allow users to use Internet resources via Presentation Server, we recommend the following as a minimum list to assist in securing your servers:

- Use some form of spyware/malware blocking software.

- Leverage a antivirus solution that can proactively monitor the Internet application's local file and registry usage (and deny where appropriate).

- Consider having a "special" bank of servers that allows for browsing and restrict it on all other servers.

- Implement some form of Internet auditing, tracking, and site-blocking solution on your network.

- Implement very restrictive Group Policy Objects.

- Attempt to *never* browse the Internet as a "privileged" account from the Presentation Servers (you may inadvertently be allowed to "break" the server due to your elevated privileges).

- Consider using a Web browser *other* than Internet Explorer (if possible).

With the list of preventative measures taken care of, let's turn our attention to a typical hardware recommendation for this solution. This hardware will be based on a single "Web site" that our internal users will visit that allows for real-time ordering from one of our part suppliers. The Web site leverages the Java Runtime Environment and Internet Explorer 6.0 or higher. Our testing has revealed that CPU utilization is less than 1 percent and memory consumption is about 36MB per user session.

- Dual processor P4 2.8GHz or faster

- 4GB of RAM (limitation of Windows Server 2003 Standard Edition)

- Teamed network cards

- RAID 1 for system

- Redundant power supplies

This server would most likely support approximately 100 simultaneous user sessions.

Server Virtualization

One of the most exciting new technologies to be introduced to server-based computing in the last few years is server virtualization. Server virtualization allows a *host* operating system to provide *guest* operating systems a completely virtualized hardware environment. For example, a single dual processor server running Windows Server 2003 as the host operating system could virtualize servers for Windows servers, Linux servers, or NetWare servers. By completely separating and virtualizing the hardware required by the guest operating system, server virtualization provides many benefits. While things would appear to be easier on the surface as far as the hardware planning for this environment, special consideration must be given to guarantee the resources needed by a particular guest operating system. The Datacenter and Enterprise Editions of Windows Server 2003 provide some of this functionality with the Resource Manager component CD that ships with the software. Additional third-party software is available to assist in "controlling" the virtualized environment; one product in particular called ArmTech is from Aurema (www.aurema.com). Aurema provides a specific toolset for "fair sharing" of resources, especially within a virtualized server context.

Server virtualization requires a special application to run on top of the host operating system. This software provides the management and hardware virtualization for the guest operating systems. Microsoft produces a relatively new offering known as Virtual Server 2005. Virtual Server 2005 is based on software created by Connectix (a company recently purchased by Microsoft) that allowed Macintosh and Windows users to virtualized x86 architecture operating systems. The biggest player in this space is definitely VMWare. VMWare offers a host of products for virtualization and management thereof, but the product that most closely relates to Microsoft's Virtual Server 2005 would be VMWare GSX Server. VMWare has been working on computer virtualization for quite some time and has developed a suite of products to aid in deploying and supporting this solution. One of our personal favorites is VMotion, which allows for uninterrupted transfer of guest operating systems from one host to another (very powerful stuff indeed!)

Server virtualization is definitely a situation when scaling up is the way to go. "Big Steel" is needed typically to see the return on investment from such a consolidation. The following would be a good list to start with and grow from there:

- Eight-way P4 2.8GHz or faster

- 16GB of RAM (the more the better, HOT ADD would useful)

- Multiple physical network cards (to allow for teaming or assigning to specific guest operating systems)

- RAID 1 for host operating system, separate RAID 5 stripe(s) for the guest operating systems

- Redundant power supplies

This setup would most likely support six or more (depending on applications) Presentation Servers and would be excellent at consolidating the other pieces of the Citrix Access Suite, such as Web Interface, Secure Gateway, and the Secure Ticket Authority.

Platform Deployment Options

Now that we have a basis to assist in selecting our hardware, we will turn our attention to select the appropriate method to deploy the hardware and the operating system to support our Citrix MetaFrame Presentation Server 3.0. Platform deployment options include manual installation, unattended or scripted installs, server cloning, and a newer approach called server provisioning. Finally, we will discuss a mixed or hybrid approach that uses the best pieces of these various solutions. Selecting the best platform deployment option for your environment involves a detailed review of the requirements for each with special emphasis on the additional software and engineer expertise required. Most environments may lean heavily on one of the following solutions, but may ultimately be categorized as a hybrid due to the nuances required to integrate into the existing networking environment.

Manual Installation

The manual installation method of platform deployment has been around as long as server deployments. It is the tried and true method that we have all used from time to time to build or rebuild servers—insert CD, follow on-screen instructions. While this option is the method we are most familiar with, there are certain advantages and disadvantages to using this for platform deployment.

Advantages:

- **No additional upfront investment in software or hardware**
- **Little additional training required**
- **Allows complete configuration of server hardware and operating system**

Disadvantages:

- **Requires manual configuration** All configuration and information is entered by hand, leaving room for human error.
- **Time consuming** This method requires the most effort on the part of the person doing the actual installation and offers no mechanism to deploy additional servers at an accelerated pace. If it takes eight hours to deploy one server, it will take 40 hours to deploy five servers.
- **Not scalable** This method is scaled linearly. In other words, the more servers to build, the more effort required to build those servers.
- **Issues with consistency** As this method relies heavily on repetitive human interaction with the installers and configuration tools, consistency of the configurations will undoubtedly become an issue.

- **Slow to recover a server** Recovering a server would involve the same time-consuming steps that installing it would. Disaster recovery from tape may be faster than a manual rebuild, but that involves the additional expense of backup agents and tape media.

- **Slow to adapt** Manual installation is slower to adapt to changes required in the environment. Every change, update, or patch would need to be applied to all servers by hand

Recommended uses:

- Pilot or proof-of-concept environments

- Labs or test servers

- Initial builds for more advanced methods such as server cloning or server provisioning

Unattended or Scripted Installs

Unattended or scripted installs offer some decided benefits over the manual installation option of platform deployment. Unattended installs have been supported for many years for both installation of Windows Server 2003 and for Citrix MetaFrame Presentation Server 3.0 (and the previous incarnations thereof).

Advantages:

- **Reduces time to production** Once scripted, the deployment process is much faster, as the installers can simply read the answer or configuration files.

- **Tested, reliable, and scalable** Many servers could be built simultaneously by a single person using the scripted method. Additionally, the resource executing the scripts could be a less-skilled resource than would be required for the manual install process.

- **Enforces best practices** Since the "choices" based on best practices are incorporated into the scripts, best practices are easily enforced.

- **Repeatable** The same scripts can be reused, and each reuse continues to return on the investment required to create them.

- **Portable between platforms** With minor changes, typically, unattended installation scripts can be ported between various hardware platforms to allow for greater adaptability in the environment.

- **Possible hardware configuration support** Typically can be used for hardware configuration as well, such as configuring the RAID controller settings.

Disadvantages:

- **Additional upfront time** This method requires greater amounts of upfront time to plan and test the scripts.

- **Higher level of technical skill** The person or team responsible for the creation and testing of these scripts will typically have a much higher level of skill with the hardware platform, operating system, and version of Presentation Server being deployed. Additionally, detailed knowledge of scripting languages will be required to create and maintain the scripts.

- **Server build time** Although faster than the manual process, this method is typically slower than other options.

Recommended uses:

- Larger environments of 10 servers or more

- Environments where server hardware is dissimilar

- Already have staff highly skilled with scripting

- Organizations that already have a standard scripted install for Windows 2003 (which could easily be modified)

- Server farms

- Inclusion into more advanced methods such as server provisioning

Server Cloning

Server cloning was derived from a similar method used to "clone" workstations for deployment to users' desktops. The concept of cloning should be familiar to anyone who has ever used Symantec's Ghost or PowerQuest's Drive Image. The principle is simple: you perform a manual install of the server (or workstation) and all the required software that an end user would need. Once the server is built and tested, you simply take a "snapshot" of the drive's contents to allow for easy duplication later. Server cloning is a widely used method, although with some supportability issues.

Advantages:

- **Reduces time to production** This method is the fastest of the options for platform deployment as outlined in this book. Servers can be "imaged" in a matter of minutes, depending on the methods used and the size of the image file(s).

- **Tested, reliable, and scalable** Similar to the unattended or scripted option, server imaging provides a pre-tested highly scalable solution for deployment.

- **Enforces best practices** Since the "choices" based on best practices are incorporated into the image, best practices are easily enforced.

- **Repeatable** The same image can be "restored" an infinite number of times.

- **Typically faster to production** Server cloning is typically faster than unattended or script-based installation due to less upfront time to develop the process.

Disadvantages:

- **Lack of portability** The primary disadvantage of this method is the lack of real portability between server hardware platforms. Once an image of a server is "fixed," it is set at that point in time, with that specific configuration on a specific hardware platform. Restoring the image to a different hardware platform will typically meet with much lower success and a greater potential for problems to arise in the future.

- **Lack of support for hardware configuration** Where the scripted install option provided some mechanism for configuration of the server's hardware, server cloning assumes that the hardware is identical and has been configured identically; for example, RAID controller type, RAID controller configuration, and RAID volume configuration.

- **Images are static** Once configured, any updates, modifications, or changes to the image will typically require the recreation of the image. This will obviously require additionally time and introduces a new task commonly referred to as image maintenance.

- **Greater skill depth required** A higher level of skill will be required, specifically with additional skills on cloning for those tasked with image creation and maintenance.

- **Additional cost** Additional costs associated with the "cloning" software and the space required to maintain the image files for the various server platforms.

- **Lack of universal support** Not all vendors support cloning. Citrix has had an off-again on-again stance to cloning Presentation Servers, although the current position is that this method is supported. Microsoft doesn't support cloning Windows when applications are installed. This lack of support may be sufficient cause to investigate other methods of deploying servers.

Recommended uses:

- Larger environments of five servers or more

- Environments where server hardware is identical

- Already have staff highly skilled with cloning workstations

- Environments in which the base image of the server would require little change over time

- Inclusion into more advanced methods such as server provisioning

Server Provisioning

Out of the need for a more complete and flexible solution for deploying server hardware (or redeploying as needed), many companies have recently started offering single-seat management solutions for hardware configuration and operating system deployment. These seemingly wondrous solutions fall into a space we typically call *server provisioning*. Some solutions are more complete than others are. Some solutions involve complete hardware configuration and management, operating system deployment and updates, and application deployment including beginning to end of life cycle management for our server solutions. Some vendors' solutions are designed only to provision the operating system and possibly install applications. The camps are fairly evenly divided between hardware vendor-specific and hardware vendor-independent. Microsoft provides solutions in server provisioning that are platform independent with products like Systems Management Server (SMS) and Remote Installation Services (RIS). Altiris originally started the whole "server provisioning" management software craze. The fine people at Altiris constructed the framework and toolset needed to allow us to automate nearly every piece in a server's life cycle. Various vendors (to include Hewlett-Packard and Dell) chose to leverage the Altiris platform instead of developing their own solution to assist in the deployment of their hardware. The benefits of these server provision solutions are too numerous to fully explore here. However, one of the major advantages of the vendor-based solution is that it allows a single seat for management of all your platforms, from Windows to Linux to NetWare. Table 3.2 lists the vendors and their solutions.

Table 3.2 Server Provisioning Vendor Solutions

Vendor	Server Provisioning Solution
Hewlett-Packard/Compaq	Rapid Deployment Pack (RDM) (based on Altiris product)
Dell	Dell OpenManage (Dell's newest products have snap-ins directly to Altiris' Deployment Server)
IBM	Remote Deployment Manager (RDM)

Advantages:

- Seamless integration with the vendor-specific hardware platform.

- Ability to use hardware-specific tools for scripting configurations of firmware, RAID controllers, and so forth.

- Pre-eXecution Environment (PXE) support to allow "diskless" booting to network resources for automation. Note: PXE requires support in both the NICs and the system's firmware. In same cases, system firmware can be "overcome" using PXE boot floppies.

- Single seat administration of the process to include reporting and asset tracking.

Disadvantages:

- **Lack of portability** These solutions are typically tied to the specific vendor and are not portable from, say, IBM to HP platforms. This has changed a bit in recent history and some effort has been made to allow for better integration, but there is still a long way to go. For now, it would be best to assume that any solution you design using server provisioning will not be portable between vendors.

- **Cost** Typically, servers that are managed using this solution require additional licensing for the management software. Additionally, the management solution normally requires some network file storage space and additionally some server resources.

- **Increased upfront time** A much greater amount of time will go into building the framework and setting up the mechanisms for hardware configuration and operating system deployment.

- **Expertise** There is a bit of a learning curve for people who are new to Altiris or IBM's RDM. The level of integration and capability comes at the price of a much deeper and broader skill set regarding hardware and scripting.

Recommended uses:

- Larger environments of 20 servers or more, or a blade-based server environment

- Environments where there is a single server hardware vendor (or nearly)

- Already have staff highly skilled with automation scripting and server cloning

- Environments that are trying to leverage a specific hardware vendor and maintain a single seat to management and deployment of server platforms

Hybrid Approach

The hybrid approach allows you to combine the best from the previous four methods described, and is the method used by most real-life implementations. For instance, a hybrid approach would allow you to use a server cloning base image due to the very fast nature of deployment and combine that with an unattended/scripted installation method to update the server to the most current hotfixes, run a security identifier (SID) changing tool, and install a few pieces of software that may have "missed" inclusion in the base image. The hybrid approach offers the greatest flexibility for server deployments but also maintains the limitations of all the various methods (we are just choosing to ignore those limitations that apply to our environment).

Two possible submethods that exist under the hybrid approach (arguably, they could exist under scripting or server cloning) are System Preparation Tool (SYSPREP) and Remote Installation Services (RIS) based installs. Both of these techniques for installing a server operating system (or workstations for that matter) were developed by Microsoft and have been supported for some time. SYSPREP has been around since the days of NT 4.0, although not supported for servers until Windows 2000. RIS has existed since Windows 2000 Server and can be used to provide a variety of "clients" an unattended installation of the platform's operating system. We chose to place SYSPREP and RIS in the hybrid approach primarily because of the "blending" of techniques they employ.

SYSPREP, for instance, is a method of cloning a server after it has been built that also uses an answer file, thus blending the benefits of server cloning and unattended or scripted installations. SYSPREP is supported for Windows Server 2003 as a method of deploying the operating system fully configured with relevant service packs and hotfixes to the waiting hardware. Due to the cloning nature of the procedure, SYSPREPPED images are typically specific to the hardware platform at hand, therefore inheriting the limitations of the server cloning method. SYSPREP is, however, a very powerful method to assist in the automation of the operating system in a very fast and consistent manner. Due to the nature of the answer file that it employs, further automation of the image after "install" is a snap. This would allow inclusion of key elements such as installation of Citrix MetaFrame Presentation Server 3.0 and various other applications or core tools needed on every Presentation Server, such as backup agents or antivirus software.

RIS can be leveraged much in the same way as Altiris or the other server provisioning tools mentioned previously. Microsoft developed RIS to allow administrators to quickly and efficiently deploy the operating systems to new workstations as they were brought onto the network. Since its inception, RIS has been extended to include support for deploying servers. RIS supports the deployment of unattended installations and images similar to SYSPREP known as RIS-PREPPED images. In a typical deployment, RIS leverages the PXE feature of most modern computers' network cards to assign a DHCP address and "present" a menu of options or to execute a series of scripts. Since RIS can leverage unattended or "cloned" images, it provides a very flexible and fast method for deploying servers. More information on RIS and SYSPREP is available in the Windows Server 2003 documentation located on the installation media. Alternatively, the most current information can be found by reading the *Automating and Customizing Installations* section of the *Microsoft Windows Server 2003 Deployment Kit* located at www.microsoft.com/resources/documentation/WindowsServ/ 2003/all/deployguide/en-us/Default.asp?url=/resources/documentation/WindowsServ/ 2003/all/deployguide/en-us/dpgACI_overview.asp.

Advantages:

- **Greatest flexibility** This method allows the use of any of the benefits of the other methods to include scripted installation, server cloning, and server provisioning.

- **Best of breed** Allows for the selection of the key capabilities from each method to allow for better integration.

Disadvantages:

- Contains all limitations of previous methods

- May increase complexity

- May increase costs due to various pieces that may or may not be implemented

Recommended uses:

- Environments of five servers or larger

- Environments with highly skilled technical staff with depth of knowledge on the pros and cons of the various methods

- Departments or divisions of an organization that deploy their own servers in separate locations with differing rules or practices

Microsoft Windows Server 2003 Hardware/Software Requirements and Recommendations

Well, now that we have figured out *how* we are going to configure the hardware and install the operating system, we can turn our attention to the actual requirements to install Windows Server 2003. This section begins by performing the same ritual required in any technical manual, you know the one—list the minimums and then point out how woefully inadequate they are when compared to actual production requirements. The difference here is that we also outline some best practices and reasoning behind the recommendations. We'll also discuss how to properly use the Microsoft Hardware Compatibility List (HCL) and the importance of conducting a hardware inventory

Hardware Requirements

We can start with a look at the minimum hardware requirements and the recommendations for deploying Windows Server 2003 as a terminal server (Table 3.3).

Table 3.3 Windows Server 2003 Hardware Requirements and Recommendations (Assumes Standard Edition)

Hardware	Minimum Requirement	Recommendation and Reasoning
CPU	133MHz	Dual processor with fastest available processor and bus speeds. Processors with larger L1 and L2 cache may improve performance for some applications through Terminal Services and should be tested thoroughly to determine the benefits. Processors that support hyper-threading may actually be a deterrent to some applications and server platforms. Review your hardware vendor's information on how to disable hyper-threading on your specific platform. Thorough testing should be performed to determine the benefit, if any, of hyper-threading on your platform.
Memory	128MB	256MB to 512MB for the operating system. Then, calculate the average memory consumed for user sessions through testing. Typical users can consume 64MB to 128MB for standard office applications. Some applications will consume more than 128MB.
Disk space	1.5GB	2GB plus page file sizing.
Disk subsystem	IDE	SCSI RAID 1 An Ultra320 RAID Controller with 128MB and 15K RPM drives would be best cost to performance ratio.
Network	Not required	Teamed 100Mbps Fast Ethernet adapters You could also consider teamed 1Gbps cards, although typically more for fault tolerance than throughput requirements.

To further the explanation of recommended server hardware configuration, let us consider the following scenario and example of hardware sizing based on some real-world business requirements. Suppose that we work for a company that has decided to provide remote office and home office access to our company's critical line of business applications. These applications consist of Microsoft Office 2003 with Outlook 2003 (to access our Exchange 2003 mail system), our company's customer relationship management system, and our clients will need access to the human resources system. We can suppose that there will be no more than 500 concurrent users on the system using these applications at any given point, and that the users will possibly leverage most of the applications at the same time.

From this scenario, we can gather the following hardware for our servers:

- Dual processor 2.8GHz Xeon 1MB cache or faster
- RAID 1 mirrored 36GB Ultra 320 15k RPM drives
- 4 GB of fast RAM
- Windows Server 2003 Standard Edition
- Teamed or multihomed 1Gbps network cards

This hardware configuration is based on the assumption of 50–75 users per server (based on previous implementations). While the server will most likely perform adequately, memory will probably be the first bottleneck we encounter. Chances are that our server hardware will support in excess of 4GB of RAM, but Windows Server 2003 Standard Edition will not. Thus begins the process of trade-offs, and for that, refer to the earlier section in this chapter on vertical vs. horizontal scaling.

One of the more important tasks to master is the use of the HCL that Microsoft provides so we can conduct a hardware inventory. This process will be especially useful to those of us who must reuse existing hardware as part of a migration to Windows Server 2003 Terminal Services and/or Presentation Server 3.0. A hardware inventory will provide very valuable information that will help in determining what hardware is suitable for the new platform during an upgrade, and provide detailed information on the difference in hardware, which will assist with the following:

- Determining what method to use to deploy the operating system
- Allows you to determine firmware version needed to support Windows Server 2003
- Differences in hardware will assist creation of load evaluators that are used by Presentation Server during load balancing

Conducting a hardware inventory can be time consuming. Emphasis should be placed on thoroughness of the inventory to the inclusion of what may seem nonessential on the surface. A thorough hardware inventory would include the following information at a minimum (and may contain more based on your environment's needs):

- Manufacturer
- Model number
- Model revision
- Warranty status
- Service tag numbers
- Serial numbers

- Computer name

- Internet protocol configuration

- Rack position

- **Central processing unit (CPU)** Number, type, speed, slot/socket architecture

- **Memory** Amount, slots available, slots used, type, error correcting (ECC)/Non-ECC, maximum supported on hardware

- **Disks** Number, size, type, speed, cache size, interface type, hot plug

- **Disk controllers** Number, number of channels per card, memory, current RAID level, write-through supported

- **Mainboard/system** Firmware version, supports Server 2003 Yes/No

- **Network cards** Number, type, speed/duplex settings, teamed Yes/No

- **Remote management cards** Number, type, firmware version, supports Server 2003 Yes/No

- Miscellaneous cards/components

Once the inventory is completed, we can cross-reference the findings with the Microsoft HCL for Windows Server 2003. Microsoft maintains this list on its Web site and the information can be viewed by navigating to www.microsoft.com/whdc/hcl/default.mspx. From this, you can actually reference all products that are designed to work with Microsoft solutions. For those of you who have better things to do with your time than surf the HCL Web site, Microsoft has created a built-in HCL Checking tool, Microsoft Windows Upgrade Advisor, which can be found on the Windows Server 2003 media. To leverage this amazingly easy to use tool, simply insert the Windows Server 2003 CD into any server for which you have questions regarding upgradeability.

- Select **Check System Compatibility**.

- Select **Check My System Automatically**.

- Select **Yes, Download the Updated Setup Files (Recommended)**.

Figure 3.2 gives you an idea of how easy and fast this tool is to use.

Follow the remaining wizard prompts and the tool will retrieve the latest information on supported hardware and software directly from the Microsoft Web site. The Upgrade Advisor then will compare that current HCL information with what is installed on this system and generate a report at the end with any known issues based on the hardware and software that the tool finds. You read that correctly, it also checks your major software packages, such as backup software, antivirus, and so forth to see if they are Windows Server 2003 compatible.

Figure 3.2 Microsoft Windows Upgrade Advisor

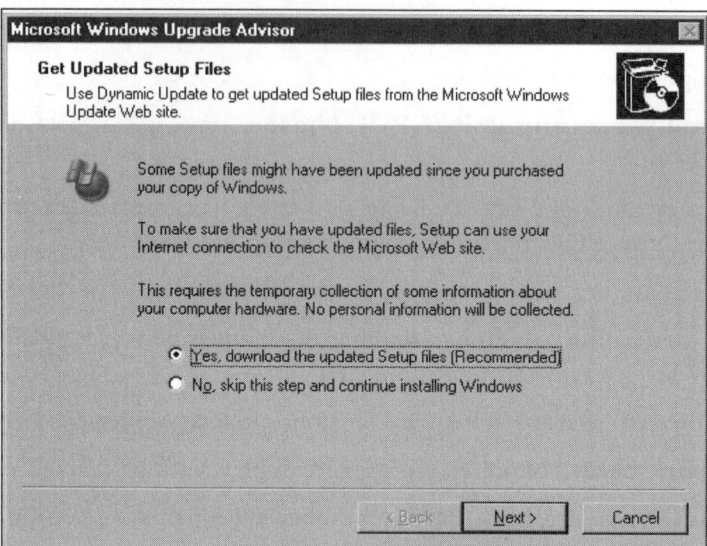

> **NOTE**
>
> Microsoft also included this tool in the Windows 2000 Server distribution. From field experience, this tool is very handy and typically very accurate. However, we have seen it report no compatibility issues only to have a server fail during upgrade. We strongly encourage you to have a good working backup of the system in question, prior to performing an upgrade based solely on the results of this tool.

Software Requirements

Once we have our hardware selected, we can focus on the underlying software requirements to support Windows Server 2003 Terminal Services and thereby allow us to install MetaFrame Presentation Server 3.0. Presentation Server 3.0 is supported on Standard, Enterprise, and Datacenter Editions of Windows Server 2003.

The first step is to choose the correct version or edition of Windows Server 2003. On the surface, this may seem like a simple affair, but after further investigation, there are several factors driving this decision. Let us begin by looking at the various "flavors" of Windows Server 2003. Web Edition is Microsoft's attempt to provide a lower cost of entry into the Windows 2003 world for those who may consider staying on their current platform or migrating to Linux. Web Edition, as the name implies, is targeted at servers destined for Web server work. This version supports up to two processors and

2GB of memory. While this edition of Server 2003 can fill many roles, there are two in particular that it cannot. The first is that Microsoft has disabled its capability to be a fully functional domain controller. The second and most important is that Terminal Services can only function in Remote Desktop for Administration mode, thus no full Terminal Services; therefore, Citrix MetaFrame Presentation Server cannot be installed. Since we have now ruled out Web Edition, let us review the options for Standard Edition.

Windows Server 2003 Standard Edition is the most widely deployed version of the platform, especially when Terminal Services is considered. Standard Edition supports up to four processors and 4GB of memory. Both full domain controller and Terminal Services modes are supported. Overall, this is a fine choice to serve as the basis for our MetaFrame Presentation Server 3.0. However, there are a couple scenarios in which Standard Edition may not fit the bill. The first is for applications that require copious amounts of memory per user session to function. For instance, if we take our 4GB maximum and subtract 512MB for the operating system, that leaves us with 3.5GB for user sessions. If the application in question consumes 128MB per session, that puts us at 28 sessions per server with no room for idle sessions and no reserve on our memory. Not a pretty place for your servers to be. We may have sufficient processor power with the available two or four processors in the server to support the application, but may quickly bottleneck at the available RAM. The second limitation is somewhat tied to the first, in that if we have a memory situation such as running low or failed memory, the ability to hot-add memory is not supported on Standard Edition. Thus, we begin the investigation of Enterprise Edition.

Windows Server 2003 Enterprise Edition is a possible candidate for deployment of Presentation Server 3.0 for a few reasons. The primary reason is for scalability. If you have application sets or an environment that supports scaling up, the eight processor and 32GB of memory support for the 32-bit version of Enterprise Edition may provide the platform you need. Additionally, Enterprise Edition supports the hot-add memory feature for dynamic growth on the fly. However, if you can't see the need for the hardware support or hot-add memory features, Enterprise Edition can be a costly platform that doesn't provide a valid cost justification over Standard Edition. Current street prices place Enterprise Edition at two to four times the cost of Standard Edition.

Datacenter Edition for Windows Server 2003 has some amazing hardware support features. However, this platform is typically reserved for vendor-assisted deployment and is usually supported directly from your hardware vendor. With that said, due to the limited support for hardware platforms, the prohibitive cost to acquire the platform, and the "requirement" for certified applications, Datacenter Edition would be a poor choice to host MetaFrame Presentation Server. One possible real-world use would be to leverage Datacenter Edition running Microsoft Virtual Server 2005 or VMWare GSX Server and build your Citrix servers on virtual servers operating as guests of this large host platform. Datacenter's extensive hardware capabilities and the Microsoft Resource Manager software that the product ships with make an excellent platform for "carving up" or virtualizing the hardware with Virtual Server 2005 or GSX Server. A single 16-CPU Datacenter server could host a dozen or more "virtual" or "guest" servers while maintaining a fairly even distribution of resources between the various "guests." The lowered overall cost of ownership is realized through the reduction in hardware to support and the flexibility of the "guests" to be moved between "physically" different "hosts" for maintenance. In fact, VMWare's VMotion toolset allows a guest to be moved "seamlessly" between hosts with no interruption in service. It becomes much easier to "realize" the fast approaching 100-percent uptime requirements with solutions like this!

Now that we have selected the edition of Windows Server 2003, let us look at some basic licensing scenarios. Windows Server 2003 allows the server to be licensed in either per-server or per-seat mode. Per-server licensing means that each server will maintain its own count of file and print client access licenses for when users connect. Per-server mode works best for environments with a single server. Per-seat mode is the method nearly all Presentation Server farms use. Per-seat mode relies on "centralized" licensing (usually performed by a domain controller) that enforces Microsoft's file and print licensing on a device-by-device basis.

Application Planning and Requirements

The introduction of applications into a Terminal Services-based environment can be challenging. To ensure proper functionality of applications and guarantee the stability of the servers upon which we intend to install the applications, several processes need to be completed. To correctly complete this series of processes, we will look at the following:

- Conducting a software inventory
- Assessing software compatibility
- Understanding the impact on the hardware resources and operating system of new applications

Conducting a software inventory can also be time consuming. However, a detailed analysis of the application environment to be deployed via Terminal Services and Presentation Server is paramount to the successful deployment or upgrade. To begin a software inventory, start with all the major applications that your users use on a regular basis, such as your office suite, your e-mail package, and any other line of business applications. Make a thorough list of the software, including version numbers, service packs, and hotfixes required by your business. You may also want to include any support information about the application vendor such as contact information, licensing models, and any support agreement numbers. Next, consider all the supporting applications that must be installed for your primary applications to function correctly. For instance, if your primary application is an Access database, then MS Access or the runtime version thereof will most likely be required to support the execution of the application. Pay special attention to the "plug-ins" and "add-ons" that are required for your applications to function correctly. An example would be a human resources system that uses Microsoft Internet Explorer as the front-end client, and requires the Java runtime environment from Sun Microsystems, Inc. and the Adobe Reader ActiveX control for viewing portable document files (PDFs) directly on the Web site. The final stage of this software inventory would include all the system-level software and services that your user sessions don't need to execute but provide us the management side of the server builds. This would include the backup agents, antivirus software, spyware removal tools, and miscellaneous reporting and monitoring pieces that will allow us to leverage other components of our environment. Remember to record all the detail you can with regard to the application version, hotfixes, and services packs required.

Once the software inventory is complete and the application dependency matrix is built, it is time to put all that hard work to use—with some more hard work! Assessing software compatibility is the next phase and is divided into two subphases. Step one is simply using the information of the various applications we have compiled and viewing the appropriate application vendor documentation and/or contacting the vendor to confirm the correct functionality and support status of the application while running on a Windows Server 2003 Terminal Services platform. While this will seem easy on the surface, many application vendors may have never heard of or tested their application on a terminal server. Which leads us to the second and more complicated phase of assessing software compatibility: we must make some decisions surrounding applications that are not supported on Terminal Services.

If the application vendor doesn't certify their application for Windows Server 2003 Terminal Services, we have a few options. First, we could upgrade to a newer version of the application that is supported on Terminal Services. Option two, if no upgrade to the application is available, we could choose a different application that provides similar functionality to the end users. Option three, we could elect not to deploy that particular application through Terminal Services and Presentation Server 3.0, instead leaving the application on the user's desktop. Alternatively, we have our personal favorite, option four. Option four is where we elect to deploy the application via Terminal Services and Presentation Server regardless of the lack of support by the application vendor. However, before we choose option four, we must first investigate the impact of the application on the hardware and the operating system.

There are many reasons why an application vendor may elect not to support their product on a terminal server. Perhaps they have never actually tested on Terminal Services and therefore choose not to certify the application on the platform. In many cases, this is the situation. Occasionally, the vendor has tested the application on Terminal Services and found that it either performs poorly or not at all. In other scenarios, the application may not maintain its settings and preferences in the appropriate locations, whether in the registry or file system, thus making the application fail to work correctly in a multiuser environment. The result is that normally applications that are not certified for the Terminal Services platform can be made to execute in a Terminal Services environment with a few minor changes. The question of "how" to make these applications work is not the point of this current discussion. On the contrary, we are tasked at this point to determine whether we as an information services infrastructure want to take on support for a noncertified application. This isn't nearly as ominous as it seems. How many times have your own internal resources resolved issues that were not resolved by the application vendor's support channel? Many companies elect to support the applications that cannot or will not be supported by the vendors. The choice is up to you.

To assist in determining whether to deploy an application via our Presentation Servers, we must also consider the impact that the application will have on the server hardware and the operating system. Let us start with the hardware discussion. If the application in question consumes a disproportionate amount of system resources, there may be grounds to place it on its own server to lower the impact that the use of the application will have on other sessions on the server. Citrix refers to this concept of isolating applications for performance, security, or other reasons as load-managed groups. This concept of load-managed groups can be extended for applications that make sufficient changes to the system as to not allow other applications to share the server. An example of this would be a previous version of an application that requires an older version of a DLL located in the system root or an application that needs to be installed multiple times, such as a financial application that writes information into the registry for a particular state that is overwritten on subsequent installs of "other" states. These are good examples of sufficient impact to the server to warrant further planning of where and how to deploy these applications.

Citrix MetaFrame Presentation Server 3.0 Initial Farm Planning

Now that we have decided how we are going to install Windows Server 2003, we are almost ready to build our MetaFrame Presentation Server. Before we can drop the CD in the drive to start the installation, though, we need to explore a few concepts surrounding the installation and configuration of Presentation Server. In this section, we will look at the items that exist "outside" the logical boundary of the farm, exploring the requirements for each. We will then turn our attention to those pieces that exist logically "inside" the farm. We will then switch gears back to the basics of hardware and software requirements for MetaFrame Presentation Server 3.0 and conclude this section with a dissection of the different methods that exist for installing Presentation Server 3.0.

Let's begin with a definition of what a "farm" is and how it relates to your Citrix deployment. A farm is a logical grouping of servers for the purposes of management, administration, load balancing, and scalability. There is no practical limit to how large a farm can grow. A farm can consist of a single Citrix Presentation Server 3.0 server or can span continents and contain thousands of servers. By definition, the farm is the Presentation Servers themselves, that through configuration we choose which farms they will participate in at any given point in time. A server can be a member of a single farm at any one time, but may change farms at any point. Most organizations regardless of size or complexity can function correctly on a single farm, although some elect to divide into multiple farms for political or economic reasons. Figure 3.3 provides a graphical overview of the farm layout from a logical standpoint.

Figure 3.3 Inside and Outside Farm Components.

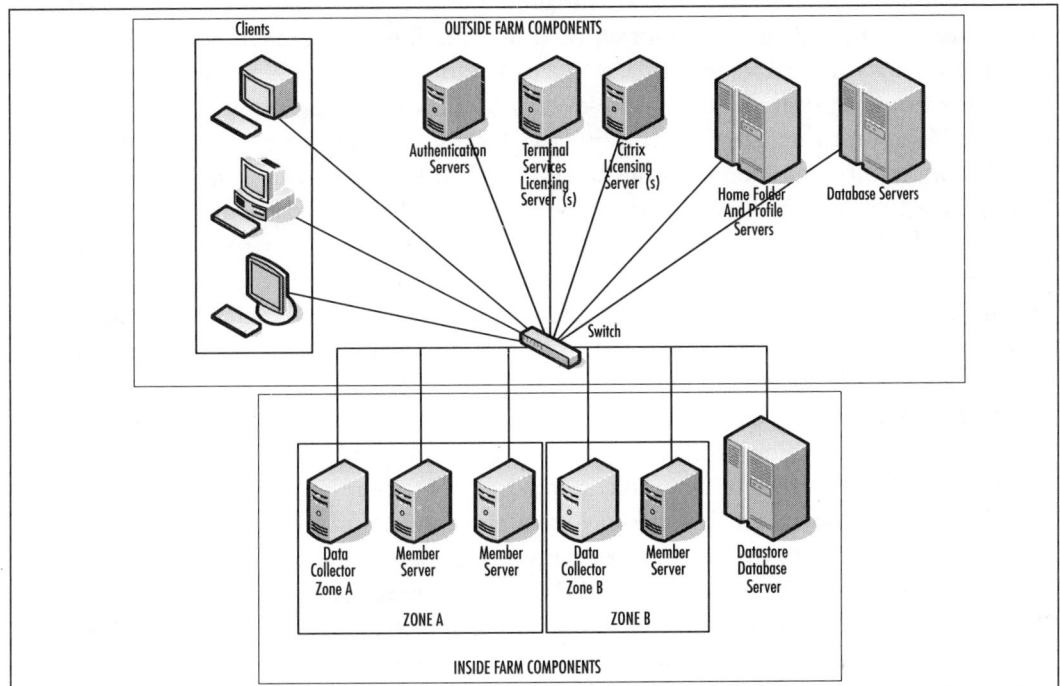

Planning Components Outside the Farm

As we begin to build or upgrade our Presentation Server farm, several components exist outside the management boundary that is the farm. The external components are present to service the underlying functionality of the farm and the user sessions that the farm hosts.

The first external component to consider is your licensing services. To legally and functionally use a Windows Server 2003-based Presentation Server farm, there are two major licenses that a user's connection will need: a Microsoft Terminal Services Client Access License and a Citrix MetaFrame Presentation Server Connection License. Both of these licenses types require backend services to issue, enforce, and manage the licensing aspect. Licensing is a very important piece in any farm design and is covered in more detail in Chapter 5.

Two of the more important pieces that exist "outside" the farm but are critical to its successful operation are the user's home folder and profile. We can begin by reviewing the importance of the home folder, especially in a Presentation Server farm, and then discuss the two types of home folders.

Aside from the typical uses for a home folder, Terminal Services (and therefore Presentation Server) leverages the home folder to maintain per-user INI files. For instance, when running a session on the Presentation Server, a user needs to "edit" an

INI file that exists in the system paths (C:\Windows), Terminal Services will copy the original file to the user's home folder and allow the user to modify the home folder version instead of the shared C:\Windows version. Additionally, Terminal Services monitors the time stamps on the INI files to assist in determining if the user needs a newer copy of the file from the system paths in the event of a major system change, such as installing a new application to update the C:\Windows INI files. In addition, the per-user file repository, user home folders, obviously serve as the dumping ground for all user created files and are typically the target of many policies for redirecting content from the users' desktop and My Documents. Home folders come in two types, normal and Terminal Services. Normal home folders are like those we have always defined for user accounts in our NT or Active Directory domains. Terminal Services home folders allow administrators to specify an alternate folder structure that only applies when a user logs in to a Terminal Services session (and not at a workstation or desktop).

The second "important" folder is the user's profile. Before we delve into the types and strategies surrounding profiles, let's review what a profile is and what type of information it contains by default. A profile is the user side of the configuration of the computer's operating system, and to a lesser extent the applications that reside on the system. A profile contains two portions of information, a file and folder structure and a registry section. If we look at the %SYSTEMDRIVE%\Documents and Settings folder for a Windows Server 2003 computer, we can examine this structure in more detail. For instance, we see the All Users profile and the Default User's profile. The Default User's profile is the template from which a user's profile is built if at login time there is no local or network copy of a profile located for the user; for example, if this is the first time the user has logged on to this server and/or network. The All Users profile contains the shortcuts and information that is common to all users that log on to this specific server. We as administrators can simplify a user's experience by "modifying" the contents of the user's profile either by editing the Default User's profile prior to the user's profile being created, using Group Policy Objects to assist in the configuration, or writing some creative scripts to configure elements of the profile for the user in the background. Let's look specifically at the Administrator's profile on our test machine. The Administrator's profile functionally is no different from another nonprivileged user's profile. It contains similar file-based and registry-based information (Figure 3.4).

Everything you see as far as files and folders would be the file-based portion of the profile. For example, the folder Desktop would contain all the items that the administrator had placed on his or her desktop of this particular server. The file NTUSER.DAT is a very special file as it contains the registry-based portion. If this user were logged in, everything that is located in the Hive Key Current User (HKCU) section would be the result of information gathered from the NTUSER.DAT file and Group Policy Objects at that current point in time.

Profiles exist in three basic types. The first is a local profile. A local profile is a profile that exists only on the computers where a user logs in. Local profiles are beneficial because they are fast to load (as they are local to the server's hard drive). However, local profiles don't typically work well in a server-based computing environment because the settings and folder information found on server1 for userA don't necessarily exist on server2 for userA, resulting in a confused user. A good example of this would be Microsoft Word. If userA ran a session on server1 and set MS Word to "autosave" every five minutes and then later ran MS Word on server2, the user would expect that the auto-save feature would be enabled and set to five minutes. In fact, the setting may not be enabled. In a local profile scenario, userA has two profiles, one on server1 and one on server2, that have no way to synchronize. What we need is a profile that follows the user around no matter where he or she runs a session.

Figure 3.4 Administrator's Profile

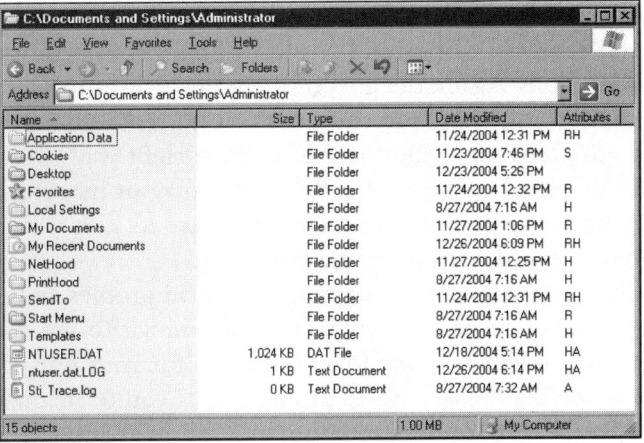

The profile that follows the user to the server he or she logs in to would be the second basic type of profile, the roaming profile. Roaming profiles are wonderful, as they allow userA to execute MS Word today on server1, and at logoff, userA's settings are copied to a network share point ready for later when userA runs a session on server2, thus allowing userA to "maintain" his or her configurations as he or she "roams" between servers. Roaming profiles have several administrative burdens. First, they tend to "grow" rapidly if not properly restricted. If we go back to our previous example of items on the user's desktop, if a user saves a 10MB file to the desktop, then that is now part of the user's profile and must be written out to the network share every time the user logs out of the a session. In addition, every time the user starts a new session and his or her profile must be copied down locally, the 10MB file comes with it. This can cause very long login and logoff times and dramatically increase network traffic with the result being unhappy users.

The second most common problem is profile "collisions" or corruption. Let's suppose that userA is running MS Word on server1 and MS Excel on server2 at the same time. UserA only has one profile available to him or her, so it is copied to both server1 and server2. If the user saves a setting or file to his or her profile on server1 and a different setting or file on server2, we have the potential for profile collisions. When userA ends his or her sessions on server1 and server2, the *last* server that writes the roaming profile out to the network share will be the copy retained. So, in this example, if userA saves a critical document to the desktop while on server1 and changes the MS Excel default save location (a registry-based change) while in session on server2, if server2 is the last to write the profile out, the user would potentially lose the critical document that was on the desktop of server1. What we need now is the ability to manipulate the profile to help minimize these profile collisions or corruptions.

This practice of minimizing profile corruption results in the third and final basic type of profile, the hybrid profile. Hybrid profiles are not "defined" anywhere in a user's account properties and there is no way to distinguish if a local or roaming profile is a hybrid without "digging" under the covers. Hybrid profiles are a culmination of techniques such as folder redirection with Group Policy Objects, login compatibility scripting to "correct" registry settings, and possibly a series of system variables resulting in multiple profile locations. Again, the goal of these practices is to reduce the profile collisions and corruption issues and present a more consistent user experience. Hybrid profiles are a fairly advanced topic and there is no "one right way" to implement them, as there are literally thousands of settings and files that may or may not need to be "redirected" based on your environments needs. The first place to start would be implementing a folder redirection policy in Active Directory.

Whether we choose to implement roaming or hybrid profiles, both types can be defined as either normal or Terminal Services profiles (similar to the concept of home folders). If you already implement some form of profile for your non-Terminal Services users, the concept of the Terminal Services profile allows you to maintain two separate profiles, one for "normal" desktop use, and one for "Terminal Services" use. The differences in the configuration of these folders exist in the account object inside Active Directory. By viewing the properties of any user account with Active Directory Users and Computers, we can see the two tabs that house the settings.

In Figure 3.5, we see the "normal" options for home folder and profile path.

In Figure 3.6, we can see the Terminal Services specific versions for these two types.

NOTE

Whether implementing local, roaming, or hybrid profiles, administrators can choose to make the profile *mandatory* (not allowing the user to change it) by renaming the NTUSER.DAT to NTUSER.MAN. Mandatory profiles are useful in environments where large groups of users will have the same settings for their applications. Mandatory profiles historically were very popular with Terminal Services and Citrix solutions, but with the advent of more powerful scripting solutions, the control of Group Policy Objects, and the increase in need for user-specific settings in many applications (thus prohibiting the mandatory option), more and more administrators are choosing the hybrid profile option. Additionally, if the folder in which the user's profile is located is renamed with a .MAN extension, the user will not be allowed to log in if the profile path is not available, in the event of a failed server or such. An example of this configuration would be similar to Figure 3.6, but the path to the profile would be \\server\tsprofiles$\administrator.man.

Figure 3.5 Typical Options for Home Folder and Profile Path

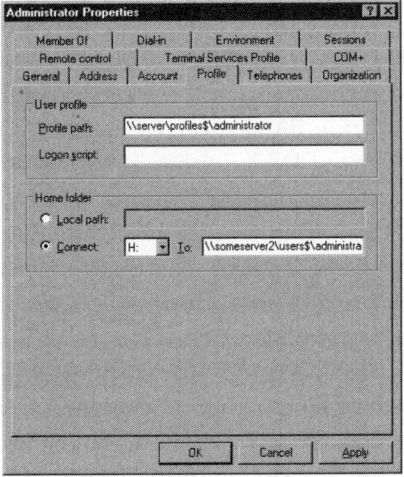

Figure 3.6 Terminal Services Profile

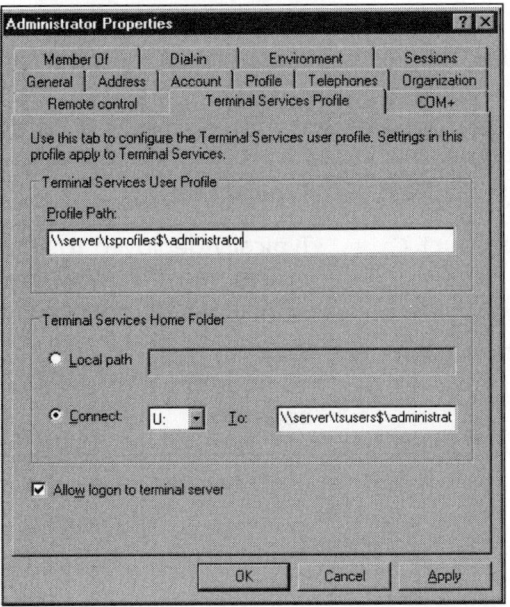

Planning Farm Components

Now that we have a basic understanding of the requirements that exist outside the Citrix farm, we can dig into the pieces that work inside the farm. We will pay special attention to a few key pieces, the *Data Collector*, the *Data Store*, the *Local Host Cache*, and the hardware and software requirements for the installation of Citrix MetaFrame Presentation Server 3.0.

MetaFrame Presentation Server is available in three versions or editions: Enterprise, Advanced, and Standard. Most companies typically deploy Enterprise or possibly Advanced due to the load-balancing capability available in these editions. In truth, there is really no difference between the media and the servers built from the media that would distinguish versions. During installation, we select a version or type in a product code. This product code directs the IMA Service as to the "level" of functionality it is to assume. Think of it as a ticket to an airplane. We may all be getting on Presentation Server Flight 3.0, but our "tickets" allow us to sit in different sections of the plane, which affords us better features and options. The product code for Presentation Server functions as the airplane ticket. Any Citrix client can connect to a seat on the plane, and where they sit determines the cost of the ticket. The same holds true for client connections to servers in a farm. If a farm has multiple editions (which most do not) of Presentation Server, the "cost" of connecting to a server is derived from the edition of software on that server. Citrix allows us to build, with production licenses, as many servers in the farm as we desire. The only limiting factor would be number of connection licenses we have.

Breaking down the editions is a fairly easy task. All versions of Presentation Server include the same basic features. The more advanced features are reserved for the more advanced platforms. Table 3.4 lists the editions, benefits, and targeted users for each.

Table 3.4 Citrix MetaFrame Presentation Server 3.0 Editions

Edition	Features Added	Typical Use
Standard	Base product	Typically deployed to small workgroups or offices, most likely where a single server would suffice (do to lack of load balancing).
Advanced	Load balancing	Small to medium-sized businesses that could leverage the high availability features of load balancing.

Continued

Table 3.4 Citrix MetaFrame Presentation Server 3.0 Editions

Edition	Features Added	Typical Use
Enterprise	Load balancing, Resource Manager, Network Manager, Installation Manager	Anyone wanting to take full advantage of the enterprise management features available, such as application packaging and deployment, SNMP-based network management, detailed current and historical performance analysis, and the benefits of load management. In addition, anyone wanting to use some of the newer features of zone preference and failover, more advanced features of *smooth roaming*, and the custom views and report center.

Before we delve into the various architectural components of the farm, we need to understand a few key protocols and services that exist to support the underlying functionality of the farm concept. Two basic types of communications exist inside a Citrix Farm, client to server and server to server. We will begin with server-to-server communication, as it is typically the easiest to understand. Presentation Servers communicate with each other using a newer framework service that Citrix introduced with Presentation Server 1.0 (also known as MetaFrame XP 1.0), Independent Management Architecture (IMA). IMA is described as a framework service due to the modular design the developers used to create the service. Each "module" or subsystem provides specific functionality within the farm. For instance, the Citrix Licensing subsystem assists in enforcing licensing, and the Program Neighborhood subsystem provides for application set enumeration based on user credentials (among other features). IMA is, in its simplest form, a collection of subsystems constituted by a series of DLLs and EXEs, tied to together under a single service. IMA could be considered the backbone of Citrix communication. IMA is also the name of the protocol used for this communication and occurs in two forms. Server-to-server communication occurs over TCP port 2512. When we as administrators open the Presentation Server Management Console (PMC) and "connect" to a particular server, the PMC-to-server communication occurs over TCP port 2513.

Independent Computing Architecture (ICA) is the client-to-server communication protocol with which we are most familiar, especially if you have worked with Citrix software at any point in the past. ICA is the presentation layer protocol that has existed essentially since the "dawn" of server-based computing. ICA operates most typically over TCP 1494 for the purposes of user sessions. Historically, ICA was also used for server-to-server communication, but that functionality has been replaced with IMA in the Presentation Server platforms. ICA only performs server-to-server communications in the event of interoperability mode, which we will discuss later. ICA also has a legacy broadcast port UDP 1604 that facilitated application and server enumeration over the network. Although this functionality still exists in the client and server pieces, it is disabled on the server side by default. Today, we use a much more network-friendly TCP or HTTP(s) unicast message to enumerate applications and servers. This function of application enumeration occurs on either the legacy UDP broadcasts or the TCP unicast from the client to the server's IMA service, specifically the Program Neighborhood subsystem. The HTTP(s) request type would be received by the XML Service subsystem.

NOTE

Although Presentation Server 3.0 supports connections on transports other than TCP, such as IPX/SPX and Network Basic Input/Output System (NetBIOS), support for these types of *Winstations* from Microsoft ceased with Windows 2000 Server. Although Microsoft has never implemented a Remote Desktop Protocol Winstation that can use any protocol other than TCP/IP, the functionality exists in the Terminal Services core to support IPX/SPX. With Windows Server 2003, Microsoft has removed that capability and only supports TCP-based connections. Thus, Presentation Server 3.0 on Windows Server 2003 can only use TCP/IP, while Presentation Server 3.0 on Windows 2000 Server can use TCP/IP, IPX/SPX, and NetBIOS.

The servers within a farm can communicate at will with each other across IMA for the purposes of updating license usage counts, server load information, and so forth. As the farm grows, this traffic grows exponentially. To help control this flow of communications, Citrix uses the concept of a *zone*. A zone is a logical grouping of servers typically associated with subnets. Each zone has a *data collector*.

The data collector is responsible for complete knowledge of the dynamic information for the zone it is a member thereof. What is dynamic information, you may ask? Dynamic information is information that changes regularly within the farm, such as user session count on a given server, number of licenses consumed, number of disconnected sessions, status of a given connection, and so forth. The data collector typically is also responsible for all load information to allow for the decision as to where to load balance an incoming session. The data collector is very important and directly impacts the users' perception of performance.

Since the data collector is so important, let's review some best practices and general information about data collectors.

- By default, the first server built in a new farm is "selected" as the data collector.

- There is a single data collector per zone.

- A single zone may contain up to 256 servers.

- Larger or busier farms (five or more servers) should isolate a zone data collector (per zone) that will service application enumeration and load-balance requests to increase performance. This server should not service actual sessions, but instead redirect users' sessions to the appropriate servers.

- The role is dynamically reassigned in the event that the data collector should fail.

- Client software and Web interface servers typically should be pointed to the data collector for their zone for application enumeration (as it will be typically faster than crossing a WAN link).

The servers within a farm all share a common repository for configuration known as the *data store*. The data store is a standard database format. The servers that are members of the given farm, which this specific data store defines, perform read/write operations against this data store database based on the configuration we enter as administrators into the Presentation Server Management Console and the server-to-server communication associated with the Independent Management Architecture service. There are two types of data store databases: local databases and network databases. At the time of creation of a new farm, the "type" of database must be considered, as it will impact the design, scalability, and cost of the server farm. The local data store databases consist of two formats, either MS Access or Microsoft SQL Desktop Engine (MSDE). The network data store databases can leverage MS SQL, Oracle, or IBM's DB2. Each type, local or network, has its benefits and disadvantages. Let's outline some of the facts and best practices around these two types to allow us to make the best design decisions for our environment.

Local data store databases:

- No additional costs associated with database software, database servers, or database client software to load

- Good for farms of up to 40 servers (we recommend no more than five servers in a farm with Access or MSDE)

Network data store databases:

- Additional cost for database server and licenses

- More flexible, as the database is separate from a Presentation Server in the farm

- More scalable through database replication

- More fault tolerant through database clustering

- Good for larger farms (five servers and larger)

Data store connections come in two flavors, direct and indirect. Depending on the type of data store database you select, you will have options here. Indirect connections are required for servers that are members of the farm where a local data store database (MS Access or MSDE) is used. Why, you may ask? Since the database exists on the first

Citrix server in the farm, all servers must communicate indirectly via the IMA service to gain information from the database. In other words, if Server1 were the first server in the farm, it would maintain the MS Access database. If Server2, a member of the same farm, needs to gain access to the farm database, the IMA service on Server2 communicates with the IMA service on Server1, and then the IMA service on Server1 fulfills the request for Server2 and returns the results via IMA (thus indirectly). As you can see, Server1 is the single point of failure and a major scalability concern. Thus, most architects agree that a direct connection method is the best in terms of scalability and fault tolerance. A direct connection requires each Presentation Server to maintain its own connection to the data store; therefore, it will require all the necessary database client software (such as the MDAC, Oracle client, or DB2). Additionally, licensing will need to be maintained for each server that will connect.

The next component to consider is the *local host cache* (LHC). The LHC is a partial copy of the data store database that every Presentation Server maintains locally to the server itself (hence the name). The partial local replica is maintained in MS Access format and is encrypted, similar to the information in the data store database. There are many reasons why a Presentation Server would want to maintain a partial copy of the data store database locally; however, two reasons sum up most of the logic behind this decision. First, by maintaining a local partial replica of the data store database, the Presentation Server could continue running based on the configuration that is last received from the data store. Therefore, in the event of failure of the server that houses the actual data store, the farm could continue functioning for up to 96 hours (based on a hard limit imposed by Citrix). The second reason is all about performance. Servers may need to frequently consult the information in the data store database. In a larger farm, this could lead to a bottleneck at the server housing the database. Therefore, with a partial replica being available locally, the IMA service can review those settings and synchronize in the background with the "master" copy of the data store. This provides much greater scalability and much less reliance on the server housing the data store database. By default, Presentation Server 3.0 maintains this database in the path C:\Program Files\Citrix\Independent Management Architecture in a file named MF20.MDB.

The Management Console for MetaFrame Presentation Server (also known as the Presentation Server Console, or PMC) is the primary tool that administrators will use to manage their server farms. This tool is automatically installed when you install Presentation Server 3.0. You may install this software on a non-Presentation Server to allow you to perform remote management. To install the PMC, your target machine must meet the following requirements:

- Java Runtime Environment 1.4.1_02 or higher
- 50MB disk space
- 25MB–80MB memory (depending on version of Presentation Server)
- 800 x 600 resolution or higher

If you are going to consider installing the PMC on machines that are not Presentation Servers, be sure to consider the need to update the PMC as you update your servers with new service packs and hotfixes from Citrix. Historically, having inconsistent management console versions can cause issues when modifying the data store database (for example, changing published applications, monitoring sessions, and so forth).

Finally, we will turn our attention to the last big "architect-level" decision that we need to consider, the "way" that user's will access our newly built Presentation Server 3.0 farm. On the surface, there are two basic methods for access the farm's resource: via a locally installed MetaFrame Presentation Server Client, or via a Web browser leveraging an optional component of the MetaFrame Access Suite called Web Interface 3.0. It is not to say that both methods could not be used. Perhaps when internal to the network our clients can use the more feature-complete locally installed clients, and when they are remote, they can access the environment through the Web browser interface provided by Web Interface. There are advantages and disadvantages to both methods, so let's review these to allow us to determine which method of access is best for users.

The locally installed clients typically have varied support for Citrix client features. Citrix basically develops the client software based on the most common operating systems that are likely to be Presentation Server clients. Based on that premise, the client for Windows 32 is the most "feature rich" developed client.

Hardware Requirements

Citrix MetaFrame Presentation Server 3.0 has no substantial hardware requirements beyond what Windows Server 2003 requires apart from some disk space requirements. The amount of hard drive space required to install Presentation Server 3.0 depends on the version of Presentation Server and the amount of additional or optional components installed. Table 3.5 outlines the disk space requirements.

Table 3.5 Disk Space Requirements for Citrix MetaFrame Presentation Server 3.0

Component	Disk Space Requirement
MetaFrame Presentation Server, Enterprise Edition	400MB
Access Suite Management Console (MMC snap-ins)	25MB
Presentation Server Management Console	50MB
Document Center	35MB
MetaFrame Access Suite Licensing	30MB

Software Requirements

There are several software requirements for the installation of Citrix MetaFrame Presentation Server 3.0. These requirements depend on the component being installed. The information in Table 3.6 is based on Windows Server 2003 except where noted.

Table 3.6 Software Requirements for Citrix MetaFrame Presentation Server 3.0

Component	Software Requirement
MetaFrame Presentation Server 3.0, Enterprise Edition	Windows Installer 2.0 (*included in Windows 2000 SP3 and higher*) Java Runtime Environment (JRE) 1.4.1_02 or later (installs this version automatically if no JRE is present) Terminal Services installed and in Application Server mode Windows 2000 Server (Standard, Advanced, or Datacenter) Windows Server 2003 (Standard, Enterprise, or Datacenter) *Although not a requirement for installation, Citrix MetaFrame Access Suite Licensing and Terminal Services Licensing are recommended to be installed and functioning correctly prior to installing Presentation Server.*
Access Suite Management Console (MMC snap-ins)	Windows 2000 Server (Standard, Advanced, or Datacenter) Windows Server 2003 (Standard, Enterprise, or Datacenter) Windows XP Professional Windows 2000 Professional .NET Framework 1.1 or later (installs this version automatically if no .NET Framework present) Microsoft Management Console 1.2 or later (for snap-ins) MDAC 2.6 or later (to allow reporting functions from Resource Manager Summary Database)
Presentation Server Management Console	JRE 1.4.1_02 or later (installs this version automatically if no JRE is present) Windows 2000 Server (Standard, Advanced, or Datacenter) Windows Server 2003 (Standard, Enterprise, or Datacenter) Windows XP Professional Windows 2000 Professional Windows NT 4.0 (Workstation or Server)

Continued

Table 3.6 Software Requirements for Citrix MetaFrame Presentation
Server 3.0

Component	Software Requirement
	The Presentation Server Management Console is installed by default during the installation of Presentation Server. This information is provided for administrators who elect to install this on a separate non-Presentation Server.
Document Center	Adobe Reader 5.0.5 with search capability or newer
MetaFrame Access Suite	Windows 2000 Server (Standard, Advanced, or Licensing Datacenter)Windows Server 2003 (Standard, Enterprise, or Datacenter)IIS 5.0 or later (* *If optional License Management Console is installed*)
Web Interface 3.0	Windows 2000 Server (Standard, Advanced, or Datacenter) Windows Server 2003 (Web, Standard, Enterprise, or Datacenter) IIS 5.0 or later .NET Framework 1.1 or later (installs this version automatically if not present) Visual J# .NET 1.1 or later (installs this version automatically if not present) ASP.NET (Windows component that will have to be manually installed)

Methods of Deploying MetaFrame Presentation Server 3.0

Finally, the great day of installation is nearly upon us. A few lingering decisions to be made and we are on our way to server-based computing nirvana. However, before we reach the Promised Land, we must decide "how" to install Presentation Server 3.0. The options we have for installation are similar to those we reviewed when discussing platform deployment options earlier in this chapter.

- Manual

- Unattended or scripted install

- Group Policy Object or Systems Management Server-based install

- Integrated into server provisioning

Manual is a great option for building your first server in the farm, as the effort to build the first server using script typically isn't justified, as the scripts would require substantial changes in order to install member servers in the farm. The manual process would typically be used to build a dedicated data collector, for instance.

Unattended or scripted installs are possible through two options provided by Citrix. The first option leverages a standard text file provided on the installation CD. Locate the installation media, browse the folders Support\Install, and locate a file named UnattendedTemplate.txt. This file can be edited with any standard text editor such as Notepad. This file provides full instructions *within* the file as to how to edit the file to accomplish the specific setup options, such as joining or creating a farm, adding a Web interface, selecting the version of Presentation Server 3.0, and so forth. It is important to note that not all options are required to have information entered. For instance, if you were editing the template file to allow for unattended installs to join an existing farm, you would not need to enter information in the create farm sections. Once the file has been edited, you can use it with a parser that Citrix also ships on the installation media in the same path as the UnattendedTemplate.txt called UNATTENDEDINSTALL.EXE. The UNATTENDEDINSTALL.EXE allows us to leverage the MSI package provided by Citrix and the unattended answer text file you just created to silently install Presentation Server. You can use the following command-line syntax to use it to install Presentation Server:

```
UNATTENDEDINSTALL.exe R:\MetaFrame Presentation Server\MPS.msi
X:\YourAnswerFile.txt
```

R:\ is the path to the Presentation Server 3.0 Install CD or the contents thereof.

X:\YourAnswerFile.Txt is the path and name of the unattended answer file we created by editing the template.

NOTE

The unattended answer file you create contains important information that most network administrators will want to keep secure. The file contains entries for the username and password for both farm creation and data store access. As there is no method to encrypt this information in a text file, you could optionally leave the entries blank. The file will still prove useful for installing Presentation Server; it will simply halt install and wait for input from the person executing the install for the "empty" answers.

When troubleshooting scripted installs, we recommend reviewing the following settings in the unattended answer file:

[Options]
RebootOnFinish=Yes
LogLevel=*v
LogFile=c:\msi.log

UILevel= BASIC_UI_NO_MODAL

In the OPTIONS section, the LogLevel=*v implies log everything and sets the level to verbose. More importantly is the path where the log is written in LogFile=C:\msi.log. Change this entry to an appropriate path based on your server's configuration, keeping in mind that some administrators choose to save these install logs to a common network share if you choose to install batches of server simultaneously.

The second unattended or scripting option involves using the command-line MSIEXEC.EXE to provide a "full string" of answers to the Windows Installer service as it reads and executes the directions in the MPS.MSI package. This is our personal favorite option, as it allows us to not have the bother of creating and maintaining an answer file. This syntax that we will review can also be leveraged to perform silent installs via group policy or Systems Management Server in the following section (in addition to the method described there).

The following list is the options that can be used as "switches" to perform a command-line install of Presentation Server 3.0 using the MSIEXEC.EXE (command-line Windows Installer Service). This example is of a server install that is joining a farm. For complete information on this process, refer to the *Advanced Concepts Guide MetaFrame® Presentation Server for Windows® Version 3.0* available from www.Citrix.com/support. It is important to keep in mind that as with the UnattendedTemplate.txt file from the previous section, not all options will be required.

```
msiexec /i mps.msi /qb- /l*v SOMELOG.log INSTALLDIR="%systemdrive%\Program
Files\Citrix\" CTX_MF_FARM_SELECTION="Join" CTX_MF_JOIN_FARM_DB_CHOICE="Direct"
CTX_MF_ODBC_USER_NAME="sa" CTX_MF_ODBC_PASSWORD="pass1"
CTX_MF_ODBC_RE_ENTERED_PASSWORD="pass1" CTX_MF_NFUSE_DEF_WEB_PAGE="No"
CTX_MF_SHADOWING_CHOICE="Yes" CTX_MF_XML_PORT_NUMBER="80"
CTX_MF_XML_CHOICE="Separate" CTX_MF_SERVER_TYPE="e" CTX_MF_PRODUCT_CODE="0D00-
06A7" CTX_MF_SHADOW_PROHIBIT_NO_LOGGING="No"
CTX_MF_SHADOW_PROHIBIT_NO_NOTIFICATION="No"
CTX_MF_SHADOW_PROHIBIT_REMOTE_ICA="No" CTX_MF_LAUNCH_CLIENT_CD_WIZARD="No"
CTX_MF_SILENT_DSNFILE="PathtoDSN\MF20.DSN"
CTX_MF_CREATE_REMOTE_DESKTOP_USERS=CopyUsers CTX_MF_ADD_ANON_USERS=No
CTX_RDP_DISABLE_PROMPT_FOR_PASSWORD="Yes" CTX_MF_TURN_FEATURE_RELEASE_ON="Yes"
CTX_MF_REBOOT="Yes"
```

Let's exam what the various "switches" are doing in a method that's a little easier to understand. We will proceed "entry" by "entry" with the plain explanation of what is occurring in the preceding syntax.

■ The Windows Installer Service (msiexec) is started and instructed to (/i) install MPS.MSI.

- During this install action, the service is to perform a quiet install (/qb-) and log (/l) everything verbosely (/l*v) to a file called somelog.log.

- Presentation Server will be installed (INSTALLDIR) to C:\Program Files\Citrix and will join the farm using a direct connection to the data store with the user sa and the password of pass1.

- Web Interface will not be the default Web site and shadowing will be enabled.

- The Citrix XML service will be installed separately from IIS and will use port 80.

- This server will function as an Enterprise Edition using the product 0D00-06A7.

- Shadowing will be allowed without logging or notification and will allow remote control of the session.

- The client CD wizard will not start at the end of installation.

- The installer can use the MF20.DSN from the path specified to find the data store so that it may read the information and join the farm defined therein.

- The members of the local users group on the target server will be copied into the built-in group remote desktop users (new security function with Terminal Services for Windows Server 2003).

- The anonymous accounts will not be created on the target server, thus prohibiting the use of anonymous connections to published applications on this particular server.

- As part of the new feature to support Microsoft's Remote Desktop Clients via Web Interface, the prompt for password feature will be disabled on the RDP-TCP connection.

- The feature release will be enabled and the server will reboot at the completion of the install.

Group Policy Objects or Systems Management Server (among others) can be used to deploy Presentation Server much in the same way that other applications may be delivered. This method requires the use of a transform file (MST) to apply to the Windows Installer package (MSI) or the use of the "switches" as outlined previously and in the aforementioned *Advanced Concepts Guide MetaFrame® Presentation Server for Windows® Version 3.0* available from www.Citrix.com/support. Citrix provides a series of transform files located on the install media in the Support\Install directory. However, the ability to "modify" these transform files is not provided by Citrix. The ability to edit the transform files will require the use of some third-party software such as Installshield's Admin Studio or Wise's Package Studio. Additionally, Wise's InstallTailor supports creating MST files by simulating the install of an MSI, and the best part is the price—

free—so it might be worth taking a look. Once the MST is created or edited, we can leverage the standard MSIEXEC command-line tools, Active Directory Group Policy Objects, Systems Management Server, or other tools to deploy Presentation Server 3.0.

Presentation Server 3.0 Pre-Install Decisions

In addition to the various other decisions that must be made during the installation of Citrix MetaFrame Presentation Server 3.0, there is a handful of very important decisions that must be made prior to starting the install procedure manually, scripted or otherwise. One of the decisions we will have to make is whether to reassign the terminal server's drives. The second decision concerns the need for interoperability with a NetWare environment. If you will need to allow users to authenticate to NetWare resources, you should install the Novell NetWare client *prior* to installing Presentation Server. While this is not a requirement, it is a strong recommendation due to a concept referred to as Graphical Identification and Authentication (GINA) chaining.

Citrix Presentation Server provides a feature that allows a user's client device drives to be available or "re-mapped" during the ICA session. When a user starts a session, the client device drives are remapped using drive letters that will not conflict with the server's logical volumes. In other words, if the server has a C: and D: drive and the client device has the same C: and D:, through a session the explorer can only report one C: and D: (those of the server in this case), and the client drives are "re-mapped" to other nonconflicting letters inside the session. Basically, the session "maps" the client's various local drives' roots to various letters inside the session. No changes are actually made to the local client drive letters or the servers in the process. However, it allows the user to use the local drives of the client through the session as if they were "on the server," similar to a normal mapped network drive only more "automatic." In the event of a drive conflict, as described previously, the server's drives (where all the applications are installed and running from) must stay their original letters, C: and D:. The client's drives would most likely be remapped to V: and U: for the client's C: and D:, respectively. Explaining to users that their client's local C: will appear as V: through a Citrix session can be a little confusing to support. Therefore, Citrix grants us the ability to change the server's drives to something other than C: and D: so there are no conflicts of drives through the session, and the C: the user sees in the session is truly his or her local client's C: as the server's drives have been reassigned prior to setup. The decision to reassign the server's drives should be made as soon as possible after the Windows Server 2003 has been built, especially prior to installation of applications and such. Anything that will write information about installation paths or application locations in the registry or in an INI file will most likely break if we reassign the server's drives after they have been installed. If we make the mistake of installing applications prior to reassigning the server's drives, typically we can simply reinstall them. Occasionally, this will unfortunately require a rebuild of the operating system, thus explaining the importance of making the correct decision up front.

When a user runs a session on a terminal server without Presentation Server, the authentication process occurs entirely using only the MSGina.DLL, the native Microsoft GINA for logging on to a Windows machine. When Presentation Server is installed, Citrix places a GINA in the "chain" of events. When a user runs a session on a terminal server with Presentation Server, the CTXGina.DLL grabs the information it needs, passing the credentials to the MSGina.DLL (hence the chaining). The CTXGina.DLL is responsible for assisting with a good deal of work at login time, such as drive mapping, printing mapping, and so forth. The GINA chaining issue can be problematic, as it allows for inconsistent login results, if a user session didn't "log in" using the correct GINA. Users don't get to "select" which GINA they will use; to the contrary, we as administrators change the GINA order when we install Presentation Server or the Novell NetWare client. On a workstation without Presentation Server, one that authenticates using the NetWare client, the GINA order is: the NWGina.DLL grabs the information first (to allow tree/context authentication and assist with all the NetWare scripts that can occur) and then hands the credentials to the MSGina.DLL to perform any subsequent authentication to the domain or local machine that need to occur. The NWGina.DLL is aware of the MSGina.DLL. The CTXGina.DLL is aware of both the NWGina.DLL and the MSGina.DLL. If you install the NetWare client after you install Presentation Server, the GINA chain will be broken and the CTXGina.DLL will fall out of play (causing great amounts of pain for users). Thus, the correct install sequence is Terminal Services, then the NetWare client, and finally the Citrix MetaFrame Presentation Server 3.0, thereby allowing the GINA chain to be preserved in the correct order of CTXGina.DLL | NWGina.DLL | MSGina.DLL.

Summary

In this chapter, we examined the aspects of hardware planning, platform deployment options, Windows Server 2003 installation planning, and an introduction to Citrix MetaFrame Presentation Server 3.0 farm design and planning. Quite a wide swath to cut in a single chapter, but our approach was more at a high-level overview of the concepts, a manageable piece of information to start us down the right path to planning.

We began with a look into hardware planning with a detailed discussion of horizontal vs. vertical scaling. We looked at the traditional bottlenecks that terminal servers face to allow us to better understand when and how to scale up or out. We followed with a planning section on building redundancies into our server hardware.

Next, we spent a great deal of time reviewing the architect-level concepts of platform deployment. We covered the "how am I going to deploy this hardware and software" question by examining the five different methods or approaches to platform deployment: manual installation, unattended or scripted installations, server cloning, server provisioning, and finally the hybrid approach. For each solution, we examined the pros and cons and looked at examples of the type and size of environment in which the given approach may work best.

Once we were able to answer the "how" question, we turned our attention to Windows Server 2003 specifications for deployment. We looked at the minimum requirements and reviewed some realistic recommendations for the hardware. We also discussed the various software requirements, such as "which" version of Windows Server 2003 is right for our environment. We also explored the challenging concept of software compatibility and the process and importance of conducting a software inventory.

Finally, we reviewed the basic concepts of farm design for Presentation Server. We looked at the components that exist outside the farm, such as licensing, home folders, and profiles, and reviewed the basic components that exist as part of the farm, such as the role of the data collector, the data store, and the local host cache. We also reviewed the hardware and software requirements to install Citrix MetaFrame Presentation Server 3.0.

In conclusion, installation planning and requirements involves more than just reading through a vendor-provided list of hardware minimums. Installation planning requires an architect-level view of all the components of your environment that will be impacted, not just the selection of the correct server hardware from which to host your Presentation Server-based applications. The primary focus of this chapter was to cement the concept that successful planning of a Windows Server 2003-based Presentation Server 3.0 farm requires a holistic approach to the complete network picture.

Solutions Fast Track

Hardware Planning

☑ Deciding whether to scale up or out is the first step and usually scaling out wins the day.

☑ Determining what redundancies to build in.

☑ Consideration for applications to be deployed.

☑ Options around Server Virtualization.

Platform Deployment Options

☑ Manual Installation – good for one off servers or test labs.

☑ Unattended or Scripted Installs – good for dissimilar hardware or pre-existing process.

☑ Server Cloning – Excellent for large deployment with identical hardware.

☑ Server Provisioning – the most flexible single method but involves additional complexities and costs.

☑ Hybrid Approach – the most flexible method of all, but requires the greatest level of technical expertise as it encompasses techniques from all platform deployment options.

Microsoft Windows Server 2003 Hardware/ Software Requirements and Recommendations

☑ Dual Processor Pentium 4 Xeon (fastest available with most L1 and L2 cache).

☑ 256-512 MB for the Operating System then plan for 64MB to 128MB per session (depending on applications).

☑ SCSI RAID 1 Ultra-320 15K drives.

☑ Teamed 100Mbps or faster NICs.

Citrix MetaFrame Presentation Server 3.0 Initial Farm Planning

☑ Where to place the terminal services licensing server.

- ☑ Where to place the Citrix Licensing server.

- ☑ Home Folder and Terminal Services Profile selection and placement.

- ☑ Choosing the version of Presentation Server 3.0 needed (Enterprise, Advanced or Standard).

- ☑ Data Store selection for the Citrix configuration database.

- ☑ Dedicated Data Collector placement.

Citrix MetaFrame Presentation Server 3.0 Hardware/Software Requirements and Recommendations

- ☑ 400MB for Enterprise Edition of Presentation Server.

- ☑ Windows Installer Requirements (2.0 or greater).

- ☑ JRE 1.4.1_02 or higher.

- ☑ Web Interface will require IIS 5 or 6 with ASP.

Frequently Asked Questions

The following Frequently Asked Questions, answered by the authors of this book, are designed to both measure your understanding of the concepts presented in this chapter and to assist you with real-life implementation of these concepts. To have your questions about this chapter answered by the author, browse to **www.syngress.com/solutions** and click on the **"Ask the Author"** form. You will also gain access to thousands of other FAQs at ITFAQnet.com.

Q: I have older hardware on which I am currently running Windows 2000 Server Standard Edition and MetaFrame Presentation Server 1.0. Will my hardware support Windows Server 2003 with MetaFrame Presentation Server 3.0?

A: The answer to this question is typically yes. However, a quick look at the section on "compatibility" would be recommended as well as a quick review of the Windows Server 2003 Hardware Compatibility List (HCL). Most environments that upgrade existing hardware from Windows 2000 Server to Windows Server 2003 will notice an actual improvement in server responsiveness, not to mention the huge benefits that Presentation Server 3.0 brings to the table over the aging 1.0 platform.

Q: I have been reading a great deal about the benefits of blade-based computing, especially for Citrix MetaFrame Presentation Server farms. Will I see any appreciable benefit to deploying a rack of blades versus a rack of 1U servers?

A: Typically, blade solutions are all about rack density. Your end users will most likely never know the difference in performance between a session running on an HP BL20p blade versus an HP Proliant 360 G4. The real benefit of blades comes from the number of servers you can fit into the same amount of space. If you consider a standard 42U rack, you could fit 42 1U HP 360s. The same 42U rack could accommodate in excess of 60 blades. Additionally, and in many cases more importantly, are the management benefits that blades force to the table (notice we didn't say "bring"). Blades typically have much better cable management and similar or lower power consumption. They also typically "share" network and fiber connections through "mezzanines" for the blade enclosure, resulting in less cabling and less numbers of switch and storage area network ports. However, where blades shine would be the server provisioning software that is invariably required to operate and configure them. The single seat administration for hardware and operating system provisioning to entire racks of servers truly begins to deliver on the promise of *adaptive computing*.

Q: I understand that the data collector maintains the "dynamic" information in the zone for the server farm. In the previous version of Presentation Server, 1.0, Citrix's documentation stated that a zone should have no more than 100 servers, even though the maximum size was 256, in order to not "overload" the zone's data collector. With MetaFrame Presentation Server 3.0, is this still the case?

A: In short, for most farms the answer will be no. With Presentation Server 3.0, Citrix rearchitected the design of the data collector. In a 1.0 farm, the data collectors will responsible for complete knowledge of all servers and zones including their own, thus creating a scalability concern. With Presentation Server 3.0, the zone data collector is now only responsible for complete knowledge of the zone it is charged with managing, thus eliminating this bottleneck. In MetaFrame Presentation Server 3.0, zones of up to 256 servers are acceptable.

Chapter 4

Upgrade and Migration Strategies for Citrix MetaFrame

Solutions in this Chapter:

- **Should I Upgrade?**

- **Mapping Out an Upgrade Strategy**

- **Migrating Older Citrix Versions**

- **License Migrations**

- **Migrating MetaFrame 1.8 Servers to MPS 3.0**

- **Migrating MetaFrame XP Servers to MPS 3.0**

☑ **Summary**

☑ **Solutions Fast Track**

☑ **Frequently Asked Questions**

Introduction

In this chapter, we examine the steps required for a successful migration to MetaFrame Presentation Server (MPS) 3.0. Because MPS 3.0 represents an evolution of the previous Citrix software versions, different steps are required depending on your starting point. For example, administrators upgrading from MetaFrame 1.8 on NT4.0 Terminal Services Edition will have a lot more work to do than someone migrating from MetaFrame XPS on Windows 2000. In either case, careful planning will lead to greater success.

The key to any migration is to map out your strategy ahead of time and weigh the pros and cons of every available path. Taking the time to understand your options can help to prevent lost time later recovering from an unforeseen migration issue. It is impossible to cover the entire scope of both operating system (OS) migration and the migration of your Citrix software here, so this chapter will deal primarily with the Citrix side of the strategy.

Should I Upgrade?

You have the hardware. You have the software. And you have the desire. Your chance to upgrade is here, and you are ready to seize it. But should you? That's the first question you need to ask. Just because it's new and shiny doesn't mean it's the best choice for your environment. Here are some simple questions to consider before you tackle migration planning:

- Are there any fixes to issues I have?
- Are there any new features that I need for my farm?
- What will it cost me in terms of money and man hours?
- What will the impact be to my users?

These probably seem like simple questions, but they do need to be asked. If you are all about the latest and greatest software, then you can probably glaze over this section and get on with the nitty-gritty of the upgrade process. For the rest of you, let's address the questions one at a time.

Are There Any Software Fixes?

Yes. MPS 3.0 incorporates quite a few fixes and updates to the MetaFrame platform. That alone isn't a reason to upgrade, unless those software fixes have an impact on your environment. Citrix publishes a list of the fixes that are incorporated with MPS 3.0 in the Readme file, which can be found on the MPS 3.0 installation CD and online at www.citrix.com. You should also take the time to read the *MPS 3.0 Administrator's Guide* and the *MPS 3.0 Advanced Concepts Guide*. There is a load of great information to be found, and taking the time to read it now could save you some headaches later in life.

Are There New Features?

Of course! MPS 3.0 is a major feature release for the MetaFrame platform. Here are a few key features of MPS 3.0:

- Microsoft Management Console snap-in for ease of Citrix management
- Zone preference settings for multisite farms
- Extended policies within the console to control almost every aspect of client connection
- Client-side microphone support for digital dictation
- Advanced Speedscreen functionality for improved user connection speed experience and server load

These are just some of the areas that MPS 3.0 improves on MetaFrame XP. For a complete list of features, please see Chapter 2 of this book and the *MetaFrame Presentation Server Administrator's Guide.*

What Will It Take?

This is a question only you can answer. The cost in time and budget depends entirely on your current situation and what the migration will consist of. If you are simply moving from MetaFrame XP FR3 on Windows Server 2003, the process is relatively simple. If for some reason you are still on Citrix WinFrame, expect it to be a lot more complicated. Take the time to consider everything involved and budget your time and money accordingly. Make sure the migration makes sense for your situation

What Will the Impact Be?

Again, this is dependent on your situation. It is possible that your users might never know a migration happened. Through proper planning and backend strategies, you can minimize the impact on your users and still be able to perform you migration tasks. Later in this chapter, we address how you can maintain user connectivity through the migration process.

Mapping Out an Upgrade Strategy

Stop! Before you pop in that CD and fire up Install Shield, take the time to understand everything involved in your migration process. What is your migration strategy? Do you have a plan to back out if things go bad? Will your users be affected by any downtime? Have you tested your migration strategy in a Quality Assurance (QA) environment? These are just some of the things you need to consider when tackling an upgrade strategy. Nothing is more important to your successful upgrade than the time you spend planning the process and execution.

Table 4.1 lists the available upgrade and migration methods depending on your base software version. Make sure you understand the options presented before deciding on a migration strategy.

Table 4.1 Migration Strategies by Current Software Revision

Current Citrix Version	Current OS Version	Migration Path
Citrix WinFrame	Citrix WinFrame (NT3.51)	Migration is not supported. WinFrame was a stand-alone product that combined NT3.51 and early Citrix ICA technology. You must configure a fresh install of Windows Server 2003 and MPS 3.0.
Citrix MetaFrame 1.8	Windows NT4 Terminal	Migration is not supported Server Edition from NT4TSE. You must configure a fresh install of Windows Server 2003 and MPS 3.0.
Citrix MetaFrame 1.8	Windows 2000 Server	Because we are focusing on Windows Server 2003 in this book, a clean install of Windows Server 2003 and MPS 3.0 will be required. For reference, a direct upgrade to 3.0 can be done on Windows 2000 Server as long as Service Pack 4 for Windows 2000 in installed. With MetaFrame 1.8, you are also presented with the opportunity to choose a Parallel Migration strategy or to use Interoperability Mode.
Citrix MetaFrame XP (any version)	Windows NT4 Terminal Server Edition	Migration is not supported from NT4TSE. You must configure a fresh install of Windows Server 2003 and MPS 3.0.

Continued

Table 4.1 continued Migration Strategies by Current Software Revision

Current Citrix Version	Current OS Version	Migration Path
Citrix MetaFrame XP (any version)	Windows 2000 Server	Again, a clean install of Windows Server 2003 and MPS 3.0 is required. The same caveats as the 1.8 on Windows 2000 migration apply, with the exception of Interoperability Mode.
Citrix MetaFrame XP	Windows Server 2003	A direct upgrade to MPS 3.0 is possible. Please make sure to read the *License Migration* section. Citrix also recommends that you install Microsoft hotfix MS03-045 prior to installing MPS 3.0.

Your QA Environment

We cannot stress enough the importance of having a QA or test bed environment. Without it, you are severely limiting your ability to test your migration strategy ahead of time. The QA system allows testing of new applications, patches, underlying system changes, and of course, major updates such as migrations to new versions. Many administrators choose to run without a QA environment, either by choice or by necessity. We consider that to be like driving a car without insurance. You might go your whole life and never have an accident. However, you could be hit backing out of your driveway. Think of QA as your IT insurance policy.

As a real-world example, a company this author worked for was in a rush to deploy a medical imaging program to its users. We did some basic QA on the server side to check the user load, but we failed to consider the network implications of the app before we deployed it. Citrix might be optimized for slow connections, but it is more than happy to use any bandwidth it can. These images were several megabytes in size each, and when we pushed it out to 50 radiologists the network came to a screeching halt.

This is one reason to make your QA environment a mirror of your live system. The closer it mirrors the existing environment, the more accurate your test results will be. This means maintaining like hardware and software revisions between the two environments. It also means using a knowledgeable pool of testers who can tell you whether the application is actually working as intended. Keep in mind that with good cloning techniques, you can duplicate your setup with a minimal amount of hardware. We will discuss backups and cloning in Chapter 15. It is good practice to QA all essential applications on a server before you begin an upgrade. You will need to use your own common sense about what is and is not essential.

Many applications also have underlying software version requirements that could be impacted by an upgrade. ODBC driver versions can also cause conflicts between Citrix and installed applications. Citrix also relies on Java technology for its Citrix Management Console, and an incorrect version can cause it to error out. A good QA environment will allow you to perform test runs of your migration strategy without impacting your live environment. This has the obvious benefit of minimizing outages and support calls.

Don't make the mistake of thinking that QA is going to solve all your problems. The unfortunate fact is that we are only human, and even the best QA is going to miss a problem. All you can do is to try to eliminate as many errors as possible ahead of time.

Migrating Older Citrix Versions

When Citrix first worked with the NT3.51 software to develop their technology platform, they decided to release a self-contained product that modified the NT3.51 source code to integrate ICA tightly into the underlying OS. They rebadged this product Citrix WinFrame, and sold it as a thin client computing solution. WinFrame boxes were licensed by server and by concurrent user count. Obviously at this point NT3.51, and with it Citrix WinFrame, is well past the point of support. Both Citrix and Microsoft discontinued support for it several years ago.

If you are still running WinFrame systems, this might be a good time to upgrade! WinFrame was a solid, reliable product. Unfortunately, the technology it is based on has long since reached its shelf life. Beyond the support issues, getting WinFrame installed on current hardware is close to impossible. Manufacturers no longer make drivers for NT3.51, and getting parts for older hardware is problematic.

As you might have guessed, there is no simple upgrade for WinFrame users. Obviously, your result is going to be Windows Server 2003 and MetaFrame Presentation Server 3.0. If you choose to use existing hardware, you will need to do a completely fresh install of Windows Server 2003 and MPS 3.0. Considering the age of any hardware you would be running WinFrame on, chances are that a parallel migration strategy would be more appropriate.

In a parallel migration, you would create an entirely new Citrix farm on hardware other than your current WinFrame servers. This would give you the chance to do a clean install of all software involved without disrupting your current user base. It also allows you to QA your new environment prior to the switchover from your current WinFrame solution.

Regardless of whether you are choosing an in-place or parallel migration, your first step will be to migrate your licenses to MPS 3.0 keys. Assuming you have maintained your Citrix Subscription Advantage, you are entitled to receive upgrade licenses in place of your WinFrame licenses. If you haven't maintained your Subscription Advantage, be prepared to pay a relatively hefty price for new licenses. In the next section, we will discuss the license migration process. Once you have your license requirements up to date, you can proceed with the initial install.

Keep in mind that Citrix MPS 3.0 uses a database for your IMA data store. This can be an access database on one of the Citrix boxes, or a database server such as a SQL box. If you choose to use an Access database, the first server you install and create the new Citrix farm on will host the database. For this reason, the first box you install should be the one you plan to use for that purpose. If it isn't, you can move the database to another server later in your migration process. However, for the easiest transition, it makes sense to do that box first.

The first server installed will also act as your zone data collector for the initial zone. If you are using a separate SQL server to host your data store, you will want to make sure and configure it prior to beginning the migration process. After the migration of your first server, the migration process can be performed in any order that makes sense to you. If your new Citrix server spans multiple sites or subnets, it makes sense to keep the plans for your zones in mind as you begin the process. Some administrators prefer migrating one zone at a time. Some prefer to do the primary servers of each zone first, and then fill in the member servers. There is not a requirement for a specific order.

License Migrations

This is a good time to talk about migrating your Citrix licenses. MetaFrame Presentation Server 3.0 introduced a new digital licensing scheme to Citrix farm management. Previously, licensing was maintained as part of the IMA data store. Citrix now has a separate license server technology called the MetaFrame Access Suite License Server. This server is managed by the License Management Console, a browser-based interface new to the release of MPS 3.0. Because licensing is so different with MPS 3.0, Citrix has released a guide for administrators entitled *MetaFrame Access Suite Licensing Guide*. This guide can be downloaded from www.citrix.com.

There are three tasks for license migration:

1. Choose a license server and install the Citrix MetaFrame Access Suite License Server and the License Management Console.

2. Using MyCitrix.com, fulfill your licenses and migrate them to MPS 3.0.

3. Download the created license file and store it on the license server.

The new license server technology lets you perform a number of different processes. You can now run historical usage reports, download the license files from MyCitrix.com, and a variety of other tasks. You can also have multiple dedicated license servers to prevent single points of failure. Planning your license server infrastructure is an important part of your upgrade considerations. Remember that if you have not maintained your Subscription Advantage, you will have to pay to upgrade the connection licenses before you can install them.

Table 4.2 shows some general guidelines from Citrix for deciding on your license servers based on your total number of Citrix servers.

Table 4.2 Deciding on Your License Servers

Total Servers	License Server Recommendations
Less than 50	A shared license server is fine for this installation.
50 to 500	A dedicated license server is recommended.
500 or more	Multiple dedicated license servers.

Another consideration to improve your license server performance is geographical concerns. If your farm or farms span multiple geographic locations, you might want to consider a dedicated license server for each region. This will improve the overall response time that your users experience. Keep in mind that if you divide your licenses between multiple farms, they are locked to that particular farm. You cannot share licenses between farms.

For example, suppose you manage three separate farms. Prior to the new license model, you would have been required to keep track of your licenses separately for each farm and maintain them on an individual basis. With the new licensing model, you can roll all of your licenses to a single group and then divide them between the farms based on need. You can even shift licenses from one farm to another if your capacity needs change.

License Migration from MetaFrame 1.8

Migrating MetaFrame 1.8 licenses is a two-step process. First, the licenses must be converted from 1.8 licensing to MetaFrame XP. At that point, you can convert the XP licenses to MPS 3.0. The XP licenses do not ever need to be downloaded or installed, but a direct migration from 1.8 to MPS 3.0 licenses is not possible. The details for the process are relatively simple, but they do need to be followed to generate a valid license file.

Here are the steps for license migration from MetaFrame 1.8:

1. Log on to your MyCitrix.com account (www.mycitrix.com).

2. Choose **Licensing | Fulfillment | Fulfill Eligible Products** and choose the program type of your license.

3. Select **MetaFrame XP Presentation Server** as the product to receive.

4. Open the MetaFrame Presentation Server Migration page and select the licenses you want to migrate. You will get a Product Fulfillment Certificate to confirm the conversion and display the resulting codes.

Once these new codes have been generated, follow the steps in the next section to migrate your new XP licenses to MPS 3.0. Once the migration is complete, you can allocate the new licenses into the license files and download those files to your license server(s).

Migrating Licenses from MetaFrame XP

License migration from MetaFrame XP to MPS 3.0 can be done directly through License Fulfillment on MyCitrix.com. Licenses can be migrated from any of the MetaFrame XP versions, with any Feature Release installed. The following steps detail the process for the license migration from MetaFrame XP:

1. Log on to your MyCitrix.com account (www.mycitrix.com).

2. Choose **Licensing | Fulfillment | Fulfill Eligible Products** and choose the program type of your license.

3. Select **MetaFrame Presentation Server 3.0** as the product to receive.

4. Open the MetaFrame Presentation Server Migration page and select the licenses you want to migrate. You will get a Product Fulfillment Certificate to confirm the conversion and display the resulting codes.

Once the new license codes have been generated, they must be allocated into license files, and the files must be copied to the appropriate license server. When you allocate licenses, you can choose to use some or all of your available licenses at a time. The file generated is a digitally signed file that contains your product licenses and the information needed by the license server.

To activate and download your license files:

1. Open the License Manager console and click on **Configure License Server**.

2. On the License Files page, select **Download license file from MyCitrix.com**.

3. Select **Licensing | Citrix Activation System | Activate or Allocate Licenses.** You will be prompted through the activation process.

4. From the menu, choose **Download License File**.

5. Decide how many licenses you want to allocate to this file. You can choose all or a portion of the licenses. Type in the name of the license server where this file will be stored.

6. Download the license file. The file will have a .lic extension. By default, the last location used by your Save As is where the license file will be placed.

7. Navigate to the Licenses Files page in the Configuration tab of the License Management Console.

8. Select **Copy license file to License Server**.

You have now successfully migrated your MetaFrame XP licenses to MPS 3.0 license files. Your MPS 3.0 servers will use the licenses provided by the license server when clients connect to their published applications.

Migrating MetaFrame 1.8 Servers to MPS 3.0

Now that you have successfully migrated your licenses to a new MPS 3.0 license server format, you can begin the process of migrating your MetaFrame 1.8 servers to MPS 3.0. Citrix provides two paths for migration from a 1.8 farm to MPS 3.0. Your first decision is going to be which path you will support.

Parallel Migration or Interoperability Mode?

When you begin your migration plan from 1.8 to MPS 3.0, two choices are available:

- **In-place migration** (Interoperability Mode) In an in-place migration strategy, you will be using the existing hardware infrastructure in the new Citrix environment. This means that any OS upgrades, Citrix software upgrades, and application changes will be made to boxes that are in your current Citrix environment.

- **Creating a new server farm** (parallel migration) A parallel migration strategy involves creating an entirely new Citrix environment. This allows you to perform all the installations, upgrades, and application configurations in an entirely clean install.

Configuring and Implementing...

Can I Do an In-Place Migration?

Interoperability Mode is only available with MetaFrame 1.8 farms. Older MetaFrame versions such as 1.0 and Citrix WinFrame 1:8 are unable to run in Interoperability Mode with MPS 3.0. This obviously limits your migration strategy to only one choice, a parallel migration. Another key factor in deciding your upgrade strategy is whether the current hardware will support the new software requirements.

It is also important to note that Citrix does not support OS upgrades. If you choose to upgrade your operating system as part of your migration plan, you will

Continued

need to install MPS 3.0 as a clean install instead of upgrading. This is why it is important to understand the total impact of your migration, and to develop a strong strategy.

Creating a New Farm for Migration

The easiest method for migrating your 1.8 boxes to MPS 3.0 is to create an entirely new farm. This is similar to a fresh installation, and avoids the limitations and problems that Interoperability Mode can present. There are several advantages inherent to this choice for migration:

- Using the multiple farms features of the Web Interface, you can provide seamless access to both the old and new farms without your users realizing there has been a change.

- Everything is installed from the ground up, giving you a chance to consider all of your application concerns.

- The new farm can be a good QA test bed until live implementation.

- All MPS 3.0 features will be immediately available.

If you take the approach of creating a new farm, there are several steps you can take to help manage users' applications while the migration process is happening.

1. Using the Web Interface, you can publish applications from multiple farms to users in a single list.

2. Load balance the applications between the old and new farms and publish the same applications in both.

3 Organize the applications so that you migrate them in logical groups where possible to lessen the reliance on the old farm.

Load Balancing Old and New Farms

Load balancing applications between old and new farms is a good method to keep your users productive while performing your migrations. If the Web Interface is already installed, it only requires a few general steps to be successful:

1. Build your new farm running MPS 3.0.

2. Make sure your applications are published in the new farm with exactly the same name as in the old farm.

3. In the Web Interface Console, configure the **Server Address** list so that servers from both farms are included and select **Use the server list for load balancing**.

4. As you upgrade your servers or install new hardware, join them to the new farm and publish applications to them. This process keeps the user impact to a minimum

Using Application Lists

Because the Web Interface provides users with application sets from multiple farms, you can configure the applications displayed to further enhance the seamless transition feeling. Once you have set up the new farm and published your applications, navigate to the **Manage MetaFrame Server Farms** page of the Web Interface Console and select the farms you want to be available to your users.

This feature makes application set migrations for large applications much easier for administrators. You can publish the apps in both the old and new farms, but the users will be presented with only the single instance of the app. They will then be load balanced between the two farms (and between servers within those farms if multiple servers host that published app) in a nonintrusive fashion. A consistent set of applications can be maintained for your user community with minimal effort or downtime.

Interoperability Mode

In some cases, it is not possible to create an entirely new farm to run MPS 3.0. For this reason, Citrix developed a process called Interoperability Mode to allow MetaFrame 1.8 and MPS 3.0 servers to coexist and communicate with each other. Interoperability Mode is not designed to be a permanent solution, and is not considered a best-practice strategy. If you choose to use Interoperability Mode, please be aware of the following disadvantages:

- Many of the management and client features of MPS 3.0 will not be available while the server is designated as running in Interoperability Mode.

- Installing and publishing new applications to the farm is problematic and not recommended during the time Interoperability Mode is running.

- You must maintain separate licensing for each product version.

- Troubleshooting and administration is significantly more difficult while in Interoperability Mode.

As you can tell, Citrix really doesn't want you to run in Interoperability Mode. In some cases, however, you may lack the hardware for a separate MPS 3.0 farm, or the Web Interface may not be a route you want to employ. Interoperability Mode is not the ideal solution, but it does provide a transition point for you to complete the migration process and get all of your servers to MPS 3.0.

Follow these steps to configure Interoperability Mode:

1. Configure the database server for your new farm. If you are using anything other than the default Access database, this server cannot be an MPS 3.0 server. If you are using Access, the first server you install MPS 3.0 on will become the data store.

2. Upgrade your first server to Windows Server 2003 and install MPS 3.0. This should not be one of your current ICA Master Browsers.

3. During the setup, make sure to name the new MPS 3.0 farm the exact same name as your MetaFrame 1.8 farm.

4. Within the MPS 3.0 Management Console on the new server, highlight the farm and select **Farm Properties**. In the **Interoperability** section, choose **Work with MetaFrame 1.8 servers in the farm**. This server is now your ICA Master Browser.

5. By default, this server also becomes the zone data collector. This can be changed later in the **Zones** section of the farm properties.

6. Reboot the server once the setup is complete. This will force a master browser election. Applications will be temporarily unavailable during this process.

Configure Client Access

Once you have enabled Interoperability Mode on your new server, make sure to publish the applications you want available to the users. Your users will also need to receive the latest Citrix ICA client so they can access the MPS 3.0 boxes. The client can be distributed through an automatic download on the Web Interface if you choose to use it, or turn on the auto-update feature on each new server. Until all of your users have received the updated client version, you cannot disable the client UDP broadcasts on your MPS 3.0 boxes.

WARNING

Don't forget to disable Interoperability Mode once you have completed your migration process. Until you do, certain features of MPS 3.0 will be unavailable to you or your users.

Why Shouldn't I Use Interoperability Mode?

Make sure you understand all of the consequences that Interoperability Mode brings. Most administrators consider it more of a headache than a help. Here are the major limitations Interoperability Mode presents:

- Active Directory user logons cannot be performed with user principal name (UPN) format. MetaFrame 1.8 does not support Active Directory, and will not display application sets or allow client connections to MetaFrame 1.8 boxes with UPN logins.

- Any application addition or modification must be done in both farms, and done exactly the same.

- Users with older client versions will not be able to locate the published applications unless you enable the UDP Broadcast Response setting in the farm properties of your MPS 3.0 farm. Make sure you have upgraded your clients before you turn off UDP response, and before you turn off Interoperability Mode.

- During the initial configuration process, the new MPS 3.0 server becomes the ICA Master Browser. This forces a browser election, which can cause hang-ups in application response. It is recommended that this initial setup be performed after hours. Additionally, if new MPS 3.0 servers are brought up in other subnets, they will take over the Master Browser duties for that subnet.

Application Load Management with Interoperability Mode

A farm running in Interoperability Mode can load balance applications across both the MPS 3.0 and MetaFrame 1.8 servers. The applications must be published with exactly the same name on both servers. Only default load evaluators may be used until all the servers are migrated.

While you are running in Interoperability Mode, application load balancing occurs in the following sequence:

1. A user selects a published application. The client software requests the least loaded server's address from the ICA Master Browser (in this case, the MPS 3.0 server).

2. The ICA Master Browser identifies the server with the lightest load among the MetaFrame 1.8 boxes, and the server with the lightest load among the MPS 3.0 boxes.

3. The master browser compares the user load on the two identified servers and sends the client the address of the one with the fewest sessions. If both have the same load, the client is directed to the MPS 3.0 server.

Once you have finished the migration process and Interoperability Mode has been disabled, you can use the Load Manager to configure the load evaluators instead. These evaluators provide you with many more options beyond the default session load.

Migrating MetaFrame XP to MPS 3.0

Migrating from MetaFrame XP to MPS 3.0 is a much simpler process than migrating from a 1.8 server farm. There is no need to run in any kind of Interoperability Mode, because MPS 3.0 is built on the same technology as MetaFrame XP.

If you are already running MetaFrame XP on a Windows Server 2003 server, you can perform a direct migration without upgrading the OS. MetaFrame XP can run on Windows Server 2003 with Feature Release 3 installed. Prior versions of MetaFrame XP were not compatible with Windows Server 2003.

Configuring and Implementing...

What If I'm Running XP on a 2000 Server?

As mentioned before, Citrix does not support an OS upgrade without a fresh install of the Citrix product. If you decide to migrate your Windows 2000 servers to 2003 as part of this process, you will obviously have to perform the OS upgrade first. This will complicate matters if you are using an Access database for your data store. Traditionally, you would want the first server you migrate to be the one that hosts your data store. However, since you will be upgrading the OS and reinstalling Citrix, this will destroy your data store.

One method for getting around this is to move your data store to a separate database server. If you already have a database infrastructure (or even a spare server), this option might make the most sense. Once you have performed the data store migration to the database server, you can simply designate another server as the zone data collector when you need to reinstall your former data store machine.

By default, the first machine you migrate to MPS 3.0 will take over the data collector duties. It has a higher ICA browser level revision than your XP machines. If you migrate a server other than the one that you want to be your data collector first, make sure to go back later and correctly configure your zones.

If you use an Access database but do not want to move it to a database server, you will need to database to a new server. Chapter 15 provides the steps required to move an Access data store from one Citrix server to another.

Checklist for Migrating an Existing Farm

Migrating an existing farm from MetaFrame XP to MPS 3.0 is relatively simple, but you have to make sure to do it in the correct order:

1. Install the MPS 3.0 license server.

2. If you use Resource Manager, you must manually update the summary database.

3. If you use MetaFrame Conferencing Manager, upgrade it to version 3.0.

4. Upgrade the MetaFrame Presentation Server Console.

5. Upgrade the Web Interface from older NFuse versions.

6. If you are using Access for your data store, migrate the data store server first.

7. Upgrade all of your zone data collectors.

8. Upgrade Resource Manager.

9. Upgrade the rest of your farm servers.

10. Upgrade your Network Manager plug-ins.

User Access During Migration

The Web Interface is the easiest method to provide users access to all of the applications during the migration process. Because the Web Interface can access all of your Citrix farms and provide a consolidated application list to your users, there is no need for multiple logins and different access methods between farms. This remains true regardless of your method of migration.

There are other ways to provide access to your users. If you choose to do a parallel migration, you can do a mass conversion of your users to the new farm by simply changing your Web Interface settings to point to the new farm. Another alternative is to push out a new Program Neighborhood program that points to the new servers. Whatever method you choose for completing your migration, be sure to weigh the impact for your user community. The most successful migration is one where the users never even know it happened.

Installing the License Server

We discussed the upgraded licensing program that Citrix has provided with MetaFrame Presentation Server earlier in this chapter. Please follow the instructions for installing and configuring your MPS .0 licensing server prior to beginning the migration process. More details about the license server installation can be found in the *MetaFrame Access Suite Licensing Guide*, which is available from the Document Center.

Upgrading Conferencing Manager

If you already use MetaFrame's Conferencing Manager in your environment, it is important that you upgrade it to Version 3.0 prior to installing MPS 3.0. You must also install and configure the Guest Attendee Web Interface after you upgrade the Web Interface server and your MPS 3.0 servers. Additional details on the process can be found in the *MetaFrame Conferencing Manager Administrator's Guide* in the Document Center.

Upgrading the MPS Console

MPS 3.0 uses a new console for the management of your Citrix environment. If you already have the Citrix Management Console for MetaFrame XP installed on workstations in your environment, you need to upgrade it to the MPS 3.0 console version. Using the older console to modify data in the farm can cause corruption. New settings from MPS 3.0 will also be unavailable for configuration.

Upgrading the Web Interface

The installation process of MetaFrame Presentation Server can wipe out any settings you have on your servers for earlier versions of the Web Interface. If you need to maintain those settings, upgrade the Web Interface component first. This can be done from the MetaFrame Presentation Server Components CD to perform just the Web Interface migration. Once this upgrade has been done, the MPS 3.0 install will not remove the Web Interface or the settings when it is installed.

Migrate Your Data Store

If you are using an Access database for your data store locally on a Citrix server, you need to migrate this server first. This will update the data store information correctly, and will make sure that this server remains the data store server. If MPS 3.0 is installed on a different server first, it may try to recreate the data store without the correct information. If you have your data store installed on a database server instead of locally on a Citrix server, you may skip this step.

Updating Your Zone Data Collectors

It is good practice to upgrade your zone data collectors first. This allows them to maintain their role as the data collector because they still have the highest software revision in their zone. They will be able to support all MPS 3.0 functionality as you upgrade your member servers.

Upgrading the Resource Manager

If you have a previous version of the Resource Manager component in your farm, you will need to upgrade both farm metric servers prior to upgrading your member servers. This will prevent you from having inconsistent data in the Resource Manager database. Because MPS 3.0 uses new metric information, the new version is required to track the metrics for both old and new servers during the migration process. These are the steps to migrate Resource Manager:

1. Perform a manual update in the Management Console to import your existing data into the summary database.

2. Turn of the summary database by clearing the **Summary Database enabled** checkbox in the Summary Database Configuration dialog.

3. Upgrade the database connection server.

4. Upgrade both farm metric servers.

5. Re-enable the summary database by checking the **Summary Database enabled** checkbox.

By following this migration path, you will maintain the integrity of your Resource Manager database throughout your migration process.

Upgrading Member Servers

Now that you have upgraded the critical servers, you can begin the process of upgrading the farm's member servers. The order of the member servers is not important other than how it impacts you and your user community. Unless you have a smaller installation base, it is best to divide them into manageable chunks. This can be divided into business lines, load-balanced concerns, or even physical convenience.

Upgrading the Network Manager Plug-ins

MPS 3.0 includes new versions of the Network Manager Plug-ins. These are used in third-party SNMP console programs like Tivoli's NetView or HP OpenView. If you are using either of these programs, you must make sure to delete all of the MetaFrame objects and symbols before uninstalling the old plug-ins and installing the new version.

Summary

The choice to migrate your servers is a serious one. MPS 3.0 provides a significant upgrade over older MetaFrame versions, and there are many reasons you could choose to migrate your environment. The first thing to identify is why you should begin the migration process and to map out your migration strategy. Once you have identified your migration plan, you can choose to perform a parallel or in-place migration.

If possible, the migration process should be tested in a lab environment before doing it live. This will help you iron out any bugs in your process, and identify areas you might need to spend more time considering. The QA process will not always find every bug, but it will help you be as thorough as possible before you begin the migration process.

The actual migration process will depend entirely on your starting point. Migrating from a small XP farm to MPS 3.0 is a much easier task than migrating from WinFrame to MPS 3.0. You need to consider the time involved, any increased costs, and the impact it will have on your user community. Although migration may make sense from a technical perspective, you may have to convince your users that it makes sense from a business perspective as well.

Be sure to follow the migration steps when you begin the process. Skipping a step could have unintended consequences to your migration. For instance, failing to migrate your Resource Manager servers prior to upgrading your member servers can lead to invalid data in the Resource Manager database. In addition, make sure to pay attention to any warnings from Microsoft or Citrix prior to the migration process and read the documentation. Product documentation is available on the MPS 3.0 CD and on Citrix's Web site.

Solutions Fast Track

Should I Upgrade?

- ☑ Are there fixes for current bugs in your environment?
- ☑ Are there improved features to benefit your user community?
- ☑ Do you have the time and budget?
- ☑ What will the user impact be?

Mapping Out an Upgrade Strategy

- ☑ Understand what your migration choices are based on your starting point.
- ☑ Try to use a test bed to try your migration strategy before implementing it in the live environment.

☑ Your test bed won't catch every error, but it will help the process.

Migrating Older Citrix Versions

☑ Citrix does not support OS upgrades with MetaFrame installs, so you will have to upgrade the servers to Windows Server 2003 first or use new hardware.

☑ You may not be able to do an in-place migration based on your starting point and your current hardware.

License Migrations

☑ Understanding and implementing the new licensing structure is very important. It has drastically changed!

☑ Follow the license guidelines from Citrix in deciding how many servers you require.

☑ If you have not maintained your Subscription Advantage, you will have to pay for the upgrade licenses.

☑ You will need to convert MetaFrame 1.8 licenses to MetaFrame XP before you can convert them to MPS 3.0.

Migrating MetaFrame 1.8 to MPS 3.0

☑ You must decide between doing an in-place or parallel migration.

☑ Citrix provides you with Interoperability Mode to allow you to run different versions at the same time.

☑ Interoperability Mode does limit functionality in your MPS 3.0 farm, and should be disabled as soon as possible.

☑ If you are performing a parallel migration, you can provide continuous application access with the Web Interface or with the Program Neighborhood client.

Migrating MetaFrame XP to MPS 3.0

☑ If you are already on Windows Server 2003, you can perform a straight upgrade to Citrix.

☑ There is a specific order you must follow to migrate your existing servers to MPS 3.0.

☑ You must use the new console software to manage any farm with MPS 3.0 installed, or you will not be able to access all of the features.

☑ Follow the checklist provided to make your migration process as smooth as possible.

Links to Sites

☑ **www.citrix.com** The primary Web site for Citrix Systems

☑ **www.mycitrix.com** The Web site used to fulfill subscription licensing and get product updates

Frequently Asked Questions

The following Frequently Asked Questions, answered by the authors of this book, are designed to both measure your understanding of the concepts presented in this chapter and to assist you with real-life implementation of these concepts. To have your questions about this chapter answered by the author, browse to **www.syngress.com/solutions** and click on the **"Ask the Author"** form. You will also gain access to thousands of other FAQs at ITFAQnet.com.

Q: What if I need to perform an OS upgrade on the server that has my Access-based data store?

A: One method is to copy the MF20.dsn file to a new server and then edit the WSID parameter to point to the new cache server instead of the old one. This keeps your existing servers able to connect. It might also be a good time to consider a separate database server.

Q: I have licenses for multiple Citrix products. How should I divide my license servers?

A: When possible, Citrix recommends having all of your licenses for the same product on the same license server.

Q: I'm running the very early MetaFrame 1.0. What is my migration process?

A: You will need to upgrade your 1.0 licenses to 1.8, then to XP, and then to MPS 3.0.

Q: Do I need to migrate my client software as well?

A: For your clients to take advantage of all of the MPS 3.0 features, they will need to be on the 8.0 client version.

Q: Can I use the SNMP plug-ins with other software?

A: Yes, you can use the included .mib files to expose the SNMP messages to any program that can receive them.

Chapter 5

Installing and Configuring Your Windows 2003 Server

Solutions in this Chapter:

- **Pre-Installation**

- **Options for Installing Windows Server 2003**

- **Installing Windows Server 2003**

- **Configuring Windows Server 2003 for Terminal Services**

- **Post Installation Updates and Tweaks**

- **What Happened? Troubleshooting Installation Problems**

- **Windows Server 2003 Checklist**

Related chapters:

- **Installation Planning and Requirements**

- **Upgrade and Migration Strategies**

- **Server Cloning and other Disaster Recovery Strategies**

Introduction

By now, you should have all the information you need to install Windows Server 2003. As indicated in previous chapters, information gathering and planning are of the utmost importance. Knowing before you start what drivers you will need, choices you must make, and information you will need will speed the process along and give you a sense of confidence.

Pre-Installation

If you have been diligent in your implementation planning, there should be no surprises during the installation process. Those who have worked with prior versions of Windows Server will find the Windows Server 2003 installation straightforward and familiar but more complex than past versions. Whether you are a seasoned Window's administrator or just beginning, planning is critical. If you do not make the right decisions during the installation process, you could be forced to start the installation over. Careful consideration and planning will save you time and a great deal of frustration. There are a number of pre-installation tasks and decisions that must be made to ensure that your server installation is successful. Here are a few items you may want to organize before you begin:

- Verify the server hardware requirements.
- Check hardware compatibility in the Hardware Compatibility List (HCL).
- Check the Windows Server Catalog to ensure your server hardware and software are compatible. The Windows Server Catalog provides information about hardware and software products that were designed for Windows Server 2003.
- Gather and make ready any third-party drivers that may be needed. Be careful to use only drivers that have been digitally signed by Microsoft, as they have been pre-tested and certified to behave well in a Windows Server 2003 environment.
- Review and download service packs and security updates.
- Review release notes in advance.
- Decide whether you will upgrade or perform a new installation.
- Know what type of installation you will perform.
- Create a DNS-compliant name for the new server.
- Know the Domain or Workgroup the server will join.
- Create a local Administrator name and password.
- IP, Subnet Mask, Gateway, DNS, and WINS addresses that will be used.
- Decide the type of file system that will be used and formatting option.

- Know the Licensing Mode you will use.
- Make sure the Product Key is available.

In this chapter, we explore in detail the installation process and the various options you have for installing Windows Server 2003. Next, we concentrate on the post-installation configuration options. We pay close attention to those options in particular that relate to Terminal Services configuration in preparation for installing the Citrix MetaFrame Access Suite.

Because the first server you build is rarely the one moved into the production environment, we highly recommend using a test server for your first attempt. A test environment is a critical tool for administrators, as it provides a safe place to test new products, upgrades, patches, and drivers *before* turning them loose on production machines. Never assume that a program, patch, or new driver is safe. Proper testing is the ultimate safeguard for your production environment. By testing offline, you can help prevent unscheduled downtime, user frustration, *and* save your valuable reputation.

Designing and Planning…

Virtual Servers

If you do not have the spare hardware to dedicate or the capital to purchase more, other options can be employed, such as EMC's VMware or Microsoft's VirtualPC. Both provide the means to run multiple "virtual machines" on a "host" computer. This method does not require dual booting. Rather, the guest operating systems behave just as "real" machines and can be turned on/off and restarted without interfering with the host computer and its operating system. This approach is inexpensive and requires only one machine with adequate resources to act as host. Whole domains can be created on one host to mimic a test lab provided the host is equipped with enough resources.

Options for Installing Windows Server 2003

One of the earliest decisions you must make is whether to upgrade an existing Windows server or perform a new "clean" installation. While upgrading will allow you to retain existing users, groups, permissions, and settings, it is always wiser to do a new installation. Since our server will be a member server in an Active Directory, we do not have to worry about users and groups. As for retaining permissions, experienced administrators know how muddled and incorrectly applied they can become over a period of time. By performing the installation from scratch, you greatly reduce the risks of corrupt files, incorrect configuration settings, and passing existing problems to the new server. You will begin with a known good server. However, a new installation will require a few more steps. You may want to take the time to back up and document your existing servers so that you can duplicate the configuration on the new server. Since the server we discuss in this chapter will become a Citrix MetaFrame server, it is not advisable to upgrade. The possibilities of something going wrong are just too great.

The next decision you must make is what type of installation to perform. If this is your first server, you will want to do an attended installation, but other options should be considered once you have built your first server and are ready to deploy others. The choices for performing a Windows Server 2003 installation are:

- **CD-based installation** This is the standard method of installing using the server's CD-ROM or DVD drive. The Setup wizard can be started by either booting directly to the CD-ROM, or by running Winnt32.exe or Winnt.exe. Use Winnt32.exe if you are starting from within an existing Windows operating system. If you are booting from a DOS diskette, run Winnt.exe. Both executables are located in the \i386 folder on the Windows Server 2003 CD-ROM.

- **Network installation** The Windows Server 2003 files can be copied to a location on your network and used instead of a CD-ROM drive. Although a network installation can be slower than a CD-based one, multiple servers can be installed at one time. This method is also used for unattended installations. To prepare for network installations, copy the \i386 directory from the installation CD-ROM to a network share. If you are performing an installation on a new server with no existing Windows operating system, you will need a network boot diskette. Once you have booted and logged in to the network, you can map a drive to the distribution server and run WINNT.EXE to begin the installation. If you are performing the installation from a server with an existing Windows operating system, map a drive to the distribution server and run WINNT32.EXE to begin the installation.

Configuring and Implementing...

Case Scenario

Want to install Windows Server 2003 from the installation CD in drive F? We know the network card will not work with the drivers in the CD, so it is important that

Continued

we have access to these files during the setup. If the drivers were available from another computer in the network, we could issue the following command at the Run prompt.

F:\i386\winnt32 /copysource:n:\nic\oem /makelocalsource

This command will tell the computer to make a local copy of the directory where the network card drivers are stored and delete it once the installation has completed.

Automating Server Installation

Once you have built your server, tested it, and are confident that the configuration is first rate, you may want to add additional servers to your farm. Even with good documentation and planning, there is always the risk that servers will not be configured uniformly using manual, attended installations, especially in fast-paced environments where administrators juggle multiple tasks at once. Luckily, there are installation options to insure that each server is configured just as well as the first, with no variations or omissions. Two popular options are unattended, scripted installs and disk imaging.

What Automated Install Is Right for You?

When choosing your automated installation method, you must consider the hardware of both the source and destination servers. Both methods are helpful when deploying multiple servers; however, unattended, scripted installs can be used on servers with dissimilar hardware, while disk imaging or cloning requires the server hardware be identical. Disk imaging will only work if the hardware abstraction layer (HAL) is the *same* on both the source and target servers. For instance, if the source server has an Advanced Configuration and Power Interface (ACPI) HAL, the target server must have an ACPI HAL as well. Note: If you force an incorrect HAL via a disk image, the server may stop responding and report a STOP 0x0000007b error. To find out what HAL your server has, go to **Start | Setup | Control Panel | System | Hardware | Device Manager**. Expand **Computer** to see the HAL version as shown in Figure 5.1.

Figure 5.1 Windows Server 2003 Device Manager

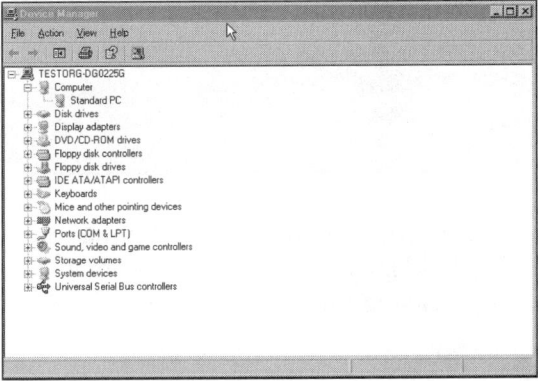

Unattended, Scripted Installs

Unattended, scripted installs use *Answer files*, which contain the unique configuration information for each server. The Answer files provide the responses to the questions asked during the installation process so that administrator intervention is not required. Windows Server 2003 includes a sample Answer file in the \i386 folder on the installation CD-ROM. The file is called *unattend.txt* and can be customized to suit your needs. Note: If you are performing an unattended installation from a CD-ROM, you must rename the unattend.txt to *Winnt.sif*. The Setup Manager wizard, located in the **\Support\Tools** folder on the Windows Server 2003 CD-ROM, provides a graphical interface for specifying setup options. To run Setup Manager, open the **DEPLOY.CAB** file, copy the contents to a folder on your hard drive, and then run **SETUPMGR.EXE**. Setup Manager creates or updates a share on the distribution server and places in it a copy of the \i386 folder from the Windows Server 2003 CD-ROM. By default, the shared folder is called *Windist*.

Setup Manager can create answer files for three types of setups: Unattended, SYSPREP, and Remote Installation Services as shown in Figure 5.2. The answer files' format and contents will depend on the type of setup you choose. When you run Setup Manager, you will be prompted for answers to the questions that are asked during an attended installation, and your responses will be placed in the Answer file, which is queried during the setup process.

Figure 5.2 Windows Server 2003 Setup Manager

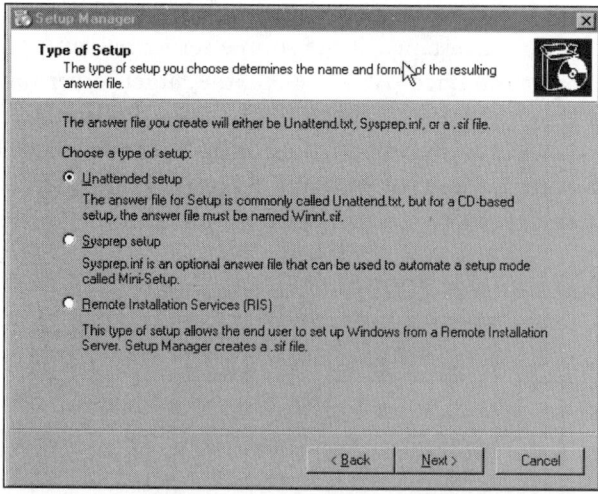

If your goal is to fully automate the installation, you must provide answers for every prompt; otherwise, administrator intervention will be required. Figure 5.3 shows the various information you can provide in the Answer file.

Figure 5.3 Setup Manager Wizard

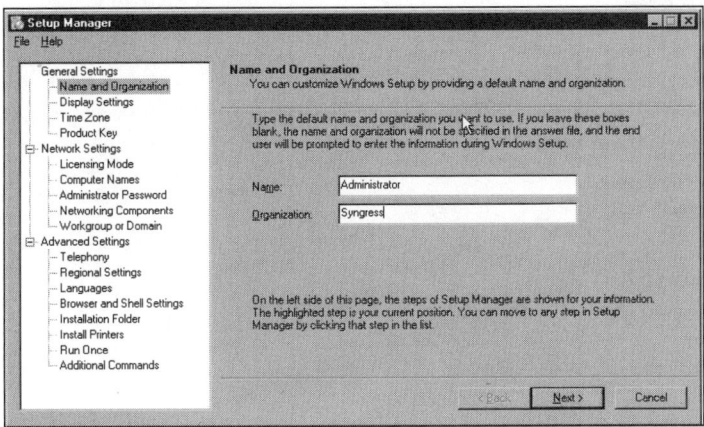

Once you have entered the information you want to provide, Setup Manager generates the unattend.txt, the unattend.udb, and unattend.bat files and places them in the \Windist folder. The unattend.udb file is the Uniqueness Database and is used to modify the answer file. The unattend.bat file is the batch file used to launch the unattended installation. The following is an example of an unattend.txt file. As you can see, it is fairly easy to decipher and could be modified manually; however, if the file format is altered, the installation process will fail.

```
;SetupMgrTag
[Data]
    AutoPartition=1
    MsDosInitiated="0"
    UnattendedInstall="Yes"


[Unattended]
    UnattendMode=FullUnattended
    OemSkipEula=Yes
    OemPreinstall=Yes
    TargetPath=\WINDOWS


[GuiUnattended]

AdminPassword=82b55c3da8a2ce77aad3b435b51404eefe52b85bc13b31dc084bb63e6335bff1
    EncryptedAdminPassword=Yes
    AutoLogon=Yes
    AutoLogonCount=12
    OEMSkipRegional=1
```

```
      TimeZone=15
      OemSkipWelcome=1


[UserData]
      ProductKey=RK39S-L08AL-D97LA-SM8DJ-8D5HL
      FullName="administrator"
      OrgName="Syngress"
      ComputerName=*


[LicenseFilePrintData]
      AutoMode=PerSeat


[SetupMgr]
      ComputerName0=CTXSYN01
      ComputerName1=CTXSYN02
      ComputerName2=CTXSYN03
      DistFolder=C:\windist
      DistShare=windist


[Identification]
      JoinDomain=SYNGRESS
      DomainAdmin=administrator
      DomainAdminPassword=dcs1947


[Networking]
      InstallDefaultComponents=No


[NetAdapters]
      Adapter1=params.Adapter1


[params.Adapter1]
      INFID=*


[NetClients]
      MS_MSClient=params.MS_MSClient


[NetServices]
      MS_SERVER=params.MS_SERVER


[NetProtocols]
      MS_TCPIP=params.MS_TCPIP
```

```
[params.MS_TCPIP]
    DNS=No
    UseDomainNameDevolution=No
    EnableLMHosts=Yes
    AdapterSections=params.MS_TCPIP.Adapter1

[params.MS_TCPIP.Adapter1]
    SpecificTo=Adapter1
    DHCP=No
    IPAddress=192.168.121.15
    SubnetMask=255.255.255.0
    DefaultGateway=192.168.121.0
    DNSServerSearchOrder=192.168.121.15,192.168.121.16
    WINS=Yes
    WinsServerList=192.168.121.12
    NetBIOSOptions=0
```

Using the Answer File

Now that we have created an answer file for an unattended installation, we need to tell the Windows Server 2003 installation process to use it. The syntax is **winnt32.exe /unattend:c:\windist\unattend.txt**, assuming you keep the default shared folder and it resides on your C: drive. Other installation options you may want to consider using are /dudisable, which disables dynamic updates, and /makelocalsource, which copies the \i386 folder to the destination hard drive.

Imaged or Cloned Installations

Imaging or cloning is typically achieved using a third-party utility such as Symantec Ghost or PowerQuest's Drive Image. This is a good choice if your servers have identical hardware. .If the source and the target server do not have identical hardware, there could be hardware and driver issues. One of the problems with creating an exact clone of your server is that it will have the same computer name, SID, and IP address as the source server. This may not be a huge issue if you are only cloning a few servers, as you could take the source server offline while you change the clone's information, but on a larger scale, it could cause chaos. Imagine if you were imaging several servers at the same time. The first to go online after imaging would cause a conflict on the network and the other servers would no longer be able to reach the source server. Luckily, Microsoft has provided a utility for exactly this reason. The System Preparation Tool, or *SYSPREP*, can be found on the Windows Server 2003 CD-ROM in the **\Support\Tools** folder.

To use SYSPREP, perform an attended installation on the source server and install any applications that will be deployed. Next, run SYSPREP on the source server. SYSPREP will delete the SID and other user and system specific information and then power off the server. The new SID and related information is regenerated when the target system reboots from the new image. When the newly imaged machine is booted for the first time, a mini-setup program will prompt for the unique information such as administrator's password, computer name, and IP address. If the sysprep.inf file (SYSPREP's Answer file) is used, administrator intervention will be bypassed. SYSPREP.inf can be generated by the Setup Manager in the same way it generated the unattended install Answer file. One of the benefits of imaging is that images can be multicast to several machines at one time.

Remote Installation Service

The Remote Installation Service (RIS) was first introduced in Windows 2000 Server to assist administrators in deploying Windows 2000 Pro to workstations. Microsoft enhanced this feature in Windows Server 2003 to include fully automated installations of Windows Server (2000/2003) as well as workstations (2000/XP). RIS uses a technology similar to imaging, but allows for different server hardware configurations while keeping the same system configuration settings and installed applications. RIS is most appropriate for smaller deployments of 75 servers or less and may require user intervention to start the installation. This feature is included in all versions of Windows Server 2003 except Windows Server 2003 Web Server. You can use RIS to install operating systems on remote boot-enabled client computers. The client computers are placed on the network and started using a Pre-Boot Execution-capable (PXE) network adapter or remote boot disk. Your environment must also include a DHCP server, a DNS server, and Active Directory.

To install RIS, go to **Start | Control Panel** and click **Add Or Remove Programs**. Click **Add/Remove Windows Components**, select **Remote Installation Services**, and then click **Next**. If prompted for the Windows Server 2003 installation files, place the Windows Server 2003 CD-ROM in the drive. Click **Finish** to complete the install and click **Yes** to restart the server.

Automatic Deployment Services

Microsoft rolled out Automatic Deployment Services (ADS) as part of its Dynamic Systems Initiative (DSI) aimed at creating self-managing environments. ADS is capable of imaging up to 128 bare metal servers simultaneously. ADS is run from a central server console, and "listens" for new servers placed on the network, and then pushes an image out to the target servers. ADS is a free download intended for Windows Server 2003 Enterprise and Datacenter versions only and is suitable for large-scale, high-speed deployments in datacenter environments.

Customizing the Installation Process

If you need more control over the installation process, Microsoft provides a number of switches or options that can be used when launching your installation via Winnt32.exe or performing automated installations. Table 5.1 lists the switches available and how you can use them. The commands can be run from the command prompt or by modifying the autoexe.com file on Setup Disk A.

Table 5.1 Command-Line Parameters

Switch	Purpose
/checkupgradeonly	Checks whether an upgrade is possible. Does not install the software.
/cmd:*command*	Launch other programs or perform additional customizations before setup completes.
/cmdcons	Add the Recovery Console item to the boot.ini file.
/copydir:*folder*	Copies specified folders to the installation directory during setup.
/copysource:*folder*	Copies directories and deletes itself afterward.
/debug[level]:[filename]	Level 0 offers basic debugging information. Use Level 4 for complete details.
/dudisable	Skips the dynamic update.
/duprepare:*path*	Path containing the CAB files with updates. Requires the use of the dushare option.
/dushare:*path*	Path to share created by dupprepare.
/m:*folder*	Look in the specified folder first to start copying files.
/makelocalsource	Copies the entire source to the hard drive.
/noreboot	Will bypass the screen at the end of the first setup wizard.
/s:*sourcepath*	To specify multiple source paths (CD-ROM, network, floppy...). Each specified path must be available or Setup will fail.
/syspart:*drive*	Will start setup to the specified drive and mark it as active. The drive can then be installed in a different computer. Requires the /tempdrive parameter.
/tempdrive:*drive*	Specifies where setup stores the temporary files.
/unattend	Automated, no-input-required upgrade of previous operating system.
/unattend:[num]:	As before but contains a text file with all the answers relating to the complete setup.
answer_file	/udf:id[,udf_file] Answers to questions that are unique to each computer.

Installing Windows Server 2003

For the purposes of this exercise, we will use Windows Server 2003 Standard Edition and assume this is a "clean" installation on a server with no existing operating system. So that you do not miss any crucial steps, we will also assume that no vendor-provided configuration software such as Compaq's SmartStart or Dell's Open Manage is being used. An attended, CD-based installation will typically take approximately two hours, although much of that time requires no intervention.

Designing and Planning...

Don't Forget to Document!

Creating documentation is not most administrators' favorite past time, but often is their saving grace. Even though this may be only be a test machine, take the few extra minutes to document the process, the choices you make, and configuration settings you select. If something goes awry during the installation or during the configuration stage, you may be able to pinpoint the problem and avoid it next time around. If things work out well, you will have a blue print for building future servers and possibly serve as part of your disaster recovery documentation.

Step-by-Step Installation

In this section, we will walk through a step-by-step installation of Windows Server 2003, Standard Edition. If you have a test server handy, you may find it helpful to follow along with your own installation. If you do, don't forget to keep a notepad and pen handy to jot down any issues or thoughts you may have along the way. Now, let's get started.

1. Since we are assuming a clean install, insert the Windows Server 2003 CD and either turn on or restart the server. The Setup wizard will immediately start and begin inspecting your server's hardware and disk space. It then loads a minimal version of the operating system into memory. At this point, you will see the familiar blue screen as the Setup wizard guides us through the Text Mode phase of the Windows Server 2003 installation.

Configuring and Implementing...

ACPI and the HAL

The Advanced Configuration and Power Interface (ACPI) is an industry specification response to global concerns about energy conservation and environmental control. ACPI specifies how a system's BIOS, operating system, and peripherals communicate with each other about power consumption. ACPI must be supported by the system's motherboard, BIOS, and operating system as well. If it is not, it could cause the installation process to hang, or if the installation finishes, you could be plagued with BSODs or systems that hang at startup and shutdown. To help prevent problems related to ACPI, update your system's BIOS prior to installing Windows Server 2003 and afterwards, check to make sure the correct HAL is installed. You can check the HAL by going to **Start | Settings | Control Panel | System | Hardware | Device Manager**. Expand the **Computer** branch.

Tools and Traps...

Configuring and Implementing

Some server vendors such as HP/Compaq and Dell provide server configuration software that assists with the operating system installation. The software prepares the system for installation by installing drivers, configuring array controllers, and installing management software. Much of the information needed during the installation is collected by the software and entered when needed, simplifying the installation and requiring less interaction.

2. The first prompt you will see asks whether your server requires third-party SCSI or RAID drivers as shown in Figure 5.4. Press **F6** if you require third-party drivers. If not, do nothing, and the Setup program will continue without intervention.

Figure 5.4 Windows Setup—Add Third-Party Drivers

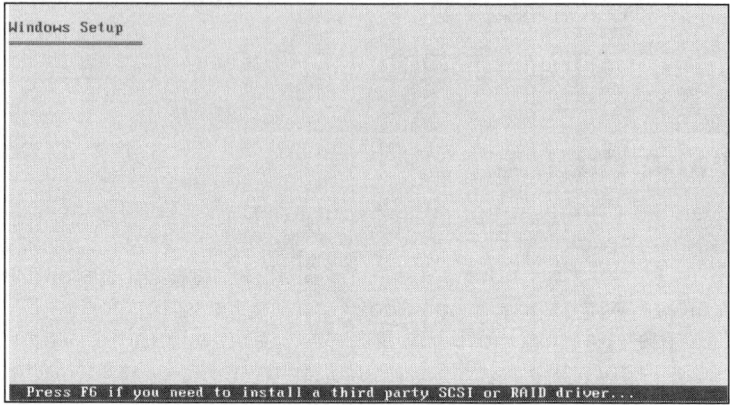

3. Setup will continue to load files into memory for several seconds. Then, you are presented with a Welcome screen and prompted for a course of action as shown in Figure 5.5. Your choices are to **Repair** a current installation, **Install** new, or **Quit** the wizard. Since this is a new installation, press **Enter** to continue the installation.

Figure 5.5 Windows Server 2003 Welcome Screen

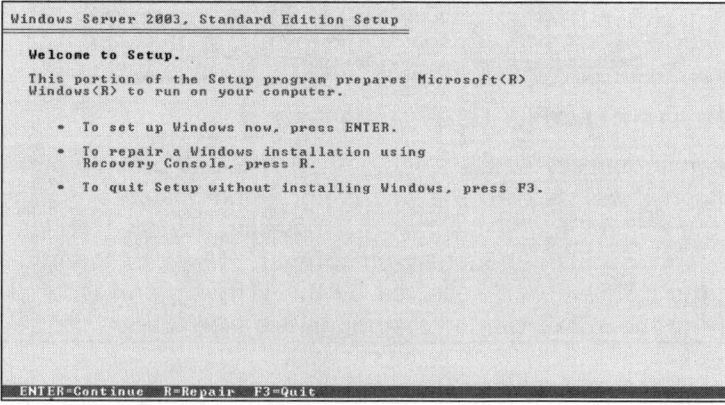

4. The next screen presents the Microsoft End User License Agreement (EULA). Press **F8** to acknowledge and continue.

5. Now you must decide how much of the hard drive to use for the system partition and how to format it. Windows Server 2003 must be installed on a single disk partition, but you are given several options with regard to this partition:

    ■ Create a new partition on a nonpartitioned portion of the hard disk.

    ■ Create a new partition on a partitioned hard disk.

- Install into an existing partition.

- Delete an existing partition and create a new one.

6. You must also decide the amount of disk space the partition will contain. We recommend that the partition that holds Windows Server 2003 should be at least 10GB. Any free space on the drive can be partitioned and formatted after the installation. Generally, to ensure better performance, the operating system should be kept on a separate disk from the applications and data. If this is not possible, install on separate partitions. Once the partition has been created, press **Enter** to continue and install Windows Server 2003. If you have reconsidered the space needed, simply elect to delete the partition and recreate it.

7. The next screen prompts you to choose the type of file system to use. In Windows Server 2003, you have a few more choices than in earlier versions (Figure 5.6):

- FAT Quick Format

- NTFS Quick Format

- FAT

- NTFS

NTFS is the recommended file format because it supports larger volumes and provides security, disk compression, disk quotas, and encryption. FAT should only be used in environments where security is not an issue. The Quick Format option is not recommended if the server on which you are installing Windows Server 2003 has existing partitions that may have held files of a sensitive nature. Select the file system and press **Enter** to continue.

Figure 5.6 Windows Server 2003 Formatting Options

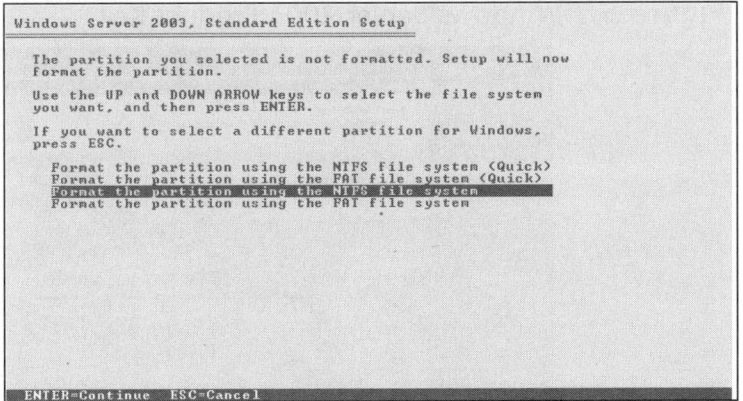

Designing and Planning...

Formatting Options

Windows Server 2003 includes two new options for formatting partitions: FAT Quick Format and NTFS Quick Format. The quick method formats in approximately a quarter of the time typically needed, but is only a high-level format. It is not recommended that you use this option if your server previously contained confidential information.

8. Once the partition is formatted, the server will reboot and Setup will enter the Graphical Mode phase. The first screen in the Graphical phase prompts you to configure Regional Settings. This provides optional formatting for currency, date and time settings, and language and keyboard settings for international or special use. If no changes are needed, press **Next** to continue.

9. You are now prompted to personalize your software by entering your name and the name of the organization. Enter the information and click **Next** to continue.

10. Next, you are prompted for the Product Key. *Without the key, you cannot continue.* There is no option to enter the key *after t*he installation and *no grace period.* If you lose your Product Key, you must contact Microsoft for a replacement. However, since you collected all your information during the planning stage, you will enter the 25–character key and then click **Next** to continue (Figure 5.7).

Figure 5.7 Windows Server 2003 Product Key

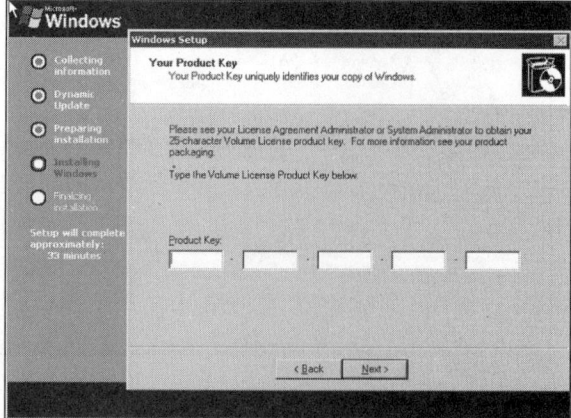

Configuring and Implementing...

Microsoft Product IDs and Activation

You can purchase a retail version of Windows Server 2003 or a volume license for Windows Server 2003. The retail version provides you a Product ID that is used to activate the operating system. It can only be used to activate one instance of Windows Server 2003. If you have a Select Agreement or Open License Agreement with Microsoft, you are provided with a Volume License ID that can be used to install as many instances of the operating system as indicated in your agreement and bypass the activation process.

11. Next, you must select the licensing mode for your server (Figure 5.8). The two selections are Per Server and Per Device or User. Per Server Mode means that you must purchase enough Client Access Licenses (CALs) to support all concurrent client connections to the server. This mode is typically used for small organizations with only a single server or for Web and Remote Access Service (RAS) servers. As in previous versions of the Windows operating system, if you are unsure of which licensing mode you need, select Per Server. Microsoft allows you to change from Per Server to Per Device or User. *You cannot change from Per Device or User to Per Server.* Per Device or Per User requires only one CAL for each device or user connecting to any server and is more typically used in larger organizations with multiple servers. For our purposes, select **Per Device or Per User** and click **Next** to continue.

Figure 5.8 Licensing Modes

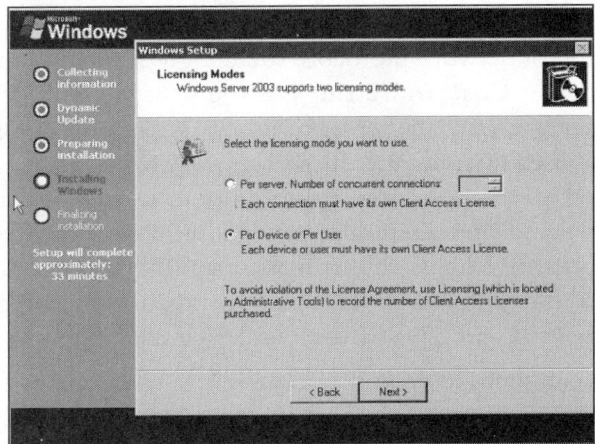

12. The next screen prompts for the server name and the administrator password. If possible, stick to a consistent naming convention for all your servers. Once you have entered this information, click **Next** to continue. Note: If the administrator password you entered does not meet the criteria for *strong passwords*, you will receive a warning message (Figure 5.9) and be given the opportunity to continue or go back and change the password. Administrator passwords can be up to 127 characters and may contain alphanumeric and special characters. Microsoft suggests that you use a strong password of at least six characters, including numbers and special characters.

Figure 5.9 Strong Password Warning

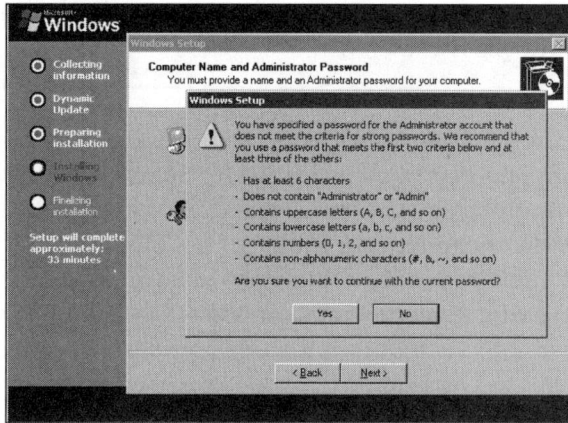

13. You are now prompted to set the appropriate date, time, and time zone for your locale. Scroll down the list, select your location, and then click **Next** to continue.

14. At this point, the network component phase of the Windows Server 2003 installation begins. The wizard detects system components and permits the selection of network protocols. You are given the option of selecting **Typical Settings** or **Custom Settings**. If you select Typical Settings, you will be asked whether you want the server to join a Workgroup or a Domain, and DHCP will be used to configure the server's network adapter. If Custom Settings is selected, you will have the opportunity to select and configure your network protocol and client. Typically, you will want to select Custom Settings and enter your IP address, subnet mask, and DNS settings. Again, since you have done a thorough job of planning your installation, enter your IP address, subnet mask, and DNS settings, and then click **Next** to continue.

15. Setup continues to copy files and register components for some time without your intervention. Notice that you are given an approximate time until completion and an indication of what stage of the install you are in. In Figure 5.10,

you can see that you have approximately 25 minutes left and are in the Installing Windows stage. This process will continue for some time until the installation enters the Finalizing Installation stage. From this point on, there are no other prompts. Once the Finalization phase ends, the server restarts and comes up to the Windows Server 2003 logon screen.

Figure 5.10 Installing Windows

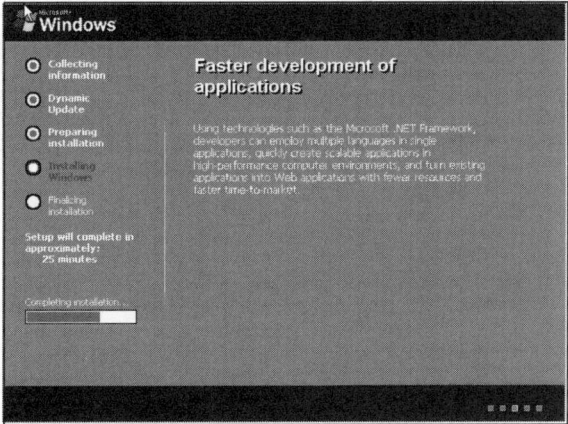

Configuring Windows Server 2003 for Terminal Services

After the initial logon, the server will display the Manage Your Server screen as shown in Figure 5.11. The Manage Your Server screen allows you to configure your server's role, whether it will be a terminal server, a domain controller, file server, or any number of other options

Figure 5.11 Manage Your Server

Once you have selected a role, the wizard will walk you through the necessary steps. Since your final destination in this exercise is a Citrix MetaFrame server, your server will need to be a terminal server. To install Terminal Server on your Windows Server 2003 server:

16.   Click on the **Add or Remove a Role** link. Then, click **Next** to continue.

17.   Select **Terminal Server** and click **Next** (Figure 5.12).

Figure 5.12 Select Server Role

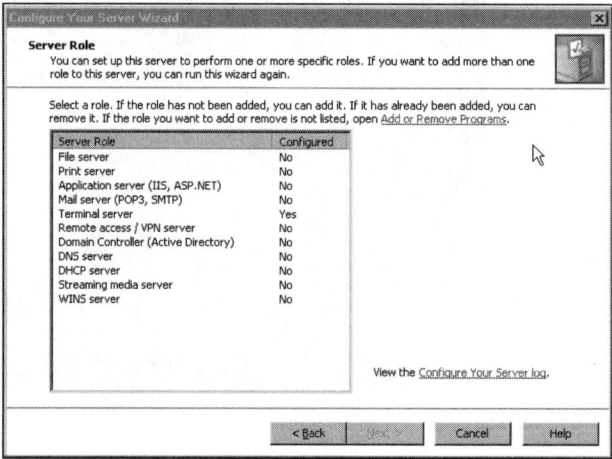

18.   Click **Next** to install Terminal Server.

19.   If there are any other open programs, close them and click **OK**.

20.   Your server will reboot and you will need to log on as administrator again.

21.   Once the installation has completed, click **Finish** to exit the Configure Your Server wizard.

22.   One of the new features in Windows Server 2003 is that you are required to assign user groups who will be allowed to use Terminal Services. To add the user groups allowed to use Terminal Services, go to **Start | All Programs | Administrative Tools | Computer Management** and expand **Local Users and Groups** (Figure 5.13). From within Groups, double-click **Remote Desktop Users** and add the Domain Users or groups that will have access via to the server via Terminal Services.

Figure 5.13 Add Users to Remote Desktop Users

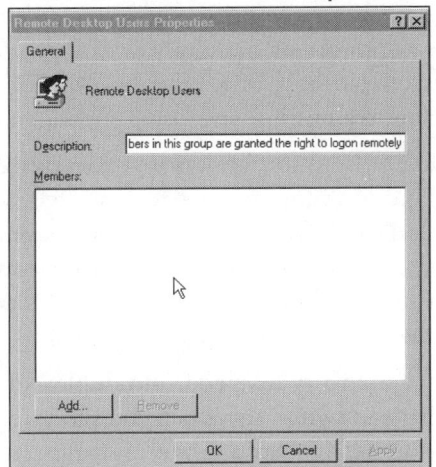

Designing and Planning…

Windows Licensing and Terminal Services

Terminal Services can be used for Remote Administrative purposes without requiring additional licenses but when used in Application mode, you must have at least one licensing server on your network. Microsoft provides a 120-day grace period during which time users can connect to the Terminal Server. Once the grace period expires, users will no longer be able to connect.

Post Installation Updates and Tweaks

Now that you have completed installing Windows Server 2003 and Terminal Server, there are a number of post installation tasks that should be completed to update and optimize your server.

1. Run **Windows Update** and install critical updates. Make sure you select Advanced so you can review the updates and remove any unnecessary ones. As of this writing, there is no service pack for Windows Server 2003, but as always, remember to test any new service pack on a test server before placing on production servers. It is also an excellent idea to check the Microsoft and

Citrix Web sites for issues related to service packs and hotfixes. If there are any known issues with service packs, the Citrix Web site will have information on any possible workarounds or simply warnings not to install. If you are an early implementer, check the Citrix User Forums for information or tips. If you find no information, try posting your own message asking for information.

2. Check the Event Logs for any errors or warnings. Pay close attention to the System Log and look for any errors associated with the installation or patching. In addition, look for any services that may have failed to start. If any are found, track down the source and correct any issues found. This is mandatory, as you do not want to go forward with the Citrix MetaFrame installation if you have existing problems.

3. Hard code the media type, speed, and duplex of the server's network card(s) and verify that the switch to which the server connects is configured correctly. Never keep the default "auto detect" settings. In addition, while you are in Network Settings, verify the server's IP, DNS, WINS, and Gateway information.

4. Verify that the computer name matches the server's Active Directory name. The quickest way to do so is to open a command prompt and type **net config rdr**.

5. Create and format any additional partitions. Even partitions that do not hold the operating system should be formatted as NTFS.

6. Move the page file to another drive or another partition and set to 1.5 times the total amount of RAM installed on the server (4095MB maximum).

7. Remove any unnecessary Windows components such as games, Accessibility wizard, and Communications.

8. Disable Automatic Updates. Updates should be done manually and only after first checking for issues and testing on nonproduction servers.

Configuring and Implementing…

Windows Software Update Service

While automatic updates are not recommended, Microsoft has provided a free utility to assist administrators in automating and deploying critical updates and security rollouts. SUS consists of a server-side component and a client agent. The server component synchronizes daily with the Microsoft Update site and downloads available updates. Administrators can be notified via e-mail when updates are ready. Once the updates have been tested, the administrator has the ability

Continued

to select updates to deploy. SUS requires a Windows 2000 or Windows Server 2003 running Internet Information Services.

9. Identify and remove any unnecessary startup applications. Often, unneeded applications can lengthen the logon process and often cause problems. Check the **Windows Startup** folders, for both *user* and *all users*. Next, go to **Start | Run**, type **REGEDT32**, and click **OK**. Check the following registry keys for unneeded applications that run at startup:

```
HKLM\SOFTWARE\Microsoft\Windows NT\Current Version\Winlogon
Value: App Setup
And
HKLM\SOFTWARE\Microsoft\Windows\Current Version\Run
```

10. Maximize memory-related settings. **Go to Start | Control Panel | Network Connections** and click **Properties**. Select **File and Printer Sharing for Microsoft Networks** and click **Properties**. Under Server Optimization, select **Maximize data throughput for network applications**. The default setting is to Maximize data throughput for file sharing. Do not leave this setting enabled, as it will increase the paging activity (Figure 5.14).

Figure 5.14 Server Optimization

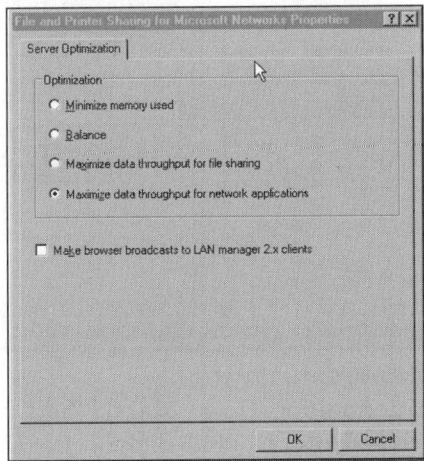

11. Set the Event Log parameters. Change the Event Viewer log parameters to a suitable size for the amount of data you will collect, and choose what action is taken when the server reaches the maximum size you set. The default is to overwrite when the top limit is reached.

12. Change My Computer name. This is a handy registry tweak for environments with larger server farms. It changes the caption under the My Computer icon on the desktop to "User Name" on "Computer Name." This helps to remind you what server you are on and who you are logged in as. Of course, you will need to enable Classic Start Menu or add My Computer to your desktop manually in order to see it, as the default desktop has nothing but the Recycle Bin on it. To enable Classic Menu, right-click on **Start**, select **Properties**, and select **Classic Menu**. This will place the My Computer, My Network Places, My Documents, and Internet Explorer shortcuts on the desktop. To change the caption beneath My Computer, go to **Start | Run** , and type **REGEDT32**, and then click **OK**. Expand the **HKEY_CLASSES_ROOT\CLSID\{20D04FE0-3AEA-1069-A2D8-08002B30309D}** key. Double-click on **LocalizedString** and change the **Value Data** to **%Username% on %Computername%** (Figure 5.15). Click **OK** and exit the registry editor. Once back to the Windows Server 2003 desktop, press **F5** to refresh the desktop. The My Computer caption should now have the logged-in user's name and the server's name. Don't forget the usual caveats when working with the registry, as it could crash your system.

Figure 5.15 Change My Computer Name

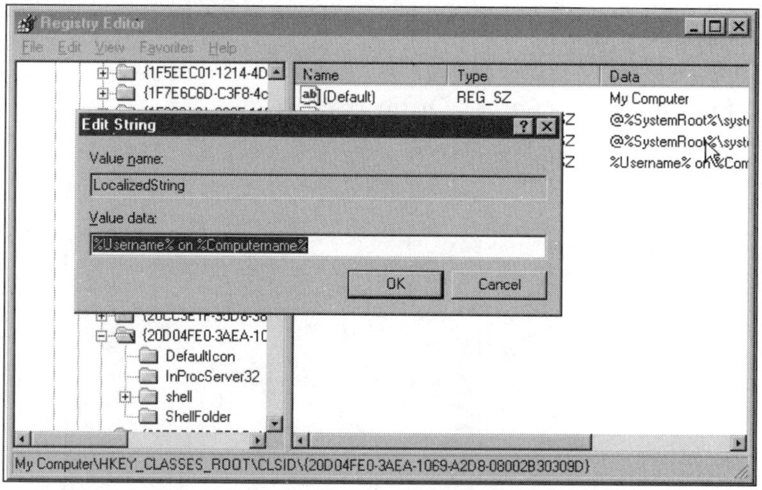

13. Enable Security Auditing. Go to **Start | Settings | Control Panel | Administrative Tools**. Double-click on **Local Security Policy**. Expand **Local Policies** and select **Audit Policy** (Figure 5.16).

14. Configure the options for how the operating system behaves in the event of an unexpected stop. To do so, go **to Start | Settings | Control Panel**. Double-click on **System**, go to the **Advanced** tab, and then click the **Settings** button. Here you can change the amount of time to display startup and

recovery options, enable administrative alerts, and select the type of memory dump to create and whether to automatically reboot in the event of a STOP error (Figure 5.17).

Figure 5.16 Enable Auditing

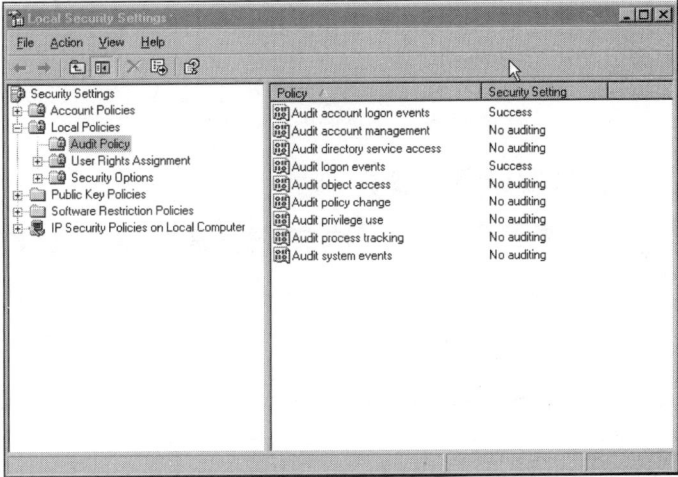

Figure 5.17 Startup and Recovery Options

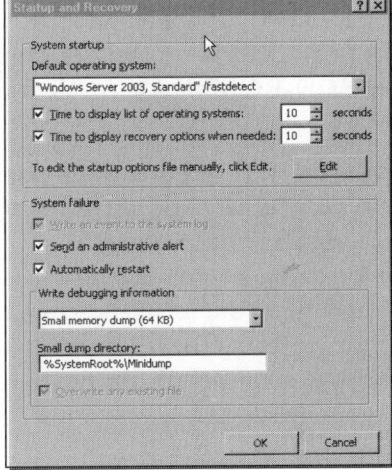

Keep in mind that a complete memory dump may take some time to complete, depending on the amount of physical RAM in the system. You may also want to make sure the server automatically reboots to limit downtime.

15. Install the Recovery Console. The Windows Recovery Console can be started from the Windows Server 2003 CD-ROM, but it is far more convenient to

use as a Startup option. To install the Recovery Console, place the Windows Server 2003 CD-ROM in the CD drive, open a command prompt, type **D:\i386\winnt32.exe\cmdcons**, and press **Enter** (where D: is the CD drive letter). Click **Yes** when prompted and **OK** to finish.

16. Rename the Local Administrator account. For security purposes, make sure you have given your Local Administrator account a strong password and then rename the account. Choose a unique name for the account that cannot be easily guessed.

What Happened? Troubleshooting Installation Problems

As long as you have taken the time to check your hardware for compatibility, your installation should go smoothly. However, things can and do go wrong. A relatively simple problem with a CD drive could slow you down unless you have thought about alternative ways to get the job done. Following are a few scenarios that are fairly common and how to work around them:

■ **Media or drive problems** First, when you get a new application or operating system CD-ROM, make a copy of it. One of the most common problems is that caused by scratched, dirty, or cracked CD-ROMs. After you have duplicated the CD-ROM, check it and make sure it is readable. If you have one that cannot be read, try it on another drive or machine. If it is the drive, you can copy the CD-ROM to a network share and perform a network installation.

■ **Network connectivity problems** This one is very common. You install the operating system but the network interface card (NIC) is not properly recognized. Setup may or may not inform you of this until you attempt to join a domain. If you are doing an attended installation, you can opt to join a Workgroup and continue the installation, but if it is an unattended installation, it may stop. If you can bring the server up as a member of a Workgroup, begin troubleshooting your connectivity. Try pinging another server on the network. If you get a response back, you have connectivity, so either it is intermittent or you possibly did not have a correct administrator name and password. Check your cable and make sure it is connected securely. If it is, try changing out the cable. If, however, you do not have connectivity, check your Network Settings. Make sure you have the proper IP address and subnet mask for your network. The quickest way is to go to the command prompt and type **IPCONFIG /ALL**. Check the network adapter and make sure it installed properly. Look in the Event Log and Device Manager for any problems. Check the driver and make sure the adapter is configured with the proper driver. Finally, check your adapter's media, speed, and duplex, and check the switch port to which your server connects. Make sure the switch port is functional and there is no type mismatch between the two.

■ **Installation hang-ups**. Hang-ups that occur during installation can be caused by a number of things. Third-party mass storage devices or incorrectly configured SCSI devices could be the problem. If this is the case, installing the correct driver or checking the SCSI configuration and termination should take care of the problem. Another source could be the system's BIOS. If the BIOS does not correctly support the Advanced Configuration and Power Interface (ACPI), Setup will hang. The solution is to upgrade the system's BIOS to fully support ACPI. Hang-ups can also be caused by Setup using the wrong Hardware Abstraction Layer (HAL) for your system. This goes hand in hand with the ACPI problem. If you don't want to wait for the BIOS upgrade or can't find an upgrade, you can try installing a different HAL during Setup. To do so, wait until you see the message **Setup is inspecting your computer's hardware configuration**, and then press **F5**. Setup will prompt you to select the desired HAL.

■ **Unattended installation problems** The most common problem that occurs in scripted, unattended installations are misspelled or missing words or characters. Check your Answer file for spelling errors, transposed letters, or anything else that may not be the right information.

Configuring and Implementing...

When Things Go Wrong

Trust us, no matter how many precautions you take, things can and will go wrong. Hopefully, not often, but they will. A good way to minimize the damage or at least give yourself a starting point for troubleshooting the problem is to document *everything*. Don't stop when the server is built; continue to document each service pack, hotfix, patch, and application that is added to your servers. Every change you make to the configuration should be documented as well. If you can, take the time to reboot after each hotfix, patch, or application you install. This way, you are more likely to catch the one that caused the problem.

■ **The dreaded Blue Screen of Death (BSOD)** The most frustrating scenario is when Setup crashes and you are left staring at a Blue Screen of Death.

Most of the time, the information given on the screen makes no sense at all to common mortals. Sometimes, you can look at the first few lines and search the Microsoft Knowledge Base to determine the answer.

Windows Server 2003 Installation Checklist

- Do the homework and make sure you have a plan and all the resources you need before beginning.

- Verify that your server hardware is supported.

- Always use NTFS and select the "normal" formatting method over the Quick Format.

- Standardize your environment, naming conventions, and server build. The best way to standardize your server build is to automate the installations by either imaging or scripted installs.

- Know your licensing mode and have your Product Key handy.

- Install Terminal Server and remember to add your user groups to the local Remote Desktop Users group.

- Run Windows Update and apply security updates. Be careful of other updates and service packs. Research and test prior to installing.

- Check all your server settings and make sure they are correct.

- Configure memory optimizations.

- Remove unnecessary applications.

- Remove unneeded startup applications.

- Check the Event Logs for problems.

Summary

The key to a successful installation and deployment is careful planning and methodical implementation. Preparation will save you time in the long run by avoiding common problems and known issues. In this chapter, we reviewed some of the planning steps and what items we should gather pre-installation. We also took a close look at the Windows Server 2003 installation process discussing both Attended and Unattended installations from either CD-ROM or over the network. Automated installations were considered and the different methods available for automating such as using scripts and server imaging, Remote Installation Services, and Automated Deployment Services. Which methods you choose depends largely on your environment, but uniformity and consistency contribute hugely to stable production environments.

We also looked at the Terminal Services installation process via the Manage Your Server Wizard, licensing issues, and adding Domain User groups to the Local Remote Desktop User group. All three tasks must be accomplished before users can connect to the server.

A good portion of this chapter explained the post-installation tasks that will help insure that your server is optimized for Windows Server 2003 and Terminal Services. Changes such as memory optimization, page file size and location, and network adapter configuration are extremely important. Other changes help to keep your environment free of unneeded components and startup applications that may affect startup and logon times.

Finally, we touched on a few of the more common problems encountered during a Windows Server 2003 installation. Most of the common problems such as incorrect drivers and incompatible hardware can be prevented with careful planning. Other problems such as media, drive, and network connectivity problems can typically be corrected or worked around with a little troubleshooting.

At this point, if you have been following along, your server should be ready for the next step: installing Citrix MetaFrame Access Suite, which we will discuss in the next chapter.

Solutions Fast Track

Pre-Installation

☑ Plan your installation and deployment carefully. Know what information you need for the installation process, choices you must make, and any third-party drivers your server might require.

☑ Before deploying production servers, create a test environment and test your installation, the applications that will be deployed, and post-installation updates and patches.

☑ Know what your options are for installing Windows Server 2003 and decide which method is best for your environment.

Options for Installing Windows Server 2003

☑ Windows Server 2003 can be installed directly from the CD-ROM or from a network share. If you have several servers to install, a network installation may save you time, as you can install multiple servers at the same time.

☑ Once you have installed and tested your server, there are multiple ways to automate additional deployments. Automated installations can be created via scripting or imaging and deployed using Remote Installation Services or Automatic Deployment Services.

Installing Windows Server 2003

☑ Partition sizes should be at least 10GB for Windows Server 2003.

☑ Always use the "normal" method of formatting for servers being redeployed.

☑ Use NTFS as the file system on both the system partition and any others.

Configuring Windows Server 2003 for Terminal Services

☑ Use the Manage Your Server Wizard to install Terminal Services, or go to Add/Remove Programs.

☑ Remember to add domain user groups to the Remote Desktop User group on each terminal server.

☑ Insure that a Licensing server is on the network, or users will not be able to connect when the 120-day grace period expires.

Post-Installation Updates and Tweaks

☑ Install necessary updates and patches.

☑ Check the Event Logs for problems.

☑ Hardcode the network adapter's media type, speed, and duplex.

☑ Verify DNS and IP settings.

☑ Remove unnecessary Windows components and startup applications.

☑ Format remaining partitions or drives with NTFS.

☑ Create an appropriately sized page file and place on a separate drive or partition.

☑ Disable Automatic Updates.

☑ Optimize memory-related settings.

☑ Enable Security Auditing.

☑ Set Event Log parameters.

☑ Configure System Failure Options.

☑ Change My Computer name.

☑ Install the Recovery Console.

☑ Rename the Local Administrator account.

What Happened?
Troubleshooting Installation Problems

☑ Check the CD-ROM and the CD-ROM drive for problems.

☑ Make sure you have network connectivity and all connections are intact for network installations.

☑ Upgrade the server BIOS and make sure the HAL is correct.

☑ Check scripts for misspellings or incorrect format.

☑ Make sure all drivers are signed and compatible with Windows Server 2003.

Links to Sites

- ☑ **www.dabcc.com** Doug Brown's Citrix site

- ☑ **www.tokeshi.com** Great Citrix site with tons of tips

- ☑ **www.thinplanet.com** A good Terminal Server/Citrix forum.

- ☑ **www.citrix.com** Citrix Support and Knowledge Base site

- ☑ **http://support.microsoft.com** Microsoft Support and Knowledge Base site

- ☑ **www.vmware.com/** Information about VMWare Workstation

- ☑ **www.microsoft.com/windows/virtualpc/default.mspx** Information on Microsoft's VirtualPC

- ☑ **www.google.com** A great search engine that can search both Web and usenet

Frequently Asked Questions

The following Frequently Asked Questions, answered by the authors of this book, are designed to both measure your understanding of the concepts presented in this chapter and to assist you with real-life implementation of these concepts. To have your questions about this chapter answered by the author, browse to **www.syngress.com/solutions** and click on the **"Ask the Author"** form. You will also gain access to thousands of other FAQs at ITFAQnet.com.

Q: I know how important it is to have a test environment, but my company does not have spare equipment or the means to purchase new equipment for a test lab. What would you recommend?

A: Find at least one machine, desktop or server, that you can use for testing. If you can, pick one with decent processor speeds and beef up the RAM. You can purchase VMWare Workstation or VirtualPC for less than $200.00 retail. Both products allow you to run multiple operating systems on one machine without dual-booting.

Q: What can I do if I cannot find my Product Key?

A: You can call Microsoft for a new one. Support calls about licensing issues are free. Without the Product Key, you will not be able to install Windows Server 2003.

Q: How can I create an Answer File for an unattended installation?

A: Use the Setup Manager, found within the DEPLOY.CAB file, located in the \Support\Tools\ folder of the Windows Server 2003 CD-ROM.

Q: How long can you use Terminal Services in Application mode without a licensing server?

A: Microsoft provides a 120-day grace period, after which time users would no longer be able to connect. If Terminals Services is used in Remote Administration mode only, no license server is needed.

Q: After installing Terminal Services in Application mode, my users still cannot connect unless they are in the Administrator group. What went wrong?

A: Before ordinary users can connect to a terminal server, they must be added to the local machine's Remote Desktop Users group. Also, check the **Remote** tab under **System Properties** to ensure that **Remote Desktop** is enabled. This option is activated by default when you install Terminal Server.

Q: I noticed that Automatic Updates are enabled by default, should I keep this setting?

A: No. Disable Automatic Updates. Any updates applied to your server should be researched for issues and tested on a nonproduction server prior to installing on your production servers. It is very common for new service packs and patches to have disastrous results.

Q: How can I find out about known issues with service packs, patches, and common applications installed on Windows Server 2003 with Terminal Services?

A: Besides the usual Microsoft and Citrix support sites, there are a number of excellent sites that provide up-to-date information and user forums. We listed a few in the *Links to Sites* section, but there are many others. Try using Google to search on Terminal Services and Citrix. You may also want to try searching the Usenet groups.

Chapter 6

Installing and Configuring MetaFrame Presentation Server 3.0

Solutions in this Chapter:

- The Installation Process
- Remapping Server Drives
- Creating the Data Store
- Installing the License Server
- Installing the Web Interface
- Installing MetaFrame Presentation Server 3.0
- Migration Checklist

Related chapters:

- Installation Planning and Requirements
- Upgrade and Migration Strategies

Introduction

At first glance, the installation process for MetaFrame Presentation Server 3.0 (MPS3.0) looks very similar to previous releases. However, with further investigation, you will find that there is more under the hood than you initially thought. MPS3.0 includes several new features, all of which should be included in your overall implementation strategy. In case you have not heard it enough, do not forget to plan your deployment! If you plan your deployment *before* putting that CD-ROM in the drive, you will save time and frustration and look like a genius to your co-workers, not to mention your boss! How can you prepare best prepare for an MPS3.0 deployment? Here are a few tips:

- If you have an existing MetaFrame farm, will you upgrade or perform a new installation? If you plan to upgrade, you need to know what is supported and what is not. Of course, if you have the luxury of time, it is always best to do a new, clean install.

Designing and Planning...

Upgrading and Migrating to MPS3.0

If you decide to upgrade and/or migrate to MPS3.0, there are a few caveats you must know before beginning. First, Citrix does not support an operating system upgrade. In other words, you cannot upgrade an existing Windows 2000, MetaFrame XP server to Windows Server 2003 and MPS3.0. If you choose to upgrade the operating system, you must do a new installation of MPS3.0. Further, you cannot downgrade a MPS3.0 server to prior versions of MetaFrame.

- Make sure that your hardware meets or, more realistically, exceeds all the requirements.

- Check the Citrix Web site for Pre-installation Update Bulletins. Often, new information regarding operating system, hardware, and software configuration will become available after the initial release. Patches and hotfixes may be recommended or warned against, and work-arounds may be provided for various software installations.

- After building and configuring your Windows Server 2003 and installing Terminal Services, download and apply any new Microsoft service packs and security updates prior to installing MPS3.0.

Configuring and Implementing…

Installing Service Packs and Updates

As mentioned in the previous chapter, it is not a good idea to configure automatic updates on production servers. Service packs and updates should be reviewed and tested in a like environment before going live. Because keeping up with Microsoft security updates has become a major task, Microsoft has come up with two methods of staying current with updates: Software Update Server (SUS) and Windows Update Service (WUS). The Windows Update Service is included with Windows 2000, Windows XP, and Windows Server 2003 operating systems. It can be configured to download and automatically install updates, to download and hold until you have reviewed the updates, or not to download at all. This method works best for desktop operating systems. The newer method, SUS, is a free utility consisting of a client agent and server component that synchronizes with Microsoft daily to download updates. Once downloaded, an e-mail notification is sent to the administrator. SUS requires Windows 2000 or Windows Server 2003 running Internet Information Services (IIS). To find out more and download SUS, go to www.microsoft.com/windowsserversystem/sus/default.mspx.

- Download and make ready any Citrix critical updates that may be needed after MPS3.0 has been installed.

- Make sure you understand what the installation will entail, what questions will be asked, and options from which you have to choose. Making these decisions on the fly could mean starting from scratch.

- Drive remapping only works on new installations; you cannot remap the drives on an upgrade. If you plan to remap drives, do so before installing MPS3.0, any components or applications, and make sure the applications you plan to deploy are capable of running from the new drive letters.

As mentioned previously, Citrix has added a few brand new features in this release that require a bit more planning than before. You will want to be prepared so there will be no surprises. For those of you familiar with prior releases of MetaFrame XP, you will find that in addition to the usual installation choices including "View Installation Checklist," "Install or Upgrade" (now known as "Product Installation"), "Citrix on the Web," and "Browse CD," you are also given the opportunity to install the "Document Center." The Document Center is a handy new online library that contains all the new Administration Guides for MetaFrame Access Suite in portable document format (pdf).

Adobe Acrobat Reader is necessary to view the documents and can be downloaded from www.adobe.com. The "Other Tools and Component" option no longer exists on the main screen, but the Console installations can be found when you drill down through Product Installations.

Under Product Installations, you will find yet another interesting addition: "Install MetaFrame Access Suite License Server." Citrix added the licensing server to simplify managing product licenses, which we all know is a nuisance. The licensing server is similar to the Windows Server 2003 licensing server in that it is a centralized location where you can manage and monitor licenses. It differs from Microsoft's version in that you can manage and monitor *all* the Access Suite products from the same location. The actual licensing process has changed as well and differs from prior versions, so be sure that you understand the new licensing features and requirements before diving in.

In this next section, we will go over, in detail, the installation process for the new features and those that have not changed (for you newbies out there). If you followed along and built a test server during the last chapter, you may find it helpful to follow along in the step-by-step installation section in this chapter.

The Installation Process

Citrix recommends the following sequence of steps to ensure that your MPS3.0 server and components run smoothly:

1. Review checklist.
2. Install the Document Center.
3. Create the data store (unless using an Access database).
4. Install the license server.
5. Install individual servers.

To customize MPS3.0, we have to add a couple of steps:

6. If upgrading, re-order data, re-order groups, and apply appropriate rights.
7. If installing new, create the appropriate folder structure, create appropriate groups, and apply appropriate rights, even to empty data folders or currently empty groups.

Reviewing the Checklist

Before beginning the installation process for MPS3.0, insert the CD-ROM, and from the Autorun screen, select **View installation checklist** as shown in Figure 6.1.

Figure 6.1 MetaFrame Presentation Server 3.0 Autorun Screen

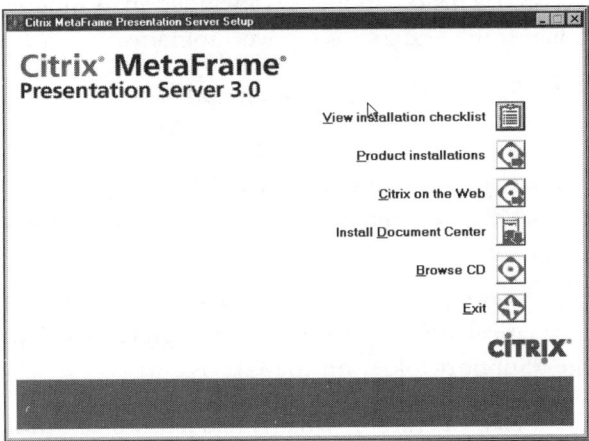

The pre-installation checklist is an actual checklist that Citrix provides that can be used online from the CD-ROM or printed out. It provides an easily accessible listing of basic information such as system requirements for each component and brief, step-by-step instructions for installing MPS3.0 and creating or joining a farm (see Figure 6.2).

Figure 6.2 Pre-Installation Checklist

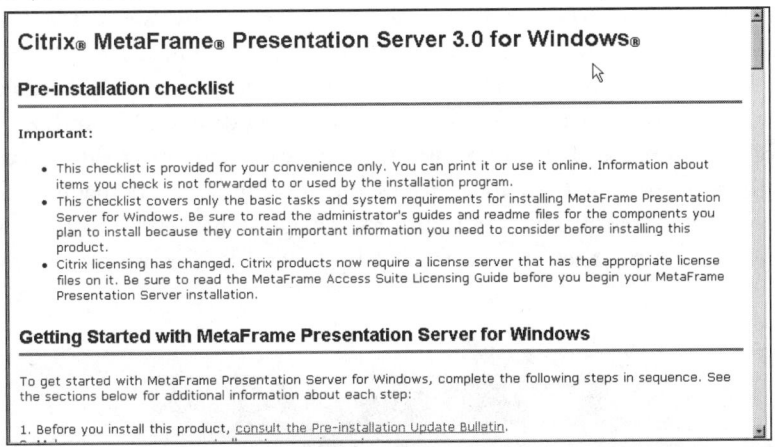

Before we begin our installation, let's browse through the checklist and see if there are any other bits of information we might need. We have already ascertained that we have met or exceeded hardware requirements for each component, but there are a few more items we will need before we begin:

■ Microsoft Internet Information Services (IIS) version 5 or later is required if the optional License Management Console is installed.

- ASP .NET is needed for the Web Interface and must be installed prior to installing MPS3.0. This component is included in Windows Server 2003 and can be installed from Add and Remove Programs.

- Adobe Reader 5.05 or later to view the .pdf documents within the Document Center.

- Microsoft Data Access Components (MDAC) version 2.6 or later in order to run reports from the MetaFrame Access Console in farms where Microsoft SQL Server data stores are used.

- Java Runtime Environment, .NET Framework, and Visual J# .NET are installed automatically by Autorun, or if you prefer, you can install them manually from the \Support folder on the CD-ROM.

Now that we have a clear picture of what is needed, we can proceed to the first step in the installation process. For the purposes of this exercise, we will assume that this is the first server in our server farm and that no license server or data store has yet been created.

Remapping the Server Drives

If you are unfamiliar with the concept, you may wonder what exactly "remap" means and why would you want to do it. The explanation lies on the client side. Users browsing My Computer from within a MetaFrame session will see server drives such as A:, C:, and D:. If they are on a machine with local drives (versus a thin client device with no drives), the local machine's drives will be mapped to V:, U:, and W:. This can be confusing for the user, and if the administrator has not locked down the server's drives, users could mistake them as their local drives and possibly cause damage to the server. For this reason, Citrix has provided a utility to reassign drive letters to the server drives, changing them to different letters and freeing up C: and D: for use on the client side.

Configuring and Implementing…

Remapping Server Drives

Remapping the server drives should be done before installing MetaFrame Presentation Server 3.0 or any of the components. If you attempt to remap the drives after installation, the utility will let you, but Citrix warns that it can cause the server to be unstable and may render the operating system inoperable. You may also want to note that the drive remapping is permanent and the drives remain remapped even if MetaFrame Presentation Server is uninstalled.

Drive remapping should only be performed on a new installation. If you attempt to remap the drives on an existing server, you will be allowed to, but any existing applications will no longer work because the registry entries for the applications will still point to the original location. If you plan to remap your server drives, do so before installing MetaFrame Presentation Server or any applications. To remap the server drives, select **Re-Map Drives** from the **Product Installation** menu. The utility opens, and next to the server's current drive designations, a drop-down box allows you to choose the first drive letter that will be used for the server's remapped drives. The default first letter is "M," but you can select other letters as long as they are not currently used (see Figure 6.3). Once you have selected the first drive letter you will use, click **OK**. The utility makes the necessary changes and then prompts you to restart the server. Once the server restarts, the drives are reassigned.

Figure 6.3 The Citrix Drive Reassignment Utility

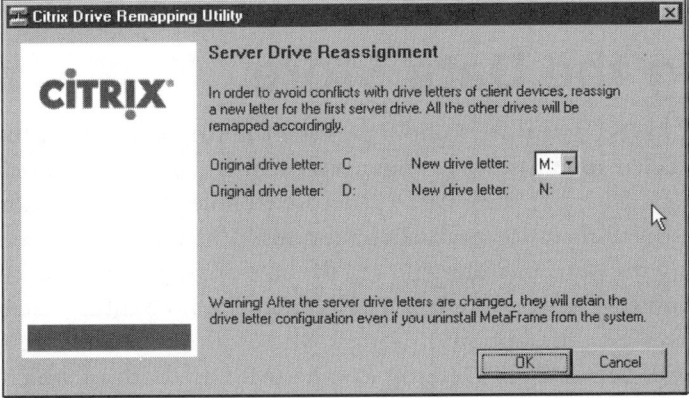

Installing the Document Center

The Document Center can be installed on any 32-bit Windows system and does not require MPS3.0. However, Adobe Acrobat Reader 5.05 or later must be installed to read the documents, as they are in .pdf format. You can get a free version of Adobe Acrobat from the Adobe Systems Web site.

To install the Document Center, access the MetaFrame Presentation Server CD-ROM, and from the main menu, select **Install Document Center**. When the Welcome screen appears, click **Next** to continue. Select the destination folder where the Document Center will be installed and click **Next**. The documents will be copied to the folder specified and when completed, you will be informed that the installation was successful and prompted to click **Finish**. Once installed, you can locate the Document Center under **Start | Programs | Citrix | MetaFrame Presentation Server | Documentation**. Double-click on **Document_Center.pdf** to access the Document Center main screen as shown in Figure 6.4.

Figure 6.4 The Document Center

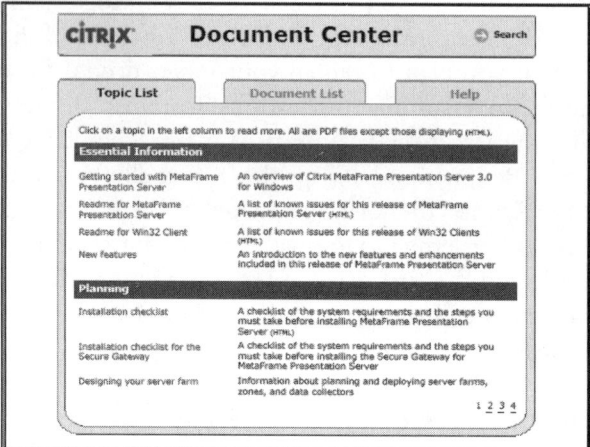

Creating the Data Store

Each farm must have a data store to hold persistent information about the servers in the farm such as installed applications, configuration settings, and other information that remains fairly static. The data store uses a database to hold the information and Citrix has allowed for several mainstream database options. Which database you choose will have a lot to do with your environment and the size of your farm. For instance, if your environment consists of only a few servers and there are no existing database servers or administrators, you have the option of using a Microsoft Access database (Jet database) or the Microsoft SQL Server 2000 Desktop Engine (MSDE), both of which are included on the CD-ROM at no extra cost. Otherwise, your database options include Microsoft SQL Server, Oracle, and IBM DB2; all more robust and scalable databases that can be used for any size farm. In the following sections, we discuss creating an MSDE and MS Access data store. If you plan to use MS SQL, Oracle, or DB2, you will need to use your database management software to create the database the data store will use. In addition, remember that MS SQL and Oracle take considerable expertise to administer. If you do not currently have MS SQL or Oracle in your environment, you may want to consider using Access or MSDE.

Unless you plan to use Microsoft Access for your data store, you will need to create the data store *prior* to beginning the MetaFrame Presentation Server installation. Then, during the installation, you will configure an Open Database Connectivity (ODBC) connection to the data store. If you use Microsoft Access, the data store database is created during the installation process.

Designing and Planning…

Data Store Considerations

Deciding which database you should use for the data store is an important decision. Before you decide, examine your current environment; how much do you expect it to expand in the next six months, in the next year to three years? Make sure the database you choose has the capability to sustain any future increase in servers, applications, and users. You may also want to keep in mind the expertise it requires to install and maintain these applications, as most higher end client/server database products require advanced knowledge to administer.

Installing Microsoft SQL Server 2000 Desktop Engine with Service Pack 3

As mentioned earlier, the Microsoft SQL Server 2000 Desktop Engine (MSDE) is included on the MetaFrame Presentation Server 3.0 CD-ROM, and although you can download and install MSDE from Microsoft, Citrix recommends that you use the version with Service Pack 3 from the MetaFrame Presentation Server CD-ROM. MSDE must be installed on the first server that will run MPS3.0 prior to installing MPS3.0.

From the MetaFrame Presentation Server CD-ROM, there are two ways that you can install MSDE. The first method assumes that you have no other instances of MSDE running on the server and that you have opted to use the default instance name "CITRIX_METAFRAME" and password "CITRIX." If you cannot use the default values for instance name and password, you will need to run the MSDE setup from the command prompt. This method requires that you install MetaFrame Presentation Server manually, which we discuss later in this chapter.

Designing & Planning…

MSDE Default Instance Name and Password

When you install MSDE with the default values, the default instance name is set to "CITRIX_METAFRAME" and the SA password to "CITRIX." Normally, this would be considered a security risk, but by default, SQL authentication is disabled so the SA password is not used. For security purposes, if SQL is enabled, you will want to create your own unique instance name and create a user account with appropriate administrator privileges.

To install MSDE with Service Pack 3 with the default values, browse to the \Support\MSDE folder on the MetaFrame Presentation Server CD-ROM. Double-click on **SetupMsdeForMetaFrame.cmd** to launch setup. No other intervention is necessary to complete the install.

If you are required to specify the instance name and password, go to the command prompt and change to the \Support\MSDE\MSDE folder on the MetaFrame Presentation Server CD-ROM. Place the server in Install mode by typing:

```
change user /install <ENTER>
```

Next, launch the setup program with the following parameters:

```
Setup.exe INSTANCENAME=<name> SAPWD=<password> <ENTER>
```

where <name> and <password> are the values you have selected for the instance name and password.

Once you have completed the installation, return to the command prompt and type:

```
change user /execute <ENTER>
```

NOTE

Placing the server in Install mode ensures that an application can be accessed by multiple users simultaneously. For applications to function, registry settings must be replicated to all users. There are two ways of placing the server into Install mode: using Add/Remove Programs to install an application, or using the commands just shown from the command line. The difference is that Add/Remove Programs creates a "shadow key" in the registry where changes to the HKEY_CURRENT_USER are monitored and propagated to each user.

Configuring & Implementing…

MSDE or MS Access?

If Oracle and Microsoft SQL Server are not viable options, should you use MS Access or MSDE? Most administrators consider MS Access a single-user database and not as reliable as SQL Server or Oracle. It is also a well-known fact that MS Access databases are easily corrupted. MSDE is a freebie provided by Microsoft to bridge the gap between real client/server database applications and MS Access. MSDE can be used as a local database or can be configured as a stand-

Continued

alone, centralized database for small farms, as it can handle up to five concurrent connections. This works well, as each MetaFrame Presentation Server only connects to the data store every 10 minutes. To use MSDE as a centralized data store, you will need to change the "setup.ini" found in the \Support\MSDE\MSDE folder on the MPS3.0 CD-ROM. Add the following lines, replacing <name> and <password> with the proper values:

```
DISABLENETWORKPROTOCOLS=0

INSTANCENAME=<name>

SAPWD=<password>
```

Next, install MSDE on a non-MetaFrame server. The setup.ini will configure the MSDE server to allow network access, create the instance name, and specify the SA password. Once the installation is complete, go to the command prompt where we will use the *osql* utility to grant user access to the MSDE server and newly created instance. You may want to create a new user for this task. From the command prompt, type:

```
C:\osql -E  -S servername\instance_name  <ENTER>
```

This command will connect to the named instance you created earlier. If you receive an error indicating the server does not exist or access is denied, check to make sure the SQLServer service has started and that the spelling of the server\instance_name is correct. If you successfully connect, the command prompt will change to `1>`.

Now, to grant access to the MSDE server for the user created previously, at the prompt, type:

```
EXEC spgrantlogin domain_name\user_name <ENTER>
```

where domain_name is the name of your domain and user_name is the name of the user created earlier. Finally, we will grant access to the newly created instance. At the prompt, type:

```
EXEC sp_grantdbaccess domain_name\user_name, instance_name <ENTER>
```

Once you have entered all the commands, type **GO** at the command prompt to process the commands and **EXIT** to disconnect from the MSDE server.

For more information on the *osql* utility, see Microsoft KB325003.

Installing the License Server

Since we are assuming that this is the first server in our server farm, we will begin our installation with the license server. Later, during the Presentation server installation, we will be prompted for the name of our license server, and since we have taken the time to plan our implementation, we *will* know its name. This is an excellent example of why the planning stage is so important!

Configuring and Implementing…

The License Server and Grace Periods

Citrix recommends that you install the license server prior to adding your first MetaFrame Presentation Server. This is an excellent recommendation because, as mentioned previously, you will be prompted for the license server name during the MetaFrame Presentation Server installation process, and because the MetaFrame Presentation Server will not accept user connections until it can contact a license server. Citrix provides a 96-hour initial grace period that will allow up to two users to connect while unable to connect to a license server. We recommend you use this period for testing your server before downloading license files. Coincidentally, MetaFrame Presentation Server licensing is not compatible with previous versions of MetaFrame, so you should not upgrade your licenses until you have upgraded or migrated to MPS3.0. Both versions can coexist in the same farm, but the licenses must be managed separately.

The license server can be installed on a server dedicated solely to licensing or share one with other applications. Whether you can use a shared server depends on the size of your farm. According to Citrix, the licensing server can co-reside if the number of machines connecting to the server is less than 50. For small environments of less than 50 servers, the licensing server can reside on the same server as MPS3.0. The only caveat is that the server must be running at least Windows 2000 Server with Service Pack 3. If the number of machines connecting to the license server is over 50 but less than 500, Citrix recommends using a dedicated server.

A default installation of the license server also installs the License Management Console. To use the console, Microsoft IIS version 5 or later must be installed. If you do not choose to install IIS, you can use the License Administration Commands from the command prompt; however, you will not be able to generate licensing reports.

Installing Internet Information Server

From the Windows Server 2003 desktop, go To **Start | Settings | Control Panel**. Double-click on **Add Or Remove Programs** and select **Add/Remove Windows Components**. From the Windows Components Wizard, highlight **Application Server** and click on **Details** as shown in Figure 6.5.

Next, from within the Application Server menu, select **Internet Information Services (IIS)**. The "Enable COM+ Access" will also be installed, as IIS and World Wide Web Services are dependent on this component (see Figure 6.6). Since we know that ASP.NET will also be needed for the Web Interface, now would be a good time to install it as well.

Figure 6.5 Windows Components Wizard

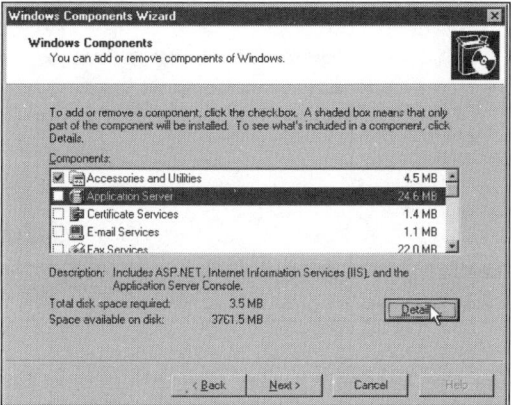

Figure 6.6 Application Server Options

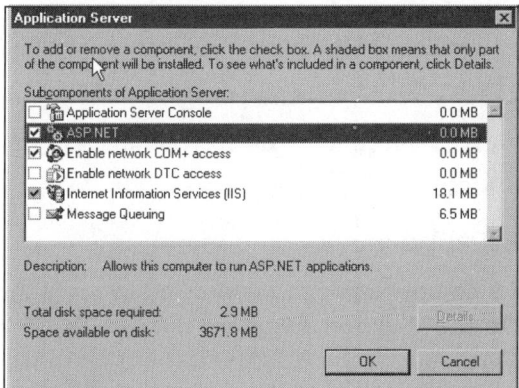

You will be prompted for the Windows Server 2003 source files. If you copied the \i386 folder to the server's hard disk or a network share, point the installation process to that folder. If not, insert the Windows Server 2003 CD-ROM. Once the installation completes, check the System Event Log for any problems or errors.

Now we are ready to install the license server. Place the MetaFrame Presentation Server CD-ROM in the drive, and when Autorun starts up, select **Product installations** from the Server Setup screen. Next, select **Install MetaFrame Access Suite License Server** as shown in Figure 6.7.

Figure 6.7 Product Installation Options

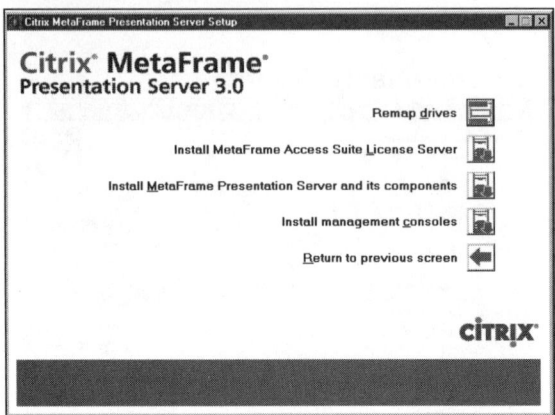

1. The MetaFrame Presentation Server Components installation begins and you are asked to accept the Licensing Agreement.

2. Click **Accept**, and click **Next** to continue.

3. The next screen informs us that there are software prerequisites that must be installed before installing MetaFrame Presentation Server. The requirements are:

   - Microsoft .NET Framework, version 1.1 or later

   - Java Runtime Environment (JRE), version 1.4.1_02 or later

   - Visual J# .NET, version 1.1 or later

   - ASP .NET (a Windows component)

All but the Windows components can be installed by setup automatically or, if we so choose, we can browse to the \Support folder on the CD-ROM and install manually. Any Windows components, such as the ASP .NET, must be installed prior to continuing with the MetaFrame Presentation Server setup.

4. The next screen allows us to select the MetaFrame Presentation Server components we want to install. Since we have decided on a shared server, we will select all the components for installation. Remember, a dedicated license server is warranted if the environment consists of more than 50 client machines. Click **Next** to continue the installation.

5. The License Server Welcome screen, as shown in Figure 6.8, appears next and warns us to close any open applications before installing. Make sure you have no applications running, and click **Next** to continue.

6. We are now prompted to accept the Citrix Licensing Agreement. Click **Accept** and then click **Next** to continue.

Figure 6.8 MetaFrame Access Suite Licensing Setup

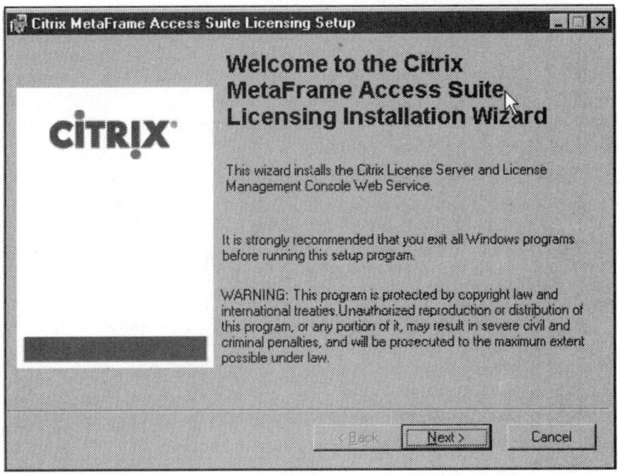

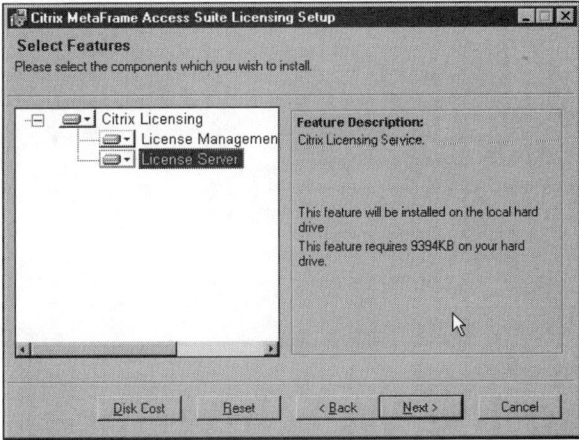

7. Now we are given the opportunity to select a different location for our files. We recommend keeping the Citrix files in the default location. Click **Next** to continue the installation.

8. We must now confirm that we want both the Management Console and the license server install. Both components are selected by default as shown in Figure 6.9. Click **Next** to continue the installation.

Figure 6.9 Select Features for Licensing Setup

9. Next, we are prompted for the location where we will store our license files. Again, leave the default and click **Next**.

10. The next screen asks if it is okay to restart the IIS Web Server service. Since this is a new server and nothing else is using IIS, click **OK**. If we were installing on an existing server, this may not be the case (see Figure 6.10).

Figure 6.10 Restart IIS Web Server Service

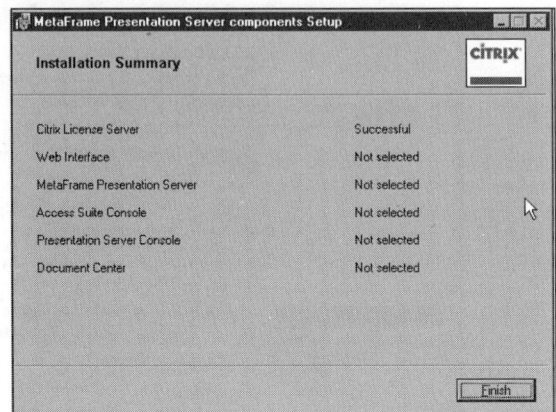

11.   On the next screen, click Next to install the license server. Once you click Next, the installation begins and completes without further intervention.

12.   On the final screen, you are presented with a Summary of the installation (see Figure 6.11). When prompted, click Finish to end the installation.

Figure 6.11 Installation Summary

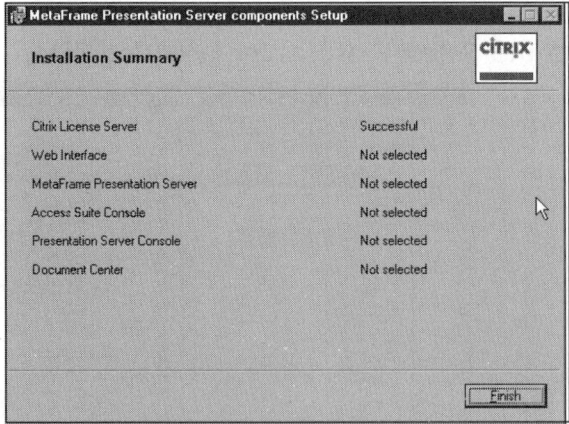

Installing the Web Interface

The Web Interface makes it possible for users to access their applications through a Web browser or through the Program Neighborhood Agent. Although accessing published applications through the Program Neighborhood Agent does not require a published Web page, it does require the technology the Web Interface provides.

Before installing the Web Interface, be sure that IIS and ASP.NET have been installed. You will also need to know the port number that is or will be used (if a new farm) for the Citrix XML service. The XML service is the communications link between the rest of the servers in the farm and the server running the Web Interface. If you have existing MetaFrame Presentation Servers and do not know the port number, open the Management Console, right-click on a server, and select **Properties**. From the Properties menu, select **MetaFrame Settings**.

The installation process for the Web Interface should look familiar by now, and if you have all your prerequisites and the information you will need, it will be short and sweet. Citrix recommends that for larger farms, the Web Interface should be run on a dedicated server running IIS, but for smaller farms, it can share hardware with MetaFrame Presentation Server. To begin the installation from the CD-ROM:

1. Select **Install MetaFrame Presentation Server and its Components**.

2. Accept the license agreement and click **Next**.

3. Click **Next** on the **Prerequisites** screen.

4. Select Web Interface from the components and then click **Next** to continue.

5. Again, accept the license agreement and click **Next**.

6. Next, we are prompted to install the MetaFrame Presentation Server Clients. If you choose to install the clients, select **Install the Clients from the Components CD-ROM** (see Figure 6.12) and browse to the ICAWEB directory. The contents of this directory will be copied to the \Citrix\ICAWEB directory off the Web server's document root. If you do not elect to install the clients at this time, be sure that you create the directory structure. Click **Next** to continue.

Figure 6.12 Location of Clients

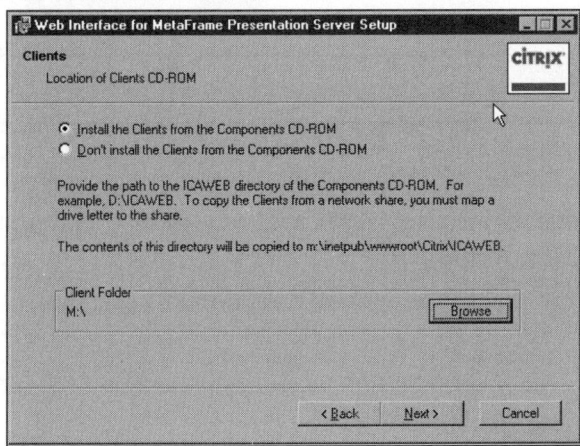

7. The next screen asks you to define the server settings. At least one server in the farm must supply the Web Interface with published application information. You will need to specify the server's name or IP address and the port that the XML service is running on as shown in Figure 6.13. Since the server we are building is the first server and will also host the Web Interface, we will leave the default settings. Click **Next** to continue.

Figure 6.13 Define Server Settings

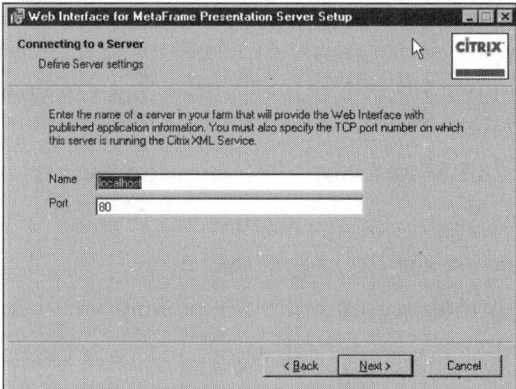

8. We are now asked to configure the default Web site. As you can see in Figure 6.14, the default location for the Login page is http://servername/ Citrix/MetaFrame/default.htm. That is a rather long URL for the users to remember. If you select **Set site's default page to the Web Interface**, the Login page URL will be http://servername—much easier to remember. Select where you want the Login page and click **Next** to continue.

NOTE

If you prefer, you can configure the location from the IIS Administrator.

9. Now that all the selections have been made, click **Next** to begin the installation of the Web Interface.

10. Once the installation process has finished, click **Finish** to complete the installation.

Figure 6.14 Default Web Page

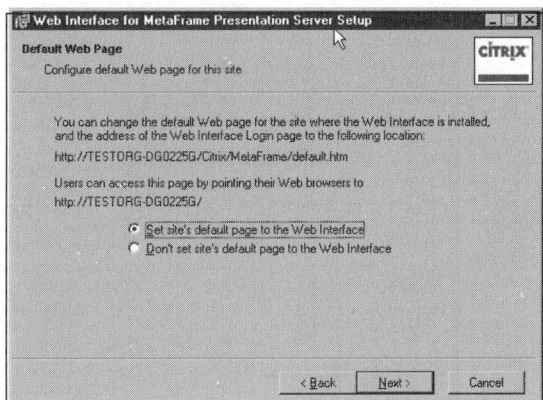

Installing MetaFrame Presentation Server 3.0

Finally, we come to step 5 in the recommended installation sequence: to install the individual servers. We have installed the Document Center, created the data store, and installed the Web Interface; now, we will install MetaFrame Presentation Server 3.0. The installation process is not too different from previous releases, but as with other components, it is a good idea to become familiar with the process and the information you will need to complete it. Next, we will step through the process of installing MetaFrame Presentation Server 3.0 and discuss in detail the information you will need and decisions you must make. By now, the installation screens and verbiage should be familiar. Here we go:

1. From the product CD-ROM Autorun screen, select **Product Installation | Install MetaFrame Presentation Server 3.0 and components**.

2. Again, accept the license agreement and click **Next**.

3. You are again reminded of the prerequisites; click **Next** to continue.

4. Next, we select the components we want to install. Since we have already installed the Document Center, license server, and Web Interface, de-select those components. If you want to install the consoles on the server, leave these selected; if not, de-select those as well and then click **Next** (see Figure 6.15).

5. The next screen warns us that we did not elect to install a license server. Our options are to either have an existing license server or plan to install one later with the product CD-ROM as shown in Figure 6.16. Select the first option indicating that we already have a license server and then click **Next** to continue.

Figure 6.15 Select the Components to Install

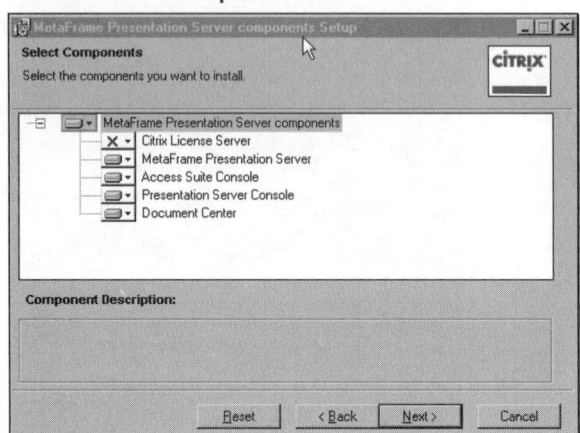

Figure 6.16 License Server Warning

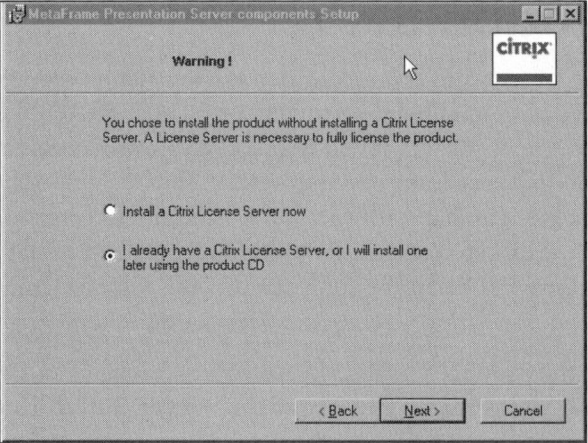

6. The installation process begins updating the system and then we are presented with the Welcome screen. Click **Next** to continue.

7. This next screen must be one of your favorites by now, and we're sure you know what to do. Accept the license agreement and click **Next** to continue.

8. At this point, you are asked to select the product edition that you are licensed to run: Standard, Advanced, and Enterprise. If you are unsure of the edition you are licensed for, check your product documentation or check with your reseller. You do not want to install options that you will not be able to use. If you have a Standard Edition Licensing, you have just the basic MetaFrame Presentation Server and components. The Advanced Edition, designed for small to medium environments, includes load-balancing functionality. If your license

entitles you to the Enterprise Edition, Load Balancing, Installation Manager, Resource Manager, and Network Manager are all included. This edition targets medium to large environments that need a single point of control for resource monitoring, application packaging and delivery, and network monitoring. For our purposes here, we will select the Enterprise Edition. Select the edition you are licensed for and click **Next** to continue (see Figure 6.17).

Figure 6.17 Product Edition Selection

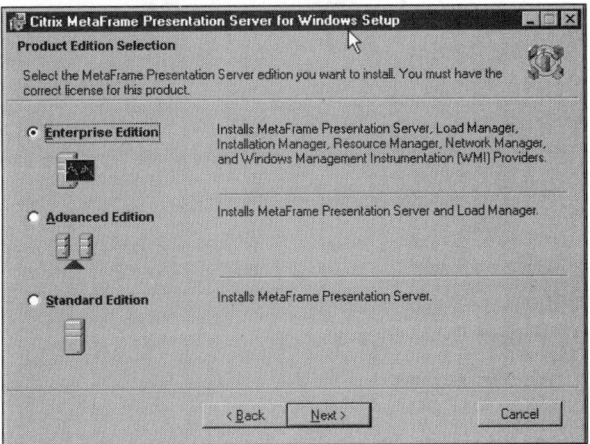

9. From the Component Selection screen, you have the opportunity to select the various components you want to install. If you selected Enterprise Edition, you will see all the available components. If you selected another edition, you will only see those components included with the edition you selected. Figure 6.18 shows the component selection for the Enterprise Edition. Citrix also includes a handy utility here that can check the disk space needed for the components you select. To see how much disk space you will need, click **Disk Cost**. When sure your server has the space required for the components selected, click **Next** to continue.

Figure 6.18 Component Selection

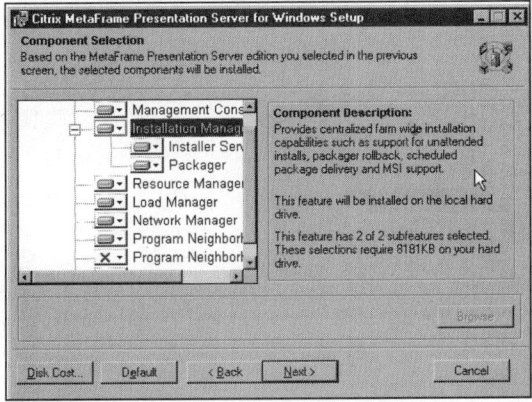

See Table 6.1 for the components included with each edition of
MetaFrame Presentation Server 3.0.

Table 6.1 Components Included with Each MetaFrame Presentation Server
3.0 Edition

Components	Standard	Advanced	Enterprise
Management Console for MetaFrame Presentation Server	X	X	X
Installation Manager			X
Installer Service			X
Packager			X
Resource Manager			X
Load Manager		X	X
Network Manager			X
Program Neighborhood	X	X	X
Program Neighborhood Agent	X	X	X
WMI Providers			X

10. Next, we are asked whether we want to install Passthrough Authentication (see
    Figure 6.19). Pass-Through Authentication allows the user's name and password
    to be passed from the local machine to the server. If you do not elect to install
    Pass-Through Authentication now and decide that you want this feature later on,
    you will need to reinstall the Pass-Through Client. Click **Next** to continue.

Figure 6.19 Pass-Through Authentication

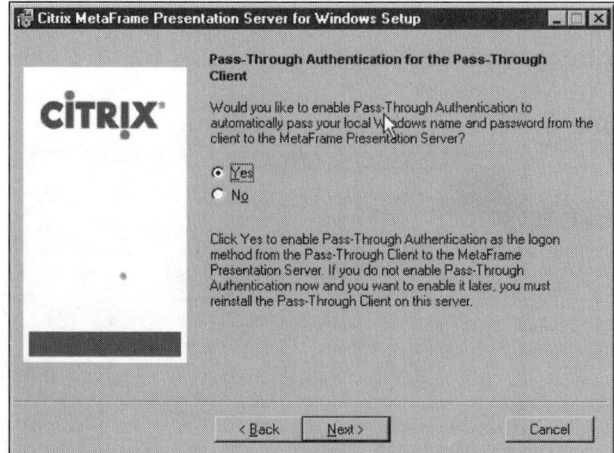

11. The next screen allows us to create a new farm or join an existing one. Because this is the first server in our farm, we will select **Create a new farm** and click **Next**. For creating the first server in the farm and adding additional servers to an additional farm, you will need to know what type of database will be used, the host name of the server where the database will run, and the logon credentials to access the database (see Figure 6.20).

Figure 6.20 Create or Join a Server Farm

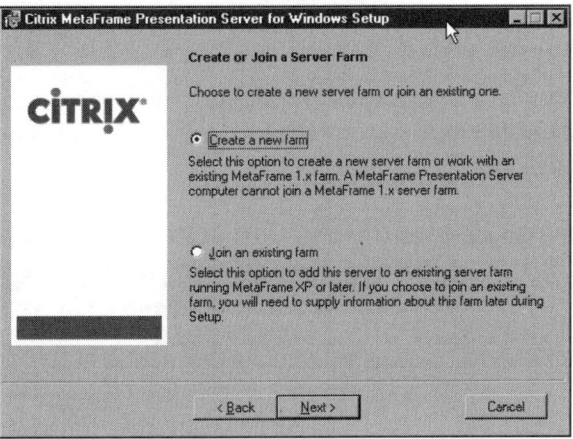

12. We are now prompted to enter the initial settings for our new farm. You will enter a new farm name and select the database to use for the data store. Farm names can be up to 32 characters in length and can contain spaces. Because we elected to use MSDE, we will select it from the Local Database drop-down. If we had arranged to use a MS SQL, Oracle, or IBM DB2 database, we would select the second option and point to a database on a separate server. A zone name is also required, and the default uses the IP subnet mask where the server resides. You can choose a different zone name if you wish (see Figure 6.21). When all selections have been made, click **Next** to continue.

Figure 6.21 Configuring the Initial Properties for the Farm

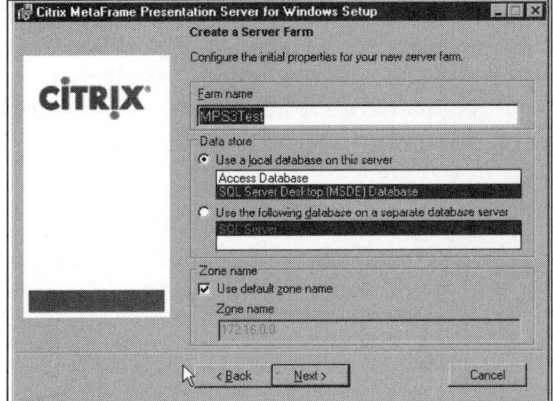

MS SQL Server, Oracle, and IBM DB2 Databases

In environments where a dedicated database server will be used, we would select the second option and select the type of database from the drop-down list. Once we have selected the database, we would select the driver to be used. If the driver needed is not in the list, you must cancel the installation and install the driver before restarting the installation.

13. We now must specify a domain user who will be the initial administrator for the farm. Enter a user name and the domain name, and then click **Next** to continue.

14. On the next screen, we must provide the host name and port number for the licensing server, or we can choose to provide this information after completing the installation (see Figure 6.22).

Figure 6.22 Identify the Citrix Licensing Server

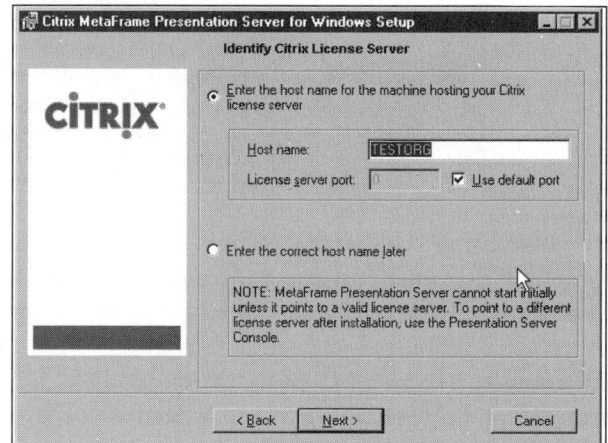

15. Next, we are warned that no licenses were found (see Figure 6.23). This is to be expected because we are creating a new farm and have just installed a new license server. To avoid issues with licensing, we recommend that you continue the product installation and use the 96-hour grace period for testing before downloading your license files. Remember, previous versions of MetaFrame licensing are not compatible, and although both versions can coexist in the same farm, the licenses must be managed separately. Select **Continue the product installation without installing licenses** and click **Next** to continue.

16. Our next decision revolves around session shadowing. Shadowing is used to monitor users' sessions and, if needed, interact with their sessions. It is a handy tool for help desk personnel and others who need to actually see the users' sessions. However, in some secure environments, shadowing may not be per-

mitted. You should check your company's policy and make sure you are compliant. During installation, as shown in Figure 6.24, we are given the option to prohibit shadowing. This option is permanent if configured during installation. Unless you are very sure that you do not want to allow shadowing, do not select this option. If you decide later not to allow shadowing, you can disable its use. Our other options with respect to shadowing are:

Figure 6.23 Warning Message: No Licenses Found!

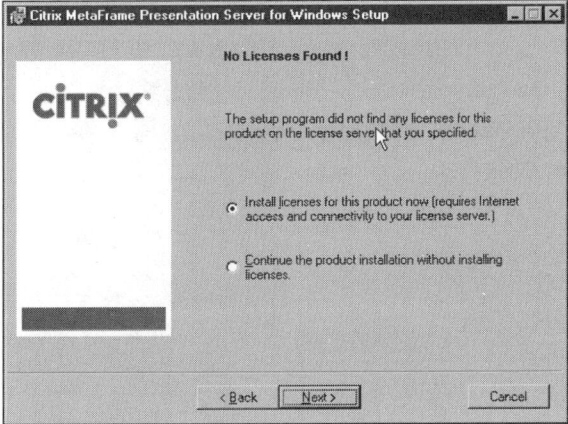

- **Prohibit remote control** This option prevents interacting with the user's session while shadowing.

- **Force a shadow acceptance popup** Users shadowed will receive a pop-up alert and must accept before shadowing is allowed.

- **Log all shadow connections** This option logs all shadowed connections to the Event Log.

Figure 6.24 Shadowing Options

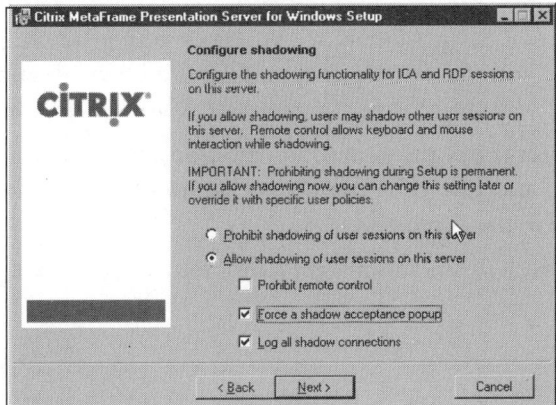

17. Next, we must configure the port used by the XML service. The XML service provides the Web Interface and ICA-connected clients with the names of the published applications available in the farm. The default setting is to share port 80 with Internet Information Server and is necessary if sending data over HTTPS. If you do not intend to use HTTPS, select an unused port. If you are unsure of which ports are currently in use, type **netstat −a** at the command prompt. Be sure that all servers in a farm use the same port (see Figure 6.25).

Figure 6.25 Configuring XML Service Port

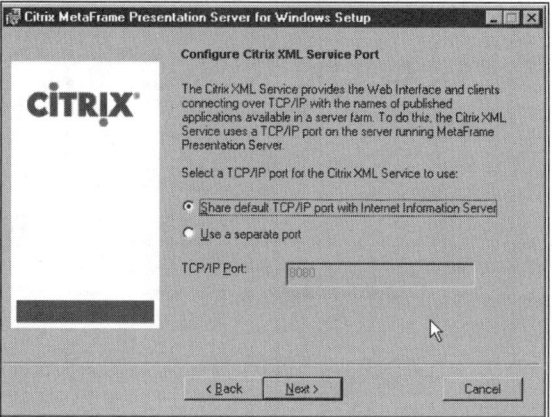

18. Setup now asks if we want to add users to the Remote Desktop group. The Remote Desktop group is a built-in group within Windows Server 2003 and users can be added at anytime. If you do not want to add the users during setup, select **Skip this step** and click **Next**.

19. The next screen (Figure 6.26) allows you to review your selections and summarizes the components to be installed. If satisfied that all are correct, click **Finish**, or click **Back** to change selections.

20. The installation now begins updating the system. Note: You may receive a pop-up warning indicating that the MetaFrame Presentation Server cannot access the Virtual Scripts Directory. You must either let setup change the settings on this directory, or exit setup and run setup again and change the port. If you do not want to change the port the XML services uses, click **Yes**.

21. Once setup completes the system update, you are informed that the installation was successful and given the options to launch the ICA Client Distribution Wizard or view the Readme.

22. The installation is again summarized and you are prompted to restart the server.

Figure 6.26 Installation Summary

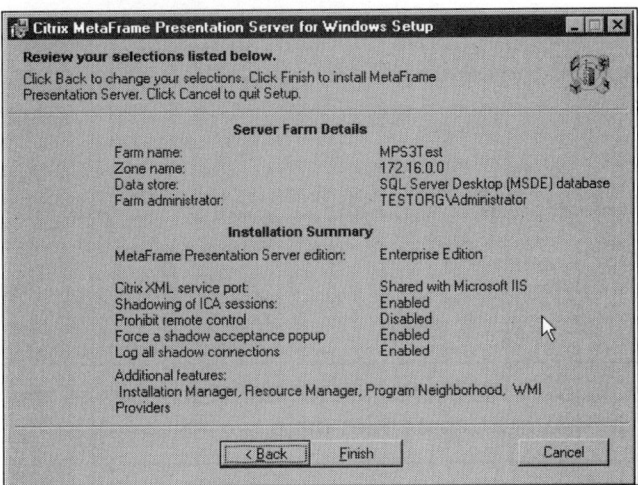

23. Once the server restarts, the installation process is complete. At this point, you can apply any Citrix MetaFrame updates that may be needed and begin testing your server.

24. When you have thoroughly tested your server and feel confident that it is in good working order, you will want to download your license files to your license server. Keep in mind that the previous versions of MetaFrame Presentation Server are not compatible with the new license server. You can run a mixed farm, but you must manage the licenses separately. If you have a mixed farm, you will not want to allocate all your licenses to MetaFrame Presentation Server 3.0. To obtain your license files, you can either download them during the installation process or as we suggested earlier, wait until after the testing phase to download them. To download the files post-installation, go to **www.mycitrix.com**:

    1. Log in with your MyCitrix username and password.

    2. In the top, left-hand corner of the page, click to select **Licensing**.

    3. Again at the top, left-hand side of the page, click on **Citrix Activation System**.

    4. Next, click on **Activate or Allocate Licenses**.

    5. On the right-hand side of the screen, enter your license code as shown in Figure 6.27 and click **Continue**.

    6. Enter the type and number of licenses you want to allocate.

    7. Enter the host name of the license server.

NOTE

The host name is case-sensitive. If you are unsure of the name, case, or spelling, type **hostname** at the command prompt on the license server.

8. Download the license file and click **Copy License File to Your License Server**.

NOTE

If you manually copy the license file to your license server, you must run **Update License Data** from the License Files page.

Figure 6.27 Allocate Licensing

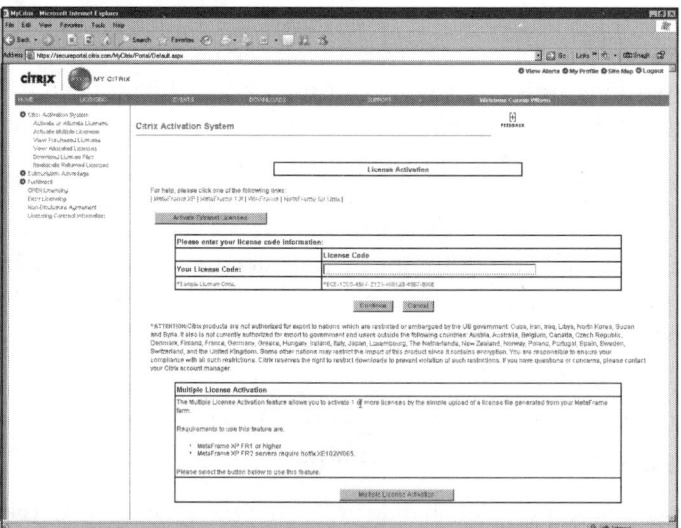

Performing an Unattended Setup of MetaFrame Presentation Server 3.0

As with the Windows Server 2003 installation, MetaFrame Presentation Server 3.0 setup can be configured to run without user intervention. There are two possible ways to make this happen:

- **Using Windows Installer transforms** When you launch the MetaFrame Presentation Server installation process, it kicks off the mps.msi file. A file with the extension .msi is a Windows Installer Package file. Inside the .msi file is a relational database that holds the install and uninstall instructions for the program with which it is associated. A transform file modifies the relational database inside the package file, providing the answers to the questions asked during installation. To create a transform file, you must have access to a utility to edit Windows Installer Packages such as the Wise Package Studio. Once you have created your transform, place the MetaFrame Presentation Server 3.0 CD-ROM in the drive, and from the command line, type **misexec /i mps.msi /L*v c:\output.log <Enter>**. If you plan to use transform files, it is best to become familiar with the Windows Installer Service. Instructions and command-line options can be found at www.microsoft.com/resources/documentation/windows/xp/all/proddocs/en-us/msiexec.mspx.

- **Creating an answer file** The answer file is similar to the one used for the unattended install of Windows Server 2003. It provides answers to the questions asked during the MetaFrame Presentation Server 3.0 installation process. A sample answer file is provided on the product CD-ROM under \Support\Install. When you have modified your answer file, go to the command line and type **unattendedinstall mps.msi answer file** (where "answer file" is the name of your modified answer file). For more information on creating answer files, visit the Microsoft Deployment and Resource Kit site at www.microsoft.com/windows/reskits/default.asp.

Upgrading to MetaFrame Presentation Server 3.0

If you have an existing MetaFrame server farm, you might want to upgrade to MetaFrame Presentation Server 3.0 instead of installing from scratch. This can be done, and Citrix supports directly migrating to MetaFrame Presentation Server 3.0 under the following conditions:

- Windows 2000 Server SP4 must be installed prior to migrating to MetaFrame Presentation Server 3.0.

- Client is running Windows Server 2003.

- Client is runnging any release of MetaFrame XP 1.0.

- If MetaFrame 1.8, you will need to upgrade to MetaFrame XP first.

Whether the upgrade process makes matters any easier or faster is a matter of debate. In some scenarios, it makes sense to upgrade rather than reinstall. For instance, if you are currently running Windows Server 2003/MetaFrame XP, the only upgrade you will need is from MetaFrame XP to MetaFrame Presentation Server 3.0. A new installation usually entails installing fresh on a new server or taking an existing server and reinstalling everything from scratch. Upgrades should work and often do, but nothing tastes as good as whipping it up from scratch, or so to speak. When upgrading the operating system or MetaFrame, there are always outdated files and drivers left over from the previous version, some of which just take up space and others that can actually cause problems. Then, there are the situations where not all the servers are configured the same; perhaps some were upgraded from previous versions and others were installed from scratch. It can be difficult to know what to expect and could be a complete nightmare. The best rule of thumb, when possible, is to start fresh. If that isn't feasible for your environment, then read on, as we will discuss the upgrade process here.

Designing & Planning...

Upgrade or Fresh Install?

Citrix and Microsoft both provide upgrade paths for their products, so why would you want to start over and perform a completely new install? While upgrading may seem like a good idea, there are a few things to think about before making your decision. First, unless you have kept your existing MetaFrame server pristine, you may have outdated or redundant data or applications stored on the server. If you choose to upgrade, do some spring-cleaning first and get things in order. Second, check any local groups created on the server and make sure they are still valid. Lastly, check NTFS file permissions to make sure they are correct. With all the time and trouble it will take to analyze the server and clean it up, it may be easier to back up any data and install fresh.

When upgrading to MetaFrame Presentation Server 3.0, you should follow the same process as you would for a new install: make a plan, read the documentation, create a checklist, gather needed updates, credentials, drivers, and information. In other words, know what to expect and be prepared. It is important to note that no one can tell you everything you need to know to ensure a successful migration. Your environment is unique, and only those who work there day after day can provide all the answers—and sometimes not.

What is the best way to proceed with an upgrade from MetaFrame XP to MetaFrame Presentation Server 3.0? First, you must consider your environment. Do you have spare hardware on which to perform testing? Again, just like a new installation, testing is extremely important. If you don't have spare equipment, can you pull one of the production servers out of the farm without impacting the environment? It would be wise to make testing a priority, right up there with planning. It would be a shame to do all the work an upgrade requires, only to have your farm fail because of unperceived issues.

Designing and Planning…

Before You Migrate…

Before you decide on a migration plan, take a few minutes to review your current environment. What operating system are the servers running on, and are there plans to upgrade in the near future? Does the current farm design suit your current environment, and can it be expanded to meet future needs? What problems, if any, do your current servers have? If there are any issues, it would be wise to fix the problems you have before attempting a migration.

The Upgrade Process

Just as with new installations, Citrix recommends a specific order for carrying out an upgrade. Primarily because Citrix licensing has changed, it is important to carry out the upgrade tasks in a specific sequence. Look at the following list while planning your upgrade. If done correctly, you will preserve configuration settings and avoid inconsistencies.

1. Uninstall any anti-virus programs before upgrading. Anti-virus programs should be installed last and can be reinstalled once the upgrade is complete.

2. Uninstall any system applications running; these too can be reinstalled once the upgrade is complete.

3. Update drivers. Check for new versions of drivers and update as needed.

4. Check for application compatibility or any problems and/or work-arounds.

5. If installing on a Windows 2000 server, be sure to upgrade to Service Pack 4 before upgrading.

6. Review the checklist for any information you may need prior to your upgrade. It is also a good idea to print the checklist and have it on hand during the upgrade process.

7. Install the license server *before* upgrading the first server in the farm.

8. Manually update the Resource Manager Summary Database, if used.

9. Upgrade the Conferencing Manager, if used, to version 3.0 prior to upgrading to MPS3.0.

10. Upgrade the MetaFrame Presentation Server Console. The console must be upgraded before upgrading because only the upgraded version can be used to change settings in the new farm.

11. Upgrade the Web Interface *before* installing MetaFrame Presentation Server 3.0. If you upgrade MPS3.0 before upgrading the Web Interface, the older version of the Web Interface will be removed and no configuration settings will be saved. Upgrading the Web Interface first will preserve your settings.

12. Next, for farms using MS Access or MSDE, upgrade the server hosting the data store.

13. Upgrade Zone Data Collectors next. Here's a tip: If you plan to run in mixed mode with a previous version of MetaFrame, configure the server running MetaFrame Presentation Server 3.0 as the Zone Data Collector.

14. Upgrade Resource Manager, if used and the farm metric servers, both primary and backup.

15. Finally, upgrade the remaining servers in the farm.

The preceding list is illustrated in Figure 6.28.

NOTE

You can upgrade the MetaFrame Presentation Server Console and Web Interface automatically by accepting the default settings of the **Install MetaFrame Presentation Server and its Components**. This setting will automatically upgrade both the console and Web Interface before upgrading to MetaFrame Presentation Server 3.0.

Removing Servers from the Farm

If it becomes necessary to remove a server from your farm, Citrix recommends uninstalling MetaFrame Presentation Server prior to removing the server. If the product is not uninstalled, the data store will still contain information about the server and it will still be in the list of servers shown in the Console. The removal process is fairly simple. First, make sure all users are logged off the server and all applications are closed. Then, from **Add/Remove Programs**, select **Change or Remove Programs**.

Figure 6.28 The Upgrade Process

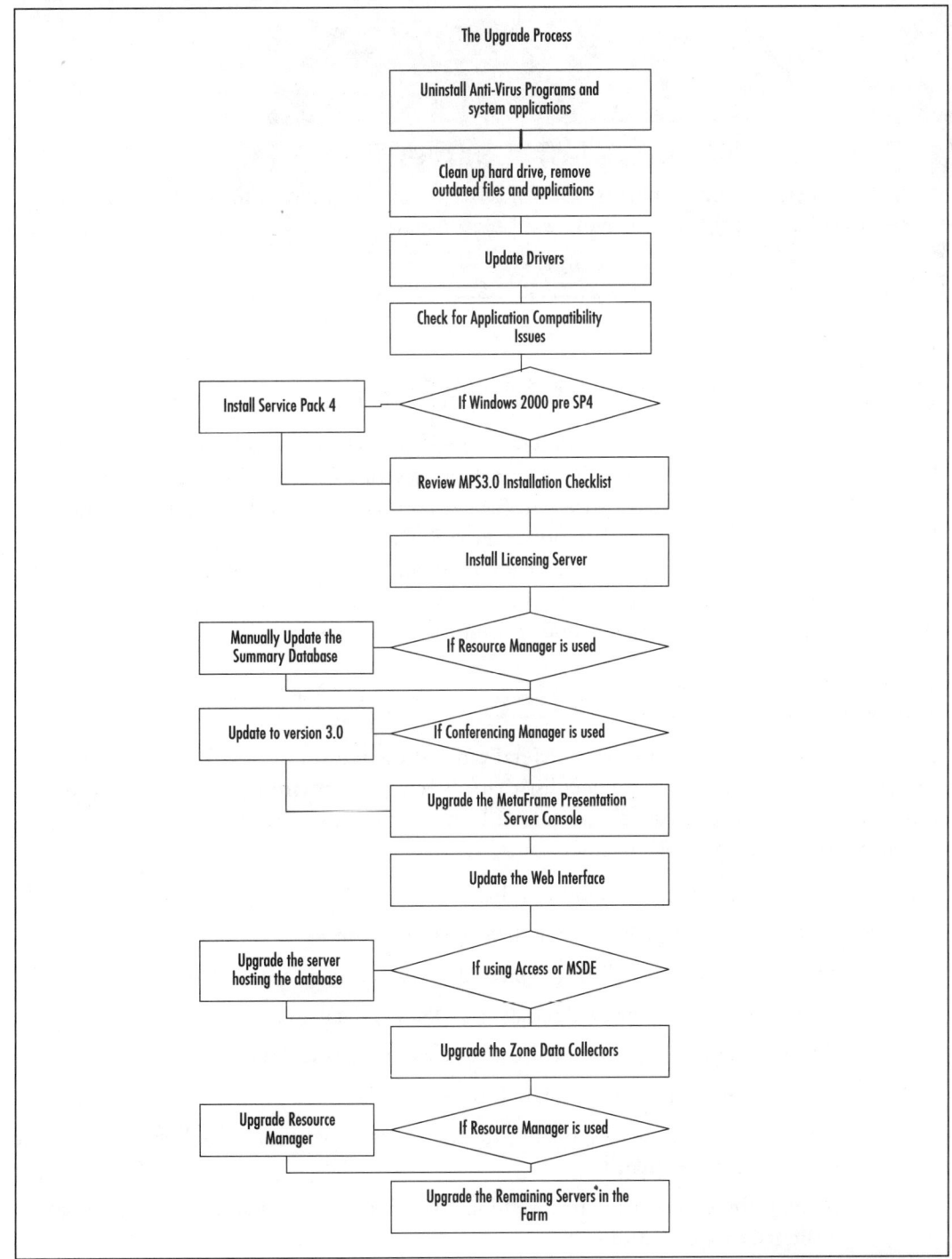

Citricks...

Forcing the Removal of a Server ...

If the uninstall process hangs or fails, which it occasionally will, you can force the removal by typing the following at the command line:

```
CTX_MF_FORCE_SUBSYSTEM_UNINSTALL ="Yes"<ENTER>
```

Downgrading to Previous Versions of MetaFrame

Currently, Citrix does not support downgrading from MetaFrame Presentation Server 3.0 to previous versions. If you must revert to a previous version, the options are few and could be messy. First, make sure you have a complete system backup of the system. Next, uninstall MetaFrame Presentation Server 3.0, and then restore from backup. A second option, also requiring a system backup, would be to uninstall the newer version and then perform a new install of the previous version and restore data afterwards. Neither method is recommended, and it might be easier to reinstall from scratch.

Migration Checklist

Before beginning your migration to MetaFrame Presentation Server 3.0, look over the migration process and create a checklist that reflects your environment, similar to the following. Having a checklist to guide you through the process can be extremely helpful when frequent interruptions distract you.

1. Read all the documentation and check for updates.
2. Download any updates or patches ahead of time.
3. Make sure you have all third-party drivers that may be needed.
4. Have authorized user credentials for OS and database.
5. Know what database you will use and where it is located.
6. Plan where each component will be installed.
7. If you will remap drives, make sure the software you will install can be installed on a drive other than C:.
8. Remap the drives prior to installing MetaFrame Presentation Server, any components, or applications.

9. Remember that you have a licensing grace period of 96 hours.

10. Know what company policy is on shadowing and select appropriate options.

11. Know what port you will use for XML and if you will use HTTPS.

12. Remember that previous versions of MetaFrame Presentation Server are not compatible with the new licensing server, so in a mixed environment, licenses must be handled separately.

13. To preserve configuration settings during a migration, remember to follow the prescribed order for upgrading each component.

14. Plan your migration strategy with your users in mind; downtime decreases productivity and increases frustration.

Summary

It is a well-known fact that "techie types" frequently scoff at reading manuals. Many prefer to tinker with things until they get the hang of it. "We don't need no stinking manual!" Reading the manual may never come into play until frustration sets in or things are so messed up that reading the manual becomes a necessity. In this case, however, even those hard-core techies will benefit from reading everything they can about the topic, particularly if migrating an existing farm.

MetaFrame historically has a reputation for being complex and difficult to manage, and this is a *new* version with enough differences that beginning without finding out as much about it as possible and making a plan could end up in disaster. Use the Installation Checklist and check the Citrix Web site for new information or updates. If you have software that is known to be problematic, check the Citrix Support forums to see if anyone else out there has run into issues—they may have found the fix.

With any luck, this chapter provided enough information to help you perform the basics of creating a new or migrating to a MetaFrame Presentation Server 3.0 farm. Depending on your environment, the process could be more or less complex. Each environment is unique and will have its own unique issues. Proper preparation and planning can help to avoid many of the common problems that arise, but others will require research and trial and error before they are resolved. Remember, practice makes perfect, and that goes for server builds as well. Find a way to perform test installations and upgrades before doing a live migration and your efforts will certainly pay off!

Solutions Fast Track

Pre-Installation

☑ Review the Installation Checklist.

☑ Be sure to read the documentation and update information before beginning.

☑ Install and perform testing before attempting to place in production.

☑ When performing the test installation, document the process, the decisions you must make, and the information that is required so you will not be surprised when building your production server.

☑ Prior to beginning the installation process for a production server, make sure you have all the required information, credentials, updates, and drivers you will need.

The Installation Process

- ☑ Review the Checklist.
- ☑ Install the Document Center.
- ☑ Create the data store (unless using an Access database).
- ☑ Install the license server.
- ☑ Install individual servers.

Remapping the Server Drives

- ☑ Remember to remap the server drives prior to installing MetaFrame Presentation Server or components.
- ☑ Remapping the drives frees up the drive letters C: and D: for use by the client.
- ☑ Drive remapping is permanent and remains changed even if MetaFrame Presentation Server is uninstalled.

Creating the Data Store

- ☑ Unless you plan to use MS Access, the data store must be created prior to installing your first server. You will be asked during the installation process for the name and location of the data store.
- ☑ A small farm of 50 or fewer servers can use MS Access or MSDE in indirect mode. Indirect mode refers the servers in the farm connecting to the data store installed on a MetaFrame Presentation Server that hosts the data store.
- ☑ Medium- to enterprise-level farms should have a dedicated server hosting the data store and use one of the true client/server database products supported, such as MS SQL Server, Oracle, or IBM DB2.
- ☑ Before deciding on a database to use for the data store, be sure your environment has the technical expertise to administer the database, and that the database you select will handle any expected growth in your environment.

Installing the License Server

- ☑ MetaFrame Presentation Server 3.0 uses a new and different licensing scheme.
- ☑ If running a server farm with both MetaFrame Presentation Server 3.0 and a previous version of MetaFrame, the licenses must be handled separately.

☑ The licensing server can be run on a dedicated server, or it can share hardware with another MetaFrame Presentation Server. Citrix recommends a dedicated server if the number of servers in the farm exceeds 50.

Installing the Web Interface

☑ Ensure that IIS version 5 or later and ASP.net have been installed prior to installing the Web Interface.

☑ Configure the default URL for the login page to http://server name.

☑ Be sure you know the XML port that will be used and if the IIS service will share it.

Installing MetaFrame Presentation Server 3.0

☑ Know if you will upgrade or perform a new installation, and understand what each entails before starting.

☑ If using a dedicated database server, be prepared with the credentials necessary to access the database.

☑ Have database ODBC drivers on hand.

☑ Remember that Citrix provides a 96-hour grace period during which testing can be performed.

☑ Once the server has been tested, download the license files from http://mycitrix.com.

Links to Sites

- www.citrix.com
- http://support.microsoft.com
- http://mycitrix.com
- http://support.citrix.com
- www.dabcc.com
- www.tokeshi.com
- www.thinplanet.com
- www.wise.com

Frequently Asked Questions

The following Frequently Asked Questions, answered by the authors of this book, are designed to both measure your understanding of the concepts presented in this chapter and to assist you with real-life implementation of these concepts. To have your questions about this chapter answered by the author, browse to **www.syngress.com/solutions** and click on the **"Ask the Author"** form. You will also gain access to thousands of other FAQs at ITFAQnet.com.

Q: What exactly is "drive remapping" and why would I want to do this?

A: Drive remapping reassigns the drive letters used by the server. For instance, if your server drives are C: and D:, they could be remapped to M: and N:. If the server drives are not remapped, the local drives of users connecting to the MetaFrame servers will be remapped to U:, V:, and W: because C: and D: are taken by the server. Users often become confused by this and assume that C: and D: are their local drives. Remapping the server drives frees up C: and D: for use by the local drives.

Q: At what point should the drives be remapped?

A: Prior to installing MetaFrame Presentation Server or any of the components.

Q: What is the Document Center?

A: The Document Center is a new feature that creates a library of all the MetaFrame Access Suite guides, in .pdf format, in one central location where they can be easily accessed when needed. The Document Center can be installed on the server or workstation.

Q: What are the benefits of using Microsoft SQL Desktop Edition over using MS Access for the data store?

A: MSDE is a scaled-down version of Microsoft SQL Server and is included free on the MetaFrame Presentation Server CD-ROM. MSDE can be used in small server farms of 50 or fewer servers in indirect mode, just as MS Access, or in very small environments as a direct connection. MSDE support up to five concurrent connections, and since the servers do not all contact the data store at the same time, there is little risk that all five connections would be in use at the same time.

Q: What are the three editions of MetaFrame Presentation Server, and how do I know which edition I need?

A: The three editions are Standard, Advanced, and Enterprise. The Standard Edition is the core product, the administrative console and the Document Center. This edition is best for small environments with little need of centralized monitoring, unattended installations, or load balancing. The Advanced Edition is the core product and Load Management. Load Management manages the user load to servers and applications. The Advanced Edition is suitable for medium to large environments where users connect to multiple servers and a way to manage the load on each is needed. The Enterprise Edition includes all that the Standard and Advanced Editions have and adds Resource Manager, Network Manager, Installation Manager, and WMI Providers. This edition is suitable for large, enterprise environments where centralized monitoring and unattended installations are needed.

Q: What is the licensing server and where should it be installed?

A: The licensing server is yet another new feature in MetaFrame Presentation Server 3.0. It is a centralized licensing utility where all the Access Suite licenses can be managed.

Q: What information do I need to know to add a new MetaFrame Presentation Server to an existing farm?

A: You will need to know what type of database is being used for the data store, whether it is a local database (MS Access or MSDE) or one on a dedicated server (MS SQL Server, Oracle, or IBM DB2), and the host name of the server where the database resides. You will also need logon credentials to access the database.

Q: If during setup, I choose to prohibit shadowing, can I turn it on later?

A: No, the decision during setup is permanent. To turn it back on, you would need to reinstall the server.

Q: What if I decide after installing MetaFrame Presentation Server that I do not want to use the same port for IIS and the XML service?

A: The port can be changed post-installation. To change the port, go to the command prompt and type **ctxxmlss /u** to unload the XML service. Next, type **ctxxmlss /rxx**, where "xx" is the port you will use. When finished, restart the XML service.

Q: I'm not sure I want to upgrade to Windows Server 2003 at this time, but I want to migrate from MetaFrame XP 1.0 to MetaFrame Presentation Server 3.0. If I decide later that I'm ready to upgrade to Windows Server 2003, will that be a problem?

A: Yes. Citrix does not support upgrading the operating system. If you choose to upgrade your existing operating system, you must perform a new install of MetaFrame Presentation Server 3.0.

Q: We have a MetaFrame XP farm running on Windows 2000 SP3 and we want to upgrade to MetaFrame Presentation 3.0. Will we lose all of our configuration settings in the process?

A: Not if the upgrade is done in the proper order. First, consider whether you will upgrade your Windows 2000 servers in the near future. If you plan to move to Windows Server 2003 and do not do it prior to installing MetaFrame Presentation Server 3.0, you will need to completely reinstall it after upgrading to Windows Server 2003. If you plan to stay with Windows 2000, you will need to apply SP4 before upgrading to MetaFrame Presentation Server 3.0. As for upgrading from MetaFrame XP to MPS3.0, Citrix provides a list of tasks that must be performed in sequence in order to retain your configuration settings.

Q: How can I remove a server from the farm and not have it show up in the MetaFrame Presentation Server Console?

A: Uninstalling the server before removing it from the farm will remove it from the list of servers in the Console.

Chapter 7

Client Configuration

Solutions in this Chapter:

- Introduction
- ICA Client Options
- Deciding Which Client to Use
- Deploying the Client to Users
- ICA Clients for Mobile Devices
- Non-Windows ICA Clients
- Securing the ICA Client

☑ Summary

☑ Solutions Fast Track

☑ Frequently Asked Questions

Introduction

Now that we have explored the server-side installations of Windows Server 2003 and MetaFrame Presentation Server 3.0, let's take a look at the client-side piece: the Independent Computing Architecture (ICA) client. As you learned in previous chapters, the ICA client allows users to access and use resources installed on the MetaFrame Presentation Server. On the server-side, protocol-specific ICA listener ports wait for users to connect via an ICA client installed on a PC or other computing device. Once the connection is made, an ICA session is established and the user can begin using the resources.

Designing and Planning...

Idle Port Listeners

Windows Terminal Server 4.0 and Windows 2000 Server created two Idle Port Listeners by default and more could be added as deemed necessary. Windows Server 2003, however, does not use Idle Port Listeners. Listener ports are created dynamically as they are needed.

As with other phases of a MetaFrame Presentation Server deployment, the client installation and configuration phase demands its share of planning and testing. Citrix provides clients for nearly every platform and device on the market as well as Web-based clients for accessing published applications via a Web browser. Before you begin your deployment, look closely at your environment and analyze both your current and future requirements. Your decisions should reflect your current environment, and the direction you perceive your environment will change and grow in the future. After analyzing your environment, you should have the answers to the following questions:

- How will your users access the resources installed on the MetaFrame Presentation Server?

- What protocol will the clients need?

- What type of devices and/or operating systems will require access?

- How will clients connect to the network?

- What resources will be provided?

- Who will access the published resources?

- How will the ICA clients be deployed to your clients?
- How will you configure and secure access?

In this chapter, we explore the decisions you must make concerning the client and look at the various methods of access, the devices, and platforms supported. We also discuss in detail the configuration, security, and management of access to the MetaFrame Presentation Server as well as how access can be secured and deployed. By the time you complete this chapter, you will have a better idea of how you will proceed and a few ideas that can improve productivity and user experience.

Device and Client Options

As mentioned earlier, Citrix provides ICA clients for virtually every platform and device on the market. Now users can access published applications and data from personal data assistants (PDAs), smart phones, and Java-enabled devices as well as desktops running Windows, DOS, UNIX, Linux, Macintosh and OS/2, and the list continues to grow. Table 7.1 provides a current listing of devices and ICA clients supported by MetaFrame Presentation Server 3.0. For the purposes of this chapter, we focus primarily on the Windows 32-bit clients and touch briefly on some of the more popular non-Windows clients.

Table 7.1 Supported ICA Clients

Platform	ICA Client
Microsoft Windows	Win32 or Win16
WinCE/Pocket PC	ARM, ARM4I, MIPS, SH-3, SH-4, x86
Macintosh (MAC)	OS X, PowerPC, 68K
Java	Java
IBM OS/2 Warp	IBM OS/2 Warp
EPOC/Symbian OS	Nokia 9300/9400, Sony Ericsson 800/900/91, Nokia 9200 Series, Psion
DOS	16 and 32 bit
UNIX	Solaris/Sparc, Linux, AIX IBM, HP UX, Solaris/x86, Sun OS, Compaq Tru64, SGI, SCO

As you can see, Citrix has made it possible to deliver published resources to a wide range of devices and operating systems. Businesses can now leverage mobile and wireless devices as well as the traditional desktops, providing business applications and data to users regardless of their location. Moreover, users can now roam across multiple wired and wireless networks and move from one device to another while maintaining their original session, without reauthenticating. This feature, called *smooth roaming*, helps to boost productivity and reduces lag time while actually reducing administrative headaches.

32-Bit Windows Clients

As you might guess, the 32-bit Windows ICA client is intended for Microsoft Windows 32-bit operating systems, which include Windows 9*x*, Windows Me, Windows NT 4, Windows 2000, and Windows XP. Citrix provides not one, but *three* 32-bit Windows clients, and you must decide which client or clients best suit your environment, the needs of your users, and the way you want to manage access to published resources. Your ICA client choices for 32-bit Windows operating systems are:

- Program Neighborhood client
- Program Neighborhood Agent client
- Web clients

Before you can decide the best client or clients for your environment, you need to thoroughly understand the differences between each client, what options each provides, and how configuration and deployment can be managed. The sections to follow examine each of the three clients and discuss features, deployment options, and management.

The Program Neighborhood Client

The Win32 Program Neighborhood (PN) client provides users with access to published resources, application sets, and individual servers in the farm via its own unique user interface (see Figure 7.1). The PN client is the only Win32 ICA client that *does not* require the Web Interface, so if you are not running a Web server or the Web Interface, this is the client to choose. You can use this client with the Web Interface, but once you look at the Program Neighborhood Agent and Web client features, you will not want to use the PN client. The downside to the PN client is that it is more complex and the only client that cannot be managed centrally or "pushed" out to the client preconfigured. It must be configured at the user's desktop and requires more administrative intervention. It could also be an issue if the users are unfamiliar with the client and the consequences of any changes they may make.

If you have not yet deployed ICA clients, Citrix strongly recommends installing the Web Interface and deploying the Program Neighborhood Agent or Web client rather than the Program Neighborhood client. Version 8.*x* of the 32-bit Windows clients can be found on the MetaFrame Presentation Server CD-ROM under \ICAWEB\language\ICA32 and \ICAINST\language\ICA32 (where *language* is EN, FR, DE, SP, or JP). Citrix recommends deploying version 8.0 or later for use with MetaFrame Presentation Server 3.0 and assures us that versions 8.9 and later are backward compatible with earlier versions of MetaFrame Presentation Server. The files that can be used to install the Program Neighborhood client are ica32Pkg.msi, ica32.exe, and wfica.cab. If you want to make sure you have the latest versions, download the clients from www.citrix.com.

Figure 7.1 The Program Neighborhood Interface

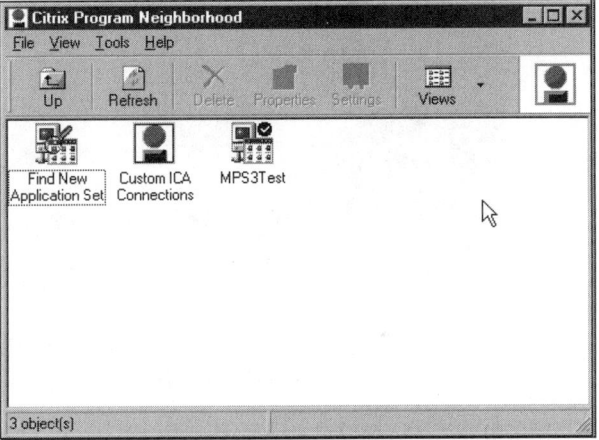

Designing and Planning…

Installing ica32.msi

If you are installing the ica32.msi package on pre-Windows 2000 machines, you must install Windows Installer 2.0 redistributable, which can be downloaded from www.Microsoft.com/ or use the ica32.exe self-extracting executable to install the client.

Installing the Program Neighborhood Client

The installation process, as you might expect, looks very similar to the installation of the other MetaFrame Presentation Server components.

1. First, we are greeted with the Welcome screen as shown in Figure 7.2. Then, setup searches for previous versions of the client. If found, Setup will prompt you to upgrade or install a new version. If no other version is found, setup continues. Click **Next** to continue the installation.

Figure 7.2 Program Neighborhood Client Welcome Screen

2. Next is the Citrix licensing agreement. We must agree to the licensing agreement before we can install the client. Click **Next** to continue.

3. Now we are prompted to choose a destination location. Here we can either browse to a new location or accept the default location. Click **Next** again to continue.

4. Next, we are prompted for an ICA client name. The default name is the computer name where the client is being installed, but this can be changed by unchecking the **Use machine name as client name** box as shown in Figure 7.3. Accept the default name or enter a new one, and then click **Next** to continue.

Figure 7.3 ICA Client Name

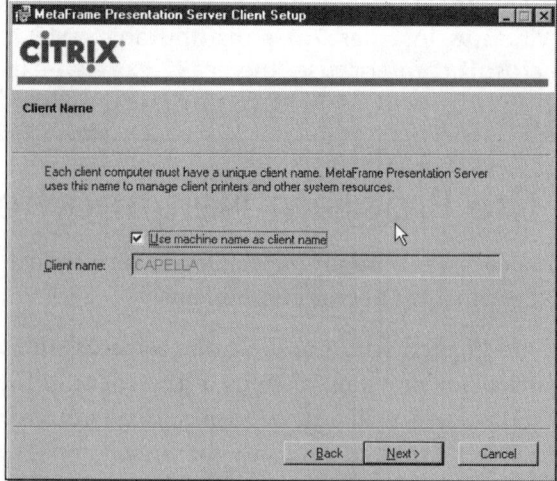

5. As setup begins updating the files, we must click **Next** once again to copy the files.

6. When setup has completed the update, you will be prompted to click **Finish** to complete the installation.

Configuring the Program Neighborhood Client

After the computer restarts, you will see a Program Neighborhood icon on the desktop. Double-click on the icon to open the Program Neighborhood Interface. On your first access, you will be prompted for a username, password, and the name of the domain to log in to. Once logged in, you will see the Program Neighborhood Interface and one icon, the Application Set Manager. Figure 7.4 shows both the logon screen and the Application Set Manager within the Program Neighborhood Interface.

Figure 7.4 The Application Set Manager

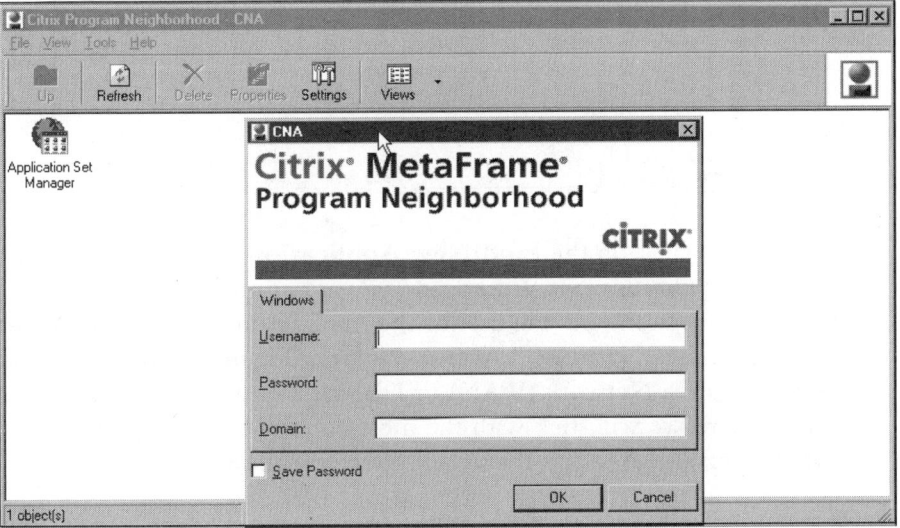

Before you can access the MetaFrame Presentation servers and applications, you must tell the ICA client how to find the servers and how to communicate with them. In Citrix terms, the ICA client locates the MetaFrame servers through "ICA browsing." Once the servers are located, the ICA client initiates an "ICA session" with the server. When the ICA session has been established, it is used as the communication link between the client and server through which screen displays, keystrokes, and mouse clicks travel.

7. Now that we know how the client locates the servers and applications, let's look at how to configure the Program Neighborhood client so that we can access the

servers and published applications. From within your Program Neighborhood window, double-click on the Application Set Manager icon. Two icons will appear and replace the Application Set Manager icon: the Find New Application Set and Custom ICA Connection icons, as shown in Figure 7.5.

Figure 7.5 ICA Connection Options

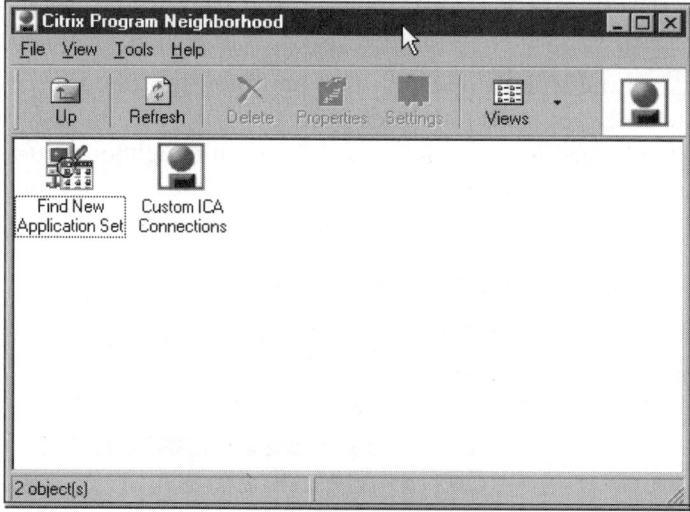

8. Next, double-click on the **Find New Application Set** icon. This starts the Find New Application Set Wizard, and you are prompted to select the type of network connection you will use for the Application Set. The default connection is Local Area Network (LAN) as shown in Figure 7.6, but we can also select Wide Area Network (WAN) or Dial-Up Networking (DUN). For our purposes here, we will stick with the most popular connection method and leave the default LAN, and then click **Next** to continue.

Designing and Planning...

Remote Connections Using RAS and DUN

Remote users can use RAS or DUN to connect to MetaFrame Presentation servers, providing RAS or DUN client software is installed on the client device and the RAS or third-party PPP server is located on the same network as the MetaFrame Presentation server. Users connecting remotely are limited to TCP/IP connections, as Windows Server 2003 Terminal Services does not support remote connections over IPX/SPX or NetBIOS.

Figure 7.6 Find New Application Set Wizard

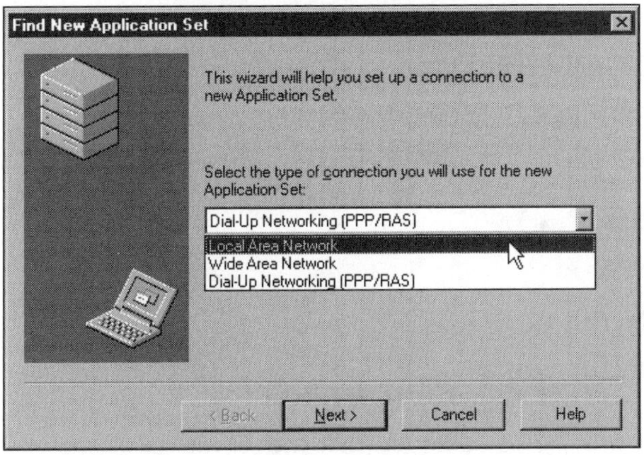

9. The next screen asks us for a description of the Application Set and prompts us to locate the Application Set to add as shown in Figure 7.7. Type in a descriptive name for the new Application Set, and then click the **Server Location** button.

Figure 7.7 Server Location

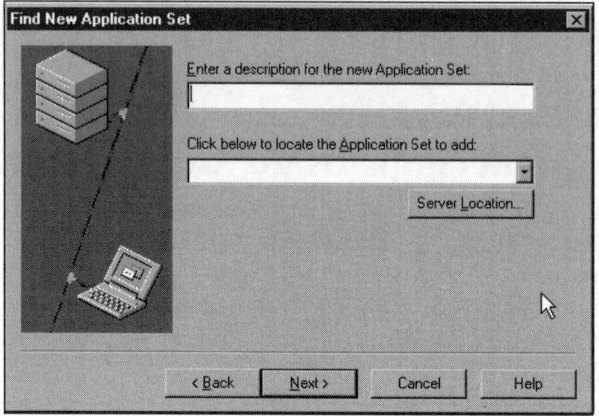

10.   The Server Location network protocol options are:

■   TCP/IP+HTTP

■   SSL/TLS+HTTPS

■   TCP/IP

■   IPX

■   SPX

■   NetBIOS

Selecting a Server Location Protocol

Our discussion thus far has assumed that the servers in question are Windows Server 2003 servers, so we will begin with the network protocols native to a Microsoft Windows network. The three options are:

■   TCP/IP+HTTP

■   SSL/TLS+HTTPS

■   TCP/IP

Which option should you use? Citrix recommends using TCP/IP+HTTP as the Server Location network protocol because it provides several advantages over TCP/IP alone. One of the primary advantages is that TCP/IP uses User Datagram Protocol (UDP) broadcasts to locate MetaFrame servers. UDP broadcasts can cause unnecessary network traffic, especially on slower networks. TCP/IP+HTTP does not. When an ICA client uses TCP/IP+HTTP to browse for a MetaFrame server to connect to, it uses HTTP encapsulated data that is sent to port 80 (by default) on the MetaFrame server.

The XML service running on the server then provides the client with the address of a server in the farm that has the desired application. Once the client has the appropriate address, the ICA session is established and the user can begin using the application as shown in Figure 7.8.

Figure 7.8 TCP/IP+HTTP Server Location Protocol

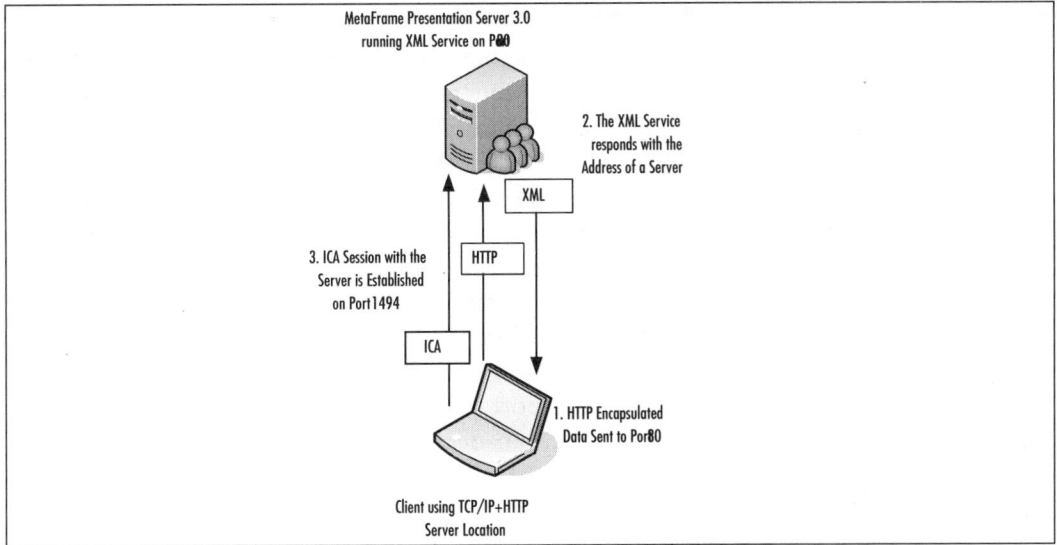

Citrix also recommends specifying servers to contact for ICA browsing. If no servers are specified in the Address List, the default name "ica" is used, and DNS or WINS will be relied on to resolve the name "ica" to a MetaFrame Presentation server address. If the name "ica" cannot be resolved, no server will be contacted.

Configuring and Implementing...

DNS Round Robin

DNS round robin can be used to map the hostname "ica" to multiple MetaFrame Presentation servers in your farm. Round robin refers to a technique that in simpler terms means "taking turns." The IP addresses of the servers are placed in a list, all resolving to the hostname "ica," and each time a request comes in to resolve the hostname, the DNS server hands out the first IP address in the list. That address then moves to the end, and the next time the request comes in for "ica," the DNS server provides the second IP address, and so on, until it loops

Continued

back around to the first address. When used for Server Location addresses, it provides a work-around to configuring the client with individual addresses. The only caveat here is when the default XML port is changed. Even though you add the DNS entries mapping the "ica" hostname to valid server IP addresses, there is no way to set a specific port number from within DNS. ICA clients attempting to connect to the farm using "ica" in the server list will receive the error message "The ICA Browser did not return any names."

Since TCP/IP+HTTP is the preferred method for ICA browsing, you may wonder why plain old TCP/IP was provided as an option. After all, TCP/IP uses UDP and produces broadcast traffic on the network and is clearly less efficient than using TCP/IP+HTTP. Citrix retained TCP/IP as an option for those environments that still have MetaFrame 1.8 servers and must operate in "interoperability mode," although it can be used in native mode as well. Native mode is when all the servers in the farm are IMA-based, which includes MetaFrame XP and MetaFrame Presentation Server 3.0. By default, farms operating in native mode do not respond to UDP broadcasts.

The default setting for TCP/IP's Address List is "Auto Locate." When Auto Locate is used, the client locates servers and applications in the farm by sending UDP broadcasts to the MetaFrame server's ICA browser on port 1604. When Auto Locate is used and the server is not configured to accept UDP broadcasts from clients, the client will not locate any servers or applications. Either the client must be configured with valid server addresses or the MetaFrame server must accept UDP broadcasts from the client.

SSL/TLS+HTTPS provides strong encryption appropriate for use over the Internet or through a proxy or firewall as well as server authentication. SSL, or Secure Socket Layer, operates between TCP and HTTP using port 443. The combination of SSL and HTTP is known as HTTPS. SSL establishes secure communications, delivers the server certificate, delivers the client certificate if there is one, verifies the integrity, and encrypts and decrypts the data. TLS, or Transport Layer Security, ensures the privacy between communicating applications and the Internet and uses port 443. If you opt to use SSL/TLS+HTTPS, the MetaFrame Presentation servers you want to communicate with must be configured to accept SSL or TLS communication.

1. Once you have chosen a Server Location protocol and pointed the client to a valid MetaFrame Presentation server, you must select an Application Set from the drop-down list. Click the down arrow just above the Server Location button, and any published Application Sets will be shown in the list. Select an Application Set and click **Next** to continue.

2. The next screen allows us to customize how we view the Application Set. We can enable or disable sound, change the default window colors, and change the window's size to suit our personal preferences unless overridden by Administrative configuration. Our window color choices include 16 colors, 256 colors, High and True color, as shown in Figure 7.9. The Window Size

options can be from 640x480 to 1600x1200, Custom Size, Full Screen, Percent of Screen, or Seamless Window. Once you have made your selections, click **Next** to continue.

Figure 7.9 Configure Window Colors

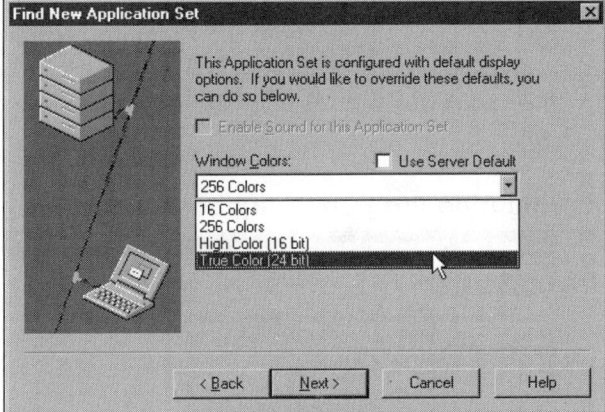

3. On the final screen, click **Finish** to complete the configuration. You should now see your Application Set icon within the Program Neighborhood Interface.

The Program Neighborhood Agent

The Program Neighborhood Agent provides "transparent integration" of published applications to the user's Desktop. This means that users can have shortcuts on their Desktops, Start menu, and System Tray that will appear as though the applications were installed locally, but the shortcuts actually point to applications on the MetaFrame Presentation server. Thus, users will not be challenged with any new access methods.

As for client management and administration, the Program Neighborhood Agent is "centrally" managed from the Program Neighborhood Agent Console. All user options such as logon method, shortcuts, shortcut placement, display, and audio settings are configured from the console and pushed out to the users. When modifications are made to the configuration, the changes are dynamically made when the client connects.

The Program Neighborhood Agent, as noted previously, requires the Web Interface to be installed. When a user clicks on a published application shortcut, the client uses HTTP or HTTPS to connect to the Web Interface where the configuration file is read and the user's Desktop is updated. The Program Neighborhood Agent console is a browser-based tool that resides within the Web Interface. To access the console, open a Web browser and connect to http://*servername*/Citrix/PNAgentAdmin, where *servername* is the name of the server running the Web Interface.

Program Neighborhood Agent Installation

The Program Neighborhood Agent can be installed using the ica32pkg.msi or the ica32a.exe self-extracting executable. Installing the Program Neighborhood Agent is much simpler than installing the Program Neighborhood client. The major difference is that the Program Neighborhood Agent is configured centrally from the Web Interface console. As mentioned earlier in this chapter, the Program Neighborhood Agent requires a Web server and the Web Interface to be installed before it can be used. During the installation, you will be asked for the URL of the server running the Web Interface as shown in Figure 7.10.

Figure 7.10 Configuring Program Neighborhood Agent

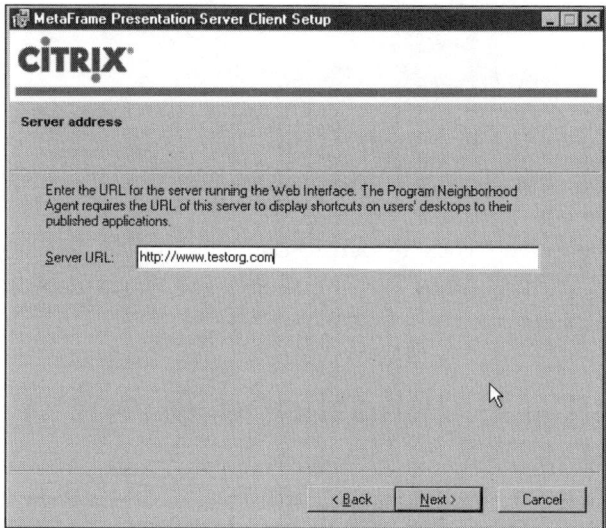

After clicking **Next** to continue, you are asked for the folder within the Start menu where you want the published resource icons placed. The next screen prompts for the client name, which can be left at the default machine name or changed to a unique client name. Next, you are asked whether you want to use the local user name and password to log on to future sessions. If you do not elect to do this during setup, you will need to run setup again and modify the configuration. Click **Next** to continue and you are presented with a summary of your choices. If all choices are correct, click **Next** again to begin copying files. Once the files have finished loading, click **Finish** to complete the installation.

Program Neighborhood Agent Configuration

The configuration file is located on the server running the Web Interface, under \Inetpub\wwwroot\PNAgent, and contains the information regarding the user environment and the settings to which they have access. You can create multiple instances of the configuration file with varying options to suit the needs of individual users or departments. Because the configuration is performed on the server side, the only change that must be made on the client side is to change the URL to point to the configuration file in the Web Interface. Each configuration file created will control only the clients pointed to its URL. Modifications to a configuration file will affect all users pointing to that particular file and no one else. Citrix provides a default configuration file, config.xml, which may be used as is or used as a template to create other files.

As shown in the default config.xml in Figure 7.11, the file is broken down into sections that allow control of various aspects of the user's experience.

Figure 7.11 Program Neighborhood Agent Console

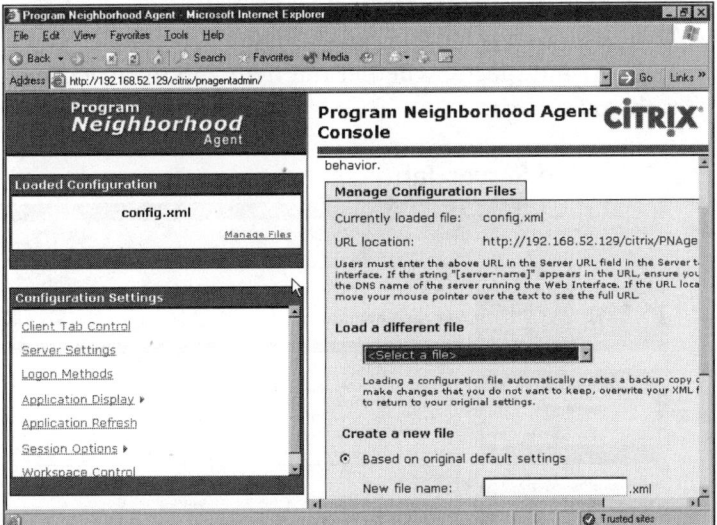

From Configuration Settings, the options you can control and manage from a central location are:

- **Client Tab Control** When the Program Neighborhood Agent is active, users will have a Program Neighborhood Agent Properties dialog box in their System Tray. The Properties dialog box by default, has five tabs that control Server, Application Display, Application Refresh, Session Options, and Reconnect Options. The Client Tab Control allows you to specify the tabs the users can see and which options on each tab they can manipulate. For example, you may not want users to see or modify the Server settings because if they change the URL, they will not be able to connect to their configuration file. Other settings that can be configured from the Client Tab Control are:

- **Application Display** allows you to specify where the shortcuts to published applications will be placed. Options are Desktop, Start Menu, System Tray, and Programs submenu. You can select one or all locations.

- **Application Refresh** tells the client when to refresh the applications that are enumerated to the client. Options are at Program Neighborhood startup, when a remote application launches, or at hourly intervals.

- **Session Options** controls the window size, color depth, and audio settings for each session.

- **Reconnect Options** allows you to set the conditions to reconnect disconnected sessions. Disconnected sessions can be reconnected automatically or manually and to active and nonactive sessions.

- **Server Tab** The Server Tab, shown in Figure 7.12, allows you to configure the server URL and specify whether the users can see or change the settings, as well as the refresh rate.

Figure 7.12 The Server Tab

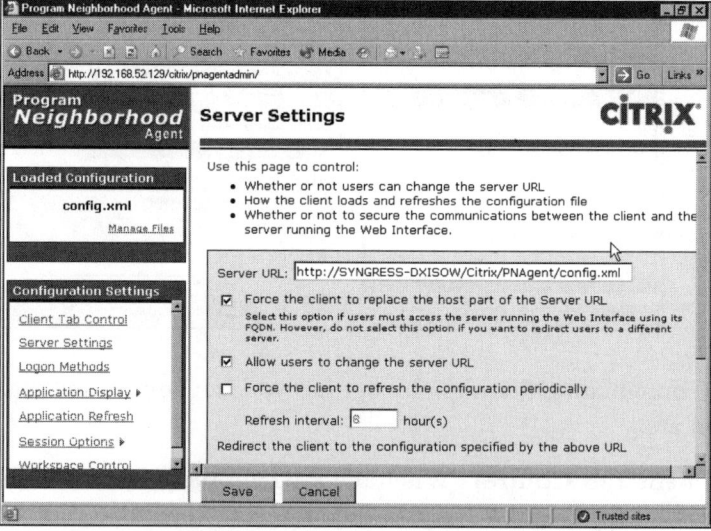

- **Logon Methods** This tab controls the logon methods users are allowed to use and the default settings (see Figure 7.13). Logon methods available include Anonymous, Smart Card, Smart Card with Single Sign On (SSO), Prompt, with or without Save Password, and Single Sign On.

Figure 7.13 Logon Methods

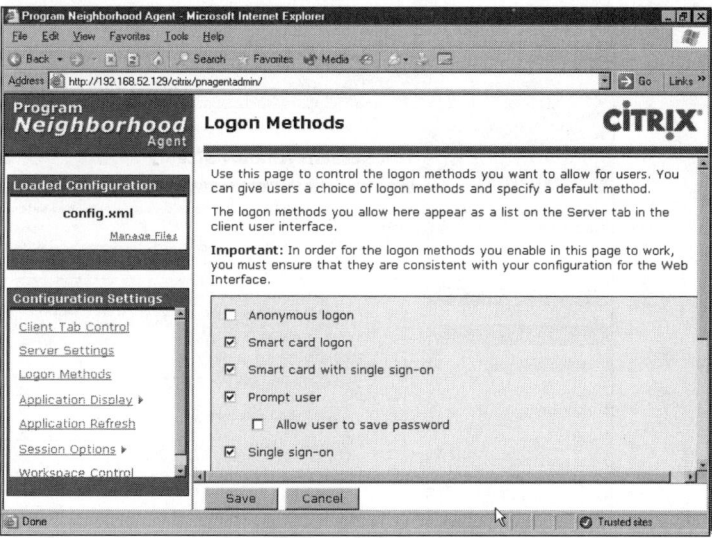

- **Application Display** From this menu, you can manage what shortcuts a user sees when logged in through Program Neighborhood Agent and whether shortcuts created by the users are retained after they log off.

- **Application Refresh** This feature allows you to force the refresh of published resources and whether the user can see and modify the settings. Options are to Refresh when Program Neighborhood Agent starts up, Refresh when a published resource is launched, or at hourly intervals. You can also specify whether the user can customize these options.

- **Session Options** From Session Options, you can specify the window size, the color depth, and audio settings. You may also specify whether the user can make the selection (see Figure 7.14).

Figure 7.14 ICA Session Window Size from the Session Options
Menu

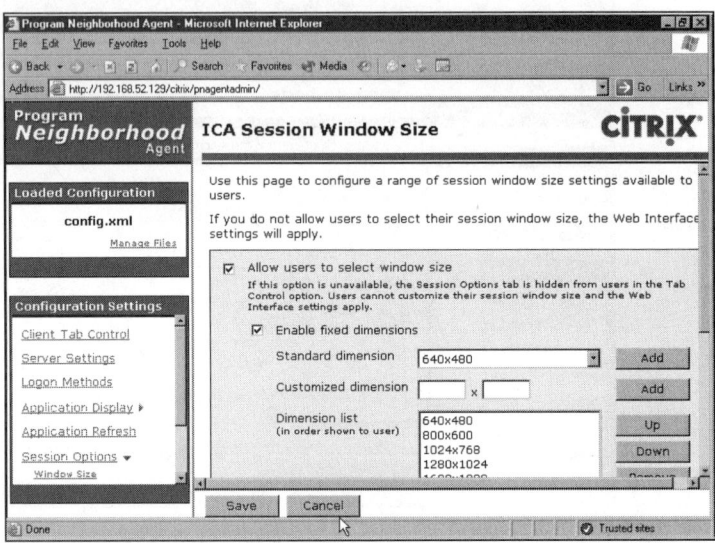

■ **Workspace Control**   Workspace Control is a new feature that allows users to
move about between wired and wireless networks and devices. A user at a
desktop computer can disconnect his session and then reconnect to his session
from a PDA or smart phone. The user can then travel across country and
remain connected to the published resources as long as he has a wireless
Internet connection. From this menu, you can control the instances in which a
user can reconnect to a disconnected session, and whether the user can override the settings as shown in Figure 7.15. Users can reconnect to sessions at
logon or by using the Reconnect button. Options include "Enable automatic
reconnection" to "Active and disconnected sessions," or "Disconnected sessions
only," and "Enable automatic reconnection using the Reconnect button," to
either "Active and Disconnected," or "Disconnected sessions only." The
Reconnect Options are only available when running Program Neighborhood
Agent or for sessions running through the Web Interface.

Figure 7.15 Workspace Control

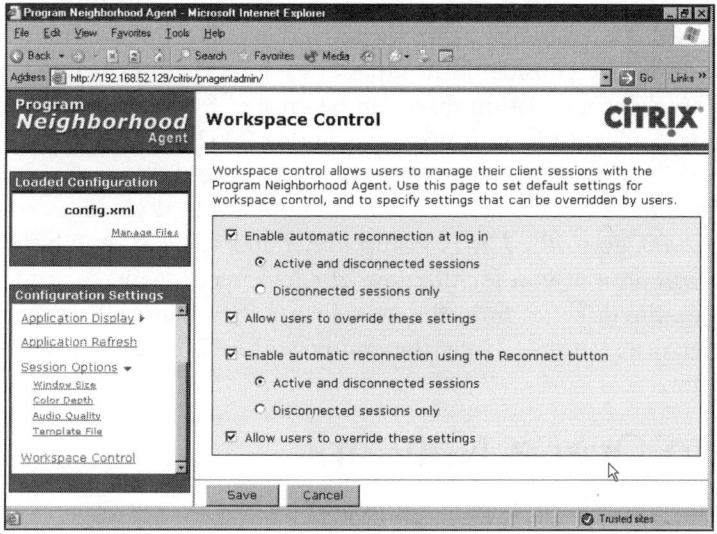

The Web Client

Citrix provides several options for installing the Web client. The full version can be installed using the ica32pkg.msi or the wficat.cab. The minimal version can be installed using the ica32t.exe self-extracting executable or the wficac.cab. Both of the minimal versions are designed for users running Internet Explorer and can be downloaded and installed on the first visit to the MetaFrame Presentation Server Web page. All client setup files are much smaller than the other ICA client files, which allows the client to download and install much quicker. Very little user interaction is necessary for the Web client. Once the license agreement is accepted, setup copies the files to the client device. The Web client configuration is centralized and accessible from the Web Interface console.

Deploying Clients to the Users

Which client you use and how you get it to your users depends greatly on your environment. In small, homogenous networks, it may be a simple matter to configure each client independently, but in large enterprise environments, this would be a huge undertaking, not to mention inefficient. Luckily, between Microsoft and Citrix, we now have several alternate means of deploying the client to users without needing to visit every desktop. In the next section, we discuss some of the ways to deploy ICA clients to users without making a house call.

Creating Client Installation Disks

Client installation disks can be created to assist in deploying the Program Neighborhood client only and should be considered in situations where the user is remote, such as with dial-up users. The client installation disks can be created from servers running Windows 2000 using the ICA Client Creator. Windows Server 2003 no longer includes the ICA Client Creator, so you must manually copy the files to the diskettes from the CD-ROM. To begin, you will need three or four 3.5-inch floppy disks. If you are creating the disks from Windows 2000, go to the Citrix group folder and select **ICA Client Creator**. The Client Creator will prompt you for the type of client needed, and then format and copy the files. To create the diskettes from the MetaFrame Presentation Server CD-ROM, go to \ICAINST\en\ica32\disks\. Copy the contents of each numbered folder to corresponding diskettes.

Deploying Over a Network

Another option is to copy the ICA client setup files to a network sharepoint and let your internal users install the clients themselves. From a support standpoint, this is not the best scenario unless you perform the installations silently or without user interaction. Fortunately, this is a possibility and you can create silent installations for all the ICA clients.

Configuring the ICA Client Silent Installation

Each of the three clients can be configured for silent installation and either pushed out to users or placed on a network share where users can launch their own installation. Each type of client, the Windows Installer Package, the self-extracting executable, and the Web clients must be configured differently. We discuss the silent installation configuration for each client next.

The Windows Installer Package

The first step in creating a silent installation is to create a network sharepoint from which to run the client. Once you have the sharepoint created, the client software must be configured and placed within the sharepoint. To configure the client and silent installation:

1. Copy the ica32pkg.msi file from the MetaFrame Presentation Server CD-ROM or download the latest from the Citrix Web site.

2. From the command prompt, type:

   ```
   msiexec /a ica32pkg.msi <Enter>
   ```

3. The Client Packager Setup starts and reminds you to close any open applications before continuing. Click **Next** to continue.

4. From the Create Client Package dialog box, you are prompted for the UNC path to the sharepoint and the compression method you will use to create the package (see Figure 7.16). Type in the full UNC path to the sharepoint and Uncompressed for ease of installation. Click **Next** to continue when finished.

Figure 7.16 Create Client Package Dialog Box

5. Now we see the very familiar licensing agreement. Accept the agreement and click **Next** to continue.

6. Next, we are prompted to select one or more clients to configure. The options are Web Client, Program Neighborhood Agent, and Program Neighborhood. If both the Program Neighborhood Agent and Program Neighborhood are selected, you will configure both wizards. At this point, we also have the opportunity to change the default path for the installation. After making your selections, click **Next** to continue.

7. From the Server Address dialog box, enter the URL to the server running the Web Interface and click **Next** to continue.

8. Next, we must tell Setup what folder within the Start menu to place the program icons. Either accept the default path or type the full path to the new location. Click **Next** to continue.

9. The next screen asks whether we will use the machine name as the client name or allow the user to provide a new name. In most cases, the client name works best. Click **Next** to continue.

10. Now we must decide if we want to use the local user ID and password to log on to the ICA session. This is called "pass-through authentication" or Single Sign On (SSO). If you disable this feature now and later decide to use it, you will need to reinstall the client. Make your selection and click **Next** to continue.

11. Next, we decide whether to permit client upgrades or to overwrite existing clients. If you elect to overwrite existing clients, you will be permitting client downgrades. Click **Next** to continue.

12. Now we come to the Select User Dialog Boxes screen as shown in Figure 7.17. Here you can decide which, if any, installation dialog boxes the user will see. For a silent installation, click **Remove All** and then click **Next** to continue.

Figure 7.17 Select User Dialog Boxes

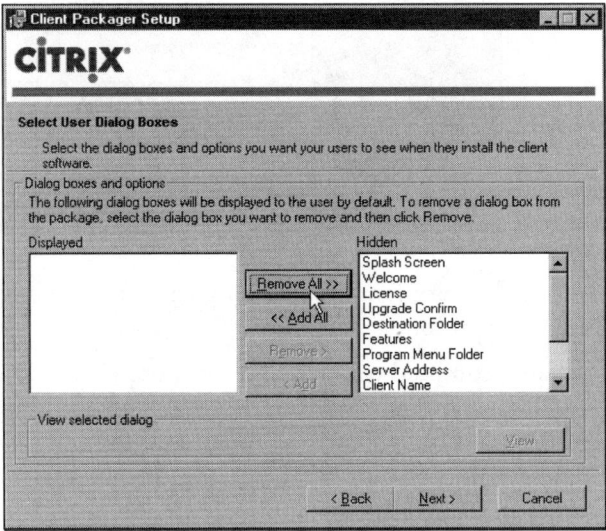

13. Next, we can review our selections on the Summary page, and when satisfied that all is well, click **Next** to continue.

14. Setup now updates the files and when completed, prompts you to click **Finish** to exit setup.

15. Now that you have configured the Windows Installer Package for the ICA clients, you can run the following from a script, Microsoft SMS, or from the command prompt to silently install the ICA clients:

```
msiexec /I ica32pkg.msi /qb- /L c:\logs\icalog.txt <Enter>.
```

16. The Windows installer will now run the setup program in silent mode. The user will see Setup begin but will not be able to interfere or cancel it as shown in Figure 7.18.

Figure 7.18 Beginning Silent Installation

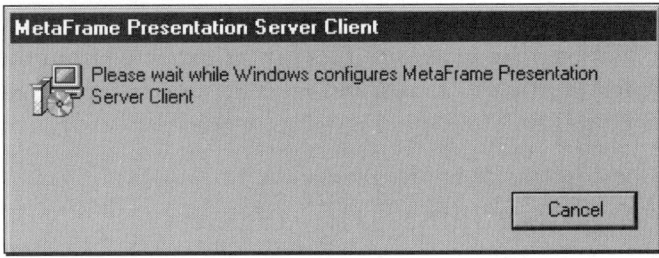

Self-Extracting Executables

To create a silent installation from one of the self-extracting executables, you must extract the contents of the files to modify them. This can be done with most standard compression utilities or with the command-line options as shown here. The catch here is that you must use a third-party application to repackage the contents so that they can be executed or redistributed. The following steps are needed to create and configure a silent installation from a sharepoint when using the self-extracting executable for the Program Neighborhood Agent.

1. From the command prompt, type **ica32a.exe –a –unpack: <Directory location>,** where *Directory location* is the path to the directory where you will extract the files.

2. Go to the directory the file was unpacked to and open the **INSTALL.INI** file. Note: .ini files can be opened with any text editor, including Notepad.exe and Wordpad.exe.

3. From within the **INSTALL.INI** file, change the following parameters so that the user will not be prompted for a response:

   ```
   ServerURL=<the server running the Web Interface>
   SetMachineNameClient=YES (yes uses the default machine name)
   Location=<Program Files> to place in the default Program Files
   directory or the path to a new location.
   StartMenu=<path to Start Menu> This may be the default user profile
   directory.
   InstallSingleSignOn=YES (yes is the default and enables pass-through
   authentication.)
   AcceptClientSideEULA=YES
   ```

When you have completed the changes, save the file and repackage.

The Web Client

Although the Web client requires very little user intervention and can be downloaded and installed from the Web site, you can limit the amount of intervention needed by suppressing the initial user prompt and the licensing agreement. The same caveat applies to the Web client; however, the individual files can be extracted from the ica32t.exe file for modification but a third-party application must be used to repackage afterwards. The modifications needed to perform a silent installation are:

1. Extract the contents of the ica32t.exe file.

2. Open the **CTXSETUP.INI** file for editing.

3. Change the **InitialPrompt** value from 1 to 0.

4. Change the **DisplayLicenseDlg** value to 0.

5. Save the file and repackage.

The Program Neighborhood Client

The Program Neighborhood client allows for more configuration options on the client side than the other clients do because it cannot be centrally managed from the Web Interface console. All of these settings are kept in ".ini" files. These files could be sorted through and modified after installation, but the easiest way to make the changes is to actually install the client making the configuration changes needed and then using the .ini files from this installation to create a new client install. As with the Program Neighborhood Agent and Web client, you will need to extract the contents of the executable and repackage them after making the modifications. To make the modifications:

1. Extract the contents of the ica32.exe file to a specified folder. We will call this folder NEWICA.

2. Go back to the ica32.exe and double-click to run the setup program just as you would during a manual installation.

3. Customize the client settings just as you would from the user's workstation, making sure you have all the settings configured as desired.

4. Next, go to the \%User Profile%\Application Data\ICAClient folder and copy all the .ini files to a new folder we will call NEWINIS.

5. Change all the file extensions in the NEWINIS folder from .ini to .src.

6. Copy all your new .src files over to the NEWICA folder where you first extracted the contents of the executable, overwriting all the existing .scr files.

7. Repackage the NEWICA folder into an executable.

Common Configuration Options

Once you have completed the initial installation and configuration of the client, many other features can be configured that are common to all the Win32 ICA clients. This section covers those features common to the clients, their function, and configuration options. The options include:

- Connection Limits
- ICA Display Settings
- Auto Client Reconnect
- Dynamic Client Name Support
- Speed Screen Browser Acceleration
- Smart Card Support
- Session Reliability
- SSPI/Kerberos Security for Pass-Through Authentication
- Digital Dictation Support
- Windows NT Challenge/Response (NTLM) Support
- Certificate Revocation List Checking
- Novell Directory Services Support

Many of the common options can be accessed and configured from the client side, from the MetaFrame Presentation Server console, from the Citrix Connection Configuration Tool, or the Web console. We discuss each of the features here and how and where they can be configured.

Connection Limits

The Connection Limits option allows administrators to limit the number of connections permitted on a per-user basis for the entire farm. If a user establishes a connection to the MetaFrame Presentation Server, whether for one published application or a full desktop, it counts as one connection. Users connecting to individual published applications will establish a connection for each application they open; thus, it is important to keep the limit high enough not to limit productivity. Note that users with multiple connections do not consume multiple licenses as long as they are connecting from the same client device. Each session, whether active, idle, or disconnected, will use server resources and should not be allowed to remain idle or disconnected indefinitely. Connection limits must be configured from the MetaFrame Presentation Server console and can be configured for regular users and/or administrators, although setting connection limits for administrators may hamper their ability to shadow users. Connection limits can also be configured as a Farm Policy from the MetaFrame Presentation Server console (see Figure 7.19).

Figure 7.19 The MetaFrame Presentation Server Console—Policies

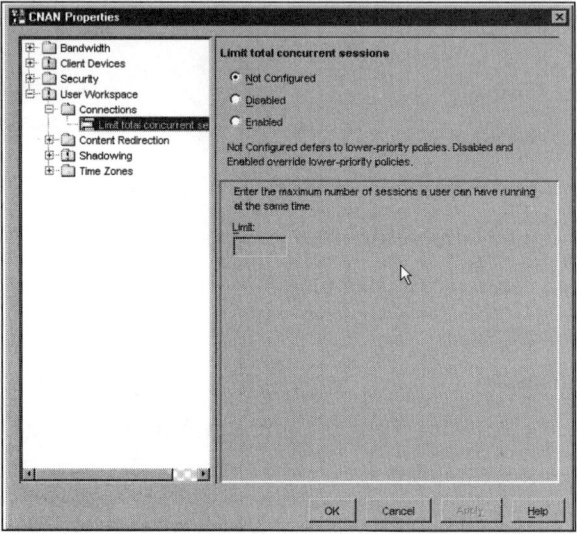

Auto Client Reconnect/ICA Display Settings

The Farm ICA Client Reconnect and Display settings must be set from the MetaFrame Presentation Server console. To access, select the **Farm**, and from the **Actions** menu, select **Properties**. Then, from the **Farm Properties** screen, select **ICA Settings**. These settings allow you to control how graphics are handled within ICA sessions, and how users reconnect to disconnected sessions. Under ICA Settings, the following options may be configured:

- **Discard Redundant Graphics Operations** This feature saves bandwidth by not sending any graphics to the client that are displayed only briefly and then immediately replaced. Typically, this type of graphic is nonessential in nature so the user won't need to see it.

- **Alternate Caching Method** The Alternate Caching Method is an algorithm that breaks the screen display down into small bits and stores them in memory. When the server sends updates to the user's screen, it only needs to send incremental changes, not the entire screen.

- **Maximum Memory** This setting controls the size of the buffer used for each ICA session. The values range from 150KB to 8192KB, and the actual amount required is dependent on the resolution and color depth.

TIP

To calculate the maximum amount of memory required for a user session, use the following formula:

```
((Horizontal x Vertical) x Depth) ÷ 8 ÷ 1024 = Maximum Memory
```

where horizontal and vertical are measured in pixels and color depth is in bytes. Therefore, if you need to calculate the amount of memory needed for an ICA session configured at 1280 x 1024 and color depth at 24, the formula would be:

```
((1280 x 1024) x 24) ÷ 8 ÷1024 = 160 = 3840KB Maximum Memory
```

- **Degradation Bias** This setting allows you to decide whether you will degrade the color resolution or the color depth if a situation occurs where the maximum memory limit has been exceeded or the client device is unable to support the requested settings. The default is to degrade resolution first. You are also given the option to notify the user of the degradation, which might help reduce the number of help desk calls (see Figure 7.20).

Figure 7.20 ICA Display Settings and Auto Client Reconnect

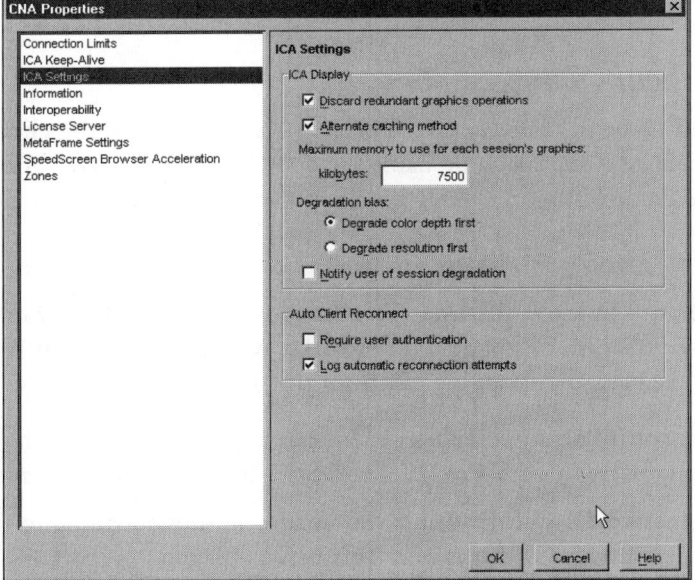

NOTE

Display settings can also be set per server from the command line using TWCONFIG. The syntax for the command is:

```
Twconfig /query

Twconfig /inherit: on |off

Twconfig discard: on | off

Twconfig /supercache: on | off

Twconfig /maxmem:nnnn

Twconfig /degrade:res | color

Twconfig /notify: on | off

Twconfig /?
```

- **Auto Client Reconnect** When this setting is enabled, the ICA client will attempt to automatically reconnect a user's broken connection. Cookies are created on the client device or within the user's profile that contain keys to user credentials and session IDs. When the client attempts to reconnect, the cookie will be examined and the session reconnected. Auto Client Reconnect is enabled by default for the entire farm, and only requiring reauthentication or logging can be enabled or disabled here.

Dynamic Client Name Support

When the client name has been set to match the machine name, the client name will automatically change if the machine name changes. If the client has not been configured to use the same name as the machine, the client name will not change.

Speed Screen Browser Acceleration

This feature helps to improve the user experience when using HTML-enabled applications over low-bandwidth or congested networks. When Speed Screen Browser Acceleration is enabled, users can benefit from the following features:

- **Background Image Delivery** Images are downloaded in the background, allowing users to click the Back and Stop button as they download.

- **Progressive Drawing** While the images are downloading in the background, users can interact with the elements in Web pages.

- **Responsive Scrolling** The users' experience is as if they are using a local browser.

- **JPEG Image Compression** Images can be compressed to save bandwidth.

- **Adaptive JPEG Image Re-Compression** The compression ratio is determined by the available bandwidth. If there is sufficient bandwidth, the images are not compressed.

Citricks…

Speed Screen Browser Acceleration

For the best results when using Speed Screen Browser Acceleration, make sure that "Play Animations in Web Pages within Internet Explorer" is disabled. Citrix also recommends using the latest version of the Microsoft DirectX runtime. Speed Screen Browser Acceleration is only available to users running Internet Explorer 5.5 or later.

Smart Card Support

Users can now access their published applications by authenticating with smart cards rather than typing in passwords. This feature will work with smart card–aware applications such as Microsoft Outlook.

Session Reliability

This feature allows a user's applications to remain open even if he loses network connectivity and then automatically resume when network connectivity is reestablished.

SSPI/Kerberos Security for Pass-Through Authentication

Kerberos, a network authentication protocol included in the Microsoft Windows operating systems, can now be used in conjunction with Security Support Provider Interface (SSPI) to provide pass-through authentication with secret key cryptography and data integrity. When using Kerberos, the client does not need to handle the password and it is not sent over the network. This greatly reduces the risk of Trojan horse attacks on the client to access user's passwords.

Digital Dictation Support

New in the 8.*x* client, Digital Dictation Support provides the ability to publish dictation software and use microphones for input from the client. Digital Dictation Support is only available with MetaFrame Presentation Server 3.0 Advanced and Enterprise versions.

Windows NT Challenge/Response Support

Windows 32-bit ICA Clients version 7.0 and later now support NT
Challenge/Response (NTLM) for security and authentication.

Certificate Revocation List Checking

This feature enhances the cryptographic authentication and overall security of SSL/TLS
connections between client and server. The ICA client must check to see if the server's
certificate is valid before allowing the user to log on. Certificate Revocation List
Checking can check for only the local certificate list or both the local and network.

Novell Directory Services Support

Novell Directory Services (NDS) support has been integrated into the Program
Neighborhood client, the Program Neighborhood Agent, and the Web Interface Users
in a mixed Windows and Novell environment can now log on and authenticate using
their NDS credentials

ICA Clients for Mobile Devices

It is becoming increasingly important for companies to become more efficient and
respond faster to opportunities in order to remain competitive. Opportunities are often
fleeting, and if not acted upon immediately could be lost. Businesses are discovering that
mobile and wireless technologies can help deliver the competitive advantage by keeping
them in touch with enterprise applications and data even when out of the office. Mobile
and wireless technologies, however, pose challenges for traditional IT departments.
Wireless networks are inherently unreliable and less secure than wired networks. For
wireless and mobile technologies to work efficiently, these problems must be overcome.
Security risks include wireless network hacking and theft of mobile devices. Theft poses
a risk if there is sensitive data stored on the device. Other challenges faced by IT departments attempting to implement mobile and wireless technologies deal with installing
applications, patching operating systems, and updating anti-virus definitions. With multiple devices and operating systems, this could create real problems.

Citrix has worked diligently to provide the capability to reduce or even overcome
the problems that wireless and mobile technologies pose to IT staff and users. Because
Citrix provides ICA clients for nearly every operating system, including those used by
Palm Pilots, Compaq iPAQs, hand-held devices, and even smart phones such as Nokia,
Psion, and Sony Ericsson, we now have the capability of providing published applications from the MetaFrame Presentation server to these devices in the same way we can
to hard-wired thin client devices and PCs. Various existing devices can now be integrated into the network instead of replacing them with standardized devices. This
approach simplifies the related IT tasks and overcomes the security and logistical chal-

lenges as well. Once the proper ICA client is installed and configured, the device is ready to access the applications and data on the network, and because the device uses the published applications and data from the network, there is no need to keep sensitive information on the device itself.

MetaFrame Presentation Server 3.0 includes new "mobile-friendly" features such as the previously discussed smooth roaming. With smooth roaming, a user in an office can move about the office, switching from device to device while maintaining the original ICA session. The same user can then switch to a wireless PDA or smart phone, keeping the same session open, and travel to a new location. If the connection is lost in route, while going under a bridge for example, the application will remain open and reconnect once network connectivity is restored, without requiring the user to reauthenticate.

Smooth roaming incorporates three features that work together to accomplish the preceding scenario. Workplace Control allows users to switch devices and continue working within their original ICA session on another device, automatically closing the original session once the user logs in to the new one. Dynamic Reconfiguration optimizes and adapts the display when the user switches to a new device. This resolves the problem of switching from full-sized screens to PDAs or smart phones. Yet another feature of smooth roaming, Session Reliability, compensates for unreliable wireless network connections by maintaining the application display even when the network connection is lost, and then automatically reconnects when the link is restored.

Other Ways to Optimize Wireless Access

In addition to smooth roaming, Citrix has worked to provide a variety of features to assist administrators in extending their networks with wireless and mobile technology. Some of the most common problems that must be addressed if wireless access is to succeed include:

- Network latency
- Lengthy login times
- Inefficient use of network bandwidth

The following are configuration recommendations that will help to improve the user experience and minimize the affects of latency on wireless networks, including server connections over satellite networks. The most convenient way to make these changes and apply them to all wireless users is to make the modifications to the wwan_template.ica file from the Web Management console. The changes will then affect all users configured to use the file from the Web Interface or Program Neighborhood Agent. Table 7.2 lists the configuration entries for the following features within the wwan_template.ica file. The changes can be made from the Web Management console and wireless users assigned to use the configuration file.

Table 7.2 wan_template.ica Optimization Settings

Module.ini Entry	Value	Explanation
OutBufCountHost	118	Affects the maximum amount of data sent from the server to the client that the connection will attempt to keep active. A higher value is not recommended.
OutBufCountClient	118	Affects the maximum amount of data sent from the client to the server that the connection will attempt to keep active. A higher value is not recommended.
OutBufLength	512	The maximum recommended packet size for ICA over TCP/IP for wireless networks. A lower value is not recommended.
ZLMouseMode	1	A value of "1" enables Mouse Click Feedback. A value of "0" disables.
ZLKeyboradMode	1	A value of "1" enables Local Text Echo. A value of "0" disables.
Compress	On	Data Compression enabled.
MouseTimer	200	Reduces the amount of small packets sent to the server. Setting the value higher could degrade interactive response.
KeyboardTimer	50	Keystrokes are combined into larger packets before being sent to the server.
MaximumCompression	On	Maximum Compression enabled.
PersistentCacheEnabled	On	Entry to enable persistent cache.
UpdatesAllowed	Off	Entry to disabled automatic client updates.
COMAllowed	Off	Disables client COM port mapping virtual channel.
CPMAllowed	Off	Disables client printer mapping virtual channel.
VSLAllowed	Off	Disables client print spooler virtual channel.
CDMAllowed	Off	Disables client drive mapping virtual channel.
ClientAudio	Off	Disables client audio virtual channel.

Limiting TCP/IP Packet Size

Citrix recommends limiting the packet size of ICA over TCP/IP for wireless networks to a maximum packet size of 512 bytes to manage latency. Typically, the default maximum packet size of ICA over TCP/IP transmitted over a wired network is 1460 bytes. Since latency corresponds to packet size, reducing the packet size will reduce the latency; however, we are cautioned *not* to reduce the packet size below 512 bytes, as it will impact throughput.

Enable Speed Screen Latency Reduction

Speed Screen Latency Reduction includes two features that help to provide a better user experience over high latency networks and wireless networks. Local Text Echo echoes the user's keystrokes on the client device as they are typed. If you have ever typed into an application on a low-bandwidth network, you have seen the how latency affects keystrokes. You will not see all the characters you type until seconds later and must stop typing to allow the characters displayed on your screen to catch up. When using Local Text Echo, the characters are echoed to the screen at the same time they are sent over the network to the server so that the user's perceived latency is much less.

The second feature of Speed Screen Latency Reduction is Mouse Click Feedback. As with keystrokes, mouse clicks will take a while to catch up on high latency networks. The user clicks a mouse button and nothing happens or he sees no indication that anything has happened. With Mouse Click Feedback enabled, the user clicks a mouse button and then sees the cursor change to the hourglass. Once the server receives the mouse click, the cursor changes back to the default.

Caching and Compression

To fully utilize limited wireless bandwidth, the data stream should be compressed to minimize the amount of data sent and received over the connection. This uses the bandwidth more efficiently and can reduce wireless network charges if they are based on the amount of data sent and received. Client-side caching, when enabled, can also reduce the amount of data sent and received over the connection. Persistent caching can reduce logon time and improve graphic performance; however, this feature is not available for ICA clients. The Windows CE client does not support this feature due to resource constraints.

Disable Client Device Mapping

Faster login speed and application performance can be attained by disabling client device mapping. Client devices that are typically mapped on a wired network are COM ports, printer mapping, client drive mapping, and audio and print spooler virtual channels. When a user logs on to the system, the operating system must discover the various client devices that will be mapped. Disabling device mapping can provide a significant performance increase over wireless connections.

Disable Automatic Client Update

If automatic client updates are enabled, the client will attempt to update at logon, increasing the time it takes the user to begin using the applications. Citrix recommends disabling the automatic update feature and updating the client when logged in to the wired network or via the Web Interface.

Non-Windows ICA Clients

Although we have primarily focused our attention in this chapter on the Windows 32-bit ICA clients, one thing that sets Citrix apart from the Microsoft RDP client is the ability to provide support for many different operating systems and devices, including non-Windows operating systems such as UNIX, Linux, and Macintosh. Microsoft's native client, RDP, does not provide support for other operating systems and lacks the capability to support some of the features the ICA client supports natively. Table 7.3 compares the two protocols, the operating systems, and some of the features supported.

Table 7.3 Comparison of ICA and RDP Supported Operating Systems and Features

Clients Supported	ICA	RDP
Windows XP, 2000, 9.x	Yes	Yes
Windows for Workgroups 3.11	Yes	Yes
Windows 3.1	Yes	
DOS	Yes	
Windows CE	Yes	Yes
Macintosh	Yes	
UNIX Solaris, DEC, HP/UX, SCO, IBM, SGI	Yes	
Linux	Yes	
Java	Yes	
Browsers	Yes	Yes
Supported Protocols		
TCP/IP	Yes	Yes
IPX/SPX	Yes	
NetBIOS	Yes	
Supported Network Connections		

Continued

Table 7.3 Comparison of ICA and RDP Supported Operating Systems and Features

Clients Supported	ICA	RDP
Local area network	Yes	Yes
Wide area network	Yes	Yes
Direct (Async) cable connections	Yes	
Direct dial-up without using RAS	Yes	
ISDN, xDSL, and VPN	Yes	Yes
Other Supported Features		
System Beeps	Yes	Yes
Stereo Audio	Yes	
Local Printing from Printer Attached to Thin Client or PC	Yes	Yes
Local Drive Mapping	Yes	Yes
Redirection of COM and LPT Ports to Client Ports	Yes	Yes
Cut and Paste between Client and Server	Yes	Yes
Connect to Desktop or Published Application	Yes	Yes
Publish Directly to User's Desktop	Yes	
Session Shadowing	Yes	Yes
Encryption	Yes	Yes
Automatic Client Update	Yes	Yes
Preconfigured Clients	Yes	Yes

Although Microsoft's newest RDP client can now support printing, drive mapping, and other functions the ICA client supports, it still does not support any of the UNIX platforms, Linux, Java, or Macintosh operating systems. Novell is supported but only if you intend to use TCP/IP and not Novell's native IPX/SPX protocol. In today's mixed environments of legacy servers and applications side by side with newer technology, organizations are looking for ways to consolidate and lower administrative costs and complexity. Citrix has addressed this issue by providing ICA clients for heterogeneous environments so that no matter what operating system or device, the user can access the applications and data needed. Complexity and administrative costs are reduced because the applications are installed centrally on the MetaFrame Presentation servers where they are administered and maintained. From the client side, the ICA client, in most cases, can be preconfigured, deployed, and updated from a central location. Users connecting to the Web Interface or Program Neighborhood Agent can be managed and updated without user intervention just as with the Windows 32-bit clients.

Securing the ICA Client

One of the biggest, if not *the* biggest, challenges that organizations face today is security, and the impact on IT departments is huge! IT must address security risks that affect systems, networks, and the organization's data. To further complicate matters, now organizations must follow a new set of legalities enforced by the Sarbanes-Oxley (SOX) Act signed in 2002. SOX now affects every publicly owned company in the areas of ethics, reporting, and auditing. Technology plays a huge part in data collection, reporting, and auditing. Thus, IT departments are scrambling to ensure that they have all the necessary controls in place for compliance. SOX also requires a corporate strategy that includes secure access to the infrastructure, to systems and networks both local and remote.

Citrix is not new to the security scene and has continued to improve the security features it offers with MetaFrame Presentation Server and the ICA clients. Citrix provides several ways to improve security between the client devices and the MetaFrame Presentation server farm. For instance, if you are running SSL on your network, the ICA client can be configured to use a compatible protocol. The ICA client can also be configured to work with firewalls or the Citrix Secure Gateway. These settings can be configured for the entire enterprise, per Application Set, or per application or custom ICA connection. Some of the ways the ICA clients support and integrate with the infrastructure security standards include:

- Connecting through a SOCKS or secure proxy server such as an HTTPS proxy server or SSL tunneling proxy server

- Integrating the ICA clients with Secure Gateway for MetaFrame Presentation Server or SSL Relay solutions with SSL and TLS protocols

- Connecting through a firewall

Connecting through a Proxy Server

What exactly is a proxy server and why do we need one? A proxy server is a server that acts as an intermediary between a client application such as a Web browser and another server such as a Web server. The proxy server is configured with certain rules that limit the access in to and out of a network. All requests in to and out of the network are intercepted by the proxy, and if the requests are legitimate, are forwarded on. Proxy servers also handle connections between ICA clients and MetaFrame Presentation servers. Citrix ICA clients support both the SOCKS and secure (HTTPS, SSL, or TLS) proxy protocols and can automatically detect and configure the client to work with the correct protocol.

Both the Program Neighborhood Agent and the Web Interface can be configured remotely to use proxy server settings, and the auto-client proxy detection is enabled by default. The Program Neighborhood client, however, must be configured at the user's workstation. In environments with multiple proxy servers, use the auto-client proxy detection feature. This feature will communicate with the Web browser to discover the information about the proxy server. It can also be helpful when configuring the client if you do not know which proxy server will be used. The auto-client proxy detection feature requires Internet Explorer 5.0 or later, or Netscape for Windows 4.78, 6.2, or later. To set or change proxy settings within the Program Neighborhood client:

1. Start Program Neighborhood.

2. Right-click either the **Application Set** or **Custom ICA Connection** you want to configure.

3. Select **Properties**.

4. From the **Connection** tab, click the **Firewalls** button

Your options on the Firewall Setting screen (shown in Figure 7.21) include:

- **Use alternate address for firewall connection.**

- **Use Web browser proxy settings** When enabled, this setting enables auto-client proxy detection.

- **Custom proxy settings** Here you can choose SOCKS or Secure and enter the proxy address and port to be used. If you were using Citrix Secure Gateway, you would configure the gateway address here as well.

Figure 7.21 Configuring the ICA Client to Use a Proxy Server

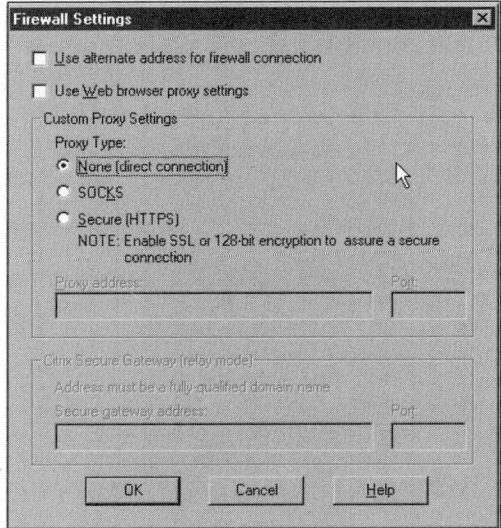

Client Deployment Checklist

As with any other application deployment scenario, it is a good idea to have a checklist to keep you on track even if you are distracted. A checklist can keep you from skipping crucial steps or leaving out important details. Once you have tested and documented the process, create a simple checklist that you can print out each time you need to perform a specified task. You will find that following the same procedure each time will make administering and supporting your environment much easier. The following is a simple checklist to help you think through the steps of selecting and configuring the clients you will deploy.

1. Take a close look at your environment, what it looks like today, what you want it to look like, and what you expect it will look like in a few years before deciding which client to use.

2. Think about how you want your users, internal and external, to access the resources published on your MetaFrame Presentation servers.

3. Decide which client options and features you will allow the user to configure, which options you do not want the user to see, and which ones you will set as default.

4. Look at each deployment method and decide which is best for your environment. Automated, silent installations may require more time before deployment but will speed up the rollout to the users.

5. Check the Citrix Web site for updates and information regarding any issues with hardware, operating systems, and applications before deciding on a client version.

6. Install and test the client on each platform you will use it on before deploying to a production environment.

Summary

The client piece may seem like a small, insignificant part of the whole picture, but in reality, it deserves just as much thought, planning, and testing as the larger pieces do. The ICA client is the key that provides access to the resources on the MetaFrame Presentation server, and it is loaded with configuration options that make the task of providing application resources to users much more efficient—as long as we take advantage of them. By carefully planning the configuration and deployment of the client, we take one more step toward providing first class service and support to our users.

In this chapter, we examined the Windows 32-bit ICA clients, the different types of clients available, and the methods of installing, configuring, and managing them. Which client you choose will depend on your environment and how you want your users to access the published resources. Citrix provides clients for numerous non-Windows operating systems as well as a variety of clients for Windows, making it easy to deploy applications to all your users even in diverse environments. You also have options as to how your users will access published applications. They can be accessed from the Program Neighborhood interface, from shortcuts integrated into the users' existing Windows Desktop, or via a Web browser.

Configuration and management features allow all but the full Program Neighborhood client to be configured centrally and pushed out to the client. Administrators can choose which options the users can see and modify, or choose to lock down the client and allow no changes. Client installation can also be automated, or as with the Web client, automatically downloaded and installed without user intervention.

Therefore, as we have seen, the ICA client is yet another important piece of the server-based computing architecture and can help simplify administration in diverse environments.

Solutions Fast Track

Introduction

- ☑ Know the requirements of your environment and plan for the future.
- ☑ Know the options and the benefits of each client and when each should be used.

ICA Client Options

- ☑ The Program Neighborhood Agent provides seamless application access by placing shortcuts to published applications on the user's Desktop, Program Files, and Quick Launch toolbar.

☑ There are two Web clients: the full version included in the Windows installer package, win32pkg.msi, and the minimized version that can be easily downloaded from a Web site.

☑ Program Neighborhood is the only client that does not require the Web Interface.

☑ Both the Web client and the Program Neighborhood Agent can be configured and managed centrally from the Web Interface console.

Deciding Which Client to Use

☑ Citrix provides clients for a variety of non-Windows environments such as DOS, Linux, UNIX, and MAC, as well as three clients for 32-bit Windows operating systems.

☑ Select the Program Neighborhood Agent or Web client if possible for centralized configuration and management.

☑ The Program Neighborhood is the right option if your environment does not include a Web server or you do not want to run the Web Interface.

☑ The Program Neighborhood Agent is a good choice if you have users on existing PCs, because shortcuts to the published applications can be placed on the user's Desktop as if they were installed locally.

Deploying the Client to Users

☑ Options for deployment include manual install from CD-ROM or diskettes, installation from a network share, and silent installations.

☑ All three clients can be configured to install silently without user intervention.

☑ The self-extracting executables must have their files extracted to configure for silent installation. Afterwards, they must be repackaged using a third-party utility.

ICA Clients for Mobile Devices

☑ Citrix provides ICA clients for nearly every device and operating system, Palm Pilots, Compaq iPAQs, hand-held devices and even smart phones such as Nokia, Psion, and Sony Ericsson.

☑ Smooth Roaming, Workplace Control, and Dynamic Reconfiguration work together to provide a seamless user experience while moving from network to network and device to device.

☑ Configuration options that can optimize wireless connections include limiting packet size, enabling Speed Screen Latency Reduction, enabling caching and compression, disabling automatic updates, and device mapping.

Non-Windows ICA Clients

☑ Citrix provides ICA clients for Sun Solaris, Sparc, HP/UX, IBM AIX, DEC, SGI and SCO UNIX, Linux, Macintosh, Java, and DOS.

☑ Although Microsoft's native RDP client has incorporated many of the ICA client features, it still does not support non-Windows clients.

☑ ICA clients for multiple operating systems and devices are important, as both new and legacy equipment can continue to be used and all devices can be managed centrally.

Securing the ICA Client

☑ The ICA client can be secured by configuring it to connect through a proxy server or firewall.

☑ Citrix supports SOCKS and secure proxy servers (HTTPS, SSL, TLS).

☑ The ICA client can be configured to auto detect the proxy server by using the browser proxy settings.

Links to Sites

■ **www.citrix.com** The official Citrix Web site.

■ **www.microsoft.com** Needs no further introduction.

■ **www.wise.com** Wise provides utilities to modify and repackage both executables and Windows Installer files.

Frequently Asked Questions

The following Frequently Asked Questions, answered by the authors of this book, are designed to both measure your understanding of the concepts presented in this chapter and to assist you with real-life implementation of these concepts. To have your questions about this chapter answered by the author, browse to **www.syngress.com/solutions** and click on the **"Ask the Author"** form. You will also gain access to thousands of other FAQs at ITFAQnet.com.

Q: Can platforms other than 32-bit Windows-based PCs access applications published on a MetaFrame Presentation server?

A: Yes. Citrix provides 16-bit Windows clients as well as clients for Linux, UNIX, MAC, and CE-based operating systems.

Q: What is the advantage of using the Program Neighborhood Agent over the full version of the Program Neighborhood?

A: First, the Program Neighborhood Agent can be centrally configured and managed from the Web Interface console. Program Neighborhood must be configured and managed from the local PC. Second, the Program Neighborhood Agent places shortcuts to published resources on the user's Desktop, Start menu, and Quick Start bar just as if they were installed locally.

Q: What is the difference between the ica32.msi and ica32.exe client installation packages?

A: The ica32.msi is a Windows Installer package and requires the Windows Installer Service to be installed on the machine prior to installing the ica32.msi package. If you do not have the Installer Service and do not want to install it, you can use the ica32.exe self-extracting executable.

Q: What is the main advantage of using TCP/IP+HTTP for the Server Location network protocol?

A: TCP/IP+HTTP does not use UDP broadcasts to locate MetaFrame servers. UDP broadcasts can cause undue network traffic.

Q: Why does the default "ica" hostname in the Server Location Protocol Address List work?

A: For the hostname "ica" to resolve to valid server addresses, you must specify those addresses in either DNS or WINS.

Q: How can I prevent my users from making changes to the configuration of their Program Neighborhood Agent?

A: Program Neighborhood Agent can be configured from the Web Interface console, and you as administrator can select which options the user will see and which ones the user can change. This goes for the Web clients as well.

Q: Can the Program Neighborhood be centrally configured and managed?

A: No, the full Program Neighborhood client must be configured manually from the desktop.

Q: Since the Program Neighborhood cannot be centrally managed, in what circumstances would it be used?

A: Some environments do not have a Web server or choose not to run the Web Interface. Both the Program Neighborhood Agent and the Web client rely on the Web Interface.

Q: How can I connect the various mobile and wireless devices my users have to the MetaFrame Presentation server farm?

A: Citrix has provided ICA clients for virtually every device and operating system on the market. Install and configure the latest ICA client for the devices and optimize the connections to overcome the latency issues.

Q: Is the any way I can optimize my MetaFrame Presentation server to compensate for the inherent latency of wireless networks?

A: Yes, you can do a number of things, including limiting the packet size transmitted, enabling caching and compression of the data stream, disabling automatic updates, and client-side device mapping.

Q: Can I incorporate our UNIX and Macintosh workstations into our network and provide them with published applications from our MetaFrame Presentation farm?

A: Yes. Citrix provides numerous UNIX ICA clients and Macintosh clients that will enable those clients to access the same published applications as your Windows clients.

Q: I know I can provide published applications to my UNIX and Macintosh users, but will I be able to centrally manage the ICA clients as I do the Windows ICA clients?

A: Yes again. If you have your UNIX and Macintosh users access the published application via the Web Interface or the Program Neighborhood Agent, you can manage the clients in the same way you do your Windows clients.

Q: In what ways can I secure the communication between the ICA client and my MetaFrame Presentation server farm?

A: The ICA client can be configured to use a SOCKS or secure proxy, a firewall, or Citrix Secure Access for MetaFrame.

Chapter 8

Printing

Solutions in this chapter:

- Creating Client Printers
- Printing in a Server Farm Environment
- Troubleshooting Printing Problems

☑ Summary

☑ Solutions Fast Track

☑ Frequently Asked Questions

Introduction

Even if everything else works perfectly, a user will not be happy if printing fails. Printing is one of the few outputs that a computer provides. It gives users valuable hardcopy versions of the work they produce. As such, the printing function is extremely important to users. Although you may be familiar with network printing, you'll quickly find that due to the myriad of options available with Citrix MetaFrame Presentation Server, printing can be one of the most complex problems to troubleshoot in your server farm.

In the three-tier architecture of a Citrix MetaFrame solution, printing can be configured in multiple ways. Local printers are connected to the client; some printers are connected to the server; others are available on the network. In addition, you must ensure the user's session recognizes the printer before its applications can print.

Understanding printing is your first step toward being able to successfully configure and troubleshoot the printing process. Even though an administrator configures printing when first deploying Citrix MetaFrame, you need to constantly manage the print environment, ranging from updating print drivers to managing the print queue.

Defining Printer Terminology

We must define printer terminology before we can get into more detail about configuring your printing environment in your Citrix MetaFrame server farm. Printer terminology is often confusing because of the repeated use of the word *print*—thus using a term to define it. Here is a list that will help you brush up on printing terminology:

- **Printer** Many people confuse the term *printer* with the physical print device. The term *printer* doesn't mean the physical print device; rather, it is a logical reference to a print device. The printer is actually the icon you see when you open the Printers folder in Control Panel. Think of this icon as the virtual representation of the physical print device.

- **Print device** The print device is the actual physical printing equipment attached to a serial or parallel communications port on your computer. It takes information from your computer in a format it understands and outputs it to hard copy.

- **Print driver** The print driver is the software that is installed on the operating system that acts as the translator between the various applications and the physical print device. The driver translates the print commands into language the printer understands in order to output the print job. Print drivers also enable special printer features and advanced functionality.

- **Print job** A *print* job is the term given to any document that has not been output to hard copy or has not yet appeared on the physical print device. Any document submitted for printing is called a *print job*. A print job can consist of one or more documents.

- **Print queue** The print queue is a staging area where submitted print jobs are lined up in the order in which they were received by the physical print device. A print queue is like a waiting line for print jobs. Print queues are usually located on print servers and are accessed via a printer share. On a Windows system, you can view your print queue by going to **Start | Settings | Control Panel | Printers** and double-clicking the name of a printer in the window that pops up; this list of names is the printer queue, as shown in Figure 8.1. It is important to note that more than one print queue can exist for the same print device. In this situation, you can have a second print queue that expedites certain print jobs, processing them first. You would offer this service to your company's executives, for example. Two or more printers can also service one print queue, thereby processing jobs faster.

Figure 8.1 Print Queue Window

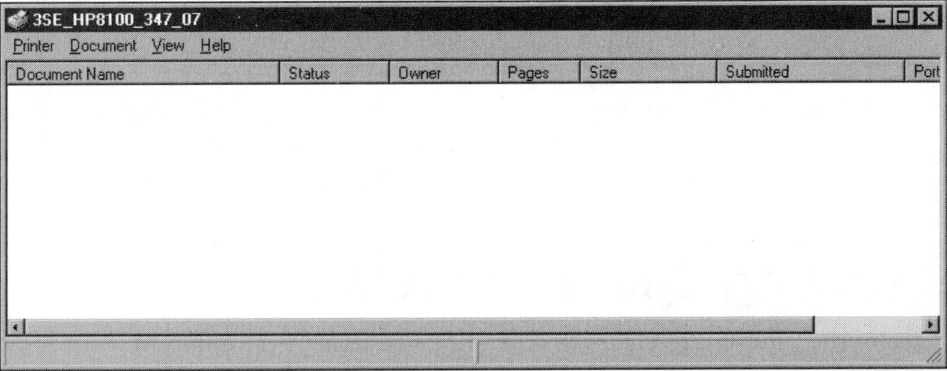

Defining Network Printing

Now that you've learned basic printer concepts, a clear understanding of how printers are used within a network environment is just as important. The following represent common printing scenarios:

- **Print server** A print server is usually a server dedicated to several printers that arc accessed by users over a network. The server's main duty is to route print jobs among computers and the physical printers attached to the print server. The print server also provides a centralized location from which you can manage print queues. Usually, every printer is associated with only one print queue, so if you have three printers, you have three queues to manage and administer on your print server. However, more than one print queue can exist for a single print device.

- **Shared Printer** A printer share is a logical printer, usually on a Windows server, that is shared and that allows multiple users to connect and print to the physical print device. Printer shares can also be made available on Windows-based workstations. It can exist in almost any environment in which the printer can be shared and is able to provide printing services to users.

- **Network printers** Network printers are physical print devices that are accessible from any location on the network. Network printers typically reside on a print server. A network printer can also be a client's local printer that is shared on the network, although this is not typically recommended, because when the computer is turned off, the printer will be unavailable. A network printer can be attached to a MetaFrame Presentation Server even if it is not a member of a farm. It is basically any printer that can be shared and accessed from any connection on shared network.

- **Local printers** A local printer is a printer that is directly connected to a computer via cable or port. It cannot be accessed from the network and is typically available only to users of that particular computer. Although printers can also be shared locally from the desktop computer to network users, this configuration is not recommended in a Citrix MetaFrame environment. Local printers can also be attached directly to servers. They can basically be attached to any computer that accepts a serial, parallel, or USB cable.

Creating Client Printers

One of the most useful Citrix MetaFrame features is its capability to make local client printers available to the user during an Independent Computing Architecture (ICA) session. When you launch your ICA session and run your applications within that session, and when you are ready to print, you can print to your physically attached printer as though you were working locally on your computer. This capability is very convenient for users because they are no longer bound to use only the network printers that an administrator installs and can take full advantage of their own local printers.

Auto-Creating Printers

As we discussed in the previous section, the ICA protocol gives you the ability to use locally attached printers within an ICA session. This feature, known as *local client printer mapping*, is available with 16-bit and 32-bit ICA clients. For local client printer mapping to work, several steps need to be properly addressed:

1. The print driver installed on the Citrix MetaFrame Presentation Server must be compatible with the print driver installed on the client computer.

2. The name of the print driver must be identical between the Citrix MetaFrame Presentation servers and the client computer. The next section on the impact of print driver names provides more information.

3. The driver must then be replicated to all Citrix MetaFrame Presentations servers so that the user can use the driver, regardless of the Citrix MetaFrame server to which he or she is connected.

Administrators can manually map printers; however once installed, Citrix MetaFrame Presentation Server also allows printers to *auto-create* mappings. The auto-created client printer now automatically makes available the client's locally attached printer the next time he or she logs in to the MetaFrame Presentation servers. This minimizes the administrative or user involvement in making local printers available within a Citrix ICA session. A user is able to identify his or her printer by the unique name that the server assigns. This name is in the following format: *Client\clientname#\printername* (see Figure 8.2), where *Client* designates it as an auto-created local printer, *clientname* is the name of the client workstation on Windows 32-bit client platforms, and *printername* is the logical name of the printer as it appears in the Printers folder in Control Panel on the client's workstation.

The auto-created client printer should automatically disconnect when the user logs off, but in some cases in which print jobs are stuck in the print queue, a printer will remain visible until either the server is recycled or the print spooler directory is cleaned. For users who don't log off but rather put their session in disconnect mode, the auto-created printer is neither deleted nor disconnected; it remains mapped and ready to service the user when he or she reconnects to his or her session. In this case, the printer remains until the session is completely logged off the server. In the event users disconnect their sessions and move to other workstations to reconnect to the same session, the auto-created printer will not work because *clientname* would not be the same on the new workstation.

Figure 8.2 The Auto-Created Client Printer Properties Window

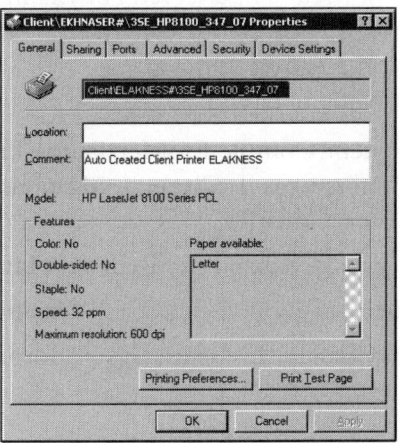

Impact of Print Driver Names

Print driver names play a big role in the success or failure of an auto-created printer. The print driver name installed on the Citrix MetaFrame Presentation Server must exactly match the name of the print driver installed on the client workstation; otherwise, the auto-creation process will fail.

In the event that the names don't match, you can manually create a mapping (described in the next section), specifically telling the server that this client print driver name should be associated with a particular server print driver. This also needs to be done when you're dealing with Windows 9x print drivers; the naming process is usually different from naming Windows NT or 2000 drivers.

Mapping Print Driver Names

We have been discussing the auto-creation feature available within Citrix MetaFrame and how sensitive it is—the slightest mismatch in print driver names can cause the process to fail. For auto-creation to work, the name of the print driver installed on the client machine must match exactly that name installed on the server. This works well when you're dealing with Windows NT 4.0, Windows 2000, and Windows XP drivers, as print driver names are usually identical, but the difference is clear when you deal with Windows 9x print drivers.

For example, a Windows 9x print driver might be named HP LaserJet 5Si/Mx, whereas the Windows NT 4.0 or Windows 2000 print driver name might be HP LaserJet 5Si. In this scenario, the auto-creation process will fail simply because the names don't match. Another problem occurs when the client is using the manufacturer's print drivers versus those available from Microsoft. The print driver names are almost always different between the native Microsoft naming conventions and those used by the manufacturer. Here is where *print driver mapping* comes in. You can locate the print driver on the local workstation by viewing the properties of the printer in Control Panel.

Mapping print driver names tells the server to associate a local driver with another name stored within the Citrix MetaFrame server. For example, the HP LaserJet 5Si/Mx client driver could be associated with the HP LaserJet 5Si server driver, thereby allowing auto-creation to complete and printing to occur.

To create a print driver name mapping:

1. Open the Management Console for MetaFrame Presentation Server by selecting **Start | Programs | Citrix | Management Consoles \ Presentation Server Console**.

2. In the left menu console, expand the **Printer Management** node.

3. Right-click the **Drivers** subnode and click **Mapping**.

4. The Mapping window appears. Select the Platform for the print driver and click **Add**.

5. Type the client name and match it with a driver name installed on the server as seen in Figure 8.3. Click **OK**.

Figure 8.3 The Add Mappings Window

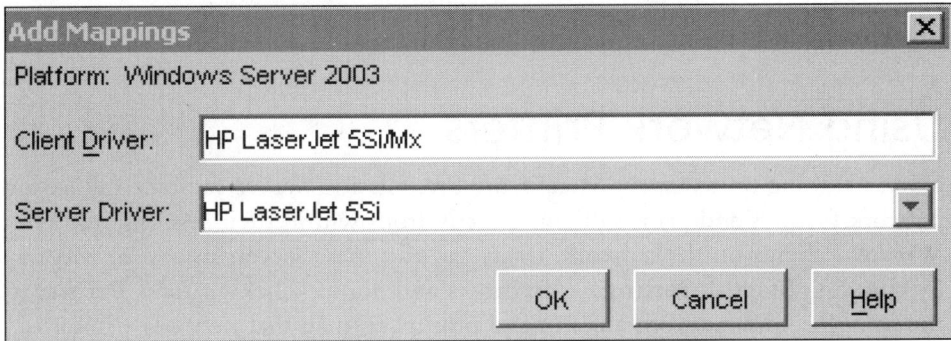

6. The mapping is now shown in the Mapping window (see Figure 8.4). Click **OK**.

Figure 8.4 The Driver Mapping Window

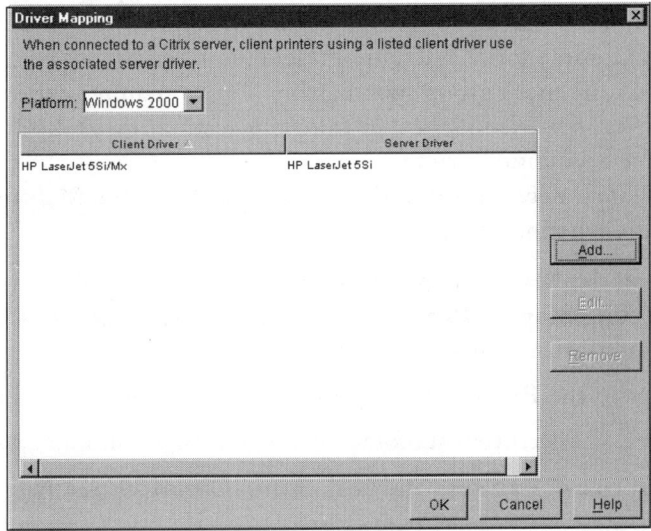

At this point, we have mapped the HP LaserJet 5Si/Mx driver to the HP LaserJet 5Si driver. Any client that has the 5Si/Mx driver will be able to print in the ICA session because the server will automatically map that driver to the server-installed driver of 5Si.

NOTE

Printer driver mappings that are configured using this utility are stored in the Wtsprnt.Inf file located on the Citrix server.

Using Network Printers

Clients logging on to Citrix MetaFrame Presentation Server can take full advantage of network printers and print to them directly from within their sessions, just as any other Windows clients on the network. Users can add these servers in one of two ways: either by choosing **Start | Settings | Printers** and double-clicking **Add Printer**, or using the *net use* command from a command prompt to map that network printer to their LPT ports. This process, however, is dependent on how the user's environment is configured. In some environments in which only published applications are available, the user doesn't have the option of mapping or adding a printer. In some other environments in which the user is presented with a desktop, that function might be locked down, either by the use of Group Policy or by simply giving the user a mandatory profile that doesn't include access to the print folder or to a command prompt.

We recommend that an administrator add these network printers in the Management Console for MetaFrame Presentation Server and enable them to auto-create based on the user's group membership. This is required when using a DOS client of WinCE client. For example, a user from the accounting group would be preconfigured to use the accounting printer.

To configure a network printer for auto-creation in the Management Console for MetaFrame Presentation Server:

1. Open the Management Console for MetaFrame Presentation Server by selecting **Start | Programs | Citrix | Management Consoles | Presentation Server Console**.

2. Expand the **Printer Management** node in the left pane of the screen.

3. Select the **Printers** subfolder. A list of printers should appear on the right.

4. Right-click **Printers** and click **Auto-Creation** (see Figure 8.5).

Figure 8.5 The Auto-Creation Option

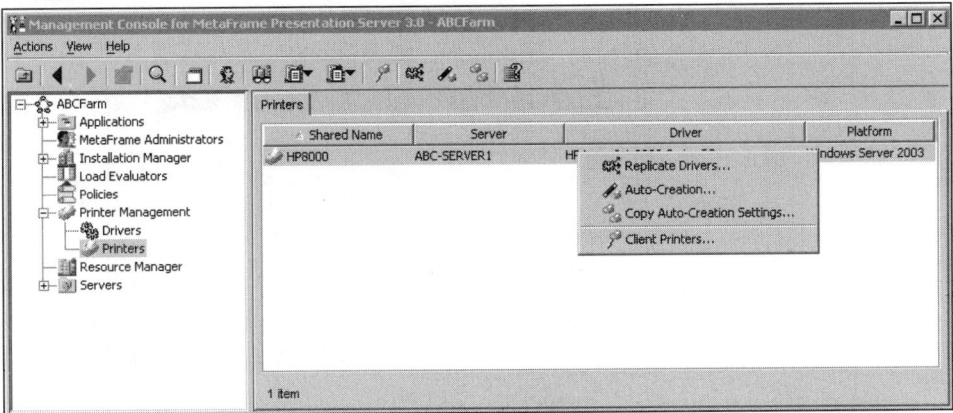

5. The Auto-Creation Settings window appears, prompting you for a user or a group with which to associate the auto-creation as shown in Figure 8.6.

Figure 8.6 The Auto-Creation Settings Window

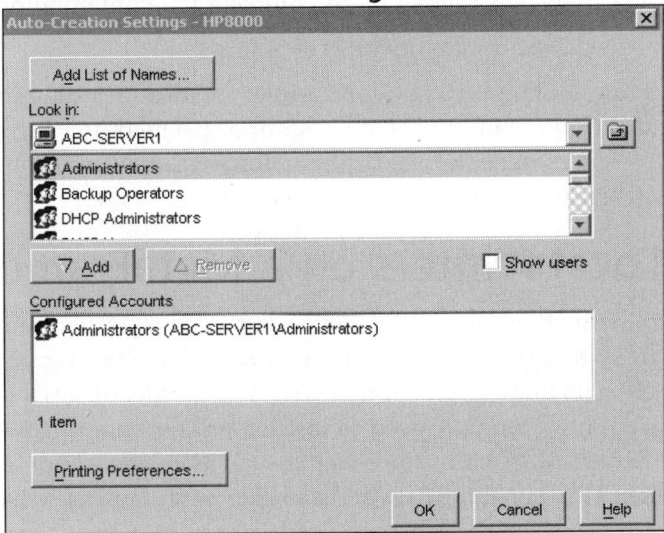

6. Select your group, or if you want to select a specific user, check the box that says **Show Users**, select your users, and click **OK**.

7. Select **Printing Preferences** to define standard options to be used for the printer selected as shown in Figure 8.7.

Figure 8.7 Printing Preferences Window

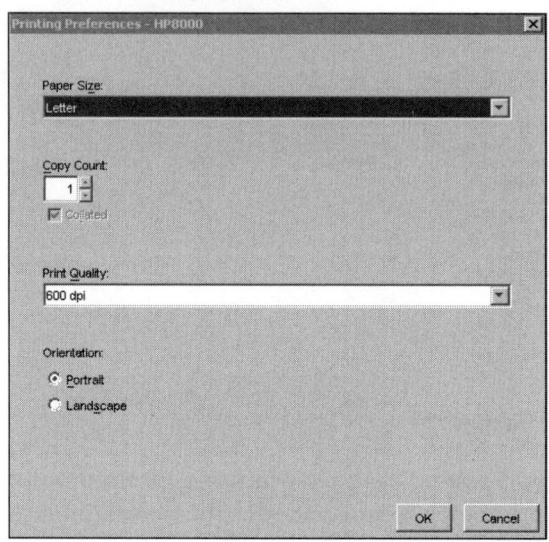

8. Once completed, select **OK** to complete the configuration of auto-created printers.

You have just configured a network printer to auto-create for a specific group or user. The next time a member of that group or a specified user logs in to the Citrix MetaFrame Presentation Server, he or she will have the option to print to this printer, and it will auto-create without any user intervention.

Using Local Printers on a MetaFrame Server

Local printers are used in Citrix MetaFrame just as in any other Windows 2000/XP workstation or Windows 2000/2003 server. Local printers are typically physically attached to the Citrix MetaFrame Presentation Server via a parallel or serial communications port. Although uncommon, you may need to install a printer on a single Citrix MetaFrame Presentation Server for specific requirements such as an application requiring a local attached printer. This can also be useful in smaller environments where network printing is not necessary except by those using a single Citrix MetaFrame server. Everything is done using the Printers folder, which is accessible by going to **Start | Settings | Printers** or to **Control Panel | Printers** and manually adding the printer. After you add the local printer, the name will appear in the Printers subnode of the Printer Management node in Management Console for MetaFrame Presentation Server. If it does not, you can right-click the **Printer Management** node and select **Update Printer and Driver Information** to immediately import new printers added.

To install a local printer on a Citrix MetaFrame Presentation server:

1. Log on to a Citrix MetaFrame server console as an Administrator or using an account with sufficient privileges.

2. Click **Start | Printers and Faxes** and double-click **Add Printer**.

3. Click **Next**.

4. Make sure Local printer is selected, uncheck the **Automatically detect and install my Plug and Play printer** check box, and choose **Next**.

5. Select the communications port to which the printer is attached (LPT1 or COM1, for example) and click **Next**.

6. Select the appropriate print driver for the device being installed, and click **Next**.

7. Assign the printer a name, determine if you want this printer to be selected as the default, and click **Next**.

8. The next window asks you whether you would like to share this printer. Select **Share as** and assign it a share name such as **localprinter**. Click **Next**.

9. Follow the wizard until setup is complete.

10. Open the **Management Console for MetaFrame Presentation Server** and make sure that the newly added printer shows up in the Printers subnode of Printer Management as detailed in Figure 8.8.

Figure 8.8 The Newly Added Local Printer

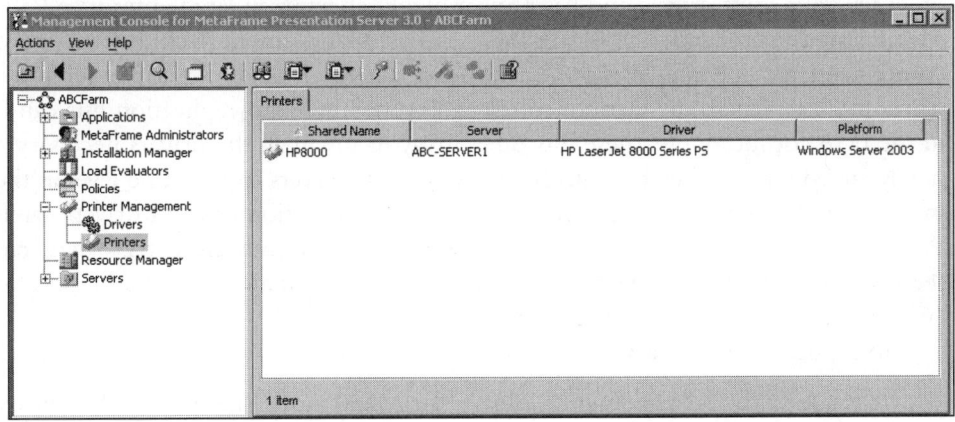

Printing in a Server Farm Environment

Citrix continues to improve printing with Citrix MetaFrame Presentation Server and provides a set of tools to make the installation and management of printers and print drivers even easier. As with most other administration and management tools, Citrix has centralized Printer Management as a node in the Management Console for MetaFrame Presentation Server, so all administrative tasks are accomplished from within the management console. You now have the ability to import an entire print server from the network and make its drivers available in your Citrix MetaFrame Presentation server. Replication of the print drivers from one server to all the servers in the farm is another great feature of Citrix MetaFrame. In addition, you can automate replication so that as soon as a new server joins the farm, replication occurs to install the supported print drivers without any additional administration required.

Replicating Print Drivers

Replicating print drivers across the Citrix MetaFrame Presentation Servers in your farm is a critical step that must be completed before a user can log on and use a particular printer. Before Citrix introduced driver replication, administrators had to manually log on to every server in the farm and install the necessary drivers. You can imagine how much of an administrative inconvenience this was, in addition to lacking any method of keeping track of what you have installed where.

Citrix recommends you dedicate a server in the farm where you would always install new drivers for print driver replication. You would then initiate replication from that server to the rest of the Citrix MetaFrame server farm. This allows a centralized point of management for your print drivers and has proven highly effective in large enterprise Citrix MetaFrame server farms. The Citrix Independent Management Architecture, or IMA, components provide a replication function that allows an administrator to replicate a print driver to all servers in the farm or to select servers only. Auto-replication lists can be saved in the IMA for future use; these lists offer a way to install all the drivers necessary on newly added servers, thereby quickly bringing these servers to the same level as the others in the farm. It is strongly suggested to manage the replication of print drivers carefully. Print driver replication can quickly become intensive on both the Citrix MetaFrame servers and the network links between them. It is recommended to avoid replicating a large number of drivers simultaneously.

To replicate a print driver:

1. Open the Management Console for MetaFrame Presentation Server by selecting **Start | Programs | Citrix | Management Consoles | Presentation Server Console**.

2. Expand the **Printer management** node.

3. Select the **Drivers** subnode.

4. In the right control pane, use the server pull-down menu to select the server from which you will replicate the drivers to the rest of the Citrix MetaFrame server farm.

5. Right-click the driver you want to replicate and select **Replicate Drivers**. If you selected **Any**, a warning message will be displayed, as shown in Figure 8.9. If multiple versions of the driver exist, it could lead to a variety of printing errors. It is recommended to use a central server as the repository by which print drivers are replicated.

Figure 8.9 Replication Driver Warning Message

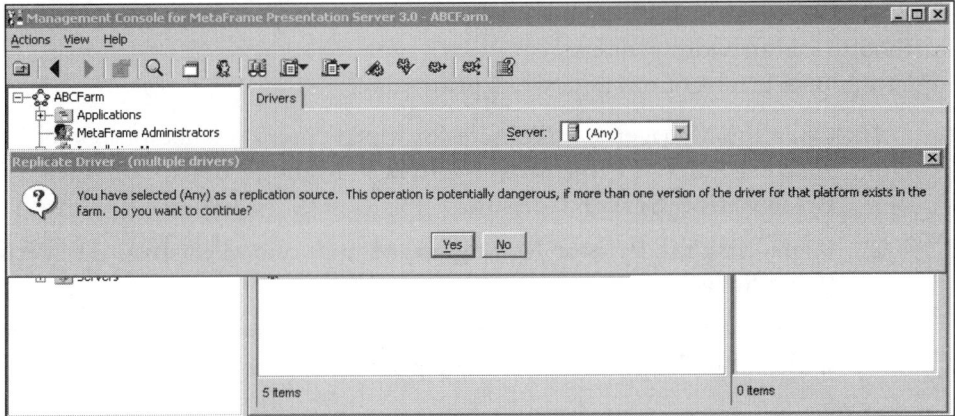

6. The Replicate Driver dialog box appears; either choose to replicate to all Citrix servers, or select one or more servers to replicate to (see Figure 8.10).

Figure 8.10 The Replicate Driver Window

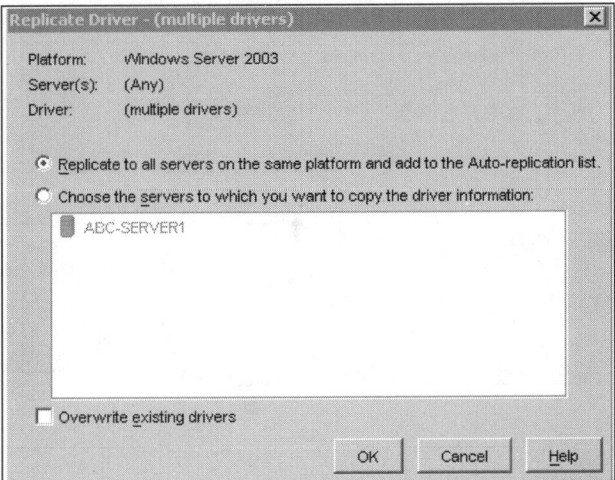

7. Once completed, you may view the **Drivers** subnode in the Management Console for MetaFrame Presentation Server to make sure that the driver has been replicated to all servers in the farm.

Importing Print Servers

Another great feature available with Citrix MetaFrame Presentation Server is the ability to import a print server from the network and make its printers readily available to users. As we have discussed, the network printers that are not installed or mapped properly within a Citrix MetaFrame Presentation server will not be readily available for use for Citrix ICA clients. Importing a network print server provides a quick and easy method to add network printers.

To import printers from a network print server:

1. Open the Management Console for MetaFrame Presentation Server by selecting **Start | Programs | Citrix | Management Consoles \ Presentation Server Console**.

2. Right-click the **Printer Management** node and select **Import Network Print Server**.

3. You will be prompted to enter the print server's name and a user account with sufficient privileges to access these printers as seen in Figure 8.11.

Figure 8.11 The Import Network Print Server Window

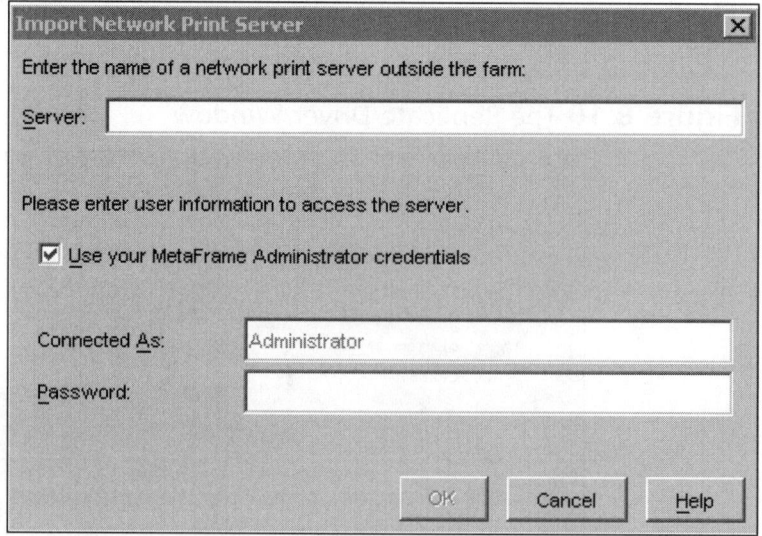

4. Once the network print server has been imported, it should be listed in the **Printer Management** node in the **Network Print Servers** tab. Verify that all its printers were also properly imported by expanding the Printers subnode and making sure the printers are all there.

NOTE

Once a network print server has been imported into the Citrix MetaFrame Presentation server farm, it cannot be re-imported. Its information is also not dynamically updated; therefore, if any changes occur on the print server, a manual refresh or update must be initiated to update the print server. Any change in the printer's properties or any newly added printers or deleted printers require an update or refresh before they take effect on the farm. To refresh or update the print server, simply right-click the server in the Management Console for MetaFrame Presentation Server and select **Update Network Print Server**.

Managing Print Drivers

Print drivers are a very sensitive issue, especially in a Citrix MetaFrame environment. Using the wrong print driver or an incompatible print driver will result in the server having symptoms that can range from a simple print spooler malfunction to a server crashing. Citrix has designed a new feature called *driver compatibility* that allows you to manage compatibility using two different methods. The options are to either allow only drivers in this list (only the drivers listed will be deemed compatible) and thus used, or to allow all drivers except those in the list (all drivers are deemed compatible except the ones listed).

This tool can be very helpful for creating compatible or incompatible drivers for use with the servers. All these tools are geared toward making your life as an administrator as easy as possible and offering you different tools that will ensure a stable printing environment at all times.

To create these driver compatibility or incompatibility lists:

1. Open the Management Console for MetaFrame Presentation Server by selecting **Start | Programs | Citrix | Management Consoles \ Presentation Server Console**.

2. In the left pane, expand the **Printer Management** node.

3. Right-click the **Drivers** subnode and select **Compatibility**. The Driver Compatibility window appears.

4. Within the Compatibility List options, select the type of list you intend to create. Your options are to either **Allow only drivers in the list** or **Allow all drivers except those in the list**.

5. Click **Add** to select a printer driver.

6. Select a driver from the drop-down menu and click **OK**. The driver appears in the driver compatibility window as shown in Figure 8.12.

Figure 8.12 The Driver Compatibility Window

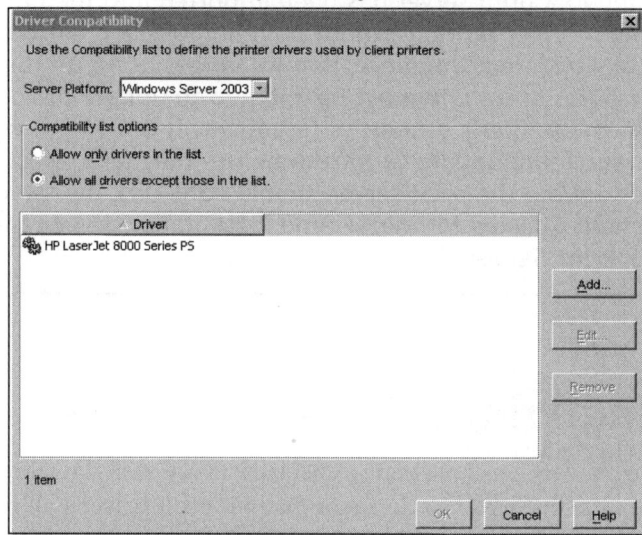

7. Repeat these steps until you have created a comprehensive list that includes all drivers required.

8. Click **OK**.

Updating Print Drivers within the Citrix MetaFrame Data Store

The Citrix IMA service on every Citrix MetaFrame Presentation server regularly scans the print registry keys and compares its information against that available in the data store. In the event that the IMA should discover a new driver, for example, that driver's information is written to the data store. This ensures that print drivers are installed and available to Citrix users and administrators.

So how do we install a print driver? That depends on the operating system you are using. If you are using Windows NT, there is one way to do it; if you are using Windows 2000 or Windows Server 2003, there are two ways.

On Windows NT 4.0 Terminal Server Edition, Windows 2000, and Windows Server 2003, you can do the following:

1. Click **Start | Settings | Printers** or **Start | Printers and Faxes** on Windows Server 2003.

2. Double-click **Add Printer** and go through the regular installation of the printer.

3. When you're done and a printer icon is created for that printer, delete the **printer icon**. This deletes the icon but preserves the files that were installed.

On Windows 2000 or Windows 2003 servers, you have an alternative and easier way to update print drivers:

1. Click **Start | Settings | Printers** on Windows 2000 or **Start | Printers and Faxes** on Windows Server 2003.

2. On the **File** menu, click **File | Server Properties**.

3. The **Print Server Properties** window opens, as shown in Figure 8.13. From this window you can add, remove, update, or view driver properties.

Figure 8.13 Print Server Properties

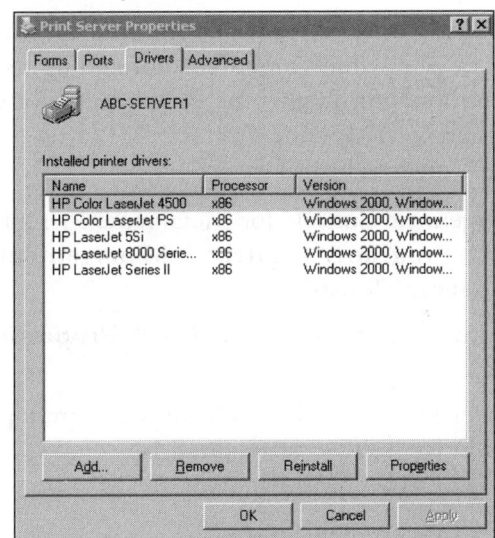

The latter method is easier and more convenient, since we don't have to go through the steps of installing each printer and sharing and assigning a name for it, and then deleting its logical representation. Simply install the driver's files. Once the print driver has been installed, open the **Management Console for MetaFrame Presentation**

Server, expand **Printer Management**, and select **Drivers**. The driver should appear in the list to the right. If it does not, wait a few minutes before refreshing the list by right-clicking the **Drivers** node and selecting **Refresh Drivers**.

Citrix Universal Print Driver

Citrix MetaFrame Presentation Server now offers the Citrix Universal Print Driver, a generic PCL4 print driver stripped of any features. Developed to minimize administrative hassles with printing, the driver is a new feature that frees you from the hassle of installing print drivers for different devices on the Citrix MetaFrame Presentation servers within your farm. This driver generates the print jobs in PCL4 format and passes the jobs to the local machine for processing. The local machine uses its locally installed print driver to output the print job.

The Universal Print Driver can be used with almost any printer. If you can print to your local printer outside the ICA session, you should be able to print to it using the Citrix Universal Print Driver. This is a wonderful capability, especially when you don't support all kinds of devices; now you can tell your users that almost any printer they can print to locally, they can print to from their ICA session. Home users with DeskJet printers that usually are not supported by administrators can now print to their DeskJets. Users who use those Xerox printers that are also usually not supported now find themselves printing.

Citrix uses the HP PCL5c driver to provide Universal Printing with 32-bit clients and Macintosh version 7 or later, which supports color and up to 600 dots per inch (dpi) resolution. Citrix continues to support the PCL4 driver for older client versions and previous versions of Citrix MetaFrame.

To configure the Universal Print Driver:

1. Open the Management Console for MetaFrame Presentation Server by selecting **Start | Programs | Citrix | Management Consoles \ Presentation Server Console**.

2. Right-click **Printer Management** and click **Properties**. The Properties window pops up.

3. Under the Printer Drivers section, you can select multiple options to use the Universal Print Driver as seen in Figure 8.14.

4. Once selected, click **OK** to continue.

Figure 8.14 Printer Management Properties Window

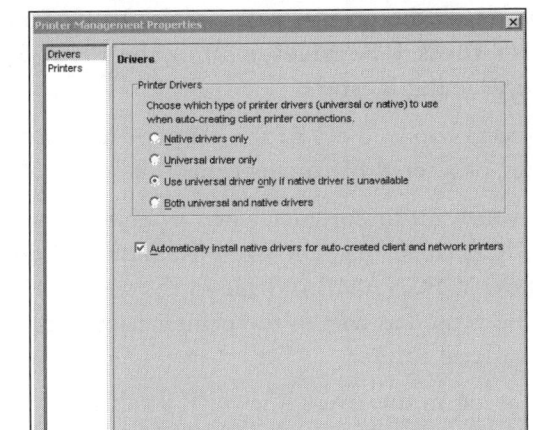

If you are still using Citrix MetaFrame 1.8 or older versions of Citrix MetaFrame XP and are interested in implementing something similar to the Universal Print Driver, there is a variety of third-party printing solutions available. These solutions can also be used with Citrix MetaFrame Presentation Server and offer many of the features that the Citrix Universal Print Driver lacks, such as the capability to print on both sides of the paper.

Troubleshooting Printing Problems

Printing problems will inevitably occur within your Citrix MetaFrame farm. Your ability to analyze and quickly troubleshoot and resolve problems is essential to ensuring a smooth operating environment. Printing continues to be improved upon within each new release of Citrix MetaFrame, especially with the introduction of the Universal Print Driver. When troubleshooting printers, you must always remember that the problem is not always related to Citrix MetaFrame. The problem may lay in many different areas such the operating system on which Citrix MetaFrame Presentation Server was installed. The problem can also exist in the print drivers installed on the local client machines; if they become corrupted, printing might not occur at all or the computer might output garbage from the printer. When you're troubleshooting printing issues, you can check a few things that might resolve your problems quickly:

- Check the print queue for any jobs that are stuck. If you find any, delete them. Then, stop and restart the print spooler service by clicking **Start | Administrative Tools | Services**, locating the **Print Spooler** service, right-clicking it, and selecting **Restart**.

- Check the physical connectivity to the printer—an Ethernet cable if it is a network printer, or a serial or parallel cable if it is a local printer.

- Another issue you want to consider when troubleshooting printer issues is verifying that the ICA client machine name is unique. To do this, view and, if necessary, edit the WFCNAME.INI file in the root of C: on the local computer. This name is used as part of the printer name and for redirecting print jobs back to the local printer.

- The Application log in the Event Viewer is a valuable tool for discovering and in many cases resolving errors that are logged both by the Citrix ICA client and the Citrix MetaFrame Presentation servers. The Event Viewer is available in Windows Server 2003 by selecting **Start | Administrative Tools | Event Viewer** and selecting the log you want to view.

These issues are common ones that you should monitor and check when you face a printing problem. When installing a new print driver within the Citrix MetaFrame server farm, be sure that the driver is compatible with Terminal Services and that it will not cause your server to malfunction. The print driver manufacturer will typically provide technical specification as to whether a driver has been approved for use with Terminal Services. Table 8.1 is a list of printing problems, their causes, and how to resolve them.

Table 8.1 Printing Problems, Causes, and Resolutions

Problem	Cause	Resolution
My server "blue screens" on printing.	Server blue screens can occur when you're using a print driver that's not supported for use on Terminal Services.	To resolve this issue, make a note of the DLL filename that appears on the blue screen, restart the server, and search for that file. When you locate it, right-click it and choose **Properties**. Try to identify the print driver with which this file is associated. After you identify the bad print driver, click **Start	Printers and Faxes**, click **File	Server Properties**, select the driver, and remove it.

Continued

Table 8.1 continued Printing Problems, Causes, and Resolutions

Problem	Cause	Resolution
Users are having problems printing large files via Citrix MetaFrame. How can I optimize the process of printing large files?		Adjust the module.ini file with the following settings: [ICA 3.0] Bufferlength=8192 [ClientPrinterPort] Windowsize=2048 MaxWindowsize=8192 See www.thethin.net for reference.
Users are reporting that their printouts are unreadable or that the printer is printing garbage.	Bad cable to the printer, or print drivers have become corrupted.	Check the physical cable to the printer and then reinstall the print drivers.
Users are reporting that they can print sometimes, but at other times, they can't.		The first thing you should check is to make sure that the client print driver is installed on all the MetaFrame Presentation servers in the farm, thereby ensuring that the driver is readily available for use, regardless of which server the ICA client attaches to. Without this driver installed, the auto-creation process will not work properly.
Users are reporting that they aren't getting their local printers mapped when they log in to the MetaFrame Presentation servers.		Verify that the installed client print driver name matches exactly that installed on the server. If it doesn't, no auto-creation will occur. You can use a mapping to associate a client print driver with a specific server printer.

Continued

Table 8.1 continued Printing Problems, Causes, and Resolutions

Problem	Cause	Resolution
The print queue is full, but printing is stalled.	The print server serves more than one physical print device. If a document is jammed or corrupted and stuck in any of the queues, printing will stall for all the physical print devices attached to the print server.	Delete the problematic print job and then stop and start the print spooler service on the print server. Users should resubmit any deleted jobs.
Users are complaining that none of their print jobs is being output.	Several things might cause this problem: an unplugged physical cable to the print device; a stuck print spooler; the printer is out of paper or out of toner; or something has physically happened to the print device.	Make sure that the actual print device isn't reporting any device errors about things such as toner, paper, or any manufacturer malfunctions. Check the print cable. Finally, check the print spooler and make sure it is not stuck. Stop and start it if necessary.

Local Client Printers Failing to Auto-Create in ICA Sessions

Local client printers failing to auto-create is probably one of the most frequently occurring issues within a Citrix MetaFrame environment. We will examine some basic troubleshooting steps that you should follow and double-check when faced with this type of issue:

- Open the Citrix Connection Configuration tool on the MetaFrame Presentation server by choosing **Start | Programs | Citrix | Administration Tools | Citrix Connection Configuration**.

- Double-click the **ICA protocol**. Click the **Client Settings** button and verify that **Connect client printers at Logon** and **Default to main client printer** are both checked. In the **Client Settings** in Citrix Connection Configuration, also verify that the following are *not* checked as seen in Figure 8.15:

  - Disable Windows Client Printer Mapping
  - Disable Client LPT Mapping

Figure 8.15 Troubleshooting Client Printing Configuration on the Citrix MetaFrame Presentation Server

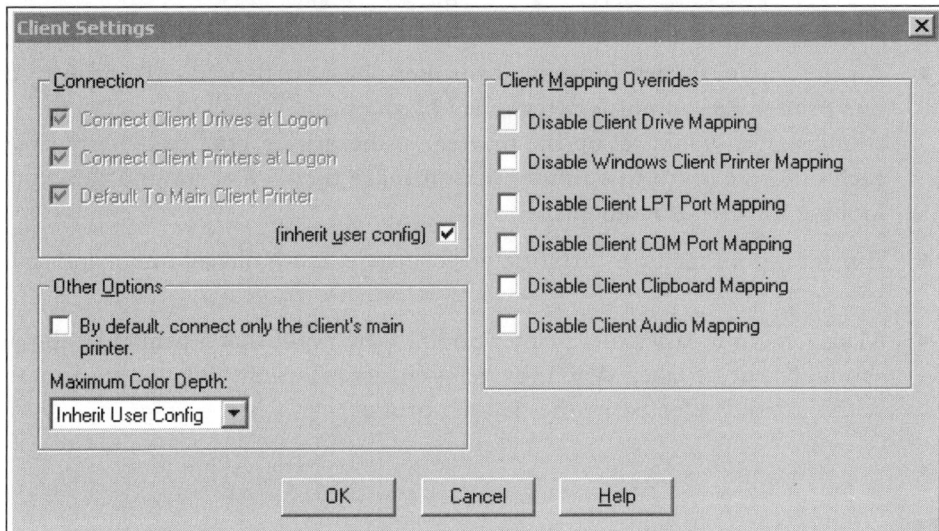

- Verify that the needed print drivers are installed on both the client workstation and on all the Citrix MetaFrame Presentation servers in the farm.

- Verify that the print driver names match exactly on both the client workstation and on the MetaFrame Presentation servers.

- Verify that *clientname* of the end-user workstation is unique.

- In the event that administrators are the only ones who can auto-create printers and regular users cannot, make sure that the users have at least READ, WRITE, and EXECUTE permissions to the following:

    - %SYSTEMROOT%\system32\spool

    - %SYSTEMROOT%\system32\printer.inf

Creating a Printer Pool

A *printer pool* offers you the ability to connect one logical or virtual printer to several physical print devices through multiple ports. Let's assume that you have three HP LaserJet 8100 physical print devices across which you would like to create a printer pool to facilitate and speed up the output of users' print jobs. When users submit print jobs, the jobs are divided among these three physical print devices. The print jobs are processed via the available port and are therefore output faster, since three physical print devices are servicing these jobs.

Some benefits of using a printer pool include:

- A printer pool speeds up the printing process, thereby decreasing the time in which print jobs are queued.

- A printer pool is very convenient for users; because they have to print to only one printer, the output is determined by the printer pool. Of course, the administrator would set up the printers in the printer pool to be very close to each other so as not to confuse users or make them chase around the office looking for their documents.

- A printer pool increases printing performance in a high-volume printing environment.

- Management is easier in a printer pool. In the event that a printer in the pool should fail or be taken down for maintenance, users are still able to print without being affected by the defunct printer.

NOTE

In a printer pool, it is recommended that all the physical print devices participating in the pool should be identical for proper printing to occur.

To set up a printer pool, follow these steps on the print server or wherever the printers are installed or are administered from:

1. Click **Start | Printers and Faxes**.
2. Add the printer with the correct driver and share the printer.
3. Once the printer is installed, right-click it and go to **Properties**.
4. Select the **Ports** tab and check the **Enable printer pooling** check box, as shown in Figure 8.16.

Figure 8.16 Enabling the Printer Pooling Option

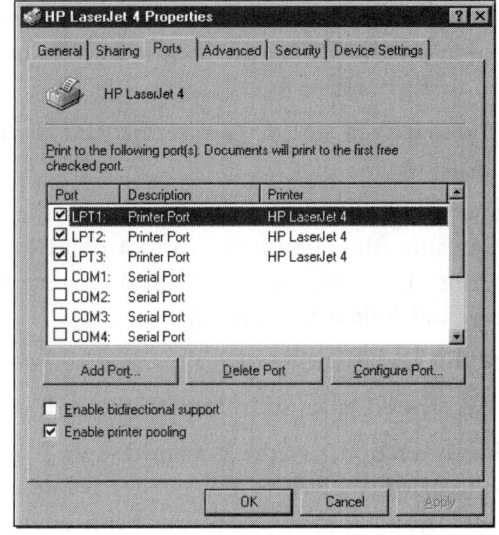

5. Select the various ports associated with the physical print devices participating in the pool. For example, if LPT1 was the original port on which the first print device was installed, select LPT2 or the port associated with another physical print device. Figure 8.16 also shows three ports selected for a single print device.

6. When you're done, click **OK** to exit the Properties window.

Creating an Expedited Print Queue

In any environment, it is often necessary to grant a group of users priority over others in terms of printing. This priority group of users could be the CEO of the company and the board of directors, for example. Expediting their print jobs and giving them priority could be necessary. It is possible to create a second print queue to a single physical print device and giving it priority printing over the other queue.

Before you create the priority queue, make sure you have already created a group in Active Directory Users and Computers and have added the users who will be granted priority-printing access to this queue. For the purpose of the example, let's assume that you have created a group named group2 and have added all the right users to it.

To create a second priority print queue and grant group1 users exclusive right to print to it:

1. Click **Start | Printers and Faxes**.

2. Right-click the printer you want to set priority for and click **Properties**.

3. Click the **Advanced** tab in the Properties window.

4. In the **Priority** section, use the Up and Down Arrow keys to set a priority. Priority is 1–99, with 1 being the lowest and 99 the highest. Set the priority level for the first printer to **1**.

5. Click the **Security** tab and make sure that the **Everyone** group has rights to print to this printer.

6. Create the second logical printer that points to the same print device and give it a different name (the same name cannot be given to more than one logical or virtual printer). (To add another logical printer, double-click the **Add Printer** icon and follow the wizard.)

7. Right-click this newly added logical printer and go to **Properties**.

8. Click the **Advanced** tab in the Properties window.

9. In the **Priority** section, use the Up and Down Arrow keys to set priority to **2**. Note that the priority given to this printer is higher than that given to the first printer; therefore, print jobs sent to this print queue will take precedence (see Figure 8.17).

Figure 8.17 The Printer Properties Advanced Tab Window

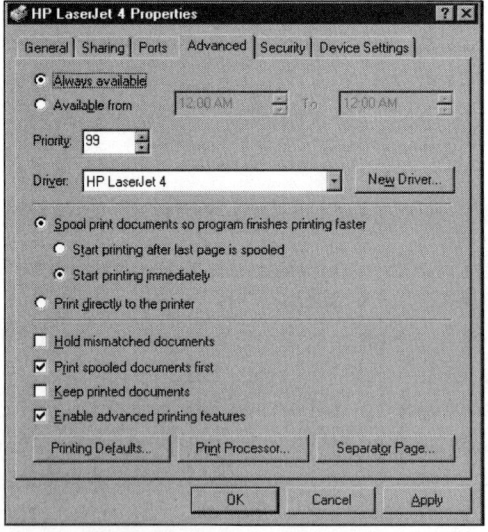

10. Click the **Security** tab, remove the **Everyone** group that was added by default, add group2, which you created earlier, and add the selected group of users who will have access to this print device as defined in Figure 8.18.

11. Click **OK** to apply the settings and close the window.

Figure 8.18 The Printer Properties Security Tab Window

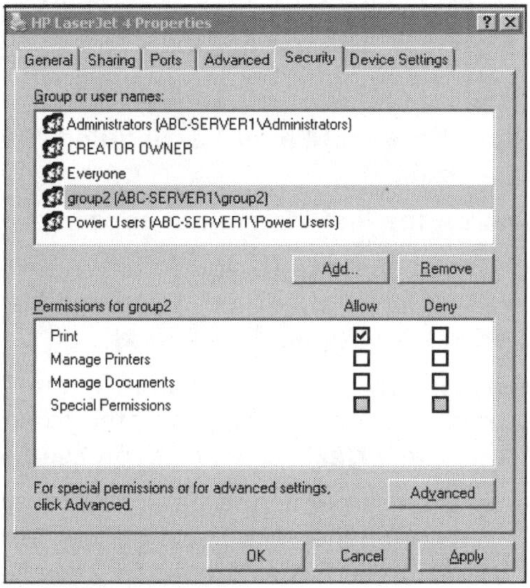

Configuring & Implementing...

Creating a Script to Clean Up the Spooler Directory

It is recommended that you clear out the print spooler files in the spooler directory using a script. This task can be automated and scheduled to run prior to the nightly reboot of the Citrix servers, for example. It is strongly recommended that you reboot Citrix servers daily due to the many instances of user mode that the Terminal server creates, which can lead to memory leaks and cause problems. You can take advantage of this reboot cycle to do some maintenance tasks such as clearing print spool files.

Follow these steps to create the script for clearing the print spool files and scheduling this job to run daily:

1. Open Notepad by going to **Start | Program | Accessories | Notepad.**

2. When Notepad opens, type the following text:

```
change logon /disable
net stop spooler
del %windir%\system32\spool\printers\*.* /q
```

Continued

3. Click **File** in the File menu and choose **Save As**.

4. Name the file (for example, **spoolerscript.bat**). Make sure that the file's extension is *.bat* and not *.txt*.

5. Click **Save**.

6. Go to **Start | Control Panel | Scheduled Tasks** and select **Add Scheduled Task**.

7. Click **Next** on the first screen that appears.

8. The second screen prompts you to browse to the location where you saved the spoolerscript.bat file. Select the file, choose how often you want the script to run, and click **Next**.

9. If you selected any option other than **When I log on** or **When my computer starts**, you will be prompted to enter time and date information and select **Next**. Otherwise, proceed to step 10.

10. Now, enter the username and password for authentication for the script. It is recommended to use a generic account you create for administrative tasks. Once completed, click **Next**.

11. Select **Finish** to complete the process. You may also configure advanced features by selecting the option provided. It is usually good to have this script run about five minutes prior to the daily server reboot schedule.

NOTE

During a user's session, her auto-created client printer is available exclusively to that user, with the exception of administrators, of course. No other user will have access to the auto-created client printer.

Summary

Printing in a Citrix MetaFrame Presentation Server environment can seem a little complicated for a new administrator until you become familiar with the various tools and features at your disposal. The auto-creation feature is one of the most sought-after features in Citrix MetaFrame and enables a user in an ICA session to print to various printers without having to install these printers—they are auto-created for the user.

Network printers can be also used within Citrix MetaFrame Presentation servers as well, and an administrator can set the users and groups for whom printers are auto-created when they log in. Local printers are another option available to an administrator; they are installed on Citrix MetaFrame servers just as they would be installed on any other Windows 2000 or Windows 2003 server.

Gone are the days when you had to log in to every server in your farm and install the same driver so you would have consistency across all servers. With Citrix MetaFrame Presentation Server, you have the option of replicating print drivers across all servers in the farm with one simple mouse click. In the event that there is a print server on your network, you can also import all its installed printers instead of having to reinstall and configure all these printers all over again.

Finally, one of the greatest features available with Citrix MetaFrame Presentation Server is the Citrix Universal Print Driver, a generic PCL5c print driver that can be used on almost any print device of any make and model.

Solutions Fast Track

Creating Client Printers

☑ The auto-created printer feature automatically makes the client's local machine available for the user to print to from within an ICA session. The user doesn't need to install anything the printer auto-creates if a set of criteria is met.

☑ Network printers can be made available for users to print to from within their ICA sessions. Network printers can be added in the Management Console for MetaFrame Presentation Server, and permissions can be set to which groups or users get these printers auto-created for them when they log on to a Citrix MetaFrame server within your farm.

☑ Local printers can be installed and attached directly to a Citrix MetaFrame Presentation server just as you would install and attach them to any Windows-based server.

Printing in a Server Farm Environment

☑ Print driver replication needs to occur to standardize the list of supported print drivers across all Citrix MetaFrame servers within the farm, so that regardless of which server a user connects to, the same set of drivers is available to service the user's printing needs.

☑ Importing a print server from your network can save time when installing network printers. After importing the print server, you need to periodically update it to make sure it is still current with regard to newly added printers or even deleted printers.

☑ The Citrix Universal Print Driver is a very simple and featureless PCL5c driver that can work with almost any print device and can be used as an alternative method to installing and replicating drivers—one driver for all devices. Citrix also includes PCL4 capability for backward compatibility.

Troubleshooting Printing Problems

☑ Always check to see if the name of the print driver installed on the client matches exactly that of the print driver installed on the server.

☑ If driver replication doesn't occur after the installation of new drivers, you could experience an issue when your user logs on to a Citrix MetaFrame server that doesn't have the right drivers installed. That user will be able to print to some servers and not to others. Always make sure that printer replication occurs.

☑ The Windows Event Viewer can be your friend in some cases for troubleshooting printer issues. Always keep an eye on the Application log within Event Viewer for any errors or error codes.

Frequently Asked Questions

The following Frequently Asked Questions, answered by the authors of this book, are designed to both measure your understanding of the concepts presented in this chapter and to assist you with real-life implementation of these concepts. To have your questions about this chapter answered by the author, browse to **www.syngress.com/solutions** and click on the **"Ask the Author"** form. You will also gain access to thousands of other FAQs at ITFAQnet.com.

Q: We have a print server on the network with many printers already installed on it. Is there an easy way to import these printers without having to reinstall all the printers?

A: Yes. You can use a feature within Management Console for MetaFrame Presentation Server called Import Network Print Server. Using this tool, you can specify the name of the print server in your network, and a wizard automatically installs the printers. You must manually reinstall the print drivers and ensure you re-import the network printer server if a printer is modified later.

Q: What do I need to do for auto-created printers to work?

A: First, you need to install the print driver on all the Citrix MetaFrame servers within your farm. Second, make sure the name of the print driver installed on the local client machine matches that which is installed on the server. Third, make sure your client machine name is unique.

Q: Where is the print driver and replication information stored in the server farm?

A: The Citrix IMA service stores the print driver and replication information and manages the replication between servers.

Q: How can I view the installed print drivers on my Windows Server 2003 Citrix MetaFrame Presentation servers?

A: You can view a list of the drivers installed on the server by choosing **Start | Printers and Faxes**. On the File menu, click **File | Server Properties** and select the **Drivers** tab. From this window, you can view, add, or delete any driver installed.

Q: Why should I consider using the Citrix Universal Print Driver?

A: The Universal Print Driver can eliminate the need to install print drivers for your various print devices. It is also a great idea to use the Universal Print Driver to give broader support to your client base, enabling users to print on devices from virtually any printer manufacturer and any model. Since the release of Citrix MetaFrame

Presentation Server, addition capabilities have been added, such as greater resolution and support for color printing.

Q: Is it a good idea to clear the files in the spool directory?

A: It is definitely recommended that you clear the spooler directory on a regular basis. We recommend that you implement a script that runs a few minutes prior to the regular server reboot. This way, when the server comes back up, there are no files in the spooler directory that could cause unstable printing services.

Q: The default number of print jobs that can be sent to the spooler is 10. Is there any way to can increase this number so the print spooler can accept more than 10 jobs?

A: Yes. Use the Citrix CltPrint.exe utility to increase the number of jobs the print spooler can accept. You can execute the utility by opening a command prompt and typing **CltPrint /pipes:nn**, and substituting the **nn** with the number of jobs the spooler can accept. You can also run the command with the **/q** syntax, which will display the current number of configured pipes.

Q: We are considering using the Citrix Universal Print Driver in our Citrix environment. Are there any disadvantages to doing so?

A: The Citrix Universal Print Driver, like any other technology, has its pros and cons. One disadvantage is that you could lose the ability to print full duplex, which means on both sides of the paper. However, the pros related to the Citrix Universal Print Driver make it a technology worth exploring. With the Universal Print Driver, you can use one print driver for almost any type of printing device, thereby offering your users the freedom to print to any piece of equipment. It frees you from the hassle of installing print drivers and making sure that you don't crash your server doing it. If you don't want to lose these features but still want to take advantage of the technology, check out a variety of third-party printing solutions available. Printing solutions include features not available with the Universal Print Driver, such as printing in full duplex and more advanced features.

Chapter 9

Network and Firewall Configuration

Solutions in this Chapter:

- Leading Users through the Firewall

- Preventing Unauthorized Access to the Network

- Various Methods to Secure Communications between Client and Server

- Citrix Secure Gateway

- Citrix Access Gateway

☑ Summary

☑ Solutions Fast Track

☑ Frequently Asked Questions

Introduction

One of the biggest challenges faced by many Citrix administrators is how to provide remote access to the farm resources without compromising the security of the network. Additionally, such access needs to be easy to use, very secure, and provide as close to local area network (LAN) performance as possible. Fortunately, Citrix has always been a company that produces products with a single goal in mind—access. Over the years, Presentation Server (and more particularly, the MetaFrame Access Suite) has become a highly secure solution for allowing remote and mobile access to your company's internal network.

In this chapter, we look at the various methods of providing secure access to our remote and mobile users. We investigate the complexities of leading user sessions through the firewall. We see how the methods of access we choose to implement will impact the firewall, the Presentation Servers, and ultimately the users themselves as they attempt to make use of the solutions we provide them. We examine many legacy methods that are still quite popular for connecting to Presentation Servers remotely, including:

- Network Address Translation (NAT)
- Port Address Translation (PAT)
- Proxy servers
- HyperText Transfer Protocol (HTTP)
- HyperText Transfer Protocol Secure (HTTPS)
- Secure Sockets Layer Relay (SSL Relay)

We spend most of our time and efforts in this chapter discussing the more modern ways of securing the communications between Citrix clients and Presentation Servers via Citrix Secure Gateway server and the new state-of-the-art Citrix Access Gateway.

Methods of Remote Access

Remote and mobile access is one of the key benefits of the MetaFrame Presentation Server Access Suite. Remote access comes in many different levels of security, and we as network architects must consider all of the pieces that must go together to form a single cohesive secure solution for our users. Today's user populations require and often demand remote access to their office computing environment. MetaFrame Presentation Server provides the solution for users, whether a traveling salesperson operating out of a hotel or a work-from-home user who is looking for the easiest and best performing access to the corporate network. There is a wide variety of remote access solutions available with Citrix. We begin with a breakdown of the most typical solutions and examine the benefits and disadvantages of each.

Table 9.1 provides a quick overview of the various options for providing remote access to your Presentation Servers (some secured and some unsecured).

Table 9.1 Recommended Remote Access Options

Remote Access Solution	Secure (1–5, 5 being most secure)	Ease of Implementation	Ease of Support	Costs
Network Address Translation (NAT) Port Address Translation (PAT)	1	Typically requires modifications to the firewall and clients to implement, and may require use of *ALTADDR* command on Presentation Servers.	Firewall rules and *ALTADDR* commands are fairly static; client support can be a challenge.	$0, all features included in product.
Proxy servers	2	Similar to PAT, typically requires firewall modification and client software.	Same as NAT/PAT plus additional support concerns with proxies.	$0, all features are included in product to facilitate use of Proxy servers. The Proxy Servers have a wide range of costs and all can work so long as they support SOCKETS (SOCKS) version 5.
HTTP/HTTPS	3*	This solution requires the servers to have an SSL server certificate in order to be secure; otherwise, it is not secure.	Modern Citrix clients default to the use of HTTP/HTTPS, so supportability is easier. The only exception would be regular exchange of server certificates to secure the servers.	$300–$800 per Presentation server per year for public SSL server certificates. Internal or private certificate authorities can be used to eliminate this cost, but will require substantially greater support for both the public-key infrastructure to support this and the deployment to the clients the root SSL certificate for the internal public-key infrastructure (more on this later in this chapter).

Continued

Table 9.1 Continued Recommended Remote Access Options

Remote Access Solution	Secure (1–5, 5 being most secure)	Ease of Implementation	Ease of Support	Costs
SSL Relay	3	Every Presentation Server would require an SSL server certificate.	Same as HTTP/HTTPS.	This is similar to the HTTP/HTTPS. SSL Relay is a legacy service developed several versions ago prior to the release of the eXtensible Markup Language (XML) service that now exists on all servers and provides the HTTP/HTTPS functionality for query farm information.
Citrix Access Gateway	5	Short implementation time and centrally deployed client and updates to clients.	Centrally managed updates and changes to the client software.	$3000+. This is Citrix's first hardware-based offering in the product line. Like all Citrix products, it is licensed per simultaneous connected user. The $3000+ price tag is for the hardware itself. More detail follows later in this chapter.

Continued

Table 9.1 Continued Recommended Remote Access Options

Remote Access Solution	Secure (1–5, 5 being most secure)	Ease of Implementation	Ease of Support	Costs
Citrix Secure Gateway	5	More complicated than Access Gateway implementation, but more seamless as of the writing of this chapter.	Once configured and functioning, support requirements are minimal.	$0*, there are no costs associated with the deployment of Secure Gateway, as all the required Citrix software components are included in the product. However, a properly designed deployment may include many new servers being added to the environment, so the cost of this hardware and the hosting operating systems and their support should be considered.

Securing Communications Between Presentation Server and Client

Let us now look in more detail at the four primary methods of securing remote access to our Presentation Servers:

- Secure Independent Computing Architecture (Secure ICA)
- Secure Socket Layer Relay (SSL Relay)
- Virtual private networking (VPN)
- Citrix Secure Gateway (CSG)

Each of these solutions has its benefits and disadvantages to deploying the solution. Let us examine these in more detail.

Secure ICA

Secure ICA is the oldest method for securing communications between Presentation Servers and clients. Back in the days of WinFrame, Secure ICA was considered an additional feature pack that would be purchased from Citrix and then licensed on your WinFrame servers to allow the administrator or users to secure the connection. Today, this functionality is built in to the product although not enabled by default. The current implementation of Secure ICA is simply referred to as *Encryption* in the Presentation Server tools and client software. Secure ICA is the legacy name, but we will continue to use it here to allow us to better differentiate the concepts. The use of the legacy name will be helpful, as we will be discussing and comparing several types of encryption in this section.

> **NOTE**
>
> Secure ICA uses symmetric key algorithms based on the work on Ron Rivest. The algorithms used today are RC5 (meaning either Ron's Code or Rivest Cipher, and this being the fifth derivation thereof). Symmetric algorithms are also known as "shared" key algorithms and are designed for speed of use. For more information, visit Ron's homepage at http://theory.lcs.mit.edu/~rivest/.

To implement Secure ICA, we must first understand how it works. Secure ICA is a feature of Presentation Server and client that allows for complete encryption of all data flowing through ICA packets between the client and server. Traffic such as screen updates, mouse movements, keyboard input, and print jobs that are redirected to the client's printers can all be encrypted. Secure ICA does not encrypt other types of data (such as Web browsing, unless it occurs within an ICA session). Secure ICA supports 40-, 56-, and 128-bit encryption settings, plus an option for 128-bit at login time only and then drops to 40-bit for the rest of the session.

NOTE

The requirements governing the use of encryption change on a regular basis. Today, the United States government has "relaxed" the restrictions of the use of 128-bit encryption continuously from outside the United States and its territories. However, prior to implementing an encryption-based solution for remote access security, check with all governmental parties involved, as several nations prohibit the use of encryption (France). Moreover, it is illegal to "export" the encryption to certain countries, especially those considered enemies of the State (Libya, North Korea, etc.).

The impact of choosing to encrypt data on modern servers and clients is negligible. Provided the server and the client have enough horsepower to perform the encryption and decryption necessary, this can be a very easy solution to securing access to your Presentation Servers. Typically, only legacy hardware or low-end thin clients will notice a difference in performance between a Secure ICA versus standard ICA session. Secure ICA can be enabled at various locations in the Presentation Server toolset, at the network interface level, at the published application level, or via Citrix policies.

Alternatively, clients can request that connections to servers or published applications be encrypted at a higher level, regardless of settings on the server.

NOTE

A user may ask for a session to be encrypted or ask for a higher level of encryption for an already encrypted session. However, if the server's connection or published applications require a minimum level, then the user will not be allowed to connect at a lower level of encryption.

Secure ICA can be implemented internally to your network or externally. It uses the same Transmission Control Protocol (TCP) port, 1494, as a nonencrypted ICA session. In many early solutions (prior to Secure Gateway or Access Gateway), many administrators would opt to use Secure ICA to encrypt their otherwise open solutions of NAT/PAT and proxy servers. Prior to Web Interface and Presentation Server policy, some administrators chose to implement multihomed servers to allow for control of when and how to encrypt data.

Figure 9.1 demonstrates a multihomed Presentation Server in which the internal network interface would not have Secure ICA enabled, but the external or demilitarized zone (DMZ) network interface would have Secure ICA 128-bit enabled.

Figure 9.1 Multihomed Presentation Server with Secure ICA

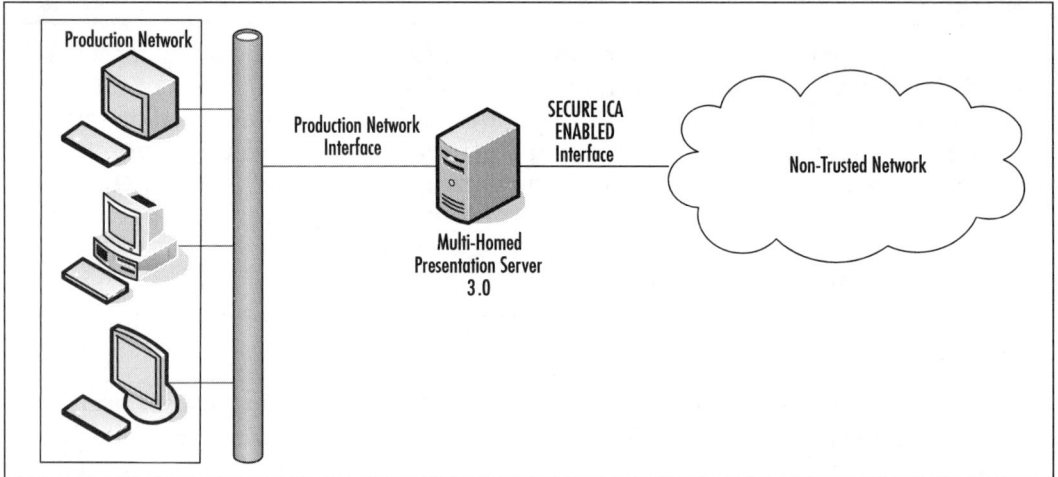

In this scenario, sessions originating from the production network would not be required to use encryption. External (nontrusted) network users would be denied connections if they didn't connect using encryption.

As previously mentioned, Secure ICA can be required on the network interface (via the Citrix Connection Configuration utility), on a published application by published application basis, or via Citrix policy. Published applications and Citrix Policy are "automatic" in allowing clients to connect with no changes required on the client end. If we configure the Citrix Connection to require encryption, then any connection created (except those already published applications with encryption or policies requiring encryption) will require a setting adjustment on the client.

Let us begin by looking at the client side. Remember, a client can request encryption at any point (even if it isn't required from the server side). For clients to request encryption, they will have to change the configuration of their application sets or their custom connections.

Figure 9.2 demonstrates the client changing the properties of a single custom connection to require encryption.

Figure 9.2 Client Enabling Encryption for a Custom Connection

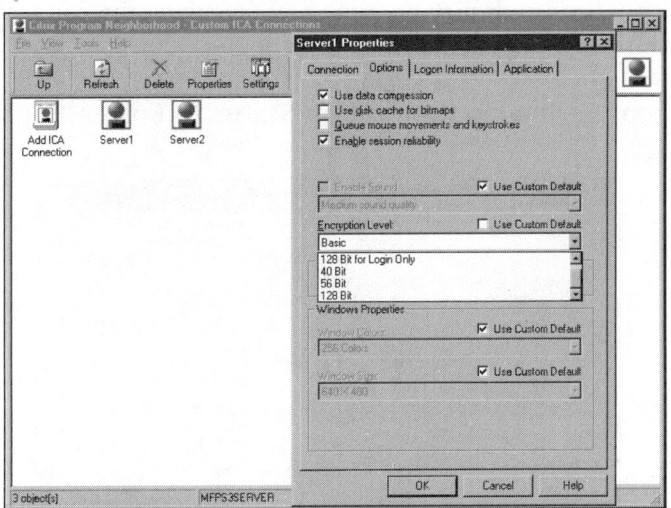

Figure 9.3 demonstrates the same concept for an application set (remember, security settings on an application set effect all applications in the set, while custom connections are set for each individual connection).

Figure 9.3 Client Enabling Encryption for an Application Set

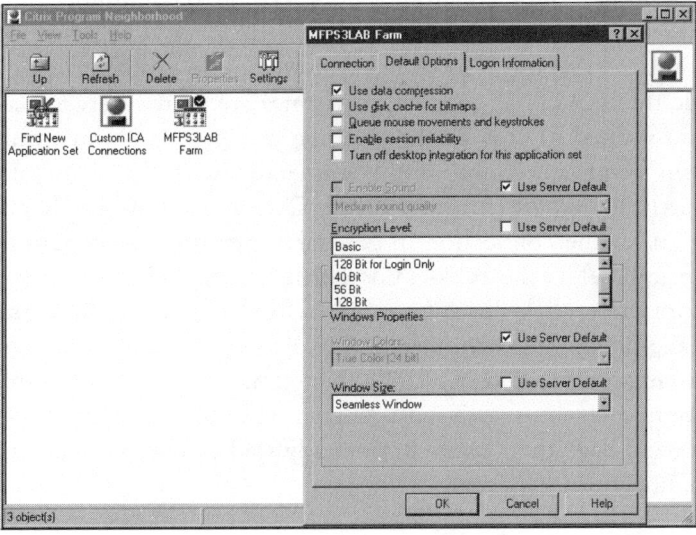

To confirm that a user is actually connected using encryption, the user simple needs to access the Program Neighborhood Connection Center in his or her system tray (Win32 clients only), click on the correct connection, and select **Properties**. The Client

Connection Status window should open and contain the encryption level as shown in Figure 9.4. Similar information may be gained by reviewing the connections in the Presentation Server Management Console.

Figure 9.4 Client Reviewing Connection Status to Ensure Encryption Is Being Used

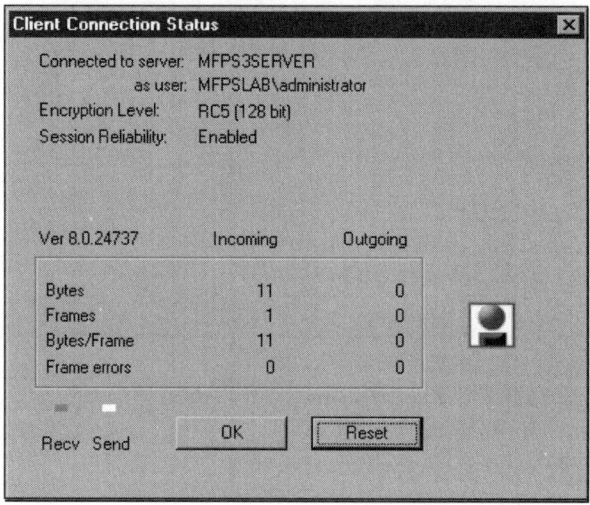

Secure ICA can be "enforced" from the server side via a number of methods. The most obvious way would be on the connection settings for ICA as we previously reviewed in Figure 9.1. Secure ICA or encryption can be enabled on a per-connection basis. By default, the ICA-TCP connection settings are shared between all adapters in the server. If you wanted to provide the scenario in Figure 9.1, you would simply create an additional connector and configure the connectors with the "internal" and "external" interfaces, respectively. For the purposes of this section, we will simply review where to enable encryption for the connection in general. Open the **Citrix Connection Configuration** tool, select the **ICA-TCP connection**, and right-click and edit the connection. From there, click the **Advanced** button from the **Edit Connection** window. Note the highlighted area in Figure 9.5 to see where to enforce this change. Remember, enforcing this setting on the connection means that all sessions that use ICA over TCP to connect to this server must be encrypted to the minimum level you specify. Clients may need to have their configuration adjusted to comply with this setting; otherwise, failed connections may result.

Figure 9.5 Encryption Settings on the ICA-TCP Connection

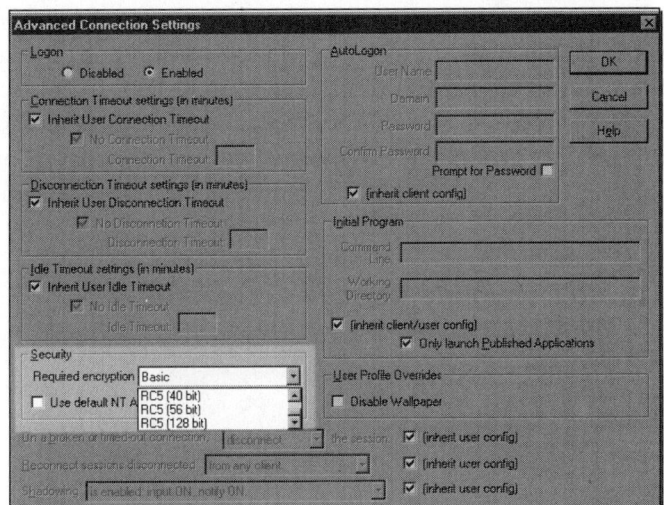

Setting the required encryption on the connection is the "oldest" of methods for encrypting a session with Secure ICA. Citrix later developed the option to allow us to publish applications and require differing levels of encryption. This flexibility allowed us to reserve the use of encryption for specific more security-conscious applications. This also allows us to publish the same application multiple times to different groups of users, and allow for some users to be forced into an encrypted session, perhaps for our chief financial officer (CFO). Enabling encryption on a given published application is a snap. Simply open the **Properties** of a given published application, navigate to the **Client Options** tab, and select the appropriate level of encryption as depicted in Figure 9.6.

Figure 9.6 Encryption Settings for Published Applications

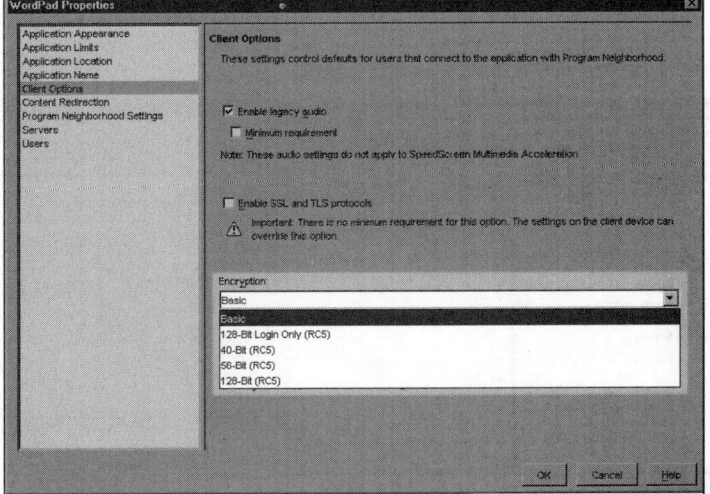

The final and arguably best method to require encryption of session data using Secure ICA is to enforce the encryption requirement through Citrix Policy. While we won't cover Citrix Policy in detail here, we will discuss using policy to affect the various sessions that would connect to our farm's Presentation Servers. In this scenario, we will configure a policy element to encrypt all session data using Secure ICA at 128-bit for the Domain Administrators group, but only when they are external to our network. The first step is configuring the policy element to require encryption as demonstrated in Figure 9.7.

Figure 9.7 Enabling Encryption through Citrix Policy

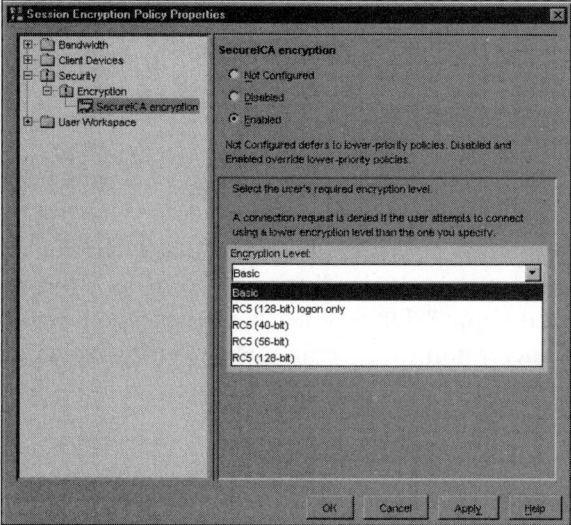

Once the policy element is enabled, we simply now need to apply it to the chosen group. Right-click the policy and select **Apply this policy to** as indicated in Figure 9.8.

Figure 9.8 Applying the Policy

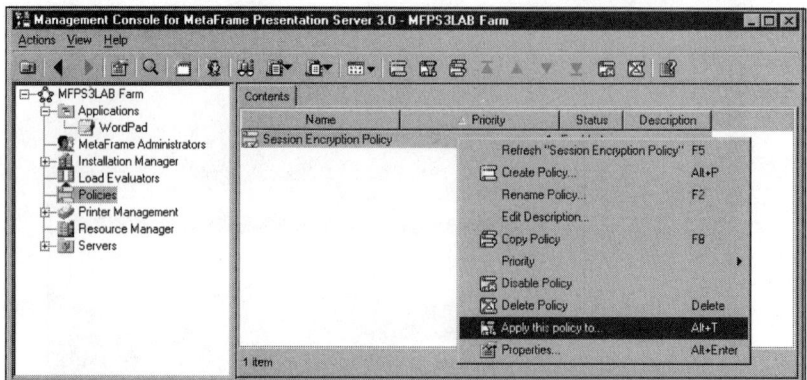

When we select **Apply this policy to**, we have several options. We can apply policy based on client IP addresses, client names, servers, or users and groups. Additionally, we can apply policy based on a combination of these "rules" to allow for greater flexibility. In Figure 9.9, we have elected to deny the policy to all sessions where the client device's IP address is in the 10.0.0.1–10.255.255.255 range. This could be especially useful if we were trying to encrypt all traffic except those sessions coming from our internal network.

Figure 9.9 Filtering by Client IP Address

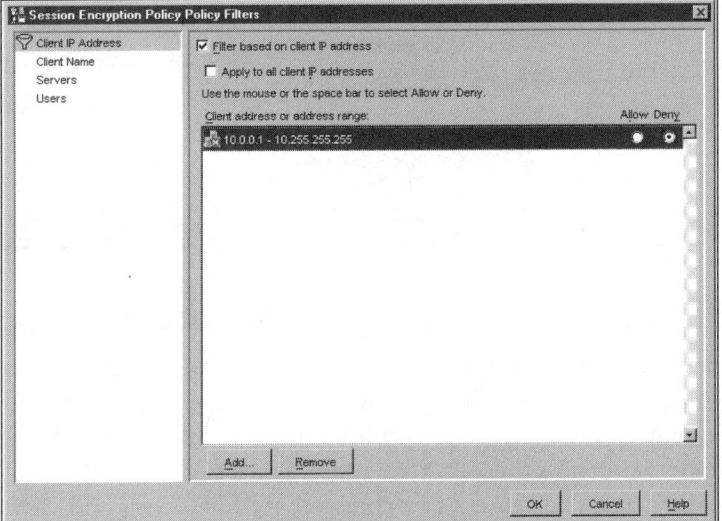

In Figure 9.10, we have elected to "filter" the policy further so that only domain admins will have the policy applied. The combination of the filters from Figures 9.9 and 9.10 would be such that only domain admins will have their sessions encrypted and only when they are not connecting from the 10.0.0.0/24 network.

Figure 9.10 Filtering by Users

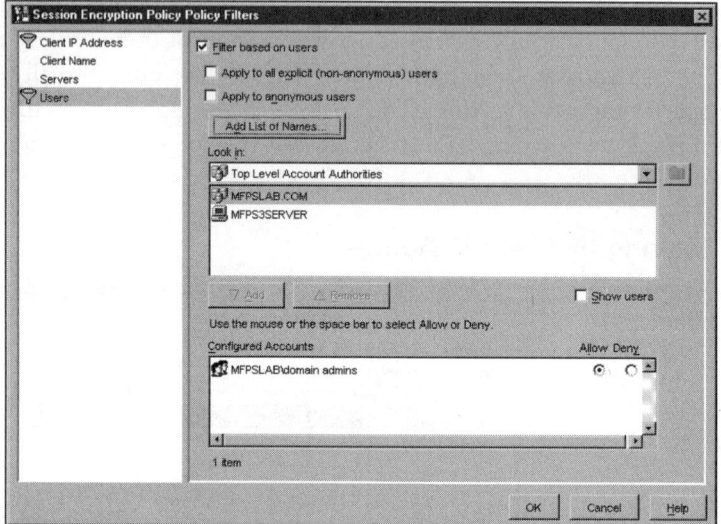

Virtual Private Networking to Secure ICA Sessions

VPN initially appears to present the "simplest" solution for providing users' remote access to our Presentation Server farms. However, this perception can be deceiving. VPN access to production networks brings with it a series of issues, some of which are specific to Presentation Servers, and others that are more generic.

Before we delve too deep into VPN connectivity for servers and clients, let us first examine the primary issues surrounding VPN as a method of accessing our Presentation Server farms.

- Installation of VPN client software

- Support of VPN client software

- Cost

- Complexity for users

- Latency and tunnel failure issues

- Split-tunneling

- Client is "part of the network"

- Worm/virus propagation

Installation of VPN client software can be a challenge for administrators and users alike. The installation programs, while typically automated, normally require administrative privileges over the computer on which the software is being installed. Additionally, the installation of the VPN client normally adds a "virtual" adapter to the workstation for the purposes of routing traffic correctly to the other end of the VPN concentrator. The existence of this VPN adapter modifies the routing tables of the local client, which, depending on the client's network, can lead to a series of issues with connectivity. Support of VPN client software is tied directly to the installation and ongoing help desk issues generated by the existence of the VPN software.

One of the largest factors to consider when deciding whether VPN access is the best method for your farm is cost. VPN client licenses are typically more costly than nearly any other alternative, and this typically doesn't include the cost associated with the hardware to install in your production network to provide the terminating end to client VPNs. Due to the higher cost associated with VPN access and the security concerns, most organizations elect to only provide access (if at all) to their internal users. Trusted business partners may be a case for this type of access, but even then, most administrators don't want to take on the support burden of a VPN client on noncompany owned and managed hardware. That said, roving access from public or untrusted computers is pretty much out as far as this solution is concerned.

For those clients who are the "right fit" for this solution, using the VPN client software can be a challenge. Probably the single biggest complaint of VPN clients is the complexity of configuring and using the actual client, and the "strange effect" the software seems to have on the computer's connectivity. This complexity is typically so high and the repetitive use of the VPN solution required in truly learning the software is so low that many users simply give up and return to the office if system access is required. This by definition is not "simple" access.

Moving past the issues that VPNs present to the clients, several issues can cause us very serious internal concerns when a user does successfully establish a VPN. Latency in the underlying network connectivity between the client and the VPN concentrator can frequently be great enough to cause the tunnel to "hiccup." This pause or drop in the tunnel is an unacceptable solution for Presentation Server sessions. ICA is a presentation layer protocol of the OSI model. The relative position of the protocol makes it extremely susceptible to breaks or drops in connectivity. Latency can for the most part be overcome with a series of technologies from Citrix called Speed Screen, discussed elsewhere in this book. Breaks or drops such as those found in VPN connectivity can cause the user's sessions (once established) to simply disappear. This can be a serious issue to troubleshoot and resolve; it is not fun for you and definitely a bad experience for your customers, also known as your users.

Another issue more related to security is the dreaded split-tunnel. Split-tunneling is a concept in virtual private networking whereby the end device establishes the tunnel to your corporate network and is able to gain access to resources outside your corporate network. In simpler terms, the external computer has simultaneous access to corporate resources and public resources. This presents serious security issues, especially in situations where a client's computing device could have been turned into a "zombie" and some external "bad guy" has leveraged your user's computer as a free ticket into the corporate network. Fortunately, split-tunneling can be disabled in most cases. However, disabling it means that the user's access outside the tunnel disappears, and all requests are sent through the tunnel to include print request, Web sites, e-mail, and so forth, much of which may be unserviceable by the corporate network. Figure 9.11 demonstrates the concept of split-tunneling.

Figure 9.11 Effects of Split-Tunneling in VPN Access

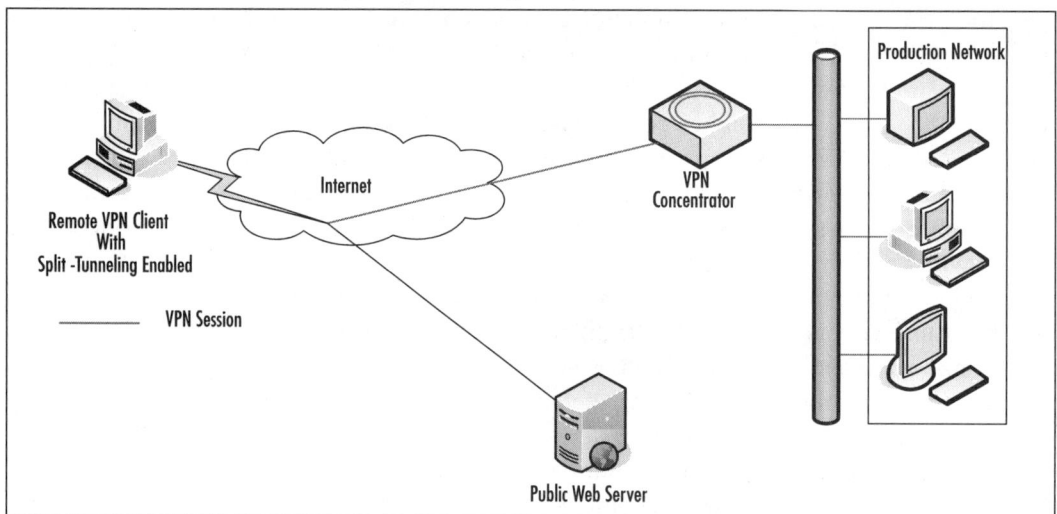

The last couple of security concerns for using VPN access as a remote access solution to Presentation Servers are based on the following simple statement, "Clients are part of the corporate network." Once a VPN tunnel is established, virtually it is as if the remote computer were actually on your corporate network, bringing with it all of the issues and concerns that exist from supporting workstations. In our corporate networks, we spend a great deal of time securing, protecting, updating, and disinfecting our workstations through of a host of services and software. While these devices are not "easy" to support and manage, they are typically within our "sphere of power" and are controllable to some extent. Computing devices in users' homes or remote trusted networks are typically outside of our management scope. The unpatched vulnerabilities, viruses, and worms that they bring to our production network the instant they establish the tunnel should be of paramount concern to all network administrators. This last concern alone had nearly halted the adoption of VPN solutions in many environments. The recent advent of SSL-based VPNs and newer "hybrid" VPNs are taking some of the sting out of VPN solutions.

That being said, VPN access does provide one major advantage to Presentation Server users: there is no need to "reconfigure" their Presentation Server client software based on the fact that they are internal or external to the network. A single set of instructions for users could be issued whether the users access the farm from inside the network or outside (as when they are outside, they will simply establish the VPN tunnel). There is a variety of solutions surrounding VPN technology, but the basic issues of support, security, and simplicity are still challenges that more or less prohibit VPN access as serious contender for the best remote access method for Presentation Servers.

Citrix Access Gateway

As this chapter was being finalized, Citrix was in the process of acquiring a company called Net6. Net6 created a hardware solution to overcome the security concerns of traditional Internet Protocol Security (IPSec) based VPNs and the inherit limitations of SSL-based VPNs. Net6's solution is based on a hardened Linux operating system that functions as a hybrid SSL-VPN. Citrix's acquisition of this solution has given Citrix its first hardware offering in the product line. It has also provided some pretty amazing feature enhancements for today's Presentation Server implementation and will undoubtedly provide even more amazing features for tomorrow's farms. As of the writing of this chapter, we are just beginning to understand how the new Citrix Access Gateway will fit into our remote access solutions, so this section will be decidedly brief. We simply couldn't omit a product (even one so cutting edge) from the discussion, as we are sure that it will play a great role in future remote access solutions.

The Access Gateway is a hardware appliance that runs a hardened Linux operating system. The server's current specifications are:

- 1U rack-mount

- Hardened Linux operating system

- 2.8 GHz processor

- 1GB RAM

- 40GB disk

- 2x 1Gbps Ethernet

- 2000 tunnels at 300 Mbps

- Supports Windows 2000, XP, and Linux clients

- Supports any application

- Supports any protocol

- Authentication support for LDAP, RADIUS, SecurID, and Local accounts

- Policy management through LDAP or Local groups

- High availability through multigateway failover

- Logging to Syslog, console, and archive to files

- Encryption support for TLS v1.0
- Ciphers: 128-bit AES
- Hashes: SHA

Additionally, the Access Gateway provides for URL-distributed client software that does not modify local routing tables and can coexist with other VPN clients. The Access Gateway provides for "Always On" roaming, so as long as the client has "connectivity," he or she will have a tunnel, and the Access Gateway provides for centralized configuration and administration and blocks the traversal of worms. Additionally, the Access Gateway is optimized for voice and video, so for users of Internet Protocol (IP) based phones, soft-phones could be leveraged from a roving user's laptop that would work as if the user were sitting at the desk in the corporate office. Ah! What a great modern world we are living in! Citrix has informed the public that the functionality of the Access Gateway will continue to increase over time. Short-term inclusions in the functionality will most likely come in the area of MetaFrame Presentation Server's Secure Gateway and the more feature-rich MetaFrame Secure Access Managers' Secure Gateway software. We suspect that in the coming weeks and months we will see this functionality included wholly in the Access Gateway, making it an even more attractive solution. The product already has a much lower cost to implement and support than traditional and SSL-based VPNs. How much better would it be if it included Secure Gateway functionality (thus saving us the cost of the hardware and operating system to run a separate server)? We discuss the software-based Secure Gateway in the next section, as currently it is the premier method of securing remote access to our Presentation Servers.

Citrix Secure Gateway

Citrix Secure Gateway (CSG) is the most commonly implemented solution for securing remote access to Presentation Server farms. There are several reasons for this solution's popularity, but the most common are ease of use for the end users, no additional software costs (this product is included as part of the MetaFrame Access Suite and Presentation Server 3.0), and the broad support of client operating systems. CSG has become the standard for remote access since its creation nearly three years ago. Secure gateway is itself a single server, but the solution requires several other components to work in concert toward a secure session for the user. A properly implemented CSG solution will include the Secure Gateway, a Web Interface server, a Presentation Server farm with published applications, and a Secure Ticket Authority. From a high-level, a typical implementation would look something like Figure 9.12.

Figure 9.12 Overview of Secure Gateway Components Placement

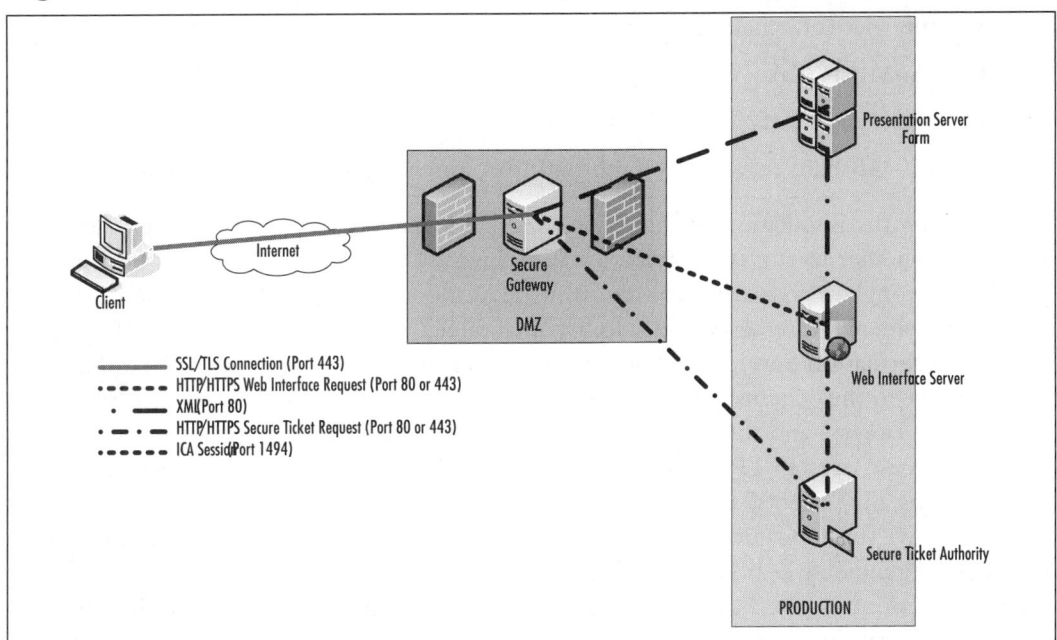

To correctly implement a Secure Gateway solution, careful planning and consideration must be given to each component. In this section, we discuss the planning and requirements for each component as it pertains to such as solution. After describing the requirements for each component, we will walk through the typical installation and configuration of that component (where applicable).

Secure Ticket Authority Installation and Configuration

We will begin with the Secure Ticket Authority (STA), as it is a component that can be built separately and its configuration is not dependent on other pieces of the Secure Gateway solution being implemented. The STA's role in life is to issue session tickets in response to connection requests from Secure Access Manager or Web Interface servers. The STA also uses the tickets as the foundation for authentication and authorization for access to published applications in the farm(s). This authentication and authorization occurs when the Secure Gateway asks the STA to validate a ticket that a session has given the Secure Gateway. Due to the "security focus" of this server role, the STA should always be deployed in a secure network—read non-DMZ! The STA need not be a member of a domain and will function quite nicely as a stand-alone server.

The STA is a relatively "light" load to place on a server, so the minimum requirements are small. Basically, any server capable of running Windows 2000 Server or Windows Server 2003 will function well as an STA. Here are the actual minimums as published by Citrix Systems:

- Windows 2000 Server Family or later with most current service pack

- Internet Information Services 5 or later

- 256MB RAM

- Network interface card (NIC)

- 150MB hard drive space (although this much higher than actually needed)

Planning the installation of the STA is simple. A few decisions need to be made regarding whether to run the service on Windows 2000 Server or Windows Server 2003. We strongly recommend running this on Windows Server 2003 because of the vast improvements in security and stability introduced with Windows Server 2003 and Internet Information Services 6. The next question is whether to secure the communication between the "clients" and the STA service. The "clients" in this scenario would be the Secure Gateway and the Secure Access Manager and/or Web Interface servers. The "client" requests are HTTP based and can be secured with a standard SSL certificate, thus allowing the "clients" to communicate with the STA using HTTPS.

Before we dig too much deeper into the configuration of the STA or Secure Gateway in general, we should briefly review certificate authorities (CAs) and the role that SSL certificates play in communications. Certificates are used to ensure that the parties communicating with each other are genuine. In today's computing world, there are three widely used types of certificates; the first is the root certificate.

The root certificate is created and issued by the CA. The purpose of the root certificate is simply to allow other devices to guarantee the authenticity of the two other types of certificates that the CA may issue, the client and server certificates. Anyone or any device may freely download and "add" the root certificate from a CA to their computer's "trusted roots." The action of adding a root certificate to a device implies that you "trust" the other certificates that the originating CA issues.

The client certificate is not as widely used today as the server certificate is. The client certificate is to allow the receiver of the communication to guarantee the caller is legitimate. Think of it this way: If a person walks up to your desk and asks you to let him into the server room, explaining that he works in IT for your company, you have no viable way of proving or disproving that statement, unless you ask to see his badge. The badge that he possesses functions as the client certificate in this case. Since you have seen other badges, you know the person who issues the badges, and you yourself have a badge, this knowledge functions as the root certificate (the one that allows you to trust). Client certificates are supported with Secure Gateway, although typically not implemented due to the cost and complexity of maintaining the infrastructure to issue and revoke these certificates.

Server certificates are our primary concern for this module. Server certificates allow you to confirm the legitimacy of the server on the other end. A perfect example of this is online shopping. Prior to purchasing the much-needed widget from eBay, you want to guarantee that the server on the other end—the one receiving your credit card information—is really an eBay server. Your Web browser does this by comparing the server certificate that the eBay Web server shows your computer with the root certificate issued by the same issuer of the server certificate. If, for instance, VeriSign issued the server certificate for the Web server we are building, we will need to ensure that the root certificate is added to the "clients" of that Web server. Most popular public CAs' root certificates are already added when you install the operating system on your computer or are updated when you apply services packs. Private CAs' root certificates could be added to your computer when you build them or through a management tool such as Active Directory if the computer exists within your management scope. Public CAs make their living by charging consumers for their services. Private CAs can typically be installed for free on many operating systems and have no cost associated with their operation other than the hardware and support needed. All of this brings us to this important point: public versus private CAs, and which to choose.

The decision to choose a public or private CA is easy, and can be based on a very simple set of rules:

- If the clients that will be "trusting" the root certificate (from the CA) are internal and under your management control, a private CA is a fine choice.

- If the clients that will be "trusting" the root certificate are outside of your management control—Internet users, remote users, home users, or trusted business partners—a public CA is the better choice.

Since the Secure Gateway and the Secure Access Manager/Web Interface server will be acting as clients to the STA, we could choose to use either a public or private CA. Either way, we would ensure that the root certificates that matched the server certificate on the STA were added to the Secure Gateway and the Secure Access Manager/Web Interface. Figure 9.13 demonstrates the legs of communication that we are specifically securing by leveraging an SSL server certificate and the relationship between root certificates and server certificates.

Figure 9.13 Using SSL Certificates to Secure the Communication to the Secure Ticket Authority

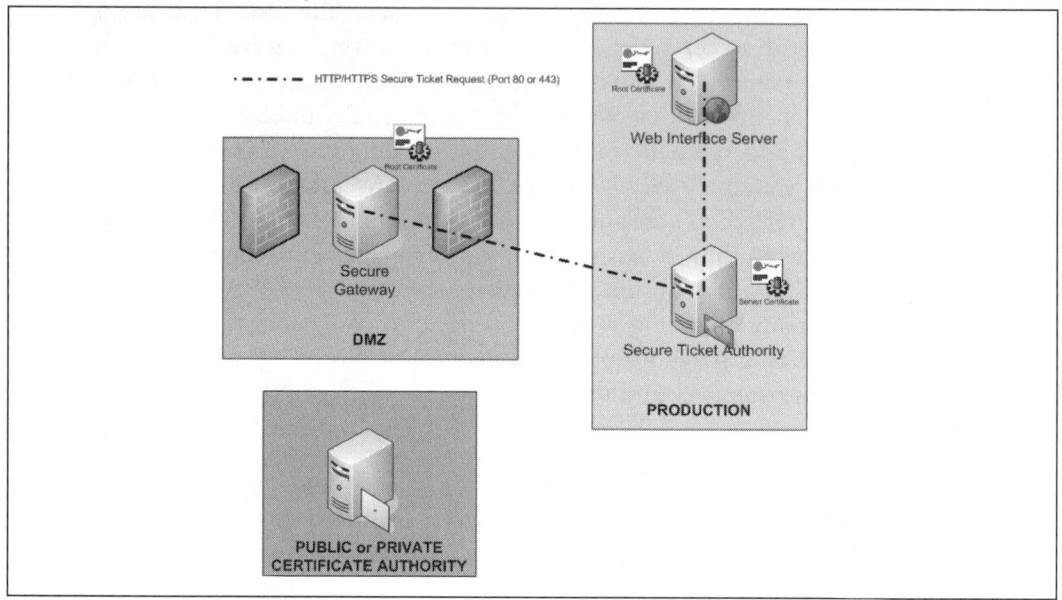

Once the decision is made as to whether to secure the network traffic between the "clients" and the STA, we now will look at redundancy considerations. A single STA is typically capable of handling the load of all but the largest environments. However, a single point of failure in our solution would be unacceptable. STAs can be load balanced or made more fault tolerant in a handful of ways. The basic rule of thumb is that the STA that issues the ticket must be the STA that validates the ticket. Web Interface provides a mechanism to load balance STAs inside the configuration, which is satisfactory for most implementations. If you elect to use Windows Load-Balancing Service or a hardware load balancer, pay special attention to the persistency, affinity, or "stickiness" of the connections. Again, it is imperative that the issuing and validating STA be the same. We review the STA load-balancing options later when we configure the Web Interface and Secure Gateway components to leverage our newly created STA.

For now, let us turn our attention to the installation and configuration of the STA itself. Once your server platform has met the requirements for installation, begin the install by inserting the Components CD that shipped with your Presentation Server software, or download the components from the MyCitrix Web site. Begin the installation by running the **CSG_STA.msi** from the CD.

The following steps and series of screenshots (Figures 9.14–9.19) illustrate the step-by-step explanation of the install process and will aid in installing and configuring the STA at any point.

Figure 9.14 Secure Ticket Authority Installation

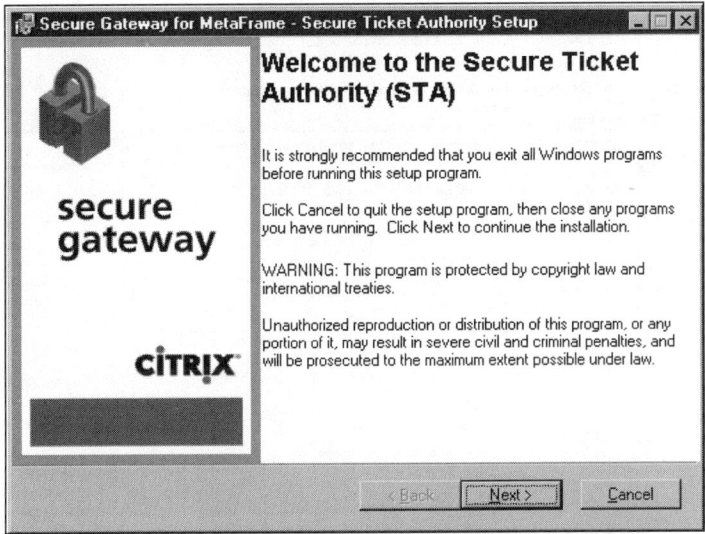

1. Click **Next**.

Figure 9.15 Secure Ticket Authority Installation License Agreement

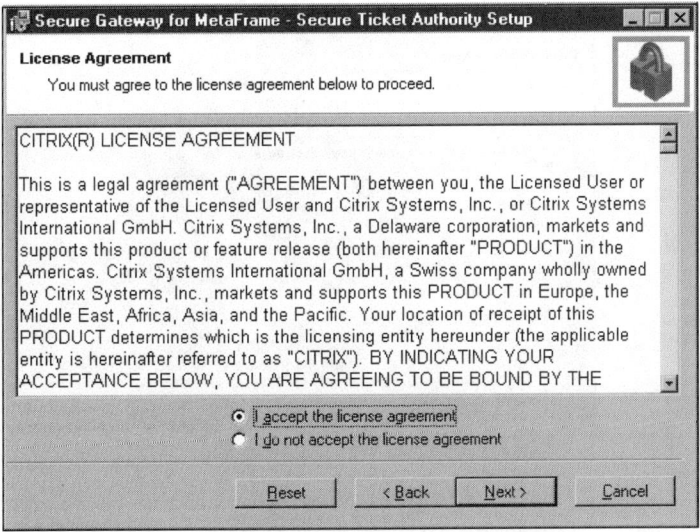

2. Select **I accept the license agreement** and click **Next**.

Figure 9.16 Secure Ticket Authority Installation Information

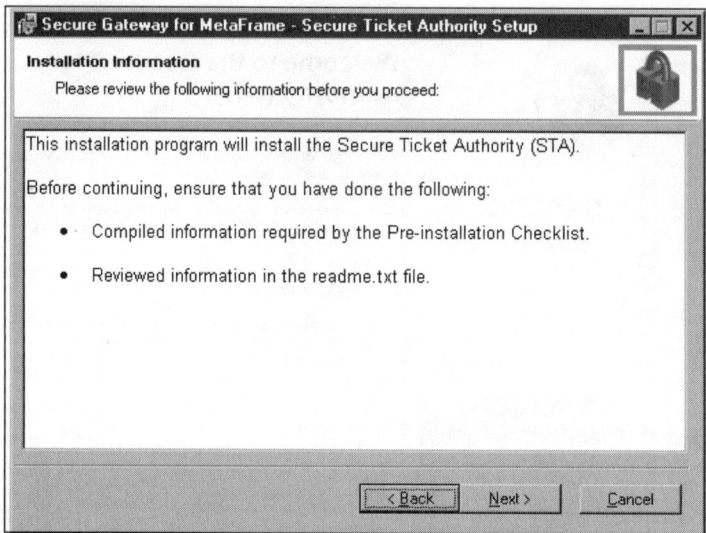

3.   Click **Next**.

Figure 9.17 Secure Ticket Authority Installation Path Selection

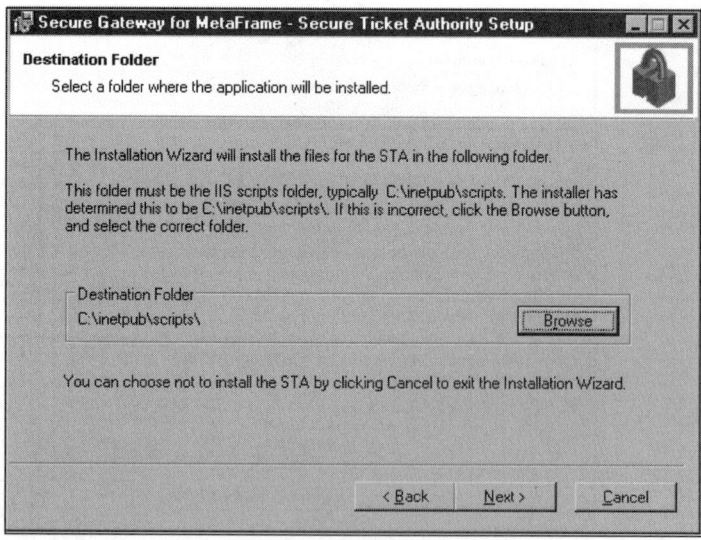

4.   The installation path should be to the Scripts directory of the installation of
     Internet Information Services (typically, c:\Inetpub\scripts). Two files,
     CtxSTA.dll and CtxSTA.config, are copied to this location. Once selected,
     click **Next**.

Figure 9.18 Secure Ticket Authority Installation Security Warning

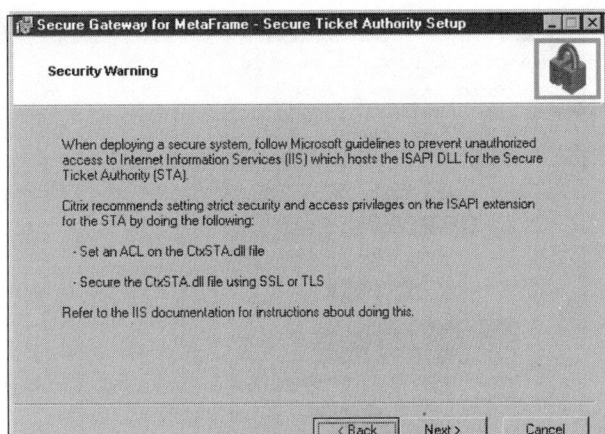

5. Once the files are copied, a security warning will appear that recommends the use of SSL (or TLS), and that an access control list (ACL or NTFS permissions) be placed on the CtxSTA.dll file. Review this warning and click **Next**.

Figure 9.19 Secure Ticket Authority Installation Review

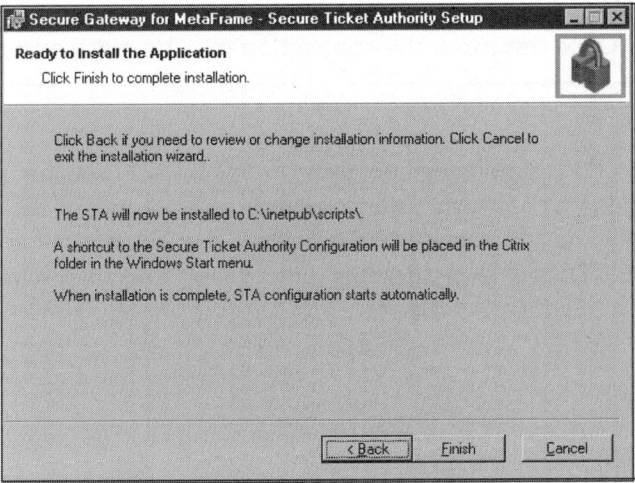

6. The final window of the installation is the review. Confirm your settings and click **Finish**.

At the end of installation of the STA, the configuration wizard will launch (see Figure 9.20). We can configure the service now or select **Cancel** and relaunch the tool later. The STA may be reconfigured at any point using the same tool.

Figure 9.20 Secure Ticket Authority Configuration—Configuration Level

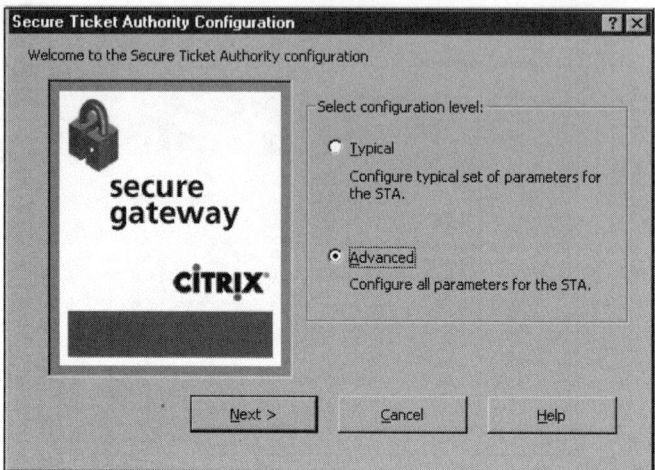

NOTE

Configuration or reconfiguration of the STA requires the Internet Information Services to be restarted. This will disrupt the ticket issuing and validation process. Those connections already completed will be unaffected; however, new connections attempted during the restart or tickets issued but not yet validated will fail. Once restarted, the connection may be reattempted.

The STA's ID is simply a name given to this STA. This name is not network addressable and need not match the computer or hostname of the server on which the STA resides. The default name is STA01, which can be changed at any point. If you are using multiple STAs for load balancing and/or fault tolerance, selecting different STA IDs is required (see Figure 9.21).

Figure 9.21 Secure Ticket Authority Configuration Parameters

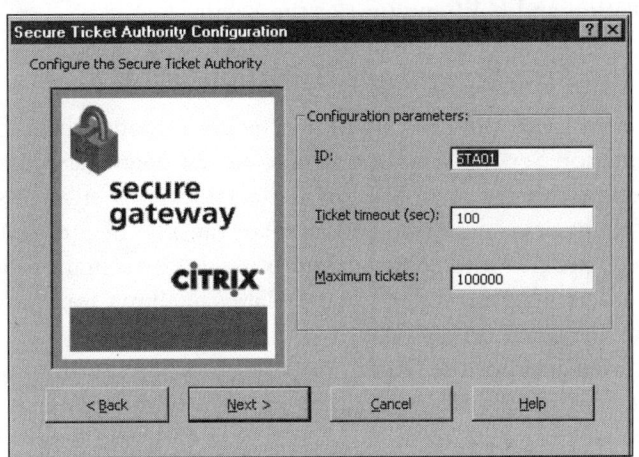

The ticket timeout defaults to 100 seconds, and is the value used to determine the "freshness" of the ticket. A ticket once issued must be used within this ticket timeout period, or the ticket will be invalidated. Most tickets are issued and validated in less than 30 seconds, so decreasing this number may assist in thwarting brute-force attacks on the STA.

The maximum tickets value defaults to 100,000 and determines the maximum number of tickets that will be allowed in this server's memory at any point. Decreasing this number will lower the amount of RAM consumed by the STA service.

Once the STA is configured (reconfigured), a restart of the World Wide Web Publishing Service will be required to enforce the new settings (see Figure 9.22). Consider other services or sites that may be hosted on this server prior to restarting this service. Once the service is restarted, the changes to the STA go into effect immediately.

Figure 9.22 Secure Ticket Authority Configuration Completion

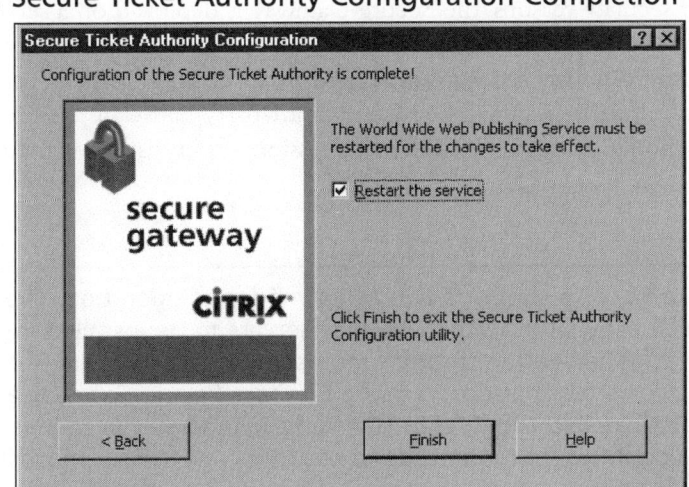

That concludes the installation and configuration of the STA. We will now shift our focus to the installation and configuration of the Secure Gateway.

Secure Gateway Installation and Configuration

The Secure Gateway service provides simplified secure remote access to your MetaFrame Presentation Server farms and Secure Access Manager access centers. The security is provided by the use of an SSL or TLS certificate to encrypt session data between the end-client device and the Secure Gateway. The Secure Gateway decrypts this traffic and then "proxies" the communication to the Presentation Servers or Secure Access Manager servers. The use of the Secure Gateway allows for a layer of defense and protection for your Presentation Servers.

Planning the installation of the Secure Gateway server is a little more involved than the STA install, but not much. For starters, the most common problem faced by implementers is the type of certificate to use for the Secure Gateway. A server certificate that is 128-bit SSL or TLS is a minimum requirement for the construction of the service. The certificate can be either public or private, although nearly all organizations use public to allow for less support concerns with the end-clients' workstations. For more information on certificates and CAs, review the previous section of this chapter on Secure Ticket Authority configuration.

Let's begin with the hardware and software requirements for Secure Gateway:

- Windows 2000 Server Family with the most recent service pack
- 512MB RAM
- 150MB hard drive space
- Network interface card (NIC)
- 128-bit SSL or TLS server certificate

Typically, for security reasons, the Secure Gateway is deployed on a server in the DMZ. This server would not have any other roles or services and is not necessarily joined to a domain. Secure Gateway servers can be load balanced and/or made highly available by using the Windows Load-Balancing Service or third-party hardware load balancers. As with STAs, care should be taken to ensure that session affinity is maintained.

NOTE

Secure Gateway also supports two other modes of operation. The first is Proxy mode, which allows for Secure Gateway servers to be installed in "chains" to allow for easier navigation through multistaged DMZs. Figure 9.23 demonstrates this concept. The second mode is where Secure Gateway and Web Interface are installed together on the same Windows server. This mode is known as Logon Agent mode. Due to security concerns surrounding IIS, we recommend separate servers for the installation and scalability of this solution. As most implementations are separate servers, the Logon Agent option will not be discussed in this chapter.

Figure 9.23 Secure Gateway Proxy Mode with Double-Hop DMZ

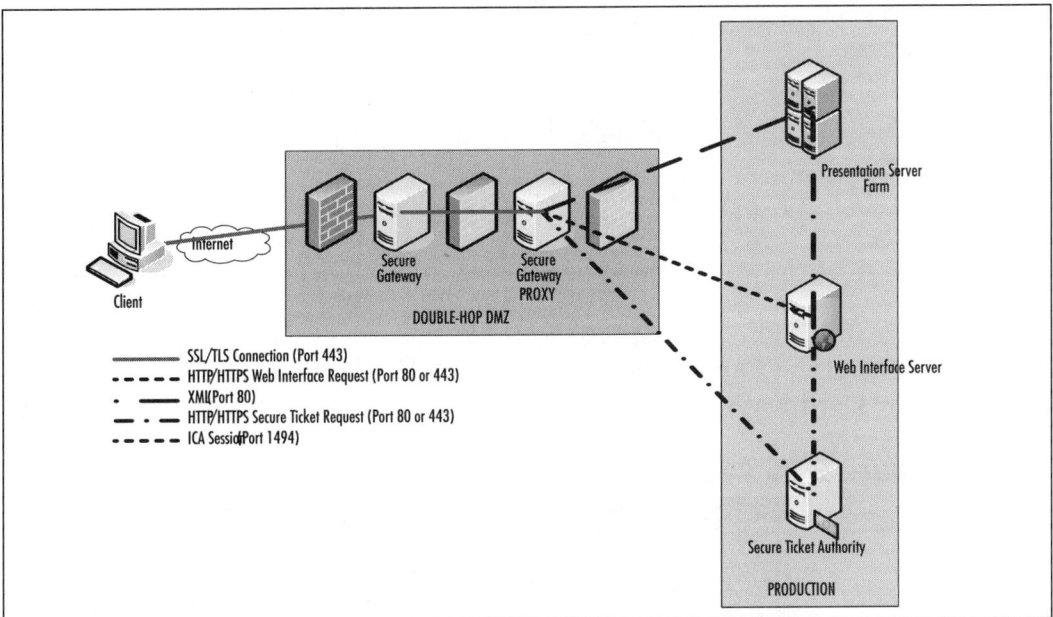

Installation and configuration of the Secure Gateway should begin with the task of obtaining a 128-bit SSL or TLS server certificate. While Secure Gateway can be installed prior to the server certificate being available, the service cannot be configured or function until the certificate has been added. While there are many ways to configure and request a server certificate, we will examine the most common methods, assume we are using a public CA (although we will be using a private CA, as the steps are nearly the same), and obtain an SSL certificate.

To obtain an SSL certificate:

1. The first step in obtaining an SSL server certificate is to generate a request from the Secure Gateway. The easiest way to generate the request is to use the Microsoft Management Console (MMC) and add the Certificates snap-in for the computer account for the local computer. To use this tool, click **Start | Run** and type **MMC**. From the **File** menu of the MMC, select **Add/remove snap-in and** complete the wizard as depicted in Figure 9.24.

Figure 9.24 Adding the Computer Account for the Local Computer's Certificates Snap-in to the MMC

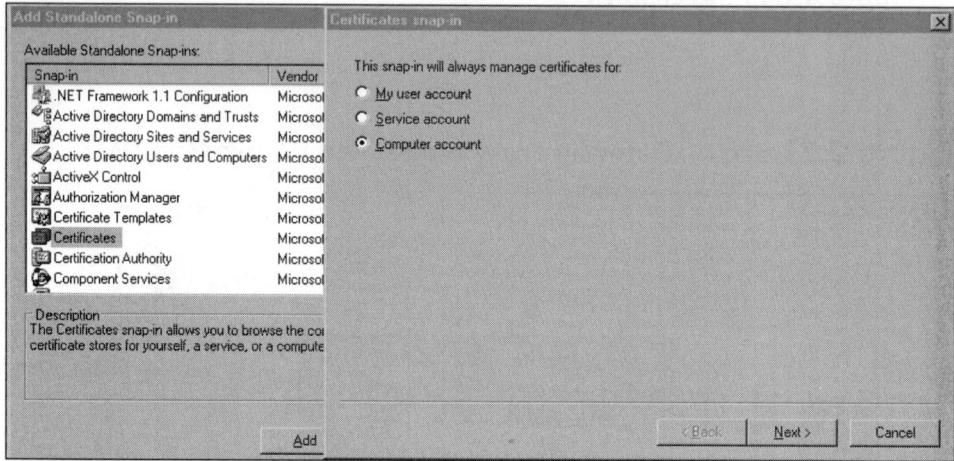

2. Once the Certificates snap-in is added, navigate the structure expanding **Personal** and **Certificates**. Right-click on **Certificates** and select **Request New Certificate** as depicted in Figure 9.25.

Figure 9.25 Requesting a New Certificate

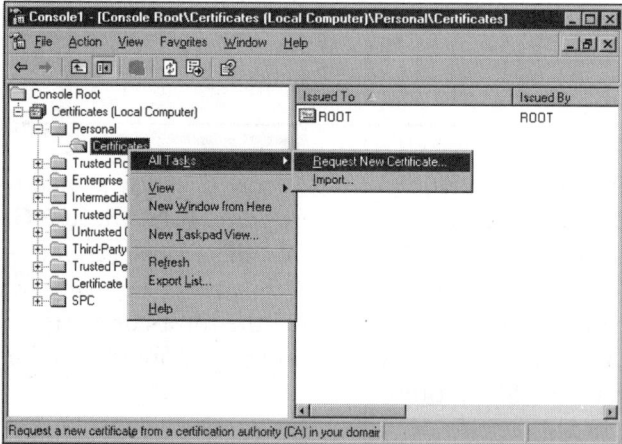

3. From there, complete the wizard with the following specifications:

    ■ **Friendly name** should be descriptive of purpose (but is not tied to DNS resolution).

    ■ **Bit length** minimum of 1024 (this is not the 128-bit key length).

- **Common name** should be the fully qualified domain name (FQDN) (for example, csg.citrix.com) and must be resolvable by DNS.

- Save the request to a file such as C:\CSG_SSL_Request.txt.

4. The next step to obtaining the certificate is to submit the request file's text to a CA. This can be accomplished online or with assistance from the many public CAs that exist. We recommend staying with a "name brand" CA to simplify the end-users' experience (as they will most likely already have the public CA's root certificate).

5. The final step is to add the certificate into the server.

Now that we have a correct SSL or TLS server certificate added to our soon-to-be Secure Gateway, we can begin the actual installation and configuration of the software. Similar to the install of the STA, the configuration will follow immediately after the install and may be completed, or cancelled and finished later. Unlike the STA install, Secure Gateway requires a reboot of the server after installation. Future configuration changes to Secure Gateway do not require a reboot, but do restart the service (breaking all active sessions).

For now, let us turn our attention to the installation and configuration of the Secure Gateway. Once your server platform has met the requirements for installation, we can begin the install by inserting the Components CD that shipped with our Presentation Server software, or you can download the components from the MyCitrix Web site. Begin the installation by running the **CSG_GWY.msi** from the CD.

The following section (and Figures 9.26–9.43) explains the install process and will aid in installing and configuring the Secure Gateway at any point.

Figure 9.26 Secure Gateway Installation Mode and Products to Secure

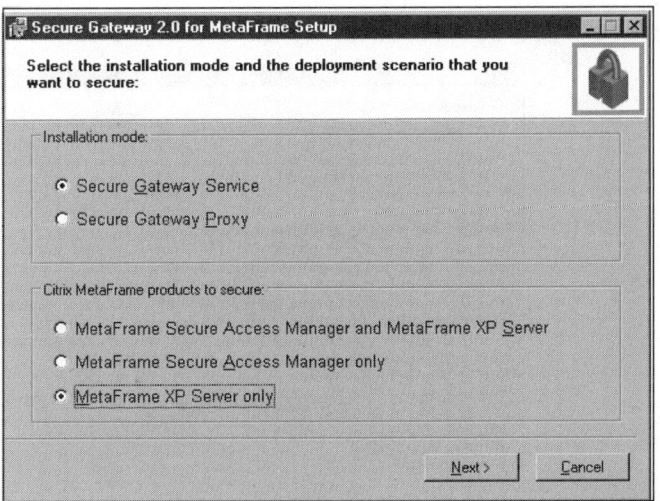

1. First, we are asked some pretty tough installation questions. Installation mode can be either Normal or Proxy. Remember that Proxy is reserved for Double-Hop or complicated DMZ traversal, so most implementations will choose Normal. The Products to Secure section allows us to use Secure Gateway for Presentation Servers (XP servers in the figure), Secure Access Manager servers, or both. For the purposes of this book, we will choose **Presentation Servers only** (Secure Access Manager's configuration can be reviewed by referencing the installation guides that ship with the Presentation Server product. Make the appropriate choices and click **Next**.

Figure 9.27 Secure Gateway Installation

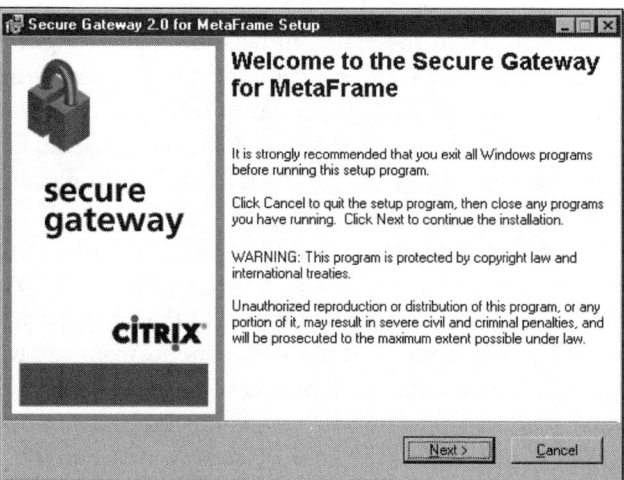

2. Click **Next**.

Figure 9.28 Secure Gateway Installation License Agreement

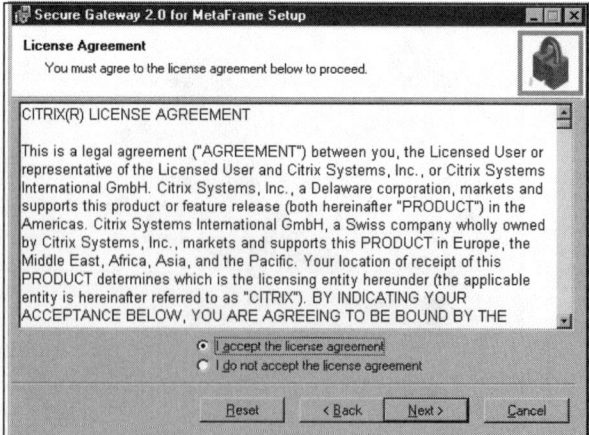

3. Accept the license agreement and click **Next**.

Figure 9.29 Secure Gateway Installation Information

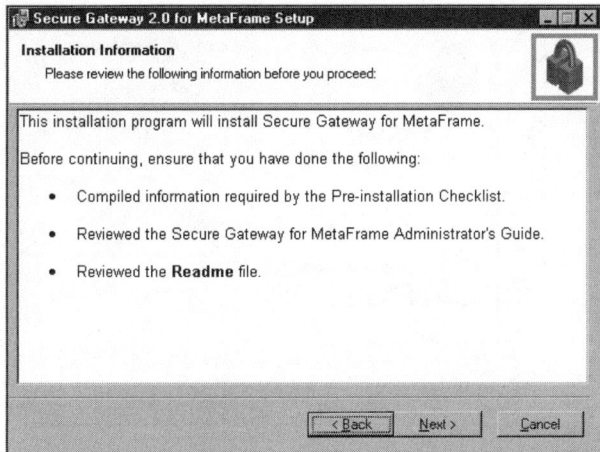

4. Click **Next**.

Figure 9.30 Secure Gateway Installation Path

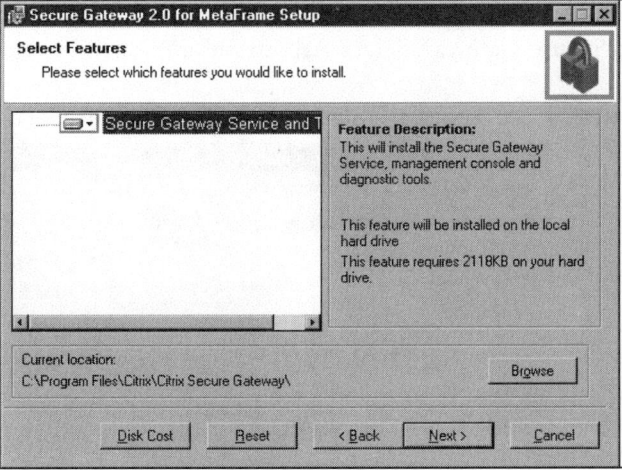

5. The Secure Gateway service is a small hard-disk footprint, consuming slightly more than 2MB. Choose the appropriate path and click **Next**.

Figure 9.31 Secure Gateway Configuration

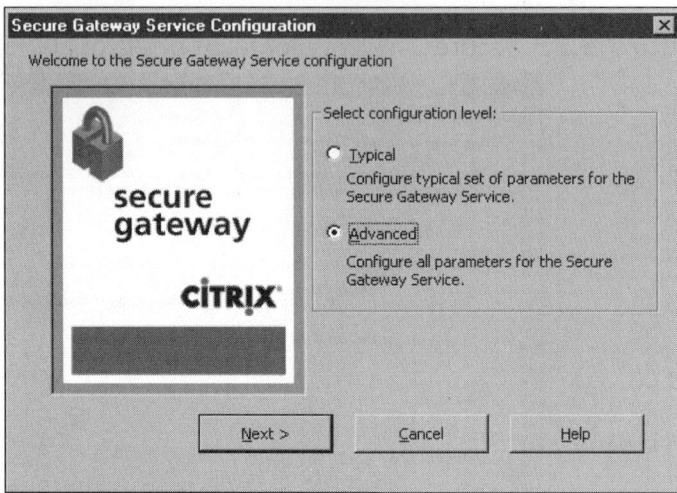

6. Immediately after the installation completes, the configuration wizard is launched. As previously mentioned, this wizard can be cancelled and resumed at a later time (especially handy if building components while waiting on an SSL certificate). We can choose Typical or Advanced; for our purposes, we will choose **Advanced**, as we can see all the configuration options available to us with Secure Gateway. Select **Advanced** and click **Next**.

Figure 9.32 Secure Gateway Configuration Certificate Selection

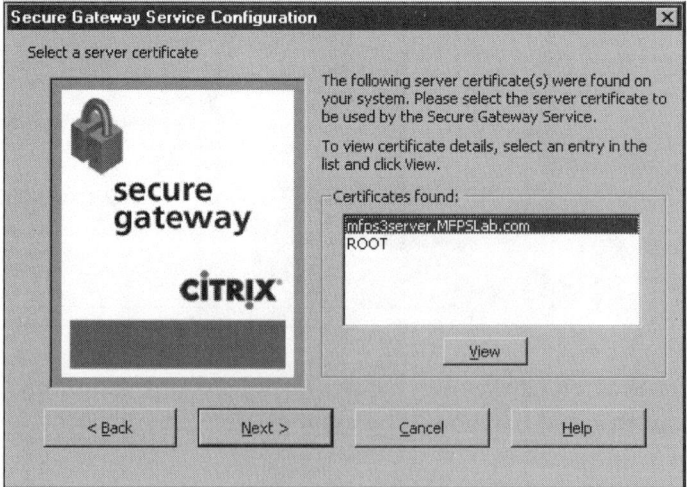

7. At this point, we must select the server certificate that we added to the Secure Gateway server. If multiple certificates are available, take care to select the appropriate one and click **Next**. If there are no certificates listed, then none are added to the server on which you are attempting to install Secure Gateway. At least one certificate must be listed to continue with the configuration wizard.

Figure 9.33 Secure Gateway Configuration Protocol and Cipher Suite Selection

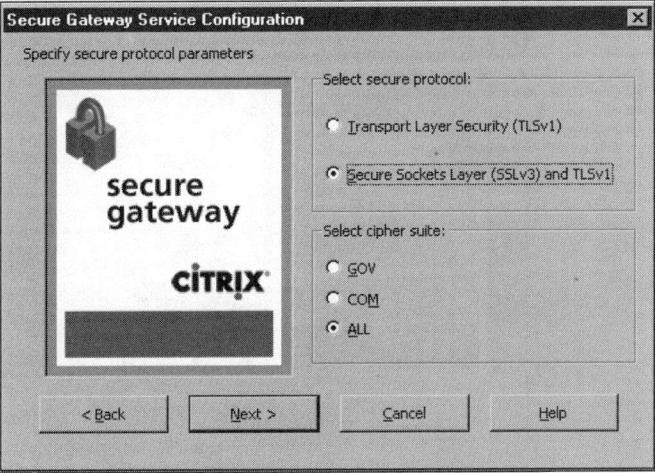

8. Select the protocol standard that you want to support based on your certificate and security needs. Most implementations will choose SSL and TLS. In addition, select the cipher suite to be used and click **Next**.

Figure 9.34 Secure Gateway Configuration Inbound Client Connections

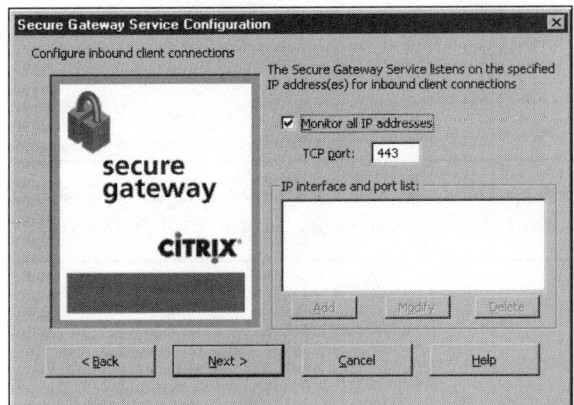

9. The default behavior of the Secure Gateway is to monitor all IP addresses (thereby all network cards with an IP stack bound to them) for incoming connections. The default SSL-based port is 443. If your server performs roles other than Secure Gateway or has multiple network cards and you want to limit those that Secure Gateway monitors, remove the check for **Monitor all IP addresses** and configure the correct information in the **IP Interface and port list**. In most deployments, the defaults are correct so we will simply click **Next**.

Figure 9.35 Secure Gateway Configuration Outbound Connections Security

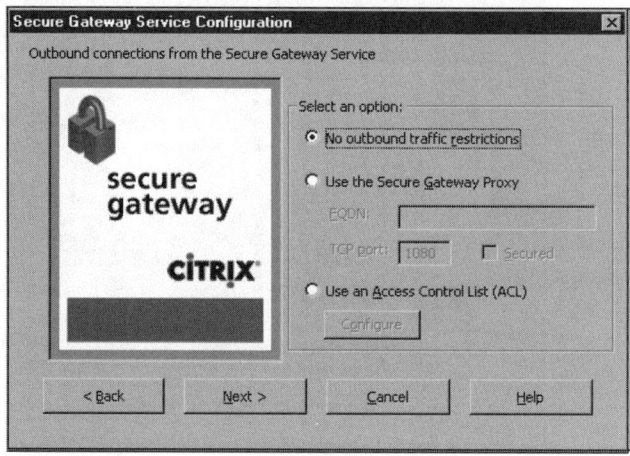

10. In a simple single-hop DMZ and most typical implementations, we will choose **No outbound traffic restriction**s. However, if you have a double-hop DMZ, then you would specify the upstream Secure Gateway that is running in Proxy mode. Additionally, Secure Gateway has the capability to restrict which IP address, subnets, or networks from which to accept traffic; this would be configured with the **Use an access control list** option. Again, for most typical deployments, select **Default** and click **Next**.

NOTE

In a double-hop DMZ, ACLs can still be implemented, but they would be created on the upstream Secure Gateway server that is operating in Proxy mode.

Figure 9.36 Secure Gateway Configuration STA Information

11.   In this window, we must list the STAs in the order in which the Secure Gateway is to contact them. To configure, click **Add**.

Figure 9.37 Secure Gateway Configuration Add STA Details

12.   Specify the FQDN (such as ctxsa.mfpslab.com), the path to the scripts directory and dll (the defaults are typically fine), and choose whether to communicate with the STA using HTTP or HTTPS (and the port number if different from the defaults). Click **OK**.

Figure 9.38 Secure Gateway Configuration STA Details Confirmation

13. Once the STA is entered, the Identifier will be "queried" from the STA. You

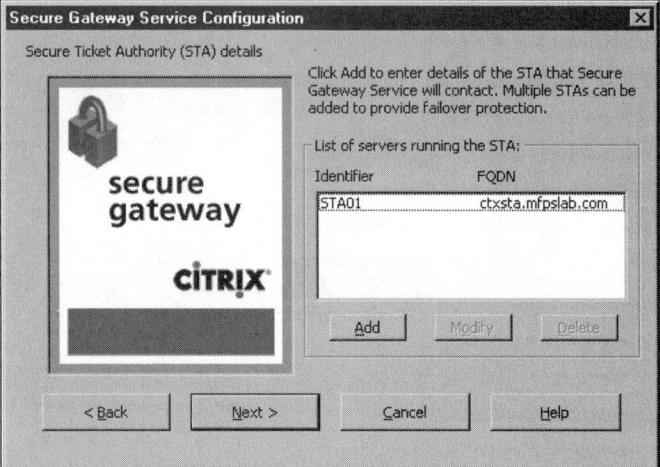

can add multiple STAs as previously mentioned, but they are contacted in the order in which they appear in the list. If the first in the list fails, it then goes to the second in the list, and so on. Confirm the configuration and click **Next**.

Figure 9.39 Secure Gateway Configuration Connection Parameters

14. The default connection parameters are typically fine. However, some environ-

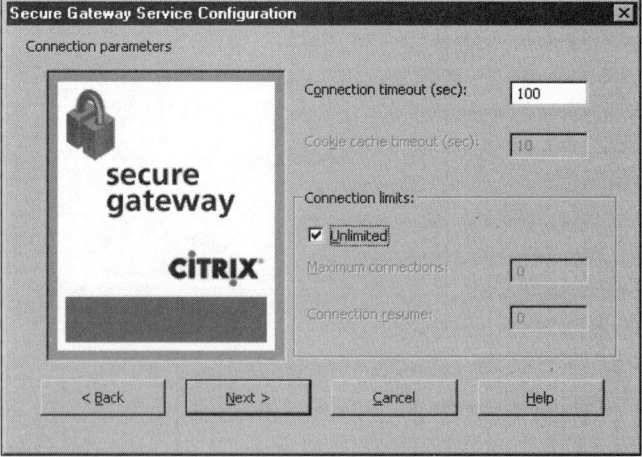

ments want to change the **Connection limits** from Unlimited to some other number more suitable for the hardware in use. If Unlimited is unchecked, you can specify a **Maximum connections** and a **Connection resume**. The

Maximum connections is just that, the value at which the server denies connections. The **Connection resume** should be about 10 percent below the maximum. The **Connection resume** is the value that the connection count must decrease to (once the maximum count has been reached) prior to new connections being accepted). Make your selections and click **Next**.

Figure 9.40 Secure Gateway Configuration Logging Exclusions

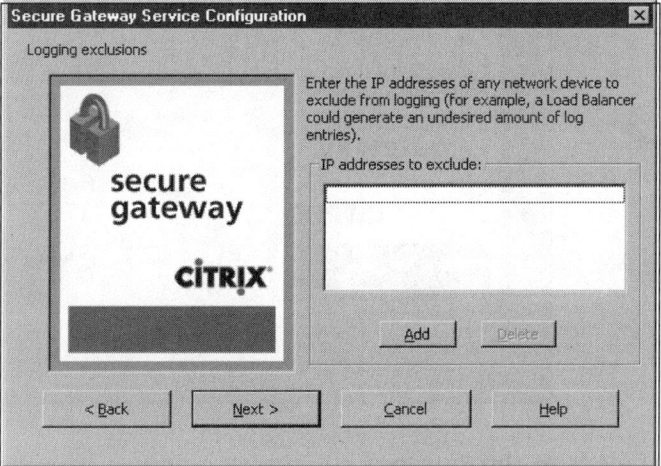

15. Logging exclusions allow us to ignore certain "chatty" devices that would otherwise generate a volume of useless entries in an otherwise usable log. Add those IP addresses to exclude and click **Next.**

Figure 9.41 Secure Gateway Configuration Logging Parameters

16. All logging for Secure Gateway is written into the server's Application log in the Event Viewer tool, and all events except informational ones are written. Set the value as you see fit and click **Next**.

Figure 9.42 Secure Gateway Configuration for Web Interface Server

17. If you install Web Interface on the same server as the Secure Gateway, choose

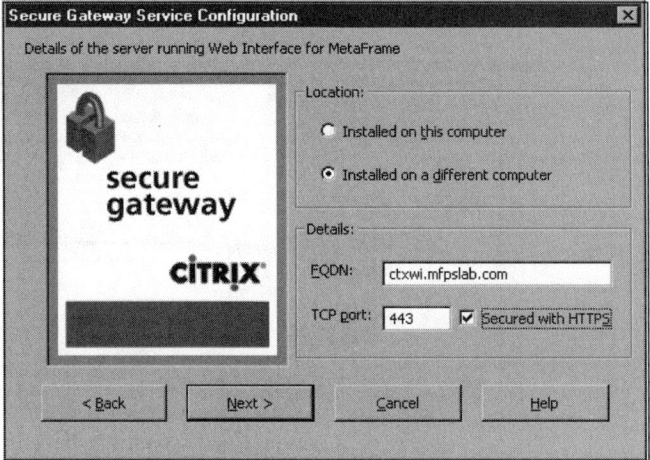

Installed on this computer. Otherwise, choose **Installed on a different computer** and specify the server's name. If the Web Interface server also has a SSL server certificate, you may opt to secure the communications between the Secure Gateway server and the Web server using HTTPS. Specify your server's name and TCP port and click **Next**.

Figure 9.43 Secure Gateway Configuration Completion

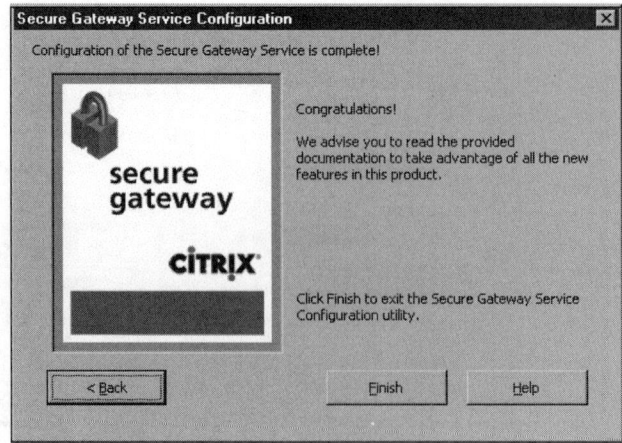

18. As previously stated, the initial install of Secure Gateway will require a reboot at the end of the configuration/installation. Subsequent reconfigurations will not require the reboot of the server, but will require the Secure Gateway service to restart, terminating all current connections. Upon completion of the service configuration wizard, click **Finish**.

After installation and configuration, Secure Gateway provides two tools for monitoring and maintaining the service. The first tool is the Secure Gateway Diagnostics. This tool, while very simple in function, can provide a wealth of information on configuration troubleshooting and issue resolution. By simply opening this tool, it will provide a detailed report of all components of the Secure Gateway service, including its capability to successfully communicate with other services, such as Web Interface. Additionally, the tool can generate reports that can be mailed to your support vendor or Citrix for further analysis and troubleshooting. Figure 9.44 demonstrates the tool.

Figure 9.44 Secure Gateway Diagnostics

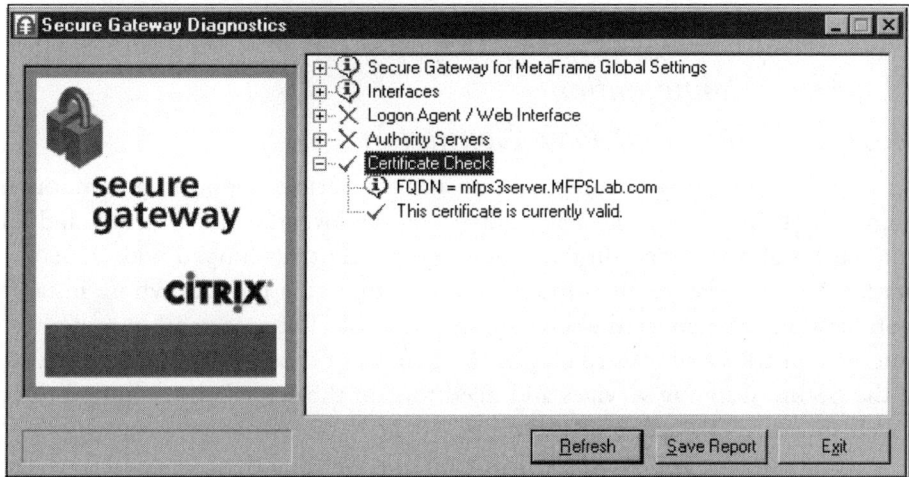

The second tool provided to manage and monitor the performance of the Secure Gateway is actually a preconfigured series of MMC snap-ins called the Secure Gateway Management Console (SGMC). The SGMC contains reporting, logging, and performance analysis from a single seat. While configuration of this service occurs through the previously detailed Secure Gateway Service Configuration tool as demonstrated at the end of installation, the SGMC is primarily an information and troubleshooting tool. Figure 9.45 provides a glimpse of the features contained in this tool.

Figure 9.45 Secure Gateway Management Console

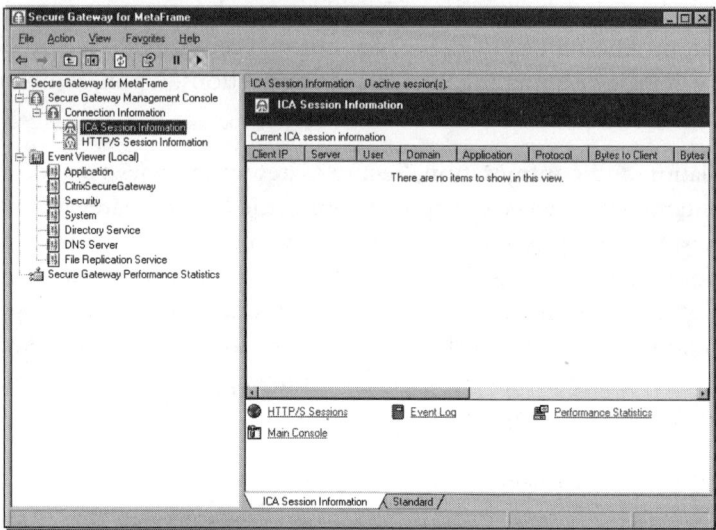

Web Interface Configuration to Allow for Secure Gateway Connections

The last step in configuring Secure Gateway and the various supporting components is to configure Web Interface to leverage our newly deployed Secure Gateway and STA. Web Interface is also included on the Components CD that shipped with your Presentation Server software. Web Interface is a feature-rich product whose installation and configuration were covered elsewhere in this book. The information presented on Web Interface in this chapter is solely for the benefit of those who want to take advantage of the Secure Gateway services and need to gain the knowledge required to configure Web Interface for such integration.

We start by opening **Internet Explorer** on our Web Interface server and navigating to **http://localhost/citrix/metaframe/wiadmin**. From the Web Interface console, we will be able to configure all the options necessary to integrate Web Interface into a newly deployed Secure Gateway solution. The first step is to expand the **DMZ settings** in the left-hand column and select the **Secure Gateway Support** option. In the right-hand column, we must enter the FQDN of our Secure Gateway server. The name entered should match the name on the server certificate used to install the Secure Gateway. The default port is 443 and should be correct unless you modified the port used by the Secure Gateway service. The next section requires us to enter the Secure Ticket Authority server information. Simply replace the **<SERVER>** section of the URL and click **Add**. Note that if you want to use SSL and have added an SSL server certificate to your STA, also change the protocol from **HTTP** to **HTTPS** before clicking **Add**. Your information should be similar to that shown in Figure 9.46.

Figure 9.46 Sample Secure Gateway Support Configuration for Web Interface

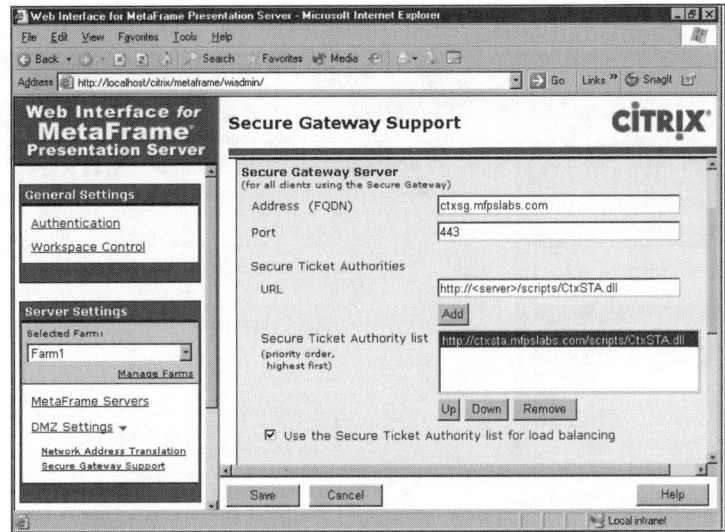

At that point, click **Save** at the bottom of the right-hand column.

Up to this point, we have given the Web Interface server the information it needs to contact the STA and direct session to the Secure Gateway, but we haven't configured the Web Interface server to know "when" to send sessions through the Secure Gateway. On the left side under **DMZ Settings**, select **Network Address Translation**. On the right, the console should change to the **Network Address Translation Settings**. Network Address Translation (NAT) Settings tends to be one of the most confusing sections of the Web Interface console. In the simplest terms, we configure this section to aid client connections to "connect" to the right name or IP based on the location of the client. In other words, if the client is inside the network and capable of "finding" the Presentation Server farm(s) through normal routing, we really don't need to "assist" the client in finding the correct path. However, if a client is outside the network, the client device may need assistance in working its way back inside.

We will use a scenario to help us better understand this configuration section. Suppose our internal network IP addressing scheme is 10.0.0.0/24 (or we are using a 255.255.255.0 mask). We know that internally the clients do not need help getting from where they are to the Presentation Servers. However, our users working remotely need some assistance. Therefore, follow the rule, "Start with what you know, and leave the unknown for last." This rule is exactly what we will use to configure these NAT settings; namely, the stuff we "know" will go in the **Specific address translation settings** section of this page. We "know" that the 10.0.0.0 network should go here and use normal translation. Therefore, in that section under **Address**, we would enter **10.0.0.0**, under

Mask, we would enter **255.255.255.0**, select **Normal**, and click **Add**. The result of the information entered should be similar to Figure 9.47.

Figure 9.47 Specific Address Translation Settings

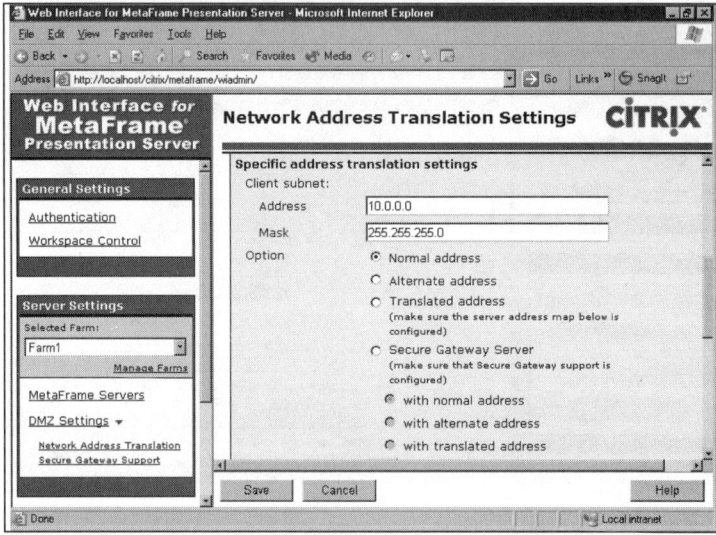

The **Specific address translation settings** map should now contain the settings as depicted in Figure 9.48.

Figure 9.48 Specific Address Translation Settings Map

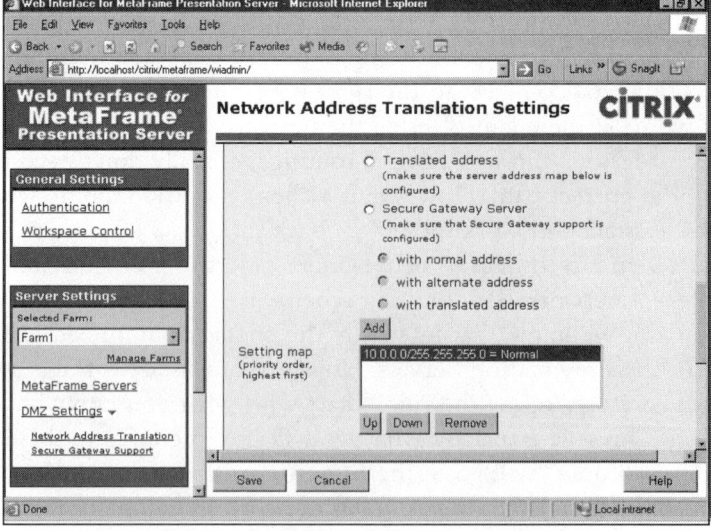

The final step is the "unknown." Since we have given the Web Interface directions on how to handle what is known, we now have tell it what to do with what is not known, namely the external or remote users. It would be virtually impossible to enter the network IDs for the entire Internet, so instead we use the **Default address translation** setting to cover all the "unknowns" and what-ifs. In this case, we would set this to **Secure Gateway Server** (leave the remaining options set to normal). Click **Save** at the bottom of the screen and then click **Apply changes** back in the main console window. At this point, we are using Secure Gateway.

Let's further expound upon our scenario for better understanding. We started with what we "knew"—the internal IP scheme—and applied that to the specific settings. We then took the "unknown" and told the Web Interface server how to handle that under the default settings. The result would be that if you were connecting from a client device with a 10.0.0.0 network IP, you would be directed to the Presentation Servers directly and would not use the Secure Gateway. If however, you were a client with any other network ID, you would be sent through the Secure Gateway, as there would be no specific settings rule, so the default would be used. You can now see how we could expand upon this by continuing to edit the specific rules with more "knowns" to allow for better control over how we communicate with our Presentation Servers.

Summary

In this chapter, we examined the aspects of providing simple secure remote access to our Presentation Server farm(s) leveraging various technologies. We explored the pros and cons to the various solutions and discussed the methods to implement most of these solutions.

We began with a thorough review of the bundled feature of encryption also known as Secure ICA. We explored the various ways of using Secure ICA from client-side settings to server-side. On the server side, we reviewed the options of connection settings, published applications, and Citrix policy to enforce the use of Secure ICA.

In the next section of the chapter, we briefly spoke of the newly arrived Access Gateway and the promise of the future that this device will bring to simplified and secure remote computing. Although the Access Gateway is a new player on the block, we believe that it will shortly replace the Secure Gateway as the primary method to provide secure access to remote users.

In the final section of this chapter, we reviewed the complete (and arguably complex) solution of Secure Gateway. We started with the planning, requirements, installation, and configuration of the Secure Ticket Authority (STA). We then planned for, installed, and configured the Secure Gateway itself, paying special attention to the areas that are typically stumbling blocks along the way. Finally, we configured the Web Interface to leverage our newly created Secure Gateway solution, using a scenario of internal and external users to guide our decision-making process.

In conclusion, user communities and corporations demand a seamless, simple, and secure remote access solution for their remote offices, work-from-home users, and mobile workforce. The Citrix Access Suite—in particular, Presentation Server, Web Interface, and the Secure Gateway—can meet that requirement.

Solutions Fast Track

Various Methods to Secure Communications between Client and Server

☑ Options include:

- Network Address Translation (NAT)

- Port Address Translation (PAT)

- Proxy Servers

- HTTP(s)

- SSL Relay

- Secure ICA

- Access Gateway

- Secure Gateway

☑ Secure Gateway is the most popular currently when paired with Web Interface or Secure Access Manager

Citrix Secure Gateway

☑ The defacto standard for allowing, controlling and securing access to your Citrix Access Infrastructure

☑ Secures traffic using industry standard SSL or TLS encryption

☑ Allows for simple and reliable access to applications and internal web resources (when partnered with Secure Access Manager)

Citrix Access Gateway

☑ Hardware-based Hybrid SSL-VPN solution

☑ Easy to implement

☑ Policy to control connections and access to network from clients that don't meet minimum requirements such as Anti-virus software

Frequently Asked Questions

The following Frequently Asked Questions, answered by the authors of this book, are designed to both measure your understanding of the concepts presented in this chapter and to assist you with real-life implementation of these concepts. To have your questions about this chapter answered by the author, browse to **www.syngress.com/solutions** and click on the **"Ask the Author"** form. You will also gain access to thousands of other FAQs at ITFAQnet.com.

Q: You mentioned that the Secure Ticket Authority is a "light" service. Could I run this on my Web Interface server(s) to save on hardware costs?

A: The answer to this question is typically yes; however, security purists would argue that the Secure Ticket Authority should be on a separate server. The service is indeed light, so light that for some clients we have taken workstation grade hardware and built two STAs (to provide the redundancy that the lower grade hardware cannot) that work just fine for many clients. At that point, you are really only out the cost of the operating system.

Q: I understand that Secure Gateway requires an SSL or TLS certificate. In an effort to save money, could I use my internal private certificate authority to generate the Secure Gateway's server certificate?

A: Yes. However, you must consider who the "customers" of this Secure Gateway will be. If you will be constructing the Secure Gateway as a remote access solution for your workforce and daily work use for the sales laptops you deploy to the field, then it can work well (as you can preinstall or add later the root certificate from your private CA). If, however, you are going to allow *any* device to connect, then distributing your internal private CA's root certificate may become a challenge. Cinsider using a public CA for a more "supportable" solution.

Q: The hardware requirements for the Secure Ticket Authority and the Secure Gateway seem very low. What would you consider the primary components for each when considering hardware builds?

A: The Secure Ticket Authority's primary consideration is memory, meaning available physical memory. The Secure Gateway's primary needs are network throughput and processor (for encryption and decryption).

Q: You mentioned that the Access Gateway might someday supplant the Secure Gateway in its role as remote access gateway. What are Citrix's plans concerning this?

A: As of today, Citrix Systems, Inc. plans to add all the features that Secure Gateway has to the Access Gateway. Citrix has stated publicly that the Secure Gateway will continue to be developed and maintained. There are currently no announced plans to discontinue the Secure Gateway solution.

Chapter 10

Citrix MetaFrame Password Manager

Solutions in this chapter:

- How Does Password Manager Work?
- Deploying Password Manager
- Configuring Application-Specific Settings
- Running the Password Manager Agent

☑ Summary

☑ Solutions Fast Track

☑ Frequently Asked Questions

Introduction

Identity and access management are hot topics in most organizations today. Few periodicals or Web sites of a business or technical nature do not reference network security, identity, and access management. If kids can hack into school systems and banks, how secure are organizations, especially the small to medium-sized ones without extravagant resources for security experts?

This is one of the major reasons why password policies have changed dramatically from what they were 10 years ago. Some of you may remember when passwords were not such a big deal; you just typed in "abc123" or something just as simple and you were through. Frequent password changes were unheard of. Ah, the good old days before hackers and Sarbanes-Oxley. Well, that has all changed. For years now, security specialists have warned us about how important it is to secure our networks and data. We were and still are told that we must have stronger security and more stringent password requirements. The new policies, although a nuisance, are intended to protect the organization and the organization's intellectual property from would-be hackers and corporate espionage.

The result has been difficult for users and has created more work for administrative staff. Even worse, it may have ultimately weakened password security. Statistics show that the average workplace user can have up to 30 passwords to remember! In the old days, that may have been simple, you would just use your favorite pet's name for every password. Now, with more sophisticated software and security in place, users must be much more creative. Passwords must be in upper- *and* lowercase letters, include numbers and special characters, and cannot be less than a given number of characters. In addition, hackers and hacking software has become so sophisticated that even the passwords we once thought to be secure are no longer. This makes passwords more difficult to remember, and since not all applications will accept the same requirements, users may have many, very different passwords. The impact on support staff has meant spending more time resetting forgotten passwords, and/or unlocking user accounts, and assisting users in remembering what password goes where. From the user's perspective, frequent calls to the Help Desk is not a good option as it reduces productivity. In many cases, the solution for users is to write the passwords down on scraps of paper or Post-It Notes. Unless an organization is extremely diligent and can afford to hire "password Nazis," passwords may be found in plain sight or hidden in obvious places such as under keyboards.

Notes from the Underground…

From the Trenches…

Imagine this scenario; a hacker is hired by an organization's competitor. The hacker is a young, very normal looking person but very computer savvy. The plan is to insert the hacker into the organization as a cleaning person. The arrangements are made and the hacker has hours alone in the offices, where, he or she can easily discover passwords without ever having to "hack" any system. Information is retrieved, passed along, and no one is the wiser. No one would ever suspect a mere cleaning person.

For reasons such as these and others, a wave of new software products have hit the market, all directed at either keeping your collective passwords in a safe place or automatically providing your passwords to the requesting applications. Citrix was no exception, and in September 2003 they added Citrix MetaFrame Password Manager to the MetaFrame Access Suite of products. Their latest release, version 2.5, offers new capabilities and enhanced application support. In the sections to follow, we hope to provide you with an understanding of how Password Manager works, and how to deploy it and manage passwords in your environment.

How Does Password Manager Work?

What exactly does MetaFrame Password Manager do? In short, it provides both password security and single sign-on (SSO) capability to not only MetaFrame Access Suite products, but applications installed locally on PCs, those accessed via the Web, applications running on other platforms such as UNIX and mainframes, even proprietary applications. Users enter their password once and Password Manager takes over and automatically feeds the required authentication information into the password-protected applications. Password Manager can also automatically detect password change requests and without user intervention, supply a new, appropriate password to the requesting application. All password-related events are monitored and logged as well. From an administrative viewpoint, Password Manager reduces the amount of support time and administrative tasks related to password changes, resets, and lockouts. From the user's point of view, it simplifies the process, increasing productivity and greatly decreasing frustration.

Implementing Password Manager is fairly straightforward, installation requires minimal effort, but to configure the individual applications and policies, you will need to do your homework. Once you have installed Password Manager Console on a centralized machine and configured the application-specific settings and policies, the client or Agent piece can be pushed out automatically to the MetaFrame Presentation servers and the users' desktops. With a bit of thoughtful planning, Password Manager can be up and running within a few days and perhaps changing the users view of the entire IT department!

In the following sections, we take a look at the key features of Password Manager, how to install and deploy Password Manager, and how it can help increase security within your organization. First, let's look at the pieces that comprise Password Manager, where they are installed, and how to go about installing them.

Password Manager Components

MetaFrame Password Manager is comprised of three main components:

- The MetaFrame Password Manager Console
- The MetaFrame Password Manager Agent
- The MetaFrame Password Manager Credential Store

The MetaFrame Password Manager Console

The Password Management Console is the administrative tool used to manage all aspects of password management. The console includes wizards to assist you in creating password policies, configuring application support, and managing Password Management Agents and credentials. The Console also provides the means to create the Central Credential Store that contains application and Agent configurations.

Figure 10.1 shows the Password Manager Console. In the left pane, the Console has five nodes:

- Applications
- Password Policies
- Password Sharing Groups
- Agent Settings
- Directory

To specify or display options for a node, select the node in the left pane and either view or specify parameters for the selected node in the right pane of the Console.

Figure 10.1 The Password Manager Console

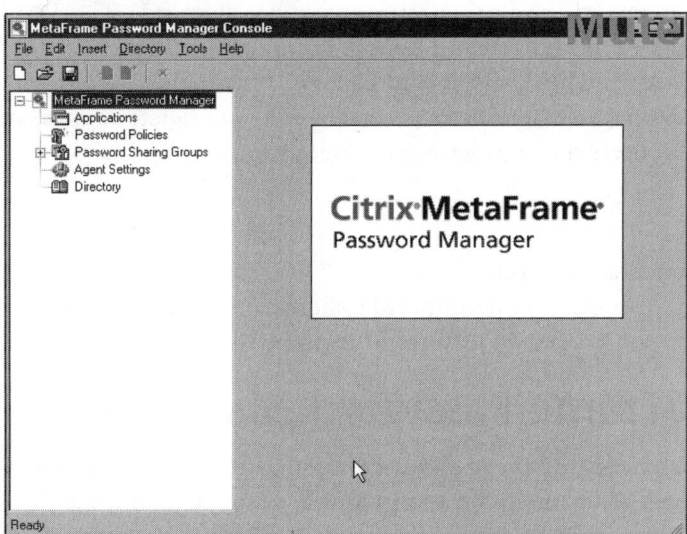

The Application Node

The Application node allows you to add Windows, Web, or host applications *identifiers* stored in application definitions. Windows, Web, and host-based applications all require different identifiers and must be defined separately. Password Manager provides us with a list of commonly used Windows and Web application definitions, but you can easily add your own or visit http://apps.citrix.com/cdn to check for application definitions created by other MetaFrame Password Manager users.

The Password Policy Node

The Password Policy node allows you to create policies that control password length, and what type of characters comprise a valid password. Password Manager ensures that your password policies are enforced throughout your organization.

Password Sharing Groups

A Password Sharing Group is a group of applications that share a common password. For instance, if your company policy allows for Windows logons and host-based systems to use the same password and a change is made to one, any password changes are propagated to all systems or applications using the same password.

Agent Settings

Numerous Agent settings can be configured to suit the security needs of your organization. We will take a closer look at the settings available later in this chapter, but this is where you will configure default policies, change synchronization settings, allow or disable viewing of passwords, and other settings for the client side. The Password Manager Agent can be used on both local and remote computers, whether or not they are connected to the network. The Agent features an easily accessible System Tray menu for easy access, a Logon Manager where users can view, edit, and delete logons, and a new logon Wizard that walks users through setting up logons for new applications.

Directory

The Directory node allows you to connect to a centralized Credential Store to synchronize and distribute application definitions, policies, and first-time use lists. We will also delve farther into the Directory features in sections to come.

The MetaFrame Password Manager Agent

The Agent is the client-side piece and is configured to interface with password-protected applications. When an application requests authentication, the Agent intercepts the request, locates the correct credentials, and passes them to the requesting application, all without user intervention. The Agent receives its configuration settings from the Credential Store where entries from the Console are stored and synchronized. In a MetaFrame Presentation server farm, the Agent is installed on each server that publishes applications requiring authentication. If individual PCs or laptops are used, the Agent is installed locally to provide authentication to locally installed applications. See Figure 10.2 for a common deployment scenario.

Figure 10.2 A Common Password Manager Deployment Scenario

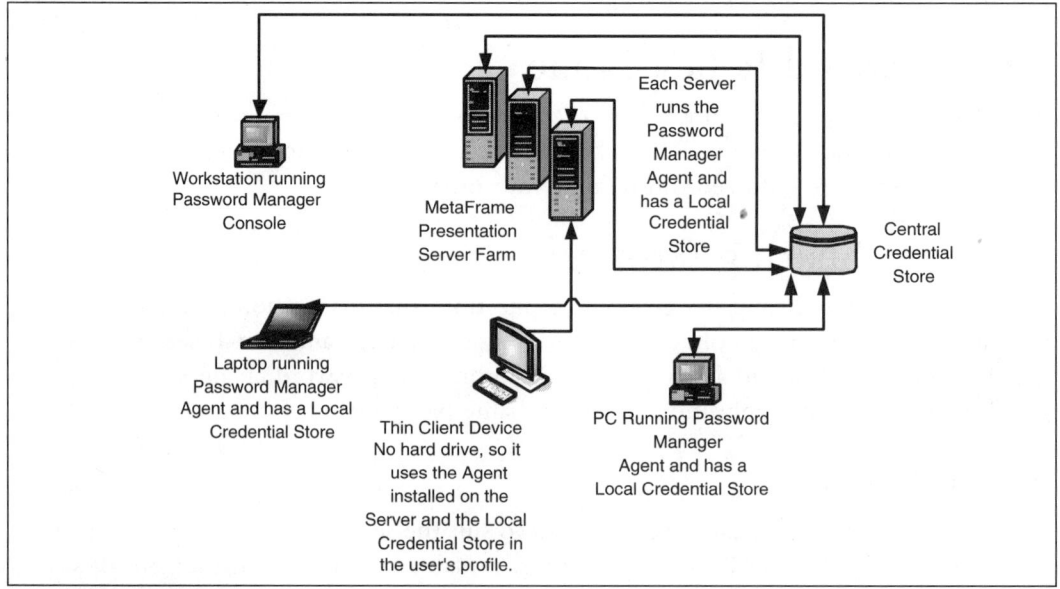

The Password Manager Credential Store

The Credential Store is just what it sounds like, a repository that stores security policies, application definitions, and credentials. Credential Stores are located both on the local machine in a binary file located in the user's profile and on a central Credential Store encrypted database. The Credential Store can reside in either an Active Directory Container or on a centralized NTFS file share. Configuration information and credentials are synchronized between the local and central stores, ensuring that both stores hold the same information. The central Credential Store is the synchronization point, and in the latest version can even use Novell public folders as the share point.

Deploying Password Manager

As always, the most important part of your deployment is the planning stage. Plan your deployment and make sure you have all the facts and figures you need before beginning the actual installation. Nothing is more frustrating to an administrator than working on a project all day only to find that you have not configured it correctly. Planning your deployment will involve a number of tasks, some you will be familiar with, and others a bit different from what you may have previously encountered. Once you have the planning taken care of, you have a series of tasks to perform before you can deploy Password Manager. Figure 10.3 provides a visual representation of the tasks that you will perform to install and configure Password Manager in your environment.

Figure 10.3 MetaFrame Password Manager Installation Process

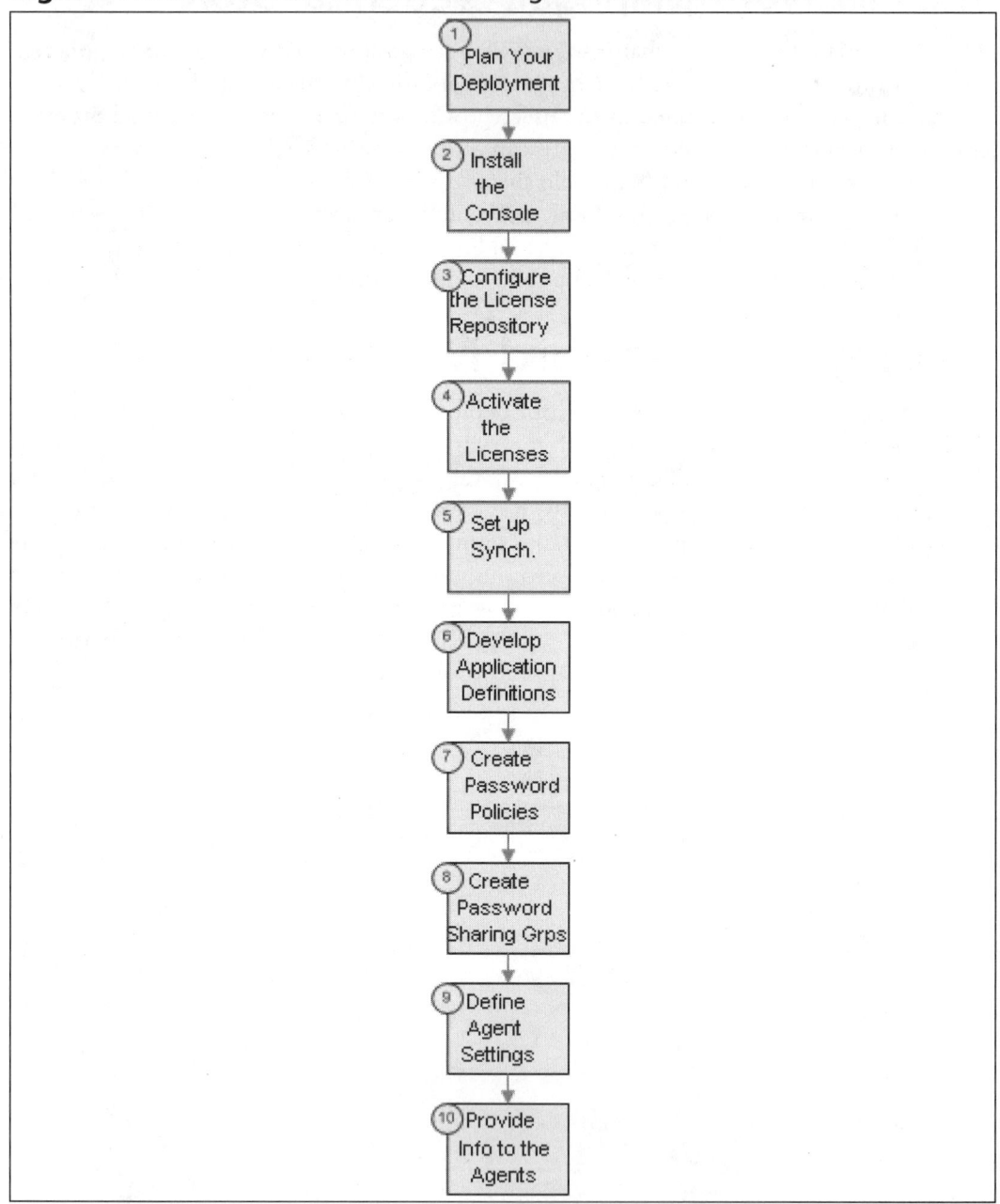

Planning Your Deployment

The first and most important step in planning your deployment is to analyze your environment. Take a close look at the applications used and how the users access those applications. Next, examine the hardware available and the applications hosted by each. Password Manager, like any other piece of software, has certain hardware and software requirements that must be met before it will run properly. The MetaFrame Password Manager Console requires the following hardware and software resources:

- 20MB (approximately) of RAM
- 20MB (approximately) of disk space
- 30MB (approximately) per user on a file share or Active Directory partition
- Microsoft .NET Framework version 1.1
- Microsoft Windows Installer version 2.0
- MetaFrame XP with SP3
- MetaFrame Presentation Server 3.0
- Internet Explorer 6.0 or later

Operating systems supported:

- Windows 2000 Server with SP4
- Windows 2000 Advanced Server with SP4
- Windows 2000 Pro with SP4
- Windows Server 2003 (32 bit)
- Windows XP Pro with SP1 (32 bit)

As you can see, the Console can be installed on either a workstation or a server, and Citrix strongly recommends that you install the Console *outside* of the MetaFrame Presentation server farm. The only caveat is that the operating system the Console resides on should match the operating system used on the servers where the applications are published or match the operating system of the machines where the Agent is deployed.

The MetaFrame Password Agent has its own hardware and software requirements. To properly install the Agent, the following requirements must be met:

- 5MB (approximately) of RAM
- 10MB (approximately) of disk space

Operating systems supported:

- Windows 2000 Server with SP4

- Windows 2000 Advanced Server with SP4

- Windows 2000 Pro with SP4

- Windows Server 2003 (32 bit)

- Windows XP Pro with SP1 (32 bit)

- Windows NT Workstation with SP6

Analyzing Your Environment and Collecting Application Information

Before you can begin configuring Password Manager, you must analyze your organization's environment, and locate and record the applications used, whether on local PCs or laptops, as published applications, Web-based applications, or from host-based systems. Application definitions must be specified within the Password Manager Console for every application that requires user authentication. All pertinent information regarding each application must be recorded, including user ID fields, password fields, domain names, executable names, and URLs. Without the proper identifying information, Password Manager will not be able to supply the credentials needed to authenticate the user automatically.

The GINA Chain

For those of you unfamiliar with the term, the *GINA* or *Graphical Identification and Authentication* is the Microsoft component that controls the Ctrl-Alt-Del dialog box used to log in to Windows. The Microsoft GINA is called MSGINA.DLL. When another application requiring authentication, such as the MetaFrame Access Suite is installed on Windows, it requires its own custom GINA.DLL to authenticate. The problem is that Microsoft operating systems can only load one GINA.DLL. The solution is to form a "chain" of GINAs, each calling the next.

Notes from the Underground…

Don't Break the Chain!

If for some reason the chain is disrupted or broken, it will prevent users from logging in and may prevent Windows from loading. Many times it will result in the Blue Screen of Death (BSOD) and a Kmode_exception_not_handled in win32k.sys error. To prevent this from happening, you may need to install or uninstall and reinstall software in a specific order to preserve the proper chaining. When using Password Manager Agent, it must be installed last so that it is called *first* by the Winlogon process.

Installing the Password Manager Console

As mentioned earlier, Citrix recommends that you install the Console on a machine that is outside of the MetaFrame farm. It can reside on a server or workstation, but the operating system must match that of the servers used in the MetaFrame farm or the machines for the Agents.

The installation of Password Manager looks much like the installation of other MetaFrame products discussed earlier in this book, so you should be very familiar with the format. When Autorun first starts, the Welcome Screen allows you to choose the product you want to install (see Figure 10.4).

Figure 10.4 MetaFrame Password Manager Autorun Screen

1. From this screen, you can choose to install the Agent, the Console, or the Console Documentation. For our purposes here, let's select **MetaFrame Password Manager Console**.

NOTE

If the Microsoft .Net Framework version 1.1 is not already installed, you will be prompted to install it. Luckily, Citrix has provided a copy on the Password Manager CD-ROM under \Support\DotNet11\dotnetfix.exe. Once you have installed the .Net Framework, you can continue with the installation.

2. On the Password Manager Welcome screen, click **Next** to begin the installation.

3. The next screen offers you a chance to accept the licensing agreement. Agree and click **Next** to continue.

4. Next, you can opt to do a Typical or Custom installation. A Typical installation installs all options for you, but for curiosity's sake and to see for ourselves what a "typical" installation entails, we'll select **Custom**, and then click **Next** to continue.

5. The Custom Setup menu allows you to install both the MetaFrame Password Manager Console and the Templates that include additional support for applications. From this screen you can also choose to accept the default installation path, or install the Password Manager Console in a different location. Once you have made your decisions, click **Next** to continue (see Figure 10.5).

Figure 10.5 MetaFrame Password Manager Console Custom Setup

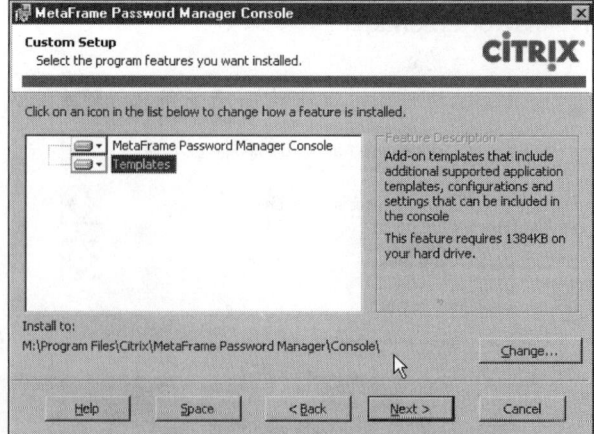

6. The next screen lets you know that the application is ready to install. Click **Install** to initialize the installation process.

7. When the installation is complete, the Installation Wizard will inform you that you have successfully installed the product and prompt you to click **Finish**.

Password Manager Licensing

The first time you open the Password Manager Console, you will be warned that you must configure your license repository before you can use MetaFrame Password Manager. Figure 10.6 shows the warning dialog box that opens when you first attempt to run the Console.

Figure 10.6 Password Manager Console License Warning

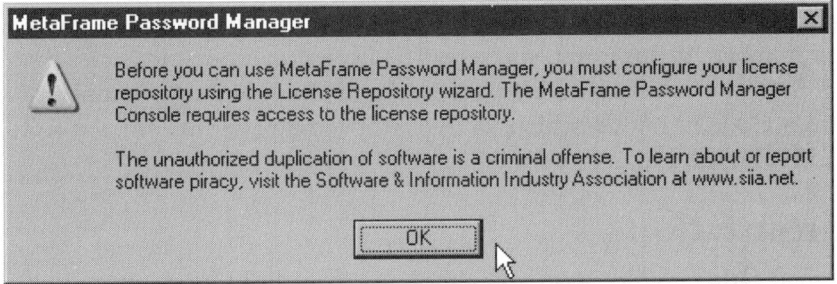

Once you click **OK**, the License Repository Wizard opens and guides you through the process of configuring your license repository. First, you need to decide where your repository will be located. Your choices, as shown in Figure 10.7, are a Microsoft Active Directory Container or a Shared Folder.

Figure 10.7 Location of the License Repository

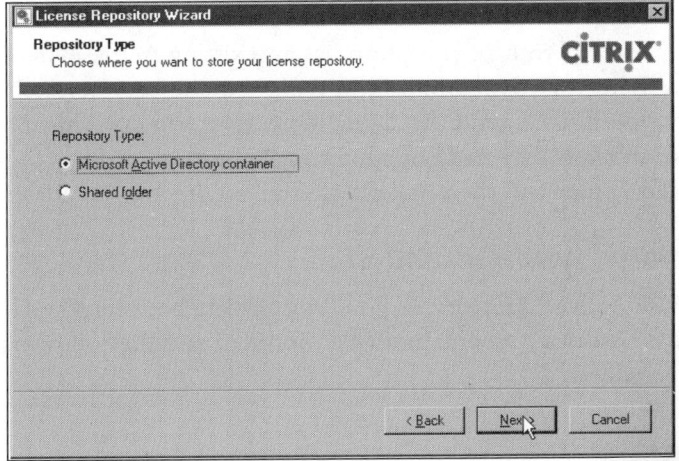

Which location you choose for your license repository is important, and each requires a fair amount of information and planning before you make your decision, as your decision will also affect synchronization between the Console and the Agent.

If you choose to use Active Directory, select **Microsoft Active Directory container**, and then click **Next**. You will then be prompted to choose an organizational unit. Once specified, click **OK** and **Finish**. Selecting a Shared Folder is much the same, but instead of specifying an organizational unit, you will specify the drive and directory where you want to locate your repository.

Once you have specified the location for your license repository, you will be prompted to add and activate licenses. You must add at least one license for the Password Manager Console to function, but you are given two days' grace to activate the license(s). The licensing process works much like the licensing process for other MetaFrame Access Suite products. You must enter the product serial number within the Password Manager License Administration Console. After adding the serial number, the Licensing Console appends several more digits, called the *Machine Code*, and the result is the license number. At this point, you copy the license number and access the Citrix Activation System at www.citrix.com/activate, paste in your license number, and receive an Activation Code in return, which you will copy and paste into the Password Manager License Administration to activate the license.

Synchronization

As mentioned earlier, the location you choose for your license repository will also be tied to the location where your application definitions, credentials, and configuration settings will be centrally stored. Synchronization occurs between the local Credential Store and the Central Credential Store in order to keep the Agent, on the client side, up to date with the most recent changes. Credentials are stored in encrypted databases and within the registry. Synchronization of data can either use an Active Directory Container or a Shared Folder.

Active Directory provides a faster, easier method of synchronization, and Password Manager Agent settings can be easily applied to individual organization units or right down to the user level. If your organization has an existing Active Directory infrastructure, using Active Directory Synchronization is a good choice. The catch is, if you do use Active Directory, you must extend the Active Directory schema. This may require specialized expertise and you may need organizational approval to do so. It is possible to start with a Shared Folder and then transfer to Active Directory at a later date.

Active Directory Synchronization

Before you can use Active Directory to synchronize data between the Console and the Agents, the Active Directory schema must be modified and the following classes and attributes must be added:

- **citrix-SSOConfig class** This setting describes the Active Directory object that contains the agent settings, synchronization state, and the entlist.ini and ftulist.ini files.

- **entlist.ini** Within this file are the application definitions that you create for each application allowing the agent to intercept and respond to password change requests.

- **ftulist.ini** The first time a user uses the Agent, the ftulist.ini file determines the Agent's behavior.

- **citrix-SSOSecretData attribute** Where the actual data resides.

- **citrixSSOConfigType attribute** Specifies the type of data.

- **citrix-SSOSecret class** This setting describes the secret data object that is used to authenticate a user.

- **citrix-SSOSecretDate** Contains encrypted credential information for applications.

- **citrix-SSOLicense class** This setting describes the object that handles licensing information.

- **citrix-SSOLicenseAttribute** Contains the actual license information.

WARNING!

Modifying or extending the Microsoft Active Directory Schema is at best, a touchy matter. Be sure that an administrator specifically experienced in the schema analyzes and makes the actual changes. Schema changes are enterprise wide and not easily reversible. Be sure to research http://support.microsoft.com for specific instructions on extending or modifying the Active Directory schema.

Shared Folder Synchronization

If you are in the testing phase of implementing Password Manager, it may be easier to configure a shared folder as opposed to setting up Active Directory synchronization. If the testing goes well, you can always configure a test environment using Active Directory and re-configure later.

The shared folder can be configured manually or by using the File Synchronization Setup Utility located on the Password Manager CD-ROM under the \Tools directory. To use the File Synchronization Setup Utility, type the following from the /Tools directory command prompt:

```
CtxFileSyncPrep /path:<pathname>/share:<sharename>
```

Where "pathname" and "sharename" are the path and share names where you want to create the directory. If you do not specify a path, the default path is %SystemDrive%\CITRIXSYNC. If you do not specify a share name, it will default to CITRIXSYNC$. Citrix recommends that you use a hidden share for the share point. The File Synchronization Utility ensures that the folder and subfolders are created correctly, with the proper permissions and security. You can opt to create the directories and permissions manually, but the utility works so well, why would you want to?

Installing Password Manager Agent

Installing the Password Manager Agent is equally as simple as installing the Console. From the Autorun screen, select **MetaFrame Password Manager Agent**. The wizard runs, prompts you to accept the licensing agreement, and then provides an opportunity to select the features you want to install. Figure 10.8 shows the choices available.

Figure 10.8 Password Management Agent Setup

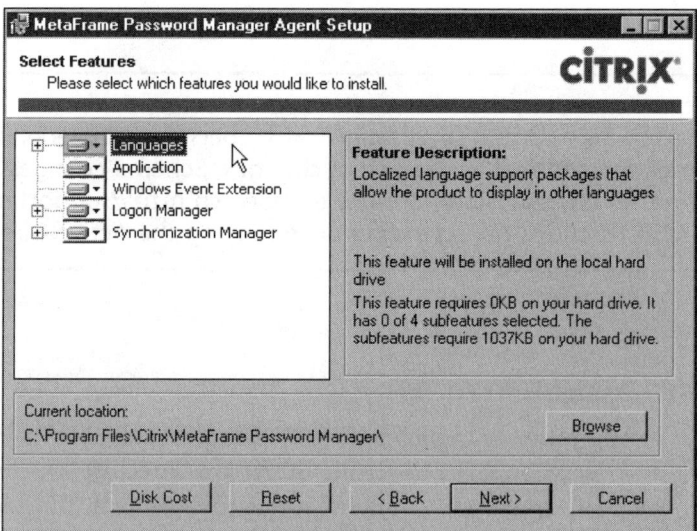

Unless you need support for various languages, expand **Languages** and disable those that are not needed. When you expand Synchronization Manager as shown in Figure 10.9, you can select the plug-in that will allow the agent to synchronize with either Active Directory or a shared folder. For the most part, the other options can be installed in full without taking up much space. Once you have selected your Synchronization plug-in, Click **Next** to continue and the wizard will complete the Agent installation.

Figure 10.9 Selecting the Agent Synchronization Plug-In

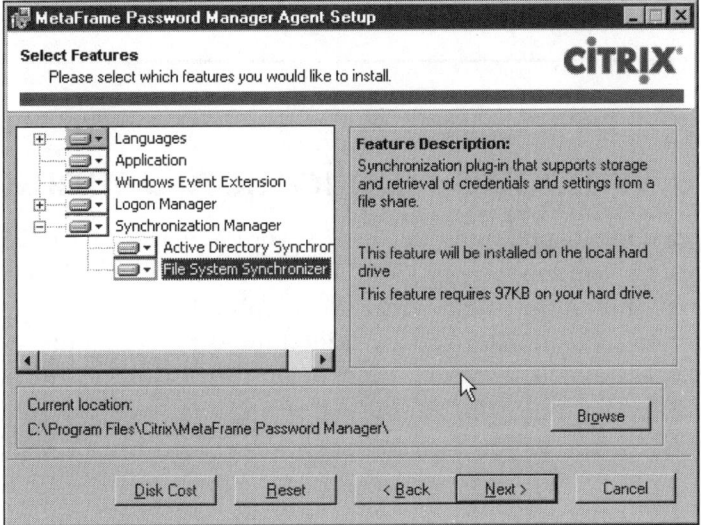

Configuring Application-Specific Settings

From within the Password Manager Console, you must use the application information you gathered during the planning stage and create a list of applications that Password Manager will monitor. As mentioned earlier in this chapter, the application information will be used to supply identifiers that the Password Manager Agent needs for each supported application. These identifiers are stored in the application definitions on the Password Manager Console and tell the Password Manager Agent how to detect logon requests and password change requests, where to enter the user's credentials, and how to submit the credential information. Common application information the identifiers include are:

- Application executable names or Web site URLs
- Password policies and error detection
- Configuration information that may include the logon window title, the form name, and where the credentials must be entered
- Logon retry policies
- Information about other required fields and the credentials needed

NOTE

Each application will require different identifiers and many will require multiple identifier sets. One application may require one form for logon credentials and another form for password changes. Both must be configured for Password Manager to handle the process.

Adding a Windows Application Definition

Citrix has provided a test application on the Password Manager CD-ROM to help illustrate how to create a Windows Application Definition. The file is called "LogonTester.exe" and can be found under the \Tools folder. Copy the executable to a temporary folder on the computer you are using for testing, and double-click to launch the application. It is a simple form with three fields: User Name, Password, and Third. Now, open the Password Manager Console and arrange both the Console and the test application on your screen so you can see both at once. To create an Application Definition:

1. From the Command Console's left pane, right-click **Applications** and select **New Windows App**. The Add Application dialog page appears as shown in Figure 10.10.

Figure 10.10 Adding a New Windows Application Definition

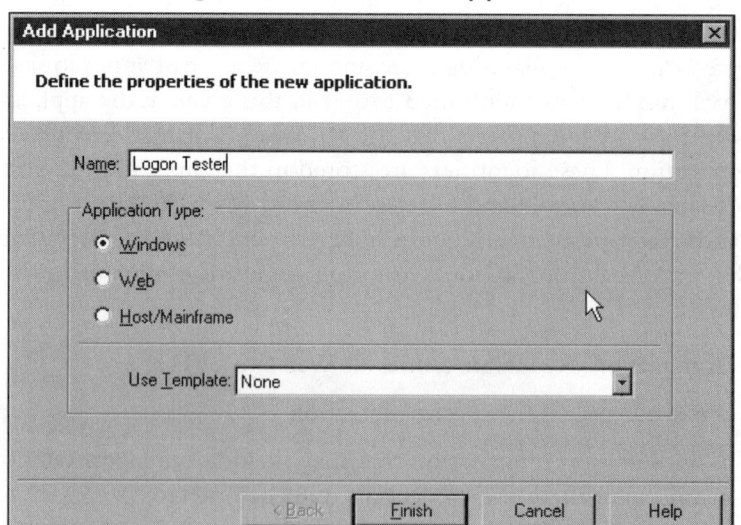

2. In the Name field, type in **Logon Tester** and make sure that the **Windows** option button is selected.

3. Click **Finish** to continue on to the Properties dialog box for Logon Tester.

4. From the **Properties** dialog box, as shown in Figure 10.11, click **Detect Fields Wizard**.

Figure 10.11 Properties Dialog Box

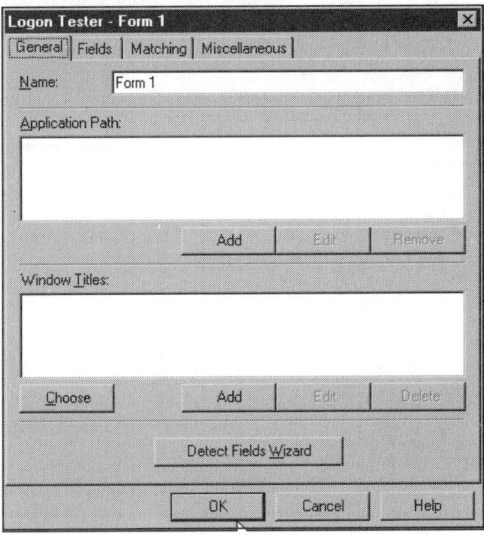

5. When the Form Wizard launches, click **Logon**. The Form Wizard will list the applications currently running on your machine and the window's title, module, and class for each (see Figure 10.12).

Figure 10.12 The Form Wizard

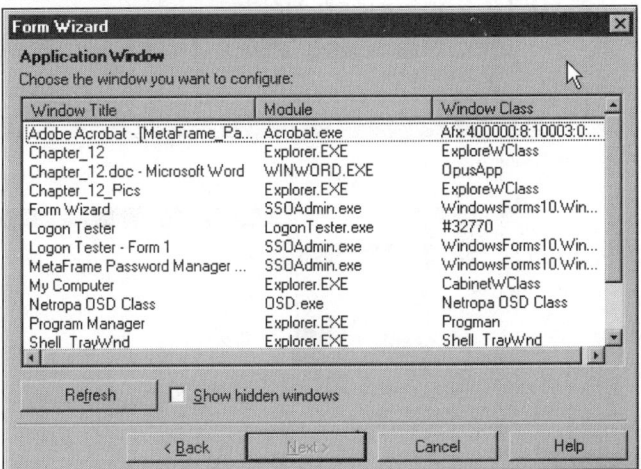

6. From the Form Wizard list, select **Logon Tester**. If you still have your Logon Tester application open, you will notice that a flashing border appears around the Logon Tester form. Click **Next** to continue.

7. The next screen displays the Logon Tester application's fields as shown in Figure 10.13.

Figure 10.13 The Application Credential Fields

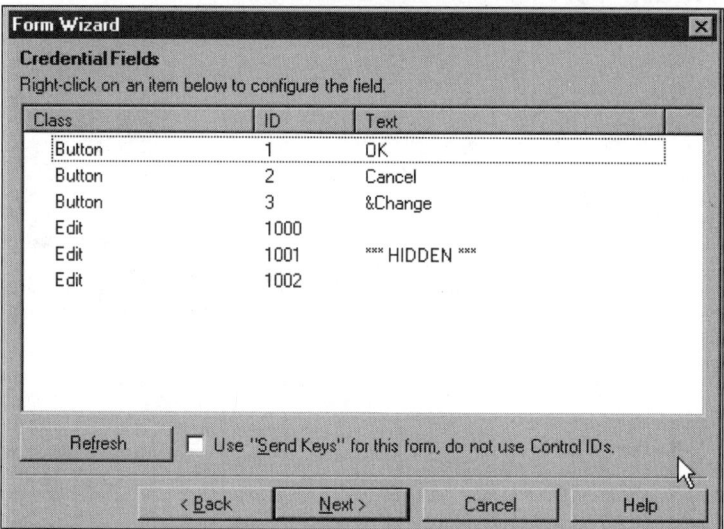

8. To configure the fields to work with the LogonTester application, right-click on the Edit class with the ID of 1000 and select **Username/ID** from the drop-down list as shown in Figure 10.14. Again, if your Logon Tester application is visible, you will notice that the User Name field border begins to flash.

Figure 10.14 Configuring Fields

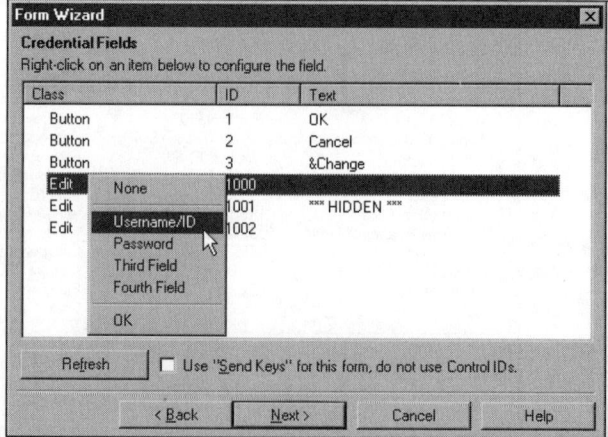

9. Next, right-click on the **Edit** class with the ID of 1001. From the drop-down list, select **Password**. You will notice that the Text column shows the word ★★★HIDDEN★★★ so the password will not be shown.

10. Finally, right-click the last **Edit** class with the ID of 1002 and select **Third Field**. Now you should see icons indicative of the fields next to each field you have edited similar to the one in Figure 10.15.

Figure 10.15 Completed Credential Form

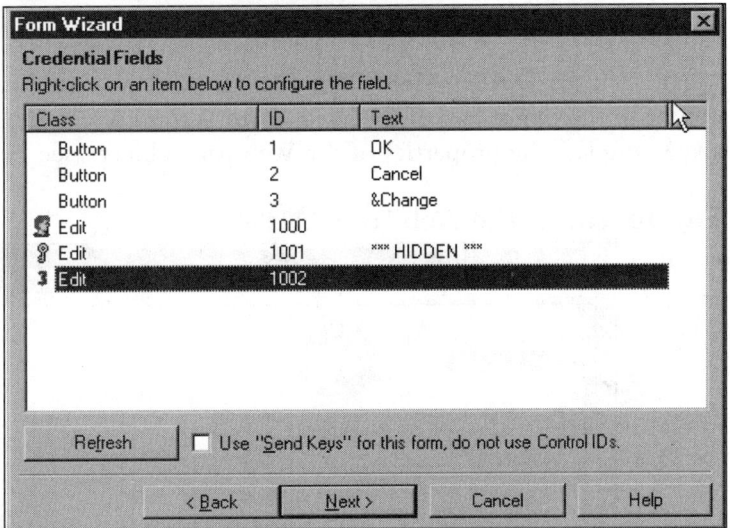

11. Once finished, click Next to continue and verify your settings, and then click Finish.

12. Again, the Logon Tester Properties dialog box appears. Click OK to close the Logon Tester Properties dialog box and then save your settings.

13. In the Password Manager Console window, you will now see the Logon Tester application listed under the Application node in the left pane.

Adding a Web Application Definition

Adding a Web Application Definition is much like adding a Windows Application Setting or Host-based definition. Most are easily configured, and Citrix even provides some templates for common settings. For our example here, create a Web Application Definition for MyCitrix.com Web site.

1. As you did to configure the Windows Application Definition, right-click on **Application** in the left pane of the Console, and this time select **New Web App**. This launches the Add Application page.

2. From the Add Application Page, insert **MyCitrix.com** in the Name field and verify that the Web option button is selected. Click **Finish** when you are through.

3. The Properties dialog box for MyCitrix.com pops up next. From the **General** tab, under **URL**, click **Add**.

4. For the URL, type **www.myctrix.com**, and then click **OK** to continue.

5. Next, click the **Detect Fields Wizard**. The Web site and the logon form appear in the upper half of the Web Form Wizard screen. The lower half of the screen displays the properties of the Web page objects (see Figure 10.16).

Figure 10.16 The Web Form Wizard

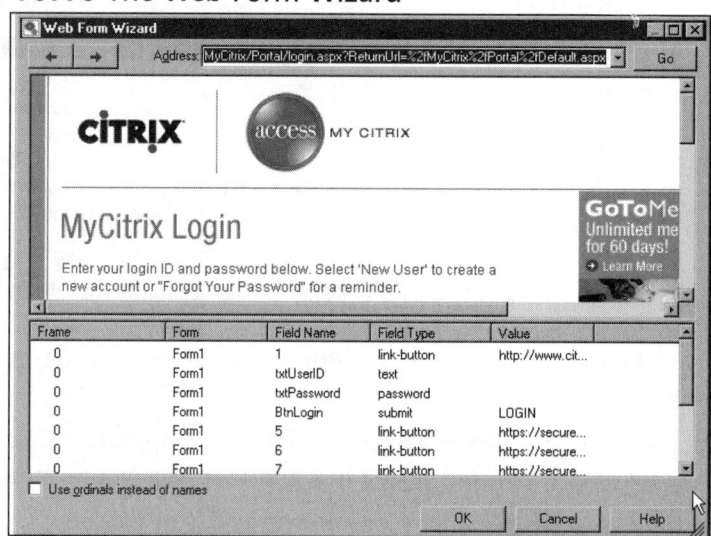

6. Much the same as you did when configuring the Windows Application Definition, we will now right-click on the various fields and select the appropriate information for each. We will start with the Field Name **txtUserID**. Right-click on the selection and from the drop-down list, select **Username/ID**. Again, you will notice that the frame around the Logon ID field begins to blink (see Figure 10.17).

Figure 10.17 Selecting the Web Form Fields

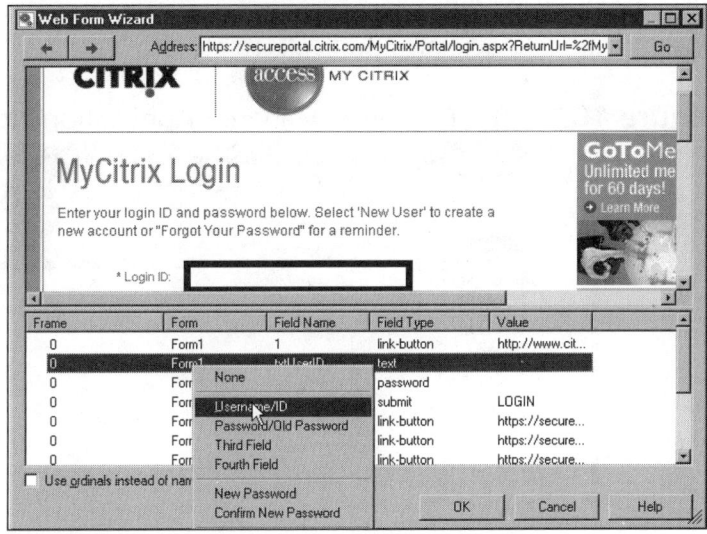

7. Next, right-click on the **txtPassword** field, and from the drop-down list, select **Password/OldPassword**.

8. Now, right-click the **Field Name** of "6," and then click **Submit**. You will notice that the New User link on the Web form begins to blink as shown in Figure 10.18, indicating that on first use, you will be prompted to create a new user account.

Figure 10.18 Creating a Link to Create a New User Account

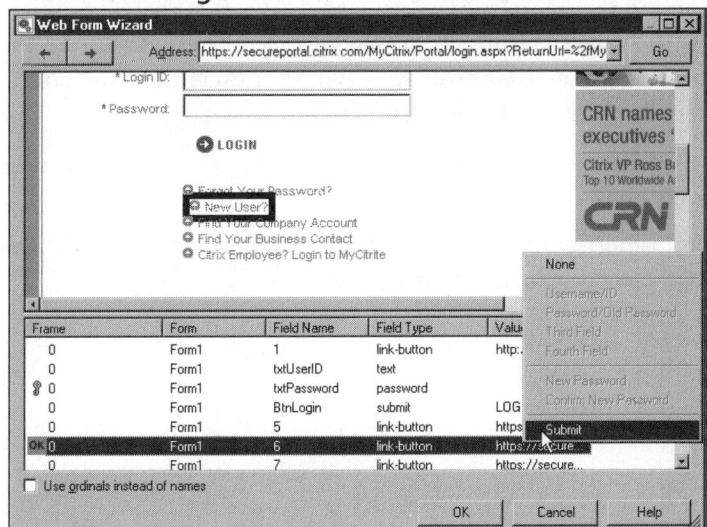

9.   Click **OK** to close the Web Form Wizard and save your configuration. Now you will notice that you have two Application Definitions under the Application Node as shown in Figure 10.19.

Figure 10.19 The Password Manager Application Node

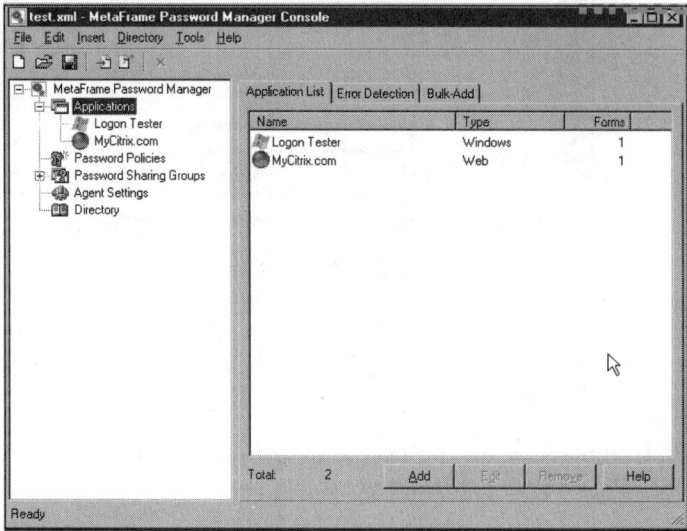

The First Time Use List

The First Time Use List is a "bulk-add" feature where you can add a list of applications that will be supplied with credential information. The first time a user logs on to a machine running the MetaFrame Password Agent, the First Time User Wizard appears and prompts the user to configure his applications. By creating the First Time Use List on the Password Manager Console, you will save users the time and frustration of configuring every application themselves.

1.   To create a First Time Use List, open the **Password Manager Console** and right-click on the **Application** node in the left pane.

2.   From the right pane, select the **Bulk-Add** tab and click **Add**. This launches the Select Applications dialog box (see Figure 10.20).

Figure 10.20 The Bulk-Add List

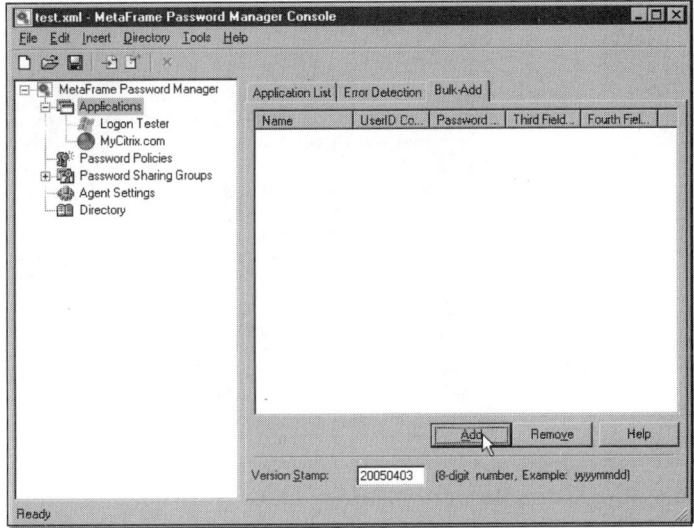

3. Within the Select Applications dialog box, you will see the Application Definitions you have defined on the console. Select the two applications we just added and click **OK**. Now both applications show up under the Bulk-Add tab and will be added to the Agent's application definitions.

Now that you have added your new Application Definitions and added them to the Bulk List, you will need to save the information to the Synchronization Point. Once again, from the Password Manager Console:

1. From the left pane, select the **Directory** node.

2. In the right pane, you should see the path to the shared folder created earlier. Right-click on the shared folder and select **Configure SSO Support**. This launches the SSO Support Wizard as shown in Figure 10.21.

Figure 10.21 SSO Support Wizard

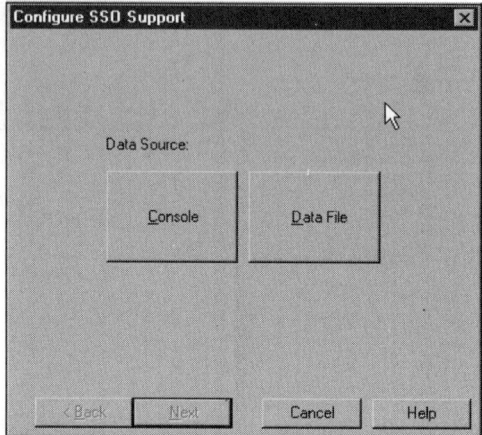

3. Select the **Console** button under **Data Source**.

4. The next screen allows you to send all applications, select only some of the applications, or to not send any applications at all. Select **Send All Applications** and check the **Create First-Time-Use (FTUList)**.

5. From the Agent Settings drop-down list, select **CITRIXSYNC** and click **Next** to continue.

6. You will now see three new objects—ADMINOVERRIDE, ENTLIST, AND FTU—under the shared folder in the right-hand pane. These objects are the files that store the information for the synchronizer.

Running the Password Manager Agent

The first time you run the Password Manager Agent, you will be prompted to provide your authentication information. You will be logged out from your current session, and when you log back in, Password Manager Agent starts up again and you are prompted to configure your authentication information.

1. Pressing the **Configure** button launches the Identify Verification Wizard.

2. A list of questions provided by the administrator appears and the user is prompted to select one, answer, and confirm.

TIP

> If this were a production environment and not a test scenario, you would create Identity Verification Questions within the Console. You might ask for "mother's maiden name" or "place of birth." The questions act as a secondary identification method for each individual user, because each user's answer will be unique, especially paired with his or her user credentials.

3. Type in your answer, confirm it, and then click **OK**.

Password Manager Agent is now ready to store your credentials and provide those credentials to the applications that require authentication all without your assistance.

Summary

MetaFrame Password Manager provides an enterprise-level single sign-on solution while simplifying user access to applications and administrative password-related tasks. Password Manager also increases security by enforcing strong password policies and placing safe-guards around credentials. Once the user authenticates once, the Password Manager Agent can provide and change passwords that meet the application's authentication requirements, all without user interaction. From within the Password Manager Console, you can create rules where even the user does not know the individual passwords needed to access applications and Web sites. In short, organizations no longer need to rely on users to create and keep safe their passwords or worry about the scraps of paper or Post-It Notes containing passwords.

Solutions Fast Track

How Does Password Manager Work?

☑ MetaFrame Password Manager is an enterprise solution for Single Sign On.

☑ Users need authenticate only once to access local applications, applications published from a MetaFrame Presentation Server farm, host-based applications, and Web-based applications.

☑ Password Manager consists of three components: the Password Manager Console, the Password Manager Agent, and the Credential Store.

Deploying Password Manager/ Running the Password Manager Agent

☑ From the Console, applications can be configured so that when the user launches an application, the Password Agent will recognize the form, fields, and type of information needed. The Agent will then pass the credentials to the applications.

☑ Password Manager Agent can also be configured to recognize password change requests and the password policies in place for the application. Password Manager Agent can automatically create a strong password and pass it to the application, all without user intervention. The user may not even need to know the password that is used.

Configuring Application-Specific Settings

☑ The MetaFrame Password Manager lowers the costs associated with administrative tasks related to passwords and application security.

☑ Users can be more productive and far less frustrated with the burden of creating and remembering passwords taken from them.

☑ In addition to the users' network authentication, they must also provide unique answers to questions configured by administration. These answers in combination with their unique IDs and passwords create a double layer of security.

Frequently Asked Questions

The following Frequently Asked Questions, answered by the authors of this book, are designed to both measure your understanding of the concepts presented in this chapter and to assist you with real-life implementation of these concepts. To have your questions about this chapter answered by the author, browse to **www.syngress.com/solutions** and click on the **"Ask the Author"** form. You will also gain access to thousands of other FAQs at ITFAQnet.com.

Q: What exactly is MetaFrame Password Manager?

A: MetaFrame Password Manager is one of Citrix's newest additions to the MetaFrame Access Suite of products. It provides password security and single sign-on access to applications that require authentication.

Q: Is MetaFrame Password Manager difficult to install, configure, and maintain?

A: It does require planning, just as any other deployment, but once you have the information needed, the rest is fairly simple to implement and maintain.

Q: What types of applications can MetaFrame Password Manager support?

A: MetaFrame Password Manager supports Windows applications installed on local PCs and laptops, applications published from MetaFrame Presentation server farms, Web-based applications, and host-based applications. That covers just about all of them!

Q: How does MetaFrame Password Manager work; does it just store passwords in a type of vault where users can open and retrieve them?

A: Not at all. There are other applications on the market today of that sort, but MetaFrame Password Manager is an enterprise solution that supplies enterprise-level security and single sign-on capabilities. The credentials are stored in encrypted Credential Stores and applied to the requesting applications without user intervention.

Q: Must I know how to write complex scripts or modify our applications, especially our proprietary ones, in order to use MetaFrame Password Manager?

A: No, that is part of the beauty of the product. There is no need for scripting or modifying your applications. Using the Password Manager Console, you provide certain details about the application such as the executable, the form name, or if it is a Web-based application, the URL and form name. Details such as these allow the MetaFrame Password Agent to identify the application requesting authentication and provide the information in the correct format.

Q: How difficult will it be to convert our users over to using Password Manager?

A: Much easier than it has been to make them remember multiple passwords. The Password Manager Agent is installed on the MetaFrame Presentation servers and/or on the users' laptops or PCs. The first time they use the Password Manager Agent, they will answer a unique question to verify their identity. From there on, passwords will be learned and applied automatically. You can also allow the users to add other applications such as frequently visited Web sites that require authentication.

Chapter 11

Security and Load Management

Solutions in this chapter:

- **Security Strategies for a Citrix MetaFrame Presentation Server Farm**

- **Encrypting Citrix MetaFrame Presentation Server**

- **Configuring Encryption on Citrix Presentation Server**

- **Using Load Manager**

☑ **Summary**

☑ **Solutions Fast Track**

☑ **Frequently Asked Questions**

Introduction

Whenever you're connecting a computer to the Internet, that computer is open to sabotage. Worms and viruses can destroy entire systems, from the operating system right down to the hardware. Intruders can access servers on the Internet and obtain the passwords for administrative functions, using them later to wreak havoc on the system. Bored or unskilled programming students, also known as *script kiddies,* can download complex scripts from a hacker's Web site and test them on any vulnerable server just to see what happens.

Among many of the destructive attacks that can take place is the theft of confidential data. This activity is especially sensitive in the areas of e-commerce and financial systems; the theft of confidential data can destroy a company's competitive edge. Even a Citrix MetaFrame Presentation server, whose traffic consists mainly of graphics transmitted to clients and keyboard and mouse clicks received from clients, can be preyed upon by a saboteur.

Keeping the server farm running well across all servers is partly a matter of managing loads in addition to ensuring that data is kept safe. If a server farm is scaled up over time, it is likely that some servers will be more powerful than others. Some will have more processing power or more disk capacity, while others will have more memory. As such, some servers will be capable of supporting more sessions than others. Ensuring equitable load management can optimize a farm.

Security Strategies for a Citrix MetaFrame Presentation Server Farm

To protect vital information from unauthorized intruders, it is vital that you secure your network and computer assets. As computer and network systems have become more common, the need for security has grown exponentially. As an administrator, you must ensure that you take into account every option that can assist in securing the computing environment. Although Citrix MetaFrame Presentation Server provides several methods to ensure security of vital information, other products and solutions are used to protect data throughout a computing environment. Options such as virus protection, intrusion detection and prevention, and firewalls are among the most common solutions used today.

Virus Protection

By definition, a *virus* is a piece of computer code that produces unwanted results; it has the unique capability to replicate itself. A virus can perform an amazing array of damage, ranging from annoying messages and extensive resource utilization to destroying files and systems and causing massive outages. In addition, virus-like programs known as *worms* have become more prevalent due to their potential impact. Worms are advanced computer viruses that replicate themselves to further infect other systems. The ability to protect computers against these types of attacks has become more a necessity than a luxury.

One of the most common threats today, virus attacks produce an astounding impact on organizations. With estimated damages being reported in the billions of dollars by various news sources, virus protection is a critical component to ensure that your networking environment is secure. Antivirus programs created by third-party software developers have become a huge component of any organization's security program.

When considering antivirus software in your Citrix server farm, you must take into account several factors. First, you must evaluate the various products along with feature sets to provide a solution to meet your organization's needs. It's very important to ensure that the software you select is supported in a Microsoft Windows Server 2003 Terminal Server and Citrix MetaFrame Presentation Server environment. This could have been difficult a short time ago, but many of the major antivirus software vendors now provide supported solutions.

In addition to using antivirus software on your Citrix MetaFrame Presentation servers, you can use various products throughout the network to protect other resources available to a Citrix MetaFrame client such as file servers, electronic mail, spam filtering, and Internet Web filtering. Limiting your users' capability to surf the Web or use e-mail can also reduce the risk of virus infection. When you use antivirus software on your Citrix MetaFrame server, you must carefully configure the application to minimize the impact to end users. Most antivirus solutions provide real-time scanning of file access, but you must carefully consider its impact to server performance. Carefully test how this software impacts the overall client experience to ensure that it's not causing more damage than good. In addition, active scanning can be performed to search the entire system for any virus. Although this is an effective tool, it is recommended that you use it after hours because it can cause severe performance degradation and interfere with your users.

Last, antivirus software use signatures to identify virus patterns while scanning. To ensure you are monitoring for the latest virus infections, you must periodically update the signatures from the manufacturer. Most software solutions available today offer scheduled automatic updates. In addition, you can manually update the signature files if needed. It is recommended that you determine an acceptable interval for updating your antivirus signatures. You should check for new signatures at least once a week and install updates only after hours, to minimize user impact. In addition, if you become aware of any new virus infections, immediately check the manufacturer's Web site for signature updates and information about the infection. Web sites maintained by industry-leading anti-virus companies are a great source to find virus removal tools in the event a system is infected.

Intrusion Detection and Prevention

Another security measure you must consider is monitoring for network intrusion. As hackers become more prevalent and savvy, you need additional tools to help protect your network environment. Intrusion detection is a strategy that any organization must at least consider in connecting the organization's computers to any public network.

Intrusion detection and prevention can be defined as the ability to monitor and react to network misuse. Many hardware and software products on the market today provide various levels of intrusion detection. Some solutions use signatures to monitor for known attacks. Some platforms provide network monitoring; others are host-based systems. While intrusion detection offers a more passive approach to potential attacks, intrusion prevention is more aggressive in responding to attacks. Some solutions react to particular alerts, such as shutting down services; others use a more passive approach by monitoring activity such as a Honeypot. You must carefully select an intrusion detection and prevention strategy to ensure that your network resources remain secure from unwanted trespassers.

Similar to virus protection, various locations and methods are appropriate to using intrusion detection. The most common use is to install an intrusion detection solution to monitor the access points from the Internet or outside world into your private networks. For example, you might want to monitor for intruders on your Web servers. There are two main types of solutions: network-based and host-based. *Network-based intrusion detection* monitors network traffic for particular signs of malicious behavior. For example, if a user is continually trying to access a port known to be used with worms or Trojans, this activity would trigger an alert. *Host-based intrusion detection* programs are software products that are installed on your servers to monitor for suspicious behavior. This solution watches for virus-like activity to prevent it before it infects anything. It is critical to determine where you should monitor for intrusion and provide the most secure solution to achieve these goals.

Firewalls

When connecting your computing resource to other networks such as the Internet, you must consider how you control access between your network and the others. In addition, some resources within your organization (such as human resources department computers that hold confidential personal information) need to be secured from internal intruders. A *firewall* is a common technique used to meet these requirements.

A firewall is traditionally used to secure one set of network resources from another network. The most common implementation of firewalls today is organizations connecting their internal private networks to the Internet. A firewall allows administrators to restrict outside individuals' access to internal resources. Although many firewall products are on the market, a firewall is more a security strategy than a single product. The solution to fit your needs might be available in a single product, but many times, multiple devices are required to completely secure a network. For example, many firewall implementations include items discussed earlier in this chapter, such as intrusion detection and virus scanning. As an administrator, you must select the options and product that best suit your environment's requirements.

To use Citrix MetaFrame Presentation Server with firewalls, you must carefully consider who and what resources need to be available to external users. For instance, if you want the Citrix Web Interface to be accessible to remote users, you must allow the appropriate services to traverse the firewall.

As an example, connecting to your Citrix Web Interface site using HTTP requires TCP port 80. For users to access this service, port 80 must be allowed to traverse your network to the server hosting the Web Interface pages. If you have elected to use SSL services to protect your Web Interface pages, TCP port 443 must be opened instead of port 80. Additionally, TCP port 1494 is used to establish Citrix ICA client sessions directly with Citrix MetaFrame Presentation servers. TCP port 2598 is also required for the Common Gateway Protocol (CDP) uses for the session reliability feature. Figure 11.1 shows a common scenario for allowing traffic for Citrix MetaFrame Presentation Server to pass through a firewall. Table 11.1 lists the most common ports associated with Citrix MetaFrame Presentation Server services.

Figure 11.1 An Example of Firewall Use for Citrix MetaFrame Presentation Server

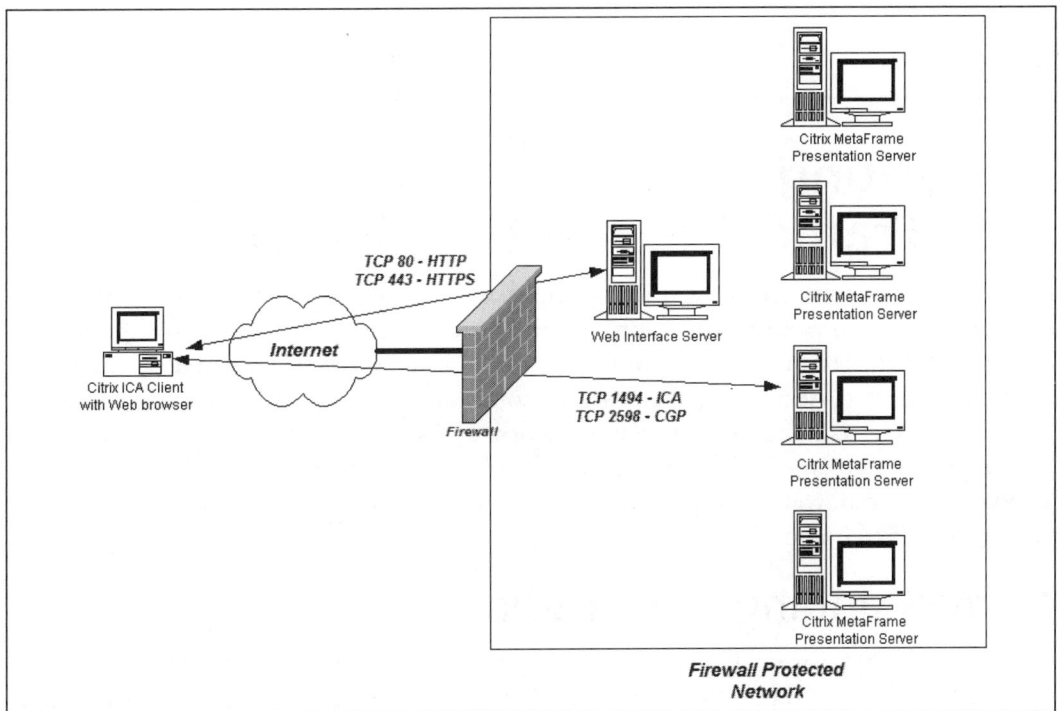

Table 11.1 Services Associated with Citrix MetaFrame Presentation Server

Port	Description
TCP Port 80	HTTP Web pages; used with Web Interface servers.
TCP Port 443	HTTPS Web pages; used with Web Interface servers using SSL technology for security or with the SSL Relay service.
TCP Port 1494	ICA session traffic; used for connecting to Citrix MetaFrame ICA connectivity.
UDP Port 1604	ICA Browser Services; used with older clients for browsing for Citrix MetaFrame Presentation server farms.
TCP Port 2512	IMA Service; used for server-to-server communication.
TCP Port 2513	Presentation Server Console; used for console communication to server farms.
TCP Port 2598	Common Gateway Protocol (CGP); used for session reliability.

Encrypting Citrix MetaFrame Presentation Server

In addition to the numerous security solutions and products available on the market today, Citrix MetaFrame Presentation Server provides built-in capability to help secure server and client communications from intruders. Using a standard technology known as *encryption*, server-to-server and client/server communication can be protected against intruders. Understanding how encryption works and where to apply it is important to ensure proper implementation of a secure server farm. Once you understand how encryption is used, you can properly set up the products and add-ons provided for Citrix MetaFrame Presentation Server.

Understanding Encryption

Encryption is the process of converting data into nonreadable text, also referred to as *ciphertext*. Ciphertext is used for transmitting confidential data. Once the data has arrived at its destination, it is then reconverted into the original data through a process known as *decryption*.

Various types of data encryption are available on the market today. Each type provides both benefits and disadvantages, including categories such as strength of security, ease of use, and standardization. The effectiveness of any security algorithm is found in its strength and the keys used to secure it. Weaker security algorithms are more easily cracked; however, if implemented properly, these options can still provide very effective solutions.

Encryption techniques are based on using keys similar to keys for your home or car. Using a key to open your car door is a method that identifies you as someone authorized to use the car. Whoever has possession of this key is able to access the car. Based on mathematical algorithms, encryption keys work the same way. If you have the correct key, you can encrypt or decrypt the data from ciphertext.

Symmetric Key Encryption

Primarily two forms of encryption are in use today. The most common form of encryption uses the *symmetric algorithm*. This method requires that each individual or device that accesses this encrypted data possess a copy of the key. Commonly referred to as *shared-key encryption* because it uses a single key for encryption and decryption, this is a relatively simple encryption technology to implement, but it might not provide the best security.

One common issue with symmetric encryption algorithms is the way the keys are transported to other users. If this type of key is obtained by an unauthorized user (such as during the encryption setup process), that unauthorized user can then easily decrypt that data, resulting in loss of data integrity. Most solutions that use symmetric keys to encrypt data also provide additional secure methods by which to negotiate and transport these keys to ensure that they are secured.

Another issue associated with symmetric keys is managing multiple identities. If you want to communicate securely using symmetric keys without all users having access to all data, you must maintain different keys for different data sets. For example, Jane at Company A wants to send data to Bill at Company B. Jane must configure communications to Bill using Key 1, and Bill must use the same key. Jane also wants to communicate with Bob at Company X. To communicate with Bob, Jane must use a different key; therefore, Key 2 is created. As the number of companies or individuals grows, so does the number of keys required to maintain communications among them. Now imagine using this technology on an enterprise scale with hundreds or thousands of sites.

The most common symmetric algorithm implementation used today is the Digital Encryption Standard, or DES. Based on a fixed 56-bit symmetric key, this algorithm creates a single key based on a binary number used to encrypt and decrypt data. Using a block cipher methodology, it uses 64-byte blocks to randomly populate a key. Currently in use by organizations such as the National Security Agency (NSA), DES offers 72 quadrillion possible encryption keys at this point. In addition, developers have created a stronger version of DES, known as Triple DES, or 3DES, because it uses the DES key by encrypting, decrypting, and encrypting again to ensure data is secure. Figure 11.2 shows an example of symmetric key processing.

Figure 11.2 Symmetric Keys

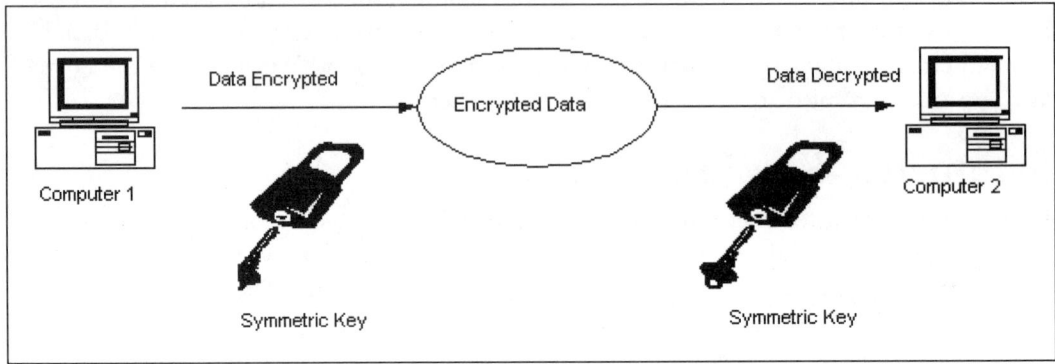

Asymmetric Key Encryption

The second method of encryption uses an asymmetrical algorithm and is commonly known as *public key encryption*. Although similar to the symmetric algorithm, this technology uses two keys to encrypt data. The first key is held privately in a secure location for the receiver to decrypt data sent to him. This validates that the receiver is authentic. The second key is freely published, is used to encrypt the data, and is commonly posted in public locations. This allows anyone to send the data, but only the holder of the private key is authorized to receive and decrypt the data. Even the public key originally used to encrypt the message cannot be used to decrypt it. This encryption technique allows you to send the public key over insecure channels and still maintain the integrity of encrypted data.

Therefore, if Tom wants to send encrypted data to Jim, he uses Jim's public key to encrypt it. Once the data is transferred to Jim, he uses his private key to decrypt the data. This methodology ensures that only Jim can access the data.

Created by and named for Ron Rivest, Adi Shamir, and Leonard Adleman, the Rivest-Shamir-Adleman (RSA) data encryption standard is the most commonly used asymmetric algorithm. It uses prime numbers to randomly generate public and private keys. A common application using RSA encryption includes Pretty Good Privacy (PGP) and Novell NetWare for a secure client-to-server communications channel. Similar to RSA, Diffie-Hellman is another common algorithm. Primarily used to transfer symmetric keys securely, Diffie-Hellman provides another form of asymmetric keys. A common example of asymmetric key encryption is using PGP to digitally sign e-mail communications. If you use a PGP signature, recipients of your messages can ensure that your e-mails are authentic. Figure 11.3 shows an example of how asymmetric keys work.

Figure 11.3 Asymmetric Keys

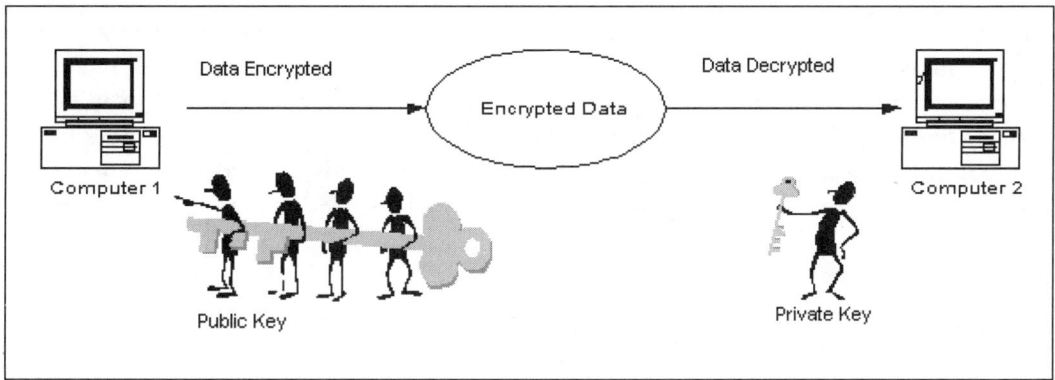

Secure Sockets Layer

Secure Sockets Layer (SSL) was created to encrypt data transmitted between a client computer and a Web server. Traditionally, Web traffic is transmitted in cleartext, potentially providing network intruders with sensitive data. Netscape developed SSL to provide a secure communications method by which to converse across the Internet. Based on RSA public/private key technology using digital certificates, SSL has become the standard for secure communication across the World Wide Web and can be used to complement your security strategy for your Citrix MetaFrame Presentation server farm.

SSL is used to confirm the identity of a server or a client machine and then encrypt all traffic between the two devices. For example, when you process a credit card transaction through a Web site, you want to ensure the identity of the receiver. SSL allows digital signatures to be used and are verified by a trusted certificate authority (CA). When you connect to a Web site using SSL, a certificate is processed, validating that the Web site is authentic. If it isn't, an error is issued, allowing you to determine whether to continue. As the process is completed, all traffic between your client and the Web site is encrypted to ensure that someone else cannot monitor the data flow.

SSL can be very useful when you're trying to secure a Citrix MetaFrame Web Interface server. Using SSL allows you to first confirm that your Web site is authentic to users. In addition, traffic such as authentication will not be sent in cleartext, increasing your security risk. To use SSL with Web sites, you connect using Secure Hypertext Transfer Protocol (HTTPS) instead of HTTP. Once this is configured, you no long have to use standard HTTP services—you can rely solely on HTTPS to ensure that your site is secured.

Encryption Strength Options

Another important factor in implementing encryption strategies is defining the strength of your solution. In addition to the encryption techniques used, the key length is a major factor in determining the strength of any algorithm. For example, 16 bits in a key provide 65,536 possible key combinations. As the number of bits increases, so does the number of key variations. When you factor the computing power of today's computers, the ability to try every combination of larger keys, such as 128 bits, can take a few years to complete.

Citrix MetaFrame has five encryption levels from which to select:

■ Basic

■ 128-bit login only

■ 40-bit

■ 56-bit

■ 128-bit

Each option provides 128-bit encryption for the logon process, and then the selected key strength is used to secure the remainder of ICA traffic throughout the session. Once a session has been established, all traffic, with the exception of a small encryption header, will be secured. This traffic includes items such as:

■ Keystrokes

■ GUI information

■ Mouse data

■ Client drive data

■ Client printer data

NOTE

The 128-bit encryption method has been banned for export to several countries. Originally, it was difficult to export 128-bit products outside the United States, but the U.S. government has relaxed this requirement, and only countries affected by a U.S. trade embargo are affected. This includes countries such as Afghanistan, Iraq, Iran, Libya, Syria, Cuba, North Korea, or Sudan.

Where Can You Use Encryption

Using a combination of symmetric and asymmetric key technologies, Citrix MetaFrame Presentation Server provides a comprehensive encryption solution to ensure secure communications. First, Citrix MetaFrame Presentation Server uses RC5, a fast block cipher developed for RSA security, as the symmetric key technology to encrypt all ICA traffic between clients and servers. To exchange these keys securely, Citrix has implemented the Diffie-Hellman asymmetric key algorithm. When an ICA client session is initiated, a unique public/private key pair is generated and passed through the communications channel. Once communication is established, these key pairs are used to arrive at the same RC5 symmetric key. Using a 1024-bit symmetric key, the client then begins processing ICA traffic and logon information.

Figure 11.4 illustrates how each of the encryption technologies is used to provide a complete solution. The communications path for initiating a connection via the Web Interface to a Citrix MetaFrame Presentation Server farm is shown.

Figure 11.4 Encryption Technologies at Work

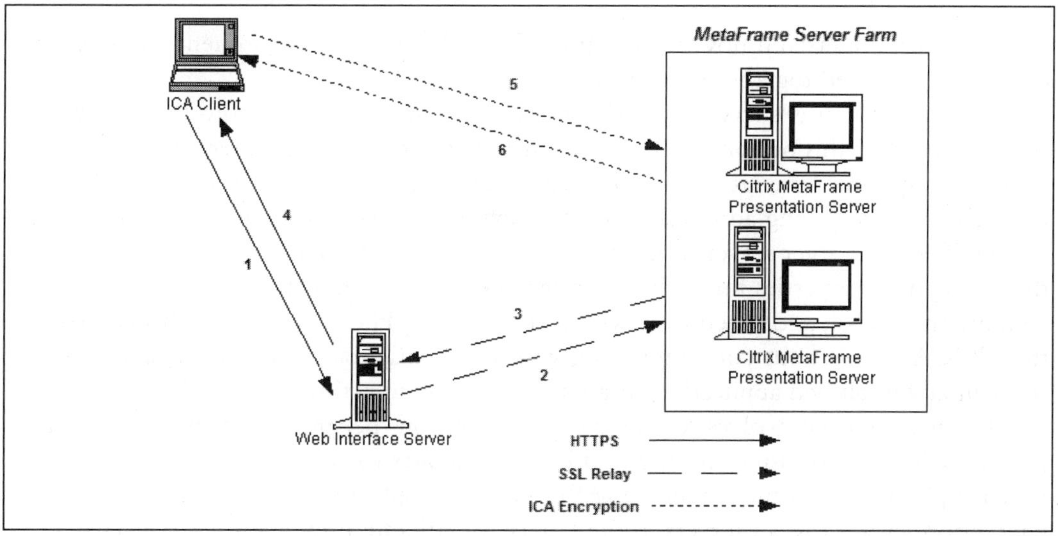

1. Client connects to a secured Web page using HTTPS.

2. The Web Interface server validates the user and requests available applications using SSL Relay service to encrypt traffic.

3. Citrix MetaFrame Presentation Server returns published applications available for this user.

4. The Web Interface server provides a Web page using HTTPS with available applications.

5. ICA client connects directly to the Citrix MetaFrame Presentation Server providing published applications.

6. A communications channel is opened using ICA encryption, and the client session begins.

Encrypting Server, Published Application, and Client Communications

Citrix offers multiple encryption techniques offering flexibility in managing secure sessions. As discussed within this chapter, encryption is a key component ensuring secure communications between the Citrix MetaFrame farm and the ICA client. There are several ways to configure encryption:

- Encrypting traffic at the server level
- Setting encryption for each published application
- Setting encryption on an individual client basis

You must understand how each option affects the overall environment and how the options can be used together successfully.

The first option is encrypting traffic for all connections coming into the server. When you select this option, all ICA sessions initiated to the configured server encrypt data to the specified strength. This option mandates that each server must be configured independently; requiring administrators to touch each server any time this setting must be modified. For larger server farms, this requirement can be very prohibitive. To adjust the encryption properties for each server, use the Citrix Connection Configuration administration tool, as defined later within this chapter. The advantage to this approach is that all ICA connections communicating with this configuration are encrypted, whether through any published application or a custom ICA connection.

The next option involves setting encryption options per published application. The primary advantage of using this method is that it applies to all servers using the published application. Any user connecting through this application will use the specified encryption level across all servers in the Citrix MetaFrame Presentation server farm. Another advantage is that you can specify different levels of encryption for each published application. For example, if a user connects to a financial application, you might require him to use 128-bit encryption. At the same time, other users connect to a word processing tool over slow network links. For these connections, you may opt to force users to use only 40-bit encryption. To configure published application encryption, you can select the encryption strength when the application is created. More detail on managing published application encryption is available later in this chapter.

If the settings were managed at the server level, as described in the last section, you would have to separate the user connections by server or configure each client independently to allow this to work. By configuring encryption for each published application, you can easily manage multiple encryption levels simultaneously, without the users knowing the difference.

The third option involves specifying an encryption level for the ICA client device. By default, the ICA client attempts to use whatever encryption strength is requested by the server. You can configure the ICA client to use different encryption strengths if the server or published application allows it. For example, if the server connection encryption strength is set to 56-bit, the ICA client cannot connect unless it is using 56-bit or higher. If you're connecting as an administrator to your Citrix MetaFrame Presentation server farm across the Internet, you might prefer to use 128-bit encryption to ensure that traffic is secured.

Using HTTPS

Encrypting the ICA client traffic secures the session information, but you must also consider accessing published applications via the Citrix Web Interface. By default, standard Web browsing with HTTP access from client devices accessing via the Web Interface transmit data in cleartext. If you want to ensure that your communications are completely secure, you must consider using Secure Sockets Layer, or SSL, on the Web server hosting the Citrix Web Interface. SSL is an industry-standard encryption technology that is application independent and works well with Web-based solutions. By configuring your Web server to support SSL technology in the form of HTTPS, client to Web server communication will now be secure. Once a server certificate is installed, the Web site can digitally sign and encrypt packets as they are sent between the client device and the Web server.

Using the SSL Relay Service

Another security issue to consider is the way in which traffic is passed between the Web Interface server and the XML service on Citrix MetaFrame Presentation servers. In a process that is similar to standard Web traffic, data is transmitted in cleartext. This becomes a security concern when traffic between the Web Interface server and the Citrix MetaFrame farm is insecure. For example, many organizations will place a Web Interface server in the DMZ, or demilitarized zone, while maintaining a Citrix server farm in a more secure network. In the event Citrix MetaFrame Presentation servers are not located in a secure network environment, the use of the SSL Relay service will help to mitigate the security concern for unencrypted traffic. Although the password is slightly encrypted, it does not provide a secure alternative to the encryption methods discussed in this chapter. To assist you with this problem, Citrix has developed the SSL Relay service. This service allows you to configure all traffic passing between Web Interface servers and a Citrix MetaFrame Presentation Server to use SSL encryption.

> **NOTE**
>
> Although encryption is available using the pass-through authentication technology for Citrix MetaFrame Presentation Server, it is highly recommended that you disable this feature. Serious security flaws have been identified with this technology, potentially providing the username, password, and domain information in cleartext. For more information, download the *Advanced Concepts for MetaFrame Presentation Server for Windows 3.0* guide from www.citrix.com.

Citrix Secure Gateway

Another methodology developed by Citrix allows the tunneling of all ICA client traffic using industry-standard security protocols such as Secure Sockets Layer (SSL) or Transport Layer Security (TLS). Citrix has developed a solution known as Citrix Secure Gateway that encrypts all Citrix client traffic such as ICA packets via industry-standard Internet encryption protocols to simplify the management of a secure infrastructure throughout your network. For example, by deploying a Citrix Secure Gateway in the corporate DMZ, the firewalls protecting your network from the Internet must only be configured to allow SSL packets to the Citrix Secure Gateway server from any ICA client. The Citrix Secure Gateway server will manage the connectivity and encryption across the public Internet and mask the Citrix MetaFrame Presentation server farm.

Not only does this provide a simplified security solution, it hides the server farm from potential intruders on the Internet. Although this offers security to the ICA clients, once the traffic passes through the Citrix Secure Gateway it is no longer encrypted. It is recommended to use one of the many other encryption techniques for the TCP\IP packets from the Citrix Secure Gateway to the Citrix MetaFrame Presentation Server farm.

The Citrix Secure Gateway is made up of the following components:

- **Secure Gateway Server** Central server that acts as "gateway" to the Citrix MetaFrame Presentation server farm. The Secure Gateway Server acts as the middleman and validates the ticket provided by the STA.

- **Secure Ticket Authority (STA)** Creates a ticket for each session offering a more secure access methodology.

- **Citrix XML Service** Provides the interface between a Citrix MetaFrame Presentation server and the Web Interface server.

- **Citrix MetaFrame Presentation Server Farm** Citrix MetaFrame server farm that provides published applications via the ICA Client.

NOTE

Citrix Secure Gateway is not found on the Citrix MetaFrame Access Suite or Citrix MetaFrame Presentation Server CD. It can be downloaded from www.citrix.com.

Clients that Can Support Encryption

To use encryption technologies, the ICA client software must be able to negotiate encrypted sessions. To accomplish this task, you must run a minimum version of 6.01 of the Citrix ICA client software. Additional enhancements continue to be released and it is recommended to use the Citrix ICA client version 8.1 or higher. Using the client upgrade database can relieve the administrative overhead of managing client versions because the database can be used to deploy the version you want to use. For more information about the client upgrade database, download the *Citrix MetaFrame Presentation Server Administration Guide* available at www.citrix.com.

Configuring Encryption on Citrix MetaFrame Presentation Server

Now that you have an understanding of what encryption technology can do and when to use it, the next step is to secure your Citrix MetaFrame Presentation server farm. Several products and techniques ensure that your environment is secured. The first step to configuring encryption options is to understand the various techniques and how they apply to your environment. For example, configuring encryption on ICA connections affects all client communication to a server; setting encryption on a single client applies only to itself. Encryption can be applied to the server, particular published applications, or even to a single client connection. In addition, traffic using Web technologies such as Citrix Web Interface servers, can be encrypted using solutions such as HTTPS and the SSL Relay.

Configuring & Implementing…

Determining the Encryption Strength to Use

When you are implementing encryption within your Citrix MetaFrame Presentation server farm, it is critical to correctly identify the encryption strength to use and where it will be configured. All encryption strengths, with the exception of basic, use 128-bit strength for the logon process. Afterward, they revert to the selected option, such as 56-bit. You might ask, "Why not just use 128-bit encryption if it's the best?" Unfortunately, the stronger the encryption algorithm, the more performance overhead is required on the server and client communications. For example, 128-bit encryption will not function properly when you use a 33.6Kbps modem connection to access a Citrix MetaFrame Presentation server. In the same manner, client performance degrades faster over inconsistent network links when you use higher strength encryption algorithms. Carefully test each option to ensure it suits your environment; it can have a major impact on the performance of your server farm if not optimized properly.

Configuring Server Encryption

The most common method for encryption data is configuring each server to request the encryption strength. Each server has the capability to specify particular connection settings for all ICA communications, including encryption strength. Configuration is completed with the following steps:

1. Open the **Citrix Connection Configuration utility** by selecting **Start | Programs | Citrix | Administration Tools | Citrix Connection Configuration**.

2. Right-click **ICA-TCP** and select **Edit**, as shown in Figure 11.5.

Figure 11.5 Selecting the Protocol to Configure

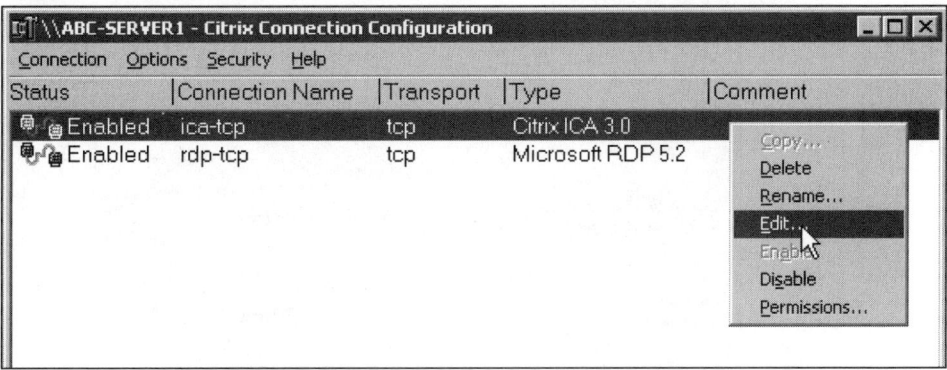

3. Select the **LAN Adapter** to configure. By default, all LAN adapters are chosen. Next, click **Advanced** to configure encryption options, as shown in Figure 11.6.

Figure 11.6 Selecting the Advanced Button

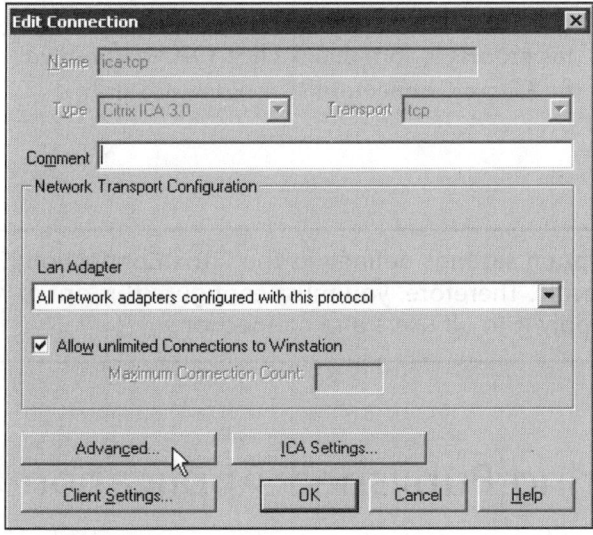

4. In the Security section, select the encryption strength to use, as shown in Figure 11.7. By default, **Basic** is the encryption strength selected.

Figure 11.7 Selecting the Encryption Strength

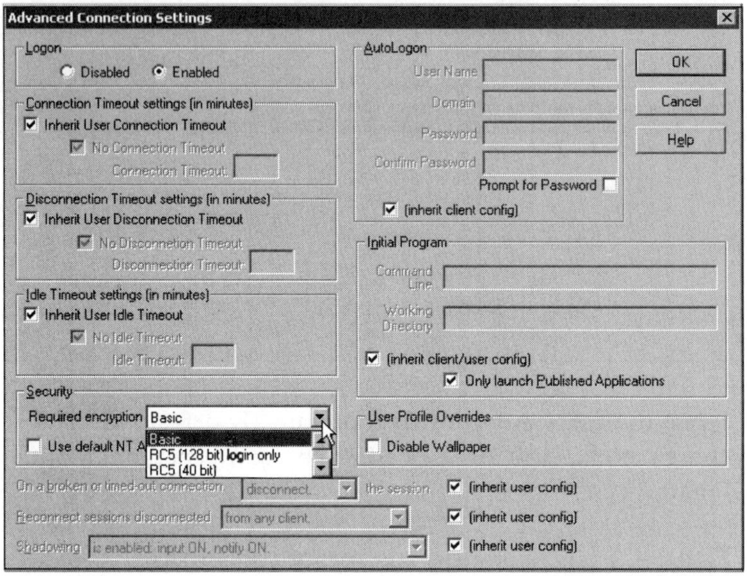

5. Once this process is completed, click **OK** to complete this configuration. Close the Citrix Connection Configuration utility.

> **NOTE**
>
> The encryption settings defined in the Citrix Connection Configuration utility are server specific. Therefore, you must configure this option on each server in your farm to apply it to all users and connections.

Configuring Published Application Encryption

In addition to configuring encryption strength at the server level, you can also set it up per published application. This method allows you to further control the applications that are encrypted and specify different levels for each if needed. To specify the encryption level, you can select the encryption strength used for the published application when you create it as shown in Figure 11.8. In addition, you can choose a minimum requirement that forces clients to connect at the specified encryption level or higher or the connection will be refused.

Figure 11.8 Specifying the Encryption Level During Published Application Setup

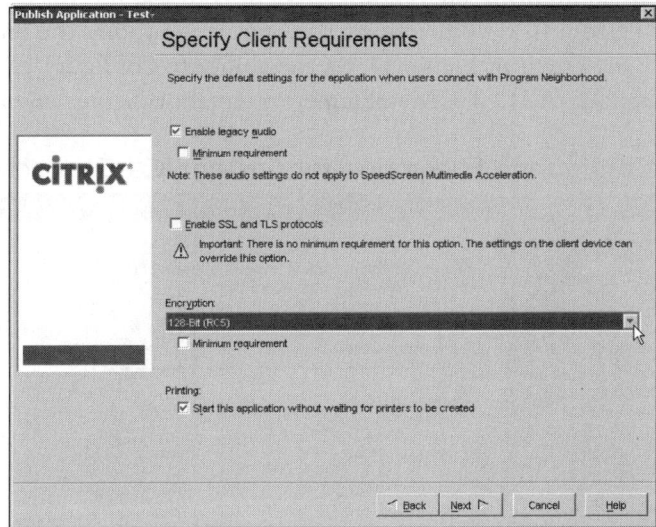

Once the published application is set up, you can go back and alter the encryption level as needed. Unlike the server connection encryption, when you specify the encryption for the published application all users connecting to this application use the encryption requirements on all servers. You do not have to change this setting more than once.

As shown in Figure 11.9, you can modify the properties of a published application from within CMC. As with the setup process for published applications, you can also specify the minimum required connection strength.

Figure 11.9 Encryption Properties of a Published Application

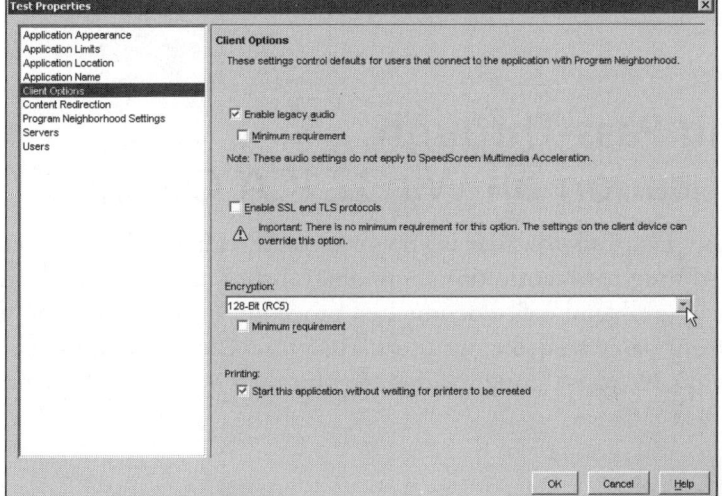

Configuring Client Encryption

Another method of configuring encryption strength is to use the ICA client itself. When you create custom ICA connections, the option to modify the encryption strength is offered. As shown in Figure 11.10, the ability to configure encryption options is consistent throughout the Citrix MetaFrame Presentation Server environment.

Figure 11.10 Configuring Encryption for Custom ICA Connections

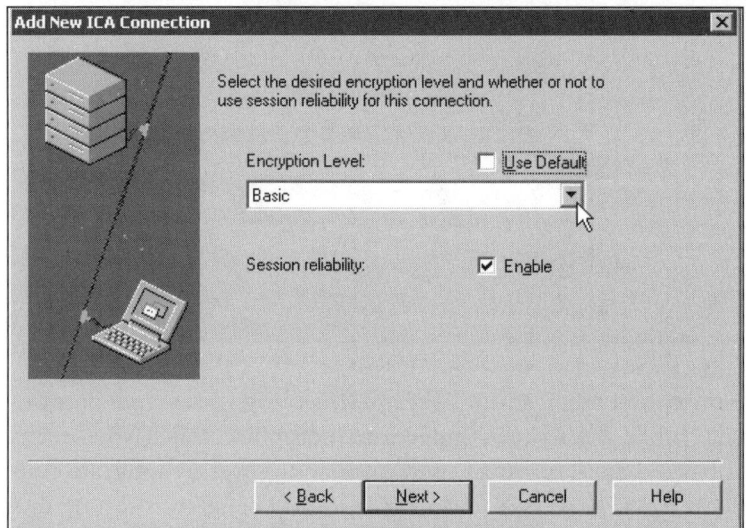

NOTE

In configuring encryption, if anything beyond Basic is selected, automatic logon will no longer be allowed.

Disabling Pass-Through Authentication on Win32 ICA Clients

Another security factor to consider is known security vulnerabilities associated with using the pass-through authentication technology. Issues have been encountered that can present a security problem; well-documented procedures can provide the username, password, and domain name to malicious users. Therefore, Citrix recommends disabling this technology. To disable pass-through authentication on a Win32 ICA client:

1. In the Win32 ICA client, select **Tools | ICA Settings**.

2. Remove the check for **Pass–Through Authentication**.

3. Delete the following files from the ICA client to prevent the feature from being enabled again: **Ssoncom.exe, Ssonstub.dll**, and **Ssonsvr.exe**.

Using HTTPS with the Citrix Web Interface

The next option available is used to secure the Citrix Web Interface. When users connect to the Web Interface home page, HTTPS can be set up and configured to secure all traffic that passes between the Web site and the ICA client. Using SSL technology, you must first request a server certificate from a trusted CA. Once this process is completed, use the Internet Manager administrative tool to configure your Web site to use HTTPS. By setting the properties on the Web server, you can manage the way HTTPS is used. For example, you can specify that only SSL connections via HTTPS can be used. You can also force 128-bit encryption as shown in Figure 11.11. Once HTTPS has been configured, type the name of your Web Interface server into the Web browser using the prefix of *https*. An example of a secured Web site is https://citrix.mycompany.com.

Figure 11.11 Requiring SSL Services

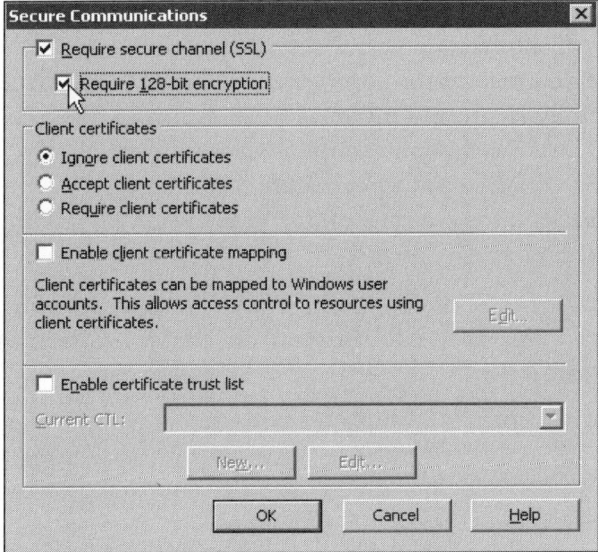

To configure an IIS Web server to use SSL technology:

1. Obtain a digital certificate from a trusted CA such as www.verisign.com.

2. Start the IIS administrator tool by selecting **Start | Programs | Administrative Tools | Internet Information Services (IIS) Manager**.

3. Select the Web server and highlight the Citrix Web Interface site. The default Web site is used initially.

4. Right-click the Web site and select **Properties**.

5. Select the **Directory Security** tab to configure digital certificates.

6. Click **Server Certificates** to initiate the wizard to configure a server certificate.

7. Complete the Web Server Certificate Wizard to assign the certificate you obtained from the CA.

8. Once the wizard has completed, click **Edit**, as shown in Figure 11.11, to require the use of SSL for this Web site. Click **OK** once you have finished.

Configuring the Citrix SSL Relay

As explained earlier in this chapter, communication between the Web Interface server and the Citrix MetaFrame Presentation server farm is not encrypted. In addition, the SSL TCP port can be used for client-to-server communication instead of TCP port 1494 to pass through a firewall. The SSL Relay service has been designed to address both these issues. To use the SSL Relay service, you must first obtain a server certificate from a trusted authority such as www.verisign.com. The same certificate used for HTTPS with the Web Interface server, as described earlier, can also be used for the SSL Relay service. Once you receive the certificate, the Citrix MetaFrame Presentation server will automatically locate and prompt for validation of the certificate. In addition to configuring the Citrix MetaFrame components, you must also configure your Web server to support SSL. Information to configure SSL technology within Microsoft Internet Information Server is available online at www.microsoft.com.

To configure the SSL Relay service:

1. Open the Citrix SSL Relay Configuration Tool by selecting **Start | Programs | Citrix | Administration Tools | Citrix SSL Relay Configuration Tool**.

2. Verify that a certificate is displayed with the server name, as shown in Figure 11.12.

Figure 11.12 Configuring Relay Credentials

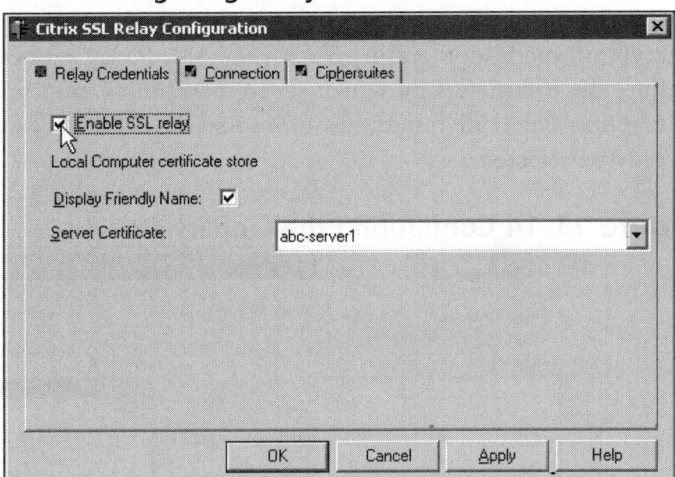

3. Select **Enable SSL Relay**.

4. Next, Select the **Connection** tab, as shown in Figure 11.13. Insert the TCP/IP address of each Citrix MetaFrame Presentation server to which this server will communicate if it has not already been populated. Specify the port for each server on which the XML service is running.

Figure 11.13 Configuring SSL Relay Connections

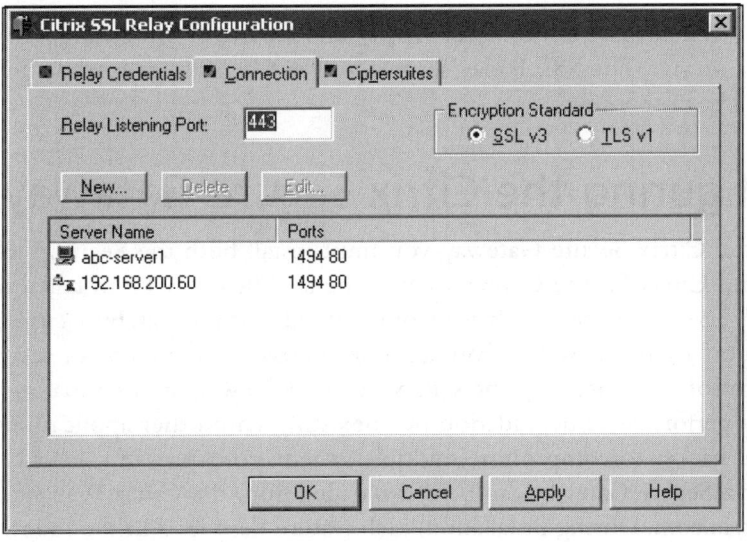

5. Select the **Ciphersuites** tab to configure the algorithms to accept from the Web server, as shown in Figure 11.14. This allows you to further define the encryption methodologies used with the SSL Relay service. Ciphersuites defines the parameters by which secure communication will occur, such as encryption type and authentication mode. By default, all options should already be selected.

Figure 11.14 Configuring the Ciphersuites

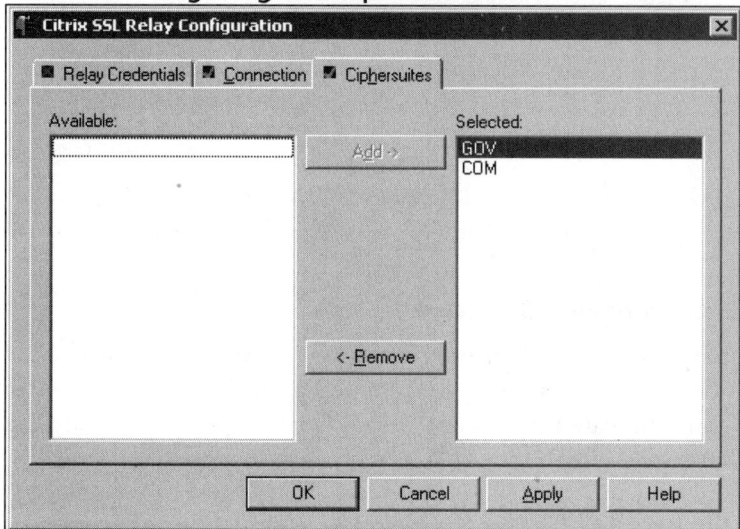

6. When that's done, select **Apply** and **OK** to finish configuring the SSL Relay service. The SSL Relay service will not be activated until after the server has been rebooted.

Configuring the Citrix Secure Gateway

To use the Citrix Secure Gateway, you must install both the Secure Ticket Authority (STA) and Citrix Secure Gateway components. They may be installed on the same or separate servers as necessary. It is recommended that the Citrix Secure Gateway be installed on a separate server from all other Citrix components for security and performance reasons. Maintaining the Citrix Secure Gateway on a standalone server can eliminate any performance degradation by coexisting with other applications and requires a potential hacker to compromise multiple systems to bypass this security measure.

Citrix Secure Gateway can be downloaded from the Citrix Web site at www.citrix.com. During installation, each feature described in the following section can be configured or left to defaults. To configure the Citrix Secure Gateway after installation:

1. Open the Citrix Secure Gateway configuration tool by selecting **Start | Programs | Citrix | Citrix Secure Gateway 1.1 | Citrix Gateway Service Configuration.**

2. You will be prompted to configure Basic or Advanced options, select **Basic**. Advanced options can be used for more granular administrative options. Click **Next** to continue.

3. You will be provided with certificates to apply to the Citrix Secure Gateway, select the applicable certificate and click **Next** (see Figure 11.15).

Figure 11.15 Configure Citrix Secure Gateway Certificates

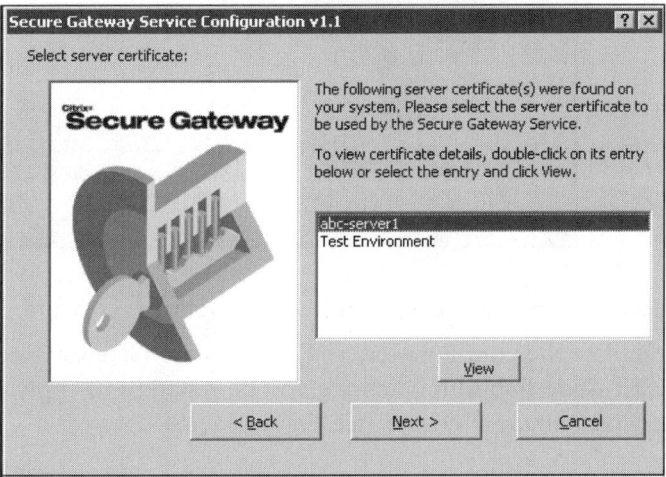

4. Administer any Secure Ticket Authorities (STA) using the **Add** button. Once completed, select **Next** to continue (see Figure 11.16).

Figure 11.16 Configure Secure Ticket Authority Parameters

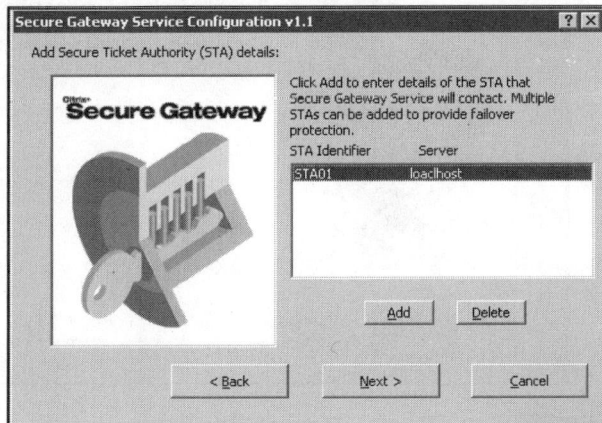

5. By default, the **Monitor all IP addresses on specified port** is selected. Unless a different port is required, select **Next** to continue (see Figure 11.17).

Figure 11.17 Citrix Secure Gateway Port Configuration

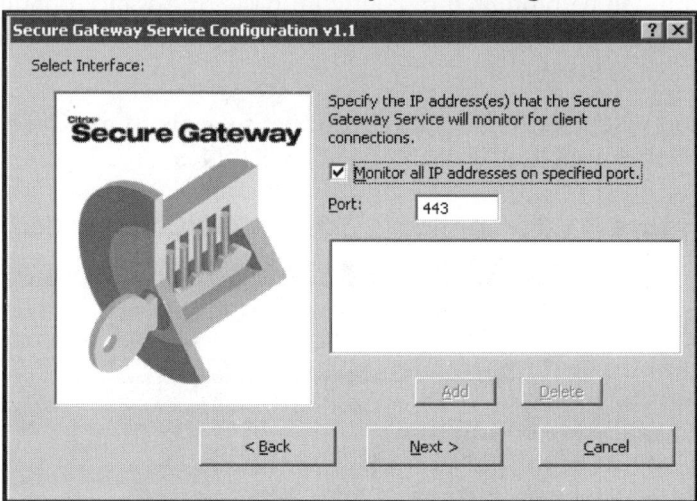

6. Select the administrative error level to log for events and click **Next**.

7. Complete the configuration of Citrix Secure Gateway by clicking **Finish**. The World Wide Publishing Service will be restarted to apply any changes made by the Configuration Wizard (see Figure 11.18).

Figure 11.18 Complete Citrix Secure Gateway Configuration

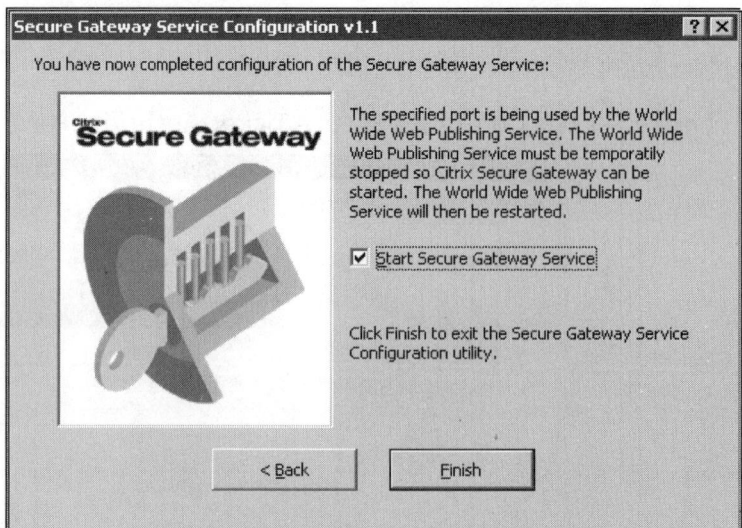

Using Load Manager

Security is an important aspect of ensuring availability, so resource management can quickly become a nightmare if it's not properly administered. The ability to dynamically direct client sessions to servers based on set requirements can greatly enhance the availability of application servers and the performance impact on a client session. As server resources become more heavily taxed, Citrix MetaFrame Presentation Server can direct client sessions to other servers to minimize the impact to users.

Load Manager is included in Citrix MetaFrame Presentation Server Advanced Edition and Enterprise Edition and is installed automatically during the MetaFrame Presentation Server installation process. This product allows you to set up and monitor load balancing between multiple MetaFrame Presentation servers within a single farm based on resource usage. For example, when accessing a published application if a server is experiencing a large amount of processor usage, new client sessions can be directed to log on to another server that is less used. Although processor usage is a common criterion to use with Load Manager, there are quite a few other parameters to select from, including memory usage, page file usage, disk activity, and number of users.

Managing Load-Balanced Applications

To appreciate how Load Manager can benefit you within a MetaFrame Presentation server farm, you must first understand how this product works. Once a user has chosen to connect to a published application, the client first contacts the MetaFrame "data collector" to obtain a list of available servers within the load-balanced server farm. The data collector maintains a list of servers available for each published application and each server's current load values as determined by load evaluators. Each server is responsible for maintaining its own load values and reporting them to the data collector. This ensures that users are directed to published applications based on the usage parameters defined by the Citrix administrator.

The data collector uses the lowest load value to determine to which server the client is directed. In this example, clients accessing the Notepad application will be directed to server NT1. After the data collector selects a server, this information is passed back to the ICA client. The ICA client then initiates a direct connection to the published application running on the designated server. If a server is currently exceeding an assigned load value, it reports itself with a load of 9999 and thereby restricts new client sessions from being initiated. Once a client connects to the designated MetaFrame Presentation server, load management no longer affects a user session. Load Manager handles only incoming client sessions and will not redirect existing client connections. For example, if a user logs in to a Citrix MetaFrame load–balanced published application and the server fails, the client session must reinitiate the connection process all over again.

Designing & Planning...

Developing Load Management Strategies

When you use Load Manager, you must give careful consideration to the load evaluators used and how they are implemented. The first step is to identify the key bottlenecks you must monitor. Common items such as CPU or processor use might be required, or you might want to stipulate a specific range of clients. You must understand what it is you need to monitor before you implement load management. The next process involves measuring the rule values to use within your environment. You must be aware of what thresholds need to be set up to enable adequate usage. In addition to these items, here are a few recommendations for using Load Manager:

1. Start by using one of the provided evaluators to familiarize yourself with how they function. Once you require more customization, try copying an evaluator and modifying the rules to meet your needs.

2. Profile the server to understand what normal use should be. This allows you to more clearly define effective thresholds for use with load management.

3. Try to minimize the number of evaluators used on your servers. Although it might be necessary to use multiple evaluators, it is recommended that you minimize the evaluators from becoming too complex.

4. Never set a load evaluator rule threshold to the maximum value a server can process. Leave the server some extra power in case it is needed.

Load Evaluators

Another item to discuss relating to Load Manager is load evaluators. Load evaluators are designed to allow administrators to manage the aspects by which a load is established. In older versions of Citrix MetaFrame, load balancing was severely limited by the capabilities of managing how load values were determined. Load Manager is the utility developed for Citrix MetaFrame Presentation Server that allows you to determine what variables to use.

Load evaluators consist of a set of rules that are used as criteria to express load values. The combination of the defined rules allows administrators more flexibility to ensure that servers are managing client sessions properly. New load evaluators can be created and customized to meet the needs based on the rules Citrix provides. They can also be assigned to published applications and/or servers as required. Default values are provided for each rule but can be modified to meet application or server needs. After an evaluator has been assigned, loads for servers are calculated using the evaluator with the highest load values.

Citrix provides two basic evaluators, default and advanced, to get you started. The *default evaluator* consists of one rule: Server User Load. This evaluator uses the default values for this rule of 100 users maximum and provides a starting point for administrators. The *advanced evaluator* is designed to calculate three different rules: CPU utilization, memory usage, and page swap. This option is designed to more closely monitor server utilization and provides a superior solution to start with. The default and advanced evaluators can be copied, but they cannot be altered or deleted.

Load Evaluator Rules

As described earlier in this chapter, rules are used within load evaluators to dictate load values. Rules are an integral part of the load management process, and provide the basics for statistically evaluating server performance based on preset values and thresholds. Each rule works independent of other rules and monitors a particular aspect of the Citrix MetaFrame Presentation server. For example, the CPU utilization rule can be used to monitor overall CPU utilization on the server. With the default values of a maximum load of 90 percent and a minimum load of 10 percent, CPU activity can be the basis for evaluator load calculations.

Within this example, two servers exist with a published application balanced between them: one with a load of 55 percent and another with a load of 35 percent. When a user accesses a published application, the data collector looks at the load from both servers with this rule and sends the new client session to the server with 35 percent. As the ICA client logs in to the server and accesses applications, the CPU resources can rise. If they rise above 55 percent, new client sessions will be redirected to the other server. If the CPU utilization rises above 90 percent, no more new client sessions will be allowed until the CPU utilization drops below 90 percent again.

Each rule can be modified to a value defined by the administrator. Most rules allow for minimum and maximum thresholds such as CPU utilization. When load reaches the maximum threshold configured, that server is no longer available for new client sessions until the threshold is no longer met. The minimum threshold defines the point at which a server reports no load. For example, by default the memory utilization rule does not report any load if utilization is below 10 percent. This allows for greater flexibility in configuring load evaluator rules.

Other rules such as the scheduling, license threshold, and IP range rules are used to enforce restrictions. Administrators can use these rules to logically allow or disable access based on a common set of criteria. For example, you could restrict users' ability to access an application after 10:00 P.M. to prevent access during backup intervals using the scheduling rule. You could also restrict certain remote clients to specific servers if requirements are dictated using the IP range rule. Table 11.2 describes each rule and provides threshold values where appropriate.

> **NOTE**
>
> Once load management is installed, Citrix MetaFrame Presentation Server automatically assigns the default load evaluator to each server.

Table 11.2 Load Evaluator Rules

Rule	Description	Load Values
Application User Load	Rule specifying the number of users available to use a specified published application on a specific server.	Default value of 100. Value range of 1–10,000.
Context Switches	Server load is calculated based on CPU context switches per second. This helps to identify CPU process switching.	By default, CPU is loaded at 16,000 context switches. No load is reported at 900.
CPU Utilization	Server load is calculated based on CPU utilization.	By default, a full load is reported at 90% utilization. No load is reported at 10%.
Disk Data I/O	Server load is calculated by monitoring disk data I/O in kilobytes per second. This helps monitor disk performance issues.	By default, a full load is 32,767.
Disk Operations	Server load is calculated by monitoring disk operations.	By default, a full load is reported when exceeding 100 disk read/writes per second.
IP Range	This rule monitors the Citrix client's TCP/IP address.	An address range can be defined to allow or disallow specific clients.
Memory Usage	Monitors overall memory utilization on a server.	By default, a full load is reported at 90% utilization. No load is reported at 10%.

Continued

Table 11.2 continued Load Evaluator Rules

Rule	Description	Load Values
Page Fault	Monitors number of page faults per second.	By default, a full load is reported at 2000 per second.
Page Swap	Monitors number of page swaps per second.	By default, a full load is reported at 100 per second.
Scheduling	Creates a schedule of allowed or disallowed times to for client access to a server or published application.	Any times can be specified.
Server User Load	Rule specifying numbers of sessions allowed per server.	Default value of 100. Value range of 1–10,000.

NOTE

It is important to understand the difference between the Server User Load evaluator and the Application User Load evaluator. Both provide similar functionality; however, the Server User Load evaluator monitors all sessions on the server. If this server is providing multiple published applications, the number of users assigned may be larger than for a single application. The Application User Load evaluator monitors only the number of users on a server running the specified application.

Creating and Assigning a Load Evaluator

Follow these steps to create and assign a load evaluator:

1. Select **Load Evaluators** from within the Management Console MetaFrame for Presentation Server 3.0. Right-click and select **New Load Evaluator**, as shown in Figure 11.19.

Figure 11.19 Creating a New Load Evaluator

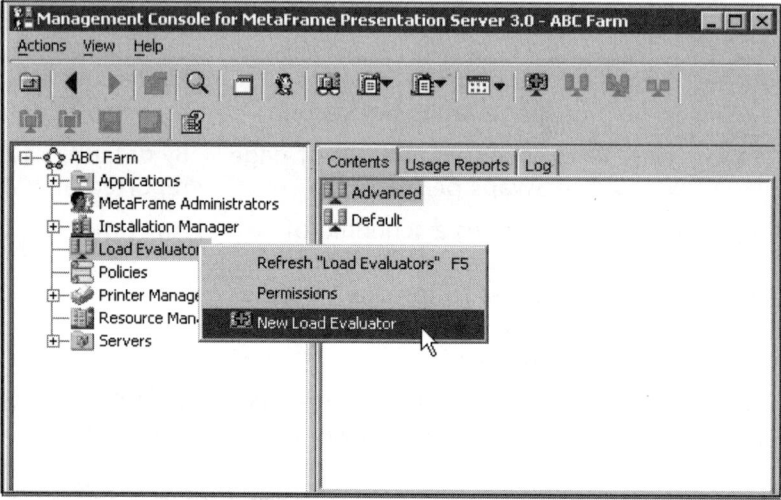

2. Next, insert a name and description to be used for this evaluator. Select from
    the various load evaluators from the left panel and click **Add**. As shown in
    Figure 11.20, modify the default values if required for each evaluator chosen,
    and click **OK** to continue.

Figure 11.20 Designating Load Evaluator Properties

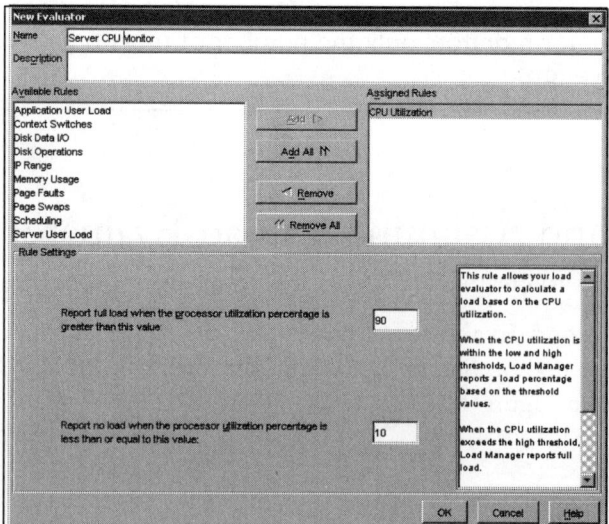

3. Once completed, the load evaluator can be assigned to a published application. Select the published application, as shown in Figure 11.21, to which to assign the load evaluator. Right-click the item and select **Load Manage Application**.

Figure 11.21 Assigning Load Evaluators to Applications

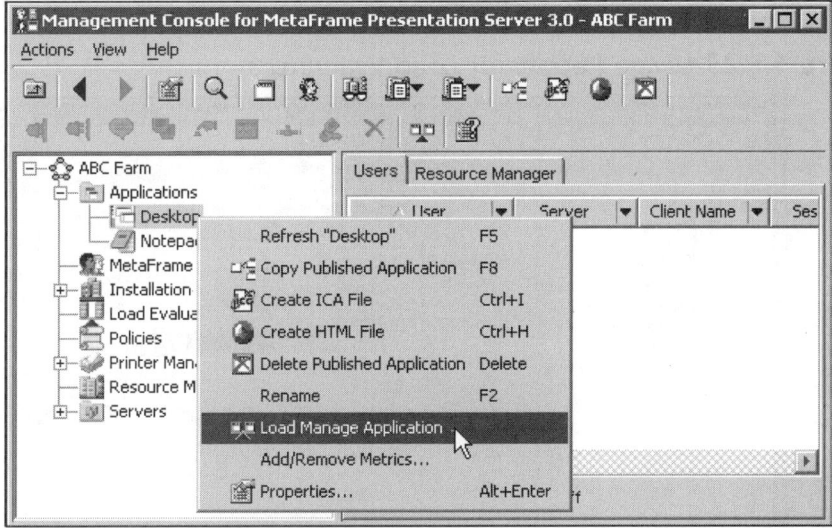

4. Finally, select the server(s) to assign the evaluator, and click **Add**. Highlight the appropriate evaluator, and click **OK** to complete this task, as shown in Figure 11.22.

Figure 11.22 Specifying Load Evaluators

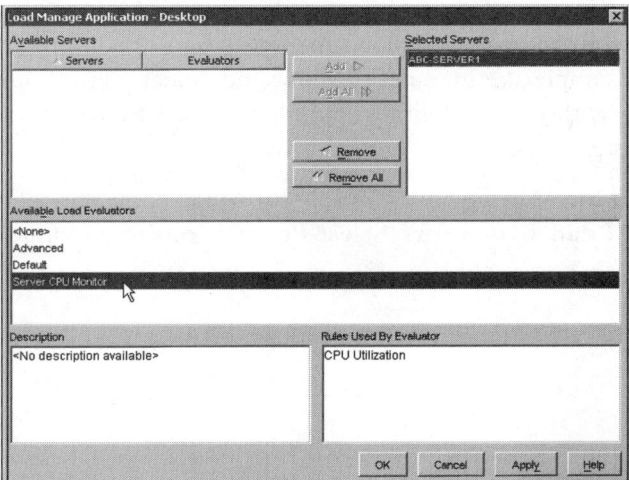

Once load evaluators have been created and assigned to a particular server or published application, you need a method of tracking them. Within the Management Console for MetaFrame Presentation Server, the load evaluator option offers the ability to identify which evaluators are assigned to applications or servers. As shown in Figure 11.23, a report is available to show evaluator assignees and can be specified by server, application, or evaluator. For example, Figure 11.23 identifies that the default evaluator has been assigned to the Notepad application located on the server.

Figure 11.23 Usage Report for Load Evaluators

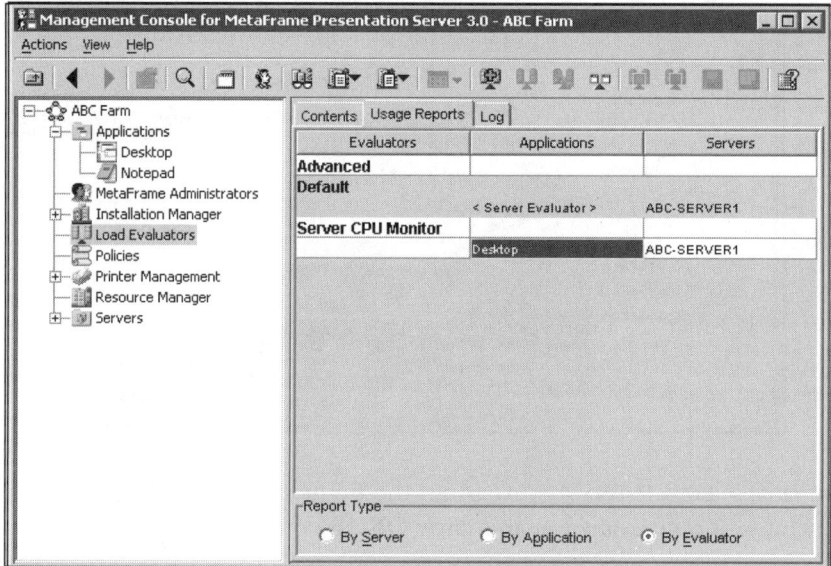

Administering Load Evaluator Permissions

To allow administrators to manage load evaluators, the Management Console for MetaFrame Presentation Server allows the delegation of administration for evaluators as required. For example, the granularity allows individual user accounts or groups to assign load evaluators without the ability to modify the rules by which load is determined.

To administer access to load evaluators:

1. Open the Management Console for MetaFrame Presentation Server and right-click **Load Evaluators**. Select **Permission**s to continue (see Figure 11.24).

Figure 11.24 Managing Permissions for Load Evaluators

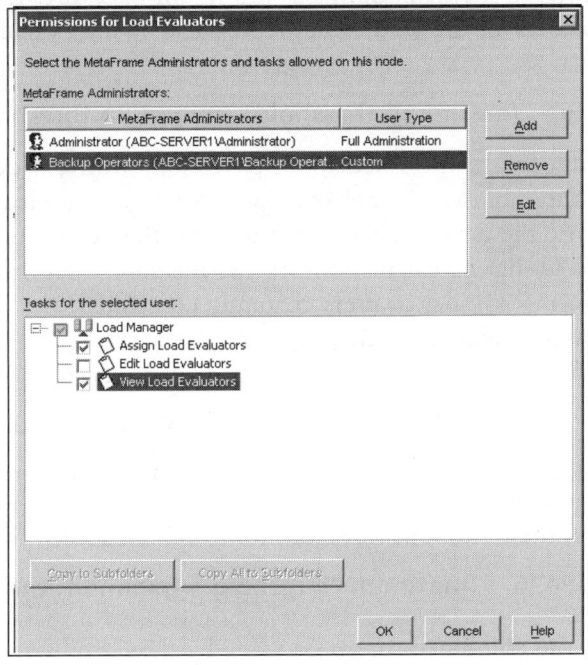

2. Click **Add** to add a user group to the permissions configuration wizard. Once selected, check the individual permission to apply.

3. Once completed, click **OK** to complete the process.

Calculating Load Values

Now that you have created load evaluators, assigned rules, and specified thresholds, you must gain an understanding of how the Citrix MetaFrame Presentation server monitors and reports these values. This understanding is critical to maintaining your server farm. You have learned how to monitor evaluators and rules assigned to specific applications and servers, but how do you tell the current load based on these rules?

Citrix MetaFrame Presentation Server uses load evaluators and thresholds that are defined to calculate the overall load for a server or application. As explained earlier in this chapter, within each rule are specified maximum and minimum thresholds. These values are used to help determine load calculations for each rule. By modifying these values, you can determine how loads are calculated and reported for user sessions.

Servers report load values to the data collector in four-digit integers ranging from 0000 to 9999. Altering the maximum and minimum load thresholds is one method of adjusting the outcome of the load values reported. The load value is calculated using the following formula:

Current rule value / (maximum threshold – minimum threshold)

Each rule must follow this calculation. The results will vary depending on the rules defined and the threshold values. For example, two servers are load managed within a single farm and use the default evaluator. Note that the default evaluator measures only user connections. Using the calculation, we can measure what the load of a particular server is based on the number of users currently connected.

Using the default values provided with this evaluator, use the preceding formula to calculate the load based on six users connected to the server:

1. Apply the default and current values to the load formula:

Current rule value (6) / (maximum threshold (15) – minimum threshold (0))

2. Subtract the minimum threshold from the maximum threshold:

Current rule value (6) / (maximum threshold – minimum threshold = 15)

3. Divide the combined threshold value by the current value:

6 / 15 = 0.4 (40%)

4. Using the method by which servers report values to the data collector, calculate 40% of 10,000. Remember that servers report values ranging from 0000–9999.

10000 x 0.4 (40%) = 4000

The load value reported to the data collector from this exercise is 4000.

Monitoring Load–Balanced Applications

Once an application has been set up with Load Manager, careful monitoring must be performed to ensure evaluators have been properly defined. Various utilities are available to facilitate this task, but the most common tool is Load Manager Monitor. As shown in Figure 11.25, Load Manager Monitor provides the ability to actively monitor load evaluator behavior and current status by graphing activity. Each rule is listed independently while also measuring the overall evaluator load based on all rules configured. Load evaluators can be used for managing load between servers for production applications and to monitor applications to better understand performance characteristics. This utility is available from within the Management Console for MetaFrame Presentation Server by right-clicking the server and selecting **Load Manage Monitor**.

Figure 11.25 Using the Load Manager Monitor

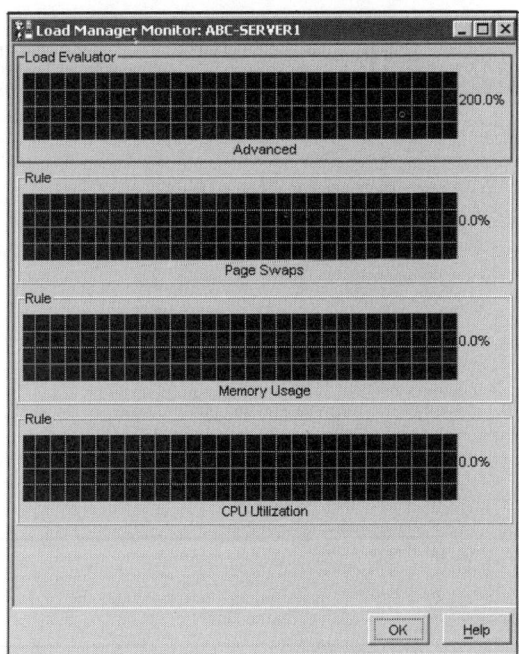

An additional utility that provides more granular detail is QFARM.exe. Installed by default with Citrix MetaFrame Presentation Server, the QFARM command-line utility allows you to monitor load evaluators in more detail than the graphical user interface. For example, load values can be displayed for each server, by application, or both simultaneously. In addition to reporting load values, this single utility can display other items, including the current zone data collector, license information, and server membership. As shown in Figure 11.26, QFARM can be a powerful utility for administering and troubleshooting load management.

Figure 11.26 An Example of Current Load Values for Published Applications and Servers Using QFARM

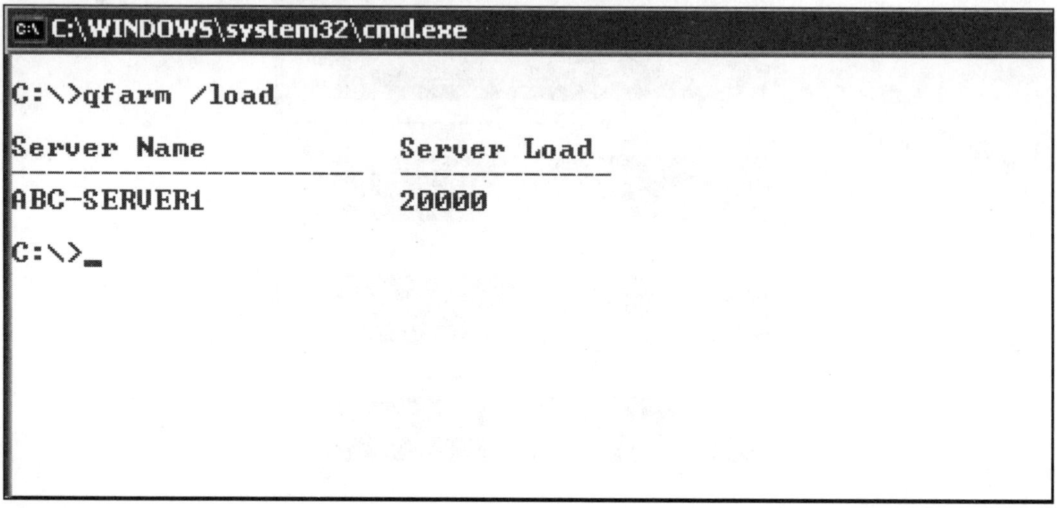

```
C:\WINDOWS\system32\cmd.exe

C:\>qfarm /load

Server Name                    Server Load
_____           _____
ABC-SERVER1                    20000

C:\>_
```

NOTE

When multiple rules are defined within a load evaluator, the rule with the greatest load is reported.

Summary

The first step in securing any computing environment is developing a comprehensive security strategy. Although Citrix MetaFrame Presentation Server provides some built-in capabilities, it might not cover every aspect of your requirements. To resolve this dilemma, you can use some common third-party solutions. The most common solution is virus protection. Used to protect against malicious computer code, virus protection is almost a requirement these days. To monitor your network resources from outside trespassers, intrusion detection software is recommended. This software monitors for unauthorized probing or use of your computing resources. Firewall software is another key component of your security strategy; it provides the gateway to other networks. To protect your internal network, a firewall is generally placed between secured resources and public networks such as the Internet.

One of the primary security mechanisms employed by Citrix MetaFrame Presentation Server is encryption technology. Based on industry-standard mathematical algorithms, encryption is used to scramble data as it is transmitted across the network to prevent unauthorized users from accessing it. Using several different technologies, including symmetric keys, asymmetric keys, and Secure Sockets Layer (SSL), Citrix MetaFrame Presentation Server works to completely secure the entire server farm. When you use Citrix MetaFrame Presentation Server, you choose from among five different encryption strengths: basic, 128-bit logon only, 40-bit, 56-bit, and 128-bit encryption. Once your system is configured properly, all traffic traversing the server farm is encrypted, with the exception of a small encryption header. This includes items such as keystrokes, mouse data, graphical data, client data, and client printing. Using a series of solutions, Citrix MetaFrame covers all the bases.

The most common configuration includes Independent Computing Architecture (ICA) encryption for server connections, published applications, and ICA client. In addition, SSL can be used via Secure HyperText Transfer Protocol (HTTPS) for the Citrix Web Interface and SSL Relay services for communication between Web servers and server farms. To support encryption technology, the ICA client device must be installed with a minimum of version 6.01 of the client software. To take advantage of the latest features, the client device should be installed with client software of 8.1 or higher.

Once you comprehend encryption technologies, you next need to learn how to configure them properly. Various tools are provided to configure encryption, such as the Management Console for MetaFrame Presentation Server, the Citrix Connection Configuration tool, and the SSL Relay Server Configuration tool. Understanding how each is used will allow you to effectively implement your encryption strategy. In addition, you must understand your Web server's configuration tool to properly configure HTTPS services for your Web Interface server pages. This configuration forces client connections to the Web Interface server to process only encrypted pages.

Another critical component in ensuring uptime of your Citrix MetaFrame Presentation server farm is the Load Manager product. With the ability to manage resources across servers to ensure availability, Load Manager is a handy tool. Based on "load evaluators," Load Manager uses rules you define to process incoming ICA client connections. The load evaluators you create continually monitor server usage and report load values to a central data collector so that client connections can be routed to the server with the least load. Rules used in load evaluators consist of items such as processor utilization, memory utilization, license usage, and memory usage, to name a few. Using the Management Console for MetaFrame Presentation Server, you can use the provided default load evaluators or create your own custom evaluator. You must then apply these evaluators to the servers and/or published applications for which you want to monitor. After you apply the rules, use the Load Monitor utility to monitor overall usage to ensure that you are getting the maximum use of your servers without overloading them. Using a predefined formula, you can monitor exact usage and monitor usage through the server farm via command-line utilities.

Solutions Fast Track

Security Strategies for a Citrix MetaFrame Presentation Server Farm

☑ Virus protection is required to protect against malicious computer code and worms. Virus protection is implemented by installing third-party software on computers in danger of getting infected.

☑ Intrusion detection and prevention software is used to monitor and react to network intruders. A variety of solutions exists, from active to passive, network-based and host-based, and signature versus anomaly monitoring.

☑ Firewalls are used to protect private networks from public resources. Firewalls are most commonly used to protect your internal network when it connects to the Internet.

Encrypting Citrix MetaFrame Presentation Server

☑ Citrix MetaFrame Presentation Server uses industry-standard encryption algorithms based on symmetric keys, asymmetric keys, and Secure Sockets Layer (SSL).

☑ Five RC5 encryption strengths are available: basic, 128-bit logon only, 40-bit, 56-bit, and 128-bit. When you set RC5 encryption, all client connections use

128-bit encryption for logon and then begin using the defined encryption strength for the remainder of the connection.

☑ To secure the entire Citrix MetaFrame Presentation Server solution, several encryption technologies are used. Symmetric and asymmetric keys are used in the form of RC5 encryption and Diffie-Hellman public/private keys to secure Independent Computing Architecture (ICA) traffic. SSL is used in the form of Secure HyperText Transfer Protocol (HTTPS) for client-to-Web server traffic, and the SSL Relay service is used to encrypt traffic between Web Interface servers and Citrix MetaFrame Presentation Servers.

Configuring Encryption on Citrix Presentation Server

☑ To configure encryption technologies, different tools are required based on how you want to implement encryption. Management Console for MetaFrame Presentation Server is used to configure published application encryption settings. The Citrix Connection Configuration utility is used to configure server connection encryption. The ICA client software must be used to configure client-specific connections.

☑ To configure HTTPS, you retrieve a server certificate from a certificate authority (CA) and apply it to your Web server. When clients connect to your Web server, they must use the prefix *https* instead of *http*.

☑ To configure the SSL Relay service, you must apply a server certificate from a CA. Once completed, you must configure the server connections that will be used along with the Transmission Control Protocol (TCP) port. By default, TCP port 443 is used.

☑ Citrix Secure Gateway provides a simplified security encryption solution to minimize security requirements and mask the Citrix MetaFrame Presentation Server farm from public networks such as the Internet. The Citrix Secure Gateway is made up of Secure Gateway Server, Logon Agent, Authentication Service, Secure Ticket Authority (STA), Gateway Account, Citrix XML Service, and the Citrix MetaFrame Presentation server farm.

Using Load Manager

☑ Load Manager provides the capability to assign incoming ICA client connections to servers based on the least load. This allows you to ensure that servers are not over-utilized.

☑ To use Load Manager, you must decide on a load evaluator, assign rules to each evaluator, and configure the thresholds for each rule. Once that's done, you assign the load evaluator to published applications or servers as required.

☑ Using the Load Manager Monitor and command-line utilities, you monitor load usage across your Citrix MetaFrame Presentation server farm.

Frequently Asked Questions

The following Frequently Asked Questions, answered by the authors of this book, are designed to both measure your understanding of the concepts presented in this chapter and to assist you with real-life implementation of these concepts. To have your questions about this chapter answered by the author, browse to **www.syngress.com/solutions** and click on the **"Ask the Author"** form. You will also gain access to thousands of other FAQs at ITFAQnet.com.

Q: If 128-bit encryption is the strongest solution, why would I use anything else?

A: With the strong encryption technology comes additional server and ICA client overhead. Although most network connections will not be affected, inconsistent WAN connections or slow dialup networking connections can be affected by the encryption strength used.

Q: Do I need to use a firewall, intrusion detection, and virus protection simultaneously?

A: Your requirements depend on how your environment is designed and your overall security objectives. You might require none of these or all three. For example, if outside computer code can be inserted into your computers via electronic mail, diskette, or another method, you might want to consider using virus protection. If your network is connected to other resources such as the Internet, you might want to consider using a firewall. The need for any of these products must be evaluated on a case-by-case basis.

Q: Why are there so many different ways to configure encryption within Citrix MetaFrame Presentation Server?

A: To meet organizations' varied requirements, Citrix has tried to provide a great deal of flexibility in how and what can be configured relating to encryption technologies. Because so many different variables are involved in using these features, you must truly understand how they all work and the overall effect to take complete advantage of the technology.

Q: Why advantage does Load Manager offer when I can point users to individual servers to separate the load between them?

A: Load Manager allows client connections to be dynamically allocated to servers in real time. This capability helps ease your administrative burden in managing all these connections. In addition, you can add and remove servers seamlessly, without having to recreate user connections.

Q: Why are rules such as IP Range used in Load Manager to determine how heavily used a server is?

A: Citrix MetaFrame XP provides the flexibility to monitor not only server resource utilization but also things such as the source network location. For example, if you want all incoming connections from a particular network to use a particular set of servers, the IP range provides this capability.

Q: To encrypt all traffic passing through the entire Citrix MetaFrame Presentation Server solution, why do you have to configure multiple items?

A: Several of the technologies involved, such as Web services, are not controlled or maintained by Citrix. Using other third-party solutions such as Netscape Web server or Microsoft Internet Information Services as a Web server requires its own method to secure them. Fortunately, industry-standard products such as SSL provide an easily implemented technology that can be used to complete these tasks.

Chapter 12

Configuring Policies (Group Policies and Citrix Policies)

Solutions in this chapter:

- Windows Server 2003 Group Policy

- Configuring Group Policy with the Group Policy Management Console

- Configuring Citrix MetaFrame Policies

☑ Summary

☑ Solutions Fast Track

☑ Frequently Asked Questions

Introduction

The successful implementation of an efficient, easy to use, and easy to manage Citrix MetaFrame Presentation Server farm does not simply rely on a correctly installed terminal server. The associated infrastructure (Active Directory, domain security and network topology) plays an undeniably essential role in supporting users, application access, and performance and reliability—all factors that determine whether an MPS 3.0 Server farm is living up to its potential.

To illustrate this point, think about these questions. How do you ensure that confidential documents used by one group of users you support are printed only on the printers at that group's location? How do you ensure that remote users connecting from a hotel's unsecured Internet connection are adequately protected from a hacker snooping around for information? How do you ensure that those same remote users are not passing viruses to your network over the Citrix Web connection from the PC they are using at the local Internet café? The answers to these questions can all be supplied via the appropriate application of a combination of Windows group policies and Citrix policies.

The goal of this chapter is to familiarize you with both Windows and Citrix policies and show you how you can configure them to work together to ensure seamless, reliable, and secure access for your users to their applications via their Citrix connections no matter where they are and how they connect.

Windows Server 2003 Group Policy

Some of us who are familiar with group policies in Windows 2000 will appreciate the enhancements introduced in Windows Server 2003 Group Policy; others who have been frustrated by Windows 2000 Group Policy will be pleasantly surprised. Although it brings with it 200 + new policy settings, Window Server 2003 Group Policy also brings with it an easier to understand management interface in the form of the Group Policy Management Console (GPMC), and modeling and testing features that allow administrators to more accurately and effectively plan domain and security policies before implementing them.

Administrators are now able to affect policies that fit their particular situations more closely and avoid more of the mistakes that result from poorly configured group policy objects (GPOs). Microsoft's new unified Group Policy model makes it possible to view and manage all GPOs across a domain, organizational unit (OU), or site, and for the first time gives administrators the "big picture" view of the networks they manage. Coupled with Windows Management Instrumentation filters, administrators can see how GPOs affect different machines based on their individual hardware and software characteristics. In addition, Windows Server 2003 Group Policy enhancements support group policy changes in the entire Windows 2000 family of operating systems, Windows XP, and Windows Server 2003 platforms.

For example, it is now possible to see how a GPO that requires machines to perform an antivirus update and scan may require more memory or simply not work for remote laptop users versus desktop users in the office on a Windows network. You could also predict how older machines with slower processors are affected versus the newer, faster machines that an IT staff rolled out (Figure 12.1). The benefit to an IT staff in the time and cost savings that Windows Server 2003 Group Policy provides is more than just an abstract factor. Knowing how a policy affects different machines on a network beforehand or as it is happening allows an IT staff to quickly identify and implement remedies to the issues that arise. This in turn translates to less downtime and increased productivity.

Figure 12.1 Different Windows Server 2003 Policies for Different OUs

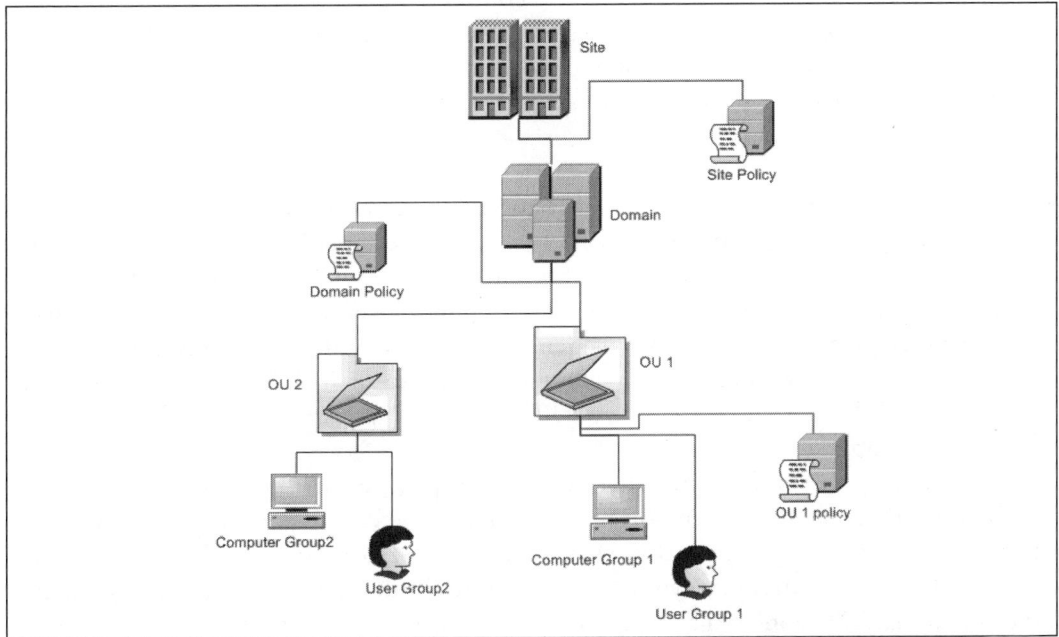

One of the primary aims of group policy was the enforcement of a consistent security stance within an organization's network. Most IT professionals know the concept of a rigidly enforced security policy across an enterprise is a fallacy. Operational demands and changing business rules and roles have made the "one solution fits all situations" paradigm outdated and a rather foolish proposition. The flexibility required of systems that support business of any kind continues to grow. Multiple GPOs must apply to individual user and computer groups, OUs, and domains. Administrators must meet the demands of in-house and remote users, customers and partners. Windows Server 2003 Group Policy goes further to aid administrators in this constantly evolving endeavor via the Administrative Templates node of the Group Policy snap-in.

The new Group Policy features also allow for backup and restore of GPOs. If an administrator has backed up his GPOs, he can restore them to user and computer groups, domains, OUs, or sites should his new GPOs produce an undesired effect.

Configuring Group Policy with the Group Policy Management Console

Group Policy is a feature used in Windows to enhance and control users' desktops and computers. It is enabled by the Windows Active Directory Service and can also be used with MetaFrame servers installed as either domain controllers or member servers. The procedures for using group policies are the same on either platform, so any procedures we discuss in this section can be used in any configuration of the two.

Group Policy was designed and is used by administrators to help centralize administration of user desktop configurations, reduce user support requirements, and enhance the security of network systems. It handles these tasks by allowing the administrator(s) to customize and control users' access to registry-based settings, security settings, and software installation and maintenance. They can automate many tasks using logon, logoff, startup, and shutdown scripts, and OS installation and Internet Explorer maintenance. User data files and folders can be redirected from the user's hard drive to network drives, where backups can be performed or preconfigured desktop displays can be pushed to new users. All these options are available, with different levels of access and control provided to different users and locations, depending on the requirements. This flexibility enables programmers to have virtually complete access to their desktops and all kinds of applications, while restricting data entry staff to only the few applications they need to perform their job.

The features and controls provided by Group Policy become even more valuable to MetaFrame administrators when you realize that your server becomes the users' desktop machines when they are using a thin client, Terminal Services client, or ICA client connection. How many times have your users broken their desktop machines through ignorance or misuse? We don't really want them doing that to our servers, do we? This is where group policies come into play.

We do not try to go into a detailed discussion of all the finer aspects and programming issues of Group Policy in this chapter. That topic could make up an entire book in itself. Instead, we focus on how to get started with group policies, how they can improve the user's experience with MetaFrame, and how they can benefit you, the MetaFrame administrator. From there, you should be able to develop your own policies and apply them in a manner consistent with your environment.

Features of the GPMC

As in Windows 2000, Windows Server 2003 Group Policy allows an administrator to configure groups of computers or users in a domain, site, or OU. Administrators would typically have read and write access to the domain system volume (Sysvol) folder to make configuration changes to user and computer accounts in a domain. Administrators use a combination of Active Directory administration tools, the Windows Server 2003 Group Policy Management Console (GPMC), and the Group Policy Object Editor to deploy and manage group policy. The GPMC includes the following features:

- **Integrated MMC Snap-In** The new MMC snap-in provides a view of an enterprise from a policy management perspective. The user interface displays GPOs and associated links in a way that makes more sense to the administrator. All administrative features such as user and computer administration, site and OU administration are integrated into the new console so we no longer have to switch to other consoles to perform the various operations involved in Windows domain management.

- **GPMC Reporting** A rich HTML-based reporting environment for GPOs and their policy settings is included.

- **Group Policy Results and Modeling** This feature allows administrators to readily see Resultant Set of Policy (RSoP) data. RSoP makes it easy for an administrator to determine the resulting set of policies for a given user or computer in both actual and "what-if" scenarios. In the GPMC, Group Policy Results displays the result of a query made directly against a computer/user. Group Policy Modeling enables what-if simulation of user/computer scenarios and can be an important tool when planning changes to a Group Policy implementation. Group Policy Modeling requires a Windows Server 2003 domain controller.

- **Support for Backup, Staging, and Testing Group Policy Objects** Using this feature, administrators can maintain GPO templates—versions of GPOs for different configurations, such as highly managed desktops, laptops, Terminal Services on Windows Server 2003, and so on. Administrators can use backup, copying, and importing features with GPOs to deploy configurations rapidly throughout an organization.

- **Enhanced User Interface in the Group Policy Object Editor** Policy settings are more easily understood, managed, and verified with Web-view integration in the Group Policy Object Editor. Clicking a policy displays text that explains its function. The operating systems that support the policy are displayed via a new **Supported On** tag.

- **Scriptable Interfaces** Operations such as backup, restore, import, copy, and reporting on GPOs can be performed via Windows scripts, which lets administrators customize and automate management. However, don't get too happy; it is not yet possible to script individual policy settings within a GPO using the scriptable interfaces.

- **Support for Cross-Forest Trusts** Administrators can manage group policy for multiple domains and sites within a given forest, all in a simplified user interface with drag-and-drop support. Cross-forest trust enables administrators to manage group policy across multiple forests from one console.

The Group Policy Management Console provides a more complete view of the operating system, computer, software, and user configurations across a domain, OU, or site. The GPMC includes all the functionality of the following administration tools in one management console:

- Active Directory Users and Computers

- Active Directory Sites and Services

- Resultant Set of Policy MMC snap-in

- ACL Editor

- Delegation Wizard

Figure 12.2 shows the GPMC.

Figure 12.2 The GPMC

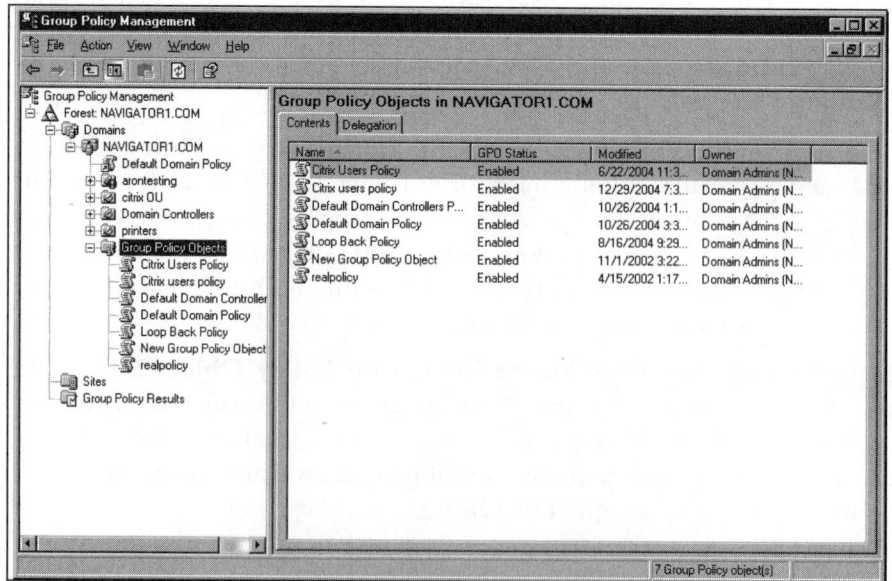

Installing the GPMC

The GPMC is a downloadable product from the Microsoft Downloads Web site. It does not come on the Windows Server 2003 CD. To install the GPMC:

1. Double-click the **gpmc.msi** package, and click **Next** (Figure 12.3).

Figure 12.3 GPMC Installation

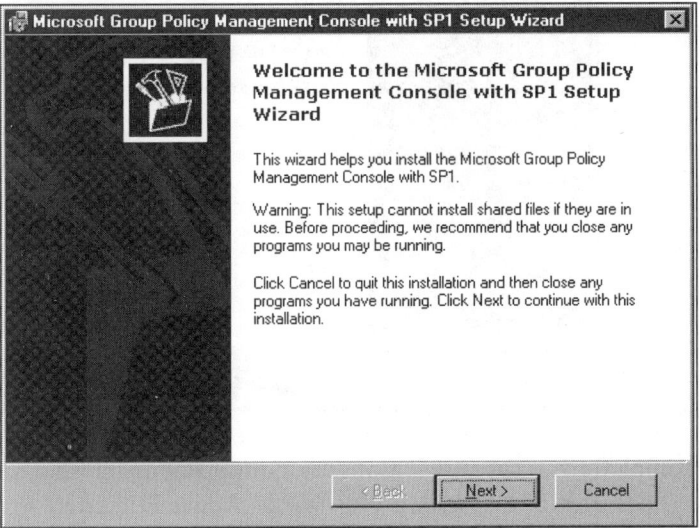

2. Agree to the End User License Agreement (EULA), and click **Next** (Figure 12.4).

Figure 12.4 Policy Management Console License Agreement

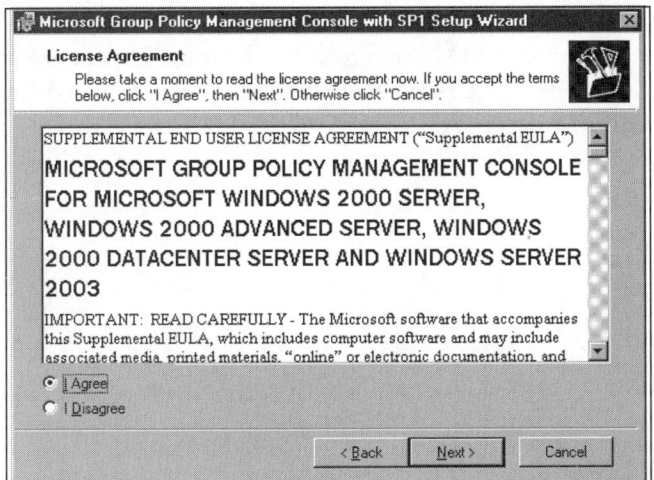

3. Click **Finish** to complete the installation (Figure 12.5).

Figure 12.5 Group Policy Finish

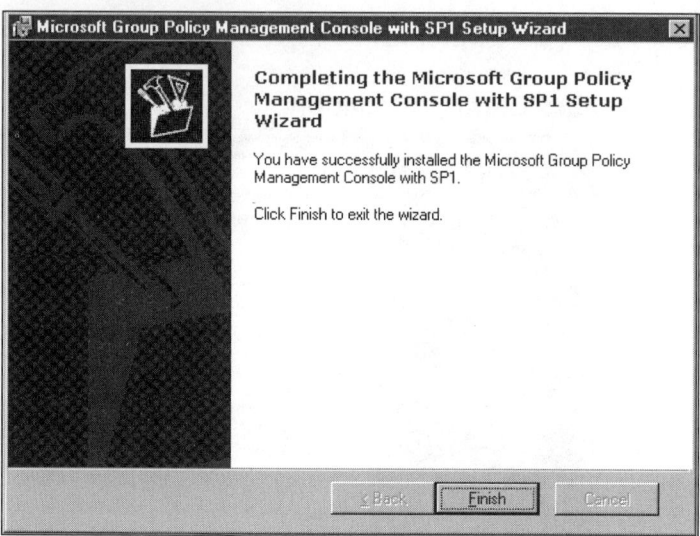

Upon completion of the installation, the Group Policy tab that appeared on the Property pages of sites, domains, and OUs in the Active Directory snap-ins is updated to provide a direct link to GPMC. The functionality that previously existed on the original Group Policy tab is no longer available, since all functionality for managing Group Policy is available through GPMC.

To open the GPMC snap-in directly, use either of the following methods:

■ Click the **Group Policy Management** shortcut in the **Administrative Tools** folder on the Start menu or in the Control Panel (Figure 12.6).

■ Create a custom MMC console. Click **Start**, **Run**, type **MMC**, and click **OK**. Point to **File**, click **Add/Remove Snap-in**, click **Add**, highlight **Group Policy Management**, click **Add**, click **Close**, and then click **OK**.

Figure 12.6 Accessing the GPMC

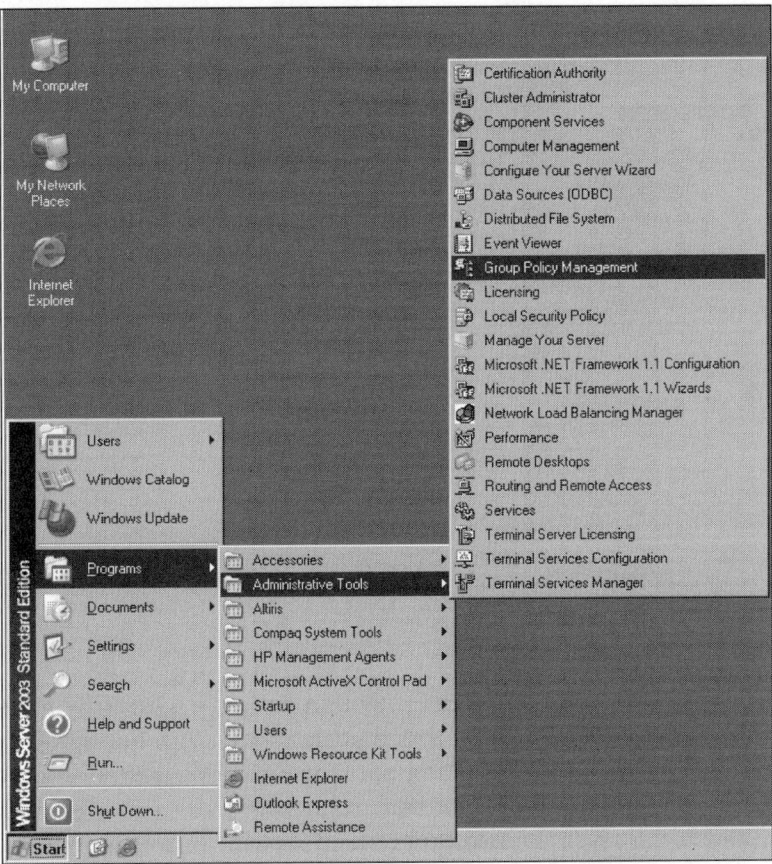

To repair or remove GPMC, use **Add or Remove Programs** in Control Panel. Alternatively, run the gpmc.msi package, select the appropriate option, and click **Finish**.

Using the GPMC

As mentioned previously, the GPMC takes the place of the administration tools usually used to manage computers and users in a Windows Server 2003 domain. Administrator can use the GPMC for the same tasks that previously required a combination of tools to perform.

Now, let's turn our attention to the components (referred to as *nodes*) and their relevance to managing MetaFrame Presentation Server 3.0 in a Windows 2003 Terminal Services environment (Figure 12.7).

Figure 12.7 GPMC Components

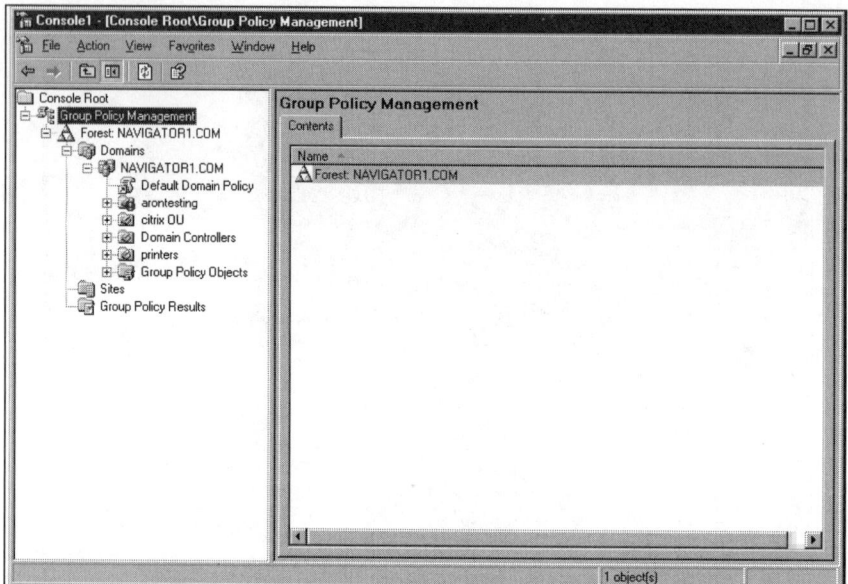

The Domains Node

The Domains node contains all the domains within an Active Directory forest, Domains nodes are identified by their DNS domain names. Administrators can choose which domains to display by right-clicking the Domains node and selecting the **Show Domains** menu option. Group policies that are meant to affect individual domains should be created at this level. Domain user accounts with Terminal Services access are frequently used to grant access to specific applications in a MetaFrame environment. Group policies that affect domains and the inheritance of these policies play an important part in configuring the environment appropriately.

The Sites Node

The Sites node contains all the sites within an Active Directory forest. As with domains, administrators can choose the sites they see by right-clicking the node and selecting the **Show Sites** menu option. No sites are displayed by default. Group policies intended to affect individual sites should be created here.

The Group Policy Modeling Node

This node is a new and powerful management feature that allows administrators to simulate policy settings applied to users and computers before actually applying the policies. This "what if" tool makes it possible to see via the **Resultant Set of Policy (RSoP)— Planning Mode**, a new feature in Windows Server 2003, what effect a policy or policies would have on any users and computers in a forest. This node only works if at least one domain controller is a Windows Server 2003 server, as the service that actually performs the simulation only exists on Windows Server 2003 domain controllers. Each policy simulation is displayed as a subnode of the Group Policy Modeling node.

Policy modeling comes in handy when first designing a MetaFrame infrastructure or when making changes to security settings that may affect access to applications. The ability to try the policies first, before implementing them, helps the administrator to avoid crucial mistakes. For example, in designing policies for remote MetaFrame users as opposed to local users, an administrator may need to make provisions for bandwidth differences or security levels between the two groups. Modeling allows the administrator to see what settings would work.

The Group Policy Results Node

Instead of showing you the **Resultant Set of Policy** for a simulation, the Group Policy Results node allows you to see the effect of policies that have actually been applied to computer and users accounts in a forest (referred to as the RSoP—Logging Mode). The results here are obtained via queries performed on the user or computer account and are displayed as subnodes in the GPMC (Figure 12.8). Group Policy Results information can only be obtained from computers running Windows XP or Windows Server 2003.

Figure 12.8 Group Policy Results

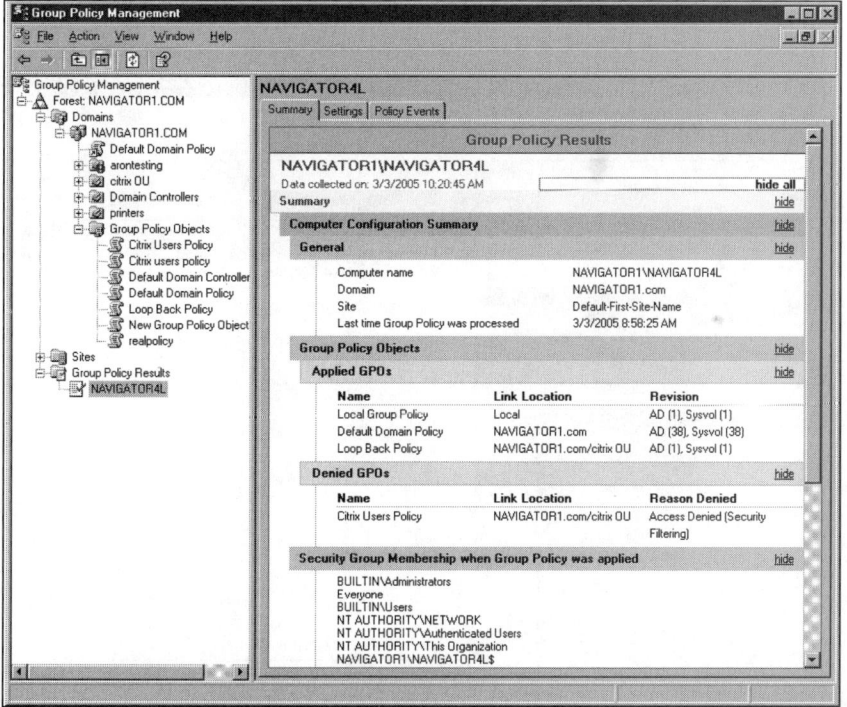

As with Group Policy Modeling, the ability to see the effect of a policy or set of policies provides administrators a roadmap of what's going on and what policy affects what user or computer in what way. For example, in troubleshooting connectivity problems, the RSoP would help to point an administrator in the right direction to identify the problem and come up with a viable solution.

Creating and Editing Group Policy Objects with the GPMC

The main purpose of the GPMC is to allow administrators to more easily create, implement, and manage GPOs in an Active Directory forest. The process of creating a GPO and applying it to a set of users or computers is called "scoping the GPO." Effectively scoping a GPO depends on three factors:

- The domain, site, or OU where the GPO is created and linked

- The security filtering configured on the GPO

- The Windows Management Instrumentation filter configured on the GPO

Let's follow the process of creating and applying a GPO:

1. Right-click a domain or OU displayed in the GPMC and select **Create and Link a GPO Here…**(Figure 12.9). It's that simple!

Figure 12.9 Creating a GPO

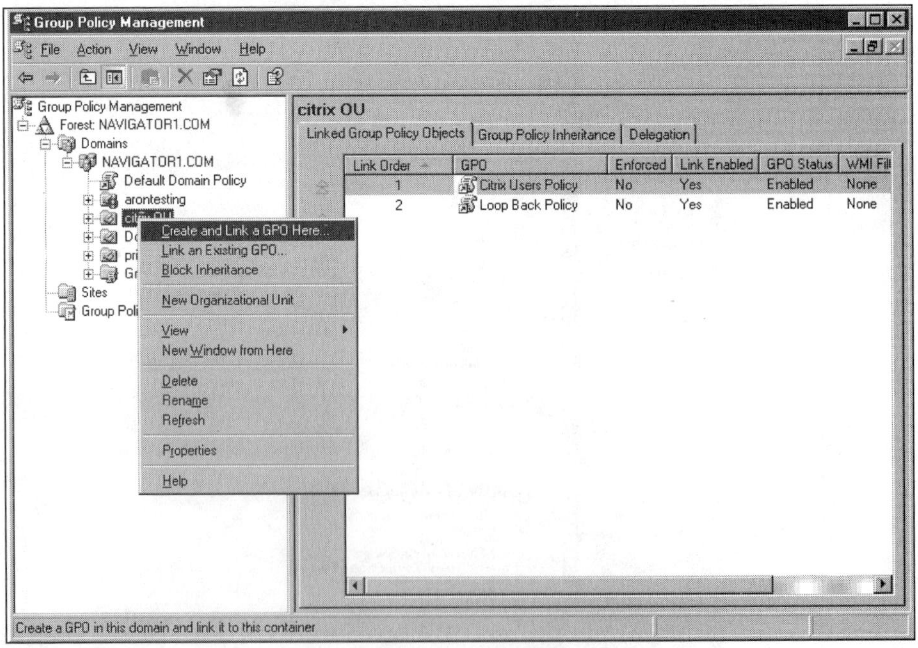

After a GPO is created and linked to a site, domain, or OU, it is referred to as the GPO's Scope of Management (SOM). When a GPO is created, it has no settings defined. GPOs are configured by using the Group Policy Object Editor. The GPO Editor can be accessed by right-clicking a GPO and selecting **Edit**. Figure 12.10 shows the details and settings that can be configured in a GPO.

Figure 12.10 Editing a GPO

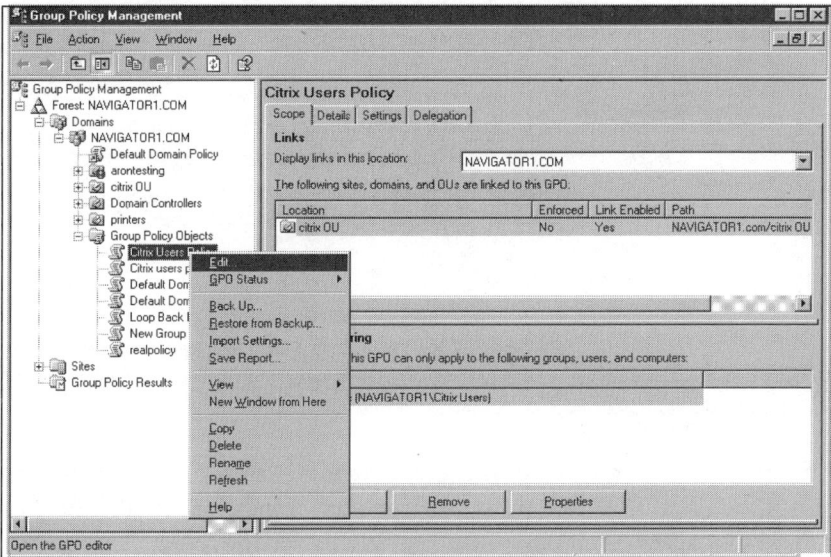

Once the GPO is created, configured, and linked to a SOM (a domain, site, or OU), it can be tweaked to have the desired effect on the SOM. This can be accomplished either by security filtering or WMI filtering, or a combination of both.

Security filtering involves setting the permissions on a GPO for a user, a user group, or a computer. The Windows Authenticated Users group—which usually contains all domain users and computers—has the default permissions of Read and Apply Group Policy for any GPO that is created and linked to the SOM they are in. However, users, groups, or computers that are normally a part of the Authenticated Users group can be excluded from the effects of a GPO by removing those permissions from them. Figure 12.11 shows the Security filter of an OU GPO.

Figure 12.11 Security Filter on a GPO

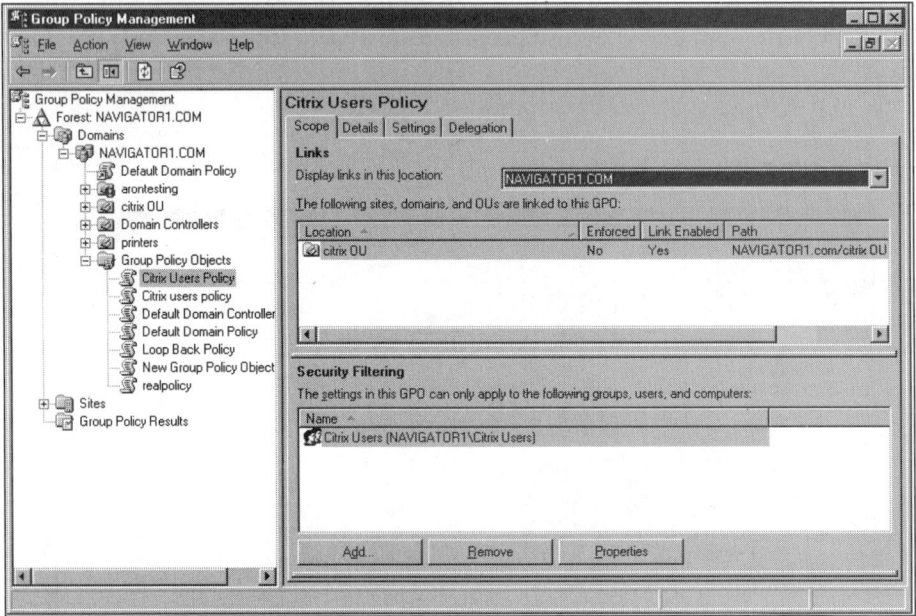

WMI filtering, however, involves using the attributes of a computer to determine application of the GPO. WMI filters are queries that search for specific attributes of a computer (hard disk space, memory, operating system version, etc.). The query information is returned as true or false responses for particular properties of the target computers. It is important to note that a WMI filter is a separate object from a GPO in Active Directory. They can be linked, however, and this is where filtering comes in. If an administrator attempts to apply a GPO that is linked to a WMI filter, the queries contained in the filter are run. If the queries return true responses, the GPO is successfully applied. If not, the GPO has no effect on the computer.

Configuring and Implementing...

Configuring GPOs in Mixed Environments

Many organizations still use multiple operating systems on client machines. It should be noted that Microsoft's WMI features have only begun to mature, and client support for WMI only exists on Windows XP. Therefore, note that when configuring WMI filters for GPOs, Windows 2000 and earlier clients will ignore the WMI filter and the GPO will always apply regardless.

Policy Design Considerations

As alluded to in the preceding sidebar, not everything configured in a Windows Server 2003 infrastructure works for every client. Many of the features of Windows Server 2003 Group Policy are not compatible with Windows 2000 and earlier clients. A compromise in design of a Citrix MetaFrame infrastructure using Windows Server 2003 that supports clients running various versions of Windows must be reached that has the most backward compatibility possible. The following tips will be useful in planning a design:

- **Create a test group that accurately represents your client base.** This give you the ability to test your deployment as any good IT professional would.

- **Take full advantage of the Group Policy Modeling feature.** The ability to see what can happen beforehand is a gift that administrators seldom have—use it wisely.

- **If possible, separate down-level clients from up-to-date clients.** Creating a separate policy for each group may bridge the gap and give you the control and security you need.

Designing and Planning…

Making Your Life Easier when Configuring GPOs

It is a good practice to separate distinct functional groups in Active Directory into OUs. User accounts and computers should be in separate OUs. For example, Executive Management at your company should be in their own OU, separate from Engineering, and so on. Their computers should also be in their own OU. This allows for more granular control. You can apply or disable GPOs to specific groups and not have to worry about exceptions to the GPO. If you take the time to design a hierarchy that makes sense with regard to your business, managing and troubleshooting Active Directory and GPOs will be much less complex.

GPO Elements of Special Importance

Since we've familiarized ourselves with Group Policy and how to navigate within the GPMC, let us now look at some GPO elements of special importance to deploying and administering a Citrix MetaFrame Presentation Server environment. In this section, we'll see how group policy plays an integral role in MetaFrame deployment—of facilitating installation of client software.

So, we've built and configured our servers and set up a farm. How then do we get the MetaFrame client software to our end users without having to track each of them down and install the software? The answer is very simple. Use group policy to install the software on the end-users' machines when they log on to the domain. The second question arises: How do we accomplish that? The answer is Group Policy Software Installation (Figure 12.12).

Figure 12.12 Group Policy Software Installation Node

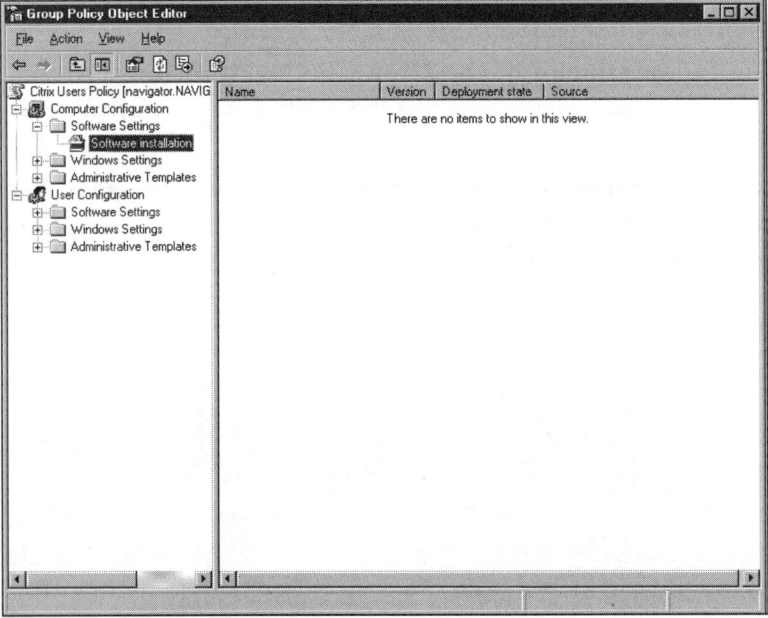

The Group Policy Software Installation node enables administrators to install and manage software across the enterprise. Administrators can specify the method of installation, the installation targets, and the parameters for the installation. Once an installation package has been created, the Winlogon service controls deployment of the application. Applications within the Group Policy Software Installation node can be managed in one of two modes: assigned or published. An assigned application is one that is installed when the computer starts up or when the user logs in to the domain. Once the application is installed, the end -user accesses the software and the installation is completed. A published application is one in which the application appears in the Add/Remove Program dialog box and the end user is able to install it from there. The Group Policy Software Installation node is reached by editing a GPO.

There are two Software Installation assignments, a per–computer assignment and a per–user assignment. The Software Installation node under the Computer Configuration GPO node is used to deploy software that is necessary for every computer in your enterprise. The software to be installed under this node is always installed in Assigned mode (Figure 12.13). Once a machine starts up on the domain, the software is installed and is available to any user that logs on to the machine. Assigned software can also be assigned to a specific end user so that when that person logs on to a computer, the software is installed even if the user logs on to different computers. The software installation follows the user. As with the computer assignment, the software installation isn't finalized until end–users launch the application.

Figure 12.13 The Software Installation Method Window

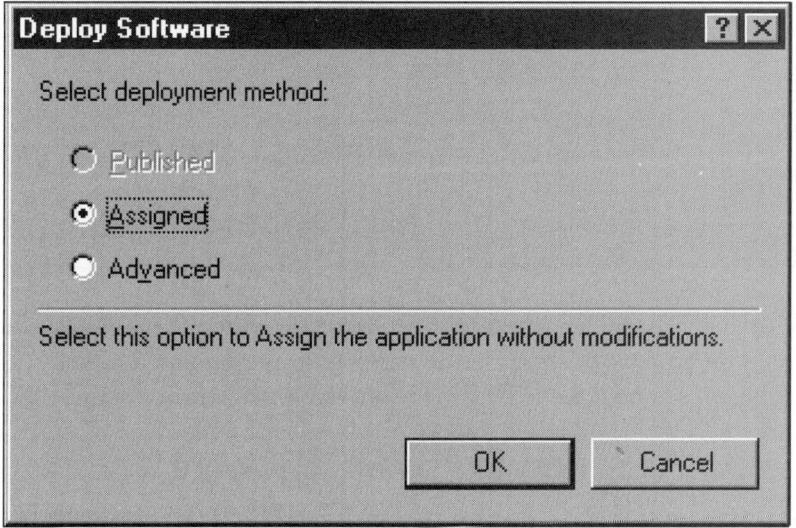

Published applications can only be installed for end users (Figure 12.14) in the User Configuration node. Published applications are meant to service the end users managed by a particular GPO. The users choose whether they want the application installed. When users log in to their computers, the published application is available for installation via the Add/Remove Programs window. The software becomes installed when the user selects to perform the installation in the Add/Remove Programs window, or opens a file that is native to the application such as a .doc file for Microsoft Word.

Figure 12.14 The Published Application Installation Method

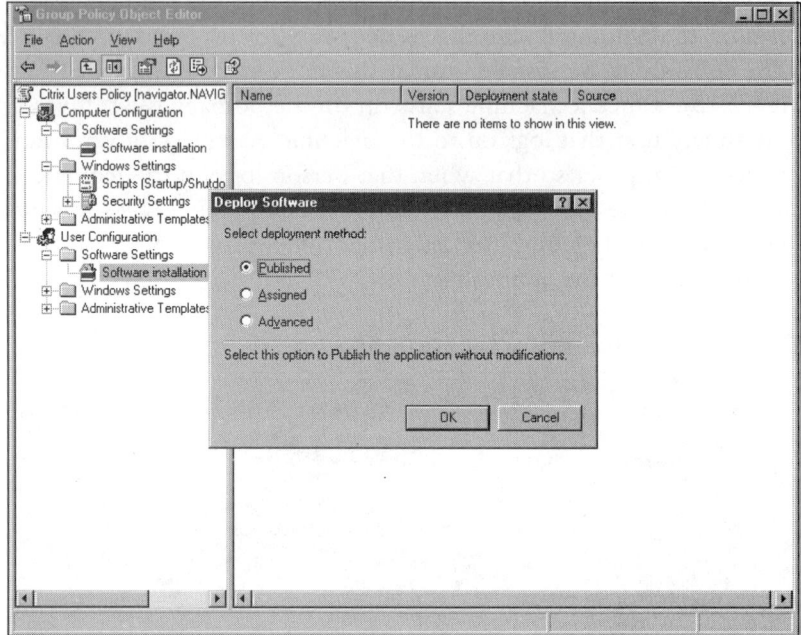

It is important for software installations of either kind to access installation packages that are located on a network share that is available to the intended target. Let us now look at creating an assigned and a published software installation.

Creating an Assigned Software Package Installation in the Computer Configuration Node

1. Right-click the **Software Installation node** under the **Computer Configuration node** and select **New Package** as shown in Figure 12.15.

Figure 12.15 Creating a New Installation Package

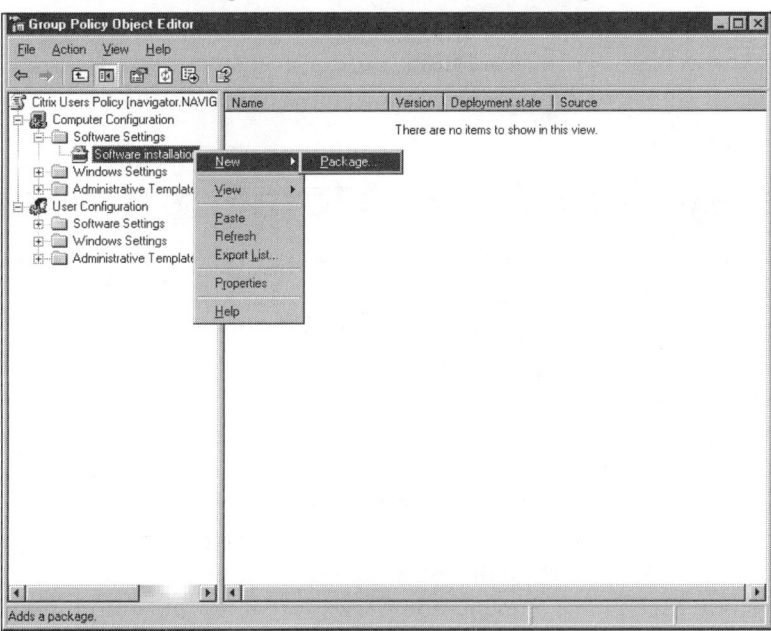

2. Browse to the network share in which the desired software installation package is stored and select the package as shown in Figure 12.16.

Figure 12.16 Selecting Installation Package

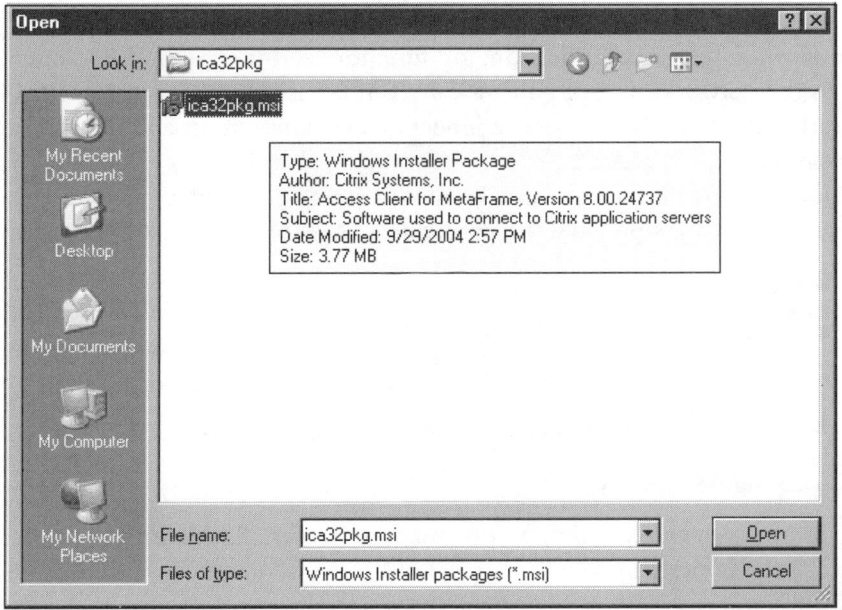

3. Click **OK** on the **Deployment Method** window that appears.

4. Click **OK** on the next window that displays the package properties to accept the defaults. A software installation package has been created. The same process is followed for the published software installation package

Configuring Citrix MetaFrame Policies

Now that we've seen what can be done to facilitate users and computers from a Windows standpoint, we are ready to delve into the added flexibility and robustness provided by Citrix MetaFrame Presentation Server 3.0 for clients.

As in earlier MetaFrame versions, administrators are able to configure policies for users and user groups. MetaFrame Presentation Server allows creation and configuration of user and user group policies, and allows administrators to create and configure policies based on server groups, IP addresses, and client names. New MetaFrame policy rules now allow more control across the board to affect features such as printing, bandwidth limits for connections, zone connection, and reliability preferences, to name a few.

At the heart of it, Citrix policies define connection settings. The new capabilities introduced by MetaFrame Presentation Server 3.0 allow an administrator to define the policies for and servers, client machines, and IP addresses he wishes. A single policy can contain multiple rules that apply different settings to all of these entities in one shot.

Creating and Configuring Policies

Administrators can create policies and configure them to meet the needs of the users they support. Policies and the rules they contain can be made to support end users based on their geographic location, job function, and the method by which they connect to the network. Citrix policies can even be used cooperatively with Windows Group Policy to secure end-user connections via encryption and deny drive mapping, for example.

Since in most scenarios it usually makes sense to use uniform criteria in designing Windows and Citrix policies, the procedures used for creating a policy are:

- Creating the policy.
- Configuring the policy rules.
- Assigning the policy to user accounts, servers, or client machines.
- Prioritizing the policies.

To configure a policy:

1. Launch the MetaFrame Presentation Server Management console and locate the Policies node.

2. Right-click the **Policies** node and select **Create Policy**.

3. Type a name for the policy and click **OK**. You have just created a Citrix policy.

Once a policy is created, it must be configured and assigned to servers, users, or client machines. A policy is inactive unless its rules have been configured and it has been assigned to an object on your network. Policies take effect once a user logs in and remain in effect for the duration of the ICA session. We mentioned earlier that a policy can contain many rules. These rules determine what happens at the user, server, or client machine level once an ICA session has been established. Policy rules exist in three states: enabled, disabled, and not configured. By default, all policy rules are not configured. All rules that are not configured are ignored when users log on to the server, so a rule only has functionality when it is enabled or disabled. Disabled rules effectively turn off or turn on a feature or setting for a user. For example, if the rule **Turn off auto client update** is enabled, the Citrix ICA client software on a connecting client machine will not be updated to the newest available version when a user logs in to the Citrix farm using that client machine (Figure 12.17).

Figure 12.17 The Auto Client Update Policy Options

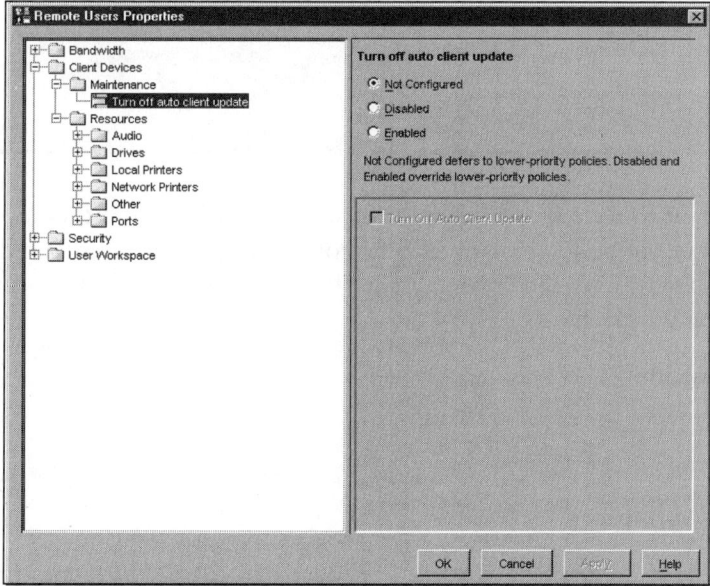

Conversely, enabled rules allow administrators to turn a feature on or off when someone logs in to the Citrix farm, and to configure the extent or support an activated feature provides. We can use the example of the **Auto creation** rule for local printers. When the rule is enabled, it allows administrators to determine how many of the clients'

attached printers will have virtual printers created for them within the ICA session (Figure 12.18).

Figure 12.18 Configuring an Enabled Policy

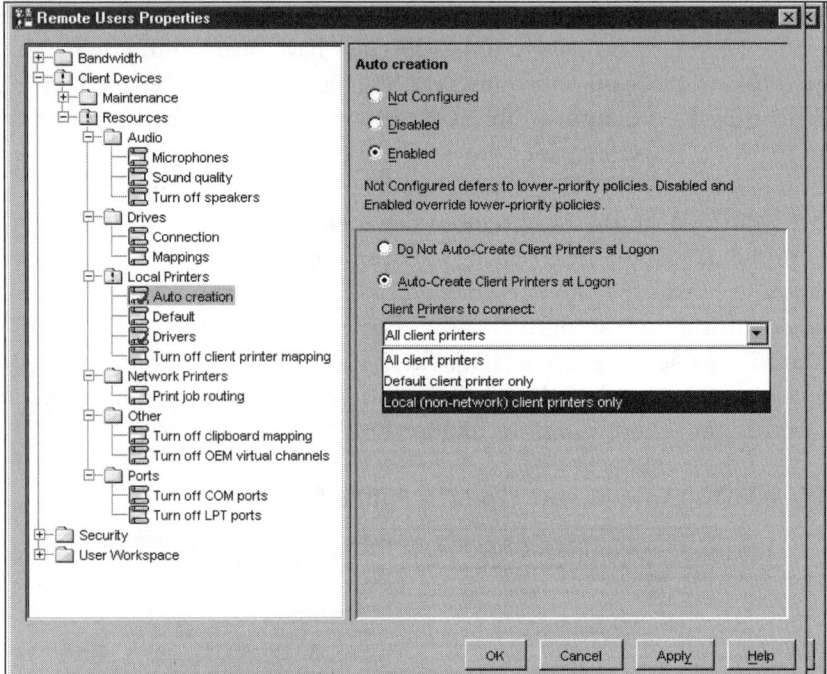

It is important to note that entire policies can be disabled, and then none of the rules contained in the policy has any effect. Policy rules can be configured for all of the following main features in Citrix MetaFrame Presentation Server 3.0 via the policy's Properties dialog window:

- Bandwidth
- Client Devices
- Security
- User Workspace

Each of these main features contains subnodes that allow configuration of options ranging from a user's audio and visual settings to the level of encryption used during the sessions (Figure 12.19).

Figure 12.19 A Main Policy Rule and Its Subnodes

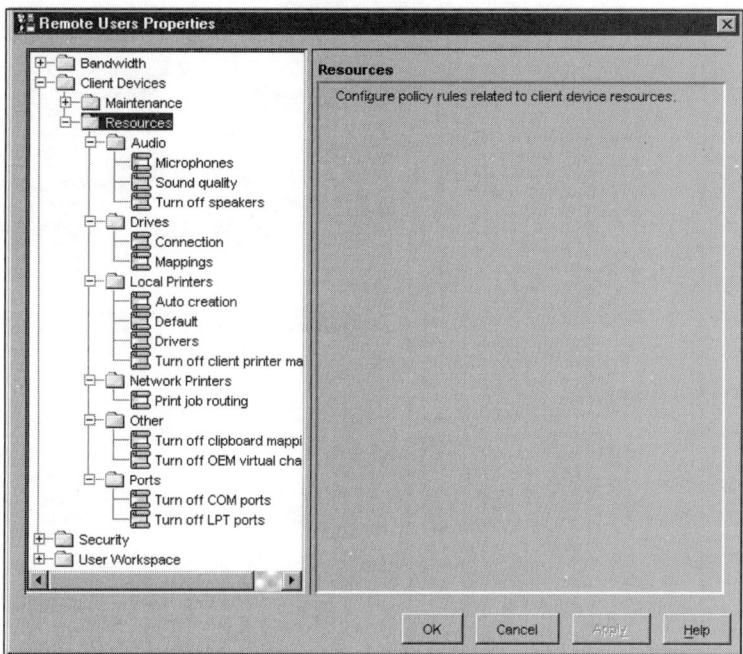

Let us look at an example of configuring policy rules by configuring a rule for printer drivers.

Configuring policy rules:

1. In the MetaFrame management console, locate the policy that you would like to configure, right-click the policy, and select **Properties**.

2. Once the Policy Properties dialog window appears, select the **Client Devices** node, navigate down to the **Local Printers** subnode, and select the **Drivers** rule.

3. Enable the Drivers rule by selecting the **Enabled** option

4. Configure the rule to allow native and Citrix Universal driver support by selecting the option shown in Figure 12.20.

Figure 12.20 Configuring the Local Printer Driver Rule

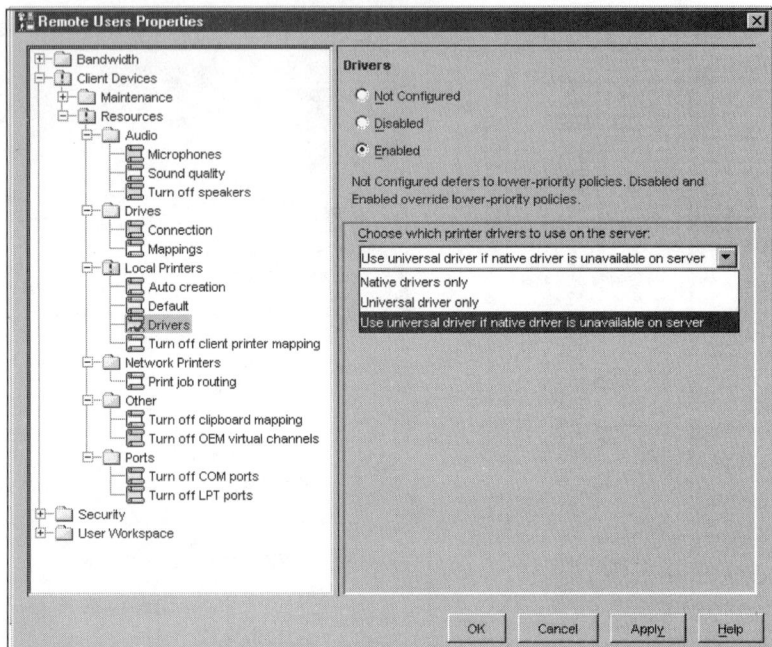

5.   Click **Apply**, and then click **OK**. You have just configured a rule.

Applying Policy Filters

The next step in using Citrix policies is the assignment of a policy to a server, user or user group, or client machine. This is done by configuring a *policy filter.* A policy filter simply says that a certain policy is to be applied to client machines, users or certain user groups, servers they log in to, and the range of IP addresses from which they access the Citrix farm. For example, a policy can be created for remote users in Cleveland who connect from the 172.16.1.0 IP address range, while a second policy can be applied to remote users from Cleveland who connect from the 192.168.1.0 IP address range. Policies are not applied to any users, client machines, servers or groups by default when they are created. They must be applied to at least one object for the policy to take effect. The following steps demonstrate how to apply a policy to a user group, a server, an IP range, or specific client names.

1.   Right-click the policy, or select the policy and click the **Actions** menu, and select **Apply this policy to** (Figure 12.21).

Figure 12.21 Applying a Citrix Policy Filter

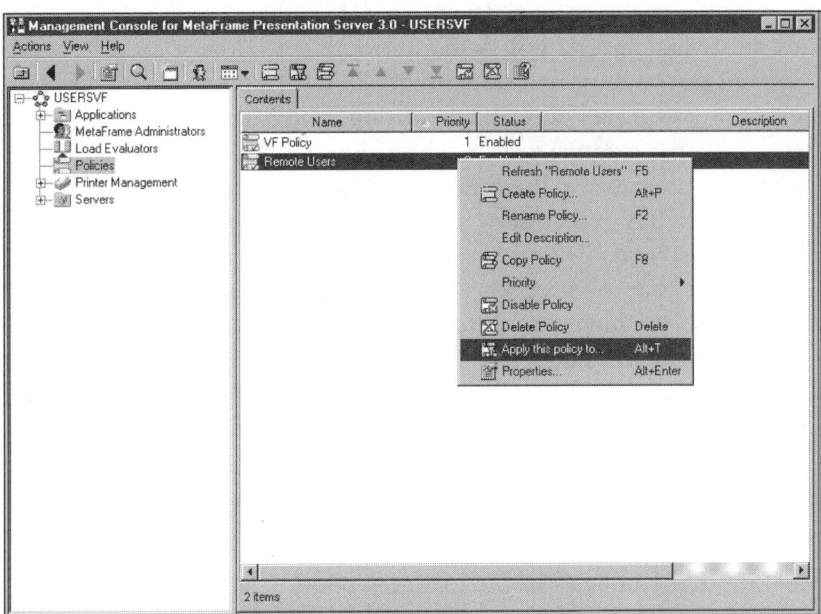

2. When the Policy Filters window appears, select **Client IP Address** to apply
    the policy to a specific IP or IP range (Figure 12.22), **Client Name** to apply
    the policy to specific client machines, **Servers** to apply a policy to a server or
    group of servers, or **Users** to apply the policy to a specific Windows domain
    user or user group.

Figure 12.22 Policy Filters

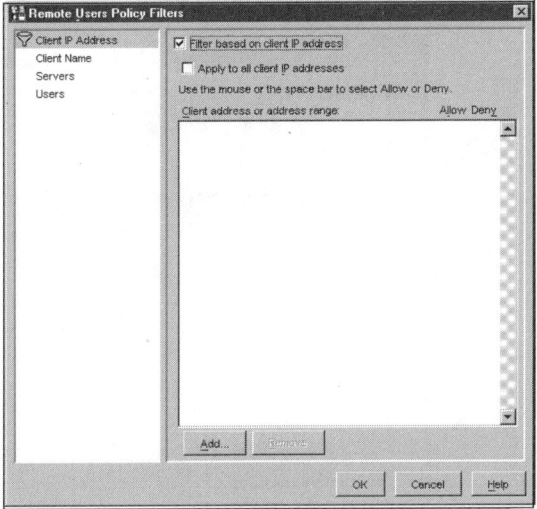

Policies can have exceptions. For example, you may wish that all employees except executives are never able to save data to their local hard drives. To accomplish this, you must first create and apply a policy that prevents mapping of local drives to all users. Then, another policy must be created that allows mapping of local drives. This policy is assigned to the Executives domain user group. You would then give this new policy precedence over the original policy. This is known as *prioritizing policies*.

Prioritizing policies sets the order of application or validity of one policy over another. When policy A has higher priority over policy B, policy A's rules are enforced on its target users, servers, or client machines. As mentioned previously, prioritizing policies is a great way to set up exceptions for special access to resources. All newly created policies have the lowest priority by default. A policy with a priority number of 1 has the highest priority. The larger the priority number, the lower the policy's priority. When a user logs in to a Citrix farm, the enabled policies that match that user's policy filter are evaluated. The highest priority policy is assessed and applied first, then the next highest policy, and so on. Policy rules that are configured as disabled take precedence over similarly ranked policies that have the same rule configured as enabled. To prioritize policies:

1. Locate the policies in the **Policies** node.

2. Right-click the policy you want to set priority for and select the **Priority** option.

3. If you want to assign the highest priority to the policy, select **Make Highest Priority**; if not, select **Increase Priority** to specify the priority you want to assign (Figure 12.23).

Figure 12.23 Setting Policy Priority

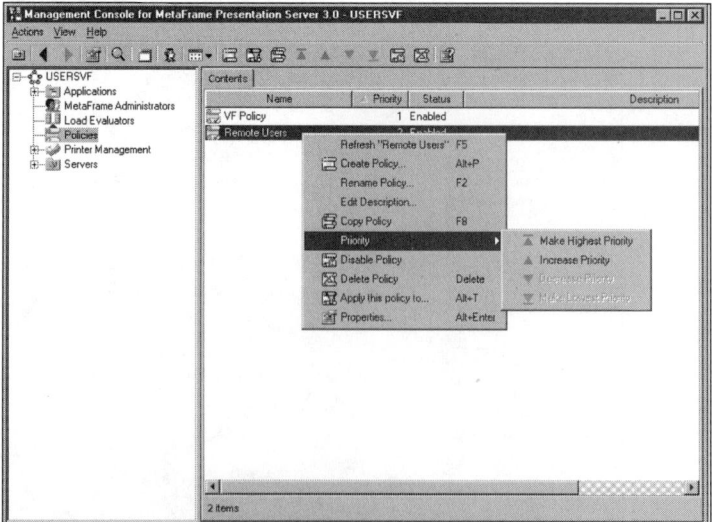

Making the Two Play Well Together

It is extremely important after all the hard work has been done to be sure that the policies created in Active Directory and in MetaFrame work to support your decided security and functionality stance. Designing policies that conflict with each other could result in the thin-client infrastructure failing to get up and running. If your infrastructure is already supporting clients, new policies that conflict with your strategy could quickly bring things to a halt. That being said, here are some points to remember:

- Microsoft Group Policy settings can override MetaFrame policy rules for connections. If the Group Policy security settings are more restrictive than the MetaFrame policy rules, Microsoft wins!

- Good Active Directory design makes it easier to apply sound MetaFrame policy rules. This seems obvious, but still bears mentioning.

- Make sure that policy inheritance is appropriately set on each GPO. You don't want to end up thinking that a policy setting applies, only to find out the hard way that it doesn't.

- Make use of the MetaFrame policy search tool. This tool is Citrix's equivalent of the Microsoft GPMC RSoP tool. It will calculate the resultant effect of multiple policies on the objects to which they are applied.

- Collaborate, compare, and contrast. Match the Microsoft RSoP with the MetaFrame Resultant Policy view. Make sure that both Citrix and Windows policies address the issue the same way.

Summary

In this chapter, we covered both Windows Server 2003 Group Policy and Citrix MetaFrame Presentation Server 3.0 policy. We saw that Windows Server 2003 Group Policy is a more mature, robust offering that adds over 200 new policy settings that affect an end-user's entire experience in a Windows Active Directory domain. We discussed the new Group Policy Management Console (GPMC) and the strength and integrity it brings to Active Directory forest management. We examined the features in the GPMC and saw how they are used. We looked at installing the GPMC and examined GPOs, and looked at the different management features on the GPO. We briefly discussed design considerations for Group Policy.

We also discussed Citrix MetaFrame policies and their uses. We looked at creating policies, configuring the rules within the policies, and applying policy filters. We also discussed the rules that govern MetaFrame policies and how they are applied and affect the users, servers, client machines, and IP address ranges to which they are applied. We talked about policy prioritization and creating exceptions to policies by changing priority between two conflicting policies.

Finally, we briefly discussed some tips for designing MetaFrame and Windows policies so that they complement each other and the built-in tools that can help accomplish this.

Solutions Fast Track

Windows Server 2003 Group Policy

☑ Includes over 200 new policy settings.

☑ Introduces more mature WMI features that enable administrators to manage different computer hardware more appropriately.

☑ New management model enables cross-forest policy management.

Configuring Group Policy with the Group Policy Management Console

☑ Integrates all Group Policy Management and domain administrative tools into one MMC.

☑ Enables administrators to model policy changes and see results in a test scenario before actually applying them.

☑ Enables the configuration of policies to match users and their functions and to match the types of client computers they use.

☑ Windows Server 2003 WMI filters are not supported in Windows 2000 and earlier operating systems.

☑ The RSoP and Group Policy Modeling tools can be used to ensure that policies have the desired effect.

☑ GPOs can be configured to deploy client software on a per-user or per-machine basis.

Configuring Citrix MetaFrame Policies

☑ MetaFrame policies can be applied to users and user groups, servers, client machines, and IP address ranges.

☑ Policies take effect at login and are active for the duration of the ICA connection.

☑ Polices exist in three states: enabled, disabled, and not configured.

☑ A Citrix policy's power lies in its rules that affect every facet of an ICA session, from desktop appearance to security and encryption.

☑ Policies can be prioritized so that exceptions to one policy can be enforced by another higher priority policy.

Links to Sites

■ **www.brianmadden.com** A well-known, well-respected Citrix and Windows Terminal Server expert. This site contains lots of useful tips that will help both the beginning Citrix administrator and the seasoned veteran.

■ **www.citrixguru.com** As the site says, "Stuff you need to know." Very useful articles and links to Citrix downloads and hotfixes.

■ **www.tek-tips.com** A bulletin board style site that allows collaboration among professionals much like a newsgroup.

■ **www.thin.net** A very useful resource for all things thin-client. Offers information on Terminal Server, Citrix, and other thin-client solutions.

Frequently Asked Questions

The following Frequently Asked Questions, answered by the authors of this book, are designed to both measure your understanding of the concepts presented in this chapter and to assist you with real-life implementation of these concepts. To have your questions about this chapter answered by the author, browse to **www.syngress.com/solutions** and click on the **"Ask the Author"** form. You will also gain access to thousands of other FAQs at ITFAQnet.com.

Q: Why can't I employ different group policies to distinguish between Windows 2000 laptops and Windows 2000 desktop computers?

A: Windows Server 2003 WMI filters are not supported on Windows 2000.

Q: Why can't I use the Group Policy Modeling feature on Windows 2003 servers in my Windows 2000 domain?

A: Group Policy Modeling requires that a domain has at least one Windows Server 2003 domain controller.

Q: Why are my clients trying to update their ICA client software even though the auto client update policy is not configured?

A: That's exactly the problem. An unconfigured policy does not turn the policy off, but defers it to a lower priority policy. To stop the clients from trying to update the Turn off client, auto update policy must be enabled.

Q: How can I ensure that my MetaFrame policy, not the Microsoft policy, is controlling my security settings?

A: Make the MetaFrame policy the most restrictive policy. This may mean relaxing Microsoft security, so do this with care.

Q: I have configured the policy to auto-create client printers on login but my printers are not added. What is wrong?

A: The Printer driver rule may be disabled in a higher ranked policy. Disabled policies and rules take precedence over lower ranked policies and rules. Enabling the rule in a higher ranked policy should solve the problem.

Q: Why does a particular application keep getting installed on every computer one of my users logs in to?

A: The application was configured for installation and assigned to that user's account, so it will follow the user and be installed on every computer he logs on to that does not already have the application.

Chapter 13

Server Cloning and Other Disaster Recovery Techniques

Solutions in this Chapter:

- **Cloning Microsoft Servers**
- **Deploying MetaFrame Presentation Server**
- **Replicating an Access Data Store**
- **Replicating a SQL 2000 Data Store**
- **Application Packaging as a Disaster Recovery Tool**

☑ Summary

☑ Solutions Fast Track

☑ Frequently Asked Questions

Introduction

If there is one rule in Information Technology (IT), it is that sooner or later you are going to need a backup copy of a server to perform a restore. Whether it's an upgrade that goes bad, corruption of key operating system (OS) files from hardware failure, or simply rolling out a number of identical servers, using smart backup strategies can drastically reduce the downtime required by any of these tasks.

In this chapter, we address several popular methods of disaster recovery (DR) for your Citrix servers. We also address using these techniques for server rollout, and for assisting you in an upgrade strategy. Citrix has some very specific requirements for successful server cloning, and there are some definite "gotchas" to be aware of before trying it. We also cover specific scenarios for backing up and restoring the most critical aspect of your Citrix environment, the data store.

Cloning Microsoft Servers

One popular term that is tossed around in the IT world is "cloning." No, we aren't talking about making mutant sheep here. A server "clone" is just that, an identical copy of an existing server. At the heart of it, you are making a copy of the software on one server and restoring it to another server. Advantages to server cloning include:

- Quick recovery of downed hardware
- Free tools provided with the OS for server cloning
- Fairly painless process to create and restore a cloned image
- Popular third-party software support for server imaging and cloning

There are a couple of disadvantages to server cloning, however:

- Requires downtime to create the clone image
- Can increase hardware costs if used as a true backup system
- Often requires identical hardware to be successful

Using Microsoft's Sysprep Tool

As mentioned previously, Microsoft provides a method to clone your servers right out of the box. The tool is called Sysprep. For prior versions of Windows, Sysprep had to be downloaded from Microsoft. Now it is included on the Windows Server 2003 CD in the Deploy.cab file, which can be found in the Support folder. Generally, you want to use Sysprep when you are making a master installation image, but it is also useful for one-to-one server cloning and replication.

Sysprep works by removing from the operating system all of the unique identifiers. It also purges the driver information for the current hardware, leaving you with a relatively clean slate from which to clone other machines. Sysprep is best used with a new, clean installation of Windows. This will help to avoid many of the potential issues that can crop up with already-loaded servers. Here are the steps to configure your Windows Server 2003 server for the Sysprep tool:

1. Delete all temporary files from the server to be cloned. This includes all temporary Internet files, anything in the TEMP directories defined in the path, and any other unwanted files.

2. Create a folder for Sysprep on the root of your server (for example, "C:\Sysprep").

3. Copy the Deploy.cab file from the Support directory on the Windows Server 2003 CD to the folder you created and extract Sysprep.exe, Factory.exe, and Setupcl.exe from it.

4. If the server is already part of a domain, remove it and place it in a workgroup. Sysprep will not complete if the server is part of a domain. You can remove the server by right-clicking the **My Computer** icon and choosing **Properties**. Highlight the **Computer Name** tab and click the **Change** button. In the Computer Name Changes window, select **Workgroup** and provide a workgroup name (usually just WORKGROUP for simplicity). Click **OK** and then **OK** again to place the server in a workgroup. The server will need to be rebooted for the process to complete. You should also remove the server account from Active Directory using the **Active Directory Users and Computers** tool.

5. Run all of the system tools to make sure you have a clean environment. Especially important to-do items are to run a full system virus scan and to perform a disk check and defragmentation. Disk defragmentation can be executed by going to **Start | Programs | Administrative Tools** and selecting **Computer Management**. Highlight **Disk Defragmenter** and select the drive you want to defragment. Click the **Defragment** button and let it go. Depending on the size and speed of the volume, the speed of your CPU, and the percent of fragmentation, this can take a long time to run.

6. Make sure your server is up to date with all of the patches and hotfixes you want applied. If you do not have a patching system in place, the easiest method is to allow Microsoft's Automatic Update to run and update your machine with the critical patches. Go to http://windowsupdate.microsoft.com.

7. Uninstall any unnecessary programs, and any programs that could be tied to the PC name, such as antivirus packages. Most programs have their own unin-

stall process, or you can use **Add/Remove Programs** in the Control Panel to uninstall the applications.

8. Clear the Administrator password by selecting **Start | Programs | Computer Management** and highlighting **Local Users and Groups**. Click **Users** and then right-click **Administrator** and choose **Set Password**. Leave the New Password fields blank and click **OK**. You can set a password option in the Sysprep.inf file, or you can simply leave it blank. If you do not define it, users can select the password during the setup process.

In addition to the preceding steps from Microsoft, Citrix also has a few requirements before you run Sysprep assuming that Citrix is already installed:

1. Remove any existing installation of MetaFrame. This can be done using **Add/Remove Programs**, or using the Citrix MPS 3.0 installation CD.

2. Remove the server name from the Management Console if it is still listed as a member server. In the Management Console, select **Servers** and look for the server name. If it exists, highlight it and right-click on it. Select **Remove Server from Farm** and click **OK** to remove the server.

Once you have completed the preceding tasks, you are ready to use the Sysprep tool. When you run Sysprep, it first searches for the Sysprep.inf file and writes those parameters to the registry. It removes the computer from a domain if it is a member, and then runs Setupcl.exe to reset the Security Identifiers (SIDs). When it is done with the SIDs, it deletes the network adapters to clear all network settings and sets the registry to run the mini-setup on the next reboot. A shutdown command is issued so that the master disk image can be created. Figure 13.1 shows a sample Sysprep.inf file.

Figure 13.1 Sample Sysprep.inf

```
;SetupMgrTag
[Unattended]

[GuiUnattended]

AdminPassword=f0d412bd764ffe81aad3b435b51404ee209c6174da490caeb422f3fa5a7ae634
    EncryptedAdminPassword=Yes
    OEMSkipRegional=1
    TimeZone=35

[UserData]
    ProductKey=XXXXX-XXXXX-XXXXX-XXXXX-XXXXX
    FullName="Test"
    OrgName="Test"
```

```
    ComputerName=Test30

[Display]
    BitsPerPel=32
    XResolution=1280
    YResolution=1024
Vrefresh=70

[SetupMgr]
    DistFolder=C:\sysprep\i386
    DistShare=windist

[GuiRunOnce]
    Command0="rundll32 printui.dll,PrintUIEntry /in /n \\server1\lj5si"

[Identification]
    JoinDomain=DOMAIN2
    DomainAdmin=Domain2\Admin
    DomainAdminPassword=4492

[Networking]
    InstallDefaultComponents=No

[NetClients]
    MS_MSClient=params.MS_MSClient
```

I've Got My Image ... Now What?

Well, the good news is that you now have a clean master disk from which to work. The next time that disk is booted in a server, the mini-setup will run and configure Windows. With this clean master image, you can begin the process of cloning your servers. There are several options that you can take advantage of using the previous steps.

Using Disk Mirroring to Clone

If you are running your OS on a hardware-controlled RAID 1 (mirrored) disk set, then using Sysprep to clone your servers is a very simple task. Please note: this generally only applies to hardware-controlled RAID 1 solutions. If you use a software RAID solution, this process may not be successful.

1. If you have already configured your Sysprep installation, execute the Sysprep.exe file and let the server power down. Do not reboot.

2. Break the mirror by pulling out one of the mirrored drives. This will cause the RAID hardware to mark the drive as missing, which breaks the mirror.

3. Power up the server and go through the mini-setup. Once the server is configured, insert a blank drive and allow the mirror set to be recreated. Most hardware RAID solutions support online disk recovery and will automatically begin recovering the mirror to the new disk in the background. You may be required to reboot and select a rebuild option from the hardware controller's menu. Consult the documentation for your RAID device before trying this process.

4. Take the mirrored drive you pulled in Step 2 and insert it into a new server. Reboot and let the mini-setup run on the new server.

5. Insert a blank drive in the new server and let the mirror set rebuild as described in Step 3.

You now have two servers that are for the most part identical. This process can be repeated as needed. Simply run Sysprep, shut down the server, break the mirror, and repeat. Servers can be rolled out in a staggered fashion on whatever timetable you require.

Designing and Planning...

What If I Have Applications Installed?

You can use the previous process with installed applications, but you need to be aware of some caveats. Some applications are dependent on the name of the machine on which they are installed. Once you have built the new server, you should do a registry search for the old server name and change it to the new name. Be aware of any .ini files used by the applications as well, as these can also contain name references.

One of the worst offenders on cloned servers is those that rely on ODBC connections. These connections will frequently need to be recreated after cloning. Many administrators prefer to remove these types of applications before cloning and reinstall them after. If you have an application packaging system in place, this can be a relatively painless process.

Other Methods for Deploying an Image

With a disk that has been Sysprep'd, you can use a variety of third-party methods for deployment of the image. Many administrators prefer to use a program such as Ghost to distribute the image to new servers. The disk image can be backed up onto removable storage such as a DVD, a network share, or just onto another hard drive. Deployment in these situations generally requires a boot disk that points to the share where the image is stored. The image can be deployed to multiple servers simply by booting them up with the disk.

Other third-party software can be used to deploy the images as well. You should investigate and decide on the option that works best for your environment. Having the clean image allows you to deploy servers as you need them and as hardware becomes available.

Using Disk Mirrors as a Backup Method

If your environment is fairly static, disk mirroring (RAID 1) can present an easy method for performing periodic backups of your servers. A mirrored set can be broken and rebuilt as necessary, and storing a drive from a broken mirror gives you an easy point-in-time backup method. Despite the ease of use, there are several immediate drawbacks:

- The server should be powered down for a clean mirror. This obviously means more server downtime.

- You incur the cost of a hot-swap drive for each server, since you are rotating three drives through the machine. Your server will always have two drives in the machine, plus the one drive in storage. As you update the mirror, you rotate the storage drive in and one of the live disks out to storage. If you require more than one point for restoration, the disk costs increase.

- Storage and labeling can become an issue. These disks need to be kept in a safe place, and under climate-controlled conditions. They have to be properly labeled as well so that the drive can be restored as needed.

- Performance can be impacted while the mirror set rebuilds. You should avoid having users on the server until the mirrored set is finished rebuilding.

- "Restores" are only to a point in time. If you made changes to the server since the last mirror creation, you will lose them.

Dollar for dollar, however, using the mirrored set as a backup method can be fairly cost effective. You do not need to purchase licenses for other backup software that you might have in the environment. It also removes the need for other online or offline storage for those backup images by removing the need for software backups of your Citrix servers. It also makes restoration in case of a failed drive array as simple as plugging in the hot-swap copy. Obviously, you have to weigh the benefits of this type of recovery versus a software backup/restore methodology and decide which applies better to your environment.

Deploying MetaFrame Presentation Server

Once you have a new server up and running, you can begin deploying MetaFrame Presentation Server. This process can be streamlined by including instructions in the Sysprep.inf to perform the install of MPS 3.0 from an administrative share or from an unattended install answer file. Both methods are discussed next.

Using Transform Files

Transform files are used to create an administrative template installation that can be used for unattended installs without requiring any configuration of an answer file. When you execute the Citrix installer and provide a path to the template file, it will record your answers and the subsequent package to the administrative share for future installations. Citrix provides several types of Transform files, which can be found in the Support\Install directory on your MPS 3.0 CD:

- **ActiveDirectoryLicensingInstallSupport.mst** is provided to install your licensing server in an Active Directory environment.

- **Join_Indirect.mst** creates an install for a farm member server that will connect through another direct server to the data store.

- **Localdb_access_create.mst** creates an admin install where the data store will be created on the local machine. This is used for new farm creation with a local data store.

- **Thirdparty_db_create_direct.mst** makes an admin install that creates a new farm and configures the data store on a third-party database server such as a SQL 2000 server.

- **Thirdparty_join_direct.mst** is used to create an install for a farm member server that connects directly to the data store, which is hosted on a third-party database system such as SQL Server.

For example, to create a template installation that will allow you to join a new server to an existing farm that uses SQL 2000 for the data store, run the following from a command prompt:

```
"D:\MetaFrame Presentation Server\mps.msi
/TRANSFORMS=d:\Support\Installation\Thirdparty_join_direct.mst"
```

This will begin the administrative installation creation. You will be prompted throughout the process to provide information for the installer to use, such as the existing farm name, the details for connecting to the data store, and so forth. These details are exactly the same information you would provide if you were performing this installation on a server. You will also specify the share point that the installation package will be created from. When it finishes, you will have a complete install package with the settings you provided in an administrative share. You can use this package to perform an unattended installation of MPS 3.0 whenever you need it.

This method is handy, but does have its drawbacks. You have to create a separate image for each of the different install types you have in your environment. These can consume 60MB or more of data, and have to be on a share that can be accessed by the install device. They also have to be recreated if your information ever changes (if, for instance, you change your data store server to a different machine).

Using an Answers File

The other method of running an unattended install with MPS 3.0 is to use an answers file in conjunction with the mps.ini install file. Citrix provides a sample answers file in the Support\Install directory on the MPS 3.0 CD. You can copy the UnattendedInstall.exe and answers file to a shared location, edit the answers to fit your installation requirements, and then run the unattended install from a command line or Sysprep answers file like so:

```
Z:\Citrix\UnattendedInstall.exe msi_file_name ini_file name
```

where msi_file_name is the name and location of the installation package for MPS 3.0, and ini file name is the name and location of your answers file. Figure 13.2 demonstrates a sample answers.ini file.

Figure 13.2 Sample answers.ini File

```
[MetaFrame License Agreement]
AcceptLicense=No

[Data Store Configuration]
CreateFarm=Yes
LocalDBType=Access
DirectConnect=No
; Leave this blank to use the default zone name
ZoneName=

[Direct Connect Settings]
DSNFilePath=
UserName=
Password=

[MSDE Settings]
```

```
InstanceName=CITRIX_METAFRAME

[Indirect Connect Settings]
IndirectServerName=
IndirectServerPort=2512
UserName=
Password=
DomainName=

[Farm Settings]
FarmName=Farm
FarmAdministratorUsername=Administrator
FarmAdministratorDomain=


[Shadowing Restrictions]
AllowShadowing=Yes
ProhibitRemoteControl=No
ProhibitNotificationOff=No
ProhibitLoggingOff=No

[Citrix XML Service]
ExtendIIS=No
; This setting applies only if ExtendIIS is No
DedicatedPortNumber=80
; This setting applies only if ExtendIIS is Yes
EnableVirtualScripts=Yes

[Update ICA Clients]
UpdateClients=No
ClientPath=

[Options]
RebootOnFinish=Yes
LogLevel=*v
LogFile=c:\msi.log
UILevel= BASIC_UI_NO_MODAL
IgnoreMCM=No
RemoveWITurnkey=No

[MetaframeServer]
ServerType=Metaframe Enterprise Server
```

```
[MFLicenseServer]
LicenseServerChoice="Point"
LicenseServerName="localhost"

[MFRDP]
DisableRDPPromptForPassword="Yes"
```

As you can see, there are many options available in the answers file. The sample
UnattendedInstall.txt found in the Support\Install directory provides even more options
for customizing the installation, and explains each setting in much more detail. Every
option that is available during a hands-on installation can be specified here, just as you
can specify them with the Transforms file. It gives you another way of performing the
installation unattended.

The benefit to using an answers file over the transform install is that edits to the
installation process require a simple edit of the .ini file to update the data. There is no
need to create the separate packages. You can simply define answers files for the different
installations and point the unattended install at the top of the answers file you want
applied. The downside is that you can inadvertently make a mistake in editing this file
that can cause the install to fail, while creating an admin install through the transform
file is (relatively) foolproof.

Deploying Your MetaFrame Package

Once you have created an unattended installation (regardless of how you choose to do
so), you can use it to install MPS 3.0 as part of an unattended installation. Figure 13.3
shows a sample of the Sysprep.inf file with the InstallFilesPath setting defined.

Figure 13.3 Sysprep.inf for MPS Deployment

```
; SetupMgrTag
[Unattended]
    InstallFilesPath=C:\sysprep\i386

[GuiUnattended]
    EncryptedAdminPassword=NO
    OEMSkipRegional=1
    TimeZone=35

[UserData]
    FullName="Test"
    OrgName="Test"
    ComputerName=TEST21
```

```
[SetupMgr]
    DistFolder=C:\sysprep\i386
    DistShare=windist

[Identification]
    JoinWorkgroup=WORKGROUP

[Networking]
    InstallDefaultComponents=Yes
```

Once the mini-setup portion of the Sysprep process completes, it will execute any commands located in the i386\oem\cmdlines.txt file. By specifying the Mps.msi package and the transforms file in cmdlines.txt, you provide everything needed for an unattended installation of MetaFrame Presentation Server. You can also define other package installs in the cmdlines.txt file, including deployment of applications that you will later publish on those servers.

Other Methods of Deploying MPS 3.0

MPS 3.0 can be deployed to cloned servers in a variety of other methods in addition to the packaged deployment we discussed earlier. Several of the more common methods are outlined here. Administrators are limited only by their tools and scripting skills in devising other ways to deploy MetaFrame.

Using SMS for Deployment

MPS 3.0 can be deployed through Microsoft's SMS software. Create an administrative share as described earlier with the source files and transform settings. Use the deployment console to push the package out using the custom transforms file to feed the install program the correct parameters.

Using Active Directory for Deployment

In this case, both the target and source servers must be in the same domain. You will also want to turn on Windows Installer Logging so that you have a record of what happens with the deployment. This is done on an individual server by adding the registry string value: **HKEY_LOCAL_MACHINE\SOFTWARE\Policies\Microsoft\Windows\Installer\Installer** and setting the value to **iwearucmopv**.

The server must be restarted after adding the key. This key is required because Active Directory does not provide any success or failure information to the admins. To install a package using Active Directory, you must create a Group Policy Object (GPO) that runs the installation under the Software installation section of Software Settings. Servers must be assigned the GPO, and when it is applied, on reboot MPS 3.0 will be deployed based on the settings you defined.

Using Installation Manager for Deployment

If you are deploying MPS 3.0 to a server already running MetaFrame XP, you can use the Installation Manager functionality of Citrix to deploy the upgrade. Using IM to deploy the upgrade is very similar to the processes discussed previously.

1. Make sure the servers are upgraded to MSI 2.0 prior to the installation.

2. Create an administrative install using the transforms file method described previously.

3. Copy the CD contents to a network share.

4. Copy the transforms (.MST) file to the folder on the share that contains the Mps.msi installer package.

5. Ensure that no users are logged on to the server.

6. Add the Mps.msi package to the IM database in the CMC. When prompted to add transforms, click **OK**.

7. Add the MST file to the package. The MST file *must* be located in the same directory as Mps.msi.

8. Deploy the package to the target servers and validate them once they have rebooted.

Replicating an Access Data Store

One of the primary weaknesses of MetaFrame is the data store. If it goes down, you have 96 hours to get it back up or your farm will cease to issue licenses. If you administer a farm with an Access data store, your options for backing up the database file are much more limited.

The Access data store runs on one of your farm servers and cannot be backed up by normal backup methods. To that end, Citrix implemented options within MetaFrame to back up the critical data store information. This command is *dsmaint*. With it, you can define parameters of the Access data store, verify the database integrity, and compact it to save space. Most importantly for our purposes, it can create a backup copy of the Access data store, and later restore that backup if it's needed.

dsmaint must be run from a Citrix server, preferably from the server that hosts the data store. The following commands are variations of *dsmaint* that are important for our purposes:

- **dsmaint compactdb /ds** Use this command to compact the database. This can be run periodically, or manually prior to a backup. While the compaction is occurring, the data store is unavailable for reads or writes.

- **dsmaint backup** *destination_ path* Backs up the Access database to the path specified.

- **dsmaint recover** Restores the backup of the Access database. This must be run on the direct server while the IMA service is not running.

- **dsmaint failover** *direct_server* Causes the specified server to become the new direct server for the machine on which it was executed. If you migrate the data store to another machine, you must issue this command on every MetaFrame server that points to the direct server.

destination_apth refers to the path to the backup data store.

direct_server refers to the new data store server

dsmaint.exe is located in the \Program Files\Citrix\System32\Citrix\IMA folder on any Citrix server. It can also be located in the \MetaFrame Presentation Server\Program Files\Citrix\System32\Citrix\IMA folder on the MPS 3.0 installation CD.

Executing *dsmaint*

dsmaint should be executed from a Citrix server. From a command prompt, you would execute the **dsmaint** command followed by the specified options. For example, to compact a local data store, follow these steps:

1. On the Citrix server that hosts the data store, click on **Start** and choose **Run**. In the provided Run line, type **CMD** and press **Enter**.

2. You should now be at a DOS prompt. Type **dsmaint.exe compactdb /ds** and press **Enter**.

3. Let the compaction run. When it is finished, you can move on to the next step if you are going to back up the data store.

Many administrators choose to script a periodic backup of the data store. A typical scripted backup would first stop the IMA data store, and then perform a database compaction. Once that was complete, it would back up the data store to a network share and restart the IMA service. Figure 13.4 shows a sample batch file that could be used in conjunction with Windows Scheduler to perform periodic local data store backups.

Figure 13.4 Sample Batch File

```
;Sample batch file for local data store backup

;First stop the IMA service
```

```
Net stop "Independent Management Architecture" /y

;Next compact the local data store file
Call "C:\dsmaint compactdb /ds"

;Then perform the data store backup to a share
Call "c:\dsmaint backup \\network\share"

;Then restart the IMA data store
Net start "Independent Management Architecture"
```

Choosing Backup Cycles

Choosing how often to back up your data store is an individual decision. If you run a farm with predictable uptime and downtime, it is possible that you can schedule the data store backup to occur every day during down periods. Because the IMA data store must be stopped as part of the process, any applications published to that server will be unavailable for new connections during the backup period.

If you run a 24x7 shop, you may have to schedule your backups at less frequent intervals. Remember that the longer the period between backups, the less valid your restore will be. If possible, your data store should be backed up after major configuration changes so that your backups can reflect those modifications.

Replicating a SQL 2000 Data Store

If your data store is maintained on a SQL server, one method of backing up the data store is to set up a distributor server and subscriber servers. This will provide you with regularly scheduled backups of the data store, and can also provide a method of load balancing the SQL connection for farms that span high latency networks. In addition, it gives you fault tolerance should a subscriber data store go down, and failover capability if you need to drop a data store offline.

The process for SQL replication is fairly complicated, and should only be attempted if you are fairly comfortable with SQL commands and configuration. The process discussed here applies to Microsoft SQL Server 2000. Consult your product documentation if you run your data store on a different SQL version. Detailed instructions for other versions of SQL Server replication can be found in the *Advanced Concepts Guide for MetaFrame Presentation Server Version 3.0* that can be downloaded from the Citrix Web site at http://support.citrix.com/docs.

Database Replication with SQL Server 2000

Prior to beginning the replication process, several conditions must be fulfilled. A new database must be created on the source server to serve as the source for all the replicas. Additionally, you must complete the following tasks prior to configuring replication:

- You must not mix Windows 2000 and Windows Server 2003 servers in the replication process. The Distributed Transaction Coordinator service is different between the two versions, and will cause the replication to fail.

- Both the publisher and subscriber SQL servers must be in the same domain.

- SQL server must be installed on the target data store servers (obviously!).

- Verify that the Distributed Transaction Coordinator is installed on the servers that will host the data store.

- If you use images to create your SQL servers, you *must* use images from different servers. If you use the same server image for all of your installations, replication will not work. It is recommended instead that you do a clean install from the CD.

- Configure the same domain login account for the SQL Server Agent, MSSQLServer, and MSDTC (or Distributed Transaction Coordinator on Server 2000). You can configure these in the **Services Manager**.

The following steps outline how to configure the Distributor server, set up replication, and publish the database to subscriber servers. Some of these steps are only required to be completed once, and some must be completed on every server in the replication scheme. Follow the instructions carefully to understand what you are doing to your environment.

Establishing the Distributor Server

Complete the following steps to configure the Distributor server. The Distributor server is the SQL server currently hosting the data store. These steps must only be completed once unless your Distributor server changes:

1. Ensure that the source and target servers are in the same Active Directory domain.

2. Open **Enterprise Manager** on the server that will be the source for replication.

3. Right-click the Replication folder and select the option for **Configure Publishing, Subscribers, Distribution Wizard**.

4. Select the current server to act as the Distributor.

5. Leave the Snapshot folder at the default.

6. On the **Customize the Configuration** page, you must choose the option **No, use the default settings**. Click **Finish**.

Enable Transactional Replication for the Distributor

Transactional Replication is the process that the Distributor uses to mark changes that need to be pushed to the Subscriber servers. The following steps show how to enable Transactional Replication. It is not on by default. This only needs to be performed once, unless you change Distributor servers.

1. Right-click the **Replication Monitor** folder and choose the **Distributor Properties**.

2. Open the **Publication Databases** tab. Select the **Trans** check box next to the database you want to replicate.

Publishing the Database

The database must be "published" so that Subscriber servers can see it. Publishing is a way to share the database using Transactional Replication so that changes are updated to the Subscriber servers. This only needs to be performed once, unless you change Distributor servers.

1. Start the **Create Publication Wizard** by right-clicking the database name and choosing **New | Publication**.

2. Select the **Show advanced options** check box and click **Next**.

3. Select the database you want to publish and click **Next**.

4. Choose **Transactional Publishing** on the **Select Publication Type** page.

5. Select the **Immediate updating** option and click **Next**.

6. Select **Servers running SQL Server 2000** and click **Next**.

7. On the **Specify Articles** page, select both **Show** and **Publish all**. Make sure you do not publish the stored procedures.

8. Click **Next,** and then name the publication. Choose not to customize the publication and click **Finish** to create it. It will appear in the Publications folder.

Setting Up the Subscribers

The final step in configuring replication is to set up the Subscriber server(s). These servers will receive the replicated data store information. This must be performed if your Subscriber servers list changes.

1. Right-click the published database and choose **Push new subscription**.

2. Select **Show advanced options in this wizard** and click **Next**.

3. Select the Subscribers for this published app.

4. Choose the database you want to replicate to.

5. Set the agent to run from the Distributor server.

6. Set the **Distribution Agent Schedule** to run "continuously."

7. Select **Yes, initialize the schema and data** and check the **Start the snapshot agent** box.

8. Choose the **Immediate updating** option.

9. On the **Start required services page**, ensure that the SQL Server Agent and MSDTC are started.

10. Select **Finish** to complete the wizard.

For further information and troubleshooting procedures, see the Citrix Knowledge Base article CTX101739.

Configuring and Implementing...

SQL Notes

If your SQL servers are Windows Server 2003 boxes, you must execute the following stored procedure for the Distributor and Subscriber servers using the Query Analyzer:

```
Exec sp_serveroption 'yourserver','data acces','true'
```

The *yourserver* option is the name of the remote server.

You must also configure the password for the SA account on all of the Subscriber servers for the replica database. Start the **SQL Query Analyzer** and execute the following stored procedure:

```
Sp_link_publication
'<Distributor>','<Database>','<Publication>',0,'SA','<PWD>'
```

> where *Distributor* is the Distribution server, *Database* is the name of the published database, *Publication* is the name of the publication to be linked, and *PWD* is the password for the SA account on the Distributor server.

Replication can also be configured for multiple subscriber servers, as well as in other SQL versions such as SQL Server 7. Consult the *Advanced Concepts Guide for MPS 3.0* from Citrix for details on alternatives.

Using Replication for Fault Tolerance

Another advantage to a replicated data store is that it provides a method for fault tolerance in case of disaster. Because the database replication is taking place on a constant basis, you can use several data store servers to bridge WANs. Each physical location can maintain its own data store, and if the data store for one site goes down, that site can be redirected to the data store for another site.

Performance for those remote servers will take a hit, but they won't be out of the water if they pass the 96-hour mark without a live data store server. You will want to measure the impact of data store replication on your WAN link, and make sure to plan accordingly for the increased bandwidth usage.

Application Packaging as a Disaster Recovery Tool

So far, we've discussed methods to clone and recover your operating system, to deploy MetaFrame, and to provide fault tolerance for the data store. That's all well and good, but without applications, your Citrix farm isn't going to be very useful. You need to consider how you will roll out your applications to these new or restored servers without significant downtime.

One method is to use application packaging. There is a variety of packaging methods out there, but they all accomplish a basic task; they create an application installation, generally known as a package, which can be executed on a machine to perform an installation. Generally, packages are created to run without any user interaction and contain all the settings required for your particular environment. Some examples of packaging programs include Microsoft's SMS, Novell's ZEN, and even Citrix's own Installation Manager technologies.

Why Should I Package?

Imagine this scenario: You have two servers in your farm with critical applications. Your boss wants to rapidly roll out four more boxes with the same apps in the same configuration. The applications are fairly troublesome to configure, and it's been a while since you had to install them. You can't find your notes. You've already tried cloning the servers with the applications intact, but they failed to work correctly. What can you do?

Alternatively, how about this scenario: Your Citrix servers are suddenly standing in two feet of water. Everything, and we mean *everything*, is blown. You have a great support contract, and within 24 hours, you have new hardware racked and ready for install. Because of their fairly static nature, your Citrix servers were never part of the backup schema for the rest of the network. You have your clone image for the OS and an admin share for MPS installation, but you're now faced with recreating by hand all the application installations. Moreover, you don't have other servers to use as a template. It's going to be a long couple of nights.

Now imagine if you had created packages of those applications when you first installed them. Sure, it was a little more work up front, but it's a lifesaver now. You clone the boxes, install MPS 3.0, and once they are in the farm you use Installation Manager to take the packages for the apps and do rolling installs. In a matter of minutes, you have four servers with the applications ready to be tested and added to your live environment.

Planning Your Packaging

You aren't limited to Installation Manager, of course. The same scenario could work with the SMS client software, ZENworks, and so forth; it's simply a matter of planning ahead when you create your environment. As administrators, we are often under the gun to get something working and get it working *now*. Sometimes, you can't spare the extra time to work through packaging complex applications. Having faced both scenarios discussed previously, we strongly recommend that you make the time sooner rather than later.

One method of creating your packages is to maintain a separate packaging environment. This can be a couple of spare servers that you were going to throw out, but now can be put to work. Create a software environment that mirrors your live server types as closely as possible, and use that for your packaging. The important thing is that the environment is identical to your live servers, so that packages behave the same way when they are deployed.

The Package Environment

Many administrators will choose to only use a couple of boxes to mirror a very large environment. With the techniques discussed earlier, this becomes very doable. Using cloning, packaging, and good notes, it becomes very easy to replicate a server in both your live and test environments. Sooner or later, you will be thankful that you took the time.

The amount of hardware you require to create your test environment really is limited to essential servers. You can use cloning and packaging to create any server combination required, and quickly dismantle and rebuild a server with little effort. Obviously, this isn't ideal for purposes like performance testing, but for simple application interaction tests it provides a method for administrators to give the application to testers in a controlled environment.

Summary

We've covered a fairly broad range of topics in this chapter, and there really is a lot more we could have covered. Cloning can be accomplished in a variety of ways, although we personally consider using Sysprep to be one of the easiest. Replication varies widely between SQL versions, and could probably be a chapter in itself. Packaging can be a complex subject based on the methods you use, and covers a broad range of technologies.

This chapter provided you with some ideas that you can carry into your own environment. The critical pieces remain the same. You do want to plan for the worst. You will need a backup eventually. In addition, you can save yourself a lot of time and headaches by planning ahead rather than scrambling to play catch-up.

Solutions Fast Track

Cloning Microsoft Servers

☑ Use Sysprep to create a clean image of the servers.

☑ Deploy the image manually by using mirrored sets, or through third-party tools such as Ghost.

☑ Cloning can also be used as a disaster recovery technique.

Deploying MetaFrame Presentation Server

☑ You can use the Sysprep.inf file to execute the installation process for MPS 3.0.

☑ MPS can be packaged and deployed using third-party tools such as SMS.

☑ If you are simply upgrading MetaFrame, you can use Installation Manager to push out the packaged version of MPS 3.0 to your servers.

Replicating an Access Data Store

☑ Access data stores cannot be truly replicated, they can simply be backed up.

☑ The backup process is a command line using the *dsmaint* command, and must be executed from a MetaFrame server.

☑ Most administrators choose to script the backup process for Access data stores.

Replicating a SQL 2000 Data Store

☑ Data store replication varies among different versions of SQL. Make sure you understand how it works for your version.

☑ Replication can also be used as a fault tolerance tool for disaster recovery and to bridge high latency connections.

☑ Replication also varies between Windows 2000 and Windows Server 2003 servers, even with the same SQL versions. It is important to understand the differences.

Frequently Asked Questions

The following Frequently Asked Questions, answered by the authors of this book, are designed to both measure your understanding of the concepts presented in this chapter and to assist you with real-life implementation of these concepts. To have your questions about this chapter answered by the author, browse to **www.syngress.com/solutions** and click on the **"Ask the Author"** form. You will also gain access to thousands of other FAQs at ITFAQnet.com.

Q: How many Citrix installations can I run at once?

A: With a powerful data store server, Citrix recommends no more than 30 installations at a time. If you are using an older database server for the data store, Citrix recommends no more than 10.

Q: Is Citrix's Installation Manager a decent packaging system?

A: It works reasonably well, but requires you to dig into the scripting to make complex changes. For simple application packaging, it works just fine. For more complex environments, a more robust packaging system such as SMS can be used.

Q: Can I use Installation Manager to deploy the application packages I create in third-party tools?

A: Installation Manager can deploy any .msi application. If you create the packages in a program that supports .msi creation, Installation Manager will work well for deployment.

Q: If I've used Sysprep to create an image, do I still need to run a SID generation tool when deploying using programs like Ghost?

A: NO! Don't do it. Sysprep already regenerated the SID, and running another SID generator on top of that can cause the image to not function.

Q: Data store replication seems like an intensive process. Do I need to do it?

A: It really depends on your environment. Many administrators will be comfortable with using the SQL tools to create incremental/full backups of the data store on a periodic basis, and rely on those for restoring the data store. Replication is more appropriate for environments with multiple remote farm sites, and situations where constant data store availability is critical.

Chapter 14

Day-to-Day Administration

Solutions in this chapter

- **Using Resource Manager as a Monitoring Tool**

- **File and Folder Management**

- **Session Management**

- **Periodic Administrative Tasks**

☑ **Summary**

☑ **Solutions Fast Track**

☑ **Frequently Asked Questions**

Introduction

Day-to-day administration of your Citrix servers is probably one of the hardest tasks an administrator has. After all, when things are working smoothly there's an understandable tendency to ignore them. As every administrator knows, however, ignoring your Citrix farm for too long can create a ticking time bomb, and nothing is worse than those 2 A.M. pager alerts that your data store has just gone red. It is important to keep an eye on your farm, and to watch for trends that can predict future issues.

Thankfully, there are plenty of tools available to do the job. If you choose to use the suite of Citrix tools, there is no additional cost beyond your base licensing. This chapter deals with some of the available monitoring tools, and best practices for using them. We also discuss administrative hurdles with files, profiles, and sessions and some common sense advice on maintaining a healthy Citrix environment.

Using Resource Manager as a Monitoring Tool

If you have Resource Manger installed as part of your Citrix configuration, you do have some out-of-the-box default monitoring applied to your Citrix servers. These are general metrics that you can further customize for your own needs. You can also configure the alert points for Warning and Critical levels, and provide notification escalation in case of serious issues. To view the default settings and change them:

1. Open the **Management Console** and expand your farm.

2. Expand the **Servers** folder and highlight the server you want to examine.

3. In the right pane, select the **Resource Manager** tab.

4. A list of the current metrics and their status will be displayed. Right-click on any of them and choose **Properties**.

5. In the **Server Metric Properties** window, select the metric you want to view or modify from the list on the left. You can then modify the properties in the right pane.

Figure 14.1 shows the Server Metric Properties window and the list of available metrics. You can modify the threshold limits of the metric you have highlighted to control when the status will change from green (operating within the defined limits) to yellow (a warning alert that the metric in question is possibly going to be a problem) to red (the metric has crossed the critical point you set).

Figure 14.1 Server Metric Properties

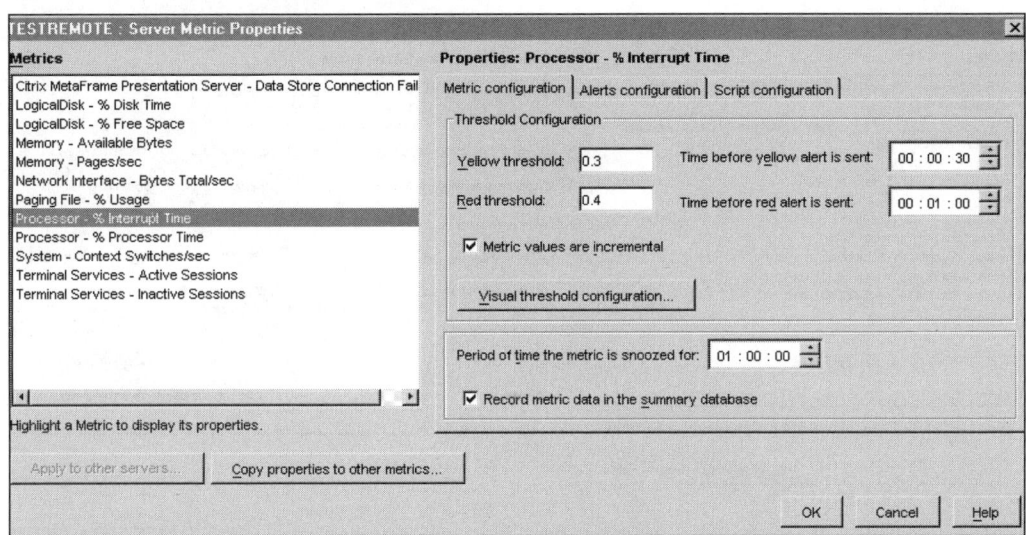

In addition to modifying the properties of the metric, you can customize the type of alert that will be sent and also define any scripts that should run in the event the metric turns red. The alert preferences are dependent on the configuration you have defined in your Resource Manger configuration. It can rely on e-mail alerts, SMS alerts, or SNMP messages. To check your current configuration for alerts in Resource Manager, highlight it in the Management Console and view the individual tabs for each technology (SMS, SNMP, and Email).

Many administrators will choose to have certain critical events send an e-mail notification that can be received by a pager to alert them of the problem. Be warned, however, that setting up these alerts can result in a lot of messages throughout the day in a busy farm if you do not narrowly define what to alert you on. Figure 14.2 shows the alert options for an individual metric that you can define.

Figure 14.2 Metric Alert Options

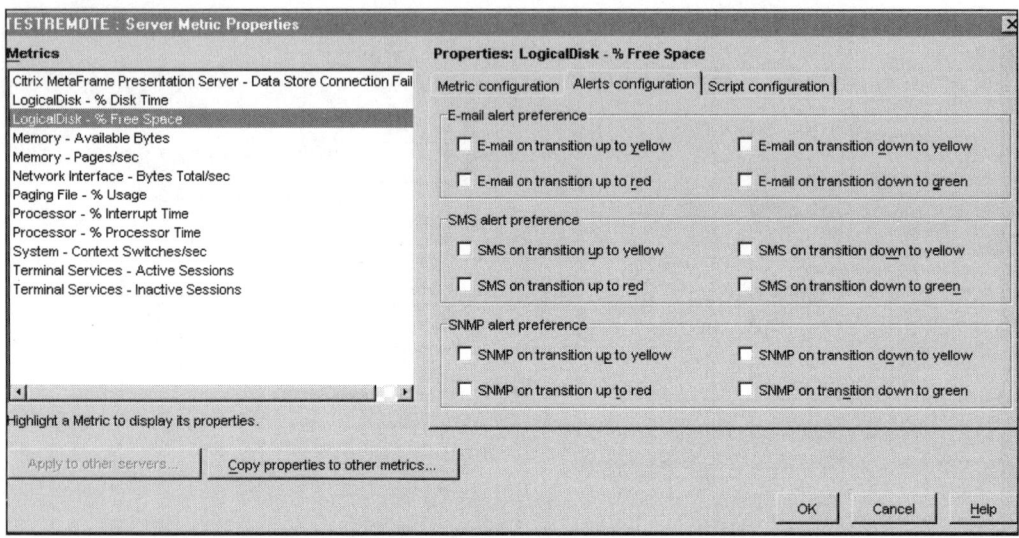

In addition to creating alerts, you can also configure a script to run on your server that can assist if a metric goes red. For instance, you have an alert set to monitor the free disk space on an application drive. It frequently fills up with temp files, and is a pain to manage. You configure a metric to monitor the free space, and when it drops below 10 percent it turns red. You also have configured a simple command file that will delete the temp files found in the application directory. To schedule the script to run:

1. Open the **Server Metric Properties** window on the server you want to run the script on.

2. Select the **Script Configuration** tab.

3. Check the box next to **Run script on transition to red**.

4. Click the **Browse** button and find the location of the command file. Note: the script must be located on the server you wish to run it on.

If you have several identical servers, you can configure them all to have the same alert settings using the **Apply to Other Servers** button in the **Server Metric Properties** window. Once you click this button, you are presented with a window where you can select all metrics or individual ones and propagate them to a server, group of servers, or even the entire farm if you choose to do so. Once you have selected the metrics and the servers you want to apply them to, click **OK** to force the changes to the targeted boxes.

Day-to-Day Monitoring

Once you have configured the metrics for your farm, you can use the Resource Manager Watcher to monitor for yellow or red alerts. To activate the Resource Manager Watcher, open the Management Console and select **Actions > Resource Manager Watcher**. You will be presented with a small monitor window that auto-refreshes and will display any server with a yellow or red alert. Double-clicking on the server will bring you to the full metrics window for that server in the Management Console and give you the exact metric that is being set off. Figure 14.3 shows the Resource Manager Watcher window.

Figure 14.3 Resource Manager Watcher

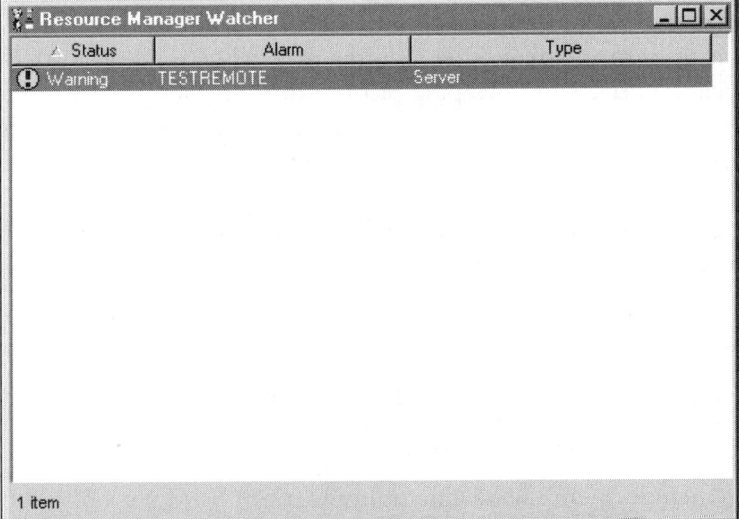

File and Folder Management

If you are lucky enough to take support calls related to Citrix, you have invariably had a customer say to you, "I saved my file to the C: drive and now it's not there." The first question a Citrix admin has to ask is, "Which C: drive?" We discussed drive remapping in previous chapters, but it is worth taking another look at here.

Should I Remap?

Citrix provides you with a method to remap your server drives as part of the install process for MetaFrame. By default they can be changed to M:\, N:\, and so forth; however, this can be altered to whatever drive scheme fits your environment. There are several reasons why you might want to have your drives remapped:

- **It eases user confusion.** Users traditionally view C:\ as a drive on their PC, and if you do not remap the server drives their local drives will be remapped instead.

- **It helps prevent garbage files on your system partition**. Because users tend to save folders to C:\, if your system drives are remapped you help to prevent user files from being mistakenly saved to your system drives.

- **It is also something of a security measure**. Some hostile programs are hard-coded to go for a C:\Windows directory, for instance. Since this isn't your system partition, it can save a crashed server.

Drive remapping does have a couple of hang-ups to be aware of. Some applications just don't like a remapped system drive. This is becoming much less common as applications are better coded, but older applications (especially 16-bit ones) had some issues if drives were remapped to anything other than the original C:\, and so forth; You also must decide to change the drive letter mapping prior to installing any applications. Remapping the drives after application installation can lead to bad pointers in the program files and registry. Most applications will break if you remap the drives after installation.

As mentioned previously, you can remap the drives as part of the install process for Citrix. You can also remap them after the installation using the installation CD, or the **driveremap.exe** command. To remap the drives using the CD:

1. Insert the MetaFrame Presentation Server installation CD. If autorun is not enabled, start the autorun process.

2. On the initial screen select **Product Installation.**

3. Choose **Remap Drives** from the list.

Citrix also includes a command-line utility that can be found on the root of the installation CD called **driveremap.exe**. It can be executed from a command line on the Citrix server to do the drive remapping. The syntax for driveremap is:

```
Driveremap.exe /drive:M
```

This specifies the M: drive as the first remapped drive letter (which is what the C: drive will be remapped to). All other drives will be remapped in order after this. Please note, because the server floppy drive is not available to Citrix sessions it is not remapped from A:. There are several other options available for drive remap as well:

- **/u** Performs the remap as a silent, unattended install. This option removes all prompts and feedback, and must be used in conjunction with the /drive option.

- **/noreboot** By default, the server reboots after drive remapping. This prevents the reboot. It is strongly recommended that you reboot as soon as possible after performing the drive remapping.

- **/dbscript:*filename*** When driveremap.exe is run on a Windows Server 2003 server, it also runs a small command utility called *Fixsecuritydatabase.cmd*. This updates the Windows Security Database after the drives have been remapped. If you copy this command file to the same directory you are running driveremap from, you do not need to specify the path. If you are executing it from a different location, however, you must specify the path to the Fixsecuritydatabase.cmd file.

It is very important that you do not attempt to do drive remapping over an ICA or RDP connection. Remapping should only be performed with direct console access, or as part of an unattended script running locally on the server.

Notes from the Underground…

Remapping Drives and Server Cloning

Remapped drives can present a challenge if you attempt to clone your servers. Many of the tools that you can use to restore a disk image will attempt to revert the mapped drives to their original settings. As an example, the Server 2003 Sysprep tool will revert the drives to C:\ and D:\. This will break your installation, and will often require a complete rebuild. If you have to clone a server with remapped drives, Citrix recommends that you use the **Newsid** utility from www.sysinternals.com. It provides an alternative to Sysprep that can be used as part of a third-party tool such as Ghost. It will also leave the drive mappings intact.

When you remap the server drives, the utility modifies certain registry entries. If you are experiencing problems with the drive remapping, check these registry keys to make sure they are set for the new drive mappings:

```
HKEY_LOCAL_MACHINE\Software\Microsoft\*
HKEY_LOCAL_MACHINE\Software\Classes
HKEY_LOCAL_MACHINE\Software\Equinox\eqn\CurrentVersion\NetRules
HKEY_LOCAL_MACHINE\SYSTEM\*
HKEY_CLASSES_ROOT\*
HKEY_USERS\*
```

The remap tool also updates the page file and the shortcut files for Default User, Administrator, and All Users to point to the new drive mapping. The first time a user logs in to the server after a remap, all drive references are updated in their profile to point to the new mappings as well.

Monitoring Disk Usage

Regardless of whether you choose to remap your server drives, you will inevitably end up with files and folders on your local drives that do not belong there. Whether these are leftover profile directories, poorly managed temp files, or even files that users mistakenly have left on a system drive, you need to pay attention to the space these wasted files take up. There are several methods to monitor your hard drive space and to alert you when it becomes a problem.

In a small environment, one of the easiest ways to check free disk space is to look. If you only have a few boxes to monitor, you can make sure to set yourself a periodic task to look at the free disk space on each of the boxes. Obviously, this isn't the most fool-proof method, since it does rely on you checking, but it can work very well when you don't want to spend the money on other products. It isn't a real-time alert either, but it is free!

You can also use Resource Manager to monitor the drive usage. One of the available metrics is % Free Space, and can be configured like any other metric to provide you alerts when disk utilization is too high. As mentioned in the previous section, if the disk space gets too low you could trigger a script to delete files that are no longer needed. Resource Manager provides real-time monitoring and alerting if your utilization goes over the threshold, and is very useful in situations where your servers can be quickly filled with files.

Automated File Cleanup and Reboot

One way to make sure your servers stay clean is to do periodic file cleanup. While it is worth the time to manually search the system drives for unwanted files, most of the unneeded files can be cleaned up through automation. Identifying directories and files that can be deleted without affecting your users can provide you with a list that can be fed through a cleanup script. Generally, this type of script is best run with a scheduled reboot to prevent deletion of files currently in use.

There are several steps to crafting a good reboot script. Generally, you would want to stop the ICA Browser Service, notify any users that the server was shutting down, give them time to get off, forcibly log off any other sessions, and then stop the spooler service. You can then delete the orphan print spooler files, remove the temp files, and reboot the server. There are obviously many ways the script could be varied, but this is the basis of a good reboot script. Figure 14.4 illustrates a basic script and explains each step.

Figure 14.4 Basic Reboot/Cleanup Script

```
REM This is a simple reboot and cleanup script
REM It will provide a walkthrough for automated reboots
@echo off
Cls
REM The first step is to stop the browser service to prevent logins
```

```
net stop icabrowser

REM Once it is stopped, all the users are messaged to please log off
Msg * This server is scheduled for a reboot in five (5) minutes. Please save
your work and log out

REM We then use the sleep command to give the users time to log out
Sleep 180

Msg * This server is scheduled for a reboot in two (2) minutes. Please save
your work and log out

REM We've given them enough warning… time to start working
REM First we stop the spooler and then we delete temp files
Net stop spooler
del %SYSTEMROOT%\temp\*.* /q
del %SYSTEMROOT%\system32\spool\printers\*.* /q
del %SYSTEMDRIVE%\temp\*.*

REM Shutdown and reboot the server
tsshutdn /reboot
```

There are many variations that can applied to the script. You could wait until the users had logged off before running the scripts. You could force their logout using a looping *logout.exe* command and then run the rest of the script. There are a myriad of ways the script can be crafted. Once it is in place, it can be scheduled to run via the windows scheduler as described here:

1. Click on **Start | Settings | Control Panel**.

2. Double-click on **Scheduled Tasks**.

3. Double-click on **Add Scheduled Task** and click **Next**.

4. Browse to the reboot script you created and then click **Next**.

5. You can schedule it to run as often as desired, and at the time specified.

6. Choose an Administrator account to run the script under.

Once you have created the scheduled task, you now have an automated cleanup solution. Again, this works best in conjunction with a periodic inspection of the drives for files that aren't in the temp directories.

Cleaning Up Profiles

One of the problems frequently seen on Terminal Services is that profiles sometimes just won't unload correctly when the users log off. This can be for a wide range of reasons, and sometimes impossible to trace down. Hung profiles create a host of problems for both the user and administrators. Because the profile is still locked in the directory, the files that would normally be deleted on a clean user exit are left in place. The next time the user logs back in, his profile may not load correctly and so he might lose his current settings. Profile cleanup is an important part of your daily maintenance.

Thankfully, Microsoft finally recognized the problems with hung profiles and released a utility called *Uphclean.exe*. At its heart, it monitors the users' sessions and makes sure they are still logged in. If it detects that they aren't, it attempts to reclaim the resources and clean any registry entries left over from the previous sessions. To install UPHClean, simply download the uphclean-setup.msi from Microsoft and execute it on the server. UPHClean does not require a reboot to take effect on Windows Server 2003. Once it is installed, it writes log events that detail the steps it takes to unload registry information.

UPHClean runs as a service, and can be stopped or started as needed. Be aware, however, that running UPHClean can slow your servers. Because it is constantly polling user data and interacting with the logoff process, it has been known to significantly increase the logoff time for users. Make sure to test it fully before releasing it to your production farm.

Lock Down Your Files

The last step to keeping your files and folders in working order is to keep your system drives as secure as possible. If users can't access the system drive, they generally can't leave files there. This ultimately will take a lot of time and patience. Applications do not always behave like we wish they would, and often require open access to places we wish they didn't. For instance, an application might require rights to an ini file located in the System32 directory. In the best of worlds, it would only need read access to this file under the user account. Poorly coded programs will often require write access as well. That is why file security can be a complex and granular task.

There are really two methods of going about securing your server. You could lock everything down and see what breaks. Generally, this means read-only access to everything in the Windows subdirectory for the users, especially in System and System32. You could also lock down all of the Program Files directories, and even the root of your system drive if you decided to. This lockdown can be done using File and Folder permissions, group policy objects (GPOs), or simply by hiding the drive entirely with a local system policy. To lock down a folder through Permissions:

1. Right-click on the folder and choose **Properties**.

2. Click the **Security** tab and select the group you want to modify.

3. Remove everything but the **List** and **Read and Execute** permissions from the user group.

Assuming the users are not members of another group with a higher permission set, they are now permitted only to execute or read the files in that folder. In many cases, you can even get away with removing the List permission, preventing the users entirely from enumerating the contents of the folder. Once the folder is locked down, launch the application in question and see if you are still able to perform all the functions. It can be a tedious job, but maintaining good file security can prevent not only unwanted files but unwanted alterations and deletions.

The second method is to leave everything wide open, and slowly start locking the folders down to check for conflicts. This is done essentially the same way as described earlier, but you are starting from a wide open system and applying security rather than removing it. This is best used on existing servers that were not properly configured before and now need to be locked down for safety or convenience. As conflicts arise, you will have to sort out the security permissions involved.

NOTE

Why can't I see my app!? When you publish an application to users, the Publish Application Wizard uses what is called the Trust Intersection to determine who can access the published application. Trust Intersection is the list of users who can access every server in the host list for the published application. This means that if certain users do not have rights to log in to a particular server in the list of hosts, they will not be able to have that published app on *any* of the servers.

This also means that if the trusts change for any reason, or if you redefine the host list and the users are no longer able to access all of the servers, they will lose the published application from their list. If you cannot change the trust relationship to accommodate the users, you will have to publish another application identical to the first, but only to the servers that the users can access.

Session Management

One of the biggest tasks in day-to-day administration is monitoring your users' sessions and trying to predict or diagnose issues. This could be anything from a suddenly slow WAN link to an overall need for increased capacity for an application suite. Citrix provides you with several tools to manage user sessions and troubleshoot potential problems in them. The biggest tool provided is the Management Console.

Session Monitoring

In the Management Console, user sessions can be monitored per application or per server. If you want to watch a specific application, open the Management Console and expand the **Applications** list. Highlight the application you want to monitor and select the **Users** tab in the right window. You will be presented with a list of all the users accessing that published application and relevant data about their session. This includes:

- Their User ID

- The server they are executing the application from

- The name of their client device

- The state of their session (Active or Disconnected)

- The amount of time their session has been idle

This information is helpful in identifying trends for an application. For instance, you have a critical business application that is used by hundreds of users over the course of a day. Often, the servers are very congested, but you don't have the budget to buy more machines. Watching the application and trending it over the course of a week, you notice that users will get on in the morning and stay on all day whether they are doing any work in the session or not. Idle times are often in the hours, and many users only log out when their day is done. With this data you can justify adding idle timeouts that will disconnect and ultimately log off these extra sessions. This frees up the resources for users actually doing work, and saves you the cost of new servers.

Another way to monitor user sessions is on a server basis. In the Management Console, expand the **Servers** list and highlight the server you want to monitor. Select the **Users** tab and you are presented with a list of sessions. Much of the information is the same as that listed previously, except that it lists the application being executed in place of the server they are executing it from. The same scenario could also apply. Monitoring these trends in your users can provide you with valuable data for future design decisions.

The Management Console also gives you a measure of control over a user session. If you highlight a connected session and right-click, you are given several options to perform on that session:

- **Disconnect** You can force the user session to a Disconnect state without the user being able to interfere.

- **Send Message** You can message the user with information such as "I am about to attempt to shadow you. Please click 'Yes' when prompted."

- **Shadow** You can shadow the user's session per the parameters for shadowing that you set when you installed Citrix.

- **Reset** You can completely reset the user's session.

- **Status** Provides you with detailed information about the traffic for that session, including the number of bytes transmitted and received, errors in the traffic, and so forth.

- **Logoff Selected Session** You can cause the session to perform a logoff, completely unloading the user information from the server and closing the user's applications.

- **Session Information** Provides you with details about the client itself. These include every process the client is executing on that server, information about the session such as color depth and resolution, and even the various Citrix Client modules loaded. This is very useful for troubleshooting user connection issues since it provides you with so many pertinent details.

As an example, you have a user that says she is hanging in Word every time she tries to open a specific file. You could monitor her session information to determine the processes she was calling and make sure something wasn't out of line. You could shadow her session to see precisely what she sees. You could even log her off if her session got stuck and she could not exit cleanly. Generally, you will get the most use out of the Reset and Logoff options as a Citrix administrator.

Using SMC Console

Citrix also provides another extremely useful session management tool called the SMC Console. This utility can be downloaded as part of the Citrix Software Development Kit (SDK) from http://cdn.citrix.com. The CDN requires registration, but is free to anyone. It allows you to actively monitor each session for a variety of information, including one very important statistic: latency.

Latency is the bane of every Citrix administrator who has to deal with remote clients. Even with the best of networks, sooner or later there will be an issue with latency. Figure 14.5 shows the SMC Console utility.

Figure 14.5 SMC Console

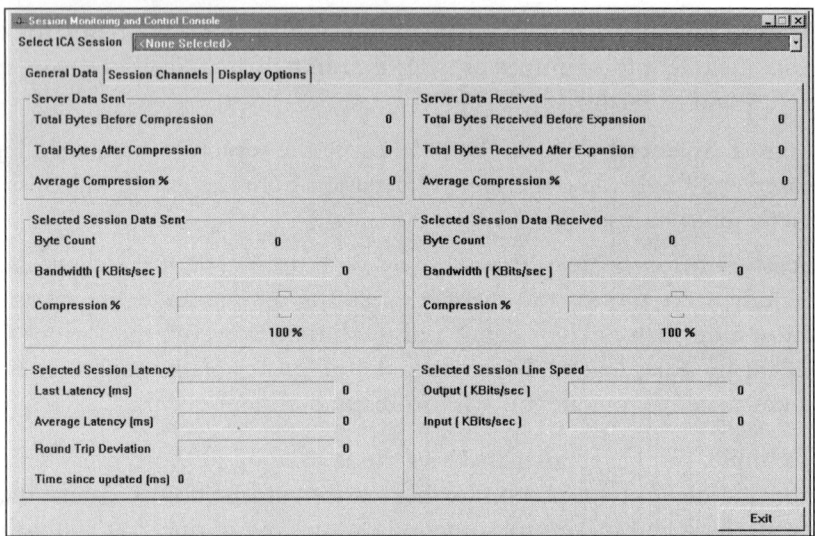

The symptoms of latency problems can be tricky to diagnose. Often, users will complain of an overall slow feel to their sessions, or that they will have long periods of what looks like a hung session followed by a burst of activity. The also have mass disconnects at their office from time to time. The networking team says it must be a Citrix issue. Here's where the console can really help.

1. Connect to the server they access and have a user from that site log in.

2. Open the **SMC Console** and select the user's session from the dropdown list.

3. Watch the user's latency numbers, both average and last. When the user has a problem have her call you so you can check the latency at that point.

4. In general, latency numbers will run around 100–200 milliseconds on a good wide area connection. If they start to top 500–600ms, you start to have problems; higher than 1000 and you will have session drops.

These latency numbers can help you trace the issue. If the office is having problems and the latency on the user sessions is through the roof, it's time to get the network team involved again. If the session latency is not a problem, you need to start looking at the Citrix servers. Perhaps they have hardware or software problems.

Another benefit of the SMC Console is that it allows you to set individual channel throttling for each virtual channel of the ICA session. You can give priority to different channels, which can increase or decrease the perceived response of the session for your users. Little-used channels can be given a very low priority, meaning they will not preempt more important data. Figure 14.6 shows the channel properties page of the SMC Console.

Figure 14.6 Channel Properties in the SMC Console

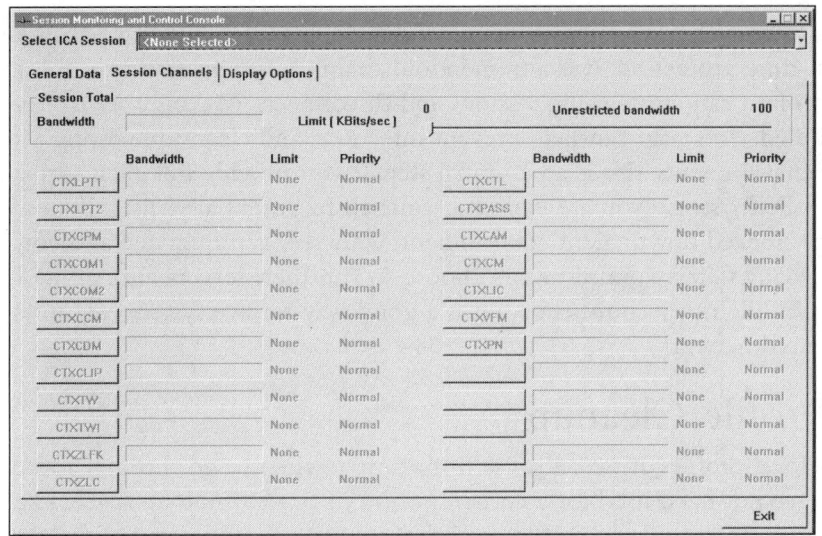

Because you can control the channel compression, you can experiment with different configurations that best suit your environment. Another key detail to this screen, however, is that it also shows you which channels are being mapped for the client. If, for instance, you are trying to troubleshoot a problem with a USB device, you can check the channel properties to make sure that it is actually being mapped by the Citrix client. If it is not, there is likely a problem with the client configuration or you have disabled the mapping on your server.

The SMC Console is just one demonstration of the source code available in the SDK. If you are a talented scripter, you can make use of the code to write your own monitoring and management applications for your Citrix environment. There are also many utilities available at various Citrix-related Web sites that can help you in your day-to-day monitoring of your Citrix environment. See the *Links to Sites* section at the end of the chapter for a few suggestions.

Periodic Administrative Tasks

The final section of this chapter covers some of the tasks that are not necessarily day-to-day administration, but should be performed on a periodic basis to make sure your servers stay in good condition. These can often be scheduled for off hours and weekends, allowing you to automate their use. These are meant mostly as suggestions, and none is critical to your server operations. They are, however, best practices as gathered through years of Citrix and Microsoft administration.

Periodic Virus Scans

If you run a virus checker on your terminal servers, it is recommended that you not enable real-time protection. It is a tremendous drain on system resources for a terminal server, and often can create hung sessions and disconnects. Making sure to have a regularly scheduled virus scan can help prevent infections and clean up existing problems. For some environments, this is an essential step. If you provide full client drive mappings to uncontrolled systems, you are exposing yourself to potential viruses. If, however, you have a fairly locked down client environment, your risk is minimized and you can scan less often. Many Citrix administrators choose to run their servers entirely without virus protection. While not recommended, it is a good way to save system resources in a tightly secured network.

User Profile Cleanup

If you use local profiles, it makes sense from time to time to go through and delete profiles that have not been used for a certain period of time to free up space. The length of time that you can consider a profile dead depends on your own environment, but if the user hasn't logged in to it in a year, it's a good guess that it can be removed. You can check this by viewing the user profiles in List mode and checking the Modified date on each one.

Along with cleaning out dead profiles, it is also important to clean out users' local temp files such as the Internet Explorer cache. This can be done manually by simply deleting all of their cache files, or through a script that runs through each profile and deletes it. If your users frequently access the Web, they will have wasted cache files.

Spyware Scanning

Unfortunately, Spyware has become a fact of our day-to-day administration. It is prevalent and vicious, and once it is in your system it is hard to remove. If your users are allowed to access external Web sites via their terminal server session, it is strongly recommended that you purchase and use a third-party Spyware removal tool such as Ad-Aware. Set it up for periodic scans and removal, and let it run prior to a reboot. This will help keep your system resources from being taken over by hijacking software.

Periodic System Reboots

We've already covered a basic reboot script, but even if you don't plan to use it you should consider periodic system reboots. Although Microsoft has done a good job of eliminating memory leaks in the core operating system, many applications can still cause them. Having a weekly or even nightly reboot schedule can keep your system from degrading over time and slowing down the user sessions.

In addition to using a scheduled task for reboots, Citrix has provided a method of scheduling reboots for MetaFrame servers. In the Management Console, highlight a server and right-click. Choose **Properties** and then **Reboot Schedule**. You are able to define the time and frequency of the reboots and the message sent to users prior to a reboot. Figure 14.7 shows the Reboot Schedule properties window.

Figure 14.7 Reboot Schedule Properties

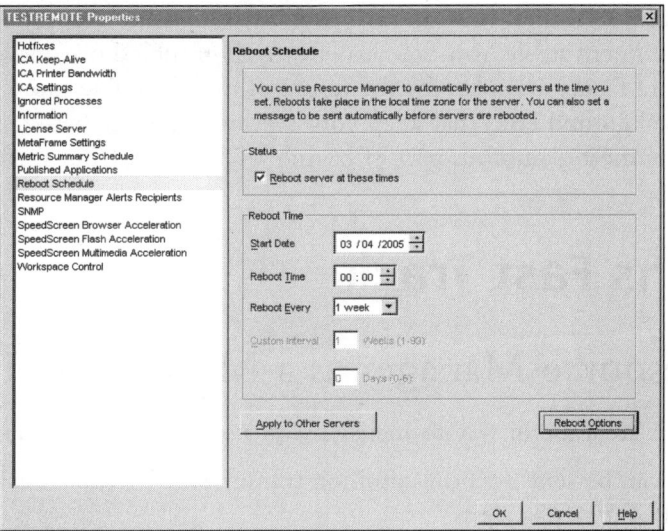

You need to make sure to define it only in one place. If you schedule the reboot in both a Citrix setting and as a local scheduled task, they will fight each other for the reboot and could cause multiple system restarts. It is best to decide on a strategy for all of your servers and apply it that way. If you choose to use the Citrix scheduler, you can use the **Apply to Other Servers** button to push the schedule to the rest of the farm and include a stagger setting so they don't all go off at once.

Summary

Day-to-day administration of a Citrix server farm can be a challenging task. Some days, it will be completely quiet, and all your sessions will be humming along happily. The next day you could have red alerts going off everywhere and management breathing down your neck. Thankfully, Microsoft and Citrix have provided tools to level out the highs and lows, and to give you indications of potential trouble.

With careful monitoring, you can save yourself from some common mistakes and keep your environment stable. You can also effectively troubleshoot and diagnose issues that your users are facing and plan for the future of the farm. The more automated you can make the background tasks that keep your servers clean, the better shape you will be in. This is not the most glamorous part of having a Citrix farm, but it is certainly the most important.

Solutions Fast Track

Using Resource Manager as a Monitoring Tool

- ☑ Metrics are a useful way to manage your user load on your server farms.
- ☑ Alerts can be sent by most common transmission methods including SMS, SNMP, and e-mail alerts.
- ☑ The Resource Manager Watcher window can be kept displayed on the desktop even when the console is minimized.
- ☑ Alert thresholds are configurable by the administrator, and can be as restrictive or open as you choose.

File and Folder Management

- ☑ Drive remapping can prevent user access to system drives.
- ☑ Several registry keys also need to be checked to make sure that they are pointed to the new drive mappings.
- ☑ Drive remap should only be performed after a clean OS install and before any applications are installed. Otherwise, you run the risk of breaking the applications.

Session Management

- ☑ Session monitoring can be performed with a variety of tools from Citrix and Microsoft.

- ☑ By monitoring an individual session, you can determine everything from the latency of the session to what channels the user is using.

- ☑ Citrix provides a tool called the SMC Console that can actively display the information about a session and the channels it is using.

Periodic Administrative Tasks

- ☑ Virus scans should be performed periodically to keep the servers clean from infection, especially in cases where the server provides e-mail services or allows local drive remapping.

- ☑ Profiles should be cleaned up periodically to prevent old files from filling up your local drives.

- ☑ Windows servers should be periodically rebooted to prevent memory leaks from slowing system performance.

Frequently Asked Questions

The following Frequently Asked Questions, answered by the authors of this book, are designed to both measure your understanding of the concepts presented in this chapter and to assist you with real-life implementation of these concepts. To have your questions about this chapter answered by the author, browse to **www.syngress.com/solutions** and click on the **"Ask the Author"** form. You will also gain access to thousands of other FAQs at ITFAQnet.com.

Q: How many Citrix servers can I reboot at once?

A: Because they access the data store when they come back up, Citrix does not recommend rebooting more than 30 servers at a time if you are using a robust database server, and not more than 10 at a time if you are using a local data store.

Q: I have a USB device that is not interacting properly with my Citrix session. How can I tell if it's even connecting?

A: Use the SMC console to look for the USB channel mapping and make sure there is activity on it. Otherwise, you may need updated drivers for your device or an updated Citrix client.

Q: How can I provide alerts to a pager?

A: The best way to manage that is to use pagers that can receive e-mail messages and set up SMTP alerts to go to that. Alternatively, you can also provide it with a group e-mail box that then distributes the alert to a list of pagers.

Q: What other tasks can I script in the shutdown process?

A: Many administrators will use the shutdown period to script in everything from profile cleanup to permission modifications. Because a restart script can be easily modified for a new task and you have a guaranteed down period, the reboot script is a great way to get your little jobs done.

Chapter 15

Troubleshooting and Helpdesk

Solutions in this chapter:

- Troubleshooting Server-Side Issues
- Troubleshooting Client-Side Issues
- Getting Help from Citrix

☑ Summary

☑ Solutions Fast Track

☑ Frequently Asked Questions

Introduction

A properly installed and configured Citrix MetaFrame Presentation server farm in a well-designed Windows Server 2003 Active Directory forest will support its configured clients as it was designed to. However, if every system built by seasoned engineers and managed by competent administrators never broke or malfunctioned we would eventually run out of jobs.

Troubleshooting and resolving malfunctions or inconsistencies in configurations is at the heart of the duties of an administrator. Although MetaFrame Presentation Server 3.0 is the most sophisticated and complete MetaFrame solution we have to date, things still do go wrong. It is an administrator's job to continue to tweak and improve his Citrix farm, as end-user requirements and network conditions change. It is also an administrator's job to take note of malfunctions or inconsistencies in functionality, track down the source, and do what needs to be done to rectify the problem.

To this end, in this chapter we cover troubleshooting issues that may arise in a Citrix MetaFrame Presentation server farm in a Windows Server 2003 Active Directory infrastructure. The issues, examples, and solutions in this chapter are real-life occurrences and problems that may be encountered with solutions that have been proven to work.

Troubleshooting Server-Side Issues

In this section, we cover issues that may arise from problems in the Windows Server 2003 operating system software or server configuration, and issues that are definitely related to Citrix MetaFrame Presentation Server. We discuss problems related to performance, connectivity, security, data store support, and application publication. Even though most of these problems are experienced by the end user, the focus of the problem is server related and thus must be dealt with at the server level.

The IMA Service is responsible for all MetaFrame server communications and serves as the management foundation for MetaFrame Presentation Server. The IMA Service is comprised of a collection of core components that define and control the execution of products in a server farm such as the farm data store. The service enables servers to exist in server farms that are independent of the physical locations of the servers and where the servers are on different network subnets. The service also allows clients to connect to the MetaFrame server via the ICA protocol. The IMA service runs on all servers in the farm as an automatic service, and its components communicate through messages passed through default TCP ports 2512 and 2513.

Since the IMA Service is of such integral importance to MetaFrame functionality, any disruption in the service could result in the dissolution of a server farm or the inability of end users to locate or connect to a single server or an entire farm as shown in Figure 15.1

Figure 15.1 IMA Service Error

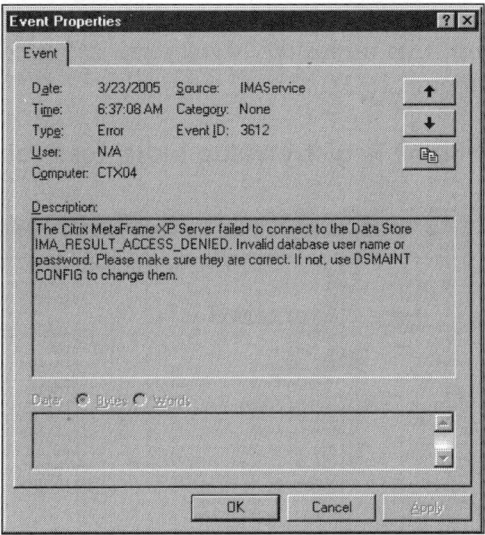

Troubleshooting issues with the IMA Service failing to start should be carried out as follows:

1. Check the Windows Services utility to see if the service is started and is running.

2. Check network communications from the server by using the *ping*, *arp*, and *netstat* commands to establish reachability, address resolution, and communication via the default TCP ports as in Figure 15.2 using *arp* to verify network connectivity.

Figure 15.2 Using *arp* to Verify Network Connectivity

```
Command Prompt                                                    _ □ ×

C:\>arp -a

Interface: 10.28.128.190 --- 0x10003
  Internet Address      Physical Address      Type
  10.28.128.1           00-00-0c-07-ac-02     dynamic
  10.28.128.85          00-08-02-19-eb-12     dynamic
  10.28.128.86          00-08-02-19-ec-94     dynamic
  10.28.128.87          00-02-a5-da-24-dd     dynamic
  10.28.128.129         00-50-8b-b9-20-df     dynamic
  10.28.128.131         00-08-02-56-18-fe     dynamic
  10.28.128.192         00-08-02-91-b6-b3     dynamic
  10.28.128.194         00-0f-20-7a-8a-32     dynamic
  10.28.129.23          00-0b-cd-ce-02-2a     dynamic
  10.28.129.24          00-08-02-91-2d-fa     dynamic
  10.28.129.63          00-0b-cd-f4-d8-b0     dynamic
  10.28.129.69          00-0b-cd-cf-1c-21     dynamic

C:\>_
```

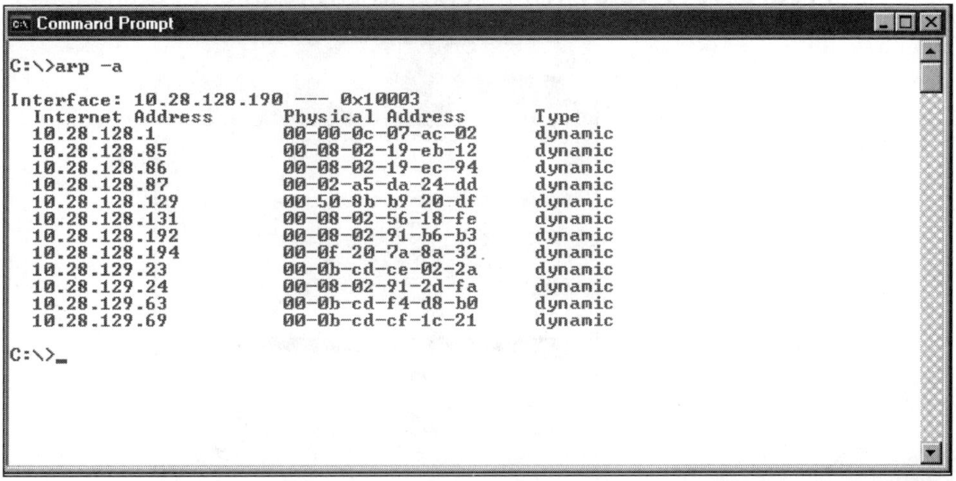

3. Check the HKEY_LOCAL_MACHINE\SOFTWARE\
    Citrix\IMA\Runtime\CurrentlyLoadingPlugin registry value for value data. If
    the value is blank, that means the MetaFrame server could not connect to the
    data store (see Figure 15.3).

Figure 15.3 Blank Registry Value Indicates Problem Contacting Data
Store

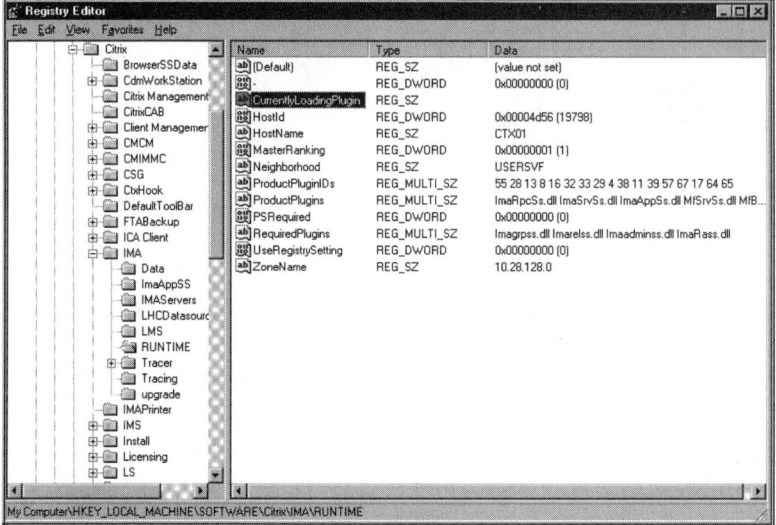

4. Check the Windows environment settings on the server for the TMP and
    TEMP values and ensure that they both point to the *<systemroot>*\temp folder
    as in Figure 15.4.

Figure 15.4 Verify Temp Folder in Environment Settings

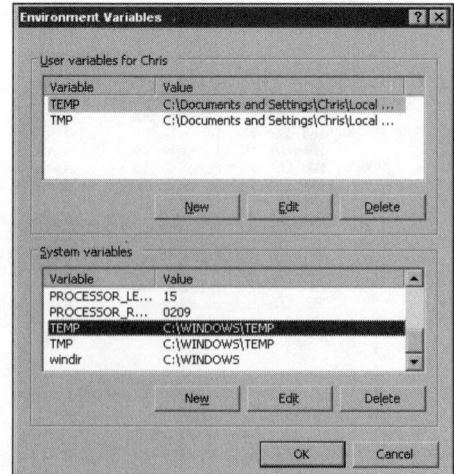

5. Enable logging of IMA events on the server by editing the
    HKEY_LOCAL_MACHINE\SOFTWARE\Citrix\IMA\Tracer registry key
    and adding values as follows:

```
Name: Log to Debugger
Type:REG_DWORD
   Data: 0x1 to enable debugging
   Name: Log to File

Type: REG_DWORD
Data: 0x1 to enable file output
Name: LogFileName
   Type: REG_SZ

Data: <full path and filename of output file>
```

Figure 15.5 IMA Tracer Registry Key

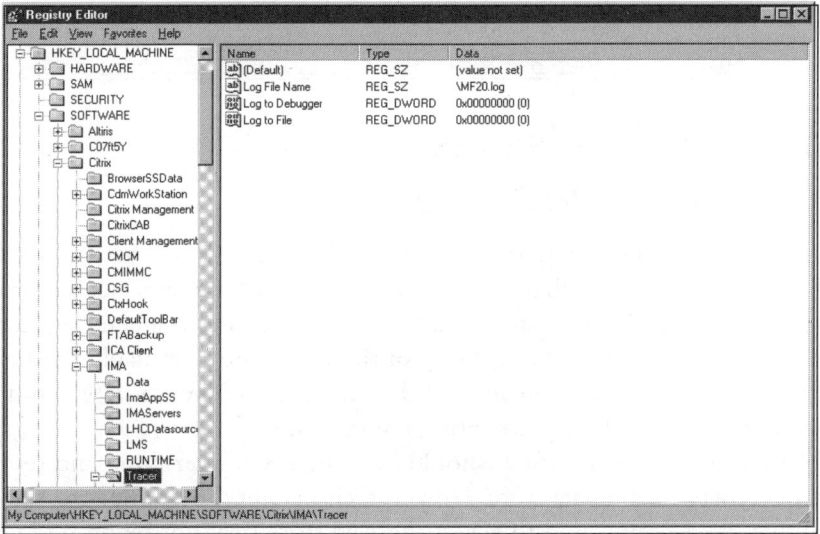

All the components of the IMA Service can be debugged using the subkeys in the
Tracer key folder. Debugging is turned on by default but the output of the debugging is
not configured. The output of the trace can be configured by setting the value of the
message values in the subkeys to 1.

The IMA Service functionality also depends on connectivity to the MetaFrame data
store. Data store connectivity depends on ODBC connectivity. The ODBC configuration and connectivity to the data store can be verified and tested via the ODBC connection test tool. The ODBC Data Source Name that the IMA is using to connect to

the data store can be verified by examining the registry at HKEY_LOCAL_
MACHINE\SOFTWARE\Citrix\ IMA\DataSourceName (see Figure 15.6).

Figure 15.6 The Local Host Cache Data Source Name in the Registry

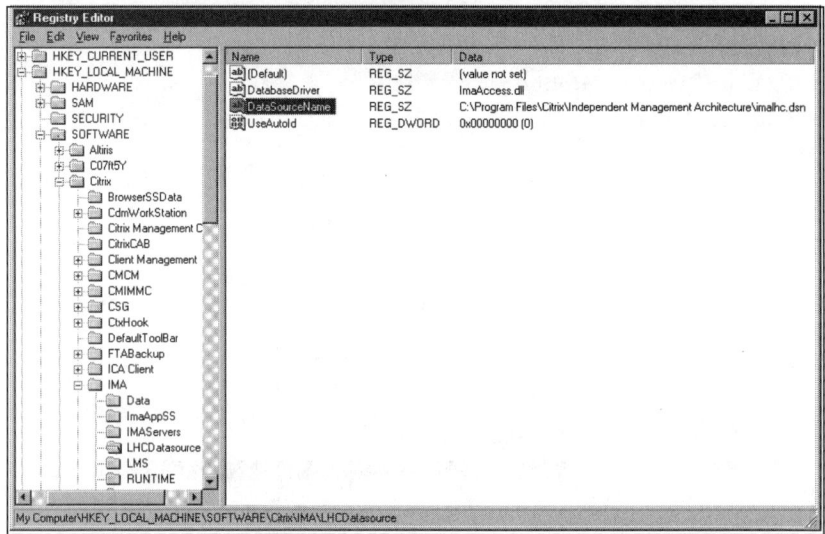

Troubleshooting Issues Related to the Data Store

We saw in the previous section that the IMA Service depends on the data store being accessible. All the information that comprises the Citrix MetaFrame server farm is contained in the data store. The data store can be a local database or a centralized database hosted on a database server. The availability of the data store is arguably the most critical factor in the existence and maintenance of the server farm. There is a 96-hour window of time before the farm will stop accepting connections.

Troubleshooting data store issues should also begin with verifying and testing the ODBC connectivity to the data store. However, an inability to connect to the data store may signal that the account used to access the data store may not be properly accessing the data store. To troubleshoot access to the data store, verify the password for the account used to access the data store by using the ODBC connection test tool. Another source of data store inoperability may be that the account used to access the data store no longer has permissions to create objects in the data store. This can be verified and resolved by checking and resetting the database permissions on the data store in particular DBMS that houses the data store. Microsoft SQL Server requires the "db_owner" permission be given to the data store access account (Figure 15.7), Oracle requires the "resource" permission to be set, and IBM DB2 requires the database "administrator authority" permission.

Figure 15.7 Data Store Account Permissions in Microsoft SQL Server

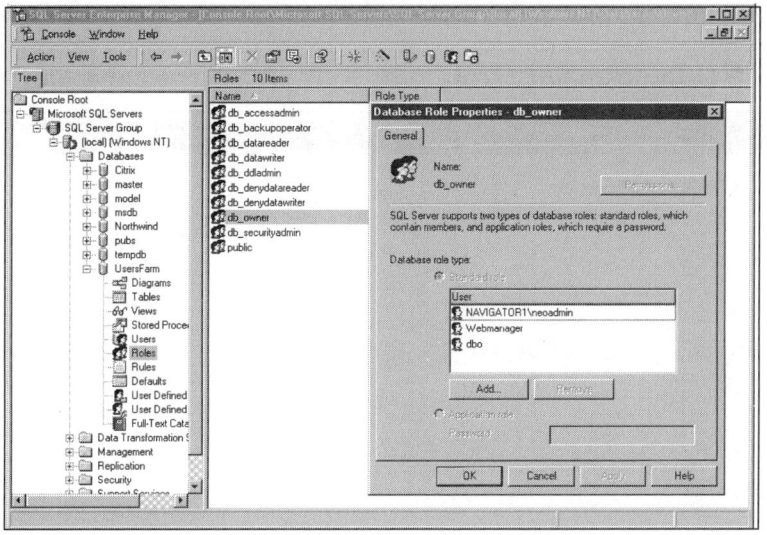

An inability to access the data store may also indicate that the data store itself or, more commonly, the server's local host cache—a subset of the farm data store that exists on each server in the farm—is corrupt. The local host cache is referenced in the server's registry in the DataSourceName registry key (Figure 15.8).

Figure 15.8 DataSourceName Registry Key Showing the Location of the Local Host Cache File

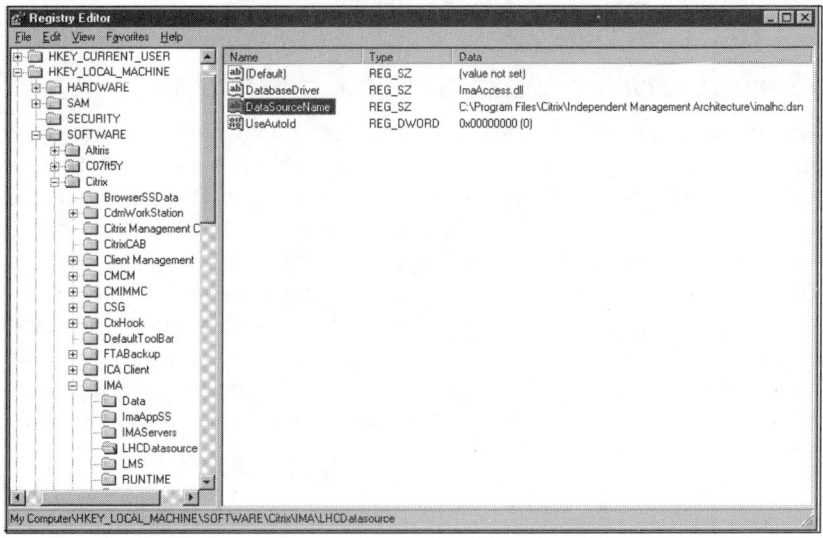

Never fear, all is not lost; the data store can be recovered. To restore the data store, use the *dsmaint recreatelhc* command to rebuild the data store (Figure 15.9).

Figure 15.9 Using *dsmaint recreatelhc* to Recreate the Local Host Cache File

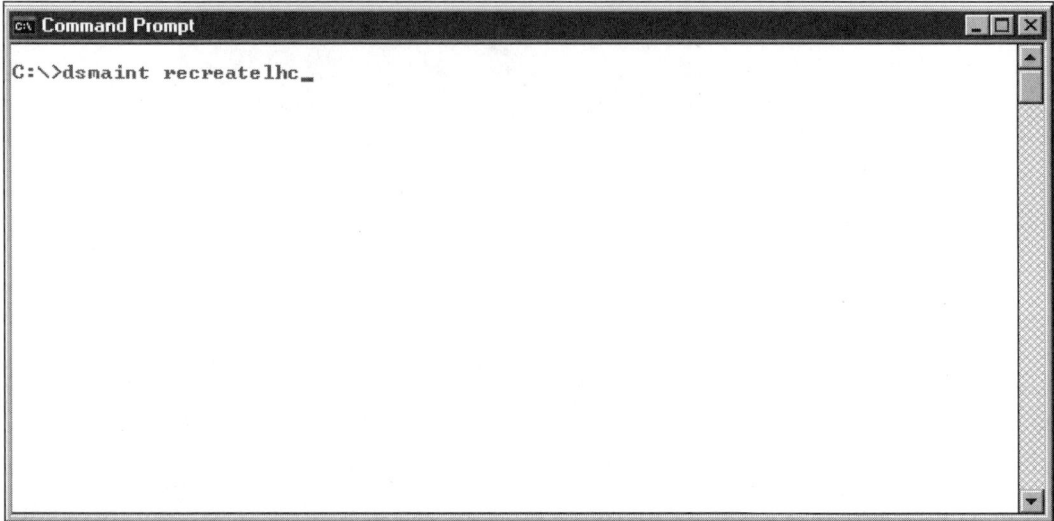

Notes from the Underground…

Recovering from a Data Store Corruption

In the event your data store somehow becomes corrupted, you may lose access to all published applications on your MetaFrame server farm. Switching your end users to RDP connections will allow them to connect to the servers in the farm.

If you are using a Microsoft SQL Server database as your data store, simply create a new database and configure a new system DSN for the new database. Then, use the *chfarm* command to create a new Citrix server farm and have all your servers join the new farm. You will have to republish your applications, but it beats reinstalling the infrastructure from scratch.

Remember, an ounce of prevention is worth more than a pound of cure. Setting up a data store where the data is replicated between two servers (a minimum) is strongly advised.

Troubleshooting Printing Issues

Perhaps the most notorious problems in a Citrix MetaFrame environment, printing problems are usually the most visible and supported issues encountered in daily MetaFrame server farm management. Citrix makes a genuine and concerted effort to support as many printers as it can either through Windows driver support or through the Citrix Universal Driver. However, some printer drivers slip through the cracks, as it is a truly daunting task to provide support for every single printing device that exists.

The main cause of printing problems in a MetaFrame environment involves client printers not mapping correctly in the ICA session. When a client initiates an ICA session with the MetaFrame server, a function referred to as *strstr()* determines what the client's attached printers are by looking at the HKEY_CURRENT_USER\Printers\ Connections registry key and comparing the printers there to the printers in HKEY_CURRENT_USER\Software\Microsoft\Windows NT\CurrentVersion| Windows:Device registry key, and maps them in the session. The strstr() function is case sensitive and thus recognizes only the printers that are named in the correct case. If the printer names do not match, that printer does not get loaded. The MetaFrame server then maps the first printer detected by the *strstr()* function as the client's default printer—whether this is true or not. The error message in Figure 15.10 illustrates the error that is generated when an incorrect printer mapping occurs.

Figure 15.10 Printer Auto-Creation Error

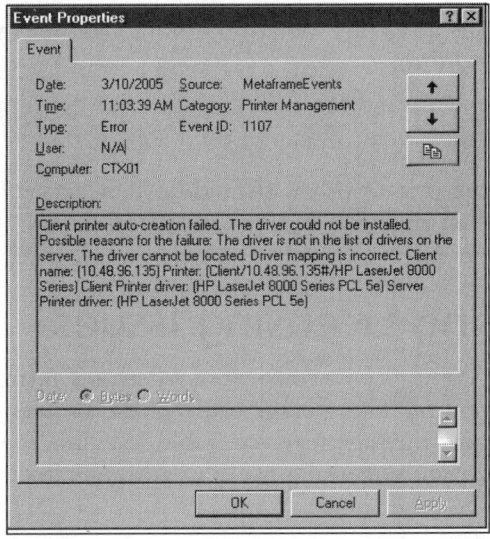

Some printing problems may also stem from simply using incompatible drivers, drivers not supported by MetaFrame, or drivers for devices that support multiple functions.

The failure of printer replication is another issue that must be addressed. If printer driver replication fails, an event is logged stating that the printer driver could not be replicated because the language monitor could not be added. This is because printer drivers with language monitor files are not standard print drivers. Only standard printers in the list of accepted printer drivers can be replicated; therefore, for the MetaFrame server to be able to support this printer, the drivers have to be loaded on each server in the farm.

Configuring and Implementing...

Replicating Nonstandard Printer Drivers

To configure replication of nonstandard print drivers the language monitor files associated with the drivers must be located by searching for the printer that needs to be added in **HKEY_LOCAL_MACHINE\SYSTEM\CurrentControlSet\ Control\Print\Environments\Windows NT x86\Drivers**. Once located, the following steps must be taken to add support for nonstandard printers:

1. In the registry, add the subkey MonitorList to the key HKEY_LOCAL_MACHINE\SOFTWARE\Citrix\IMAPrinter.

2. Add Multi-String values, where the Value Name is the name of the language monitor.

3. In the Multi-String Editor, add the name of the language monitor dependent files, each filename on a separate line.

Replication of the printer driver should now be possible. You can check the status of the replication by using the **qprinter /replica** command.

Troubleshooting Licensing Issues

Problems with licensing come from two sources: Microsoft Terminal Services licensing or Citrix MetaFrame licensing. The specific cause of the problem is often difficult to diagnose based on the error message received. Table 15.1 lists the common problems, the possible sources associated with licensing issues in a MetaFrame server farm, and their possible resolutions.

Table 15.1 Common Licensing Issues

Error Message	Possible Source	Possible Resolution
There are no licenses installed for the use of this MetaFrame Presentation server.	No license server is installed.	Install a license server.
	A valid license file is not installed on the license server.	Install a valid license file on the server.
	The correct MetaFrame Presentation server edition is not set.	Set the correct MetaFrame server edition in the server properties.
Cannot contact the license server.	Loss of network connectivity to the license server.	Locate and resolve the source of the network connectivity problem.
	Correct license server is not configured in MetaFrame farm properties.	Enter the name of the correct license server in the farm properties.
The MetaFrame Presentation server is in the grace period. There are 96 hours remaining before the system stops accepting connections.	Correct license server is not configured in MetaFrame farm properties.	Enter the name of the correct license server in the farm properties.
	The Citrix licensing service is not running.	Start the Citrix license server in the Services application on the server.
Can't Connect to license server. Verify that the license server is running.	The Citrix licensing service is not running.	Start the Citrix License server in the Services application on the server.
	License server not reading the license file correctly.	Stop the Citrix Licensing, Citrix Licensing WMI, and License Management Console services. Remove all license files except citrix_startup.lic.

Continued

Table 15.1 continued Common Licensing Issues

Error Message	Possible Source	Possible Resolution
		Restart the services. Stop the service again, restore the license files, and restart the services.
Your Terminal Services temporary license will expire in x days. Please contact your system administrator to get a permanent license.	The TS licenses are installed incorrectly	Remove the licenses and contact Microsoft Licensing for assistance to reinstall them properly.
The terminal server cannot issue a client license.	Not enough TSCALs installed	Install more TSCALs.
	Incorrect licensing mode	Switch to the correct licensing mode in the TS Licensing console.

As we can see, the sources of the error messages can be different even though the same message is reported.

Troubleshooting Issues Related to User and Group Access

User access is the whole point of Citrix MetaFrame Presentation Server. Troubleshooting user access can be very tricky. Criteria such as domain authentication and trusts, group membership, Group Policy, and Local Security policy all affect user access to a MetaFrame server farm.

User authentication issues can stem from domain authentication issues such as incorrect user account credentials, disabled accounts, inter-domain trust issues, and inter-forest trust issues. Inappropriately applied or configured group policy objects (GPOs) are also a server-side source of connectivity problems. The steps to troubleshoot these issues are as follows:

1. onfirm that a domain controller is within reach on the network.

2. Use the Active Directory Users and Computers tool to check user account validity.

3. Verify trusts between domains by using the Active Directory Domains and Trusts tool.

4. Verify GPO configuration and assignment via the Group Policy Management Console

Another important fact to note is that Windows 2003 Terminal Server access is configured differently from Windows 2000. In Windows 2000, Terminal Services access was configured via the "Allow log on locally" local security policy. Not so in Windows Server 2003. Access to Windows Server 2003 Terminal Services is granted via membership in a new local user group called Remote Desktop users (Figure 15.11).

Figure 15.11 Remote Desktop Users Group Allows Terminal Services Access

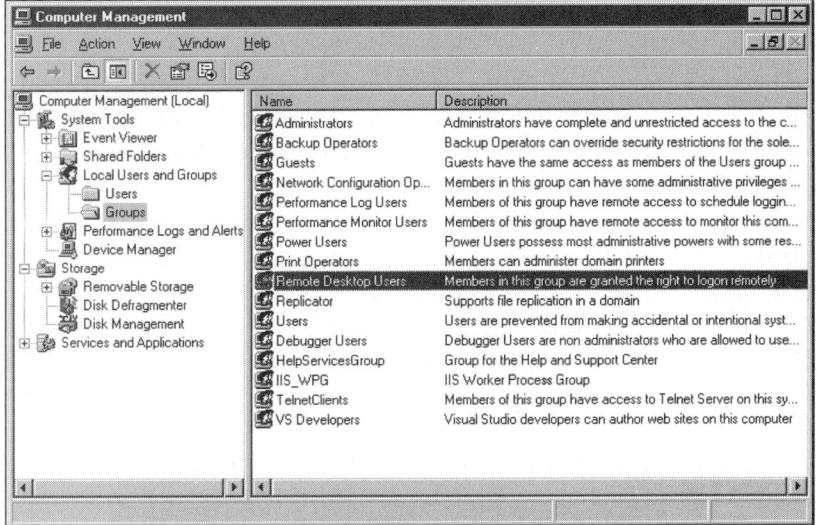

This group must also be added in the permissions for the RDP and ICA connections in the Terminal Services Configuration administrative tool (Figure 15.12).

Figure 15.12 Adding Remote Desktop Users to ICA Connection So They Can Log in to the Server

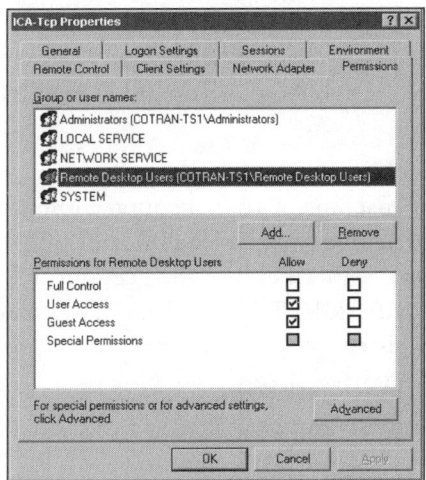

Troubleshooting Client-Side Issues

In the previous sections we discussed common server-side issues that, even though they affect the client, are remedied at the server. In this section, we discuss problems that are uniquely client based and must thus be rectified at the client station.

Client Access Issues

The most common client access issues are those that involve accessing the server and logging in to an ICA session. The most basic sources of client access issues stem from network connectivity problems that the client may be experiencing. If a client complains of not being able to access his applications, the first thing to check is network connectivity. If the client is on the LAN, begin by checking the physical elements of his network connection; for example, the network cable. Perform a connectivity test with the server by using the *ping* utility from a command prompt. Attempt to connect to the server via an RDP session. If network connectivity can be verified, the connectivity issue concerns either the server or the client software.

Figure 15.13 displays the error message most commonly seen when there is a problem initiating a connection from the client if a problem in the client software such as corrupting on the ICA is preventing network access.

Figure 15.13 ICA Client Error

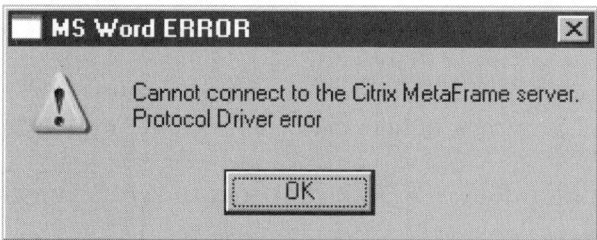

To troubleshoot and rectify the issue, perform the following on the client machine with a valid domain account. It may be that you are logged in locally or with a restricted domain account.

1. Verify that the account you are logged in with has at least Power User rights on the local client machine. A user account without enough permission to modify the local machine's registry will not be able to initiate a connection with the MetaFrame server because the account will not be able to update the HKEY_LOCAL_MACHINE\SOFTWARE\Microsoft\MSLicensing key in the workstation registry.

2. If the user is not in the local Power Users or Administrators group, add the account to one of these groups or log in as a domain administrator and use the

regedt32 utility to assign Full Control permissions to the user account or the group to which the user account belongs (Figure 15.14).

Figure 15.14 Setting Permissions on the MSLicensing Key in the Registry

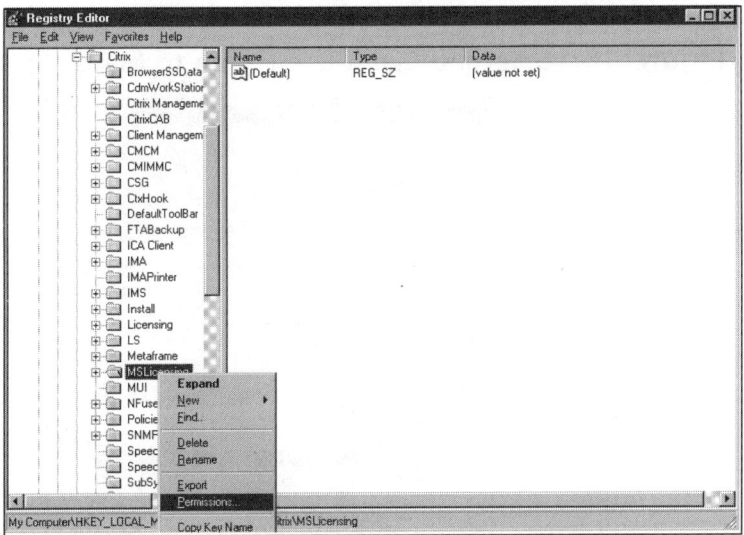

In some cases, the client software is operating properly, a client has good network connectivity, and is able to browse the list of applications and MetaFrame servers but is not able to initiate an ICA connection as Figure 15.15 shows.

Figure 15.15 Client Access Error as a Result of Configuration Issues

Some common client configuration errors include:

- Incorrect application name

- Incorrect encryption level set on the client

- Incorrectly configured Program Neighborhood Agent (PNAgent)

- Incorrect connection type

- No alternate server location configured

Addressing the client configuration issues as follows can rectify these issues:

1. Correct the spelling of incorrectly spelled application names so they match the application names on the server.

2. Set the encryption level on the client to match the level on the server for that application (Figure 15.16).

Figure 15.16 Setting Client Encryption to Match Server Encryption

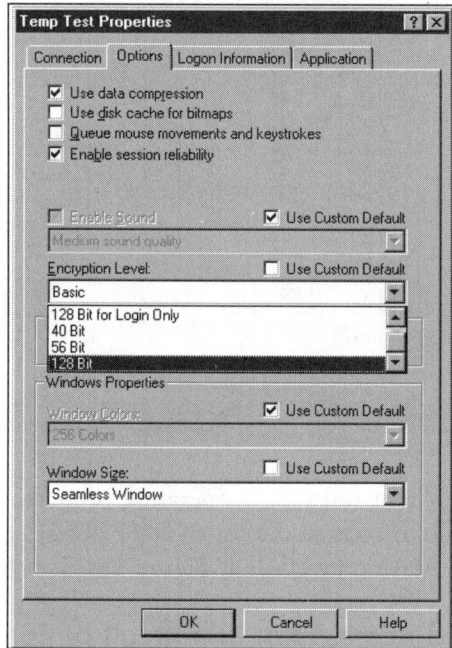

3. Remove the PNAgent from the client machine's Startup folder, or reconfigure the PNAgent to point to the correct URL for the Citrix Web Interface.

4. Edit the connection type in the ICA connection properties on the client to LAN connection or WAN connection depending on the type of connection (Figure 15.17).

Figure 15.17 Configuring Client Connection Type

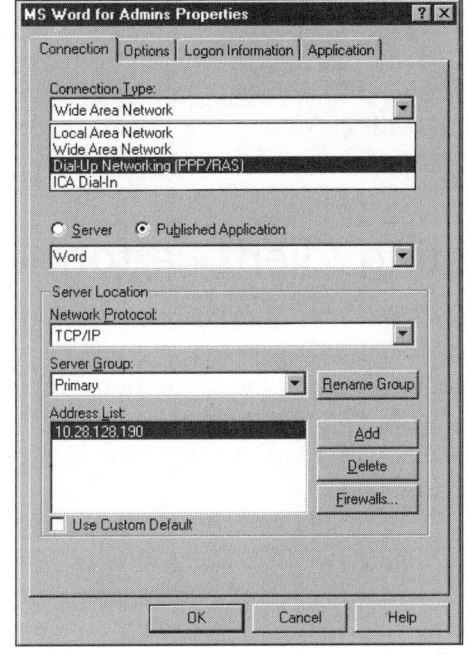

5. Make sure that the users and groups that need to access the applications are configured to access the application.

6. Edit the Appsrv.ini file on the client machine to include the UseAlternateAddress=1 and TcpBrowserAddress=x.x.x.x flags where x.x.x.x is an alternate IP address that the client can use to connect to the application should the primary connection fail.

Notes from the Underground…

Finding the Source of Client Connection Problems

MetaFrame Presentation Server allows logging of Transport drivers during ICA connections and connection attempts. If you are having problems with client disconnecting and need to find the source of the problem, one method of troubleshooting is to use the ICA runtime file *Wfcrun32.exe* to generate a log. This can be done by clicking the **Start** button, selecting **Run**, and entering:

Continued

> **Wfcrun32 /c:0x00000040 /e:0x00100000 /logfile:<log file path> <connection name>**
>
> Where <connection name> is the name of the ICA, *0x00000040* specifies that the logging is for the Transport driver and, *0x00100000* tells to log any Auto Client Reconnect related information. If an error is encountered, it is included in the log file together with an error code. The log file is readable in Notepad for easy troubleshooting.

Troubleshooting Client Performance Issues

One may think that because Citrix MetaFrame is a server-based computing infrastructure that any performance or client experience issues are strictly within the realm of the servers, the network connection, and the application. This statement holds true to a great extent. However, the client machine can play a significant part in the ICA experience. The ICA client does come with features that enable it to compensate for challenges in the infrastructure to a limited degree.

The ability of the client to influence the performance of an ICA connection does not just have to do with the actual ICA client software. The actual operating system and its features can affect the performance of a client connection or whether a client can connect at all. For example, if clients are operating on a network with drastic changes in bandwidth or network reliability problems, Session Reliability can be configured on the client to keep the application window available to the client while the ICA software is attempting to restore connectivity behind the scenes. To keep users, continue to click links or type text while the connection is being restored; mouse pointers become hourglass icons until the application connection is restored.

On the client, session reliability can be set at the Application set level or the custom ICA connection level. Enabling or disabling the **Enable session reliability** option at the client overrides the session reliability settings for the server farm. Session reliability is configured on the client via the following steps:

1. Right-click on the **Custom ICA connection** or on the **Application set icon** and select **Properties**.

2. Select the **Options** tab in the **Properties** window and check the box **Enable session reliability** (Figure 15.18).

Figure 15.18 Enabling Session Reliability Maintains Application Windows when Client Is Disconnected

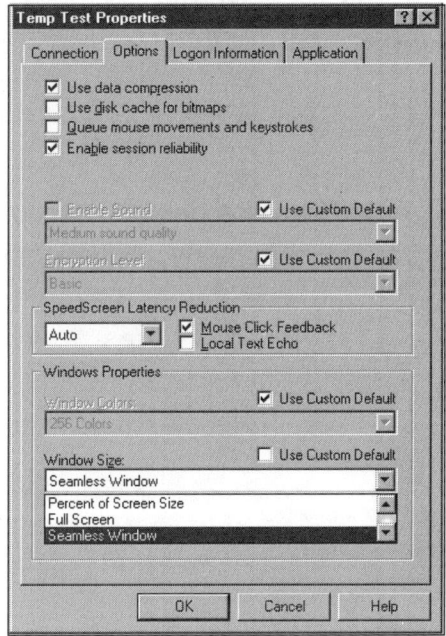

In conjunction with session reliability, another feature that may alleviate some support woes as far as client connection performance is concerned is the Auto Client Reconnect feature. Clients who are disconnected as a result of unreliable networks can use Auto Client Reconnect to detect unintended disconnections of ICA sessions and automatically reconnect users to the affected sessions. When this feature is enabled on a server running MetaFrame Presentation Server, users do not have to reconnect manually to continue working. The client attempts to reconnect to the session until there is a successful reconnection or the user cancels the reconnection attempts. Even though Auto Client Reconnect is enabled by default on client connections, reconnection does not occur if users exit applications without logging off. Clients can only reconnect to disconnected sessions.

In some scenarios, it may be better to not have the Auto Client Reconnect feature enabled. If clients have been restricted to one login session per user, having the client attempt to reconnect repeatedly actually prevents reconnection if the end user is also trying to reestablish connectivity simultaneously. The end user may receive a message stating that he is already logged in to the application, and the client software does not see the ICA connection as disconnected so it stops attempting reconnection.

One way to solve this problem is to educate your user population about the built-in features of the client. The other way is to disable the Auto Client Reconnect feature from the client altogether:

1. Locate the Appsrv.ini file **C:\Program Files\Citrix\ICA** folder on the client.

2. Open the **Appsrv.ini file** using Windows Notepad and add **TransportReconnectEnabled=Off** under the **[WFClient]** section as shown in Figure 15.19.

3. Save the file and exit Notepad.

Figure 15.19 Disabling Auto Client Reconnect in the Appsrv.ini File

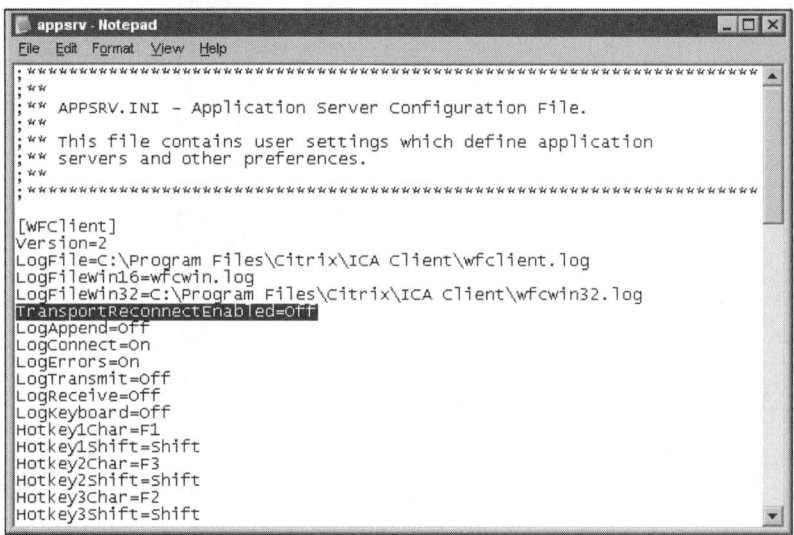

Configuring and Implementing…

Configuring Cookie Time Limit for Auto Client Reconnect

Depending on the type of connection the client machine has to the MetaFrame server, attempts to reconnect via the Auto Client reconnect feature may frequently fail because the time permitted for the cookie associated with the connection to persist is too short. The time interval value for the cookie can be extended from its default of five minutes via one of two ways. If the change is only for a specific client or group of clients, editing the value in the HKEY_LOCAL_MACHINE\ System\\CurrentControlSet\\Control\\Citrix\\

Continued

AutoClientReconnect\MaxDuration registry key to extend the time interval will suffice. If the change must be made for the entire farm, then the *acrcfg* utility must be used from the MetaFrame server or the server that hosts the data store with the following syntax:

acrcfg /farm /inherit:off
acrcfg /farm /duration:<*time interval in milliseconds*>

NOTE

Extending the time interval too long may compromise farm security, so be careful!

Getting Help from Citrix

Okay, so we've looked at some common and uncommon problems and ways to troubleshoot and even resolve them. What do we do when the solution isn't readily apparent or available? The answer to that is get help. Where else should we get help from but the same place that consultants, support engineers, and Citrix Enterprise architects the world over get support from? That's right, Citrix itself.

Collecting Information to Report to Citrix Technical Support

So, Citrix Technical Support has been or is going to be contacted. What kind of information will they need to help troubleshoot or resolve an issue? This section addresses collecting just the type of information that will be useful to a Citrix support engineer.

System Information

The place most support engineers start is with the current state of the machine in question. To acquire the current state of a computer running Windows 98 through Windows Server 2003, use the **winmsd** command. The **winmsd** command will give you the following statistics and more (see Figure 15.20):

- Operating system name and version
- Physical memory available in the system
- Pagefile location and size
- Pagefile available

- BIOS version
- System model and manufacturer

Figure 15.20 System Information Aids in Troubleshooting

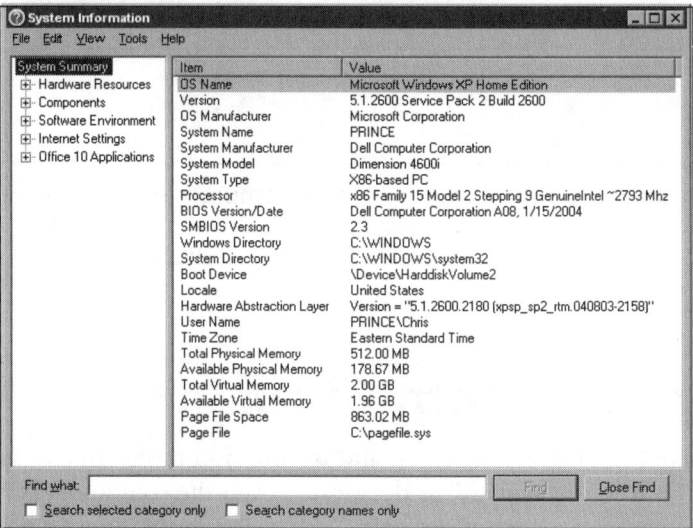

Installation Logs

If you are troubleshooting a MetaFrame Presentation Server installation, Citrix Technical Support will require an installation log file to troubleshoot the problem. Citrix recommends that if your MetaFrame Presentation Server installation does fail, attempt a second installation using the following command line to create a log file:

```
Msiexec /i <CD>\MF\mps.msi /l*v %SystemDrive%\msi.log
```

Where <CD> is the CD drive letter (for example, D:) containing the MetaFrame Presentation Server CD. If the MetaFrame Presentation Server CD was copied to a hard drive or network share, you can also replace <CD> with the full path to the installation image on the share. The preceding command line creates a log file named Msi.log in the root of the system drive.

ODBC Traces

If you are troubleshooting an IMA service problem or a data store problem, ODBC trace information might be requested by Citrix Technical Support or the DBMS vendor support team. The procedure to enable ODBC tracing depends on the database server software you are using. The following procedures detail how to activate ODBC tracing for Microsoft SQL Server.

1. Launch the ODBC Data Source Administrator.

2. Click the **Tracing** tab.

3. Type a path for the log file in the **Log File Path** box.

4. Click **Start Tracing Now** to begin tracing. Click **Stop Tracing Now** to end tracing.

ICA Client Logs

As we saw in the section on troubleshooting client issues, the ICA client can be made to generate a Transport Driver log of the ICA connection or connection attempt by using the following command:

```
Wfcrun32 /c:0x00000040 /e:0x00100000 /logfile:<log file path> <connection name>
```

The log file generated by the ICA runtime client provides output to a text file similar to the following message that could aid in the resolution of the problem:

```
03-28-2005  13:13:00:906 MS Word: Protocol Driver Error: (10060)
```

Summary

In this chapter, we looked at troubleshooting server-based and client-based issues in a more holistic fashion, as problems in a Citrix MetaFrame environment do not always readily reveal their sources. We began by discussing problems and what an administrator or even a client could expect to see while the issue is occurring. We broke down our problems to server issues and client issues.

We examined problems with the IMA service, the data store, printing and printer driver replication, user access, and performance issues. We also discussed the indications of the problem source, ways to resolve the issues, and methods of troubleshooting that will reveal the source of the problems.

Finally, we talked about what type of information should be given to Citrix Technical Support in the event we need to contact them for assistance.

Solutions Fast Track

Troubleshooting Server-Side Issues

☑ The operation of the IMA Service can be detected by looking for network activity on ports 2512 and 2513.

☑ The most common server-side issues are concerned with Terminal Server licensing and MetaFrame data store access.

☑ Each MetaFrame server in a farm operates using a subset of the data store called the local host cache.

☑ Printer replication of nonstandard printers can be accomplished if the language monitors of the printer drivers are added to the MetaFrame server registry.

Troubleshooting Client-Side Issues

☑ Client access issues may be caused by client permission issues on the local client machine.

☑ Client access problems may also stem from application set or custom ICA connection configuration errors.

☑ The ICA client has built-in features that are designed to help counteract challenges in a client network infrastructure or connection type.

Getting Help from Citrix

☑ Citrix Technical Support will most probably require the current system state information to begin troubleshooting.

☑ An administrator can generate logs from a client or a server that is experiencing a problem via command-line utilities.

☑ Other vendors such as your DBMS vendor may need to be involved in troubleshooting efforts with Citrix.

Frequently Asked Questions

The following Frequently Asked Questions, answered by the authors of this book, are designed to both measure your understanding of the concepts presented in this chapter and to assist you with real-life implementation of these concepts. To have your questions about this chapter answered by the author, browse to **www.syngress.com/solutions** and click on the **"Ask the Author"** form. You will also gain access to thousands of other FAQs at ITFAQnet.com.

Q: My IMA Service does not start when the other services on my system start, but starts a few minutes later. Why?

A: The IMA Service has a six-minute window from system start in which to start connecting to the data store.

Q: Why can I connect to my Windows 2000 MetaFrame server but not my Windows 2003 MetaFrame server with the same account?

A: The account may not be a member of the Windows 2003 Remote Desktop User group. Add the account to the group to enable access.

Q: My users complain that they get kicked out of their applications, but when they immediately try to reconnect they are told that they are already logged in for a few minutes after getting kicked out. Why is this?

A: There may be two issues here. The first is that the network connections form your client to the server farm may be faulty, which is why they are losing their connections. Troubleshoot and rectify any network connectivity issues first. The second issue may be that the client ICA session is registering as disconnected on the servers, and so the Auto Client Reconnect feature may be reconnecting the client. Have the user exit the application correctly, wait for the ICA Connection Center icon in the system tray to disappear, and then try to connect again.

Q: Why can't my new users start an ICA session at all?

A: They may not have a high enough level of access on their local machine to update the HKEY_LOCAL_MACHINE\SOFTWARE\Microsoft\MSLicensing registry key on their workstations. Add the users to the Power Users or Administrators group on their local machines.

Q: One of my MetaFrame servers is unavailable to users even though it is visible in the server farm. How can I fix this?

A: The server may have a corrupt local host cache file. To resolve the issue, stop the IMA Service on the server. Rename the current local host cache file. Use the command dsmaint recreatelhc at a command prompt to create a new imalhc.mdb file. Restart the IMA Service.

Chapter 16

Network Management and Resource Monitoring

Solutions in this chapter:

- **Baselining**
- **Resource Manager**
- **Network Manager**
- **Management Pack for Microsoft Operations Manager 2000**

☑ **Summary**

☑ **Solutions Fast Track**

☑ **Frequently Asked Questions**

Introduction

Network management and resource monitoring is a vast topic that is open to many interpretations. Management and monitoring can include everything from server performance to network performance to end-to-end session analysis. This rather large topic of discussion should also include *baselining*. Baselining is the process of determining the "normal" operational ranges for the various components of your access infrastructure during a typical usage period. Due to the magnitude of this subject, we have elected to focus on the features that Citrix Presentation Server 3.0 brings to the table with regard to management and monitoring. While we will be discussing these "Citrix-specific" solutions, this is by no means meant to be the definitive list of management and monitoring toolsets available for Windows Server 2003 Terminal Services and Presentation Server 3.0.

In this chapter, we start by further discussing baselining and the impact it has on the monitoring and management of our access infrastructure. We then look at a series of management features in Presentation Server 3.0 Enterprise Edition. These features (Resource Manager, Network Manager, and the Management Pack for Microsoft Operations Manager 2000) are only available in Presentation Server Enterprise Edition. However, for those of you using Advanced or Standard, this section is still important for the baselining discussion. This chapter shows you some of the amazing benefits of Presentation Server 3.0 Enterprise Edition and may serve as a catalyst in moving your access infrastructure up to the top-of-the-line edition.

Baselining

As previously stated, baselining is the process of determining the "normal" operational ranges for the various components of your access infrastructure during a typical usage period. Baselining as a process also needs to include some reporting or storage mechanism for the data collected from the various components over time. Baselining is essential to all aspects of network management and resource monitoring and thus is the roundabout focus of this chapter. Baselining can be used to assist in troubleshooting, act as the foundation for trend analysis, and can aid in the creation and use of service-level agreements—baselining is important.

From a troubleshooting standpoint, a properly baselined access infrastructure can provide invaluable data. The ability to reactively pull information from your resource management system concerning a component of your access infrastructure for the purpose of contrasting its current performance can be of tremendous benefit. Now, imagine leveraging that data in your management systems to proactively report and potentially fix an issue when it arises. Suppose one of your Presentation Server 3.0 servers is experiencing unusually high memory use, causing session performance to decrease on that server. Wouldn't it be nice if you were the first person who knew about this situation instead of the last? To continue that thread for a moment, consider the following scenario. After properly baselining our access infrastructure, we have determined that our Presentation server's processor use typically hovers around 65 percent. We also discovered during our baselining exercises that a legacy application on the system occasionally fails, causing processor use to increase to 100 percent. We have determined that the runaway process, oldbrokenapp.exe, can simply be terminated when this occurs and the user can restart the application. Because of our baselining, we know the normal tolerances and thus can determine when something is out-of-band. In this case, we could have our resource management system execute a script when processor use is above the normal range and kill any instance of the oldbrokenapp.exe process it finds. Network monitoring and resource management can aid you in those troubleshooting situations.

If we look at trend analysis, baselining arguably becomes even more important. Trend analysis is basically a process of "predicting the future" based on occurrences in the past. If we leverage our management and monitoring system to maintain the historical performance of our access infrastructure, we can make excellent use of that data in this divination process. An administrator could export the data captured in the management systems database into software suited for trend analysis, such as Microsoft Excel. This allows for a great deal of insight into the use patterns of your access infrastructure, including the peaks, lows, and the basis for predicting future capacity needs based on current use and predicted growth. Without a properly baselined environment, guesses at future needs are just that, guesses.

Some people cringe when they hear the phrase, "service level agreements" (SLAs). For the rest of you, we need to define what an SLA is so you can join in the cringing fun! An SLA is basically a contract that states the minimum satisfactory levels of performance for some entity or system. On the surface, SLAs don't appear to be all that heinous, but once you dig a little, you can quickly see why everyone cringes. In an access infrastructure or Presentation Server environment, many pieces and processes are frequently outside the control of the systems administrator. The typical SLA will most likely contain response time to a condition. For example, if we were managing the Presentation server farm for a call center, the call center management team would most likely want to know the response time from when a call comes in to the time it takes for the call center application to retrieve the end-customer's information (or response time) to be covered in an SLA. Again, doesn't seem so unreasonable so far—but then we look under the covers.

As the administrator of the Presentation server farm, you are dependant on the network infrastructure for all your session data. You are also dependant on the authentication servers, file servers, and most importantly, the database servers that house the customer records. It is possible that all of these components are out of your control, thus making it very difficult to support an SLA. Baselining can provide the historical information to document how well the terms of an SLA are being met. Baselining and the continuous monitoring and reporting of our management system can provide the hard facts when an SLA turns into a legal situation, which can occasionally happen. Without a baseline and the ability to retrieve performance information about the various access infrastructure components at any point, agreeing to and standing by a SLA can be very difficult to do.

We now see how important it is to have a baselined environment, so how do we perform a baseline? An excellent question indeed. And like most good technical questions, there is a variety of answers, so we can now turn our attention to several different ways of creating a baseline or point of reference.

The key thing to remember is that a baseline is a "living" thing, and must be created and recreated on a regular basis. Typically, baselines should be created before and after any major upgrade to your systems, including hardware, software, or hotfixes. Also consider creating before and after baselines when other major components of your network will change (client devices, client versions, backend databases, authentication servers, etc.). Once you figure out how often to create a baseline, we can then turn our attention to the tools needed for the task. There are as many tools as there are ways to create a baseline, ranging from simple to complex, from free to "not free." For the purposes of this chapter, we focus on Presentation Server's tools, although the concepts and to a lesser extent the tools we discuss could serve as a starting point for baselining other components of your network.

Of the tools available to us "out of the box" on our Windows Server 2003 Terminal Servers, Task Manager, Network Monitor, and Performance Monitor are the first we will discuss. Task Manager can be used for basic "real-time" information about important server resources such as processor and memory use. While Task Manager provides no mechanism to create a record for trend analysis or to support an SLA, it can be useful for quick information and aid in troubleshooting. Figure 16.1 shows us just some of the information that Task Manager can provide. In addition to the Performance tab, the Processes, Networking, and Application tabs can be very useful for general server information gathering.

Figure 16.1 Task Manager Used to Gather Performance Information

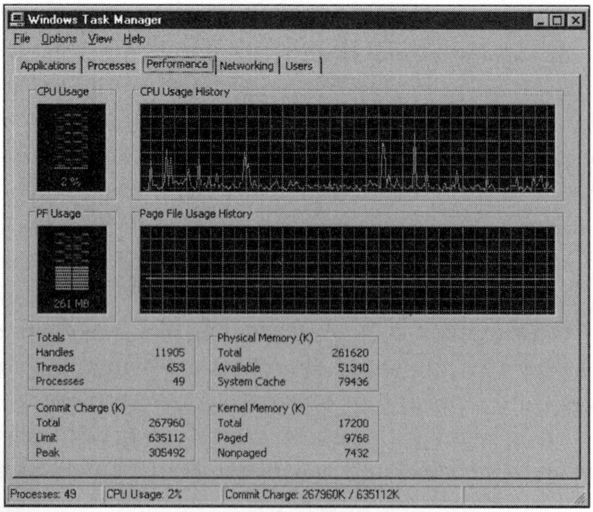

Network Monitor consist of two components, a Network Monitor application and a Network Monitor driver that is added to the various network interface cards (NICs) that aid in capturing the traffic. This additional Windows component can installed through the **Add or Remove Programs | Add/Remove Windows Components** tool under the Details of the Management and Monitoring Tools section. Network Monitor is primary designed to assist in troubleshooting but can also aid in traffic pattern analysis (see Figure 16.2). The primary limitation of Network Monitor is the lack of a "promiscuous" driver for the network card(s). In other words, the card won't listen for all traffic on the network; instead, only traffic destined for the computer running Network Monitor or traffic originating from the computer is monitored. For a more complete solution to network monitoring and the ability to "promiscuously" observe and record network traffic, consider the Sniffer line of products from Network General, or Ethereal for a free network monitor.

NOTE

Remember to enable port mirroring if you are in a switched network. Switched networks by design only send traffic to ports that the traffic is destined to go. If you are performing traffic analysis and capturing but not "getting anything," make sure you have enables the switch(es) to "copy" all traffic to the port into which your monitor is plugged.

Figure 16.2 Network Monitor in Action Capturing Network Traffic

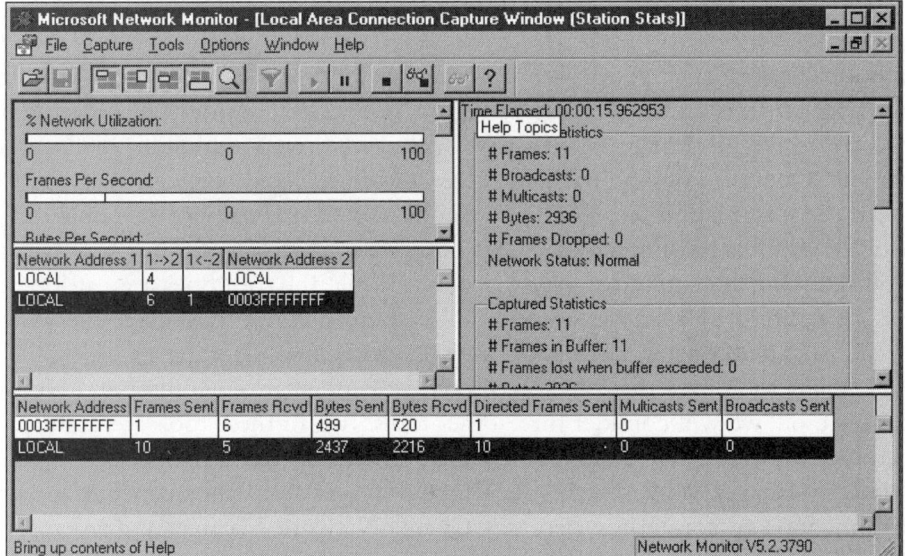

Performance Monitor can be a more useful tool for resource monitoring and analysis. Performance Monitor has the capability to define what types of information you want to gather data about. Performance Monitor has two main sections, the System Monitor and the Performance Logs and Alerts. The System Monitor is an excellent way to monitor all the various metrics that ship with Windows Server 2003, and the additional ones that are installed when Presentation Server 3.0 is added. Figure 16.3 demonstrates the System Monitor in action, collecting real-time information on processor, disk queue length, and pagefile use.

Figure 16.3 Performance Monitor's System Monitor in Action

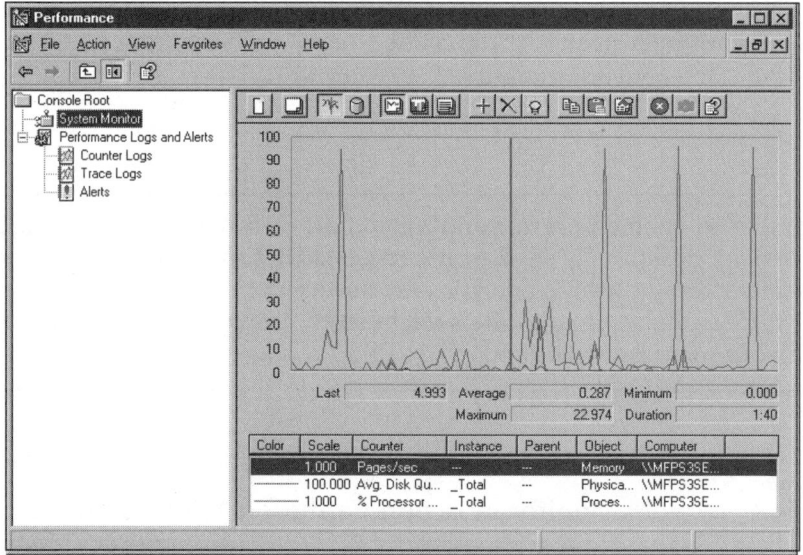

Additionally, Performance Monitor has the capability to "record" what it captures to Counter Logs (as seen on the left side of Figure 16.3). The Counter Logs give us the ability to create the baseline reports that we will need as we continue to manage our environment. Counter Logs are basically "jobs" of pre-selected counters that will capture and record the information to a file. They can be started manually or scheduled to occur automatically. The biggest limitation of this otherwise very powerful free tool is the lack of centralized reporting and cross-server analysis. While the tool does a great job on the server it is executing, in a larger farm it could become a chore to manage the various "logs" and make usable sense from what they record.

While many tools exist that can pick up where Performance Monitor and Network Monitor leave off, we will consider three other tools. Two of these tools are produced by Citrix and are features of Presentation Server 3.0 Enterprise Edition—Resource Manager and Network Manager. While Citrix's Resource Manager and Performance Manager share a similar function and common system ties, Citrix's Network Manager and Microsoft's

Network Monitor are quite different products. Resource Manager (RM) has the capability to record and monitor metrics, but RM's capabilities go far beyond basic monitoring as we will see in the next section. Network Manager is a plug-in to allow Presentation servers to integrate better with an existing Simple Network Management Protocol (SNMP) based solution such as OpenView or NetView. Therefore, Network Manager is primarily concerned with SNMP communities and traps versus Network Monitor's, well, network monitoring. The third tool, Microsoft Operations Manager (MOM), is produced by Microsoft. While we aren't immediately concerned with MOM's feature and capabilities, we are concerned with the extensible nature of the product. This extensibility is what allows other companies, such as Citrix, to create management packs to extend the capabilities of MOM. The Presentation Server 3.0 Management Pack for Microsoft Operations Manager 2000 does this very thing.

We discuss each of these three solutions in the remainder of this chapter. We begin with Resource Manager, as it can in many ways leverage the other components if they are installed, specifically Network Manager.

Resource Manager

Resource Manager is a complete management and monitoring solution for Presentation Server 3.0 that is included with the Enterprise Edition. Resource Manager has the capability to provide end-to-end reporting and analysis for the Windows platform on which Presentation Server 3.0 is installed and for Presentation Server itself. Resource Manager can provide the following features and benefits to a Presentation server deployment for farms as small as a single server to farms encompassing thousands of Presentation servers.

- Real-time monitoring
- Trend analysis
- Resource planning and provisioning
- Real-time troubleshooting and root-cause analysis
- Real-time and historical reporting
- Cost center billing and report generation

Definitions

Before we dig too far under the covers of Resource Manager, we will need to understand some key terms and concepts prior to being able to fully leverage this fantastic service. The first is a *metric*.

Metrics

For those who have used Microsoft's Performance Monitor, you will have a good understanding of what a metric is and its purpose in management and monitoring of servers. A *metric* is an instance of an individual *counter* that belongs to an *object* that may be monitored. That was a mouthful... so let's explain a little further. An *object* is some resource of the system that can be monitored, such as processor, memory, and the Citrix IMA service to name a few. If we choose the Processor object, we then have several *counters* that apply to that object. For the Processor object we have Interrupts per Second, % Processor Time, and % Privileged time—again, to name a few. If we select the % Processor Time counter for the Processor object, we then can select the *instance* for this particular system. The *instance* could be viewed as the "end thing" being monitored; for example, in a dual-processor server, you will have three *instances*—processor one, processor two, and total (the average for both processors). Let's assume that we want to monitor the instance *Total*. By putting all that together—the *Total instance* for the *% Processor Time Counter* of the *Processor object*—we have defined a metric! Our job will be to determine what metrics we want to monitor, and configure our servers accordingly. Don't worry, Citrix provides a base set of these that are consider important for all servers, and we will expand that list to include a few more as we work through this section.

Alerts

An *alert* is an action we will configure the server(s) to perform when a metric is outside a range that we configure for normal operations. For instance, perhaps from the previous example, we can configure an alert to send an e-mail when the % Processor Time is above 80 percent for our servers.

Resource Manager Local Database

Out of the box, all Presentation Server 3.0 Enterprise Edition servers maintain a *local database* that the server uses to track the metrics configured on that server, the "tolerance" ranges for those metrics, and any *alert* configurations that may exist. This local database, again, is enabled by default and additional configuration is necessary to leverage the data the database contains. The Independent Management Architecture (IMA) (and the Resource Manager subsystem thereof) is responsible for the maintenance of this database. The database is a standard Microsoft Access database that is maintained in C:\Program Files\Citrix\Citrix Resource Manager\LocalDB (where C:\ is the drive on which Citrix is installed on the server). When the IMA service is running, the RMLO-CALDATABASE.MDB will have an LDB lock file in place. Additionally, a local system data source name (DSN) called RMLocalDatabase will be configured on each Enterprise Edition server. There is no need to compact or maintain this database, as IMA does this automatically once a day or whenever the IMA service is restarted. Figure 16.4 demonstrates the location of this database.

Figure 16.4 Resource Manager Local Database Location

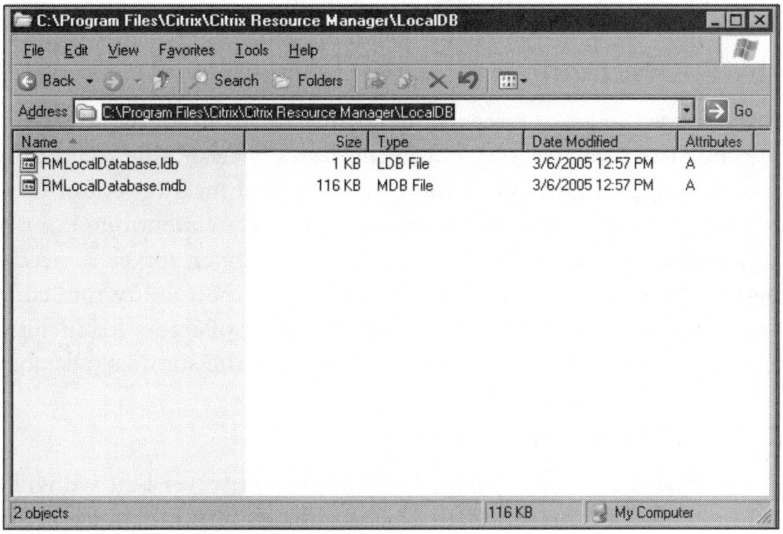

The data contained in this database is used for Current Reports, which we discuss later in this section. Additionally, the data is maintained for 96 hours in this database and then purged in a First-In-First-Out (FIFO) fashion. The individual servers "collect" their own metric information every 15 seconds and commit it to the local database. The server also compares the value of these collected metrics against the preset thresholds that are maintained in the local host cache. If the metric is in an alert state it changes the status indicator (light) to correspond with the state of the metric and can perform the following tasks depending on the configuration of the alert:

- Notification
- Script execution
- E-mail
- SNMP trap
- Short Message Service (SMS) page

Resource Manager Summary Database

The *summary database* is not enabled by default during the install of the Presentation Server software. The summary database's role is to maintain the historical information "long term" that would otherwise be purged after the 96-hour window from the RM local database. The summary database allows for the recording of all the monitored metrics in addition to additional information about sessions, users, and processes that have executed on the servers in the farm. We discuss the configuration of the Resource Manager summary database in detail later in this chapter.

Farm Metric Server

The *farm metric server* is the first server in the farm that has Resource Manager installed on it. Typically, the farm metric server is also the data collector. The role of the farm metric server is to interpret farm-wide metrics, such as application count or session count, and process them as part of its own summary data. As mentioned in the preceding section, this information in addition to the metrics for a given server is saved in the summary database. The farm metric server assumes the responsibility for "collecting" this information from the farm member servers and the data collectors for inclusion in the daily "summarization" prior to the data being written to the summary database.

Database Connection Server

The *database connection server* is one particular Presentation server that we will designate during the configuration of the summary database that is responsible for actually communicating with and writing data to the actual backend server that will house the summary database. This server will be the only server in the farm (although more than one can be configured, only one is used) that "knows" how to locate and communicate with the database maintained on a SQL or Oracle server. As we will see later during the configuration of the summary database, a local system DSN will be created manually on the database connection server to "point" to the backend data source.

Farm Metric Server

The *farm metric server* is the first server in the farm that has Resource Manager installed on it. Typically, the farm metric server is also the data collector. The role of the farm metric server is to interpret farm-wide metrics, such as application count or session count, and process them as part of its own summary data. As mentioned previously, this information is in addition to the metrics for a given server that are saved in the summary database. The farm metric server assumes the responsibility for "collecting" this information from the farm member servers and the data collectors for inclusion in the daily "summarization" prior to the data being written to the summary database.

Configuring Metrics and Alerts for Individual Servers

The first step in leveraging Resource Manager with or without the summary database being configured is to establish the metrics that you want to track. This process is easier than establishing the thresholds for those metrics; in short, this initial step is more art than science. However, you can leverage Resource Manager and/or Performance

Monitor in the creation of this baseline to allow you to more accurately establish the metrics and their thresholds that you will track.

NOTE

There are two general types of metrics, Application and Server. "Application metrics" is really a misnomer. Only concurrent instances of an application can be tracked using Application Metrics. Additionally, Application Metrics only work with 32-bit applications. DOS and 16-bit applications execute with NT Virtual DOS Machines (NTVDMs) and Windows on Windows (WoW) processes; thus, the true name of the executable is obscured under the "virtual" environment. For these reasons, we will focus our efforts in this module to Server metrics and simply refer to these as metrics to avoid confusion. Additionally, remember that Server metrics are just that, server metrics, and are not farm-wide settings.

To view or edit the Resource Manager metrics, open the **Presentation Server Console**, expand the **Servers node**, select a server (typically a member server of the farm considered "typical" of the servers in the farm), and select the **Resource Manager** tab on the right, as shown in Figure 16.5.

Figure 16.5 Default Resource Manager Metrics

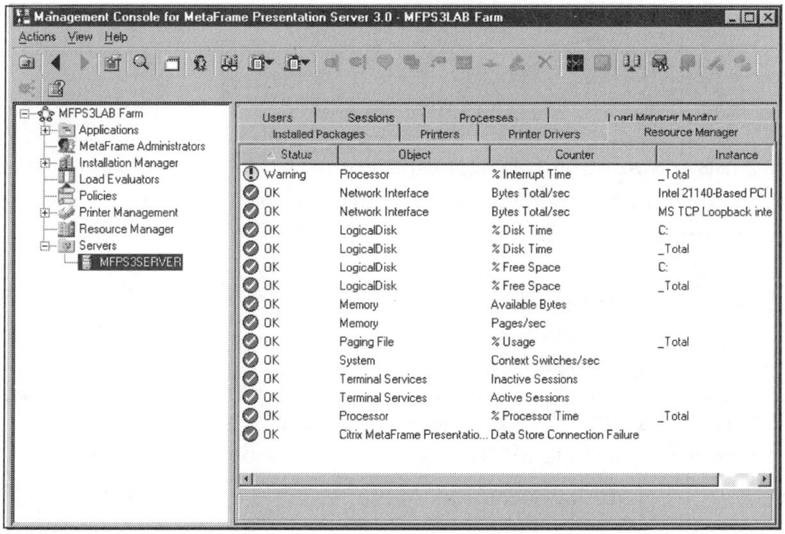

By default, Citrix Resource Manager tracks the metrics as viewed in Figure 16.5. To add new metrics, simply right-click anywhere in the right pane of the **Presentation**

Server Console where the Resource Manager metrics are listed and choose **Add/Remove Metrics** from the list of options. The Add/Remove Metrics window should come up and allow you to select from the object list. As previously described, a metric is an instance of a counter of an object. Now, choose the object from the list, select the desired counter(s), and then select the metrics. Be careful to only select the metrics that you truly want to track for system performance. Having your servers track too many metrics will decrease overall system performance and can lead to voluminous amounts of data being retained in the summary database. Figure 16.6 depicts the Add/Remove Metrics window.

Figure 16.6 Adding or Removing a Metric

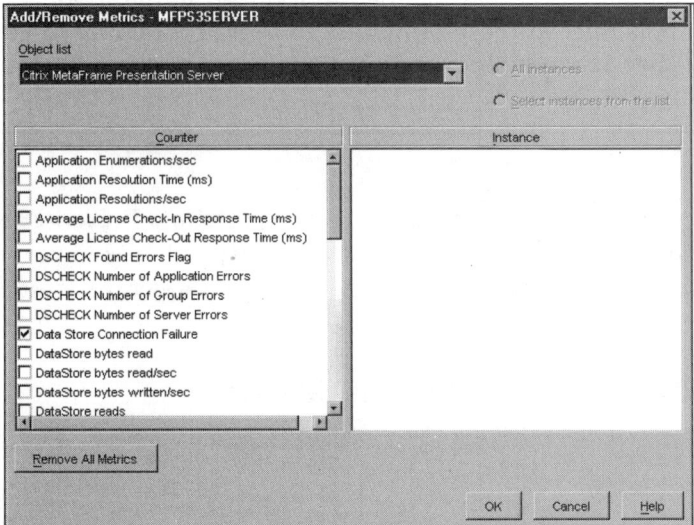

Table 16.1 lists the minimum objects and counters to track on your servers. Again, take care not to "over-track" metrics; keeping the number of tracked metrics under 50 is considered a best practice for most implementations.

Table 16.1 Recommended Metrics to Track

Object	Counter	Instance or Notes
Citrix MetaFrame Presentation Server	Data Store Connection Failure Zone Elections	default default
ICA Session	Latency – Session Average	Use this for troubleshooting mostly and remove when not in use, as an instance per session will be monitored.

Continued

Table 16.1 continued Recommended Metrics to Track

Object	Counter	Instance or Notes
Logical Disk	% Disk Time	Total and each separate volume (C:, D:, etc.)
Memory	% Committed Bytes in Use	default
	Pages per sec	default
Network Interface	Current Bandwidth	All Cards
Processor	% Privileged Time	All Instances
	% User Time	All Instances
System	Processor Queue Length	default

The metrics in Table 16.1 are in addition to the default metrics that Citrix configures during the installation of Presentation Server 3.0 Enterprise Edition. Once you add new metrics, the server will prompt you to configure those metrics. Metric configuration is, at least initially, a tweaking process. You can elect to not configure the metrics for now, as we will work through this process next.

To configure a metric or set of metrics, simply right-click on any metric in the list (ideally, the one you want to configure) and choose **Properties**. This will open the metric configuration window as seen in Figure 16.7.

Figure 16.7 Configuring Metric Thresholds

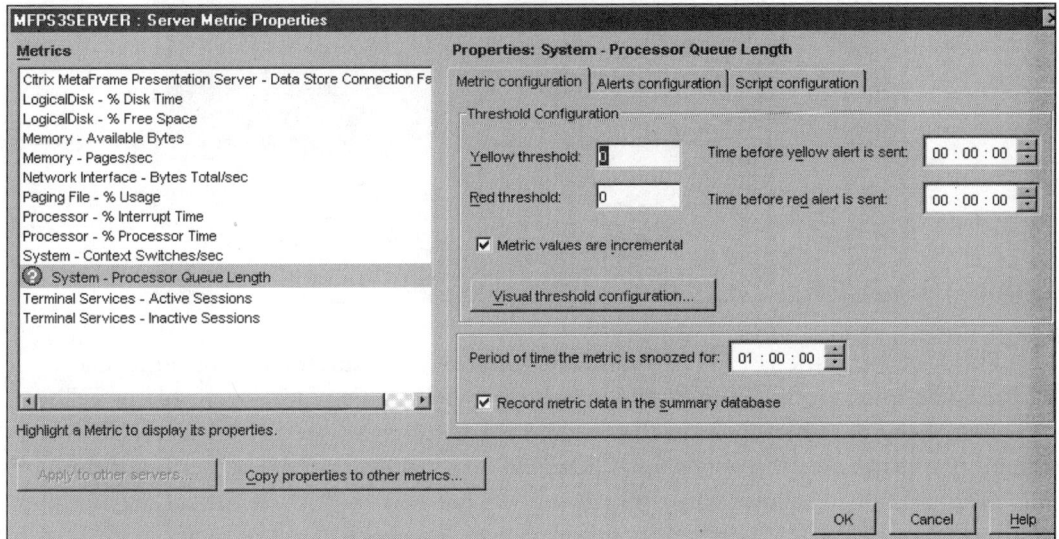

Each metric has both yellow and red thresholds as configured on the right. Yellow represents the warning state, meaning something is slightly out of ordinary but not considered catastrophic yet. Red is reserved for those metrics that indicate a severe state that will need immediate attention. As we have stated several times, choosing the correct values to enter into the Threshold Configuration is definitely a challenge that we all face. The reality is that no two Presentation Server environments are identical; every environment has its own specific server hardware, operating systems, applications, and so on. Add to that the nuisance of differences in patch levels, software configuration, and usage patterns within various applications and you can quickly see why this will present a "tweaking" exercise for your environment. As a general rule of thumb, however, you can use the Visual Threshold Configuration window to get good idea of what your current environment looks like so you can make a more educated guess as to the values to enter. Figure 16.8 illustrates the handy nature of the Visual Threshold Configuration feature. We would select a "typical" server on a "typical" day to aid in correctly configuring these metrics.

Figure 16.8 Visual Threshold Configuration

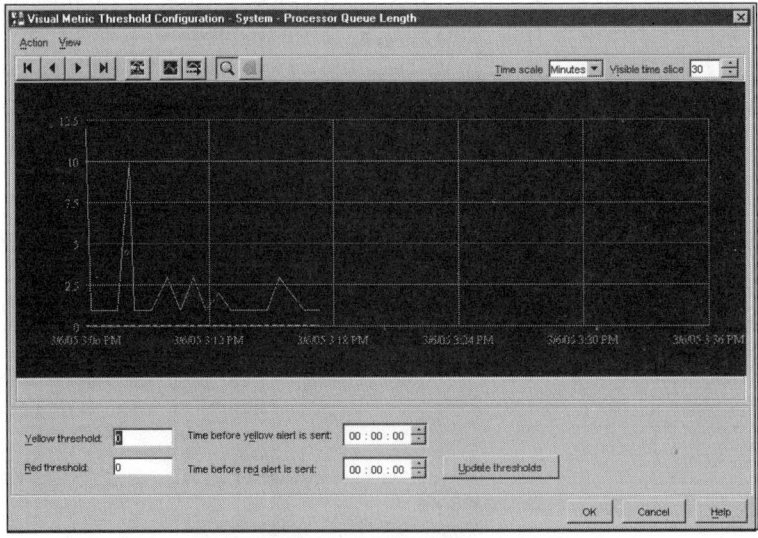

This leads us to the last few settings for configuring the thresholds. For both yellow and red, you must specify a time value by which to determine if a metric is red or yellow. When entering the time, consider that the server "reads" metrics every 15 seconds. Most administrators choose 30 seconds for yellow and 60 seconds for red. The period of time the metric is snoozed allows you a very handy feature. Any metric may be snoozed or put to sleep at any point. If a metric is in an alarm state and you have alerts configured, snoozing or sleeping it is recommended unless you want to be continually notified of the issue. Moreover, snoozing and sleeping metrics can be useful during maintenance windows where the work being performed will affect the metrics. Consider that erring on the higher side for threshold values is probably better than the low side. Next, we will be setting up alerts, so unless you want your pager and e-mail to "go wild" because of an incorrectly configured metric, start a little higher than you may think.

Configuring alerts is a two-step process. Step one is to configure the individual metrics you want to be alerted on and the method to be alerted with. The second step is to enable alerting and configure the alerting methods. Alerts can be sent to e-mails, SNMP traps, or Short Message Service (SMS) pages. The Alerts tab of a given metric's properties allows for the configuration of these options. Basically, enable the way you want to be alerted when that particular metric enters an alert state, such as the transition to red. As a best practice, it is considered good etiquette to notify that the alert state is over by sending confirmation of the transition back to a green state. Figure 16.9 illustrates the available options.

Figure 16.9 Individual Metric Alert Options

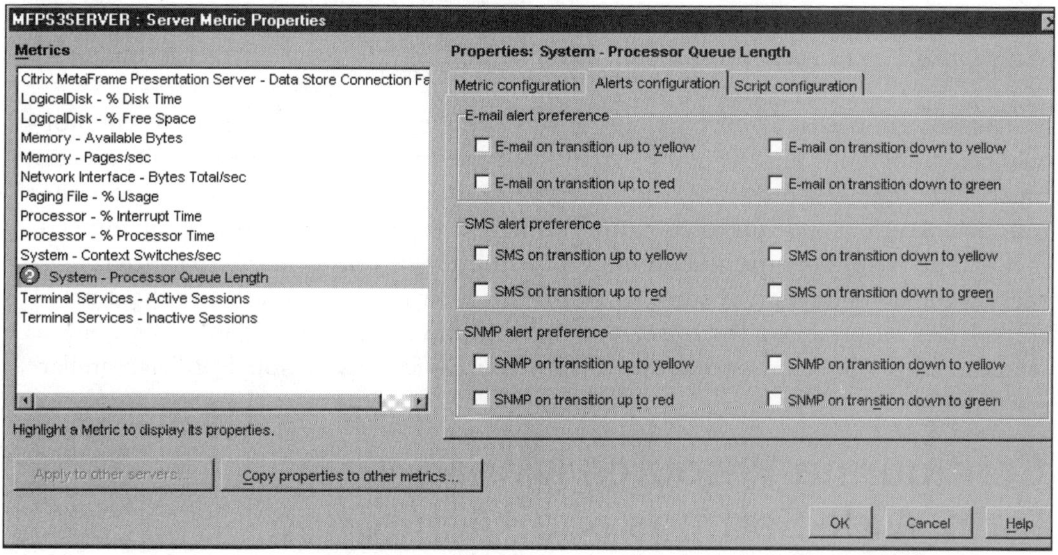

The last Configuration tab allows for a script to be executed at the point when a particular metric transitions to an alarm state (yellow or red). This can be particularly useful in killing "runaway" processes that are known issues on the server farm. For instance, let us assume you have determined that a particular legacy application causes the System—Processor Queue Length metric to enter an alarm state when it doesn't close correctly. You could create a script that is executed when this metric exhibits an alarm state that kills the bad process. In this example, we created a script called Fix_Bad_App.CMD and configured the server's metric as in Figure 16.10 to execute this script.

Figure 16.10 Script Configuration for Metric Alert States

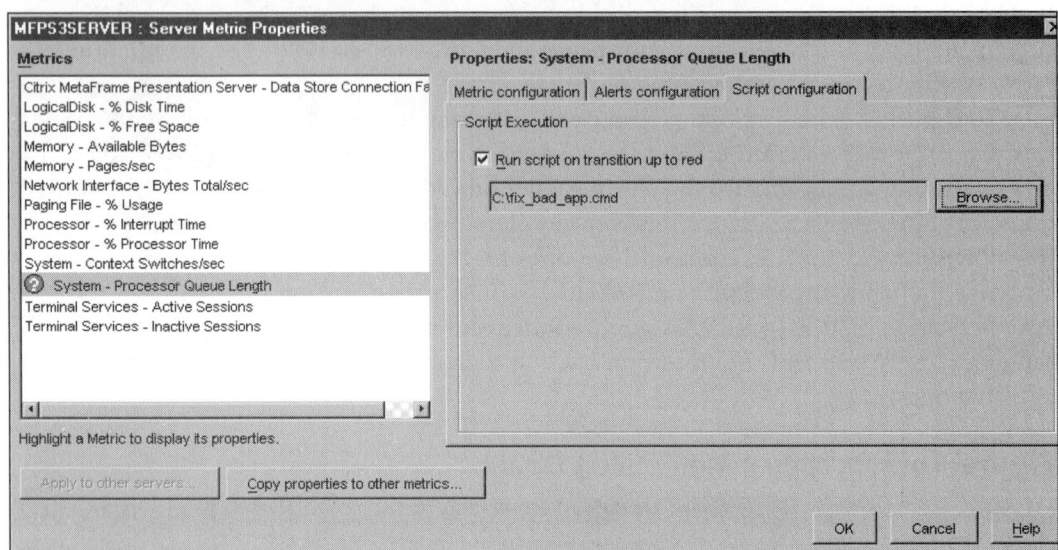

As you can probably tell, configuring and tweaking your servers' metrics will probably take some time. Fortunately, Citrix has provided two features to make this process much faster. The first option as seen in Figure 16.10 is the **Copy properties to other metrics**, which allows you to copy the configuration of a given metric to any other metric. The second option, and even more useful, allows you to **Apply to other servers** the configuration of some or all of your metric configuration. For those managing larger farms, the ability to replicate metrics and their configuration from one server to all is a huge time saver, especially if you are fortunate enough to have similar server builds.

Configuring Resource Manager Farm-Wide Settings and Monitoring

Monitoring Resource Manager can be a rather simple task. Once the metrics have been successfully configured, an administrator only needs to simply wait and observe the "status" of the given metrics. The metric status can be viewed under the Resource Manager tab for each individual server, but a better way to monitor would be to view the Watcher tab under the Resource Manager Node as you can see in Figure 16.11.

Figure 16.11 Resource Manager Node Watcher

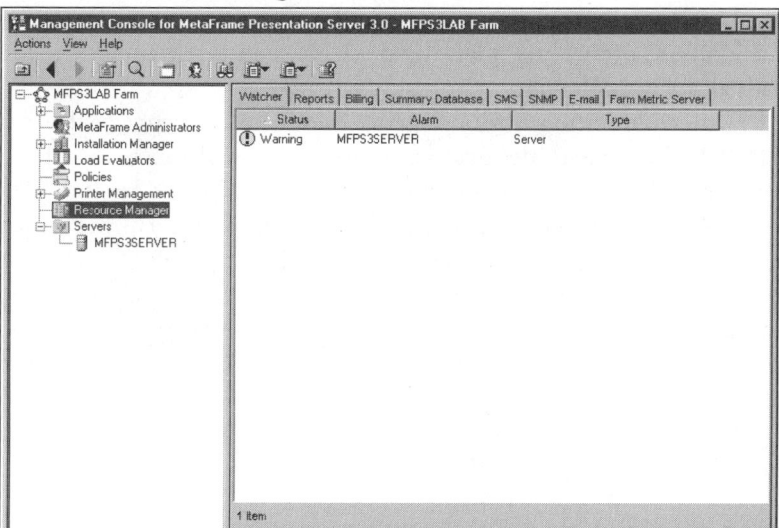

Additionally, Citrix provides the ability to view the "watcher" information in a separate window, to allow you to perform other tasks in the Presentation Server Console. Simply choosing the **Action** menu and selecting **Resource Manager Watcher** will open the Watcher in a separate window.

From either the Watcher tab of the Resource Manager node or the Watcher window, the minute a status change to yellow or red is in effect, you will see it appear. You will be notified of the status, the server on which it is occurring, and the metric type in question (server or application). To gather more information, simply double-click the offending notification and it will drill immediately to the Resource Manager tab of the server in question to allow for further diagnosis. At this point, simply double-click the metric in question and a real-time graph will appear as in Figure 16.12.

Figure 16.12 Real-Time Metric Monitor

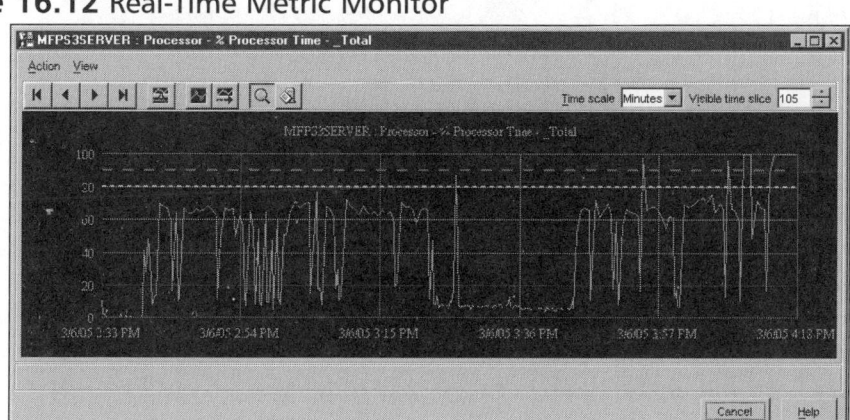

Not to get too far ahead of ourselves, but for a "quick" report on what is really going on, simply select the **Action** menu, select **Generate reports from graph via mouse**, use the mouse pointer to "pick the peak," and an instantaneous report will be generated with all relevant details.

The next farm-wide setting is found in the Resource Manager node, Farm Metric Server tab. This tab allows us to designate the server that will function as the farm metric server. It also allows us to dictate which server will be the backup server. The designation of *primary* and *backup* is a special relationship with farm metric servers. If the primary farm metric server becomes unavailable, the backup will take over the responsibility. However, if the primary returns to a responsive state, the backup will continue to function and become the primary and the primary will be relegated to the backup role. Typically, once you have set this, you are done with viewing the contents of this tab. As a final note, the data collector typically is the farm metric server (as both roles fall to the first server in the farm that is capable of filling the role). Figure 16.13 demonstrates this configuration.

Figure 16.13 Farm Metric Server Configuration

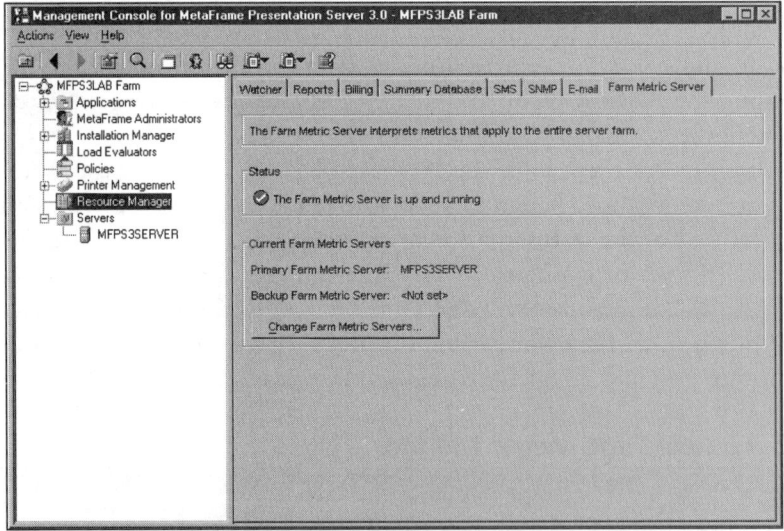

The next three tabs we will discuss are the SMS, SNMP, and Email tabs on the Resource Manager node in the Presentation Server Console. Basically, these are the settings for the various "methods" of alerting that a metric will use if it is configured to report an alert state. If you have configured your metrics to send SNMP traps, you will need to configure the farm-wide setting of the SNMP community to send those traps to. SMS paging is the ability to use a "paging gateway" to send alerts to pagers. Must people have e-mail enabled phones today, so we will forgo any further discussion of SMS. Instead, we will look to configuring e-mail for alerting. E-mail actually has two options, SMTP or MAPI. By right-clicking the Resource Manager node, you can choose whether to use MAPI or SMTP for your e-mail that will be going out as alerts. The default method is MAPI, but we prefer SMTP, as MAPI requires a MAPI profile to exist on the server that will be sending the alerts (or in other words, potentially all servers!). We like to use SMTP and configure our internal mail servers to accept relays from our Presentation servers. Alternatively, you can configure SMTP to "authenticate" so that you are not opening relaying operations. Figure 16.14 shows the SMTP configuration option.

Figure 16.14 SMTP Alert Configuration

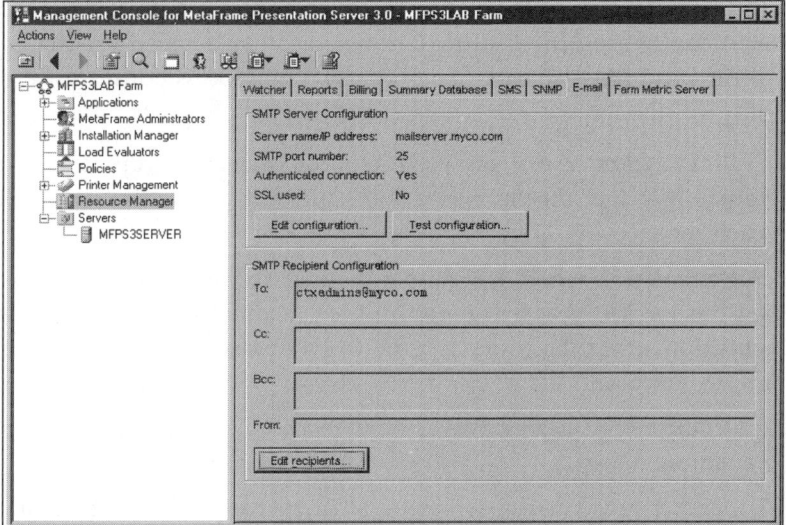

Configuring Resource Manager Summary Database

Now that we have seen the benefits of Resource Manager from a short-term basis, when we are limited to 96 hours of data, we naturally want to extend that period of time and be able to "look into the past" to diagnose problems, predict trends, and provide scaling information. The summary database allows us to do all that and more. As previously stated, the summary database is not enabled by default, so in this section we discuss the requirements of the summary database and how to enable it.

The configuration of the summary database consists of a few components. First, you will need a backend database in which to store all the summary information. Next, you will need to configure a Database Connection server. The Database Connection server is nothing more than a singled-out Presentation server that has Resource Manager installed in the correct drivers or software to allow it to talk to the backend database (be that MDAC revision or Oracle client). The final step is to configure the Resource Manager node in the Presentation Server Console.

Backend Database Server

- Microsoft SQL 7 or newer (with the latest service packs recommended)
- Oracle 7 or newer (with the latest updates recommended)

Database Connection Server

- Requires the appropriate client software to communicate with the backend database server.

We should first look at the process of how information gets to the summary database prior to configuring the feature. Through a rather detailed process, information is written into the summary database once per day. The process consists of the following steps:

- Each Presentation server running Resource Manager "summarizes" the Resource Manager metric information and adds it to a flat text file maintained on each server every hour.

- Each Presentation server will send a message to the Database Connection server once a day (when depends on the schedule) informing the Database Connection server that there is a file to be uploaded and merged in to the summary database.

- The Database Connection server requests the files from the member Presentation servers.

- The member Presentation servers send the flat text files to the Database Connection server.

- The Database Connection server writes the files to the summary database once per day (timing based on the schedule).

Now we can turn our attention to the actual steps to configure and enable the summary database. We begin with the assumption that our backend database guys have the wherewithal to create a database for us to store our summary database information. With that aside, the first step is to designate the Database Connection server and install the appropriate database client software. (For our demonstration we will be using Microsoft SQL 2000 with SP3a, our Presentation Server has a recent MDAC so we will forgo the installation of the database client.) Using the information provided by our database administrators, we will create a system DSN on one of our Presentation servers. To create this system DSN, simply navigate to the **Administrative Tools** folder from the **Control Panel** and open the **Data Sources (ODBC)** tool. Select the **System** tab and click **Add**.

Choose SQL as your driver (see Figure 16.15).

Figure 16.15 Create New Data Source for Database Connection Server

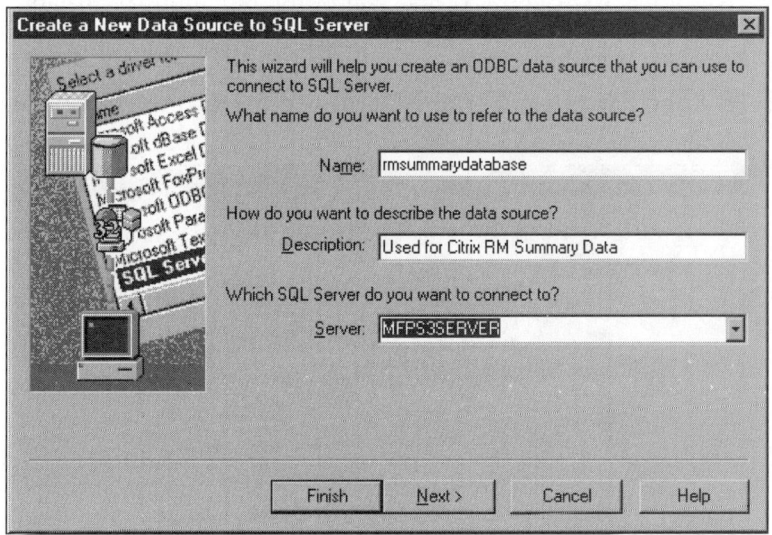

The most important step here is the name of the DSN. The Resource Manager software expects the DSN to be named rmsummarydatabase—the description is optional—and then specify the SQL server to contact (see Figure 16.16).

Figure 16.16 Create a New Data Source for Database Connection Server to SQL Server

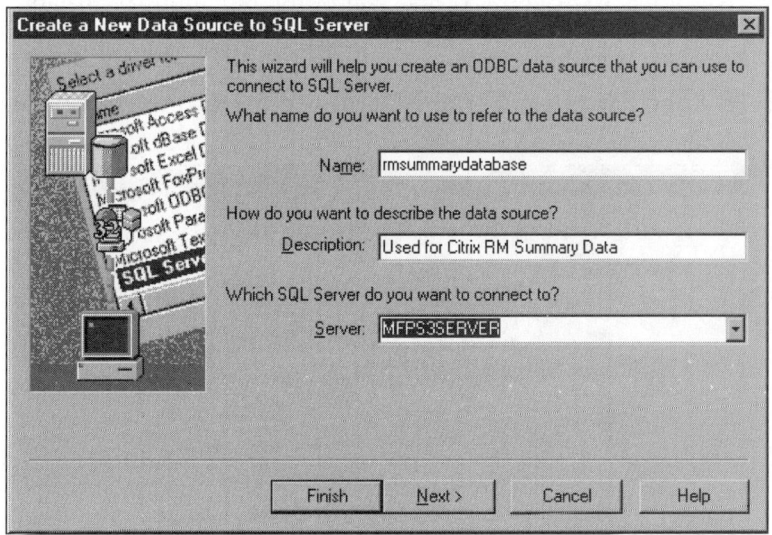

Windows Integrated and SQL authentication are both supported by Resource Manager. We have elected to use SQL authentication, so the client configuration should be the defaults (either Named Pipes or TCP/IP) (see Figure 16.17).

Figure 16.17 Choosing Authentication for Database Connection Server

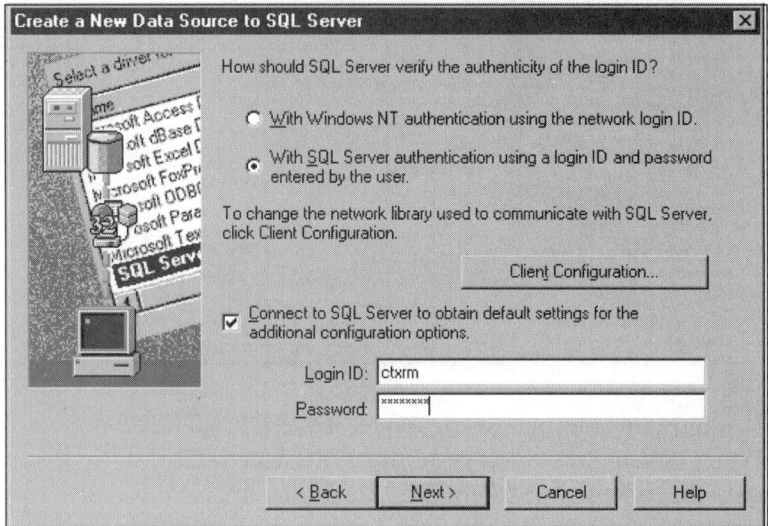

Confirm the database is set correctly. In this example, our SQL server has a database named Citrix_Resource_Manager_DB that will house our summary database data (see Figure 16.18).

Figure 16.18 Specifying the Default Database for Database Connection Server

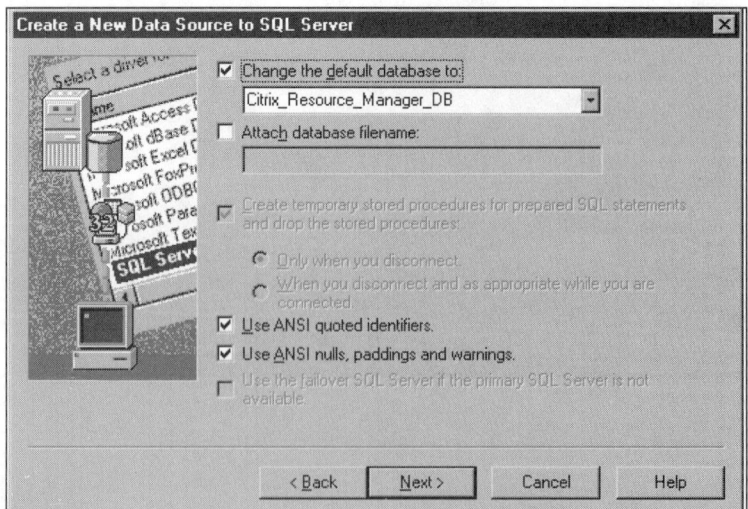

Typically, you can accept the defaults on the SQL options (see Figure 16.19).

Figure 16.19 Setting SQL Options for Database Connection Server

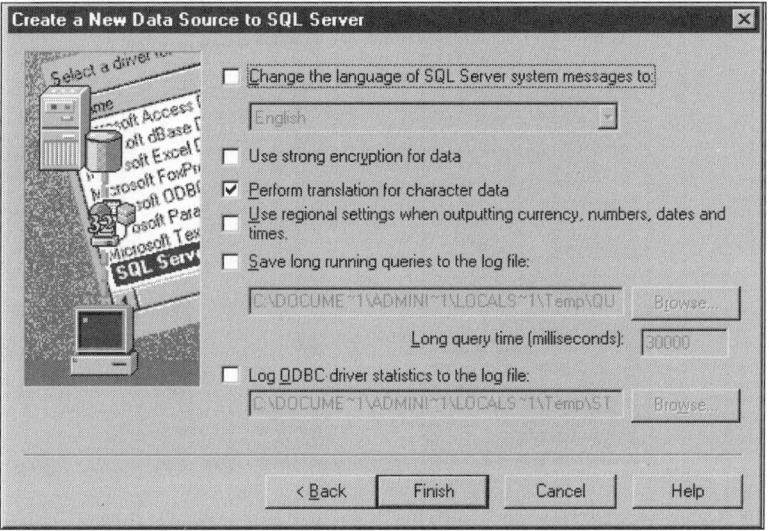

Confirm your settings and choose to **Test Data Source** (see Figure 16.20).

Figure 16.20 Confirming DSN Settings for Database Connection Server

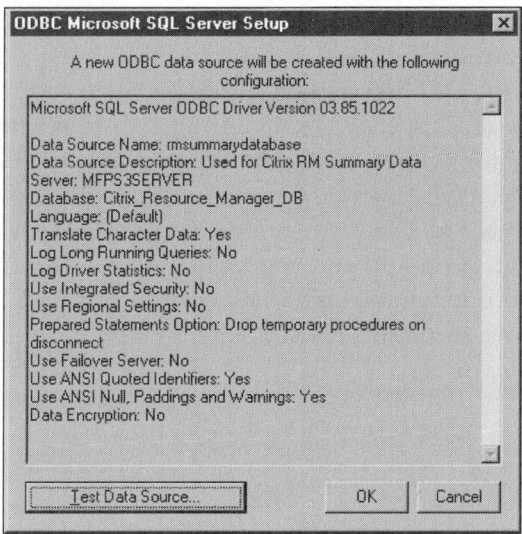

The test should complete successfully (see Figure 16.21). If not, confirm your configuration settings and consult your database administrator.

Figure 16.21 Testing the New DSN for Database Connection Server

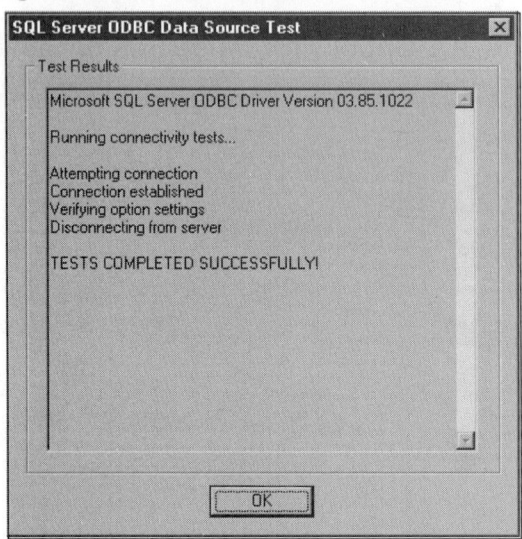

We are in the home stretch of configuring the summary database. From here to completion, we will be configuring the farm-wide settings to inform all our other Presentation servers which server is the Database Connection server. This is performed in the **Presentation Server Console | Resource Manager node | Summary Database tab**; at the bottom of the window, simply click **Configure**.

Step one is to check the **Summary Database enabled** option. Step two is to enter the **Database Connection Server** name and then enter the username and password that can leverage the DSN created on the server for access to the backend database. Additionally, you can specify the update time, or leave the default of midnight, whichever works better for your environment. Try to avoid scheduling the summary database update cycle near Presentation Server reboot schedules or backup jobs that may be occurring. Additionally, you can configure that an alert be sent at the end of the update (most administrators do not) and you can adjust the retention intervals. The default retention period is indefinite for all information, meaning your backend database will continue to grow. We recommend setting these values to something more realistic; say 1–2 years (see Figure 16.22).

Figure 16.22 Testing Summary Database Authentication Access from the Configuration Tool

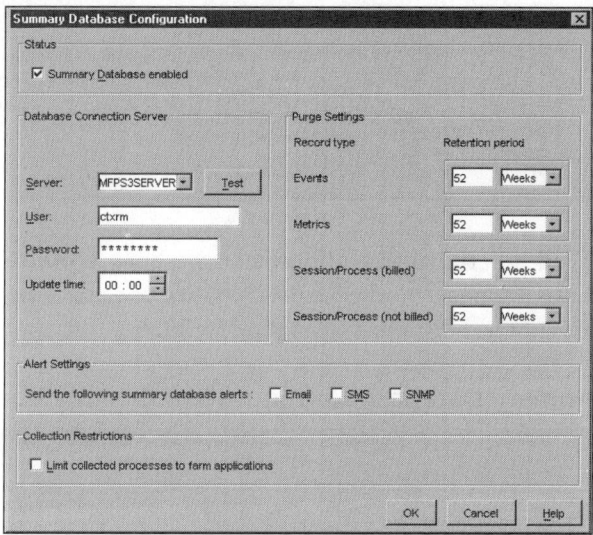

The last thing to do before clicking OK is to test the connection to the database server. The results should be similar to Figure 16.23; if not, confirm your settings on the previous page.

Figure 16.23 Testing Summary Database Authentication Access from the Configuration Tool Results

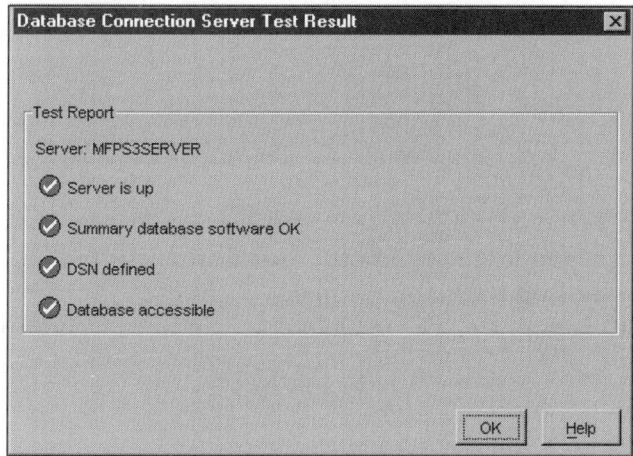

After the test, simply click **OK** on the **Test Result** window and **OK** on the **Summary Database Configuration** window. You will be prompted to click **OK** a third and final time to "fully enable" the Summary Database as shown in Figure 16.24.

Figure 16.24 Warning to Enable/Disable Summary Database

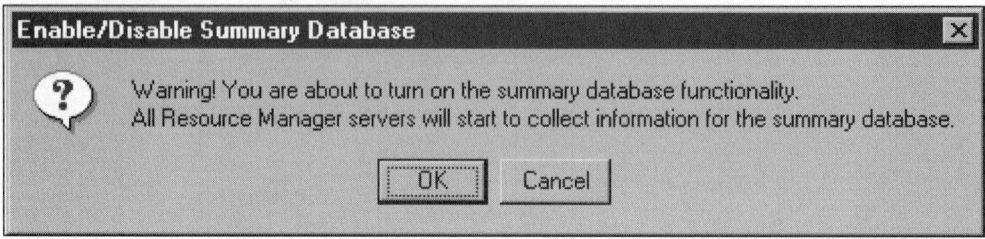

The final test of full functionality will be when we click **Update Now** at the bottom of the Resource Manager node, Summary Database tab. After clicking **Update Now**, the status lights should be similar to Figure 16.25.

Figure 16.25 Summary Database Configuration Completed and Fully Tested

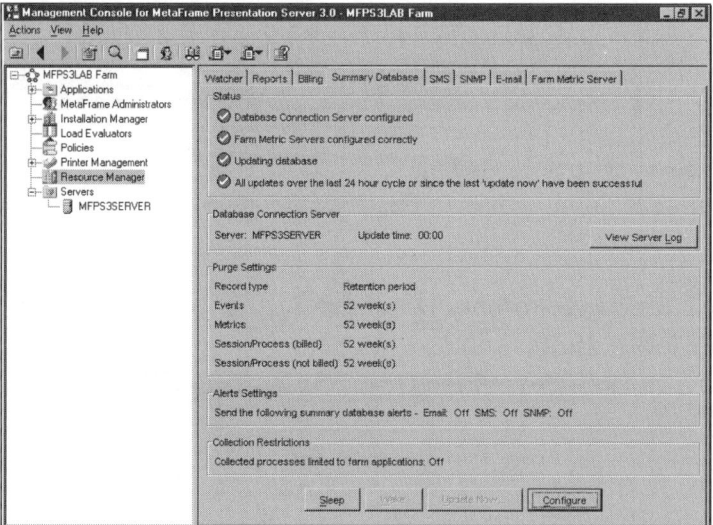

The last option would be to review the server log that contains changes in metric status and serves as a report for the update and "summarization" process. To view the log, click the **View Server Log** button on the middle-right of the **Summary Database** tab in the **Resource Manager** node. The results will be similar to Figure 16.26.

Figure 16.26 View Server Log Tool

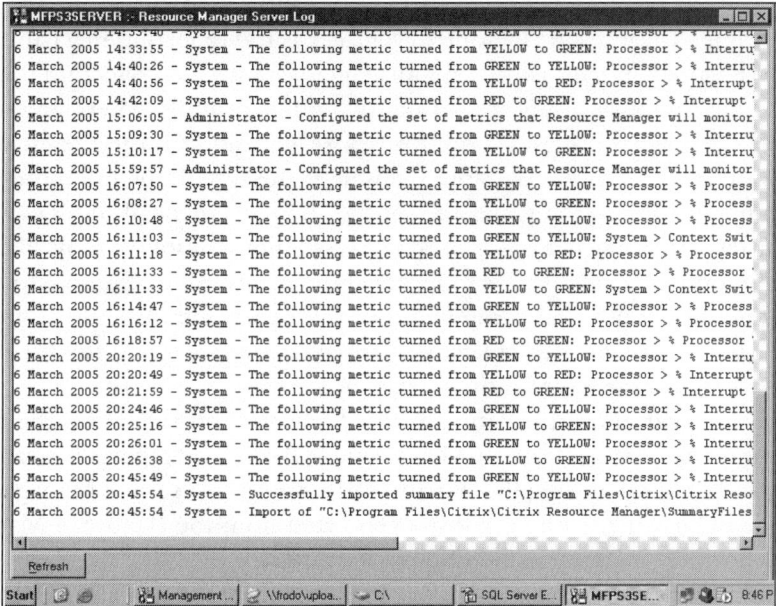

At this point, we have successfully implemented one of the major features of Resource Manager, the summary database. The last concept to discuss about configuration of the summary database is the retention and database size issue. As previously stated, the default retention period is Indefinite, meaning that our backend database will continue to grow. The size of the summary database is dependant on the following factors:

- Number of Presentation servers being monitored

- Number of metrics

- Number of sessions per day

- Number of processes executed during a session

- Retention period of summary database information

As a rule of thumb, estimate 10MB–15MB per 100 servers monitored per day (for a typical farm; your results may vary). Consider these numbers when determining your summary database retention strategy. Your retention strategy should be based on the reporting needs and billing and cost centers if you leverage these features. Now we can turn our attention to reporting and see how the summary database can begin to really pay off!

Resource Manager Reporting

One of the strongest features of Resource Manager is the reporting mechanism and capabilities. We wouldn't want all that performance data we are collecting to go to waste! Reporting can be accomplished using two different tools, where previously there was only one. The primary "legacy" tool for report generation is the Presentation Server Console. However, the new Access Suite Console is the way more and more administrators will begin and continue to generate reports. The movement of the Resource Management reporting mechanism into the Access Suite Console is most likely a glimpse of the future. Citrix's goal is to leverage the Access Suite Console to provide single-seat administration for all components of the Access infrastructure. Obviously, leveraging Resource Manager to collect performance metrics for all the various components of the access infrastructure is the next logical step.

We can begin with the Presentation Server Console. This method is the method of report generation since the release of MetaFrame XP 1.0. The reports basically break down into two broad categories; those generated from the Resource Manager Local Database, called Current reports, and those generated from the Resource Manager summary database, which are aptly named Summary reports.

The Current reports consist of Current Process, Current User, and Server Snapshot. The Summary reports consist of Process Summary, User Summary, and Server Summary. Regardless of which report you generate, you will have the ability to export the report to a comma-separated value file (CSV) or a HyperText Markup Language (HTML) file. The HTML option is great for managers and "quick reports," but the CSV is very powerful when imported into a spreadsheet application. The only downside to this report generation and saving is that there is no mechanism to automate this process through the Presentation Server Console.

As a general overview, the Process reports are excellent for determining per-user breakdowns of processor and memory use per process. This is one of our favorite and most used reports. The User reports are useful in tracking particular users' habits. The final report type, Server is also one of our favorites, as it contains all the "gory" details of the metrics we spent hours configuring. Figure 16.27 shows a sample report for Current User. We intentionally picked the "least detailed" report so it would be more viewable as an insert.

Figure 16.27 Current User Report Generated from Presentation Server Console

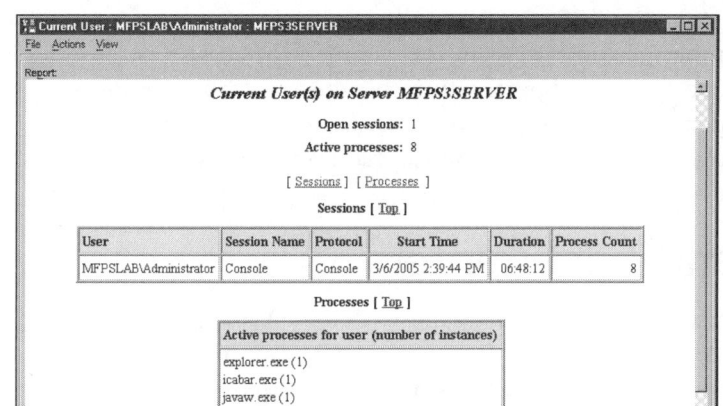

The wonderful thing about the reporting functions via the Presentation Server Management console is that once exported, a saved report can be viewed at any time. Additionally, the Historical Summary reports (and to a lesser extent the Current reports) allow you to specify time windows from which to generate a report. Imagine how powerful that can be for troubleshooting a user who says that his Word session was slow yesterday around 3 P.M!

Well, as nice as the reporting is in the Presentation Server Console, we need to press ahead and look at the awesome new reporting features in the Access Suite Console. We must warn you, though, once you see the power of the new reporting component, you will very likely never use the Presentation Server Console to generate another report!

The Access Suite Console reporting allows you to create report "templates" that can be scheduled for execution and create very nice reports in CSV or HTML format. Additionally, the automatically generated reports can be saved to a network share and are viewable by all parties concerned. We can't tell you how many times administrators have asked us for an easy way to allow their senior management team to "see the status" of the farm from a single location. Now, we can simply generate report "jobs" that periodically dump HTML reports to a share on a Web server that would be viewable by anyone through a standard Web browser. Oh, and did we mention, the reports look *much* better!

So, let us begin by opening the **Access Suite Console** and navigating to the **Reports Center** on the left-hand side. From there, the details pane on the right will present us with the three common tasks: Generate Report, Generate Specification, and Schedule Report. The toolset can be a little confusing initially, but the key to understanding the tools is the definitions of what they do. A *Specification* is a set of rules for connecting to the summary database, and once information is queried from the database how to save it to file or send it to e-mail. A single Specification can allow for many reports to be generated. A *Report* is just the type of information you are looking to query through the specification from the summary database. The *Schedule* is simply pairing the Report and the Specification together in a schedule job to generate a report or series of reports. This ability to automate the report generation process is very powerful, to say the least. Additionally, you can have a report generated and e-mailed on a scheduled basis.

Billing and Cost Centers

The last major section to be discussed in Resource Manager is billing and cost centers. Now that we have a summary database established, we have the ability to create fee schedules for our servers' usage and organize our user populations into cost centers to allow for more detailed analysis and comparison of perhaps various departments' use of the farm and its resources. While this feature set could be leveraged to create actual invoices to allow for direct billing of system resources to various business units, most administrators who implement this do so as a means to document and better understand the usage patterns within their organization.

The first step to using this feature is to generate a Fee Profile. This can be done in the **Presentation Server Console | Resource Manager node | Billing tab**. Click on the **Fee Profiles** button and let's create a new profile. Multiple profiles can be created and typically would be to allow you to better associate the costs of the equipment, maintenance, and licensing for the various hardware platforms in your deployment. In other words, you probably will have a fee profile for the really old servers that differs from the really new servers.

Name the fee profile whatever is descriptive of the solution it will support. In the details window, you can specify the currency to be used for billing and specify the billing details based on resource usage. A typical fee profile's properties may look similar to Figure 16.28.

Figure 16.28 Fee Profile Creation

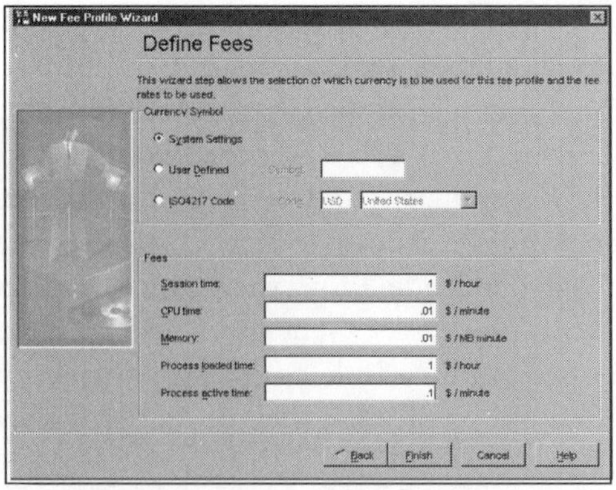

The next step is optional, but most administrators elect to create cost centers. A *cost center* is a logical grouping of users (typically by department) to allow for greater separation when the actual reports are generated. We like to create cost centers based on the departments in which our clients will be helping to "pay" for the access infrastructure. If there isn't such a system in your organization, consider using cost centers like groups in Active Directory. The real benefit of creating cost centers is that you can "link" a fee profile to the cost center to facilitate billing report later.

Once we have generated a fee profile and optionally created our cost centers (and associated a fee profile with the cost center), we can then generate billing reports based on cost center or domain. If your organization doesn't have clear cost-center divisions, consider using the By Domain option and generating the report based on group membership. Once generated, billing reports can be saved as CSV or HTML or printed.

Select **By Cost Center** and the billing wizard should start. You will see a screen similar to that of Figure 16.29.

Figure 16.29 Billing Reports by Cost Center

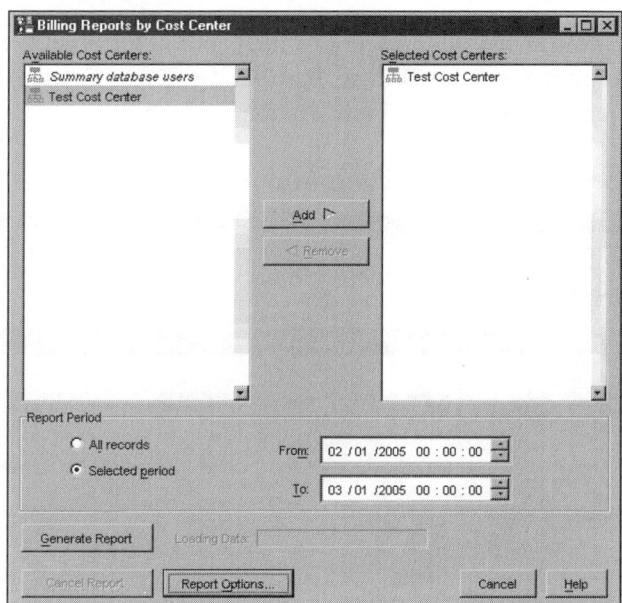

Select the cost center(s) that you want to generate billing reports for and select the report period, typically one month. Prior to selecting Generate Report, click the **Reporting Options** to all for more detailed report creation. Select the level of detail you desire; for full reporting, configure the Reporting Options as shown in Figure 16.30.

Figure 16.30 Reporting Options

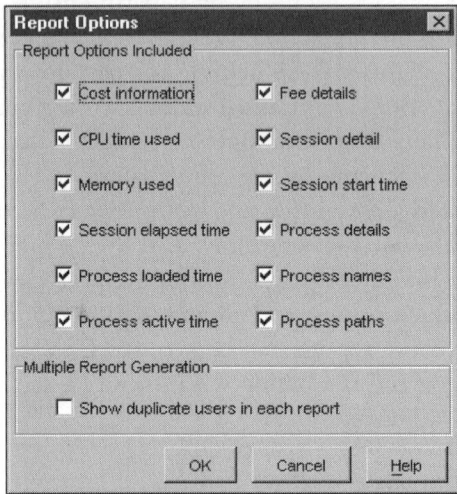

Once you have completed your selections in Report Options, click **OK** and then select **Generate Report** from the **Billing Report by Cost Center** window. We have included a sample (empty) report in Figure 16.31.

Figure 16.31 Sample Report—Billing Reports by Cost Center

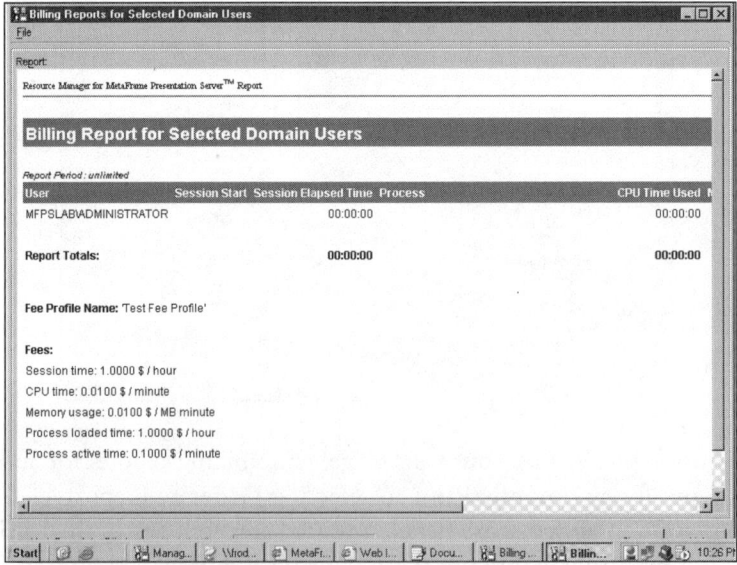

Billing by Domain offers similar options and configuration to by Cost Center billing. These options are self-explanatory with the exception that billing By Domain

allows you to pair any domain user or group with any fee profile, even if that user or group is part of a cost center that has a different fee profile defined.

Resource Manager Miscellaneous Settings

Just when you thought we had covered everything you could ever want to know about Resource Manager, there are two final items that we need to discuss. Both of these features are "out of the way" as far as the rest of RM's configuration, so that is why we saved them for last. The first is *Ignored Processes* and the second is *Reboot Schedule*.

Ignored Processes is a special tab in the Properties of each individual server. The Ignored Processes functions as a list of processes and services that Resource Manager should "ignore" and not track or record any metrics on in either the local database or the summary database. By default, the systems are configured to ignore the basic processes that exist on every Windows terminal server. If however, you have additional processes, especially system-level services, that you would like to exclude from the list, this is the place to add those in. Once you have defined the processes you want to ignore, this list can easily be Apply to Other Servers using that feature. Figure 16.32 demonstrates this server configuration tab.

Figure 16.32 Ignored Processes for Resource Manager

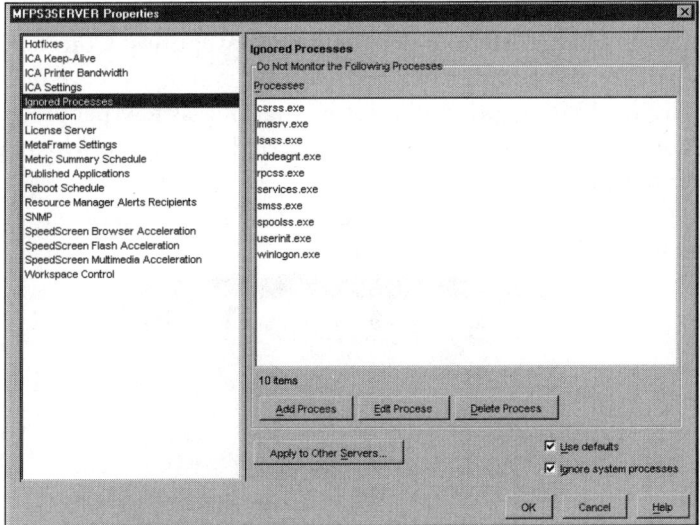

The final component of Resource Manager (considered by some to be a feature of Enterprise Edition) is the Reboot Schedule. This is also a tab under the individual server Properties. From this tab, you can enable the automatic reboot of your Presentation servers to clean up memory and improve overall system performance and stability. As throughout the Presentation Server product, you have the ability to replicate your configuration to other servers through the Apply to Other Servers option. Figure 16.33 shows you the options for reboot times and scheduling.

Figure 16.33 Reboot Schedule

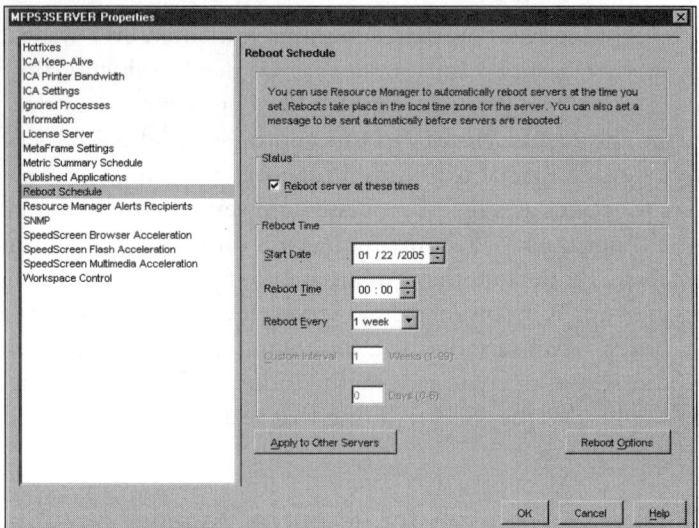

Additional settings are available under the Reboot Options. Consider enabling the message send capability and adding your own custom text as we have done in Figure 16.34. Additionally, disabling logins will assist in angering as few people as possible prior to the server reboot—nobody likes to have just started a session only to be logged out a few minutes later for a reboot!

Figure 16.34 Reboot Schedule Options

> **NOTE**
>
> As a final thought to the rebooting of servers, most engineers agree that a rebooted server is a happier server. The question is frequency. How often should you reboot your Presentation servers? The answer is as often as you can without interrupting business need. If you have an outage window once a week, reboot them once a week. If your business is 9 to 5, reboot them nightly, as it won't impact production and your servers will be "fresh" for the morning rush. Both Windows Server 2003 and Presentation Server 3.0 have come a long way from the Windows NT 4.0 Terminal Server Edition days of what seemed like "hourly reboots." However, as we always say, "a reboot a day keeps the phone calls away!"
>
> Additionally, many administrators will create custom reboot scripts instead of using the Reboot Schedule features of Presentation Server 3.0 Enterprise Edition. The reboot script that you can create allows you to do much more to a server than simply reboot it. There are several good examples of reboot scripts on various Web sites. We recommend at a minimum that your custom reboot scripts do the following:
>
> - Disable logons
> - Send messages frequently
> - Perform logoffs of active sessions
> - Perform logoffs/resets of disconnected sessions
> - Clear the temp directory
> - Clear the spool directory
> - Write a log of the tasks completed
> - Reboot the server

Network Manager

Network Manager is component of Presentation Server 3.0 Enterprise Edition that allows for integration with third-party SNMP management consoles. There are two basic components to the system, a SNMP Agent for MetaFrame Presentation Server and the Network Manager Plug-ins. Network Manager allows for your Presentation servers to more easily integrate into your existing enterprise systems management tools.

Requirements

The following sections list the requirements for the installation and use of Network Manager. Keep in mind that the installation requires changes to both the Presentation Server and the SNMP Management console.

Presentation Server Requirements

- Enterprise Edition of Presentation Server
- Installation and configuration of Microsoft's SNMP Service
- SNMP Agent for MetaFrame Presentation Server

SNMP Management Console Requirements

- Network Manager plug-in for specific platform
  - HP OpenView 6.2 on Windows 2000 SP1 or higher
  - Tivoli NetView 6.0 on Windows 2000 SP1 or higher
  - CA Unicenter
  - TNG 2.4.2 on Windows 2000 SP1 or higher
  - TND 3.1 on Windows 2000 SP1 or higher
- The Citrix Management Information Base (MIB) is copied to the Management Console automatically during the install of the Network Manager plug-in.
- Optionally, many clients will install the Presentation Server Management Console on the SNMP Management Console to allow for single-seat administration.

Installation and Configuration of the Network Manager Components

Now that we have defined the requirements, we can begin with the installation and configuration section. We will first look at the Presentation Server-side installation and configuration procedure. We will then turn our attention to the SNMP Management Console/Collection Server side of the install.

Presentation Server-Side Installation and Configuration

The first step is to install and configure the Microsoft SNMP Service on the Presentation servers that will participate in the Network Manager-SNMP community. This additional Windows component can installed through the **Add or Remove**

Programs | Add/Remove Windows Components tool under the **Details** of the **Management and Monitoring Tools** section. Once installed, the SNMP Service can be configured by opening the Properties of the service through the **Control Panel | Services | SNMP Service**. There we will configure a few basic settings. First, we will configure the **Traps** tab, as this is the primary "affiliation" with an SNMP community and the single most important tab to make SNMP work. Figure 16.35 shows the basic configuration; simply enter the community name as defined on the backend SNMP Management Console, click **Add to list**, and enter the correct IP or name to reach the backend SNMP collection server (the one that the Management Console will contact). In this case, we have a backend SNMP collection server with the IP address 192.168.131.70 that is accepting traps from the community name NM_Community.

Figure 16.35 Configuring the SNMP Traps Tab to "Join" the Community

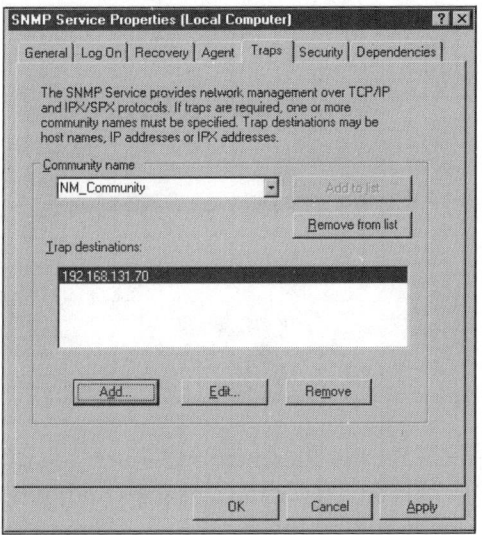

Next, we will configure the Security tab. Many administrators simply ignore this tab, as typically it is not required to make the local SNMP Service on our Presentation servers talk to the SNMP collection server. However, there are many well-known "security concerns" with SNMP, so anything we can do to help tighten the security of this aging protocol, the better. The two critical pieces to configure here is to accept traps *only* from specified communities (and those should be read-only) and to accept SNMP packets *only* from the SNMP collection servers (and possibly the SNMP management console). In this example, we are accepting traps only from 192.168.131.70, and the only accepted community name is NM_Community. While SNMP security is rather primitive, it is better to restrict who has access to this information than to simply leave it unconfigured. Figure 16.36 depicts the previously described configuration.

NOTE

For additional security with SNMP, consider using fully qualified domain names (FQDNs) to further restrict access. It will simply add an additional layer of "spoofing" required.

Figure 16.36 Configuring SNMP Security

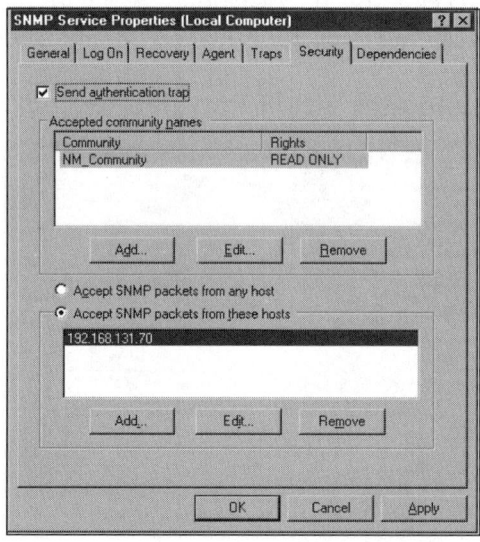

The last steps to perform on the Presentation Server side of the house are to enable the SNMP Agent for Presentation Server to send traps and optionally to enable Resource Manager to leverage this configuration for trapping purposes. You can enable the SNMP Agent at the farm level (thereby setting this for all servers in the farm), or you can enable it on an individual server basis. Open the **Presentation Server Management Console** and select the **Properties** of the farm. From the **Farm Properties** window, select **SNMP** and check **Enable SNMP Agent on all servers**. (If a warning comes up about enabling SNMP on all servers, simply click **OK**, as it is warning that the Microsoft SNMP is required to be installed and configured on all servers). At this point, you can choose what information you would like to send as traps to the SNMP collection server (based on the configuration of the Microsoft SNMP service from earlier), including logons, logoffs, disconnects, and session thresholds exceeded based on the Session Limit Per Server number you provide. Figure 16.37 shows a fully enabled SNMP Agent farm-wide.

Figure 16.37 Enabling SNMP Agent on All Servers in the Farm

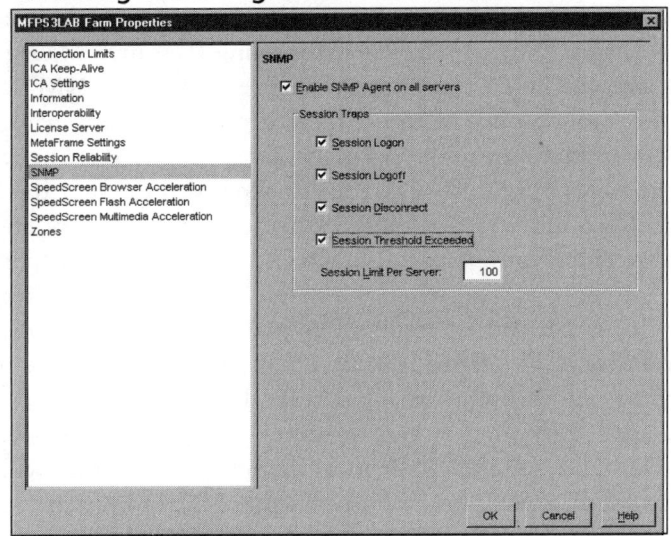

If you elect not to enable the SNMP Agent on all of you Presentation servers, you can choose to enable it on a server-by-server basis. Open the **Presentation Server Management Console** and select the **Properties** of the individual server from the farm by expanding the **Servers** node. From the server's **Properties** window, select **SNMP** and uncheck **Use farm settings**. This will allow you to then check the **Enable SNMP Agent**. The remaining options are the same as they were at the farm level. Figure 16.38 shows the settings for the individual server method.

Figure 16.38 Enabled SNMP Agent for an Individual Server

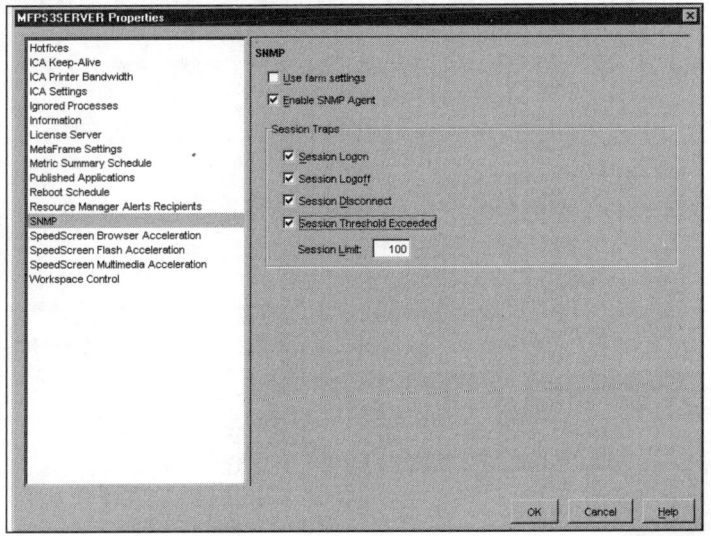

The final Presentation Server-side modification for SNMP is deciding whether to allow Resource Manager to leverage the Network Manager configuration to send traps. Once Network Manager (NM) is configured, enabling Resource Manager to use the SNMP service is simple. The configuration to enable RM to use NM occurs in two places. First, we must configure RM to use the correct community name. Open the **Presentation Server Management Console** and select the **Resource Manager** node. Click on the **SNMP** tab and click **Edit** to allow you to enter the correct SNMP community name. Keep in mind that the Presentation server will not check to see if the information you are entering is correct. The second step is to enable/configure which metrics we want to send a trap on when the state changes (say from green to yellow). The community string that you entered will be used by all Presentation servers that we configure to trap a metric. Configuring which metrics to trap is a little bit more challenging. Typically, we will configure all our servers the same, so the steps we are about to show you can be applied to other servers the same way we did in the Resource Manager section. Basically, select a server from the Servers node that will characterize the typical settings for all servers (or as closely as possible). From there, look to the right pane of the window and select the **Resource Manager** tab. At this point, you can right-click any of the metrics you see in the right-hand details pane and select **Properties**. This will open the **Server Metric Properties** window that will allow us to select the appropriate metric on the left and then click the **Alerts Configuration** tab on the right. In Figure 16.39, we demonstrate setting the % Processor Time metric to send a trap when the status transitions up to red or down to green (meaning we want to know when things are *really* bad and when they return to normal).

Figure 16.39 Enabling Individual Resource Manager Metrics to Use SNMP Agent

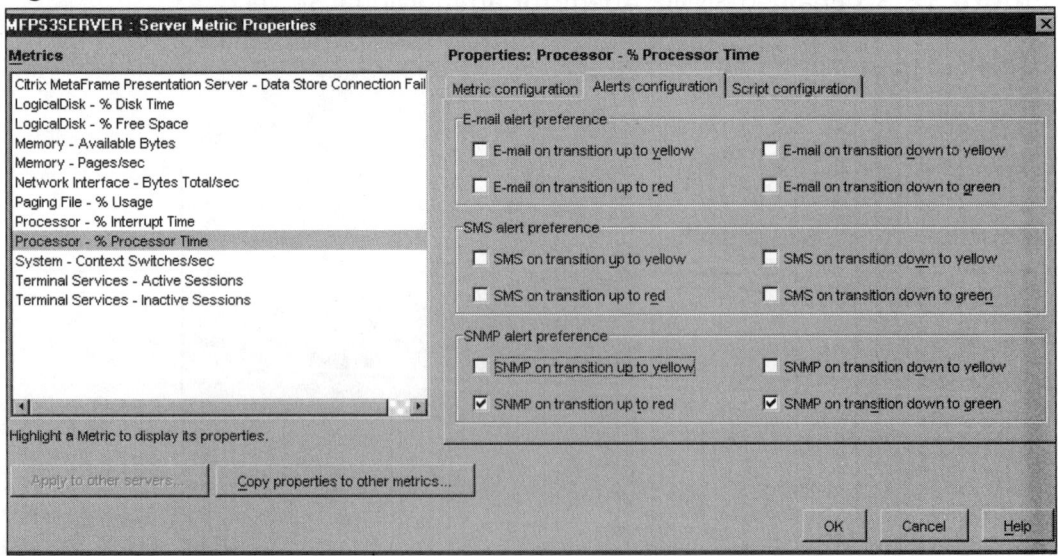

> **NOTE**
>
> Remember that the process of settings SNMP alerts is on an individual Resource Manager metric by server basis. In other words, if you want more than that metric to trap, you have to configure each metric that you want to trap on that specific server. Then configure the next server, and so on. Also remember that you can use the **Apply to other Servers** option once you configure your initial server to save a great deal of time and effort!

SNMP Management Console/ Collection Server Installation and Configuration

Now that we have configured the Presentation Server-side of the house, we can change focus to what "updates" we need to make to the SNMP Management Console/collection server side of the community. As previously mentioned, Citrix's Network Manager supports the following platforms:

- HP OpenView 6.2 on Windows 2000 SP1 or higher

- Tivoli NetView 6.0 on Windows 2000 SP1 or higher

- CA Unicenter

    - TNG 2.4.2 on Windows 2000 SP1 or higher

    - TND 3.1 on Windows 2000 SP1 or higher

For the purpose of illustration, we will be using HP OpenView to demonstrate the NM installation and configuration. The process is fairly simple and is basically two main steps. Step one is to install the appropriate Network Manager plug-in on the SNMP Management Console. The second step is optional, but most administrators also install the Presentation Server Management Console on the SNMP Management Console to provide single-seat administration. Simply put, the "tools" to manage the Presentation server itself are rather limited, and we will need access to the Presentation Server Console to fully administrator the farm and its servers from a single seat.

Let us begin with the installation of the Network Manager plug-in for the SNMP Management Console. As previously mentioned, we will be using HP's OpenView to demonstrate this installation. The first step in this process is to insert the Presentation Server Components CD into the SNMP Management Console. The autorun should automatically start, but if it doesn't, simply browse the root of the CD and double-click the **autorun.exe**. Select **Network Manager Console Plug-Ins** and the select the correct SNMP plug-in to install. Simply follow the Install wizard. At this point, you have enabled the Network Manager plug-in and you will be able to read the Presentation Server "specific" traps being sent to the management console.

> **NOTE**
>
> The SNMP Services will be stopped in order to add the Network Manager plug-in!

Optionally, you can now install the Presentation Server Management Console. The installation can be found on the Presentation Server CD. Refer to Chapters 3 and 76 for details on installation requirements for the Presentation Server Management Console.

Management Pack for Microsoft Operations Manager 2000

Microsoft Operations Manager (MOM) is a system-wide management toolset created by Microsoft to provide a more complete view into the interdependencies of the various components that make up our modern Microsoft-based networks. MOM at its most basic is a framework toolset that allows for easy extension by Microsoft and third-party vendors through the introduction of *Management Packs* to the MOM system. MOM provides real-time monitoring and problem resolution to a variety of Microsoft-based systems, from Windows 2000 to 2003, from Exchange to SQL, and nearly every Microsoft product in between. MOM can be used for performance monitoring, event management, alerting and reporting, and trend analysis all from a single seat of administration. Additionally, MOM contains a very broad range of Knowledge Base articles with links to the Microsoft Support center to aid in fixing common or known issues in a hurry. Citrix developed the Presentation Server Management Pack for Microsoft Operations Manager 2000 to allow MOM to have a more complete picture of the Citrix Services running on top of Windows Terminal Services (which MOM was already capable of monitoring). To follow suit with Microsoft's framework, the Presentation Server Management Pack contains links to Citrix Knowledge Base articles in addition to monitoring and reporting the help of the Presentation servers and the new licensing server. Installing the Management Pack is a fairly simple process and we will cover that momentarily… for now, let us review the requirements for the installation.

Requirements

The following are the requirements for the installation and use of the Presentation Server Management Pack for Microsoft Operations Manager 2000. Similar to Network Manager's installation, there are two sides to the installation. The MOM server/console will need to have the Management Pack imported (a fairly easy task), and the Presentation servers will need to have the MetaFrame Presentation Server Provider installed (otherwise, it is consider "unmanaged").

Presentation Server and/ or Licensing Server Requirements

- Presentation servers will require the MetaFrame Presentation Server Provider.
- Licensing servers will require the Licensing Server Provider.
- Installation of MOM Agents (providers) in order to be "managed."
- 56MB of hard drive space

MOM Server/Console Requirements

- Microsoft Operations Manager 2000 with Service Pack 1 or higher
- Installation of Presentation Server Management Pack for MOM
- Configuration of rules

NOTE

Once installed, the Presentation Server Management Pack for MOM cannot be uninstalled. It is strongly recommended that you backup your MOM database and server prior to importing any management packs.

Installation and Configuration of the Management Pack for MOM

Now that we have defined the requirements, we can begin with the installation and configuration section. We will first look at the Presentation Server-side installation and configuration procedure. After we have completed that task, we will install the Presentation Server Management Pack for MOM by importing it through the MOM Console. After the import, we will briefly touch on the configuration.

Presentation Server–Side Installation and Configuration

The first step is to install and configure the Microsoft SNMP Service on the Presentation servers that will participate in the Network Manager-SNMP community. This additional Windows component can be installed through the **Add or Remove**

Programs | Add/Remove Windows Components tool under the **Details** of the **Management and Monitoring Tools** section. Once installed, the SNMP Service can be configured by opening the properties of the service through **Control Panel | Services | SNMP Service**. There we will configure a few basic settings. First, we will configure Traps tab, as this is the primary "affiliation" with an SNMP community and the single most important tab to make SNMP work.

For further information on optimizing the Microsoft Operations Manager configuration, refer to Citrix's *Installation Guide - Citrix MetaFrame XP Management Pack for Microsoft Operations Manager 2000* available at http://support.citrix.com/kb/entry!default.jspa?categoryID=215&entryID=166&fromSearchPage=true.

Summary

In this chapter, we examined some of the basics of network monitoring and resource management. While a vast subject to discuss, we narrowed our focus to those solutions that were immediately of value or directly connected to the use of MetaFrame Presentation Server 3.0.

We began with a discussion centered on baselining. We discussed the importance of creating a server baseline. We also looked at the major uses of baselining, such as troubleshooting, trend analysis, and capacity planning. We looked at some of the "quick" ways to gather information from a Presentation server such as Task Manager and Performance Monitor.

Next, we spent a great deal of time investigating Citrix's Resource Manager, a component of Presentation Server 3.0 Enterprise Edition. We looked at how Resource Manager could be used to provide real-time monitoring, trend analysis, planning and provisioning, troubleshooting, reporting, and billing. We defined *metrics*, configured metrics, discussed monitoring metrics, and discovered a few of the limitations of metrics. We looked at the different methods of sending alerts such as e-mail, SNMP, and SMS. We looked at the type of information stored in the local database and the differences with the summary database. We also looked at generating reports from the two different databases. We then turned our attention to configuring and managing the summary database. The last topic of discussion for Resource Manager was the concept of a fee profile and the ability to generate billing based on the fee profile(s) and cost centers.

We explored the Network Manager component of Presentation Server 3.0 Enterprise Edition. We reviewed the requirements on both the Presentation server and the backend SNMP Management Console. We then configured the Presentation server to use Microsoft's SNMP Service and discussed the installation of the Network Manager plug-in on the SNMP Management Console.

We looked at Microsoft Operations Manager from a high-level view. We then briefly discussed the requirements for installation and integration of your Presentation servers into an existing Microsoft Operations Manager deployment.

In conclusion, baselining and thorough network and resource monitoring are critical tasks that must be considered with any deployment of MetaFrame Presentation Server. We discovered and discussed the primary tools available with Presentation Server Enterprise Edition to aid administrators in network management and resource monitoring.

Solutions Fast Track

Baselining

- ☑ Process of creating a "model" of server and application performance
- ☑ Useful for troubleshooting, performing trend analysis and scaling

Resource Manager

- ☑ A comprehensive tool to provide system and application level performance tracking
- ☑ Can be leveraged for real-time monitoring, historical reporting, troubleshooting and trend analysis

Network Manager

- ☑ SNMP Plug-in that is included with Presentation Server 3.0 Enterprise Edition
- ☑ Can provide real-time SNMP traps for selected SNMP monitoring platforms such as HP's OpenView

Management Pack for Microsoft Operations Manager 2000

- ☑ A free component of Presentation Server
- ☑ Allows for more complete monitoring and reporting of Presentation Servers and their applications through the common Microsoft Operations Manager framework

Frequently Asked Questions

The following Frequently Asked Questions, answered by the authors of this book, are designed to both measure your understanding of the concepts presented in this chapter and to assist you with real-life implementation of these concepts. To have your questions about this chapter answered by the author, browse to **www.syngress.com/solutions** and click on the **"Ask the Author"** form. You will also gain access to thousands of other FAQs at ITFAQnet.com.

Q: I have Presentation Server 3.0 Advanced Edition and Enterprise Edition servers in my farm. Can I add the Resource Manager component to all of my servers to gather the historical data and process tracking?

A: Unfortunately no, as only Enterprise Edition supports Resource Manager. Resource Manager can be installed on a non–Enterprise Edition server, but the Independent Management Architecture (IMA) will not start the Resource Manager subsystem. The best solution would be to perform an in-place upgrade on your Advanced Edition servers.

Q: I use a different SNMP collection server that is Linux based and is open-source freeware. Can I leverage the Network Manager features in this solution?

A: The basic functions of SNMP from the terminal server to the SNMP collection server will function, but the advanced features available via the Network Manager Plug-in will not work correctly. Consider using or deploying the supported products listed in the requirements section for Network Manager in this chapter.

Q: I am using the current reports that ship with Presentation Server 3.0 in both the Presentation Server Management Console and the Access Management Consoles. I have been asked to provide reporting on the Presentation servers that is not available in either of these tools. What can I do to generate the reports required?

A: Not a problem; providing you are using the summary database, this can be fairly easy. The summary database that Citrix uses is a standard database that can be queried using whatever toolset you are most familiar with that is supported by the backend database type. For instance, if you are using Microsoft SQL Server as your database, you can leverage any supported scripting or application-based solution. Additionally, Citrix provides templates for Crystal Reports that can be excellent starting points for developers accustomed with this solution. These templates can be downloaded at http://support.citrix.com/kb/entry.jspa?entryID=621&categoryID=202.

MetaFrame Access Suite Licensing

Solutions in this chapter:

- **Access Suite Licensing Overview**
- **Planning Your Deployment**
- **Installing the Licensing Server**
- **Managing and Monitoring**
- **Customizations**
- **Troubleshooting**
- **Checklist**

  Related Chapters: Installing MetaFrame Presentation Server 3.0

- ☑ **Summary**
- ☑ **Solutions Fast Track**
- ☑ **Frequently Asked Questions**

Introduction

Those of you familiar with previous versions of MetaFrame know how annoying adding licenses to your servers can be. Fortunately, the licensing process has continued to evolve, and with the latest release of MetaFrame Presentation Server 3.0, Citrix has made the most dramatic change in the licensing process thus far. MetaFrame Presentation 3.0 has centralized license management for the MetaFrame Access Suite by creating a stand-alone licensing server. The licensing server can be installed on any server with adequate resources and does not require a dedicated server. Management and monitoring of licenses has changed as well and can now be accessed via a Web-based management console that provides real-time usage information, historical usage information, and current license inventory.

In prior versions of MetaFrame, license information was stored in the IMA data store. In MetaFrame Presentation Server 3.0, Citrix moved licensing information to its own database and provided the means to back up the database to the network, or if your license server fails, you have the option of retrieving the license information from MyCitrix.com. Gone are the days of manually re-entering and activating licenses. In, fact, in the new licensing scheme, activation is no longer necessary. Instead of license activation, license files are downloaded from MyCitrix.com and placed on the license server.

If that were not enough, the new centralized license server can provide licenses across the network and between server farms, thus eliminating the need to design your farms around licensing. A single license server can manage and monitor licenses for all your Citrix products in multiple farms.

In the sections to follow, we discuss in detail the new Citrix Licensing scheme and provide you with the information you will need to plan your deployment, install your licensing server, and simplify your license-related administration tasks.

Access Suite Licensing Overview

As mentioned in previous chapters, every MetaFrame Presentation Server 3.0 farm must include at least one license server. The license server stores the license files for the MetaFrame Access Suite products that specify the parameters for the product usage. The license files replace the Activation Code that earlier MetaFrame Server products required for license activation.

The licensing architecture consists of three new licensing components:

- **The Citrix Licensing Server** The licensing server is required to use any of the MetaFrame Access Suite products. It can be installed on a dedicated server or share space with other products on the same server. Where you install the licensing server will depend on the size of your environment and the resources available on the server hardware.

- **The License Management Console** License administration has been moved from the Citrix Management Console to its own Web-based administration tool where license availability information and real-time and historical license reports can be obtained. The caveat is that the management console requires Microsoft IIS and must be run on the same machine as the license server. If you cannot run IIS, you must use command-line tools to manage your license server.

- **The License Allocation Process** The final piece is the license allocation process that involves obtaining the license files containing product usage information from MyCitrix.com, and storing them on the licensing server.

How It Works

Just like previous versions of MetaFrame Presentation Server, a user connecting to the farm is allocated one license from the pool of purchased licenses. To put it more accurately, the user's *device* is issued a license. Once the license is issued, the user can connect to multiple published applications without requiring any further licenses, *as long as the user remains on the same device.* If the user connects from multiple devices without disconnecting or logging off from the previous device, each device will consume a license. Aside from the new licensing process, the rules have not changed from the previous version.

In a MetaFrame Presentation Server 3.0 environment, the IMA Service checks the IMA data store for configuration information. Along with other fairly static information traditionally stored in the IMA data store is the name of the license server and the TCP port associated with it. By default, the TCP port number for the licensing server is 27000, although you can modify your configuration and change the port number.

When a user connects to the farm and MetaFrame Presentation Server 3.0 (or other Access Suite product), the MetaFrame server requests a license from the license server. If the user credentials are valid, the MetaFrame server and licensing server agree to allow the license to be checked out and then agree to continue further communication on another port chosen at random. This port can be reconfigured to use a hard-coded port if needed. When the user logs out, opens another session, or disconnects from a session, the MetaFrame server again contracts the license server to report the event so that the license server can keep track of available licenses and which users have checked out licenses to each particular product. Every 120 seconds, whether a license is requested or not, the two servers exchange a brief communication, called a "heartbeat," to verify that both servers are still functional and awaiting further requests. Note: The licenses requested on behalf of the authenticated users are actually assigned to the user's device. Thus, any subsequent requests to connect to a specific MetaFrame product will not consume another license as long as the user connects from the same device. If the user connects to a different product, such as Conferencing Manager, a second license will be checked out and assigned. Figure A.1 shows a typical deployment scenario in which a single MetaFrame Presentation Server 3.0 farm points to a single licensing server. The licensing server in this case is running Microsoft IIS and the Web-based management console.

Figure A.1 Typical Deployment Scenario

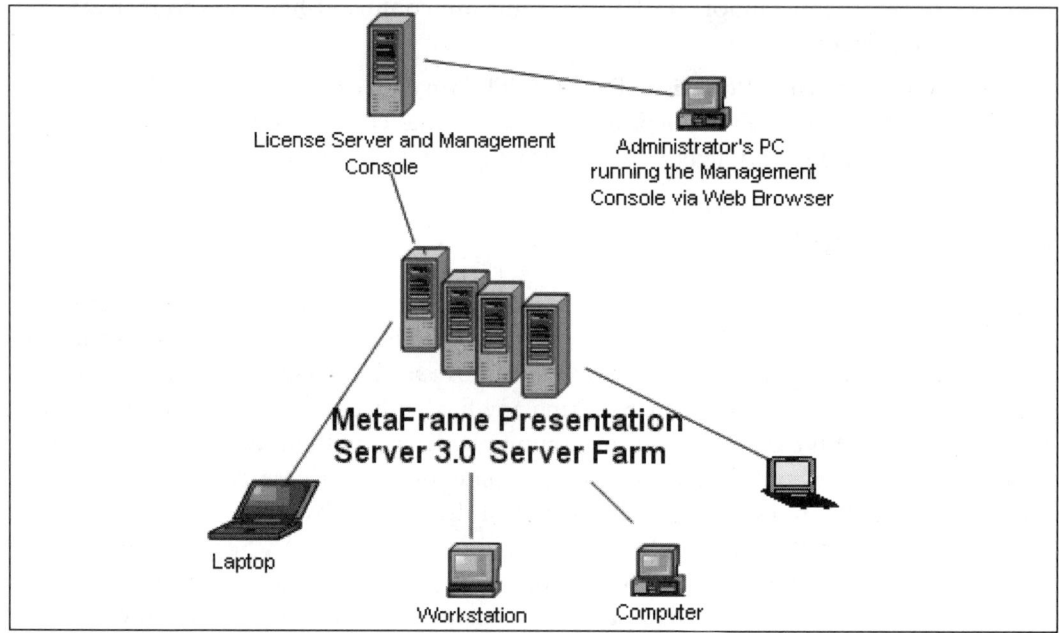

Each farm must have at least one licensing server, and that server must provide licenses for each Access Suite product running in that farm. For instance, if you plan to run Conferencing Manager in farm "A," licenses for Conferencing Manager must be stored on the licensing server to which farm "A" points. You can have multiple server farms pointing to the same licensing server or to multiple licensing servers. How you choose to deploy your farm and licensing servers will depend on the size of your environment, usage, and physical location.

Planning Your Deployment

As with any other deployment, planning is key. If you have prepared yourself with the knowledge and tools you need, you are less likely to run into show-stopping issues and unfortunate surprises. A few things you must consider when planning your deployment include:

■ System requirements

■ How many machines will connect to your license server

- The physical location of your licensing server or servers
- Future plans for growth
- Firewalls and security

In the sections that follow, we discuss these and other considerations you should address prior to beginning the actual installation of your licensing server. To simplify matters, plan your strategy; proceed with your installation carefully and methodically, and then test the installation *before* downloading your license files from MyCitrix.com.

System Requirements

In addition to specific hardware and operating system requirements, you must also consider whether you will install your licensing server on a dedicated or shared server. If you will share the server with other applications or services, you must determine what resources each will require and be sure there are sufficient resources left for the licensing server. Another factor in determining whether to choose a dedicated or shared server is the size of your environment. How many servers will connect to your licensing server, how many concurrent users, and how many Access Suite products will you provide licensing for? The answers to these questions are crucial for sizing your servers and determining whether to use dedicated or multiple licensing servers in your farm. Next, we describe the recommended hardware and software requirements.

Memory

Memory requirements for the licensing server itself are minimal and do not increase dramatically unless the server is deployed in large environments. If you plan to deploy in a large environment, it would be wise to consider dedicated servers and/or multiple licensing servers. Memory usage can increase incrementally with the number of concurrent users and the size of your license file. In most cases, however, a minimum of 512MB of RAM should be sufficient.

TIP

If you plan to run the Web-based console, you will also need to install and run Microsoft IIS. Therefore, (1) you must calculate the amount of resources needed for Windows Server 2003, (2) the resources required for IIS, (3) the resources need for the licensing server and Web Console and (4) if it is a shared server, the amount of resources the other applications will require to perform efficiently.

Disk Space

The licensing server itself takes up very little disk space, but if you plan to use the Web-based management console, you will need to run Microsoft IIS. Other considerations are the log files that the licensing server creates. You must factor in the maximum size of the logs, the length of time you choose to keep the logs, and the amount of license activity. The more licenses are checked in and checked out, the more entries will occur in the server logs.

CPU

Processor speed is the most important consideration for optimal licensing server performance. Citrix recommends at least a 1-GHz CPU. In addition, the licensing server is a single-threaded program and cannot take advantage of multiple CPUs, so if given the choice of multiple, slower CPUs or one fast CPU, go with the single, fast CPU.

Previous chapters described the system resources needed to run Windows Server 2003, IIS, and the licensing server in more detail, but just as a reminder, we have listed the basics in Table A.1. The resources in Table A.1 are based on the Windows Server 2003, Standard Version.

Table A.1 CPU Components and Resources

Component	Recommended Resources Needed
Computer and processor	550-MHz or faster processor recommended
Memory	256MB or more recommended; 4GB maximum
Hard disk space	1.25GB to 2GB of available hard-disk space
Display	Super VGA supporting 800 x 600 or higher resolution monitor recommended
Other	A CD-ROM or DVD-ROM drive

Bandwidth Requirements

Licensing-related traffic requires only small amounts of bandwidth primarily associated with the check in/check out process. Other than the license check in/check out, only the checks or "heartbeats" between the licensing server and the MetaFrame product server consume any bandwidth. The latter only occurs approximately every 120 seconds. Citrix has provided a formula to calculate the bandwidth required for both processes; 1 kb multiplied by the number of logons per second. The number of logons per second is recorded in the Management Console.

When to Use a Shared or Dedicated Server

Aside from the system requirements, you must also consider the number of servers that will be connecting to your licensing server. If your environment is small and there are sufficient resources on a shared server, you need not install a dedicated licensing server. However, if the other applications on the server demand more resources, you will see a decrease in performance in both the other applications and the licensing server. Citrix has provided a rule of thumb to follow in determining when to use a dedicated versus a shared licensing server. Table A.2 lists their recommendations.

Table A.2 Recommendations for Shared versus Dedicated Licensing Servers

Number of Servers	Recommendations for Servers
50 or fewer	Shared licensing server is appropriate for smaller environments.
50–500	A dedicated licensing server is recommended for medium to large environments.
500+	A dedicated licensing server is recommended for each MetaFrame Access Suite product.

Multiple Licensing Servers

Multiple licensing servers should be used in large environments of 500 or more servers. In this case, Citrix recommends installing one dedicated licensing server for each MetaFrame Access Suite product you use in your environment. There are other scenarios in which multiple licensing servers are recommended, such as when your servers are placed at different sites and need a local licensing server, or if you choose to segment departments within your company for security purposes.

Fault Tolerance

In environments in which it is critical for systems to remain available, you should consider implementing fault tolerance in the event of a license server failure. Fault tolerance can be implemented in various ways depending on the size or your environment and the resources it controls. One of the simplest ways to implement fault tolerance is to provide a backup license server. If your primary license server fails, you can manually point your servers to the backup server. Citrix provides a four-day grace period in the event of a failure, which should give you enough time to manually switch the license server or repair the primary.

Installing the License Server

Because you will be prompted for the name of the licensing server before you install MetaFrame Presentation Server or any of the other Access Suite products, Citrix suggests that you install the licensing server first. MetaFrame Presentation Server 3.0 will accept connections from administrators, but users cannot connect until the license server has been installed. If you do not immediately download your licensing files from MyCitrix.com, you are given a 96-hour grace period during which time users can connect.

As we mentioned earlier, the license server can be installed on a server dedicated solely to licensing, or shared with other applications. The licensing server can even reside on the same server as MetaFrame Presentation Server 3.0. The only caveat is that the server must be running at least Windows 2000 Server with Service Pack 3. A default installation of the license server also installs the License Management Console, but you must have Microsoft Internet Information Server (IIS) version 5 or later installed. If you do not choose to install IIS, you can use the license administration commands from the command prompt; however, you will not be able to generate licensing reports.

Notes from the Underground…

The License Server and Grace Periods

Citrix recommends that you install the license server prior to adding your first MetaFrame Presentation server. This is an excellent recommendation because, as mentioned previously, you will be prompted for the license server name during the MetaFrame Presentation Server installation process, and because the MetaFrame Presentation Server will not accept user connections until it can contact a license server. Citrix provides a 96-hour initial grace period that will allow up to two users to connect while unable to connect to a license server. We recommend you use this period for testing your server before downloading license files. Coincidentally, MetaFrame Presentation Server licensing is not compatible with previous versions of MetaFrame, so you should not upgrade your licenses until you have upgraded or migrated to MetaFrame Presentation Server 3.0. Both versions can co-exist in the same farm, but the licenses must be managed separately.

To install your licensing server, place the MetaFrame Presentation Server 3.0 CD-ROM in the drive and when Autorun starts up, select **PRODUCT INSTALLATIONS** from the Server Setup Screen. Next, select **Install MetaFrame Access Suite License Server** as shown in Figure A.2.

Figure A.2 MetaFrame Presentation Server 3.0 Product Installation Options

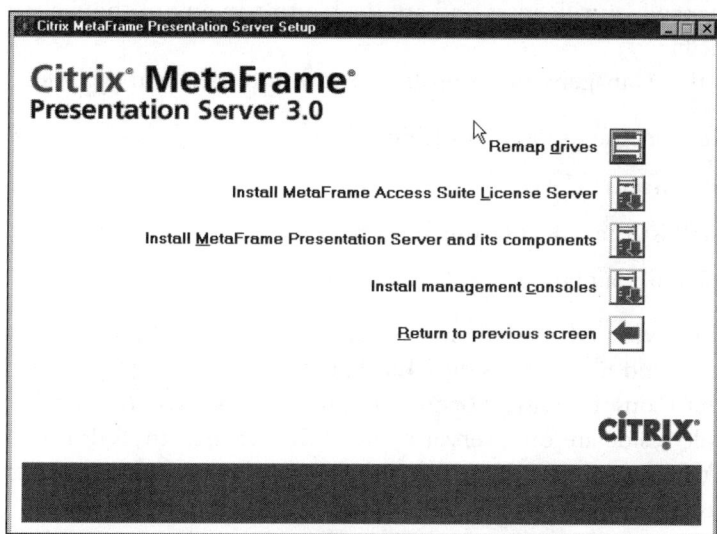

As we learned in Chapter 7, "Installing and Configuring MetaFrame Presentation Server 3.0," a few other components must be installed prior to installing the MetaFrame Presentation Server and licensing server:

- Microsoft .NET Framework, version 1.1 or later
- Java Runtime Environment (JRE), version 1.4.1_02 or later
- Visual J# .NET, version 1.1 or later
- ASP .NET (a Windows component)
- Microsoft Internet Information Server 5 or later

Once these components have been installed, the installation of the licensing server and Web Console can be continued. Rather than run through the complete installation process again, please refer to the section in Chapter 7 that provides step-by-step coverage of the license server installation and license file download process. When you have your licensing server up and running and the other MetaFrame products you will provide for your users installed, you can begin managing and monitoring your licenses.

Managing and Monitoring

Using the Management Console allows you to monitor and manage your Citrix licenses. The Management Console as stated earlier, is a Web-based utility that interfaces with the licensing server and can be run via a Web browser from anywhere on the network. The Management Console provides an easy, GUI method of monitoring and managing your licenses; without the Management Console, you can only use the command line to manage your licenses and are unable to run any of the real-time or historical reports available.

Some tasks the Management Console allows you to perform include:

- Monitor license use and availability

- Monitor license alerts

- Report historical license use and maintain reports

- Secure and maintain access to the Management Console

To begin using your Management Console to manage and monitor your license, use your Web browser and navigate, using a URL, to the server where the licensing server and Management Console reside. For instance, if the server where your licensing server and Web Console reside are on a server named "Betelgeuse," the URL you would use would be (don't forget to type the URL in lowercase letters as it is case sensitive) http://betelgeuse/lmc/index.jsp

Monitoring License Usage and Availability

The Current Usage Page displays important information about your farm and/or product licenses. To view the Current Usage Page, click **View Current Usage Data** from the **License Console Welcome Page**. From the Current Usage Page, you have the ability to monitor:

- The current license inventory

- The number of licenses available for use

- The number of licenses currently in use

- Current license expiration

- The percentage of licenses available for use

- Subscription Advantage expiration alerts

To view detailed information about your licenses, click on the **Complete License Inventory**. You can also view your expired licenses from this page.

Monitoring Usage Alerts

Alerts, or warnings, can be configured that will notify you of licensing events such as:

- Licenses nearing their expiration date
- Subscription Advantage renewal dates
- When you are running low on available licenses
- When your MetaFrame server is unable to communicate with the licensing server

You as administrator can configure the expiration and renewal alerts or thresholds by specifying the number of days before they expire or require renewal, and reminders as the time becomes more critical. Alerts will always appear at the top of the Current Usage Page and will provide more information by clicking the **Details** button. Note: You must refresh the Current Usage Page to update the alerts, as they *do not* update automatically.

Configuring the Alert Thresholds

To configure your expiration and renewal alert thresholds:

1. Go to **the License Management Console Welcome Pag**e. At this point, you will see the License Files page.
2. Click on **Threshold Options**, and then click **Change**.
3. From the Change page, you can:

- Specify an alert to appear when the license usage exceeds your specified percentage.
- Specify alerts to appear prior to your Subscription Advantage expiration date.
- Specify alerts to appear before your licenses expire.

4. Once you configured the alerts, click **Change** to complete the process.

Current and Historical License Reporting

Unlike past versions of MetaFrame Presentation Server, the new license server will allow you to create reports or current and past license activity. Usage logs are generated and kept for the length of time you specify, and can be used to create reports based on license availability, consumption, or license use for one or more MetaFrame Access Suite products.

The License Management Console allows you to specify the type of report you want to generate, which can be based on a date range, summary period, or data type. The appearance of the reports can also be modified, allowing you to change the type-face, line weight, and color scheme. In our experience, this is a very helpful feature, as management wants the reports they receive to be easy to read and easy to look at.

Generating a Historical Report

Starting again from the Management Console **Welcome Page**:

1. Select **Generate Historical Reports**; you should now see the Usage Log Page.
2. Click **ADD**, and from the list of Usage Logs, choose the one that will provide the information you require for your report. Click **ADD** again to load the log. You now have the option to produce reports based on products and licenses or Summary Reports based on past licensing activity.
3. After selecting the log and type of report you want to generate, click **Generate Report**.

Changing the Visual Appearance of the Report

1. Go to the **Welcome Page | Generate Historical Reports**, and from the **Usage Logs** page, select **Chart Settings**.

2. To modify the colors, fonts, and line weights of the reports, click **Change**.

3. Once you have made all the visual changes you require, click **Submit All Changes**.

4. After generating the report, you can view and save the report. The default file extension is .RIF (Resource Interchange File format). To import into Microsoft Excel, simply change the file extension to .CSV (Comma Separated Value).

License Report Maintenance

As discussed earlier, one of the disk sizing factors you need to consider is the log files generated by your licensing server. If you have a large farm with a lot of check in/check out activity or several products, your logs could grow quite large in a short time. To keep your license server running optimally as well as preserving disk space, be sure to check your logs frequently. Consider archiving or compressing the files, backing them up to another location or limiting the information the logs actually gather. You also have the option to overwrite the log, just as with your Microsoft Event Logs, but in our experience, as soon as you do, there will be something you wish you could look at again and examine. Changing the location of the file logs is easy, and once they are copied to the new location, you can compress and back them up for future reference. To change the location the logs are saved to:

1. From the **Welcome Page**, select **Configure License Server**.

2. From the **License Files** page, select **File Locations** and then click **Change**.

3. In the **Usage Log** path box, type in the new path and filename, and then click **Change** to complete the operation.

Securing Your License Server

As with any other component of your network, it is important to secure access to your License Management Console. Like the MetaFrame Presentation Server Management Console, you are allowed to add and remove authorized users who may perform administrative duties on a granular level. By default, the Licensing Console uses the credentials used when installing the license server. To add authorized users who can log in to and perform administrative tasks, or to delete or modify user accounts:

1. Go to the **Welcome Page** and select **User Administration**.

2. Click **Add New User** and then type the user's domain and username in the **User** box.

3. Select the administrative tasks you want to grant permissions for, and then click **Submit**.

WARNING

While not the most intuitive error message (more like a Microsoft error message), a user who does not have sufficient permissions to perform certain tasks or access certain areas of the License Management Console will receive the error `HTTP Error 403`.

Customizations

Some customizations to your licensing server may be needed under certain circumstances. Some of the most common reasons for customization include:

- Changing the port used to communicate to and from the MetaFrame Presentation server.
- Changing the server name reference in the license files.

The following section provides a brief overview on these common customization scenarios.

Changing Port Numbers

As mentioned previously, the license server uses TCP port 27000 to communicate with the MetaFrame product servers. If for some reason this port is already in use on your network, you will likely want to change it. If you need to change the port number, you will need to change the port number on *both* the licensing server and in all of your license files. If you fail to change both, the license server and MetaFrame product servers will be unable to communicate. To change the port number, you will need to do *both* of the following procedures.

Changing the License Server Port

1. First, back up all of your license server files. Typically, they are stored in C:\Program Files\Citrix\Licensing\MyFiles. Licensing files will all have the file extension .lic.

2. Remove the Read-Only attribute from the license files.

3. Edit each of the licensing files and modify the SERVER line by changing the port number after the hostname or the ANY keyword. Re-save the file with the .lic extension. An example of the command would be:

```
SERVER this_host HOSTNAME=Betelgeuse 27900 or
SERVER this_host HOSTNAME=ANY 27900
```

4. Once all the license files on a license server have been changed, go to the command line and run the following command to cause the licensing server to re-read the license files:

```
lmreread -c "C:\Program Files\Citrix\Licensing\MyFiles"
```

Note from the Underground…

Writing Scripts with the .lic Extension

If you support a large environment and have many license files to modify, you might consider writing a script that will search all documents with the .lic extension and replace the specific lines. Alternatively, if your scripting skills aren't great or you just don't have the time, try some of the new shareware utilities such as Actual Search and Replace by Divlocsoft, or one of the UNIX-like shareware utilities such as PowerGrep. Both are reasonably priced and easy to use.

Changing the License Console Port Number

Depending on your environment, you may also need to change the port number used by the Web Console. By default, the Web Console uses port 8082, but if this port is already used on your network, you will need to change it.

NOTE

The Apache Tomcat servlet engine uses port 8082, which is why the Management Console uses port 8082. The Management Console for the Licensing service uses the Apache Tomcat servlet engine and is tied to Tomcat.exe.

To change the port number used from 8082, edit the **Server.xml** file found under C:\Program Files\Citrix\Licensing\LMC\Tomcat\conf. After making the necessary change, restart the License Management Console from the Windows Services panel.

Changing the Server Name Reference in the License Files

If you change your license server name or move your license files to a server with a different name, the license files will no longer function. This may also happen if you entered the wrong license server name when you allocated your licenses. If any of the preceding occurred, you will need to create new license files that match the new server name by "rehosting" the files.

To rehost your license files:

1. You will need to access the Citrix Activation Site by logging on to **www.MyCitrix.com** and navigating to **View Allocated Licenses**.

2. Enter your **License code**, and in the License Server **Name** box, enter the name of the license server to which you originally allocated your licenses.

3. From the drop-down **Product List**, select the product for which the licenses were originally allocated.

4. Next, select **Filter Products**. You will be presented with a list of your allocated licenses.

5. Select all the licenses you want to rehost, and then click **Return**. You will be shown a list of licenses and asked to verify that you want to return them.

6. When you have verified the list, click **Confirm**. This will bring up a page showing the list of returned licenses and will allow you to choose those you want to rehost.

7. Select the licenses you want to rehost, and then type in the hostname of the license server that will host the license files. Remember, you must type the hostname exactly as it appears on the server, and it is case sensitive.

8. Once you have filled in the hostname and verified that it is correct, select **Generate**. The new license files will be generated using the new hostname, and you will be prompted to confirm the new hostname. Click **Confirm** to continue.

9. Download the new license, and file then from the MyCitrix.com page, click **Copy License File to your Citrix license server**.

Troubleshooting

As you can imagine after reading the preceding sections, numerous things can go wrong and prevent your licensing server from functioning properly. Typical signs of licensing problems are users receiving warnings indicating that the server is out of licenses, or you may find entries in the licensing server log or the Windows Event Logs. If this happens, you do have a 96-hour grace period to remedy the problem or failover to a functioning backup server. Often, the problems will begin post-installation, and with a bit of troubleshooting can be fixed before the grace period expires. Here are a few tips for troubleshooting post-installation licensing problems:

- If you recently moved your license files to a new server or changed the license server name, check the license files under **C:\Program Files\ Citrix\Licensing\MyFiles**, and make sure that all license files have the correct hostname. Be sure the hostname is spelled exactly as it is on the server and in the exact same case. If you misspelled the hostname or moved the files to a new server with a different name, you will need to log on to MyCitrix.com and rehost the license files as described previously.

- If you changed the port number used by the licensing server or the Management Console, you will need to check the license files to make sure they bear the same port number as the license server, and check the Server.xml to make sure it reflects the new port number assigned to the Management Console.

- Check for problems on the license server and make sure the IIS service and the Citrix Licensing and License Management Console services are running.

- Check the license server logs and the Event Logs for problems that may help diagnose the problem.

- Check for connection problems between the licensing server and the MetaFrame Presentation server.

- Check your MetaFrame Presentation servers to make sure there are no problems indicated in the Event Logs or incorrect settings in the Presentation Server Console.

Checklist

As with any other deployment, planning is crucial. Before you begin, make sure you have the knowledge, resources, and utilities you will need to carry out your task. Here are a few suggestions that may help you in your deployment and management of the license server:

- ☑ Check your hardware and make sure you have a server that will accommodate the licensing server. Be especially careful if you are sharing a server with other applications.

- ☑ Check your network for ports in use and, if necessary, change the ports on the licensing server, license files, and/or Management Console.

- ☑ Install and test your license server before allocating your licenses.

- ☑ When allocating your licenses, be certain of the license server hostname, and when allocating, be sure to type the hostname exactly as it is on the server, including the correct case.

☑ Be sure to monitor your license server logs to make sure they do not grow too large. Move the files to another location, compress, backup, or overwrite the logs as needed.

☑ Configure alerts to inform you of license shortages, expirations, or Subscription Advantage renewal dates.

☑ Monitor your license server and occasionally create historical reports that can be compared against older reports. This will help give you a sense of license, product, and server usage.

Summary

In this chapter, we outlined some of the characteristics and benefits of the new MetaFrame licensing server, and some of the more common customizations that can be made to take some of the mystery out of deploying your license server. We showed how the new Citrix licensing works, and how the licenses for the MetaFrame Access Suite can all be managed from a centralized location, reducing the administrative workload.

Server customization is an important piece in the new licensing scheme, and we hope that the few, more common customizations we addressed will assist you in getting started. As stated previously, when customizing your server, be careful to make sure all entries match before deploying, or you'll end up with other problems. Most of the problems we have seen were due to misspellings, incorrect case, or omissions and can be easy to troubleshoot. However, the time it takes to double check your work is well worth it and can greatly reduce the stress of administration.

Index

Syngress: *The Definition of a Serious Security Library*

Syn·gress (sin‑gres): *noun, sing.* Freedom
from risk or danger; safety. See *security.*

Microsoft Log Parser Toolkit
Gabriele Giuseppini and Mark Burnett

Do you want to find Brute Force Attacks against your Exchange Server? Would
you like to know who is spamming you? Do you need to monitor the performance
of your IIS Server? Are there intruders out there you would like to find? Would you
like to build user logon reports from your Windows Server? Would you like
working scripts to automate all of these tasks and many more for you? If so,
"Microsoft Log Parser Toolkit" is the book for you...

ISBN: 1‑932266‑52‑6

Price: $39.95 U.S. $57.95 CAN

CYA: Securing IIS 6.0
Networking professionals responsible for configuring,
maintaining, and troubleshooting Microsoft's Internet
Information Server 6.0 will find this book indispensable. They operate in high-
stress environments where competitive business demands often run counter to
"best practices." Design and planning lead times are non-existent and deployed
systems are subject to constant end-runs. But at the end of the day, they are held
accountable if things go wrong. They need help. They need to guarantee they've
configured their network professionally and responsibly. They need to CYA.

ISBN: 1‑931836‑25‑6

Price: $$39.95 US $59.95 CAN

CYA: Securing Exchange Server 2003 and Outlook Web Access
The down and dirty guide to configuring, maintaining,
and troubleshooting essential Exchange Server 2003 features. Network engineers
operate in high-stress environments where competitive business demands often
run counter to "best practices." Design and planning lead times are non-existent
and deployed systems are subject to constant end-runs. But at the end of the day,
they are held accountable if things go wrong. They need help. They need to
guarantee they've configured their network professionally and responsibly. A
highly portable, easily digestible road-map, ensuring that the reader has in fact
covered his a**.

ISBN: 1‑931836‑24‑8

Price: $$39.95 US $59.95 CAN

SYNGRESS®